THE MYTH OF PELAGIANISM

A British Academy Monograph

British Academy Monographs showcase work arising from:

British Academy Postdoctoral Fellowships
British Academy Newton International Fellowships

THE MYTH OF PELAGIANISM

Ali Bonner

Published for THE BRITISH ACADEMY
by OXFORD UNIVERSITY PRESS

Oxford University Press, Great Clarendon Street, Oxford OX2 6DP

First edition published in 2018

British Library Cataloguing in Publication Data
Data available

Library of Congress Cataloging in Publication Data
Data available

Typeset by Mach 3 Solutions Ltd

ISBN 978-0-19-726639-7

For Jenifer Bonner

Contents

List of Abbreviations

ACO	*Acta Conciliorum Oecumenicorum*
BA	Bibliothèque Augustinienne
CCSL	Corpus Christianorum Series Latina
CPL	*Clavis Patrum Latinorum*
CSEL	Corpus Scriptorum Ecclesiasticorum Latinorum
HÜWA	*Die handschriftliche Überlieferung der Werke des heiligen Augustinus*
Ep, Epp	Epistle, Epistles
MGH, AA	Monumenta Germaniae Historica, Auctores Antiquissimi
PL	Patrologia Latina
PLS	Patrologia Latina, Supplementum
SC	Sources Chrétiennes
TU	Texte und Untersuchungen zur Geschichte der altchristlichen Literatur

Acknowledgements

I would like to thank the Arts and Humanities Research Council for funding my PhD, and the British Academy for funding my postdoctoral research. I would also like to thank the Principal and Fellows of Jesus College, Oxford, for awarding me a Junior Research Fellowship and giving me three years of warm hospitality and access to all the college's resources, as well as the research facilities and many seminars of Oxford. I would like to thank Owen McKnight, librarian of the Celtic Library maintained in Jesus College. I would also like to thank the President and Fellows of Hughes Hall in Cambridge for their support. Whilst I take sole responsibility for the contents of this book, I would like to thank Professor Thomas Charles-Edwards for being my British Academy mentor during my postdoctoral fellowship; Thomas' support and his critical comments were invaluable to me. I would also like to thank Professor Kate Cooper for her wise advice and support. I would like to thank Dr Conrad Leyser for his generous help in all things academic. I would like to thank Professor Paul Russell for his critical comments on drafts of parts of this book, from which I benefitted greatly. For her unfailing help and support I owe an immense debt of gratitude to Dr Rosalind Love, who embodies scholarly academic values at their very best. All her students gain immensely from her generosity and wisdom. Finally, I would like to thank the British Academy for supporting my postdoctoral research, and this publication.

Introduction

Pelagius was a Briton who went to Rome some time in the early 380s AD, initially probably to study law.[1] Whatever the original plan was, he became a scriptural adviser to Christians in Rome; he wrote about how to live a Christian life and composed commentary explaining the meaning of books of the Bible.[2] In AD 415, he was twice tried and acquitted on a charge of heresy by ecclesiastical councils in Palestine.[3] Following a third investigation, the Pope in office at its conclusion announced that he was acquitting Pelagius but then changed his position, with the result that Pelagius was condemned as a heretic in AD 418.[4] He was characterised by his opponents as leading a separatist movement that was dangerous to Christianity, termed 'Pelagianism', and his name became a byword for wilful arrogance. In the 1,600 years since, Pelagius has never ceased to be a controversial figure, and the account of him disseminated by his opponents has never been seriously questioned.

Two characteristics of Pelagius' writings combine to make him distinctive among alleged authors of heresy. First, a number of his works survive, allowing direct comparison of the ideas attributed to him by his opponents and the actual content of his writings. For most alleged heresiarchs this is not the case; the narrative about a heresy in surviving texts is usually written by the winning side in

---

[1] Pelagius a Briton: Augustine, *Ep.* 186.1.1 (ed. Goldbacher, CSEL 57, p. 45); Marius Mercator, *Commonitorium lectori aduersum haeresim Pelagii et Caelestii* (ed. Schwartz, *ACO* 1.5.3, p. 5). Pelagius spent some years in Rome before he left (by August AD 410): Augustine, *De gratia Christi et de peccato originali* 2.8.9 (ed. Urba and Zycha, CSEL 42, p. 172).

[2] Pelagius wrote about how to live a Christian life: Pelagius, *Ad Demetriadem* 2 (ed. Greshake, p. 58). Pelagius wrote a commentary on the Pauline Epistles: Anon., *Praedestinatus* 1.88 (ed. Gori, CCSL 25B, p. 52); Marius Mercator, *Commonitorium super nomine Caelestii* (ed. Schwartz, *ACO* 1.5.36, p. 67).

[3] Pelagius tried and acquitted twice: Augustine, *De gestis Pelagii* 1.1-2 (ed. Urba & Zycha, CSEL 42, pp. 51–2); Augustine, *De gratia Christi et de peccato originali* 2.9.10 (ed. Urba & Zycha, CSEL 42, pp. 172–3).

[4] Pope Zosimus acquitted Pelagius: Zosimus, *Ep. Posteaquam a nobis* (ed. Günther, CSEL 35, pp. 103–8). Pope Zosimus condemned Pelagius: Augustine, *Ep.* 194.1.1 (ed. Goldbacher, CSEL 57, p. 176); Marius Mercator, *Commonitorium super nomine Caelestii* (ed. Schwartz, *ACO* 1.5.36, p. 68).

the struggle to shape Christian belief.[5] Second, throughout the medieval period, Pelagius' writings were just as widely available as the account of Christianity proposed by his opponents; this too is unusual. These two facts make the case of Pelagius paradigmatic in analysis of the process of heresy accusations.

The evidence in this book shows that Pelagius did not propound any new doctrine. So how did he come to be characterised as the author of new and heretical ideas? Several aspects of the context contribute to answering this question. One important factor was the upsurge of interest in the Pauline Epistles in the Latin West during the later 4th century. From the 370s onwards a series of commentaries on the Pauline Epistles were composed in Latin, testifying to a developing interest in these New Testament books; the commentaries that survive reveal debates in the Latin West about the proper interpretation of Paul's letters.[6] 'Grace' and 'predestination' were words that recurred in the books attributed to the apostle Paul; their correct interpretation mattered not only because the words of Scripture held great authority for Christians but also because very different brands of Christianity followed from different interpretations of these words.[7] As will be seen in the course of this book, these two terms were understood differently by Christian writers in the late 4th and early 5th centuries. The Latin word *gratia* had a range of possible meanings in Christian discourse.[8] In Christian contexts it is usually translated as 'grace' because it was primarily used to refer to gifts from God. God's grace denoted many things because He bestowed many gifts on mankind. In relation to the question of how Pelagius came to be characterised as teaching new and heretical ideas, the point to note is that the meaning of these words in Scripture was being debated in Christian literature at the time, and the way in which these terms were understood had important consequences for Christianity's message.

---

[5] A. Cameron, 'How to Read Heresiology', in *The Cultural Turn in Late Antique Studies*, ed. D. B. Martin and P. Cox Miller (Durham, 2005), p. 195.

[6] These were Marius Victorinus', the commentary by the unknown author named Ambrosiaster, an anonymous commentary identified by Hermann Josef Frede, the commentaries on selected Pauline letters by Jerome and Augustine, and Pelagius' commentary.

[7] On different Christianities, see R. A. Markus, 'Between Marrou and Brown: Transformations of Late Antiquity', in *Transformations of Late Antiquity. Essays for Peter Brown*, ed. P. Rousseau and E. Papoutsakis (Farnham, 2009), pp. 12–13; É. Rebillard, *In Hora Mortis: Évolution de la pastorale Chrétienne de la Mort aux IVe et Ve Siècles dans L'Occident Latin* (Rome, 1994), pp. 231–2; P. Brown, '*Gloriosus Obitus*: The End of the Ancient Other World', in *The Limits of Ancient Christianity*, ed. W. E. Klingshirn and M. Vessey (Ann Arbor, MI, 1999), p. 290; A. Cameron, 'The Violence of Orthodoxy', in *Heresy and Identity in Late Antiquity*, ed. E. Iricinschi and H. M. Zellentin (Tübingen, 2008), p. 103.

[8] In secular usage the Latin word *gratia* had a different set of meanings again. In secular contexts, *gratia* is usually translated as 'favour' and it carried a sense of reciprocity, and a return for favours given or expected. For example, it was used in the context of the client–patron relationship which was based on mutual favours and mutual advantage.

The theological issues at stake in interpreting the words 'Grace' and 'Predestination'

Interpretation of the words 'grace' and 'predestination' brought to the fore two questions. First, was human nature damaged by Adam's sin in the Garden of Eden to such an extent that no human could desire virtue unless caused to by the inspiration of God's grace because Adam's sin was passed down physically to all other humans? If the answer to this question was yes, then according to this model the sin transmitted from Adam to all humans was termed 'original sin', and this grace was termed 'prevenient grace' because it was prior to, and caused, human inclination to virtue.[9] An absolutist account of prevenient grace said that it initiated and caused all human virtue. Thus the answer given to this first question defined Christianity's account of man's nature.

If grace was interpreted as prevenient in an absolutist way, it followed that God caused all human goodness. This in turn meant that since God selected to whom he would give his prevenient grace, its recipients were predestined to salvation in the sense that it was preordained by God's selection that they would reach heaven. Predestination was in this way interpreted as preordainment by God. So in addition to the first question about whether or not human nature was unavoidably inclined to sin, the interpretation of grace as an absolute form of prevenient grace generated the second question: was access to heaven determined solely by God or did man play some part in his own salvation? The answer given to this defined Christianity's account of how Christians attained salvation. These two questions were intertwined, since it was because of original sin that man could only act virtuously if prevenient grace caused him to do so. Prevenient grace and predestination interpreted as preordainment were essentially the preparation and effect of the same supposed phenomenon, which was God's control of man. Because the doctrines of original sin, an absolutist account of prevenient grace, and predestination interpreted as preordainment were so closely linked, they will on occasion be referred to hereafter as 'the triune'.

There were, however, other interpretations of the words 'grace' and 'predestination' available in Christian literature of the second half of the 4th century and the early 5th century. Grace did not have to be interpreted as prevenient. Nor did it have to be interpreted as prevenient in an absolutist way; it could be understood as being sometimes prevenient. Prevenient grace could then be acknowledged as one among many facets of God's grace. Likewise, an alternative interpretation of the word 'predestination' understood it as God's foreknowledge of autonomous human actions. In this interpretation of predestination, man had genuine freedom of action and his decisions were not predetermined by God. In Christian literature this freedom was described as 'free will'.[10] Thus the interpretation of the

---

[9] The literal meaning of 'prevenient' is 'coming before/in advance'.
[10] The modern English phrase 'effective free will' highlights a situation in which man has free will over his good actions as well as his bad ones.

words 'grace' and 'predestination' in Scripture determined the anthropology of Christianity (its account of human nature) and the soteriology of Christianity (its account of the means of access to salvation), as well as the conception of God, and man's relationship to God, that lay at the heart of Christianity. These facts are important aspects of the background to Pelagius' condemnation.

The argument of this book is that 'Pelagianism' never existed. What does this statement mean and what are the proofs of this argument? It means that the notion of 'Pelagianism' was a composite fiction created for polemical purposes; it was a bundle of tenets, some of which were ideas in circulation at the time but had no link to Pelagius, and others of which were created by drawing unwarranted inferences from Pelagius' writings, and reading into his works doctrines that he rejected. The statement that 'Pelagianism' did not exist contains three elements. First, it identifies the fact that the character and content attributed to 'Pelagianism' by its opponents bears no relation to the reality of Pelagius' writings as they survive. There is evidence that some of the ideas that were assembled under one heading and attributed to Pelagius were indeed in circulation around the Mediterranean in the early 5th century, but only one idea that appears in the list of tenets drawn up by Augustine of Hippo as comprising 'Pelagianism' is present in Pelagius' surviving writings. What was declared heretical was a distortion and misrepresentation of what Pelagius himself taught. The second element in the statement that 'Pelagianism' did not exist is the recognition that all the doctrinal tenets of Pelagius' teaching were already present in ascetic literature before he began to write; they were assumptions taken for granted because they had never been questioned. Thus what Pelagius taught was not something doctrinally separate from the ascetic movement. Third, there was no 'Pelagian' movement; there is not sufficient homogeneity of ideas among surviving writings calling for ascetic imitation of Christ's way of life in the early 5th century to enable a movement or group to be identified as a separately cohering entity. And not only was there insufficient homogeneity of doctrine to link the various writers described as 'Pelagian', but there was also not enough to differentiate these individuals from other Christians, to separate them from the rest of the Church, because an ascetic approach to Christianity based on imitation of Christ's way of life could be argued to have been the standard approach held by all 'serious' Christians at the time.

Five principal arguments make up the case that 'Pelagianism' did not exist. There is no hierarchy among them and they are given in no particular order. The first argument presented is the profound disjunction between what is found in Pelagius' writings and what is found in the account disseminated by Pelagius' opponents of both the tenets comprising 'Pelagianism' and the spirit of 'Pelagianism'. Pelagius did not teach the fourteen tenets ascribed to 'Pelagianism' by Augustine, nor did he express in writing the attitude of arrogance attributed to him, either in his own character or in the approach to Christianity that he advocated, as these appear in his writings. The second argument is that the doctrine in Pelagius' writings is no different from what had already been stated in ascetic paraenetic literature for many decades before Pelagius began to write; his teaching was not separate from the ascetic movement. Evidence from the writings of proponents of asceticism proves this point; the main examples examined in this book are Athanasius' *Life of Antony* and the Latin translations of it, and the writings of Jerome, as well as a section of the *Commentary on the Pauline Epistles* attributed to the author known as Ambrosiaster. The third argument, which has been widely accepted for some years now, is that there was no coherent school, programme or movement that can accurately be identified as constituting 'Pelagianism'. The tenets bundled together for polemical purposes by Pelagius' opponents had in most cases no necessary link joining them together. The fourth strand in the case for the non-existence of 'Pelagianism' lies in the inability of scholars to agree on a definition of 'Pelagianism' or on criteria by which to classify texts as 'Pelagian' (or not). The history of scholarship on 'Pelagianism' shows that when examined, the concept does not withstand scrutiny; it cannot be defined, nor are there criteria by which a text can be classified as 'Pelagian'. The fifth argument lies in the identification of motive and means, which is supporting evidence in the argument that 'Pelagianism' was a deliberately invented fiction. Interactionist theory from sociological analysis provides comparative examples and offers an important perspective on the process at work in the condemnation of 'Pelagianism' and its supposed heresiarch.

The conclusion reached in this book is not just a question of terminology. In all the historical senses in which the term 'Pelagianism' is used, its referent did not exist as an historical reality, and the term is therefore misleading because inherently it introduces into scholarship the assumption that there was some sort of historical reality corresponding to the term, however diffuse. In fact much evidence, both manuscript and textual, can only be understood when it is grasped that 'Pelagianism' was an invention created for specific polemical purposes. Even if one discards the account of 'Pelagianism' that bears no relation to Pelagius' actual teaching but seeks to retain 'Pelagianism' as a theological term to mean the doctrines that human nature is innately good and that man has effective free will, this runs into the problem that it entails describing as 'Pelagian' a large number of Christian writers of ascetic exhortation who wrote before Pelagius himself did. So used, the term would be anachronistic, and such a use would also be misleading in the respect that since these ideas were regularly expounded decades before he began to write, Pelagius clearly did not invent them. In addition, such a use of the term 'Pelagianism' would be misleading because it would obscure the historical process that was at work in the 5th century, which was the defence of an understanding of the Christian message that was widely held at the time, in response to newly prominent interpretations of the Pauline Epistles which threatened that understanding of the Christian message. It would obscure the fact that the list of tenets was invented specifically to veil this fact, and to bring Pelagius into disrepute and thus suppress his defence of beliefs about man's goodness and effective free will that were of longstanding and were widely held among Christians.

I came to this enquiry via the manuscript transmission of Pelagius' works and the apparent contradiction between the evidence of the manuscripts and the received narrative about Pelagius. At first sight it seemed that the large number of surviving manuscript copies of Pelagius' writings might pose problems for the official account of Pelagius—namely, that his teaching was inimical to Christianity and was expelled from mainstream Christian teaching in AD 418. In fact, after studying the manuscript transmission of Pelagius' works, it became clear that in and of itself the large number of surviving copies of the texts does not have straightforward theological implications. Pure numbers do not have a simple theological meaning, though the scale of transmission had clear historical effects. The numbers of manuscript copies are in some respects an unreliable indicator, and they are of restricted significance in theological terms. It was other aspects of the manuscript transmission of Pelagius' works, along with other types of evidence in manuscripts such as marginalia, titles and attributions, that led towards further areas of study. Manuscript evidence alone, however, cannot prove that 'Pelagianism' never existed; it merely points towards lines of enquiry. It is the five lines of argument set out in Chapters 1–6 of this book that make the case. Evidence in manuscripts may then make more sense, indeed it may only be explicable once it is understood that 'Pelagianism' never existed, but it cannot of itself constitute an argument; it can only support the case corroboratively. It is not the case that the number of surviving manuscript copies of his works shows that Pelagius did not write heretical propositions; instead the reverse is the case: it is the fact that Pelagius was restating the central propositions of asceticism as they had traditionally been expressed for almost a hundred years—that is, it is because Pelagius was part of the ascetic movement that there are so many surviving manuscript copies of his works. In the West the ascetic movement evolved into the coenobitic monastic movement, which controlled the transmission of texts for the next thousand years. The writings of the ascetic movement were foundational for monastic communities, and this is one reason why so many copies of Pelagius' works were made and survive.

In Chapter 7 I examine the manuscript transmission of Pelagius' works, and I also look at three further myths that are bound up with the myth of 'Pelagianism', corollaries of the original foundation myth. First, the myth that Pelagius' teaching was expelled from mainstream Christian teaching. Second, the myth that his teachings were anathema to and dangerous to Christian belief. Third, the myth that the question of the relationship between divine prevenient grace and human free will was ever resolved.

The fact that 'Pelagianism' never existed is not just a reclassification of Pelagius under the larger heading of the ascetic movement, relevant only to scholars of patristics. This revision is relevant for historians because the paradigm of 'Pelagianism' both encodes a false account of the process that took place in the identification of the alleged heresy, obscuring the actual process that occurred, and presents a false account of the nature of Christianity in the 4th and 5th centuries. Following Christianity's legalisation, Christians produced a mass of epistolary, pamphlet, homiletic and tractate discussion, argument and polemic that was largely uncontrolled; the true picture was one of criss-crossing networks of influence sometimes driven by desire for authority and status in this life as well as salvation in the next. There was little control of teaching on Scripture. Patrician Romans employed lay scriptural advisers as they had done philosophers and experts in rhetoric; Roman senators felt themselves free to discuss Scripture as they pleased in their own homes. Exegesis was an arena for competition for authority, partly resulting from the competitive structure of rhetorical educational practices, and partly due to competition for Church office. Land ownership brought authority, and the increasing transfer of land to the Church effected a concurrent transfer of authority with it.[11] This shift in the pattern of landholding gave to Christian argument and exegesis a significance they did not previously possess. Meanwhile, heresy-hunting was driven by the self-construction of authority.[12] Heresy accusations were about human authority as much as God's word. In 1970 Gerald Bonner distinguished between two different uses of the term 'Pelagianism': one was its use by dogmatic theologians as a convenient shorthand label; the other referred to an historical movement.[13] I hope to show that it is entirely possible to do without the term 'Pelagianism' altogether. It is more historically accurate to use alternative terminology which avoids introducing false assumptions into discussion, and to reclassify Pelagius as a spokesman for the ascetic movement, a writer whose views are doctrinally indistinguishable from those of other advocates of the ascetic movement in late antiquity.

Furthermore, the impact of the successful promulgation of the myth of 'Pelagianism' was far reaching and enduring. A great deal of textual evidence only becomes comprehensible once it is appreciated how Christian writers were forced to create convoluted arguments in order to condemn the caricature of Pelagius while at the same time asserting the principles that he taught. Manuscript evidence in particular reveals the knots Western Christianity got itself tied into as a result of the creation of the myth of 'Pelagianism' with its toxic associations. The historical effects of this myth were significant.

A further misconception triggered by the myth is the reputational see-saw paradigm that exists for some between Pelagius and Augustine of Hippo. It is as if Pelagius and Augustine sit at either end of a reputational see-saw; if the reputation of one goes up, that of the other must go down. Augustine's legacy has been seen by some as at stake in any treatment of Pelagius. By contrast, I would argue that a key to understanding this controversy is to locate it within the bigger picture, both

[11] S. Wood, *The Proprietary Church in the Medieval West* (Oxford, 2008), p. 3.

[12] E. Iricinschi and H. M. Zellentin, 'Making Selves and Marking Others: Identity and Late Antique Heresiologies', in *Heresy and Identity in Late Antiquity*, ed. E. Iricinschi and H. M. Zellentin, (Tübingen, 2008), pp. 10–11; V. Leonard, 'The Origins of Zealous Intolerance: Paulus Orosius and Violent Religious Conflict in the Early Fifth Century', *Vigiliae Christianae* 71 (2017), passim; K. L. King, 'Social and Theological Effects of Heresiological Discourse', in *Heresy and Identity in Late Antiquity*, ed. E. Iricinschi and H. M. Zellentin (Tübingen, 2008), p. 35.

[13] G. Bonner, *Augustine and Modern Research on Pelagianism*, The St Augustine Lecture 1970 (Philadelphia, PA, 1972), pp. 1–2; repr. in Bonner's *God's Decree and Man's Destiny: Studies on the Thought of Augustine of Hippo* (London, 1987), no. XI, p. 1.

of human discussion of man's relationship to the divine, and of the development of Christian thought and interpretation of Scripture. What this wider perspective shows is that the controversy over prevenient grace and free will was an accident waiting to happen. This debate about how to interpret the Pauline Epistles was going to happen whether or not the individuals Augustine and Pelagius had existed.[14] Looking at the bigger picture, individuals diminish in importance, and any notion of blame or error on either side falls away. These two figures represented in their day two approaches to Scripture; but the debate was eternal to the human condition. For Christians in the West, Augustine and Pelagius subsequently became emblematic of two sides of an argument, but the see-saw paradigm is a misconception; it embodies a failure to grasp the abiding nature of the questions raised in the controversy across the history of Western civilisation.[15]

The aim of this book is therefore to show that 'Pelagianism' never existed and was a fiction created for polemical purposes, and thereby to reveal a more historically accurate account of late antique Christianity and the process that took place when Pelagius was condemned as a heretic.

The canon of Pelagius' surviving writings

The arguments in this book are based on Pelagius' teaching as it appears in his surviving writings. My view is that the corpus of work that can definitively be attributed to Pelagius is small. I include in the list of his surviving works the four letters: *Letter to Demetrias* (*Ad Demetriadem*), *Letter to Celantia* (*Ad Celantiam*), *On Virginity* (*De uirginitate*), and *On the Divine Law* (*De diuina lege*), plus the *Statement of Faith* (*Libellus fidei*), because these can unarguably be attributed to Pelagius.[16] I discuss the letter *To a Mistress of a Household* (*Ad quandam matronam*) in Chapter 4.

I do not include the *Commentary on the Pauline Epistles* (*Expositio in Epistolas sancti Pauli*) on the grounds that Souter's edition cannot be taken as accurately representing Pelagius' original text because there are so many unidentified interpolations in the text Souter published.[17] Hermann Josef Frede showed that Pelagius' *Commentary on the Pauline Epistles* was revised at least once, by

---

[14] See R. A. Markus, 'Pelagianism: Britain and the Continent', *Journal of Ecclesiastical History* 37 (1986), p. 198, where he wrote of: 'Elements crystallised out of a pre-existing, undifferentiated range of acceptable doctrinal options.'

[15] On the perennial nature of this debate, see N. D. Jackson, *Hobbes, Bramhall and the Politics of Liberty and Necessity* (Cambridge, 2007), pp. 276–304.

[16] Celantia was a patrician Roman matron for whom Pelagius wrote a letter of ascetic paraenesis.

[17] T. De Bruyn, *Pelagius's Commentary on St Paul's Epistle to the Romans*, Oxford Early Christian Studies (Oxford, 1993), pp. 27–35. Souter remarked that it might prove impossible ever to get to the bottom of the alterations and interpolations that occurred during the transmission of the pseudo-Jerome version of the *Commentary on the Pauline Epistles*: A. Souter, *Pelagius's Expositions of Thirteen Epistles of St Paul*, 3 vols, Contributions to Biblical and Patristic Studies: Texts and Studies 9 (Cambridge, 1922–31), vol. 1, p. 318.

an unknown individual, in the 5th century.[18] During the Middle Ages, catenas of commentary were inherently open traditions, intended for interpolation and accretion. Study of Cambridge, Trinity College B.10.5, s. viii, makes clear how easily interpolations entered commentaries; two sets of annotations crowd the margins and interlinear spaces in this copy of the Pauline Epistles. The transmission of Pelagius' *Commentary* probably included shifts back and forth between its transcription as the main text of a manuscript, and use of it along with several other commentaries to create annotations on a main text of the Pauline Epistles, which is what was happening in Trinity College B.10.5, or happened in the creation of its exemplar, or at some earlier point in its transmission ancestry. Equally the process could run back in the other direction, with compilation of a main text commentary from an annotated biblical text (such as the Trinity College manuscript). Such reuse would have given many opportunities for alteration and for readers to add their own thoughts; this process did not require one individual to have set out to revise Pelagius' *Commentary*. In the 5th century or at any time thereafter, someone may have annotated Pelagius' text or annotated a copy of the Pauline Epistles, drawing on both Pelagius' comments and his own thoughts. There are comments in the Trinity manuscript beside the siglum for Pelagius that do not appear in Souter's edition. Souter himself detailed the way Zmaragdus of St Mihiel and Sedulius Scottus in the 9th century included passages from Pelagius' *Commentary* beside the name 'Pilagius' in their compilations of exegesis.[19] Such compilations and the copying of them would have afforded opportunities for interpolation and alteration. These factors make it impossible, as things stand, to identify Pelagius' original text, and so Souter's edition of the *Commentary* is not included in this study as evidence of Pelagius' teaching.

I also consider hearsay concerning Pelagius' teaching as reported by his opponents inadmissable as evidence. Quotations from otherwise lost works by Pelagius preserved in Augustine's writings may be admissable as long as it is borne in mind that they may be paraphrases and are necessarily seen out of context, without surrounding argumentation.

---

[18] H. J. Frede, *Ein neuer Paulustext und Kommentar*, 2 vols, Vetus Latina. Die Reste der altlateinischen Bibel. Aus der Geschichte der lateinischen Bibel 7–8 (Freiburg, 1973–4), vol. 1, pp. 193–7.

[19] Souter, *Pelagius's Expositions*, vol. 1, pp. 333–9.

1

The Caricature of Pelagius' Teaching and its Disjunction from the Reality of Texts Written by Pelagius

There is a profound disjunction between, on the one hand, the account of both the tenets and the spirit of 'Pelagianism' disseminated by Pelagius' opponents and, on the other, what is found in Pelagius' writings.[1] Judging by his surviving writings, Pelagius taught only half of one of the fourteen tenets attributed to 'Pelagianism' by Augustine in his *On the Deeds of Pelagius* (*De gestis Pelagii*), and he did not express in writing anywhere the attitude of arrogance attributed to him. Furthermore, Augustine admitted openly in writing that he did not care whether or not Pelagius taught the tenets that he attributed to Pelagius. The disjunction between the caricature 'Pelagianism' promulgated by advocates of the triune and what is found in Pelagius' writings means that one of the respects in which the term 'Pelagianism' is unhistorical lies in the fact that it attaches Pelagius' name to what was a synthetic collocation of ideas that had almost no connection to Pelagius. Thus the term is misleading in the respect that it falsely associates Pelagius with these tenets and makes him their originator. François-Joseph Thonnard observed that Augustine made full use of all the devices of rhetoric in order to make his case.[2] All the participants in the controversy were the products of training in rhetoric.

---

[1] O. Wermelinger, 'Neuere Forschungskontroversen um Augustinus und Pelagius', in *Internationales Symposion über den Stand der Augustinus-Forschung. Vom 12. bis 16. April 1987 im Schloß Rauischholzhausen der Justus-Liebig-Universität Gießen*, ed. C. Mayer and K. H. Chelius (Würzburg, 1989), pp. 189–91.

[2] F.-J. Thonnard, 'Saint Jean Chrysostome et Saint Augustin dans la Controverse Pélagienne', *Revue des Études Byzantines* 25 (1967), pp. 199–200, wrote of Augustine: 'His method ... is that of the perfect rhetorician, putting all the resources of his art at the service of the defence of the catholic faith'; 'Sa méthode .... C'est celle d'un parfait rhéteur mettant toutes les ressources de son art au service de la défense de la foi catholique'. François Refoulé noted: 'The extremely free way in which Augustine uses his opponents' writings'; 'La façon extrêmement libre dont Augustin utilise les écrits de ses adversaires': 'Datation du Premier Concile de Carthage Contre les Pélagiens et du *Libellus fidei de Rufin*', *Revue des Études Augustiniennes* 9 (1963), p. 47.

A selection of tenets was attributed to what was identified as 'Pelagianism' by its opponents. Several contemporary lists of propositions survive.[3] The most comprehensive list of tenets is the one given by Augustine in his *On the Deeds of Pelagius*, and its compendious character makes it the most relevant for this survey. In this, Augustine listed fourteen tenets which he presented as constituting 'Pelagianism':

> Which [propositions] the bishops said that Pelagius rejected and condemned as opposed to the truth. The whole of this heresy is, after all, found here .... Which Pelagius replied were not in his books nor had he ever said such things, and he anathematized those who thought such things not as heretics, but as fools ....

1. Adam was created mortal so that he was going to die, whether he sinned or not.
2. The sin of Adam harmed him alone and not the whole human race.
3. The law leads to heaven in the same way as the Gospel.
4. Newborn infants are in the same state as Adam before his transgression.
5. The whole human race does not die through the death or transgression of Adam, and the whole human race does not rise through the resurrection of Christ.
6. Even if they are not baptised, infants possess eternal life.
7. If wealthy persons who have been baptised do not renounce all their possessions, they have no merit, even if they seem to do something good, and they will not possess the kingdom of heaven.
8. God's grace and help is not given for individual actions, but consists in free will and the law and teaching.
9. God's grace is given in accord with our merits, and for this reason grace itself is located in the human will, whether one becomes worthy of it or unworthy.
10. Only those people can be called children of God who have become entirely without sin.
11. Forgetfulness and ignorance are not sinful, because they do not come about willingly, but necessarily.
12. A choice is not free if it needs the help of God, since everyone has their own will either to do something or not to do it.
13. Our victory is not the result of God's help, but of free will.
14. From Peter's statement: *We are sharers in the divine nature* [2 Pet. 1:4], it follows that the soul can be as sinless as God.[4]

---

[3] For example, another list is given in the canons of the Council of Carthage (1 May AD 418): *Concilium Carthaginense A. 418* (ed. Munier, CCSL 149, pp. 67–78).

[4] Augustine, *De gestis Pelagii* 35.65 (ed. Urba and Zycha, CSEL 42, pp. 119–21), 'Quae illum contraria reprobare et anathematizare dixerunt. In hoc enim potius tota haeresis ista consistit .... Quae ille neque in libris suis esse neque talia umquam se dixisse respondit et eos qui talia saperent non tamquam haereticos, sed tamquam stultos anathematizauit ....

   1.   Adam mortalem factum, qui siue peccaret siue non peccaret, moriturus esset.
   2.   Quod peccatum Adae ipsum solum laeserit et non genus humanum.
   3.   Quod lex sic mittat ad regnum, quemadmodum et Euangelium.
   4.   Quod infantes nuper nati in illo statu sint, in quo Adam fuit ante praeuaricationem.
   5.   Quod neque per mortem uel praeuaricationem Adae omne genus hominum moriatur, neque per resurrectionem Christi omne genus hominum resurgat.
   6.   Quod infantes, etsi non baptizentur, habeant uitam aeternam.
   7.   Quod diuites baptizati, nisi omnibus abrenuntient, si quid boni uisi fuerint facere, non eis reputetur neque regnum Dei posse habere.

Only one part of one of these fourteen tenets is attested in the surviving writings of Pelagius. Each proposition will be taken in turn, and evidence will be presented from Pelagius' writings to show whether or not he asserted it.

1. 'Adam was created mortal so that he was going to die, whether he sinned or not.'

In *On Virginity*, Pelagius referred explicitly to the fact that Adam died as a result of his sin. In a discussion of how failure to obey God's positive as well as his negative injunctions would incur punishment, Pelagius wrote:

> For I do not want you to flatter yourself on the grounds that there are some things that you have not done, since it is written: *Whoever keeps the whole law but fails in one point has become guilty of all of it* [Jas. 2:10]. Adam sinned once, and died: do you suppose that you can live, when you are frequently committing the very act which killed another, though he had perpetrated it only once? Or do you suppose that he had committed a great crime, because of which he was deservedly condemned to undergo a more severe punishment? Let us see then what it was he did: he ate of the fruit of the tree contrary to the commandment given to him. What then? Did God punish a man with death because of the fruit from a tree? No, not because of fruit from a tree but because of his rejection of a commandment.[5]

Pelagius then repeated the idea that Adam's sin caused his death. After a list of divine commandments, he concluded that if his addressee did not observe them all, then God would reject him:

> If you reject him in any respect, if he spared Adam, God will spare you also. Indeed there would have been greater reason for him to spare Adam, who was still ignorant

---

8. Quod gratia Dei et adiutorium non ad singulos actus detur, sed in libero arbitrio sit et in lege atque doctrina.
9. Quod Dei gratia secundum merita nostra detur et propterea et ipsa gratia in hominis sit posita uoluntate, siue dignus fiat siue indignus.
10. Quod filii Dei non possunt uocari, nisi omnino absque peccato fuerint effecti.
11. Quod obliuio et ignorantia non subiacet peccato, quoniam non eueniant secundum uoluntatem, sed secundum necessitatem.
12. Quod non sit liberum arbitrium, si indigeat auxilio Dei, quoniam propriam uoluntatem habeat unusquisque aut facere aliquid aut non facere.
13. Quod uictoria nostra ex Dei non sit adiutorio, sed ex libero arbitrio.
14. Quod ex illo, quod ait Petrus: *Diuinae nos esse consortes naturae* [2 Pet. 1:4] consequens sit, ut ita possit esse anima sine peccato quemadmodum Deus.'
[5] Pelagius, *De uirginitate* 7.2 (ed. Halm, CSEL 1, pp. 232–3), 'Nolo enim tibi in hoc tibi blandiaris, si aliqua non feceris; quia aliqua feceris cum scriptum sit: *Qui uniuersam legem seruauerit, offendat autem in uno, factus est omnium reus* [Jas. 2:10]. Adam enim semel peccauit, et mortuus est: et tu te uiuere posse existimas, illud saepe committens, quod alium cum semel perpetrasset, occidit? An grande illum commisisse crimen putas, unde merito poena damnatus sit acriore? Videamus ergo quid fecerit: contra mandatum de fructu arboris edit. Quid ergo? Propter arboris fructum Deus hominem morte multauit? Non propter arboris fructum, sed propter mandati contemptum.'

and inexperienced, and did not have the example of anyone who had previously sinned, and died for his sin, to deter him.[6]

In *On the Divine Law*, Pelagius wrote that Adam was punished for his sin:

> Thus Adam, after enjoying familiarity and conversation with God, easily believed the devil when the devil seduced him, and as a result, overcome by desire for one apple, lost Paradise; and because he presumed to possess one good thing through transgression, he lost many good things at the same time .... I ask you, after so many proofs and so many deaths, whence grows in us this feeling of immunity from punishment for our sin?[7]

2. 'The sin of Adam harmed him alone and not the whole human race.'

Pelagius wrote that Adam's transgression damaged all his descendants:

> So I want you to know in full what I believe that you already know in part, that our Lord, the word of God, came down from heaven for this reason, so that through his assumption of our human nature, the human race, which was lying prostrate since the time of Adam, might be raised up in Christ; and the new man rewarded for his obedience with a salvation as great as the destruction that befell the old man through disobedience.[8]

Pelagius taught that Adam's sin established for his descendants an example and habit of sin so strong that it almost seemed part of human nature.[9] In this way it indeed harmed all his descendants. This was why it was important to remind people that inclination to sin was not, in fact, innate. By contrast, Augustine taught that Adam's sin damaged human nature, and all humans inherited 'original sin' (*peccatum originale*) from Adam, transmitted through the procreative act.

---

[6] Pelagius, *De uirginitate* 7.3 (ed. Halm, CSEL 1, p. 234), 'Quem si in aliquo contempseris, si pepercit Adae, parcet et tibi. Immo illi magis parcendum fuerat, adhuc rudis et novellus erat, et nullius ante peccantis et propter peccatum suum morientis retrahebatur exemplo.'

[7] Pelagius, *De diuina lege* 4.4 (ed. Migne, PL 30.109C–D), 'Sic Adam cum diabolo facile credidit seducenti, post familiaritatem et colloquium Dei, unius pomi cupiditate superatus, perdidit paradisum, et quia per transgressionem unum habere praesumpsit, multa simul bona amisit .... Rogo post tot documenta et tot mortes, unde in nobis crescit impunitas delinquendi?'

[8] Pelagius, *De diuina lege* 1.1 (ed. Migne, PL 30.105D), 'Ad plenum ergo te scire cupio, quod ex parte nosse te credo, ob hoc Dominum et Dei uerbum descendisse de caelis, ut assumpto naturae nostrae homine, humanum genus, quod ab Adam iacebat, erigeretur in Christo; tantumque nouo homini per obedientiam praestaretur salutis, quantum ueteri per inobedientiam perditionis acciderat.' See also Pelagius, *Ad Demetriadem* 8 (ed. Greshake, p. 84), 'Long habituation to sinning drew a sort of darkness over human reason'; 'Humanae rationi uelut quandam caliginem, longus peccandi usus obduxit'.

[9] Pelagius, *Ad Demetriadem* 8 (ed. Greshake, p. 84), 'Nor is there any other cause that creates our difficulty in living well other than the long habit of doing wrong which has infected us from childhood and corrupted us little by little over many years, and ever after holds us in bondage and addiction to itself, in such a way that it seems to have acquired the force of nature'; 'Neque uero alia causa nobis quoque difficultatem bene uiuendi facit, quam longa consuetudo uitiorum, quae nos, cum inficit a paruo, paulatimque per multos corrupit annos, ita postea obligatos sibi et addictos tenet, ut uim quandam uideatur habere naturae.'

3. 'The law leads to heaven in the same way as the Gospel.'

Pelagius was clear that the Gospel led to salvation much more than the law, since after Christ's coming mankind were 'under grace' (*sub gratia*). He argued that if men were able to lead holy and righteous lives before Christ's advent, then it had to be possible for men to do so after Christ's coming:

> How much more must we believe that we are able to do this after the light of his coming, we who have been renewed through the grace of Christ and reborn as better men; we who have been purified and cleansed by his blood, roused by his example to pursue more perfect righteousness, we ought to be better than those who lived before the time of the law, better even than those who lived under the law, as the Apostle says: *Sin will have no dominion over you. For you are not under the law but under grace* [Rom. 6:14].[10]

Pelagius also made this clear in *On the Divine Law*:

> Because the present time of grace is different, in which the fullness of perfection has arrived; the time of the law was different, the time of the prophets was not the same as now, as the Lord says: *You have heard that it was said to the men of old* [Matt. 5:21], that they should not kill, but I give you more perfect commandments, which the reader will find set forth in order in their appointed place in the Gospel. For from the time when the son of God became the son of man, from the time when the old leaven of the Jewish tradition was made the new scattering, from the time when the lamb is eaten not metaphorically but in truth, from the time when according to the Apostle: *The old things have passed away and all things are made new* [2 Cor. 5:17], from the time when it was commanded to set aside the image of earthly man and take up the form of the heavenly man, since that time, having died with him, we live, and by his power we have risen again in Christ alongside him.[11]

Pelagius paired the teachings of the law with the Gospels suggesting that both of them were required in order to achieve righteousness (*iustitia*).[12] He also

---

[10] Pelagius, *Ad Demetriadem* 8 (ed. Greshake, p. 86), 'Quanto magis post illustrationem aduentus eius nos id posse credendum est, qui instaurati per Christi gratiam et in meliorem hominem renati sumus, qui sanguine eius expiati atque mundati, ipsiusque exemplo ad perfectiorem incitati iustitiam meliores illis esse debemus, qui ante legem fuerunt, meliores etiam, quam fuerunt sub lege, dicente Apostolo: *Peccatum in uobis non dominabitur, non enim sub lege estis, sed sub gratia* [Rom. 6:14].'

[11] Pelagius, *De diuina lege* 10.2 (ed. Migne, PL 30.116B–C), 'Quia aliud nunc tempus gratiae, in quo plenitudo perfectionis aduenit; aliud fuit legis, aliud prophetarum, dicente Domino: *Audistis quia dictum est antiquis* [Matt. 5:21], ne occiderent, ego autem perfectiora praecipio, quae in ordine Euangelii digesta suo loco lector inueniet. Ex quo enim filius Dei, filius hominis factus est, ex quo uetus fermentum Iudaicae traditionis est factum noua conspersio, ex quo agnus non in figura, sed in ueritate comeditur, ex quo secundum Apostolum: *Vetera transierunt, et facta sunt omnia noua* [2 Cor. 5:17], ex quo iussum est imaginem terreni hominis deponere, et assumere formam caelestis, ex eo commortui uiuimus, et uirtutibus consurreximus in Christo.'

[12] Pelagius, *De uirginitate* 8.2 (ed. Halm, CSEL 1, p. 234), where Pelagius warned against un-Christian behaviour: 'If they either say or think anything improper against the teachings of the law and the apostles'; 'Si contra legalia et apostolica instituta indecens aliquid aut loquantur aut cogitent'.

asserted: 'Indeed anything that goes against the Gospel of Christ is unrighteous'.[13] Furthermore, it was axiomatic in Pelagius' writings that imitation of Christ saved Christians, and this made them dependent on the teachings of the Gospels.[14]

4. 'Newborn infants are in the same state as Adam before his transgression.'

The idea that newborn infants were in the same state as Adam before his sin is not asserted in Pelagius' surviving writings. The only evidence that Pelagius taught that infants did not require baptism comes from the accusations of his opponents. They read into his assertion of the goodness of human nature the entailment that infants were in the same state as Adam before his transgression. They then drew from this the further entailment that Pelagius taught that infants did not require baptism, on the grounds that the idea that infants lacked sin deprived the sacrament of infant baptism of any purpose.

Pelagius' response to this accusation when it was put to him at a synod was to deny that he had made the statement and to anathematise it.[15] In his *Statement of Faith*, composed as part of his defence for his third trial, he asserted that baptism was necessary and should use the same wording for infants as for adults.[16] This perhaps looks like a response to this hostile entailment being read into his defence of the goodness of human nature. This tenet therefore reveals the degree to which a bogus set of statements were attributed to Pelagius and made synonymous with his name. Both tenets 4 and 6 in Augustine's list of the constituent theses of 'Pelagianism' refer to this one issue, and this doctrine has been attributed by many scholars to Pelagius and taken as a defining tenet of 'Pelagianism', which shows how far understanding of Pelagius' teaching has been determined by his opponents' account of it.[17] The fact that in his surviving writings Pelagius only mentioned infants in his *Statement of Faith* after he had been accused of heresy for denying the need for infant baptism suggests that he was responding to a criticism of his teaching. This was an example of how the polemical context determined the

---

[13] Pelagius, *De uirginitate* 17.2 (ed. Halm, CSEL 1, p. 248), 'Iniustum quippe est quicquid contra Christi Euangelium uenit'.

[14] Pelagius, *De uirginitate* 7.3 (ed. Halm, CSEL 1, p. 233), 'Humble and gentle, you should live by the example of Christ'; 'Humilis ac mitis Christi uiua exemplo'.

[15] Augustine, *De gestis Pelagii* 11.24 (ed. Urba and Zycha, CSEL 42, pp. 77–8). See also Pelagius' statement quoted by Augustine: Augustine, *De gratia Christi et de peccato originali* 2.19.21 (ed. Urba and Zych, CSEL 42, p. 181), '"Who is so impious as to forbid the common redemption of the human race to an infant of any age?"'; 'Quis ille tam impius est, qui cuiuslibet aetatis paruulo interdicat communem humani generis redemptionem?'

[16] Pelagius, *Libellus fidei* 7 (ed. Migne, PL 45.1718), 'We believe in one baptism, which we say must be celebrated using the same wording of the sacrament for infants as is used for adults also'; 'Baptisma unum tenemus, quod iisdem sacramenti uerbis in infantibus, quibus etiam in maioribus, asserimus esse celebrandum.'

[17] B. R. Rees, *Pelagius. Life and Letters*, 2 vols (Woodbridge, 1998), vol. I, pp. 77–81; R. F. Evans, *Pelagius. Inquiries and Reappraisals* (London, 1968), pp. 118–19.

nature of the debate, which proceeded through accusation and counter-accusation. Pelagius stressed the importance of baptism as a sacrament of cleansing from sin and second birth. It was a hostile entailment read into his writings to suggest that this might make more sense for an adult than for an infant, and once again a doctrine that Pelagius did not assert was attributed to his writings.

Caelestius was a Christian from a noble family who was linked to Pelagius by Pelagius' opponents through their description of Caelestius as Pelagius' 'pupil' (*discipulus*).[18] He was tried for heresy three years before Pelagius, at an ecclesiastical council held in Carthage in North Africa, on charges similar to those later levelled against Pelagius. According to the account of some of the proceedings of the council, included by Augustine in his *On the Grace of Christ and on Original Sin*, Caelestius appears to have raised the issue of infants as a way to attack the notion of original sin, by drawing out a consequence of the doctrine which might offend peoples' sense of justice and thus turn them against the idea (because it entailed that God condemned infants to hell).[19] While Augustine could see malign intent in babies, others found the idea of evil in infants at best counter-intuitive and at worst a damaging idea.[20] Caelestius' move was then countered by adducing an entailment from the assertion of the goodness of human nature, that if infants lacked sin then infant baptism would have no purpose, since there would be no sins to remit; and this was then turned into the accusation that Pelagius denied infant baptism.

However, Pelagius asserted the good of human nature because he believed that in order to encourage Christians to moral behaviour he had to convince them that it was within their capacity and depended only on their choosing it. Thus he offered his critique of the idea of original sin through a positive presentation of his own perspective and not through attacking the position of his opponents. Brynley Rees pointed out that in the surviving fragments of the writings of Julian of Aeclanum, a Christian who wrote texts opposing aspects of the triune after Pelagius' condemnation, there is a justification of infant baptism that does not depend on the existence of original sin.[21] As things stand, there is no way of knowing what Pelagius' understanding was of the reasons for infant baptism. What is clear is that he did not deny the need for it, and that tenets 4 and 6 were entailments read into his writings with hostile intent, that are possible, but not necessary, entailments of Pelagius' assertion of the goodness of human nature.

[18] Caelestius' noble birth and pupil of Pelagius: Marius Mercator, *Commonitorium lectori aduersum haeresim Pelagii et Caelestii* (ed. Schwartz, *ACO* 1.5.3, p. 6).

[19] The record preserved by Augustine of some of the proceedings of the Council of Carthage (held late in AD 411 or early in AD 412) offers an account of Caelestius' answers to questions put to him: Augustine, *De gratia Christi et de peccato originali* 2.3.3–4 (ed. Urba and Zycha, CSEL 42, pp. 168–9).

[20] Augustine, *Confessiones* 1.7.11 (ed. Verheijen and Skutella, CCSL 27, p. 6).

[21] Rees, *Pelagius* vol. I, pp. 79–80.

5. 'The whole human race does not die through the death or transgression of Adam, and the whole human race does not rise through the resurrection of Christ.'

Pelagius wrote that the example of sin that Adam established caused mankind to die spiritually, and Christ raised mankind from this destruction.[22] He also wrote that Christians were saved through the cleansing of Christ's passion: 'God our Lord and Saviour, when he thought fit to take manhood upon himself for the sake of the salvation of the human race'.[23]

6. 'Even if they are not baptised, infants possess eternal life.'

As discussed with regard to tenet 4, the issue of unbaptised infants possessing eternal life is not dealt with in Pelagius' surviving writings. He drew a distinction between eternal life and the kingdom of heaven in so far as he wrote that there were many mansions in heaven, and that different levels of goodness would receive different levels of reward in the afterlife. This was expressed in his letters when he wrote about the vocation to virginity, and it appears to have been intended as a means to differentiate the special reward given those who dedicated themselves as virgins.[24] It would perhaps have afforded room somewhere for unbaptised infants, but in his surviving writings Pelagius did not mention infants until he was accused of teaching something he had not written, which forced him to deny having written it, and to anathematise hostile entailments read into material he had not written—namely, alleged quotations from the writings of Caelestius.

7. 'If wealthy persons who have been baptised do not renounce all their possessions, they have no merit, even if they seem to do something good, and they will not possess the kingdom of heaven.'

There is no evidence that Pelagius taught that wealth was an impediment to achieving salvation. The reverse seems to be the case. When he wrote a letter of advice to the young Roman patrician girl Demetrias about how to live a life dedicated to following Christ's injunctions, at no point did he advise her to distribute

---

[22] Pelagius, *De diuina lege* 1.1 (ed. Migne, PL 30.105D), see n. 8.

[23] Pelagius, *De uirginitate* 3 (ed. Halm, CSEL 1, p. 227), 'Dominus et Saluator noster Deus, cum propter humani generis salutem hominem dignaretur adsumere'. See also Pelagius, *Ad Demetriadem* 8 (ed. Greshake, p. 86), concerning Christ our Lord and Saviour, '[We] who have been purified and cleansed by his blood'; '[Nos] qui sanguine eius expiati atque mundati'; Pelagius, *De diuina lege* 4.2 (ed. Migne, PL 30.109A), 'Those ... who have been redeemed by Christ's passion'; 'Qui ... Christi passione redempti sunt'.

[24] Pelagius, *Ad Demetriadem* 17 (ed. Greshake, p. 118), 'In the kingdom of heaven there are different dwelling-places according to an individual's merit'; 'Dispares sunt in regno coelorum pro singulorum merito mansiones.'

her fortune to the poor, nor did he establish poverty as a future goal, nor did he denigrate her wealth.[25] When Pelagius wrote a letter of advice to Celantia, a Roman matron, he did not tell her to give away her wealth. Nowhere in his surviving writings did Pelagius advise anyone that they should give away their property. With regard to the ability of the rich to enter heaven, he did not suggest either to Celantia or to Demetrias that they should in any way diminish their wealth as he set out for them how they should live in order to reach heaven. He was explicit in his letter to Demetrias that everyone in every station in life was called to righteousness and could thereby attain eternal life: 'In the matter of righteousness we all of us owe one obligation: virgin, widow, married woman, a person in the highest station in life, the middle station, or the lowest rank, all are commanded equally to fulfil the commands.'[26] Pelagius told Demetrias that she could expect to enter the kingdom of heaven if she maintained her virtuous behaviour, and, since his advice was explicitly predicated on her living within her ancestral household, he was clearly not suggesting that she had to embrace poverty in order to enter the kingdom of heaven. Access to every area in the kingdom of heaven would be determined by how closely a person had imitated Christ, but nowhere did Pelagius suggest that poverty was part of that imitation.

What Pelagius did do was seek to downgrade the social status of wealth. He sought to elevate spiritual riches above material wealth by asserting that they had a more real value because they determined attainment of and status within the kingdom of heaven. In his letters of advice he redefined nobility as spiritual and unrelated to nobility of birth. In his rejection of earthly social status, Pelagius condemned the social order in strong words: 'It was not the equality of nature that was responsible for worldly nobility but the ambition of greed.'[27] This is the only sentence in Pelagius' surviving writings reminiscent of the anonymous tract *On Riches* (*De diuitiis*) in the Caspari Corpus, which took

---

[25] Demetrias was a young girl from one of the most powerful patrician families in Rome, the Anicii. In around AD 413 her family commissioned Pelagius to write a letter of advice and encouragement to her on the occasion of her dedication of herself to a life of ascetic renunciation.

[26] Pelagius, *Ad Demetriadem* 10 (ed. Greshake, p. 92), 'In causa iustitiae unum debemus omnes, uirgo, uidua, nupta, summus, medius et imus gradus aequaliter iubentur implere praecepta.' Pelagius repeatedly made it clear that righteousness led to eternal life: *Ad Demetriadem* 11–12 (ed. Greshake, p. 100), 'For he wants us always to be hungering and thirsting for righteousness here, so that in the future we may receive satisfaction from the repayment for our righteousness .... This must be said to all universally who desire the promises of eternal life'; 'Vult enim nos esurire hic semper ac sitire iustitiam, ut in futuro iustitiae retributione satiemur .... Hoc omnibus in commune dicendum est, qui immortalis uitae promissa desiderant.' Pelagius, *Ad Celantiam* 2 (ed. Hilberg, CSEL 56, p. 330), 'Having learnt the Lord's will, surrounded by worldly honour and the allurements of riches, you may come to love the moral values that belong to you more, and so that established in your marriage, you may be able to please not only your husband, but also him who allowed marriage itself'; 'Cognita Domini uoluntate inter honorem saeculi et diuitiarum illecebras, morum magis diligas suppellectilem atque ut possis in coniugio constituta non solum coniugi placere sed etiam ei, qui ipsum coniugium indulsit.'

[27] Pelagius, *De uirginitate* 16.1 (ed. Halm, CSEL 1, p. 246), 'Mundanam nobilitatem non naturae aequitas praestitit, sed cupiditatis ambitio.'

a dim view of wealth.[28] In his comment, however, Pelagius cast a critical eye on secular nobility, not wealth per se. Pelagius wrote this comment in a letter to the unknown addressee of *On Virginity*, clearly not a girl of patrician stock.[29]

If other Christian writers, animated by enthusiasm for ascetic values, extended critique of worldly status to include criticism of wealth per se, that does not imply that Pelagius did so. Once again, the tenet listed by Augustine cannot be found in Pelagius' surviving writings.

8. 'God's grace and help is not given for individual actions, but consists in free will and the law and teaching.'

As already noted, in Christian literature the word 'grace' could be used to refer to any gift from God. It is useful here to set out some of the different aspects of God's grace to which reference is made in Christian texts from this period. At least seven possible aspects of God's grace were referred to. First, there was the grace of creation, which included man's endowment with free will; the extent of this free will was at issue, whether it was free will to evil only, or 'dual' or 'effective' free will—that is, to virtue as well as to sin.[30] Second, the grace of God's teaching was

---

[28] The Caspari Corpus refers to six letters published by Carl Paul Caspari in 1890, which he explicitly identified as 'Pelagian'. No consensus has emerged about the authorship of the letters (or about whether one or more authors composed them).

[29] Pelagius, *De uirginitate* 14 (ed. Halm, CSEL 1, p. 244), 'Acquaint yourself with how the daughters of nobles of this world conduct themselves, with the manners which they are accustomed to show and the disciplines with which they train themselves .... So you too think about your origin, consider your lineage, pay attention to the honour of your noble stock. Recognise that you are not only the daughter of a man but the daughter of God as well, graced with the nobility of divine birth'; 'Cognosce quomodo huius saeculi nobilium filiae se gerant, quibus adsuescant moribus, quibusue se disciplinis instituant .... Et tu ergo originem tuam respice, genus intuere, gloriam nobilitatis aduerte. Agnosce te non hominis tantum, sed et Dei filiam et diuinae natiuitatis nobilitate decoratam.'

[30] Augustine's later position, which he came to after he composed his *On Free Will* (*De libero arbitrio*) and which differed from the position expressed in *On Free Will*, was that man always had free will to evil, but God caused all human virtue. Augustine argues that man always has free will to evil: Augustine, *De gratia et libero arbitrio* 2.4 (ed. Chéné and Pintard, BA 24, p. 100), 'Therefore let no one blame God in his heart, but let everyone blame himself when he sins'; 'Nemo ergo Deum causetur in corde suo, sed sibi imputet quisque, cum peccat.' Augustine argues that God causes all human virtue: Augustine, *Ep.* 194.3.9 (ed. Goldbacher, CSEL 57, p. 183), 'It remains, I say, that the faith itself, from whence all righteousness takes its beginning, on account of which it is said to the Church in the Song of Songs: *You will come and you will pass through from the beginning of faith* [S. of S. 4, LXX]; it remains, I repeat, that we not attribute faith itself to the human will, which they extol, or to any preceding merits, because any good merits there are begin from faith, but rather that we admit that it is a gratuitous gift of God, if we have in mind true grace, that is, without any merits'; 'Restat igitur ut ipsam fidem unde omnis iustitia sumit initium, propter quod dicitur ad Ecclesiam in Cantico canticorum: *Venies et pertransies ab initio fidei* [S. of S. 4, LXX]; restat, inquam, ut ipsam fidem non humano, quod isti extollunt, tribuamus arbitrio, nec ullis praecedentibus meritis, quoniam inde incipiunt bona quaecumque sunt merita; sed gratuitum Dei donum esse fateamur, si gratiam ueram, id est sine meritis, cogitemus'; *Ep.* 194.5.19 (ed. Goldbacher, CSEL 57, p. 190), 'And so what is the merit of man before grace, by which merit he receives grace, since only grace produces in us every good merit of ours and since, when God crowns our merits, he only crowns his own gifts?'; 'Quod est ergo meritum hominis ante gratiam, quo merito percipiat

regularly referred to, which included all Scripture and Christ's example. Since they were gifts from God, all of these things could be described as God's grace. Third, there was the grace of Christ's passion which washed away the sins of mankind. This gift was made available to man in a fourth aspect of grace, the grace of the sacrament of baptism, as demonstrated by Pelagius' use of the term 'grace' to refer to baptism in *On Virginity*.[31] Fifth, there was the grace of salvation. Sixth, the word 'grace' was used to describe an individual gift given by God, such as that of healing, eloquence or wisdom. Seventh, there was prevenient grace, which consisted of the Holy Spirit pouring into a person to cause them to love virtue and to choose it.

The implicit assumption within tenet 8, however, was that there was only one correct interpretation of the word 'grace', which was an absolute form of prevenient grace; and further, that all Christians had to subscribe to this interpretation of grace and the absolute prevenience of God's grace in causing all their good actions. Augustine's view of grace was that it was always a free gift; if grace was given in return for anything at all then it simply was not grace, which was by his definition always gratuitous. Augustine derived this interpretation of *gratia* from the Latin word *gratis*, meaning free, on the basis of biblical citations that made this connection.[32] This interpretation of the word *gratia* diverged from everyday

---

gratiam, cum omne bonum meritum nostrum non in nobis faciat nisi gratia et, cum Deus coronat merita nostra, nihil aliud coronet quam munera sua?'; Augustine, *De correptione et gratia* 11.32 (ed. Chéné and Pintard, BA 24, p. 342), 'Of course it happens in us, through this grace of God for receiving the good and for holding onto it with perseverance, not only that we are able to do what we want, but also that we want what we are able to do'; 'Fit quippe in nobis per hanc Dei gratiam in bono recipiendo et perseueranter tenendo, non solum posse quod uolumus, uerum etiam uelle quod possumus'; Augustine, *De praedestinatione sanctorum* 21.43 (ed. Chéné and Pintard, BA 24, p. 596), 'As long as they admit that, albeit at much greater length than they wanted, albeit to the distaste and boredom of those with understanding, we did what we have done, that is, we have taught that even the beginning of faith, just like continence, patience, righteousness, piety and the other things ... is the gift of God'; 'Dum tamen etsi multo diutius quam uellent, etsi cum fastidio ac taedio intelligentium, fateantur nos fecisse quod fecimus, id est, etiam initium fidei, sicut continentiam, patientiam, iustitiam, pietatem, et caetera ... donum Dei esse docuisse.' Augustine argues that God controls human wills: Augustine, *De gratia et libero arbitrio* 20.41 (ed. Chéné and Pintard, BA 24, p. 184), 'If divine Scripture is examined carefully, it shows that not only the good wills of men which God himself makes out of bad ones and which, once made good by him, He directs towards good acts and towards eternal life, but also those wills which preserve what is created of the world, are in the power of God in such a way that He causes them to be inclined where He wants, when He wants, either to offer benefits to some or to impose punishments on others, just as He himself judges, according to a judgement that is indeed most hidden, but is without doubt most just'; 'Scriptura diuina si diligenter inspiciatur, ostendit non solum bonas hominum uoluntates quas ipse facit ex malis, et a se factas bonas in actus bonos et in aeternam dirigit uitam, uerum etiam illas quae conseruant saeculi creaturam, ita esse in Dei potestate, ut eas quo uoluerit, quando uoluerit, faciat inclinari, uel ad beneficia quibusdam praestanda, uel ad poenas quibusdam ingerendas, sicut ipse iudicat, occultissimo quidem iudicio, sed sine ulla dubitatione iustissimo.'

[31] Pelagius, *De uirginitate* 16.2 (ed. Halm, CSEL 1, p. 246), 'We are all made equal by the grace of the divine water'; 'Omnes per diuini lauacri gratiam aequales efficimur'.

[32] Augustine, *De natura et gratia* 4.4 (ed. Urba and Zycha, CSEL 60, p. 235), '[Christ's grace] is not given in return for merits, but is given for free; for this reason it is called grace. *They have been justified*, he says, *for free by the blood of Christ* [Rom. 3:24]'; '[Christi gratia] non meritis redditur, sed gratis datur; propter quod et gratia nominatur. *Iustificati*, inquit, *gratis per sanguinem ipsius* [Rom. 3:24].'

Roman secular usage in which *gratia* commonly meant favour, with an implication of mutual reciprocity. It diverged also from the meaning of *gratia* in texts associated with Roman law. Jill Harries documented how in legal usage *gratia* was a 'morally ambivalent concept' which had negative connotations in which 'favour' meant favouritism or improper influence, and referred to a type of injustice.[33]

Examination of Pelagius' writings shows that he referred to other aspects of God's grace besides free will, the law and teaching. For example, he referred to Christ's passion wiping away mankind's sins as grace and to the help of God's grace, and he was clear that grace was something that Christians received over and above instruction and example: 'What can Christians do, whose nature has been renewed in a better condition by Christ, and who are assisted by the aid of divine grace as well?'[34] Pelagius also referred to the 'help of the Holy Spirit' (*auxilium Sancti Spiritus*).[35]

In a passage in Pelagius' *On Free Will* (*De libero arbitrio*) quoted by Augustine, Pelagius wrote of God's daily help, but Augustine refused to accept the statement and read into it an account of grace that did not describe the action of the Holy Spirit causing goodness but a grace that merely made goodness more easily achieved:

> 'But although we have free will within us that is so strong', he says, 'and so steadfast for avoiding sin, which the creator implanted in human nature universally, again on account of his inestimable kindness we are defended daily by his own help'. What need is there of this help, if free will is so strong, so steadfast for avoiding sin? But even here he wants the help to be understood as for this purpose, that the thing may be done more easily through grace, which, even if less easily, he nevertheless thinks may be done without grace.[36]

It is noteworthy that Pelagius here offered a compromise with Augustine's stress on the constant need for God's grace by specifically referring to 'daily help' (*auxilium cotidianum*).

Three patrician Romans who were living as ascetics in Palestine—Melania the Younger, her mother Albina and her husband Pinianus—wrote to Augustine in AD 418 apparently to try to persuade him to have the charges against Pelagius

---

[33] J. D. Harries, *Law and Empire in Late Antiquity* (Cambridge, 1999), pp. 163–6. Harries offered a clear example of the negative sense of *gratia* in her reference (p. 203, n. 43) to Ambrose, *De officiis* 2.24.125 (ed. Davidson, p. 336), in which Ambrose commented of bishops' hearings: 'Partiality should be entirely absent; the merits of the case should determine the judgement'; 'Gratia absit, causae merita decernant.'

[34] Pelagius, *Ad Demetriadem* 3 (ed. Greshake, p. 66), 'Quid Christiani facere possunt, quorum in melius per Christum instaurata natura est, et qui diuinae quoque gratiae iuuantur auxilio.'

[35] Pelagius, *Ad Demetriadem* 25 (ed. Greshake, p. 152).

[36] Augustine, *De gratia Christi et de peccato originali* 1.28.29 (ed. Urba and Zycha, CSEL 42, pp. 148–9), '"Cum autem tam forte", inquit, "tam firmum ad non peccandum liberum in nobis habeamus arbitrium, quod generaliter naturae humanae creator inseruit, rursus pro inaestimabili eius benignitate cotidiano ipsius munimur auxilio". Quid opus est hoc auxilio, si tam forte, tam firmum est ad non peccandum liberum arbitrium? Sed etiam hic uult intellegi ad hoc esse auxilium, ut facilius fiat per gratiam, quod etsi minus facile tamen putat fieri praeter gratiam.'

dropped. In his reply to them, Augustine referred to their report of a visit they had made to Pelagius, when Pelagius had repeated his assertion of the need for daily help and made the further concession that God's grace was needed for every action:

> You wrote to me that you had conferred with Pelagius, so that he condemned in writing whatever was said against him, and so that he said in your hearing: 'I anathematize anyone who thinks or says that the grace of God by which *Christ came into this world in order to save sinners* [1 Tim. 1:15] is not necessary, not only at every hour and at every moment, but also for every action of ours, and those who try to do away with this doctrine deserve eternal punishment.'[37]

The context of the meeting of Melania, Pinianus and Albina with Pelagius must have been the spring or summer of AD 418, after Pelagius had sent his written defence to Pope Innocent, which contained his *Statement of Faith*. In this statement, Pelagius still maintained, at the last hour in the face of excommunication, the irreducible minimum which he did not feel able to disavow—namely, the existence of human free will—but he chose compromise by adding a rider noting the constant need for God's help: 'We confess free will in such a way that we say that we always have need of God's help'.[38] These three pieces of evidence—the quotation from his *On Free Will*, the testimony of Melania, Pinianus and Albina, and Pelagius' assertion in his *Statement of Faith*—suggest that Pelagius was not uncompromisingly opposed to the doctrine that there was an aspect of God's grace that was required every day to help man to be virtuous. However, he felt the need also to confess free will alongside grace. This tenet therefore seems to be another case of a thesis being read into Pelagius' teaching which cannot be found in his writings, and which instead runs counter to the surviving textual evidence. Augustine's objection was that 'the grace of God by which *Christ came into this world in order to save sinners* [1 Tim. 1:15]' was not explicitly prevenient grace. Tenet 8 implicitly asserted that Augustine's interpretation was the only correct understanding of God's grace and its operation. It is nevertheless clear that what Pelagius was accused of publicly was not the real reason for his indictment, which was his assertion of the goodness of human nature and effective free will. The list of tenets could simply have contained these two principles. It did not do so because that would have made visible the true process at work in the accusation of heresy made against Pelagius.

---

[37] Augustine, *De gratia Christi et de peccato originali* 1.2.2 (ed. Urba and Zycha, CSEL 42, p. 125), 'Scripsistis mihi cum Pelagio uos egisse, ut quaecumque aduersus eum dicerentur scripto damnaret, eumque dixisse audientibus uobis: "Anathemo qui uel sentit uel dicit gratiam Dei, qua: *Christus uenit in hunc mundum peccatores saluos facere* [1 Tim. 1:15], non solum per singulas horas aut per singula momenta, sed etiam per singulos actus nostros non esse necessariam et qui hanc conantur auferre poenas sortiantur aeternas."'
[38] Pelagius, *Libellus fidei* 13 (ed. Migne, PL 45.1718), 'Liberum sic confitemur arbitrium, ut dicamus nos semper Dei indigere auxilio'.

Support for the idea that Pelagius sought compromise, and characterised the relationship between God's grace and man as one of co-operation, comes in his *On the Divine Law*. In this letter he directly addressed two points of doctrine involved in the controversy. In both cases his approach was cautious and inclined towards moderation. First, he discussed the criticism that stress on free will 'made grace ungrateful' (in the sense that God's grace would receive no thanks, *gratiam faciat ingratam*). Pelagius accurately identified the point Augustine was making in his criticism of him—namely, that it was necessary for man to remain grateful to God and to acknowledge God's gifts. Pelagius sought to answer this criticism directly:

> But someone will say: 'If everything is expected to come from our own efforts, then grace performs nothing'. I do not want anyone rashly and under the title of ignorance to make grace ungrateful, lest he should turn his faith into a stumbling-block and the cause of his salvation should be made into an occasion for his destruction. If reasoning about this thing is pursued with moderation, only then will it be an aid to life, reasoning which would perhaps have hurled him to his death through presumption. But grace indeed dismisses sins for free, but with the consent and the will of the believer.[39]

In this passage, Pelagius presented a model of co-operation. Grace here seems to encompass Christ's redemption of man's sins through his passion, which was another facet of God's grace (not mentioned in tenet 8), over and above aspects of grace such as man's created nature, the law, and Christ's teaching. Pelagius' characterisation of the process of achieving virtue identified two agents: God's grace and human will. The suggestion that Pelagius denied that God's grace was given for individual actions was something read into Pelagius' writings with hostile intent. Not mentioning something does not equate to denying it. The burden of the surviving evidence therefore suggests that Pelagius sought compromise as long as God's justice, founded on human responsibility, was maintained.

The second point of doctrine in the controversy that Pelagius addressed in *On the Divine Law* was predestination. Without using the word 'predestination' (*praedestinatio*), he raised the problem that if interpreted as preordainment it might preclude the universality of God's salvific will, an objection that many ecclesiastics in southern Gaul later held to be crucial:

---

[39] Pelagius, *De diuina lege* 2.2–3 (ed. Migne, PL 30.107A–B), 'Sed dicit aliquis: "Si totum ex nostro labore exspectatur, ergo gratia nihil praestat". Nolo quisquam ignorantiae titulo gratiam Dei temere faciat ingratam, ne fidem suam uertat in scandalum, et fiat ei causa salutis interitus et perditionis occasio. Cuius rei ratio si cum moderatione quaeratur, tum demum proficiet ad uitam, quae per praesumptionem forte praecipitasset ad mortem. Sed gratia quidem gratis peccata dimittit, sed cum consensu et uoluntate credentis.' The phrase *gratiam facit ingratam* showed that Pelagius understood the argument that it was important that man should never cease to be grateful to God. This passage in *On the Divine Law* was a direct response to Augustine's argument that grace had to be given free (*gratis*) for it to be grace: Augustine, *De gestis Pelagii* 14.33 (ed. Urba and Zycha, CSEL 42, p. 89), 'Since the name of grace itself and the meaning of its name is destroyed if it is not given gratuitously'; 'Ipsum quippe gratiae nomen et eius nominis intellectus aufertur, si non gratis datur'.

This first I want to ask you and to hear your answer, whoever you are that proposes this argument: if the choice is made by God himself, who also makes the calling, why did he want to call more when he was going to choose only a few out of the many? Surely out of the two called you want that one to hold his place whom God has appointed by his choice, and conversely the other to fall whom God does not protect by the power of his choice. But if this is how things are, on this account neither good nor bad actions belong to us, and the result will be that neither fault will be punished nor good deeds praised …. Secondly, if you consider to be saints only the few whom you say have been chosen, you say that those who have been called are reprobate; how then does the same apostle Paul summon *those called to be saints* at the start of his letters, as he does at the beginning of his book to the Romans, saying: *To all God's beloved in Rome, called to be saints* [Rom. 1:7]? If Christ died for a few, it is just that a few keep his commandments. But if all of us who believe receive the sacrament of his passion in baptism without discrimination, if all of us equally renounce the devil and the world, if to all of us who do not live rightly the punishment of hell is promised, then we ought all of us with the same diligence both to avoid what has been forbidden, and to fulfil his commandments.[40]

In this passage, Pelagius raised questions in a direct and reasoned manner, and avoided attacking his opponents. The passage suggests that there were two motivations behind his defence of free will: first, the desire to maintain the transparency of God's justice; second, the desire to maintain the message of God's universal salvific will. These could both be characterised as objections to exegetical interpretations of the Pauline Epistles that made prevenient grace absolute and omnipotent, and therefore interpreted predestination as preodainment rather than foreknowledge. Despite these concerns, Pelagius' writings show that he acknowledged the need for God's grace, even for individual actions; that he explicitly characterised one aspect of grace as the 'help of the Holy Spirit'; and that he proposed a synergistic model of the relationship between God's grace and human free will.

---

[40] Pelagius, *De diuina lege* 7.1 (ed. Migne, PL 30.112D–113A), 'Hoc primum quaerere a te et audire uolo, quisquis es qui ista proponis: si ipsius Dei electio est, cuius est et uocatio, quid uoluit plures uocare, qui paucos de pluribus erat electurus? Certe de duobus uocatis illum uis stare, quem Deus electione statuerit, et illum contra cadere, quem Deus electionis uirtute non muniat. Quod si ita est, nec bona ad nos pertinent hac ratione, nec mala; et sic erit, ut nec culpa poenam habeat, nec benefacta laudentur …. Deinde si paucos quos dicis electos, solos sanctos existimas, qui uocati sunt, reprobos dicis; quomodo idem apostolus Paulus in epistolarum suarum principiis *uocatos sanctos* uocat, sicut in fronte codicis ad Romanos loquitur, dicens: *Omnibus qui sunt Romae in caritate Dei uocatis sanctis* [Rom. 1:7]? Si pro paucis passus est Christus, iustum est, ut pauci mandata Christi custodiant. Si autem indiscrete omnes qui credimus, sacramentum in baptismo passionis accipimus, si omnes aequaliter renuntiamus diabolo et mundo, si omnibus haud recte uiuentibus gehennae poena promittitur, omnes debemus eadem diligentia et cauere prohibita, et explere praecepta.'

9. 'God's grace is given in accord with our merits, and for this reason grace itself is located in the human will, whether one becomes worthy or unworthy.'

This tenet comes closest to being something that Pelagius taught, since the first part of it—that God's grace was given in accord with merit—was something that Pelagius asserted: '[James] shows how we ought to resist the devil, if we are indeed servants of God, and by doing his will we may merit divine grace and may resist more easily the evil spirit with the help of the Holy Spirit.'[41] The additional statement attributed to him by his opponents—namely, that grace was therefore located in the will—was not something that Pelagius wrote, nor is it a necessary entailment of the idea that some aspects of grace might be merited.

In fact Pelagius frequently referred to several aspects of grace. Of the many possible referents of the word 'grace', the issue for Augustine was that Pelagius' references to it might not refer to Augustine's interpretation of the word, which for him was the most important aspect of grace. Prevenient grace was inextricably bound to its twin, predestination interpreted as preordainment. Augustine described prevenient grace and predestination as two stages in one process.[42] Both were causally tied to original sin because original sin made human nature so weak that it was unable to choose virtue unaided, and on every occasion it required prevenient grace to cause it to choose virtuous action. Thus these three doctrines formed a mutually dependent triune. So closely bound together were they that although it is possible to separate out two questions at issue—namely, whether human virtue was caused by man's effective free will or by prevenient grace or by some combination of the two, and whether human nature was innately capable of goodness or inherently inclined toward sin as a result of damage done to it by Adam's transgression—they could also reasonably be described as one question, at base. Augustine referred to there being one fundamental point of disagreement: 'The whole dispute with these people turns on this point: that we should not,

---

[41] Pelagius, *Ad Demetriadem* 25 (ed. Greshake, p. 152), 'Ostendit quomodo resistere debeamus diabolo, si utique subditi simus Deo, eiusque faciendo uoluntatem diuinam mereamur gratiam, et facilius nequam spiritui Sancti Spiritus auxilio resistamus.'

[42] Augustine, *De praedestinatione sanctorum* 10.19 (ed. Chéné and Pintard, BA 24, p. 522), 'If it is examined and questioned why someone might be worthy, there is no shortage of people who would say that this is due to the human will. But we say that it is due to divine grace or predestination. Between grace and predestination, however, there is only this difference, that predestination is the preparation for grace, while grace is its actual bestowal now .... For this reason, the predestination of God which directs toward goodness is, as I said, the preparation for grace, while grace is the effect of that predestination itself'; 'Si discutiatur et quaeratur unde quisque sit dignus, non desunt qui dicant, uoluntate humana: nos autem dicimus gratia uel praedestinatione diuina. Inter gratiam porro et praedestinationem hoc tantum interest, quod praedestinatio est gratiae praeparatio, gratia uero iam ipsa donatio .... Quocirca praedestinatio Dei quae in bono est, gratiae est, ut dixi, praeparatio; gratia uero est ipsius praedestinationis effectus.'

through a perverse defence of nature, make the grace of God which lies in Jesus Christ our Lord, of no effect.'[43]

That Pelagius asserted that the human will worked alongside the action of the Holy Spirit is also shown by a passage in *On Virginity*, in which Pelagius told his addressee that the Holy Spirit chose those who possessed merit:

> While the whole multitude of believers receives similar gifts of grace and all rejoice in the same blessings of the sacraments, those to whom you belong have something peculiar to themselves over and above what the rest possess; they are chosen by the Holy Spirit out of the holy and spotless flock of the Church as holier and purer offerings on account of the merits of their will.[44]

At issue is not whether Pelagius referred constantly to a direct causal relationship between human merit and the reward of the grace of salvation; he certainly did.[45] At issue is the fact that this had been a presumption within Christianity for centuries (as will be detailed in Chapters 3 and 4) until a change occurred. After much study of the Pauline Epistles in the Latin West in the last decades of the 4th century, and scrutiny of their references to predestination, to God's grace and to God's control of man as a potter controls clay, the issue became which way the trigger worked—whether the action of the Holy Spirit triggered human goodness which earned merit, or whether human free decisions created merit which triggered the action of the Holy Spirit to work in the virtuous individual. The first half of tenet 9 does refer to something that Pelagius genuinely taught, although the suggestion that he invented either the idea of a causal relationship between human effort and God's reward of grace, or the idea of man's effective free will, is false. It is also false to suggest that Pelagius did not argue for co-operation between the inspiration of the Holy Spirit and the human will.

The second half of the tenet, 'and for this reason grace itself is located in the human will, whether one becomes worthy or unworthy', attributed to Pelagius the further idea that there was never any other sort of grace than that which was a consequence of the unaided action of the human will. The attribution of this view to him was unwarranted since, as has been seen, Pelagius certainly referred to many aspects of God's agency through his grace, and he did not deny prevenient grace. In his statement to Melania the Younger, Pinianus, and Albina, Pelagius acknowledged the role of grace in every human action every day, and Augustine objected that it was unclear which type of grace Pelagius meant when he made

---

[43] Augustine, *De natura et gratia* 67.81 (ed. Urba and Zycha, CSEL 60, p. 296), 'De qua re cum istis tota uertitur quaestio, ne gratiam Dei, quae est in Christo Iesu Domino nostro, peruersa naturae defensione frustremus.'

[44] Pelagius, *De uirginitate* 1.1 (ed. Halm, CSEL 1, p. 225), 'Cum uniuersa turba credentium paria gratiae dona percipiat, et isdem omnes sacramentorum benedictionibus glorientur, istae proprium aliquid prae ceteris habent, cum de illo sancto et immaculato Ecclesiae grege, quasi sanctiores purioresque hostiae, pro uoluntatis suae meritis a sancto Spiritu eliguntur'. For a discussion of the semantic range of the Latin word *uoluntas*, see Chapter 3, n. 12.

[45] See, for example, Pelagius, *De uirginitate* 1–2 (ed. Halm, CSEL 1, pp. 225–6); 4.1 (ed. Halm, CSEL 1, p. 228); 8.3 (ed. Halm, CSEL 1, p. 236).

this assertion. Augustine then attributed to Pelagius' writings a doctrine that was not in them and which Pelagius rejected, in this case a denial of God's grace. As much as Augustine was certain that Pelagius had not meant prevenient grace, it is impossible to know that Pelagius excluded the grace of the inspiration of the Holy Spirit prior to virtuous action. Furthermore, Augustine insisted that Pelagius had to acknowledge the absolutist account of prevenient grace that Augustine proposed, in which prevenient grace was always the sole cause of virtue. While Pelagius did not acknowledge in writing the role of prevenient grace in the way that Augustine wanted him to do, his discussion of the issue in *On the Divine Law* points to a compromise model of co-operation between the Holy Spirit and man. In this regard it is noteworthy that Pelagius drew attention to the interpretative nature of discussion of Scripture, prefacing his readings with such comments as: 'I think that this should be understood to this effect'.[46] This suggests that he acknowledged that what he wrote was simply one possible way to explain a passage, and sought to avoid dogmatic interpretation of Scripture.

10. 'Only those people can be called children of God who have become entirely without sin.'

Pelagius stated that all Christians were reborn as children of God through baptism:

> We are all made equal by the grace of the divine water, and there can be no distinction amongst those who have been created by a second birth, through which the rich man as much as the poor man, the free man as much as the slave, the noble as much as the man of low birth, is made a son of God.[47]

He reminded Demetrias that she was a daughter of God.[48] He also explained that the phrase 'children of God' was used in Scripture in order to instil in Christians a sense of their own worth and the value of Christ's teaching. He did not limit this to a subset of Christians.[49] He did not suggest that Demetrias was without sin; he stressed the opposite: 'As long as we are in this body we should never believe that we have attained perfection.'[50] Pelagius told the anonymous addressee of *On Virginity* that she should remember that she was a daughter of God and act appropriately as befitted her high status. He did not tell her that she should act well in order to gain the status of child of God, but so as to make visible a status she already possessed: 'Present yourself in such a way that your heavenly birth may

---

[46] Pelagius, *De uirginitate* 2 (ed. Halm, CSEL 1, p. 227), 'Quod ita intelligendum puto'.

[47] Pelagius, *De uirginitate* 16.2 (ed. Halm, CSEL 1, p. 246), 'Omnes per diuini lauacri gratiam aequales efficimur, et nulla inter eos potest esse discretio, quos natiuitas secunda generauit, per quam tam diues quam pauper, tam liber quam seruus, tam nobilis quam ignobilis Dei efficitur filius'.

[48] Pelagius, *Ad Demetriadem* 19 (ed. Greshake, p. 124), 'Through baptism you have been reborn as a daughter of God'; 'Per baptismum in Dei filiam renata es'.

[49] Pelagius, *Ad Demetriadem* 19 (ed. Greshake, pp. 124–6).

[50] Pelagius, *Ad Demetriadem* 27 (ed. Greshake, p. 160), 'Quamdiu in hoc sumus corpore, numquam nos ad perfectum peruenire credamus.'

be visible in your person and your divine nobility clearly shine out.'[51] Pelagius addressed her as a daughter of God but presupposed that she was not perfect when he advised her to keep improving in her imitation of Christ: 'Reckon as wasted all the time in which you have failed to notice an improvement in yourself.'[52]

11. 'Forgetfulness and ignorance are not sinful, because they do not come about willingly, but necessarily.'

The suggestion that forgetfulness and ignorance were not sinful is not found in Pelagius' surviving writings.

12. 'A choice is not free if it needs the help of God, since everyone has their own will either to do something or not to do it.'

Pelagius did not write that the help of God made the will unfree. He acknowledged continuously the need for God's help, such as when he paired free will and God's help in his *Statement of Faith*.[53] In *On the Divine Law* he also twice explicitly asserted the co-operation of divine grace and the human will, expressed in the word 'consent' (*consensus*): 'We comprehend that our calling has a standing according to the honour of the one who calls us, yet also that it rests upon the consent of our will'.[54] Pelagius also acknowledged the help of God's grace in the passage from his *On Free Will*, already cited in relation to tenet 8.[55] In these passages already examined, Pelagius asserted man's need for God's help and man's co-operation with God, and he raised the concern that predestination interpreted as preordainment, as opposed to God's help, might limit human responsibility and God's universal salvific will.

   The exact content of the term 'help' (*auxilium*) was at issue. Augustine used the words 'to help' and 'to co-operate' freely in an indeterminate manner. He argued that Pelagius located God's help in nature and free will or in the law and teaching: 'So that plainly when God helps man *so that he turns from wrong and does good* [1 Pet. 3:11], he is believed to help by revealing and showing us what should be done; not by co-operating with us and breathing love into us so that we do what we know must be done.'[56] Yet elsewhere Augustine characterised the help

---

[51] Pelagius, *De uirginitate* 14 (ed. Halm, CSEL 1, p. 244), 'Ita te exhibe, ut in te caelestis natiuitas appareat et ingenuitas diuina clarescat.'

[52] Pelagius, *De uirginitate* 19 (ed. Halm, CSEL 1, p. 250), 'Omne tempus in quo te non meliorem senseris, hoc te aestima perdidisse.'

[53] See n. 38.

[54] Pelagius, *De diuina lege* 1.2 (ed. Migne, PL 30.106A), 'Colligimus uocationem nostram iuxta uocantis dignationem, etiam nostrae uoluntatis stare consensu'; for the second assertion of co-operation in this letter, see n. 39.

[55] See n. 36 (for Pelagius' *De libero arbitrio*, quoted by Augustine).

[56] Augustine, *De gratia Christi et de peccato originali* 1.3.3 (ed. Urba and Zycha, CSEL 42, p. 127), 'Vt uidelicet cum adiuuat Deus hominem: *Vt declinet a malo et faciat bonum* [1 Pet. 3:11], reuelando

of grace differently: as a force that caused good action by driving a person rather then co-operating with them or helping them: 'For *those who are children of God are* governed and *driven by this Spirit* [Rom. 8:14], not by their own will.'[57]

Thus the statement that Pelagius did not acknowledge God's help was untrue. It was the nature and role of God's help that was at issue because it equated to the nature and role of grace itself. Nor did Pelagius teach that God's help rendered man unfree. This was an argument about the meaning of the word 'grace' and the extent of God's control of man. It was perhaps also a conflict over authority, as represented in the authority to interpret Scripture, and whether authority lay with the episcopacy alone or with lay preachers and monks also. This possibility is suggested by Augustine's comment: 'A new heresy has now been introduced, not by bishops or priests or by any clerics, but by certain supposed monks'.[58]

13. 'Our victory is not the result of God's help, but of free will.'

As already noted, Pelagius explicitly wrote that God helped man, and stated that Christ was the cause of man's victory over death. In another passage from his *On Free Will* quoted by Augustine, Pelagius described human virtue as the result of co-operation between man and God:

> 'For God helps us', he says, 'through his revelation and teaching, when he opens the eyes of our heart; when he discloses to us what is to come so that we are not absorbed with the present; when he exposes the snares of the devil; when he enlightens us with the gift of his heavenly grace, which comes in many forms and cannot be explained in words.'[59]

---

et ostendo quid fieri debeat adiuuare credatur, non etiam cooperando et dilectionem inspirando, ut id quod faciendum esse cognouerit faciat.'

[57] Augustine, *De gestis Pelagii* 3.6 (ed. Urba and Zycha, CSEL 42, p. 57), 'Hoc enim *Spiritu*, non uiribus propriae uoluntatis reguntur et *aguntur qui filii sunt Dei* [Rom. 8:14].' Augustine repeated the word 'driven' (*to be driven, agi*) four times, and distinguished between being governed and being driven, the latter entailing complete control by God: Augustine, *De gestis Pelagii* 3.5–8 (ed. Urba and Zycha, CSEL 42, pp. 56–9).

[58] Augustine, *De gestis Pelagii* 35.61 (ed. Urba and Zycha, CSEL 42, pp. 115–16), '<Inlata est> etiam modo haeresis non ab episcopis seu presbyteris uel quibusque clericis, sed a quibusdam ueluti monachis'.

[59] Augustine, *De gratia Christi et de peccato originali* 1.7.8 (ed. Urba and Zycha, CSEL 42, p. 131), quoting Pelagius' *De libero arbitrio*, '"Adiuuat enim nos Deus", inquit, "per doctrinam et reuelationem suam, dum cordis nostri oculos aperit; dum nobis, ne praesentibus occupemur, futura demonstrat; dum diaboli pandit insidias; dum nos multiformi et ineffabili dono gratiae caelestis illuminat."' Augustine interpreted Pelagius' words as referring only to God's law and teaching, and not to the inspiration of the Holy Spirit. Characteristics of Augustine's account of prevenient grace were that it was, by definition, always chronologically prior and always omnipotent in the sense that it determined all outcomes. This passage was noted by Gerald Bonner (citing J. B. Mozley), 'How Pelagian was Pelagius? An Examination of the Contentions of Torgny Bohlin', in *Studia Patristica* 9, *Texte und Untersuchungen zur Geschichte der altchristlichen Literatur*, Band 94, ed. F. L. Cross (Berlin, 1966), p. 351.

14. 'From Peter's statement: *We are sharers in the divine nature*
[2 Pet. 1:4], it follows that the soul can be as sinless as God.'

In Pelagius' surviving writings there is no statement that man's soul could be
as sinless as God. This thesis was an inference read into his positive account of
man as created in God's image and his advice to his addressees to pursue perfect
righteousness. It seems unlikely that Pelagius wrote that a person could achieve
sinlessness in one of his works that do not survive, such as his *On Nature* or his
On Free Will, because if he had done, Augustine would have quoted the passage.
In *On the Divine Law*, Pelagius acknowledged that few people observed God's
commandments.[60] In his *Letter to Demetrias* Pelagius explicitly denied perfectibility.[61] He argued at length that the key to Christian virtue was constant striving
to make progress and that any other approach led to slipping backwards, citing
Phil. 3:13–14: *Brethren, I do not consider that I have made it my own; but one
thing I do, forgetting what lies behind and straining forward to what lies ahead, I
press on toward the goal for the prize of the heavenly call of God.* Pelagius advised
Demetrias to consider that she was starting afresh every day, because if she ever
stood still she would lose what she had achieved up to that point.[62]

Together this evidence shows the disjunction between, on the one hand, the tenets
attributed to Pelagius by his opponents and, on the other, what can be found in his
surviving writings. It suggests that when considering the tenets attributed to Pelagius,
it is important to draw a distinction between what he was attacked for teaching, such
as the possibility of human sinlessness, and what is found in his writings. The possibility of sinlessness was a hostile entailment read into his paraenesis, but it was not
a step that Pelagius himself took. As will be seen in Chapter 3, Jerome had for years
asserted the same goal of perfection in the same manner as Pelagius did, without
anyone reading this suggestion into his writings. The two axioms that Pelagius stated
and defended in his *Letter to Demetrias*, his careful manifesto for his position, were
that human nature was innately inclined to goodness, and that man had to have effective free will in order to make God's punishment and reward just.

The origins of the fourteen tenets

The fourteen tenets advanced as the constituent theses of 'Pelagianism' were
either false inferences read into Pelagius' writings with polemical intent, or
ideas discussed in ascetic Christian discourse around the Mediterranean to which

---

[60] Pelagius, *De diuina lege* 7.2 (ed. Migne, PL 30.113B), 'But if only I could agree that there are a few
who keep God's commandments; but I fear that they are few who truly believe in God's judgement';
'Sed utinam consentiam paucos esse, qui Dei mandata custodiant; uerum timeo, quia pauci sunt, qui
Dei credant in ueritate iudicium.'

[61] See n. 50.

[62] Pelagius, *Ad Demetriadem* 27 (ed. Greshake, pp. 160–2).

Pelagius did not subscribe, and for which he was not responsible. Apart from the idea that grace was given in accord with merit, none is present in Pelagius' surviving works, and seven of the fourteen are flatly contradicted in his surviving writings. Pelagius' prosecutors conflated statements they presented as written by Caelestius with Pelagius' teachings. Augustine saw it as crucial to his critique of Pelagius that Pelagius' and Caelestius' views were indistinguishable, and he emphasised this point repeatedly. Yet at the moment of victory in the summer of AD 418, when Pelagius and Caelestius had been excommunicated, Jerome wrote to Augustine to applaud his achievement of the condemnations, and congratulated him on his suppression of the 'Caelestian heresy'.[63] This was a strikingly odd choice of words at that juncture.

In the list of fourteen tenets in his *On the Deeds of Pelagius*, Augustine conflated a number of different positions and attributed them all to Pelagius, arguing that Pelagius lied when he disowned the statements put to him at the councils of Jerusalem and Diospolis.[64] Augustine's insistence that Pelagius was lying about what he really taught is pervasive in his writings about Pelagius; the whole of Augustine's *On the Deeds of Pelagius* repeated the idea that what Pelagius taught in private was different from what he published in writing: 'We are still concerned about the ambiguity of those words of his, lest perhaps something may be hidden in that ambiguity and he may later explain to his disciples that he said this without prejudice to his own doctrine, saying something of this sort'.[65] Augustine made it clear that most of the tenets he listed were found in writings which he attributed to Caelestius: 'There follow the objections raised against Pelagius which are said to be found in the teaching of his pupil Caelestius'.[66] Caelestius' writings do not survive now, except in fragments attributed to him by his opponents in polemical

---

[63] Jerome, *Ep.* 143.1.2 (ed. Hilberg, CSEL 56, pp. 292–3), 'With your co-operation and at your instigation the Caelestian heresy has been silenced'; 'Cooperatoribus et auctoribus uobis heresis Caelestina iugulata est'.

[64] Augustine, *De gestis Pelagii* 6.19 (ed. Urba and Zycha, CSEL 42, p. 72), 'It would seem to remain instead that we should believe Pelagius lied in an episcopal court'; 'Restare uidebatur ut Pelagium potius in episcopali iudicio crederemus fuisse mentitum'.

[65] Augustine, *De gestis Pelagii* 10.22 (ed. Urba and Zycha, CSEL 42, p. 75), 'Adhuc sumus de istorum uerborum eius ambiguitate solliciti, ne forte quid in ea lateat atque hoc se dixisse sine praeiudicio sui dogmatis exponat postea discipulis suis ita disserens'; Augustine, *De gestis Pelagii* 21.45 (ed. Urba and Zycha, CSEL 42, pp. 99–100), 'But those who know well what Pelagius was accustomed to teach ... how can they not hold him suspect, when they read not a simple confession condemning his past errors, but a defence such as suggests that he had never thought otherwise than was approved in his answers by that court?'; 'Illi autem qui bene sciunt quae Pelagius docere consueuerit ... quomodo possunt eum non habere suspectum, quando eius non simplicem confessionem praeterita errata damnantem, sed talem defensionem legunt, quasi numquam aliter senserit, quam isto iudicio in eius est responsionibus approbatum?'

[66] Augustine, *De gestis Pelagii* 11.23 (ed. Urba and Zycha, CSEL 42, p. 76), 'Haec enim sequuntur obiecta Pelagio, quae in doctrina Caelestii discipuli eius referuntur inuenta'; 35.63 (ed. Urba and Zycha, CSEL 42, p. 118), 'Among these propositions also which Caelestius had said or written which were levelled as objections to Pelagius, on the grounds of their being doctrines of his disciple'; 'Ex his etiam, quae Caelestium dixisse uel scripsisse tamquam dogmata discipuli eius sunt obiecta Pelagio'.

works, which may have been paraphrased in a misleading way. Augustine argued that Caelestius had been franker and had given away the truth about Pelagius' teaching, which Augustine considered to be the same as Caelestius': 'Indeed in this error Caelestius showed himself more frank'; and: 'Notice, therefore, what Caelestius said very openly, and there you will see what Pelagius hid from you.'[67]

Augustine also stated explicitly that it did not matter to him whether Pelagius held, taught or had written works affirming any of the theses that Augustine attributed to him:

> It may be doubtful or unclear whether Pelagius or Caelestius or both of them or neither of them, or others either with them or in their name, held or still hold such propositions. It has nonetheless been made quite clear by this court that these things were condemned and that Pelagius would have been condemned at the same time if he had not himself condemned them. Now after this judgement, when we argue against opinions of this sort, we are certainly arguing against a condemned heresy.[68]

More than once, Augustine stated his unconcern about the truth regarding what Pelagius actually taught:

> Regardless of the sense in which Caelestius may or may not have affirmed them, regardless of the sense in which Pelagius may or may not have held them, let us rejoice and give thanks and praise to God that these statements that are so evil, produced by such a new heresy, have been condemned by an ecclesiastical court.[69]

The characterisation of Pelagius and 'Pelagianism' as arrogant and deceitful

While the fourteen tenets listed in On the Deeds of Pelagius were the doctrinal theses attributed to Pelagius, there was also a discrepancy between the character ascribed to Pelagius' writings by his opponents and the spirit visible in them. Augustine maintained that 'Pelagianism' was founded on arrogance, ingratitude and pride.[70] He repeatedly used the words 'self-exaltation' (elatio), 'arrogance'

---

[67] Augustine, De gratia Christi et de peccato originali 2.2.2 (ed. Urba and Zycha, CSEL 42, p. 167), 'Caelestius quidem in hoc exstitit errore liberior'; 2.6.6 (ed. Urba and Zycha, CSEL 42, p. 170), 'Attendite itaque quid Caelestius apertissime dixerit, et ibi uidebitis quid uobis Pelagius occultauerit.'
[68] Augustine, De gestis Pelagii 14.30 (ed. Urba and Zycha, CSEL 42, p. 84), 'Vtrum ea Pelagius an Caelestius an uterque an neuter illorum, an alii siue cum ipsis, siue sub nomine illorum senserint, siue adhuc sentiant, sit dubium uel occultum. Satis tamen hoc iudicio declaratum est esse damnata, et Pelagium simul fuisse damnandum, nisi haec etiam ipse damnaret. Nunc certe post hoc iudicium, quando contra huius modi sententias disputamus, aduersus damnatam haeresim disputamus.'
[69] Augustine, De gestis Pelagii 35.65 (ed. Urba and Zycha, CSEL 42, p. 121), 'Quomodolibet ea Caelestius posuerit aut non posuerit uel Pelagius senserit aut non senserit, tanta mala tam nouae huius haeresis illo ecclesiastico iudicio damnata gaudeamus et Deo gratias agamus laudesque dicamus.'
[70] That 'Pelagianism' was arrogant and characterised by pride and ingratitude: Augustine, Ep. 186.11.37 (ed. Goldbacher, CSEL 57, p. 76), 'Lest ... they destroy others through their damnable presumption'; 'Ne ... alios perdant praesumptione damnabili'; Augustine, Ep. 194.2.3 (ed. Goldbacher, CSEL 57, p. 178), 'They do not understand that they do not strengthen human judgement but puff it up with pride so that it is carried off amid vanities'; 'Non intellegunt non se firmare humanum arbitrium sed

(*superbia*), 'to boast' (*iactare*) and 'to praise oneself' (*gloriari*) to characterise Pelagius.[71] None of these characteristics are evident in Pelagius' extant works. A recurring theme in his writings was the need for a Christian to possess humility, and to avoid arrogance and self-exaltation.[72] There is no sign of arrogance in *Letter to Demetrias*; it is a paraenetic piece about personal responsibility and dedicated effort to live by Christian values. By contrast, it was Jerome who thirty years before had advised Eustochium to cultivate a 'holy pride' (*superbia sancta*).[73] Augustine constantly used heavily coloured language to paint a picture of Pelagius' arrogance. His project in *On the Deeds of Pelagius* was to persuade the reader that Pelagius lied at Diospolis, repeating the words 'suspect' (*suspectus*) and 'suspicion' (*suspicio*).[74] Augustine simply did not believe Pelagius when he professed to acknowledge the role of God's grace in human goodness, the issue being which aspects of grace Pelagius acknowledged and whether one aspect had absolute priority. There are no grounds for assuming that Pelagius was lying when he denied making the statements put to him and anathematised them. The alternative possibility, that Pelagius was telling the truth, needs to be considered.[75]

---

inflare, ut per inania feratur'; Augustine, *De gestis Pelagii* 30.55 (ed. Urba and Zycha, CSEL 42, p. 109), 'A letter of fleshy bloated conceit and pride flies about … so that in that letter is read only human arrogance, unhappy, deceiving itself as if it were a conqueror'; 'Epistola carnalis uentositatis et elationis uolat … ut sola in epistola legatur infelix et se ipsam decipiens uelut uictrix humana superbia'; Augustine, *Ep.* 188.2.4 (ed. Goldbacher, CSEL 57, p. 122), concerning Demetrias' being influenced by Pelagius' letter *Ad Demetriadem*, 'In that way … she might learn (may it not be so) to be ungrateful to God'; 'Ita … discat Deo esse, quod absit, ingrata.'

[71] For example, use of the words *iactare*, *gloriari*, *elatio* and *superbia* with reference to Pelagius: Augustine *De gestis Pelagii* 29.53–30.55 (ed. Urba and Zycha, CSEL 42, pp. 106–10).

[72] Pelagius, *Ad Celantiam* 20 (ed. Hilberg, CSEL 56, pp. 346–7), 'Hold nothing more important than humility …. That pride is much more ugly, which hides beneath certain signs of humility. For in some way I do not understand, vices are more foul when they are hidden by the outward appearance of virtues'; 'Nihil habeas humilitate praestantius …. Multo illa deformior est superbia, quae sub quibusdam humilitatis signis latet. Nescio quo enim modo turpiora sunt uitia, cum uirtutum specie celantur'; 22 (ed. Hilberg, CSEL 56, p. 348), 'But what profit is there in weakening the body with abstinence, if the spirit swells with pride? …. They afflict their bodies for this purpose, so that they might break the pride of their spirit, so that as if from the summit of their contempt and their arrogance they may descend to fulfil God's will, which is accomplished most fully in humility'; 'Quid autem prodest tenuari abstinentia corpus, si animus intumescat superbia? …. Eo affligunt carnem suam, quo animae frangant superbiam, ut quasi de quodam fastigio contemptus sui atque arrogantiae descendant ad implendam Dei uoluntatem, quae maxime in humilitate perficitur.' Pelagius, *Ad Demetriadem* 20 (ed. Greshake, p. 130), 'For how many fashion arrogance in place of freedom, adopt flattery instead of humility …. Yet especially fleeing that false humility, [you should] pursue that humility which is real, which Christ taught, in which no arrogance is contained'; 'Quam enim multi superbiam libertatis loco ducunt, adulationem pro humilitate suscipiunt …. [Debeas] praecipue tamen fictam humilitatem fugiens, illam sectare, quae uera est, humilitatem, quam Christus docuit, in qua non sit superbia inclusa.'

[73] Jerome, *Ep.* 22.16 (ed. Hilberg, CSEL 54, p. 163), 'Learn in this regard a holy pride'; 'Disce in hac parte superbiam sanctam'.

[74] Augustine, *De gestis Pelagii* 10.22 (ed. Urba and Zycha, CSEL 42, p. 75), 'suspectus'; 21.45 (ed. Urba and Zycha, CSEL 42, p. 100), 'suspectus'; 30.54 (ed. Urba and Zycha, CSEL 42, p. 106), 'suspicio'. The same purpose animated Augustine's *De gratia Christi et de peccato originali*.

[75] It is not easy to assess the evidential value of some of the apparent excerpts from proceedings

The root of the dispute lay in the many possible aspects of grace and whether one particular aspect of God's grace, the prevenient causation of all moral goodness in man through the action of the Holy Spirit, was paramount. For Pelagius the problem with absolute prevenient grace (that is, always prevenient rather than sometimes prevenient) was that it left obscure the reason why God chose to breathe into some and not others, and it compromised the universality of His salvific will. In contrast, Augustine was comfortable with the doctrine that all humans deserved damnation.[76] On these questions it was a matter of where a Christian felt the emphasis should lie, whether on the transparency of God's justice or on inscrutable divine power and control of man on the Pauline analogy of a potter shaping clay. But this was not the ground on which Augustine chose to accuse Pelagius of heresy, and the fact that Pelagius' opponents were not prepared to debate the real points at issue, and instead accused Pelagius of a long list of other tenets, is instructive. The two material issues at stake hovered in the background of some of the tenets, but the truth is that the fourteen tenets were a diversion.

Of the fourteen propositions attributed to Pelagius, only half of tenet 9 was something Pelagius genuinely asserted. This fact raises questions as to why the other tenets were attributed to Pelagius at all, and why he was not charged with advocating just the two propositions at issue: the goodness of human nature and effective free will. Without pre-empting the discussion of motive and means in Chapter 6, the argument of this book is that the answers to these two questions

---

possibly quoted by Augustine. He gave the impression that he was suggesting that Pelagius denied writing that God's grace was given in accord with merit. This was part of a sentence read to Pelagius that included the corollary: 'Because if God gives grace to sinners, he would appear unjust'. Because the second half of this statement is clearly untrue, Pelagius could truthfully have denied saying or approving of this statement, as he could truthfully have denied making the other statements bundled together with the idea that grace was given in accord with merit. Alternatively, the proposition that God gives grace according to merit may not have been a quotation, and may instead have been an entailment that Augustine read into a different statement attributed to Caelestius that was put to Pelagius. In this situation, because Pelagius anathematised the statements put to him, not the unwarranted entailment Augustine may have later read into Caelestius' alleged propositions with polemical intent when he composed *On the Deeds of Pelagius*, once again Pelagius would not have lied when he answered as he did. At first sight, Augustine's work reads as if Pelagius had indeed denied writing that the grace of God was given in accord with merit, but, checked carefully, it becomes apparent that Pelagius may not have done this. Augustine found the idea that grace was given in accord with merit objectionable, but this may not have been a proposition put to Pelagius as unacceptable by a synod. Furthermore, there is the possibility, acknowledged by Augustine himself, that the propositions read out as having been written by Caelestius were not in fact written by Caelestius (or Pelagius) but were fake statements made up by the prosecution or written by others not associated with Caelestius (or Pelagius): Augustine, *De gestis Pelagii* 14.30 (ed. Urba and Zycha, CSEL 42, p. 84).

[76] Augustine, *Contra duas epistolas Pelagianorum* 2.7.13 (ed. Urba and Zycha, CSEL 60, p. 474), 'When in accord with God's intention one is called and another is not called, the calling is given as a free gift, and the beginning of this gift is the calling itself; one who is not called is paid back with evil because all are guilty as a result of the fact that through one man sin entered the world'; 'Cum secundum propositum Dei uocatur alius, alius non uocatur, uocatio datur gratuitum bonum, cuius boni est uocatio ipsa principium, non uocato redditur malum, quia omnes rei sunt ex eo, quod per unum hominem peccatum intrauit in mundum.'

are respectively that the other tenets were there as distraction and smear, and that the tenets were necessary to obscure the real process being effected, which was the installation of a different anthropology and soteriology into Christian doctrine. If Augustine had simply stated the two issues in dispute, he would have risked failing in his project to install as orthodoxy the interlinked doctrines of original sin, prevenient grace, and predestination interpreted as preordainment.[77] Instead, the tenets are based on the presumption that the triune was agreed Church teaching and that denial of the triune was heresy. In this way the tenets covertly asserted that the triune was established doctrine.

Conclusion

The fourteen tenets were a fabrication. There were two real points at issue. First, an allegedly obligatory choice between two poles, with effective human free will, on the one hand, and divine prevenient grace, on the other, as each being respectively the sole cause of human virtue. The second, another purportedly binary choice, concerned the anthropology of Christianity—namely, whether human nature was inherently inclined to evil as a result of the transmission of original sin from Adam to the rest of humanity, or whether it was inclined to moral goodness as a result of man having been created in God's image, and was capable of both good and evil. The tenets were designed, and the myth of 'Pelagianism' was created, in order to obscure the attempt to install as dogma particular choices between these alleged binary options.[78] The process that took place during the condemnation of 'Pelagianism' can be described as the invention of heresy in order to relocate orthodoxy. It could perhaps also be described as the crystallisation of alternative positions on these two fundamental questions from pre-existing approaches, when

---

[77] For a discussion of the concept of orthodoxy, see A. Le Boulluec, *La notion d'hérésie dans la littérature grecque IIe–IIIe siècles*, 2 vols (Paris, 1985); É. Rebillard, 'Sociologie de la Déviance et Orthodoxie: Le cas de la controverse pélagienne sur la grâce', in *Orthodoxie Christianisme Histoire*, ed. S. Elm, É. Rebillard and A. Romano (Rome, 2000), pp. 239–40; L. Ayres, 'The Question of Orthodoxy', *Journal of Early Christian Studies* 14:4 (2006); J. R. Lyman, 'Hellenism and Heresy', *Journal of Early Christian Studies* 11:2 (2003); A. Cameron, 'The Violence of Orthodoxy', in *Heresy and Identity in Late Antiquity*, ed. E. Iricinschi and H. M. Zellentin (Tübingen, 2008), pp. 102–14; S. Elm, P.-A. Fabre, É. Rebillard, A. Romano and C. Sotinel, 'Introduction', in *Orthodoxie Christianisme Histoire*, ed. S. Elm, É. Rebillard and A. Romano (Rome, 2000), pp. viii–xxv; D. Julia, 'La production de l'orthodoxie: questions transversales', in *Orthodoxie Christianisme Histoire*, ed. S. Elm, É. Rebillard and A. Romano (Rome, 2000), pp. 393–404.

[78] Averil Cameron has drawn attention to the similarities between apologetics and heresiology, and written of: 'The language of binary opposition that is standard when labeling one's enemies as "the other": the language of disqualification': A. Cameron, 'Jews and Heretics – A Category Error?', in *The Ways that Never Parted*, ed. A. H. Becker and A. Y. Reed (Tübingen, 2003), pp. 348–50. She has also drawn attention to the process of construction taking place when boundaries between correct belief and false belief are demarcated, and to the usefulness of binary oppositions as a strategy in such a construction process, when: 'Each "side" is in flux or under construction': A. Cameron, 'Apologetics in the Roman Empire – A Genre of Intolerance?', in *"Humana Sapit". Études d'Antiquité Tardive Offertes à Lellia Cracco Ruggini*, ed. J.-M. Carrié and R. L. Testa (Turnhout, 2002), p. 223.

a binary choice was imposed.[79] These questions had not been examined closely before; the scrutiny they received from the second half of the 4th century onwards, combined with the assumption that every word of the Bible was the word of God and exact literal truth, and competition for authority in interpreting Scripture because such authority conferred status and employment, drove this controversy. The reason why his opponents could not accuse Pelagius on the grounds of what he actually asserted was that this would not have secured his conviction for heresy. As will be seen in Chapter 6, in order to create rules it is imperative to secure the conviction of an actual individual for breaking those rules. To accuse Pelagius on the basis of his position on the two questions at stake would have started a discussion that would have laid bare the choices being made and revealed the supporters of each position; it might have allowed Christians to choose. Conversely, adherents of the triune believed that these doctrines were the word of God and true, and so rhetoric was used in the service of establishing God's truth and driving out alternative interpretations of Scripture.[80]

The argument of this book is not that Pelagius did not defend the goodness of human nature and effective free will, since he undoubtedly did. This book makes three points about the heresy accusation against Pelagius. First, specific objectionable theses were attributed to Pelagius that he did not teach, in order to bring into disrepute his objections to the triune and secure his conviction for heresy. 'Pelagianism' was invented. The aim was to separate supporters of effective free will from Pelagius by associating him with unambiguously objectionable theses, and repugnant characteristics such as arrogance and deceit, thus isolating him, and tarring with the accusation of arrogance anyone who continued to object to the triune. Second, Pelagius did not suggest anything that was not already in wide circulation in Christian discourse. Third, the process at work was not the eruption of a new heresy, 'Pelagianism', but rather the imposition of choices imposed according to a binary analysis of the relationship between human free will and God's grace and of Christian anthropology. Prior to the imposition of this binary choice, differing responses to these questions existed in Christian discourse. However, to facilitate the installation of the triune, its supporters had to define the situation as a threat, and as an either–or choice between good and evil, between piety and impiety.[81]

---

[79] On the '"tightening" of what constituted orthodoxy', see E. Clark, *The Origenist Controversy. The Cultural Construction of an Early Christian Debate* (Princeton, NJ, 1992), p. 245.

[80] In an important discussion of the social and theological effects of heresiological discourse, Karen King drew attention to the way in which a rhetoric of orthodoxy and heresy produced divisions and obscured the issues under debate: K. L. King, 'Social and Theological Effects of Heresiological Discourse', in *Heresy and Identity in Late Antiquity*, ed. E. Iricinschi and H. M. Zellentin (Tübingen, 2008), pp. 28–49.

[81] Cf. Susan Wessel's analysis of Cyril of Alexandria's successful strategy against Nestorius, and her concluding comment: 'The formation of Eastern Christian doctrine thus proceeds not according to the ineluctable structures of dogmatic history but according to a complex historical and cultural process fuelled by the claims of adversaries competing to appropriate the Christian past': S. Wessel, *Cyril of Alexandria and the Nestorian Controversy: The Making of a Saint and of a Heretic* (Oxford, 2004), p. 302.

This distinction between the specific theses listed in synodal condemnations of 'Pelagianism' and the two underlying questions that were being decided is critical. What was new was an enforced decision in favour of one side of a prescribed binary divide, and also the characterisation of advocacy of effective free will and innate human goodness as arrogant and deceitful in its concealment of its arrogance.

In sum, there is no evidence drawn from Pelagius' own writings that associates the list of tenets attributed to 'Pelagianism' with Pelagius. It follows that to use his name to identify this set of propositions is unhistorical and misleading. The next problem with the concept of 'Pelagianism', which will be addressed in Chapters 2 and 3, is the lack of differentiability between Pelagius' writings and other ascetic paraenesis. The evidence shows that all of the doctrines Pelagius expounded had been set out by Christian writers before him. There are further problems with the concept of 'Pelagianism', such as the fact that no one individual held the collection of views bundled together by Pelagius' opponents under the title 'Pelagianism', and also that there was no 'Pelagian' movement. Pelagius' opponents created the impression that there was an organised party, and until quite recently this has been widely accepted to have been the case. In reality, this was part of the myth of 'Pelagianism', designed to make it seem alarming; the perception of threat it generated then required a legislative response. These further problems with the concept of 'Pelagianism' will be considered in turn.

2

Pelagius did not Invent Anything: All the Teachings in His Writings Had Already Been Widely Disseminated in Ascetic Paraenesis

An important respect in which 'Pelagianism' is a myth is that Pelagius' writings, as visible in the surviving works that can be attributed to him with certainty, did not assert any propositions that had not already been asserted in ascetic paraenetic literature for decades before Pelagius began to write. Thus in terms of doctrine, his writings are not differentiable from other ascetic literature. He was in no way the first Christian writer to argue explicitly for the goodness of contemporary human nature and man's effective free will, or to advertise a direct causal relationship between Christian virtue in this life and reward in the next. In Chapter 1, evidence was presented to show that Pelagius did not assert the propositions attributed to 'Pelagianism', except for the statement that grace was given in accord with merit. In this chapter it will be shown that Pelagius did not originate the two ideas which he did assert—namely, the goodness of contemporary human nature and effective free will—and that he did not originate the idea that grace was given in accord with merit. Indeed, as will be seen, other authors made statements that show a much closer affinity with some of the fourteen tenets attributed to Pelagius by his opponents than anything that can be found in Pelagius' output; and other authors also show a closer affinity with further criticisms levelled at 'Pelagianism' by its opponents, besides those contained in the lists of theses drawn up in formal synodal indictments.

To prove this, it is necessary to compare Pelagius' writings with other works of ascetic paraenesis written either before he began to write or during the years when he was writing. Many 4th- and 5th-century Christian ascetic texts expressing the same ideas as those propounded by Pelagius have never been described as 'Pelagian', and those dating from the 4th century could not be so described without anachronism. The only distinctive elements in Pelagius' teaching were, first, that he defended what had previously been unquestioned assumptions that had underpinned ascetic Christianity, in a context of polemic; and, second, that he was subsequently labelled a heresiarch, not for his actual teachings, which were standard in ascetic paraenetic literature, but for a synthetic collocation of theses designed to bring him into disrepute. This latter process was the invention of heresy in order to relocate orthodoxy.

The evidence for this argument lies in ascetic literature already in circulation before Pelagius began his literary career. There was a great deal of such literature already in circulation in Greek and Latin when Pelagius began to write, such as Athanasius' *Life of Antony* and Evagrius of Antioch's translation of it; Jerome's letters, tracts and exegetical works, as well as his *Lives* of Paul, Hilarion and Malchus; Sulpicius Severus' *Life of Martin of Tours*; and the anonymous *Historia monachorum* translated into Latin by Rufinus of Aquileia between AD 404 and 410. This chapter is Part I of an examination of ascetic literature previous to or contemporary with Pelagius, and it will look at Athanasius' *Life of Antony*, and compare the two Latin translations of it to Athanasius' Greek original. Chapter 3 includes Part II, which discusses the writings of Jerome, as well as Part III, which examines relevant material in selected other Christian literature circulating in the late 4th and early 5th centuries, including the commentary on the Pauline Epistles by the author known as Ambrosiaster.

In Chapters 2 and 3 the evidence is set out under similar headings for ease of comparison. Section 1 examines the texts for their doctrinal position on ideas for which Pelagius was criticised, starting with the two key teachings that Pelagius asserted: that human nature was still inclined to goodness even after Adam's expulsion from Eden, and that man had effective free will. Then the texts are examined with regard to a third idea asserted by Pelagius for which he was censured—that God's grace was given as a result of merit. After that, further ideas for which 'Pelagianism' was criticised by its opponents are considered. These were not the fundamental doctrinal questions at stake, in the way that the first three points were. That ends the analysis of the texts with regard to ideas for which Pelagius was criticised. Section 2 turns to the doctrines advocated by Pelagius' opponents, to see whether or not the texts ever referred to original sin, prevenient grace, or predestination as preordainment; and also whether they characterised human nature as sinful, and man's will as weak and in need of external assistance in order to act virtuously. Section 3 is an analysis of the use in these texts of the word 'grace' (χάρις and its Latin equivalent *gratia*). Section 4 looks at a supposed hallmark idea associated with 'Pelagianism' by scholars—namely, stress on the need to obey all God's commandments. Finally, Section 5 examines the overall message conveyed by the text or author in question.

This evidence will show that the writers discussed had already asserted everything that Pelagius later taught, and that all the ideas he expressed had been freely canvassed for decades in Christian literature that has never been labelled heretical.

Part I

The Doctrinal Assumptions in Athanasius' *Life of Antony* and the Two Latin Translations of it

The date of Antony's birth is uncertain, but it is known that he died in AD 356. Athanasius lived from around AD 295 to 373, and his *Letter to the Monks in the Foreign Country about the Blessed Antony the Great* was written between AD 356 and 373, probably during the 360s since Evagrius of Antioch's translation of Athanasius' text had been made by AD 374.[1] Thus the material in these texts had been in circulation for at least thirty years when Pelagius began to write.[2] Philip Rousseau highlighted Antony's teaching role in Athanasius' Greek *Life of Antony*, and how instruction was seen as the task of leading ascetics. A significant part of Athanasius' *Life of Antony* consists of Antony's direct speech, advising monks about the ascetic way of life. Ascetic paraenesis was therefore showcased by Athanasius long before Pelagius began to offer guidance.[3] Christine Mohrmann drew attention to the doctrinal discourse contained in the speeches that Athanasius gave to Antony, and Athanasius' own meditation on the essence of the ascetic life. She observed that Athanasius composed a considered doctrinal exposition, and she also identified a process of systematisation of the practice of the ascetic life taking place in Athanasius' *Life of Antony*, which had 'speculative' elements, a process which only reached maturity in the theology of Evagrius of Antioch.[4] Thus the theological and doctrinal assumptions that underpinned asceticism were systematised during the production of these texts, which were carefully considered statements of their writers' positions.

The anonymous Latin translation of Athanasius' *Life of Antony* antedated Evagrius' translation, and was very faithful to the Greek text, often translating it literally with calques on Greek words. Evagrius was intentionally freer in his rendering of the Greek.[5] His translation became popular and was far more influential than the anonymous version, of which only one manuscript copy now survives.

---

[1] Athanasius, *Letter to the Monks in the Foreign Country about the Life of the Blessed Antony the Great*, Ἐπιστολὴ πρὸς τοὺς ἐν τῇ ξένῃ μοναχοὺς περὶ τοῦ βίου τοῦ μακαρίου Ἀντωνίου τοῦ μεγάλου. Hereafter this work is referred to in the main text as the *Life of Antony*.

[2] Assuming that Pelagius started to write *c.* AD 404.

[3] P. Rousseau, 'Antony as Teacher in the Greek *Life*', in *Greek Biography and Panegyric in Late Antiquity*, ed. T. Hägg and P. Rousseau (Los Angeles, CA, 2000), pp. 89–106.

[4] C. Mohrmann, 'Introduzione Generale', in *Vita di Antonio*, ed. G. J. M. Bartelink, Vite dei Santi 1 (Milan, 1974), p. lxxxii.

[5] Evagrius, *Vita Antonii* Preface (ed. Migne, PL 73.126).

By comparing passages from the three versions of the *Life of Antony* relevant to the doctrines that were at issue in the controversy surrounding Christian teaching on human nature and free will, it will become clear, first, what the assumptions of the ascetic movement were in the 4th century; second, whether in terms of doctrine the Latin translators added or subtracted anything from Athanasius' original; and, third, whether Pelagius proposed anything new.

In all three versions of the *Life of Antony*, some passages bear a striking resemblance both to Pelagius' teaching in his letters and also to teaching that his opponents attributed to Pelagius but which is not found in his writings. Athanasius' Greek text and the Latin translations contain statements for which Pelagius was later condemned, including material relating to the issues of the goodness of contemporary human nature, free will, the efficacy of merit in the attainment of salvation, man's pursuit of and ability to achieve perfection, and the ease with which imitation of Christ's way of life could be achieved. A selection of such passages will be examined, and in each case the texts will be considered in the chronological order of their composition, looking at Athanasius' original first, followed by the anonymous translation, and lastly Evagrius' version.

Section 1: Ideas for which Pelagius Was Criticised

The Two Key Doctrines Asserted by Pelagius: the Innate Goodness of Human Nature Even after Adam's Sin, and Man's Effective Free Will

In support of his argument for the goodness of human nature and free will, Athanasius stressed the will, habit and effort as the causes of human virtue and thus the means to reach heaven. As a result, the following three ideas are closely bound together in Athanasius' *Life of Antony*, and they often occur in the same passage, so that it is sometimes necessary to consider them together:

1. The innate goodness of human nature even after Adam's sin and the achievability of goodness by means of willing;
2. the will, habit and effort as the causes of human goodness;
3. free will.

1. The innate goodness of human nature and the achievability of goodness by means of willing

Athanasius

For the argument of this book, the single most important point that Athanasius made was his unequivocal assertion of a positive anthropology. He expounded his understanding of contemporary human nature as inherently inclined towards moral goodness in an emphatic manner; he stressed that virtue was achievable because virtue was man's natural state. One lengthy speech that Antony made to his monks on the subject of the innate goodness of human nature is particularly important evidence:

> 'Do not be afraid, hearing about virtue, or receive the word as something foreign to you. For it is not far from us, nor does it originate outside of us, but the deed is within us and the action is easy, if only we are willing .... And so, virtue only needs us to be willing, since it is within us and it is created by us. For virtue is produced when the spirit has the mind orientated according to its nature. It has it orientated according to its nature whenever it remains as it was created; it was created very good and very well disposed. This is why Joshua, son of Nun, said to the people, exhorting them: *Set your heart straight toward the Lord, the God of Israel* [Josh. 24:23]. And John said: *Make straight your paths* [Matt. 3:3]. For the soul to be well disposed is for its mind to be orientated according to its nature, as it was created. On the other hand, whenever it deviates and is distorted from its natural state, then this is called the wickedness of the soul. Therefore this thing is not difficult. For whenever we abide as we were created, we are in a state of virtue. But whenever we think about bad things, we are judged to be wicked. If doing this thing was supplied from outside of us, it would be difficult; but if it is within us, let us guard ourselves against foul thoughts, and let us keep the soul for the Lord as if we had received it as a deposit, so that he may recognise his handiwork, because our soul is in the same state as he created it.'[6]

---

[6] Athanasius, Ἐπιστολή 20.2–9 (ed. Bartelink, SC 400, pp. 188–92), Μὴ φοβεῖσθε δὲ ἀκούοντες περὶ ἀρετῆς μηδὲ ξενίζεσθε περὶ τοῦ ὀνόματος. Οὐ γὰρ μακρὰν ἀφ' ἡμῶν ἐστιν οὐδ' ἔξωθεν ἡμῶν συνίσταται, ἐν ἡμῖν δέ ἐστι τὸ ἔργον καὶ εὔκολόν ἐστι τὸ πρᾶγμα, ἐὰν μόνον θελήσωμεν .... Οὐκοῦν ἡ ἀρετὴ τοῦ θέλειν ἡμῶν μόνου χρείαν ἔχει, ἐπειδήπερ ἐν ἡμῖν ἐστι καὶ ἐξ ἡμῶν συνίσταται. Τῆς γὰρ ψυχῆς τὸ νοερὸν κατὰ φύσιν ἐχούσης ἡ ἀρετὴ συνίσταται. Κατὰ φύσιν δὲ ἔχει, ὅταν ὡς γέγονε μένῃ· γέγονε δὲ καλὴ καὶ εὐθὴς λίαν. Διὰ τοῦτο ὁ μὲν τοῦ Ναυῆ Ἰησοῦς παραγγέλλων ἔλεγε τῷ λαῷ· Εὐθύνατε τὴν καρδίαν ὑμῶν πρὸς Κύριον τὸν θεὸν Ἰσραήλ [Josh. 24:23]. Ὁ δὲ Ἰωάννης· Εὐθείας ποιεῖτε τὰς τρίβους ὑμῶν [Matt. 3:3]. Τὸ γὰρ εὐθεῖαν εἶναι τὴν ψυχήν, τοῦτό ἐστι τὸ κατὰ φύσιν νοερὸν αὐτῆς ὡς ἐκτίσθη. Πάλιν δὲ ὅταν κλίνῃ καὶ ἐν διαστροφῇ τοῦ κατὰ φύσιν γένηται, τότε κακία ψυχῆς λέγεται. Οὐκοῦν οὐκ ἔστι δυσχερὲς τὸ πρᾶγμα. Ἐὰν γὰρ μείνωμεν ὡς γεγόναμεν, ἐν τῇ ἀρετῇ ἐσμεν· ἐὰν δὲ λογιζώμεθα τὰ φαῦλα, ὡς κακοὶ κρινόμεθα. Εἰ μὲν οὖν ἔξωθεν ἦν πορ̣ιστέον τὸ πρᾶγμα, δυσχερὲς ὄντως ἦν· εἰ δὲ ἐν ἡμῖν ἐστι, φυλάξωμεν ἑαυτοὺς ἀπὸ λογισμῶν ῥυπαρῶν, καὶ ὡς παραθήκην λαβόντες, τηρήσωμεν τῷ Κυρίῳ τὴν ψυχὴν ἵν' αὐτὸς ἐπιγνῷ τὸ ποίημα αὐτοῦ, οὕτως οὖσαν τὴν ψυχὴν ὥσπερ πεποίηκεν αὐτήν. The meaning of the Greek word θέλειν encompassed both 'to wish' and also 'to be willing'. I have translated it as 'to be willing' here because to translate it as 'to wish' seems inappropriate given that in this passage Athanasius described an action that was clearly thinking, using the word λογίζεσθαι meaning 'to reckon', 'to calculate'. 'To wish' might perhaps suggest an emotion rather than a faculty of willing that was the result of a process of thought. The range of possible meanings of θέλειν, however, should be borne in mind.

Athanasius here explicitly asserted that virtue was not distant from man, nor did it come from outside of him, when he wrote: "'Nor does it originate outside of us'".[7] This statement ruled out any external force as the cause of human virtue. Virtue came from within and therefore was not difficult to achieve; the sole agency lay in human volition. The key ideas Athanasius expressed here that are relevant to the later controversy are that the human soul was inherently purely good; a soul was in its natural state when it was in the state in which it was created; a person could achieve for himself this condition of the soul according to its nature, and could regain the state of his soul as it was when God created it. If it was possible to return a soul to God in the same state as it was created by Him, this implied that there could be no taint of sin in that soul. This then excluded the possibility of any sin being transmitted down from Adam as part of the human condition. This was therefore an anthropology entirely at odds with any notion of original sin. Agency in the achievement of human virtue lay exclusively with the individual; effective free will was assumed. Athanasius' Antony had no 'original' sin.

Another passage showing that Athanasius taught that the soul could be made pure during this life came when he described the purity of soul that Antony achieved through ascetic endeavour.[8] Athanasius asserted that this purity was the natural state of the human soul. 'According to its natural state' (κατὰ φύσιν) is a phrase that recurs in Athanasius' discussion of virtue. A third passage in which he asserted that complete virtue was achievable came when he discussed Antony's ability to see the future. Here again, Athanasius stated explicitly that the soul could be cleansed completely in this life and he referred once again to the natural state of the soul; the achievement of the return of the soul to its 'natural' condition as it was created by God was what led to the gift of foresight, and the ability to see further than the demons was given by God. This return of the soul to its natural state was achieved by ascetic effort; the gift of foresight, on the other hand, was given by God to the virtuous person, and thus the model was one of co-operation. Athanasius prefaced these statements by saying that this was what he believed about foresight, leaving room for alternative explanations of the origin of such special vision, but his statement in this passage about the purifying of the soul and its being settled 'according to its natural state' was expresssed in exactly the same terms as elsewhere in his *Life of Antony*:

'But if once it also matters to us to be able to see the future, we should cleanse our mind. For I believe that when the soul has been cleansed in every way and

---

[7] Athanasius, Ἐπιστολή 20.3 (ed. Bartelink, SC 400, p. 188), [Ἀρετὴ] οὐδ' ἔξωθεν ἡμῶν συνίσταται.
[8] Athanasius, Ἐπιστολή 14.2–4 (ed. Bartelink, SC 400, pp. 172–4), 'Antony emerged as if from an inner sanctuary, as one who has been initiated into mysteries and who has been inspired by the divine .... As for his soul, its condition was pure .... For neither was he disturbed when he saw the crowd nor did he rejoice because he was greeted by so many people, but he was entirely calm, as one governed by reason and stable according to his natural state'; Προῆλθεν ὁ Ἀντώνιος ὥσπερ ἔκ τινος ἀδύτου μεμυσταγωγημένος καὶ θεοφορούμενος .... Τῆς δὲ ψυχῆς πάλιν καθαρὸν τὸ ἦθος .... Οὔτε γὰρ ἑωρακὼς τὸν ὄχλον ἐταράχθη οὔτε ὡς ὑπὸ τοσούτων κατασπαζόμενος ἐγεγήθει, ἀλλ' ὅλος ἦν ἴσος, ὡς ὑπὸ τοῦ λόγου κυβερνώμενος καὶ ἐν τῷ κατὰ φύσιν ἐστώς.

established according to its natural state, having become transparent, it is able to see more and further than the demons, because the Lord reveals these things to it.'⁹

The anonymous translator

The anonymous translator rarely departed from Athanasius' words. His translations of certain words are sometimes noteworthy, but, since his Latin was not adept and his translation does not appear to have enjoyed wide circulation, it is not possible to assume either that he reflected contemporary Latin Christian vocabulary or that he introduced vocabulary into Latin Christian discourse. He translated Athanasius' 'virtue' (ἀρετή) as *uirtus deifica*, which gave an overtly religious connotation to what was in Athanasius' Greek a moral term used by philosophers, and constituted an addition to Athanasius' wording, which was not the anonymous translator's usual practice.¹⁰

All the elements of Athanasius' account of contemporary human nature and how virtue was created were present in the anonymous translation. The translator's literal rendering of the Greek made Athanasius' statements plain for a Western Latin reader. Virtue came from within a person: '"It is not distant from us nor is it created outside of us, but is a work inside us and is an easy thing when we want to achieve it."'¹¹ It was the responsibility of man to achieve his own virtue: '"Therefore it is our task to want spiritual virtue, because it is within us and is created by us."'¹² Virtue was created when a soul had its rational faculty 'according to its natural state': *secundum proprietatem* expressed Athanasius' κατὰ φύσιν.¹³ The soul was created 'good and very upright' (*bona et recta ualde*).

---

⁹ Athanasius, Ἐπιστολή 34.2 (ed. Bartelink, SC 400, p. 228), Εἰ δὲ ἅπαξ καὶ τοῦ προγινώσκειν ἡμῖν μέλει, καθαρεύωμεν τῇ διανοίᾳ. Ἐγὼ γὰρ πιστεύω, ὅτι καθαρεύσασα ψυχὴ πανταχόθεν καὶ κατὰ φύσιν ἑστῶσα, δύναται, διορατικὴ γενομένη, πλείονα καὶ μακρότερα βλέπειν τῶν δαιμόνων, ἔχουσα τὸν ἀποκαλύπτοντα Κύριον αὐτῇ.

¹⁰ The literal meaning of *uirtus deifica* is 'virtue which makes divine'. If this is what the anonymous translator intended to say then it was a strong statement, although one possibly not entirely unwarranted by the overall message of Athanasius' text. It is also possible, however, that the anonymous translator simply intended to add a Christian religious connotation to his translation of Athanasius' word 'virtue' (ἀρετή). This is made more likely by the fact that in Latin *uirtus* encompassed morally neutral meanings such as 'courage', 'power' and 'worth', as well as 'virtue' in the sense of moral goodness. Elsewhere, however, the anonymous translator rendered Athanasius' ἀρετή simply as *uirtus*. For example, on one occasion he used *uirtus* and *uirtus deifica* as synonyms: see n. 64. This supports the view that he did not intend *uirtus deifica* to be understood with the specific meaning that virtue could make man divine, but rather he wanted to add a general implication that this virtue was pleasing to God and therefore linked to the attainment of salvation. Hence I have translated it as 'sacred virtue' and not as 'virtue that makes us divine'.

¹¹ Anon. trans., *Vita Antonii* 20.3 (ed. Bartelink, p. 48), '"Non est enim longe a nobis, neque extra nos constituta est res, intra nos est autem opus, et facile est res ista cum uoluerimus."'

¹² Anon. trans., *Vita Antonii* 20.5 (ed. Bartelink, p. 48), '"Ergo uirtutem religionis uelle nostrum opus est, quia in nobis est et ex nobis constituitur."' The anonymous translator used *uelle* ('to want') to translate Athanasius' θέλειν ('to be willing', 'to wish').

¹³ Anon. trans., *Vita Antonii* 20.5 (ed. Bartelink, p. 48), '"For virtue is created when the soul has its rational faculty according to its natural state"'; '"Anima enim intellectum suum dum habet secundum proprietatem, uirtus constituitur"'; cf. Athanasius, Ἐπιστολή 20.5 (ed. Bartelink, SC 400, pp. 188–90), Τῆς γὰρ ψυχῆς τὸ νοερὸν κατὰ φύσιν ἐχούσης ἡ ἀρετὴ συνίσταται.

As in Athanasius' text, proof of man's control of his own moral condition was provided by biblical citations, and it was possible for individuals to have their soul in the same condition as it was when God created it, and for God to recognise it as His creation. On one occcasion the anonymous translator added mention of man's 'natural state' where it was not present in Athanasius' Greek text, and he equated this with mental health, so that the mind's health was assumed to be the same thing as virtue.[14] Thus man's natural state was virtue, and, given that he so rarely altered Athanasius' text, it is noteworthy that the anonymous translator departed from the Greek original in order to repeat this equation.

Evagrius

Evagrius also retained Antony's speech to the monks telling them that virtue was achievable in his version of the *Life of Antony*. He reproduced Athanasius' idea of the innate goodness of man's present-day nature, and stated explicitly that the origin of all virtues was the 'natural purity of the spirit' (*naturalis animae puritas*). He relayed Athanasius' statement that virtue was something that came from within a person. Evagrius added the idea that no one could make the excuse that goodness was external to him:

> 'I beg you, do not fear the word virtue, as if it were something unattainable, nor let this endeavour, which depends on our judgement, seem something alien to you or remote from you. Inborn nature inclines man to this effort, and it is something that only awaits our will .... The virtue that is within us only requires the human mind. For who can doubt that the natural purity of the spirit, were it not tainted by filth from outside, would be the fount and source of all virtues? A good Creator must necessarily have created it to be good .... For to have an upright soul means that its original soundness is not stained by the blemish of any vices. If it changes its nature, then it is said to have gone astray, but if it preserves its good condition, then this is virtue. The Lord has entrusted our soul to us: let us keep what has been entrusted to us in the same state we received it. No one can put forward as an excuse that what is born in him is external to him'.[15]

---

[14] Anon. trans., *Vita Antonii* 73.3 (ed. Bartelink, p. 140), 'And Antony said: "And so when the mind is healthy and established in its natural condition, there is then no need of literacy"'; 'Et Antonius dixit: "Quamdiu mens sana est ergo, et in proprietate est constituta, opus enim non sunt litterae"'; cf. Athanasius, Ἐπιστολή 73.3 (ed. Bartelink, SC 400, p. 322), 'Antony said: "He whose mind is healthy has no need of literacy"'; Ἔφη ὁ Ἀντώνιος· ᾧ τοίνυν ὁ νοῦς ὑγιαίνει, τούτῳ οὐκ ἀναγκαῖα τὰ γράμματα.

[15] Evagrius, *Vita Antonii* 15 (20) (ed. Migne, PL 73.136C–137A), '"Nolite, quaeso, uirtutis tamquam impossibile nomen pauere, nec peregrinum uobis aut procul positum uideatur hoc studium, quod ex nostro pendet arbitrio. Huius operis homini inserta natura est, et eiusmodi res est, quae nostram tantummodo exspectat uoluntatem .... Virtus quae in nobis est, mentem tantum requirit humanam. Cui enim dubium est quia naturalis animae puritas, si nulla fuerit extrinsecus sorde polluta, fons sit et origo omnium uirtutum? Bonam eam necesse est creauerit bonus creator .... Siquidem hoc est rectam esse animam, cum eius principalis integritas nulla uitiorum labe maculatur; si naturam mutauerit, peruersa tunc dicitur; si bona conditio seruetur, et uirtus est. Animam nostram commendauit nobis Dominus, seruemus depositum quale accepimus. Nemo causari potest extrinsecus situm, quod in se nascitur"'. I have translated Evagrius' word *arbitrium* in the first sentence of this passage as 'will', although

One key sentence here stated the two ideas that Pelagius asserted: '"Inborn nature inclines man to this effort, and it is something that only awaits our will."' According to Evagrius, as to Athanasius, virtue was not foreign to human nature, or distant. As Athanasius had done, Evagrius asserted that the spirit was naturally pure; but significantly, he added the explicit statement that all impurity came from outside a person, and that the spirit was the 'fount and origin of all virtues'. Evagrius therefore strengthened the assertion that there was no stain on the soul and that moral virtue originated within the individual. He reproduced Athanasius' idea that an individual could return his soul to God in the same state in which He had created it. As with Athanasius, these statements did not simply omit to mention original sin but expressly ruled out its possibility. Evagrius left out, however, Athanasius' phrases 'in its natural state' (κατὰ φύσιν) and 'it is in us and comes from us' (ἐν ἡμῖν ἐστι καὶ ἐξ ἡμῶν συνίσταται). On the question of effective free will, in this passage Evagrius assumed that an individual controlled his virtue; this was the premise underlying his use of the word *seruemus* ('let us keep'). He referred to this positive anthropology again when he retained Athanasius' statement that it was possible to preserve the soul in the same pure state in which it was born.[16]

Pelagius

Several of these were assertions for which Pelagius was later condemned on the grounds that they were new ideas invented by Pelagius that were heretical. These passages in the three versions of the *Life of Antony* are therefore important evidence for the argument that Pelagius did not invent any new ideas but simply repeated longstanding tenets of Christian ascetic paraenesis.

Two of the ideas in this speech by Antony are fundamental to Pelagius' *Letter to Demetrias*. First, the idea that man's nature was innately good was the cornerstone of Pelagius' argument: 'There is, I say, a kind of natural sanctity (as I would put it) in our souls'. He referred to 'the good of nature', 'the riches of nature' and 'that treasure-store of the soul'.[17] Like Athanasius, Pelagius argued

---

arbitrium in Latin usually means 'judgement'. I have done this partly because *liberum arbitrium* is usually translated as 'free will', and partly because in the next sentence Evagrius seems to equate *arbitrium* with *uoluntas* ('will' or 'desire'). In my references to Evagrius' text, the first chapter numbers given are according to the text in Patrologia Latina 73 (Rosweyde's text). The numbers in brackets follow the chapter numbers given in Patrologia Graeca 26 (Montfaucon's text).

[16] Evagrius, *Vita Antonii* 17 (34) (ed. Migne, PL 73.142C), '"But if by chance someone should want to acquire this ability to know the future, let him have a pure heart; because I believe that a soul that serves God, if it perseveres in the purity in which it was born, can know more than the demons. Such was the soul of Elisha"'; '"Sed si forte aliquis hoc libenter assumat, ut futura cognoscat, habeat purum cor; quia credo animam Deo seruientem, si in ea perseuerauerit integritate qua nata est, plus scire posse quam daemones. Talis erat anima Elisaei"'. It is noteworthy that Athanasius and Evagrius referred to the 'pure' state of Elisha, since Pelagius was later criticised for adducing Old Testament figures described in the Bible as perfectly righteous in order to support his argument that virtue was innate in human nature.

[17] Pelagius, *Ad Demetriadem* 4 (ed. Greshake, p. 68), 'Est enim, inquam, in animis nostris naturalis quaedam, ut ita dixerim, sanctitas'; 3 (ed. Greshake, p. 66), 'Naturae bonum'; 6 (ed. Greshake, p. 80), 'Naturae diuitiae'; 'Ille thesaurus animae'.

that this derived from God's creation of man's soul. Second, the sentence to which Augustine principally objected in *Letter to Demetrias* was the one in which Pelagius advised Demetrias that her spiritual riches had to come from within herself and could not come from anyone else: 'No one can confer spiritual riches on you except you yourself .... Riches which, unless they come from you, cannot be in you.'[18] Pelagius' phrase: 'Quae nisi ex te in te esse non possunt' conveyed the same principle as Athanasius' ἐν ἡμῖν ἐστι καὶ ἐξ ἡμῶν συνίσταται, rendered by the anonymous translator as: 'In nobis est et ex nobis constituitur'. Indeed, so close is the similarity of phrasing between Athanasius' *Life of Antony* and Pelagius' *Letter to Demetrias* in the combination of the two prepositions *in* and *ex* that Pelagius' words should perhaps be viewed as a reworking of Athanasius'.

It is noteworthy that when questioned at Diospolis as to whether it was possible for a person to obey the commandments, the condition that Pelagius appended to his answer, 'If he should want it' (*si uelit*), seems to render exactly the sense of Athanasius' phrase, ἐὰν μόνον θελήσωμεν, with a third-person singular in place of a first-person plural, the verbal form being dictated by the circumstances in which the sentence was spoken. These two parallels between Athanasius' text and Pelagius' wording are so close that it is possible that Pelagius was intentionally recalling Athanasius' words in his phrasing.[19]

Likewise, Evagrius' assessment of man's nature and moral capability was exactly the same as Pelagius' was later. Evagrius gave the same account as Pelagius, but the latter was condemned as the originator of an arrogant and heretical position. As Evagrius had done forty years earlier, Pelagius argued against trying to excuse a lack of virtue on the grounds that man's nature inclined him to sin: 'Why do we make pointless evasions, advancing the frailty of our nature as an argument against the one who commands us?'[20] This underlines the similarity of the approach to Christianity propounded by the two authors.

---

[18] Pelagius, *Ad Demetriadem* 11 (ed. Greshake, p. 98), 'Spiritales uero diuitias nullus tibi, praeter te, conferre poterit .... Quae nisi ex te in te esse non possunt'; Augustine, *Ep.* 188.2.5 (ed. Goldbacher, CSEL 57, p. 123), 'You perceive, I am sure, how great is the ruin in these words which must be guarded against. For assuredly the statement: "These good things cannot exist except within you", is said very well and most truly; that is clearly nourishment; but that he says: "They can only come from you", this is completely poisonous. Far be it that a virgin of Christ should gladly hear these things, who piously understands the poverty that is characteristic of the human heart, and for this reason knows that she is not adorned there except by the gifts of her bridegroom'; 'Cernis, nempe, quanta in his uerbis sit cauenda pernicies. Nam utique, quod dictum est: "Non possunt esse ista bona nisi in te", optime et uerissime dictum est; iste plane cibus est; quod uero ait: "Non nisi ex te", hoc omnino uirus est. Absit ut haec libenter audiat uirgo Christi, quae pie intellegit propriam paupertatem cordis humani et ideo illic nisi sponsi sui donis nescit ornari.'

[19] The two parallels are: 'Nisi ex te, in te esse non possunt' with ἐν ἡμῖν ἐστι καὶ ἐξ ἡμῶν συνίσταται; and: 'Si uelit' with ἐὰν μόνον θελήσωμεν.

[20] Pelagius, *Ad Demetriadem* 16 (ed. Greshake, p. 114), 'Quid tergiuersamur incassum, et praecipienti naturae opponimus fragilitatem?'

The ideas that virtue was natural to man and that it came from within an individual were therefore both well established in ascetic literature before Pelagius made these assertions.

Conscience as proof of the retained goodness of human nature even after Adam's sin

Athanasius

Athanasius adduced conscience as evidence to show that virtue came from within man and as a result was achievable:

> 'And be confident that purely through shame at our sins being known, we will cease from sinning and cease entirely from holding anything impure in our hearts. For who wants to be seen committing a sin? And who, when he has sinned, does not prefer to lie because he wishes to escape being found out?'[21]

The anonymous translator

The anonymous translator did not use the word 'shame' but he conveyed Athanasius' point about no one wanting to admit to, or be seen, behaving immorally, and that this would prevent the monks from sinning.[22]

Evagrius

Evagrius added sentences to Athanasius' account, strengthening the argument that shame would prevent sin by mentioning 'conscience' and 'shame' (*conscientia* and *pudor*) once each, 'to blush' (*erubescere*) once and 'to be thrown into confusion by shame' (*confundi*) twice.[23] Evagrius used conscience as part of the

---

[21] Athanasius, Ἐπιστολή 55.10–11 (ed. Bartelink, SC 400, p. 284), Καὶ θαρρεῖτε ὅτι, πάντως αἰσχυνόμενοι γνωσθῆναι, παυσόμεθα τοῦ ἁμαρτάνειν καὶ ὅλως τοῦ ἐνθυμεῖσθαί τι φαῦλον. Τίς γὰρ ἁμαρτάνων θέλει βλέπεσθαι; Τίς ἁμαρτήσας, οὐ μᾶλλον ψεύδεται, λανθάνειν θέλων;

[22] Anon. trans., *Vita Antonii* 55.10–11 (ed. Bartelink, p. 112), '"For if we are in a situation where this is in full view because our neighbours, knowing our sins when we narrate them, throw us into confusion, then we will not commit sin nor will we have any bad thoughts. For who wants to be seen sinning? Or who does not lie after he has sinned, wanting to hide it?"'; '"Si enim hoc ante oculos habuerimus, quia proximi nostri scientes peccata nostra nobis narrantibus confundunt nos, non committemus peccatum, neque cogitemus aliquid aduersum. Quis enim peccans uult uideri? Aut quis post peccatum non mentitur, uolens latere?"'

[23] Evagrius, *Vita Antonii* 28 (55) (ed. Migne, PL 73.151B–D), 'So that leaving judgement to the Saviour we might keep watch on our own consciences by cross-examining ourselves. Antony also used to say that the path to virtue was a wide one, if each person were either to watch what he was doing or to report all his thoughts to the brothers. For no one can sin, Antony used to say, when he is going to report all his sins to someone else and endure the shame of revealing his wicked deeds in public. Finally no sinner dares to sin in front of another person; even if he does sin, he wishes to avoid a witness to his sin and prefers to lie and deny it, and to increase his original fault by adding the fault of denial. "And so", he used to say, "we are put to shame as it were before our own eyes in both thought and deed .... And just as those who have sex with prostitutes are thrown into confusion with shame if

argument that it was possible to achieve virtue, rather than as proof that human nature was inclined to goodness, but these ideas were closely linked and his argument that virtue was achievable was predicated on his earlier argument that human nature was inclined to goodness.

Pelagius

In the same way as Athanasius and Evagrius had done, Pelagius adduced conscience as proof of the soul's inclination to goodness even after Adam's expulsion from Eden. Following Evagrius' lead, Pelagius' words to Demetrias were an elaboration of Antony's words to his monks, adapted to suit his young aristocratic female addressee.[24]

2. The will, habit, and effort as the causes of human goodness

Athanasius

Athanasius stressed the importance of habit, stating that Antony could bear his strict asceticism easily because he had inculcated in himself the habit of virtue: 'He bore the hard work easily. For the willingness of the spirit, maintained for a long period of time, created in him a virtuous permanent condition.'[25] Athanasius repeated this picture of habit as the foundation of virtue: '[Antony] refused to be annointed with oil, saying that it was more fitting for the younger ones to practise asceticism with zeal and not to seek things that would make the body flaccid, but they should make it habituated to labours'.[26]

From the moment of Antony's hearing Matt. 19:21: *If you wish to be perfect, go and sell everything you possess and give it to the poor and come, follow me*

---

others are present, so we too blush to write it down if we do this"'; 'Vt concesso examine Saluatori, proprias conscientias nosmetipsos iudicantes intueremur. Necnon dicebat magnam esse ad uirtutem uiam, si singuli uel obseruarent quod gererent, uel uniuersas mentium cogitationes fratribus referrent. Non enim posse aliquem peccare, cum relaturus esset ad alium quaecunque peccasset, et subire pudorem in publicum turpia proferendi. Denique nullum peccantem coram alio audere peccare; etiamsi peccet, tamen testem uitare peccati, mentiri magis et negare, et uetus delictum nouo inficiandi augere delicto. "Igitur quasi sub oculis", aiebat, "nostris, et cogitatu confundimur et actu .... Et quomodo meretricibus membra miscentes, confunduntur ad praesentiam caeterorum, ita et nos erubescemus ad litteras, si haec agamus."'

[24]   Pelagius, *Ad Demetriadem* 4 (ed. Greshake, p. 66), 'Why is it, I ask you, that we either blush or fear at every sin we commit, displaying our guilt for what we have done at one moment by the blush on our countenance, at another by its pallor, and with an anxious mind we avoid any witness to even our smallest offences and are tormented by pangs of conscience?'; 'Quid illud, obsecro, est, quod ad omne peccatum aut erubescimus aut timemus et culpam facti nunc rubore uultus, nunc pallore monstramus, ac trepidante animo in minimis etiam delictis testem fugimus, conscientia remordemur?'

[25]   Athanasius, Ἐπιστολή 7.5 (ed. Bartelink, SC 400, p. 150), Ῥᾷον τὸν πόνον ἔφερεν. Ἡ γὰρ προθυμία τῆς ψυχῆς, πολὺν χρόνον ἐμμείνασα, ἕξιν ἀγαθὴν ἐνειργάζετο ἐν αὐτῷ.

[26]   Athanasius, Ἐπιστολή 7.8 (ed. Bartelink, SC 400, p. 152), Ἀλείφεσθαι δὲ ἐλαίῳ παρῃτεῖτο, λέγων μᾶλλον πρέπειν τοὺς νεωτέρους ἐκ προθυμίας ἔχειν τὴν ἄσκησιν καὶ μὴ ζητεῖν τὰ χαυνοῦντα τὸ σῶμα, ἀλλὰ καὶ ἐθίζειν αὐτὸ τοῖς πόνοις.

and you will have treasure in heaven, Athanasius continually stressed Antony's enthusiasm for his ascetic way of life: 'At that time moreover he started his way of living and he would measure his intention according to how he would not turn back to the possessions of his parents nor remember his family, but instead would focus the whole of his desire and all his zeal on extending his asceticism.'[27] This stress on effort was the single most repeated message in Athanasius' text, with the words 'zeal' (σπουδή) and 'enthusiasm' or 'eagerness' (προθυμία) and their derivatives recurring very frequently throughout the *Life of Antony*.[28] The word 'choice' (προαίρεσις) occurs only a few times, as if in Athanasius' thought the initial choice was taken as read and it was the determination to continue in this resolve in the face of the devil's temptation that mattered. His account of Antony's life was wholly centred on Antony's personal battle with the devil and his minions; the narrative presented a straight contest between Antony's zeal, on the one hand, and the devil, on the other. Athanasius had Antony say to the devil: '"You will not stop my enthusiasm (προθυμία) like that, devil."'[29] Thus Athanasius' narrative was founded on Antony's own will to resist evil and to pursue virtue.

Athanasius' stress on effort is unquestionable, but analysis of his position on the will and that of the anonymous translator and Evagrius depends to some extent on what exactly Athanasius meant by προθυμία and how it was translated in the Latin versions of the *Life of Antony*. This reflects the fact that how the mind worked was explored in the controversy of the early 5th century, so that questions such as what exactly the will was, whether it was a separate faculty, and what its relation was to desire and to other emotions were posed by the debate about free will. The Greek word προθυμία had a range of meanings encompassing 'readiness', 'willingness', 'eagerness', 'will', 'desire' and 'purpose'. σπουδή ('eagerness', 'zeal', 'enthusiasm') is relatively straightforward since 'zeal' is an unproblematic English equivalent. Athanasius paired 'zeal' (σπουδή) and 'desire' (πόθος) in a way that suggested that they were almost synonyms.[30] He did not, however, explore how the mind worked. He presented a single message in his *Life of Antony*: that an individual's effort to please God achieved the only valuable outcome of a person's

---

[27] Athanasius, Ἐπιστολή 3.5 (ed. Bartelink, SC 400, pp. 136–8), Ἐκεῖ τοίνυν τὰς ἀρχὰς διατρίβων, τὴν διάνοιαν ἐστάθμιζεν, ὅπως πρὸς μὲν τὰ τῶν γονέων μὴ ἐπιστρέφηται μηδὲ τῶν συγγενῶν μνημονεύῃ· ὅλον δὲ τὸν πόθον καὶ πᾶσαν τὴν σπουδὴν ἔχῃ περὶ τὸν τόνον τῆς ἀσκήσεως.

[28] *Zeal* (σπουδή) and *eagerness* (προθυμία): see for example Athanasius, Ἐπιστολή 4.1–2 (ed. Bartelink, SC 400, pp. 138–40); 7.8 (ed. Bartelink, SC 400, p. 152); 11.1–2 (ed. Bartelink, SC 400, p. 164); 13.6 (ed. Bartelink, SC 400, p. 170); 15.3 (ed. Bartelink, SC 400, p. 176); 16.3 (ed. Bartelink, SC 400, p. 178); 18.2 (ed. Bartelink, SC 400, p. 184); 46.5 (ed. Bartelink, SC 400, p. 260); 50.3 (ed. Bartelink, SC 400, p. 270); 54.8 (ed. Bartelink, SC 400, p. 280); 91.2 (ed. Bartelink, SC 400, p. 368); 93.1 (ed. Bartelink, SC 400, p. 372); 54.7 (ed. Bartelink, SC 400, p. 280), 'zeal to make progress', ζῆλος προκοπῆς.

[29] Athanasius, Ἐπιστολή 11.4 (ed. Bartelink, SC 400, p. 166), Οὐκ ἐμποδίσεις ἐν τούτῳ μου τὴν προθυμίαν, διάβολε.

[30] Athanasius, Ἐπιστολή 3.5 (ed. Bartelink, SC 400, pp. 136–8), 'He kept the whole of his desire and all his zeal directed toward extending his asceticism'; Ὅλον δὲ τὸν πόθον καὶ πᾶσαν τὴν σπουδὴν ἔχῃ περὶ τὸν τόνον τῆς ἀσκήσεως. Cited at n. 27 above.

life, which was entry into the kingdom of heaven. A presumption of effective free will underpinned Athanasius' narrative, which was an act of marketing for a way of life built on a theology that he appears to have taken to be unproblematic in terms of doctrine, although in practice he identified a potential for arrogance that needed to be comprehensively forestalled. There is no evidence that he saw this danger as a doctrinal rather than just a practical problem. Athanasius used a nexus of words to convey his central message, which hinged on personal responsibility: προθυμία ('ready willingness', 'eagerness'), σπουδή ('zeal') and its derivatives, and πρόθεσις ('resolve', 'purpose', 'intention').

This message was reinforced by the teaching that Athanasius portrayed Antony giving to the monks. Antony's instructions all presupposed that the monks were the agents of their moral choices, while at the same time he advised the monks to pray for help continually. Athanasius emphasised the monks' own agency by using personal pronouns in association with verbs to create a reflexive meaning, suggesting the monks should train *themselves*, and that they should carry out Antony's instructions in order to train their own spirits:

> [Antony instructed them] to learn by heart the instructions in the Scriptures and remember the deeds of the saints so that their souls would be trained by the saints' zeal as they remembered the commandments .... '*Examine yourselves, test yourselves* [2 Cor. 13:5] .... But let us examine ourselves, and let us hasten to supply what we lack.'[31]

The monks were to 'mould themselves'.[32] This use of personal reflexive pronouns emphasised personal responsibility for virtue. This message of their own agency was repeatedly hammered home to the monks: "'Live as if you are going to die each day, paying attention to yourselves"'.[33] Just before his death, Antony again stressed the monks' ability to guard *themselves* against evil.[34] In his final words he repeated this use of reflexive personal pronouns to stress the monks' personal responsibility for controlling themselves and for their own salvation: "'But rather you also, be eager always to bind yourselves fast, principally to the Lord, and then to the saints"'.[35] Athanasius also described faith as inherently a process of action,

---

[31] Athanasius, Ἐπιστολή 55.3–8 (ed. Bartelink, SC 400, pp. 282–4), [Antony instructed them] Ἀποστηθίζειν τὰ ἐν ταῖς γραφαῖς παραγγέλματα, καὶ μνημονεύειν τῶν πράξεων τῶν ἁγίων πρὸς τὸ τῷ ζήλῳ τούτων ῥυθμίζεσθαι τὴν ψυχὴν ὑπομιμνησκομένην ἐκ τῶν ἐντολῶν .... Ἑαυτοὺς ἀνακρίνετε, ἑαυτοὺς δοκιμάζετε [2 Cor. 13:5] .... Ἑαυτοὺς δὲ ἀνακρίνωμεν, καὶ ἃ ὑστεροῦμεν, ἀναπληροῦν σπουδάζωμεν.

[32] Athanasius, Ἐπιστολή 55.13 (ed. Bartelink, SC 400, p. 286), "'Moulding ourselves in this way"'; Οὕτω δὲ τυποῦντες ἑαυτούς.

[33] Athanasius, Ἐπιστολή 91.3 (ed. Bartelink, SC 400, p. 368), Ὡς καθ' ἡμέραν ἀποθνήσκοντες ζήσατε, προσέχοντες ἑαυτοῖς. 20.9 (ed. Bartelink, SC 400, p. 190), "'Let us guard ourselves from impure thoughts"'; Φυλάξωμεν ἑαυτοὺς ἀπὸ λογισμῶν ῥυπαρῶν. 27.4 (ed. Bartelink, SC 400, p. 210), "'Rather, let us pay attention to our own resolve of asceticism"'; Τῇ δὲ προθέσει τῆς ἀσκήσεως ἑαυτῶν μᾶλλον προσέχωμεν.

[34] Athanasius, Ἐπιστολή 89.6 (ed. Bartelink, SC 400, p. 364), "'And so instead keep yourselves pure, away from contact with these people"'; Καθαροὺς οὖν μᾶλλον ἑαυτοὺς ἀπὸ τούτων φυλάττετε.

[35] Athanasius, Ἐπιστολή 91.5 (ed. Bartelink, SC 400, p. 368), Σπουδάζετε δὲ μᾶλλον καὶ ὑμεῖς ἀεὶ συνάπτειν ἑαυτούς, προηγουμένως μὲν τῷ Κυρίῳ, ἔπειτα δὲ τοῖς ἁγίοις.

using the phrase 'the action of faith' (ἡ διὰ πίστεως ἐνέργεια); and he glossed this as requiring efforts at self-control by the individual: '"And that our faith is active, see now we apply ourselves to our faith in Christ"'.[36] Thus Athanasius made Antony the archetype of human endeavour and initiative in the achievement of virtue. He did this through his use of a carefully selected and relentlessly repeated vocabulary of personal effort and determination, and this language was predicated on a presumption of individual human agency in the achievement of virtue.

Furthermore, Athanasius set out a clear picture of how virtue was created and engendered. One way in which virtue was created in men was by Antony causing the monks to love virtue through his encouragement. When he talked to them: 'Their love of virtue increased', and the practice of a coenobitic community was presented as founded on mutual encouragement.[37] Athanasius' narrative was predicated on this model, in which the monastery was pictured as orientated towards virtue: 'A multitude of ascetics, the single thought of all of them directed toward virtue.'[38] This model of help and encouragement mirrored the relationship between Antony and Jesus depicted by Athanasius after Antony had proved his determination to resist evil. Thereafter when the demons tempted Antony: 'Antony was encouraged by the Saviour'.[39]

The anonymous translator

Where Athanasius wrote προθυμία, the anonymous translator used *prompta uoluntas* (a 'ready will' or a 'ready desire'). This translation represented a potential shift from a contingent quality of emotion, to a word that could mean either a contingent quality of emotion or a decision-making faculty. It is noticeable that no clear distinction was drawn in the anonymous translator's use of the word *uoluntas* between 'will' and 'desire': the same word was used in contexts that clearly required two different meanings, reflecting the fact that the Latin word encompassed these two separate semantic denotations.[40] Matching Athanasius' repeated use of the word προθυμία, the anonymous translation of the *Life of Antony* continuously presented 'will' or 'desire' (*uoluntas*) as the determinant of

---

[36] Athanasius, Ἐπιστολή 78.2 (ed. Bartelink, SC 400, p. 334), Καὶ ὅτι ἐνεργής ἐστιν ἡ πίστις ἡμῶν, ἰδοὺ νῦν ἡμεῖς ἐπερειδόμεθα τῇ πίστει τῇ εἰς τὸν Χριστόν.

[37] Athanasius, Ἐπιστολή 44.1 (ed. Bartelink, SC 400, p. 252), Ὁ ἔρως τῆς ἀρετῆς ηὔξανεν.

[38] Athanasius, Ἐπιστολή 44.4 (ed. Bartelink, SC 400, p. 254), Πλῆθος μὲν ἀσκητῶν, ἐν δὲ τῶν πάντων εἰς ἀρετὴν τὸ φρόνημα.

[39] Athanasius, Ἐπιστολή 52.1 (ed. Bartelink, SC 400, p. 274), Ὁ δὲ Ἀντώνιος παρεκαλεῖτο παρὰ τοῦ Σωτῆρος.

[40] Uses of the singular *uoluntas* that can only mean 'desire': Anon. trans., *Vita Antonii* 5.6 (ed. Bartelink, p. 16), 'The enemy kept suggesting to him desire for pleasure'; 'Inimicus suggerebat lenitatis uoluntatem', translating Athanasius, Ἐπιστολή 5.6 (ed. Bartelink, SC 400, p. 144), Ὁ μὲν ἐχθρὸς ὑπέβαλλε τὸ λεῖον τῆς ἡδονῆς. 19.5 (ed. Bartelink, p. 46) also translating ἡδονή, twice; 23.3 (ed. Bartelink, p. 54) translating ἡδονή. Use of singular *uoluntas* as 'will': Anon. trans., *Vita Antonii* 46.5 (ed. Bartelink, p. 96), 'But he himself stood without any trembling, showing the ready will of Christians'; 'Ipse autem sine aliquo tremore stabat, ostendens Christianorum promptam uoluntatem', translating προθυμία, Athanasius, Ἐπιστολή 46.5 (ed. Bartelink, SC 400, p. 260).

virtue. Because the significance of this is that *uoluntas* was the seat of agency in the anonymous translator's *Life of Antony*, I shall use the translation 'will' in my analysis, but it should always be remembered that it could in many cases be translated as 'desire'.[41] The point to note is that in his narrative, *uoluntas* was the effective agent in virtue and it was internal to each individual. It is interesting to see how the anonymous author translated Athanasius' assertion of the importance of habit; he characterised habit as the maintenance of will over time:

> Indeed because he remained for a long time with a ready will in himself, a good disposition toward sustaining his asceticism had been created in him, so that if he received to himself from others some opportunity for sacred virtue, he applied and demonstrated great perseverance in this too.[42]

The result of this was that the anonymous translator's narrative was about *uoluntas* almost more than it was about Antony himself, because Antony was made the embodiment of the human will to succeed in the pursuit of virtue, reflecting Athanasius' Antony who was the archetype of human endeavour, expressed in the omnipresent word 'eagerness' (προθυμία).[43] In his dramatic face-to-face duels with the devil, the anonymous translator's Antony presented this battle as a struggle between his 'will' and the devil, so that the hero himself credited his will with being the determining factor at work in his resisting evil and pursuing virtue: "'You will not impede my ready will in this.'"[44] Thus it was the 'will' (*uoluntas*) that was good or bad, and humans controlled their will.

As in Athanasius'original, this emphasis on the role of the 'will' or 'desire' was placed alongside statements that God co-operated with and helped man in this struggle to reject evil and choose virtue. It was important for the message of the need to fight that God would help Christians in their struggle, and this help was shown being given to Antony throughout his life. Because in Athanasius' narrative 'a ready will' (προθυμία) was what Antony contributed on his side of this paradigm of co-operative action, for most of the anonymous translator's text, 'will' is

---

[41] The Latin phrase most commonly used to denote the concept of free will was *liberum arbitrium*, meaning 'free judgement' or 'free decision'. For English-speakers, translation into English on this subject is muddied by the fact that the English phrase 'free will' has come to be the standard translation for what in Latin is 'free judgement' (*liberum arbitrium*).

[42] Anon. trans., *Vita Antonii* 7.5 (ed. Bartelink, p. 22), 'Prompta uero uoluntate multum temporis manens in eo, ingenium bonum sustinentiae in eum fuerat operata, ut si sibi aliquam occasionem uirtutis deificae ab aliis accepisset, multam et in hoc contulisse et ostendisse instantiam.'

[43] Most often 'will' (*uoluntas*) translated Athanasius' προθυμία. For the role of *uoluntas* as the translation of Athanasius' προθυμία, see: Anon. trans., *Vita Antonii* 13.6 (ed. Bartelink, p. 36), for Athanasius, Ἐπιστολή 13.6 (ed. Bartelink, SC 400, p. 170); 15.2 (ed. Bartelink, p. 38), for Athanasius, Ἐπιστολή 15.3 (ed. Bartelink, SC 400, p. 176); 16.3 (ed. Bartelink, p. 40), for Athanasius, Ἐπιστολή 16.3 (ed. Bartelink, SC 400, p. 178); 18.2 (ed. Bartelink, p. 44), for Athanasius, Ἐπιστολή 18.2 (ed. Bartelink, SC 400, p. 184); 50.3 (ed. Bartelink, p. 102), for Athanasius, Ἐπιστολή 50.3 (ed. Bartelink, SC 400, p. 270); 54.8 (ed. Bartelink, p. 110), for Athanasius, Ἐπιστολή 54.8 (ed. Bartelink, SC 400, p. 280); 46.2 (ed. Bartelink, p. 96), for Athanasius, Ἐπιστολή 46.2 (ed. Bartelink, SC 400, p. 260).

[44] Anon. trans., *Vita Antonii* 11.4 (ed. Bartelink, p. 32), "'Non impedies promptam uoluntatem meam in hoc.'"

the most appropriate meaning for *uoluntas*, since it so often occurs in the phrase *prompta uoluntas* in this context of the co-operative model. However, across the whole of his version of the *Life of Antony*, the anonymous translator gave mixed messages about what he understood by the term *uoluntas*. In the following passage he asserted that the Lord co-operated with man, and shortly afterwards used *uoluntas* to translate 'desire' or 'pleasure' (ἡδονή):

> 'And so let us stick to our sacred endeavour, my sons, and not yield. For the Lord is our co-worker in this, as it is written: *God co-operates for the good with all who want what is good* [Rom. 8:28] .... But we will not have any lust for a woman or other sordid desire (*uoluntas* for ἡδονή) at all, fighting always, and keeping before our eyes the Day of Judgement. For the very great fear and recall of torments dissolves the blandishment of desire (*uoluntas* for ἡδονή) and rouses a mind though it is already heading downwards toward sin.'[45]

Both in Antony's final words of advice to his monks: 'Hurry with earnestness to maintain your ready will', and in the author's summation of Antony's life: 'He preserved such an unvarying ready will toward ascetic endeavour', the message of the preceding narrative about the agency of the human will was repeated.[46] When Athanasius wrote that Antony told his monks that they should pursue their asceticism 'with eagerness' (ἐκ προθυμίας), the anonymous writer translated this as *ex uoluntate*.[47] It is not relevant to the argument of this book whether or not this prominent role for the will in the anonymous translator's Latin version of the *Life of Antony* triggered the controversy over its role in the Christian message of salvation. What is relevant is that this key role for *uoluntas* was not something Pelagius invented.

Evagrius

It is interesting to see how Evagrius translated Athanasius' statement that 'willingness of spirit' (προθυμία τῆς ψυχῆς) maintained over a long period created a virtuous habit. In Evagrius' version of this statement the voluntariness of this readiness was the key aspect; he described it as the dedication of 'voluntary' servitude (*uoluntariae seruitutis studium*): 'Because the long-term dedication of voluntary servitude to the work of God had turned habit into nature.'[48] Where the

---

[45] Anon. trans., *Vita Antonii* 19.1–5 (ed. Bartelink, p. 46), '"Adhaereamus ergo, filii, studio deifico, et non acediemur. Habemus enim in hoc Dominum cooperarium ut scriptum est: *Omni uolenti bonum Deus cooperatur in bono* [Rom. 8:28] .... Concupiscentiam autem mulieris aut alterius sordidae uoluntatis omnino non tenebimus, contendentes semper et ante oculos habentes diem iudicii. Maximus enim timor et tormentorum commemoratio dissoluit lenitatem uoluntatis et animam iam declinantem excitat.'"

[46] Anon. trans., *Vita Antonii* 91.2 (ed. Bartelink, p. 172), '"Festinate instanter custodire uestram promptam uoluntatem"'; 93.1 (ed. Bartelink, p. 174), 'Tantam aequalem custodiuit in studio deifico promptam uoluntatem'.

[47] Anon. trans., *Vita Antonii* 7.8 (ed. Bartelink, p. 22).

[48] Evagrius, *Vita Antonii* 7 (5) (ed. Migne, PL 73.130D), 'Quia uoluntariae seruitutis longum in Dei opere studium, consuetudinem in naturam uerterat.' Cf. Athanasius, Ἐπιστολή 7.5 (ed. Bartelink, SC

anonymous translator opted for *prompta uoluntas* to translate προθυμία, Evagrius made explicit and emphasised the role of the will: the fact that Antony chose this way of life of his own free will, and his resulting action.

In Antony's long speech to the monks about the achievability of virtue, Evagrius repeated the explicit assertion that the human will caused human virtue. He nowhere mentioned God's agency in human virtue; on the contrary, three times he stated explicitly that human will caused human virtue, and he used the terms *uoluntas* (here best understood as meaning 'will') and *arbitrium* ('judgement'), so that when Pelagius began to write thirty years later, these ideas expressed in this vocabulary would have been familiar to Latin readers. Athanasius' phrase 'if only we wish it' (ἐὰν μόνον θελήσωμεν) was repeated twice by Evagrius, first as: 'Which depends on our judgement' ('Quod ex nostro pendet arbitrio') and second as: 'Which only awaits our will' ('Quae nostram tantummodo exspectat uoluntatem'), so that Evagrius particularly stressed the role of the will in the pursuit of righteousness, using the terms *arbitrium* and *uoluntas*.[49]

Moreover, Evagrius translated Athanasius': 'each will be judged on these things: if he has kept the faith and if he has kept the commandments truly' using the words 'every individual prepares for himself' (*unusquisque sibi praeparat*) to emphasise human control of this process: '"Each person prepares for himself in advance either torments or glory depending on this: whether he neglects the commandments of the Scriptures, or carries them out."'[50]

Thus in this passage Evagrius altered Athanasius' text in order to stress that each individual was the author of his own destiny in relation to salvation. He made this statement more than once, using the same vocabulary. Antony urged pursuit of Christian virtues: '"Striving after these things, we shall prepare for ourselves in advance a dwelling-place in the land of the peaceful, as it says in the Gospel."'[51] Compare this with Antony's comment in Athanasius: '"Having obtained these things, we will find them there in return, making us welcome in the

---

400, p. 150), 'For the willingness of the spirit, maintained over a long period of time, created in him a virtuous permanent condition'; Ἡ γὰρ προθυμία τῆς ψυχῆς, πολὺν χρόνον ἐμμείνασα, ἕξιν ἀγαθὴν ἐνειργάζετο ἐν αὐτῷ.

[49] Evagrius, *Vita Antonii* 15 (20) (ed. Migne, PL 73.136C–D), '"I beg you, do not fear the word virtue as if it were something unattainable, nor let this endeavour, which depends on our judgement, seem something alien to you or remote from you. Inborn nature inclines man to this effort, and it is something that only awaits our will"'; '"Nolite, quaeso, uirtutis tanquam impossibile nomen pauere, nec peregrinum uobis aut procul positum uideatur hoc studium, quod ex nostro pendet arbitrio. Huius operis homini inserta natura est, et eiusmodi res est, quae nostram tantummodo exspectat uoluntatem."' Cited in n. 15.

[50] Evagrius, *Vita Antonii* 17 (33) (ed. Migne, PL 73.142B), '"In hoc unusquisque sibi praeparat, seu tormenta, seu gloriam, si uel negligat Scripturarum mandata, uel faciat."' Cf. Athanasius, Ἐπιστολή 33.6 (ed. Bartelink, SC 400, p. 228), '"Each individual is judged on this, whether he has kept the faith and has kept the commandments truly"'; Ἐν τούτοις ἕκαστος ἔχει τὴν κρίσιν, εἰ τὴν πίστιν τετήρηκε καὶ τὰς ἐντολὰς γνησίως ἐφύλαξεν.

[51] Evagrius, *Vita Antonii* 15 (17) (ed. Migne, PL 73.135D), '"Haec sectantes, mansionem nobis in terra quietorum, secundum Euangelium [cf. John 14:2], praeparabimus."'

land of the gentle.'"[52] Athanasius' Antony did not express the individual's direct control over his own salvation as explicitly as Evagrius' Antony. Evagrius used the prefix *prae-* ('in advance', 'pre-') here in *praeparare* ('to prepare in advance') to highlight how man was the author of his own punishment or reward. Later it came to embody the vexed and controversial question of the temporal priority of God's agency in words such as *praedestinatio* ('predestination'), *praeueniens* ('prevenient'), *praeordinatio* ('preordainment'), and *praescientia* ('foreknowledge'). Yet here, before the timing of agency became problematical, Evagrius was able to use *praeparare* with reference to man's agency without any hint of controversy. This statement potentially contradicted any assertion of the agency of prevenient grace. In Evagrius' *Life of Antony*, man controlled his own choices and his own fate.[53]

Evagrius was well aware of the role of will as a mental faculty. When explaining to the monks that the devil was powerless to harm them, Evagrius' Antony switched to addressing the devil directly as if he were present, and Evagrius added some sentences to the original text, in one of which Antony told the devil: '"If possibility followed will, it would be enough for you simply to wish it.'"[54] This statement was not in Athanasius, whose Antony spoke only to the monks in this episode, to explain that evil spirits could not harm them. By contrast, Evagrius' analysis developed this idea of the demons' weakness by adding this assertion, which made a technical philosophical point. Like Athanasius, Evagrius consistently used the idea of special powers (particularly powers relating to demons) as gifts from God in order to highlight man's dependence on God and man's need of His help against evil. This statement to the devil was intended as an assertion of the devil's weakness in comparison to God, and as a reason to adopt Christianity. It should be read in its context, following Antony's statements about how much the devil wanted to harm them, and as part of the marketing strategy of the text; it should not be taken as a statement that will was not enough for man in choosing virtue. It does reflect, however, the development of the discussion of will in Evagrius' version of the *Life of Antony* as compared with Athanasius' text. For Evagrius, 'will' (*uoluntas*) was at times something like a faculty of the mind. Only to the extent that Evagrius portrayed man as needing God as his helper and co-worker in the rejection of evil was human willing on its own insufficient for virtue in Evagrius' narrative. The key factor in his account of the determining of

---

[52] Athanasius, Ἐπιστολή 17.7 (ed. Bartelink, SC 400, p. 182), Ταῦτα κτώμενοι, εὑρήσομεν αὐτὰ πρὸ ἑαυτῶν ἐκεῖ ποιοῦντα ξενίαν ἡμῖν ἐν τῇ γῇ τῶν πραέων.

[53] Evagrius omitted one clause in Athanasius' text concerning virtue: 'It is within us and it is created by us' (ἐν ἡμῖν ἐστι καὶ ἐξ ἡμῶν συνίσταται). The significance of this clause is not that its omission meant that Evagrius did not assert all the central theses proposed by Athanasius; it is that this phrase about the interiority of virtue was one that Pelagius echoed to Demetrias in the work that was his clearest statement of the principles he asserted, and it was a phrase in Pelagius' letter to Demetrias to which Augustine particularly objected: see n. 18.

[54] Evagrius, *Vita Antonii* 16 (28) (ed. Migne, PL 73.140C), '"Si uoluntatem sequitur possibilitas, tantum tibi uelle sufficiat"'; cf. the whole passage at Athanasius, Ἐπιστολή 28.6–10 (ed. Bartelink, SC 400, pp. 214–16).

salvation was human initiative and willing. This was the same model of co-operation as Athanasius put forward, but Evagrius introduced greater clarity about the process and about certain concepts involved in it. Importantly, in all three versions of the *Life of Antony*, the rejection of evil was not differentiable from choice of moral virtue; the two were synonymous.[55]

Pelagius

Like Athanasius and his Latin translators, Pelagius located the determinant of virtue within the individual and his overarching theme was the need for effort. The difference was that where Athanasius and Evagrius had been able to work from a presumption of effective free will, Pelagius had to defend this principle. Also like Athanasius and Evagrius, Pelagius stressed habit as the means by which to inculcate righteous actions.[56] The evidence presented suggests that Pelagius' stress on habit as fostering virtuous behaviour was a well-established idea.

3. Free will

Athanasius: choice (προαίρεσις) as equivalent to free will

Athanasius attributed to Antony what Athanasius described as the unexpected view that neither the length nor the solitariness of ascetic endeavour were its most important attributes: 'He did not think it worthwhile to measure the path of virtue by duration, or the degree of isolation undertaken, but by desire for it and deliberate choice of it.'[57] The most valuable aspect of Antony's virtue was that it was freely chosen. Jerome later put it succinctly when he argued that free will gave virtue its value. For Athanasius, 'choice' (προαίρεσις) contained a presumption of freedom of choice, and this sentence shows how effective free will underpinned Athanasius' ascetic programme. Athanasius took this freedom of choice as read and as unproblematic, because this principle had not been questioned before the discussion of it in the Latin West in the early 5th century. He used the term προαίρεσις with a meaning that contained the sense of autonomous free determination that made it equivalent to the more technically specific sense of the phrase *liberum arbitrium*, which emerged in the Latin West from the examination of the

---

[55] In consequence, the distinction between single and dual predestination would be impossible in this schema. Similarly, Pelagius felt the logical flaw in the suggestion that when God chose to make one individual able to act virtuously, he did not *ipso facto* also choose *not* to make another individual act virtuously—that is, the lack of a positive choice was logically at the same time also a choice to make an individual morally bad: Pelagius, *De diuina lege* 7.1 (ed. Migne, PL 30.112D–113A), see Chapter 1, n. 40.

[56] Pelagius, *Ad Demetriadem* 13 (ed. Greshake, p. 104), 'The mind ... uses the advantage of long habit in order to gain the ability to live well'; 'Animus ... longae consuetudinis beneficio utitur ad bene uiuendi facultatem.'

[57] Athanasius, Ἐπιστολή 7.10 (ed. Bartelink, SC 400, p. 154), Οὐ γὰρ ἠξίου χρόνῳ μετρεῖν τὴν τῆς ἀρετῆς ὁδόν, οὐδὲ τὴν δι' αὐτὴν ἀναχώρησιν, ἀλλὰ πόθῳ καὶ τῇ προαιρέσει.

issue that occurred there at the start of the 5th century. For Athanasius, the devil's aim was to separate Antony from his choice:

> And in short, he [the devil] stirred up in his mind a great dustcloud of thoughts, wanting to separate Antony from his right choice. But when the enemy saw that he was weak in the face of Antony's resolve, and instead that he was himself cast to the ground by Antony's fixedness.[58]

Athanasius established this model of Antony's 'right choice' and 'resolve' (ὀρθή προαίρεσις, πρόθεσις) at the start of his biography of Antony.[59] He also characterised the asceticism of other monks as the result of choice.[60] The word 'purpose' or 'resolve' (πρόθεσις) recurs in the narrative, and it too contains the implicit presumption of individual agency and effective free will.[61] From the opening sentences of the *Life of Antony* onwards, however, this was conceived of as a co-operative project between man and God: 'Rightly will a person praise this resolve, and as you pray God will bring it to completion.'[62]

Athanasius also described effective free will in action when he discussed the process of rejecting evil. Antony told the monks that Christ had stopped demons from quoting Scripture so that they could not mix truth with their evil:

> 'And also so that he would accustom us never to pay attention to such things, even if they should seem to be speaking truths. For it is unseemly that we should be taught by the devil when we have the Scriptures and the freedom given to us by the Saviour'.[63]

The implication of this passage was that this rejection of the devil was made possible by the Scriptures and by Christ's coming, which gave man the positive 'freedom' (ἐλευθερία) to be able to reject the devil.

---

[58] Athanasius, Ἐπιστολή 5.3 (ed. Bartelink, SC 400, p. 142), Καὶ ὅλως πολὺν ἤγειρεν αὐτῷ κονιορτὸν λογισμῶν ἐν τῇ διανοίᾳ, θέλων αὐτὸν ἀποσχίσαι τῆς ὀρθῆς προαιρέσεως. Ὡς δὲ εἶδεν ἑαυτὸν ὁ ἐχθρὸς ἀσθενοῦντα πρὸς τὴν τοῦ Ἀντωνίου πρόθεσιν καὶ μᾶλλον ἑαυτὸν καταπαλαιόμενον ὑπὸ τῆς ἐκείνου στερρότητος...

[59] Athanasius, Ἐπιστολή Preface 3 (ed. Bartelink, SC 400, p. 126), 'But I know that when you have heard about it, you also will not only admire the man but also will wish to imitate his resolve'; Οἶδα δέ, ὅτι καὶ ὑμεῖς ἀκούσαντες, μετὰ τοῦ θαυμάσαι τὸν ἄνθρωπον, θελήσετε καὶ ζηλῶσαι τὴν ἐκείνου πρόθεσιν.

[60] Athanasius, Ἐπιστολή 14.7 (ed. Bartelink, SC 400, p. 174), 'He persuaded many to choose the solitary life'; Ἔπεισε πολλοὺς αἱρήσασθαι τὸν μονήρη βίον.

[61] Athanasius, Ἐπιστολή 12.3 (ed. Bartelink, SC 400, p. 168), 'And so, increasing his resolve in intensity more and more'; Μᾶλλον οὖν καὶ μᾶλλον ἐπιτείνας τὴν πρόθεσιν. Athanasius, Ἐπιστολή 27.4 (ed. Bartelink, SC 400, p. 210), '"Rather, let us pay attention to our own resolve of asceticism"'; Τῇ δὲ προθέσει τῆς ἀσκήσεως ἑαυτῶν μᾶλλον προσέχωμεν.

[62] Athanasius, Ἐπιστολή Preface 1 (ed. Bartelink, SC 400, p. 126), Ταύτην μὲν οὖν τὴν πρόθεσιν δικαίως ἄν τις ἐπαινέσειε καὶ εὐχομένων ὑμῶν ὁ θεὸς τελεώσειεν.

[63] Athanasius, Ἐπιστολή 26.3–4 (ed. Bartelink, SC 400, p. 208), Καὶ ἵνα καὶ ἡμᾶς συνεθίσῃ μηδέποτε τοῖς τοιούτοις προσέχειν, κἂν δοκῶσι τἀληθῆ λέγειν. Καὶ γὰρ ἀπρεπές, ἔχοντας ἡμᾶς τὰς γραφὰς καὶ τὴν παρὰ τοῦ Σωτῆρος ἐλευθερίαν, διδάσκεσθαι παρὰ τοῦ διαβόλου.

The anonymous translator

It is again instructive to see the vocabulary the anonymous translator used to render key words in Athanasius' text. When Athanasius' Antony stated that the value of ascetic effort lay in the desire and choice that led to it, the anonymous translator expressed this as: 'He used to say that the proof of sacred virtue lay in the individual's desire for it and in his good will'.[64] Athanasius' 'choice' (προαίρεσις) became 'a good will' (*bona uoluntas*), prefiguring the stress on the 'will' in Latin ascetic discourse.

Evagrius

Where Athanasius assumed effective free will, and his anonymous translator simply rendered that assumption into Latin using the word *uoluntas*, Evagrius consistently went a step further and made explicit reference to the voluntariness of virtue. As has been noted, where Athanasius wrote that longstanding habit engendered virtue, Evagrius wrote of the voluntary quality of long-maintained servitude, emphasising the role of the will and the resulting action. Where Athanasius stated at the outset that the achievement of salvation was a process of co-operation between man and God, and made God the subject of the verb 'to accomplish' (τελεῖν) in relation to the monks' resolve, Evagrius retained the co-operative model and translated 'resolve' or 'intention' (πρόθεσις) as *uoluntas*: 'Everyone will rightly marvel at your will (*uoluntas*), and God will grant the desired result to your prayers.'[65] Thus Evagrius strengthened the role of the 'will' (*uoluntas*), and in his text the will was the agent of salvation. When Athanasius' Antony stated that the value of ascetic endeavour lay in the individual's desire and choice of it, Evagrius altered this sentence to feature the notions of merit (*merita*) and free choice (*spontaneus*): 'For this reason he did not weigh the merits of endeavour by length of time, but with love and freely-chosen servitude always, he would urge his desire to advance in fear of God, as if he was just starting out.'[66] This

---

[64] Anon. trans., *Vita Antonii* 7.9–10 (ed. Bartelink, pp. 22–4), 'He did not judge it proper that the path of virtue should be valued according to the time spent on it. Nor in the seclusion into which a person withdrew for its sake, but instead he used to say that the proof of sacred virtue lay in the individual's desire for it and in his good will'; 'Non enim dignum arbitrabatur ut in transacto tempore deputari possit uirtutis uia. Neque enim in secessum, quod secessit propter illam, sed indicium uirtutis dicebat esse deificae in desiderio et uoluntate bona.' *Desire* (πόθος) was translated as *desiderium*, suggesting that the anonymous translator was here using *uoluntas* in the sense of 'will' when he translated Athanasius' word 'choice' (προαιρέσις) as 'a good will' (*bona uoluntas*). As Athanasius did, the anonymous translator drew no formal distinction between a contingent emotion such as 'desire' (*desiderium*) and the will as a faculty. He could perhaps have translated Athanasius' 'choice' (προαιρέσις) with Latin *optio*, but he chose *uoluntas*. For a discussion of Athanasius' understanding of how the mind worked, see pp. 41–2.

[65] Evagrius, *Vita Antonii* Preface (ed. Migne, PL 73.126), *uoluntas* meaning 'will', 'resolve', 'intention', 'desire': 'Hanc uoluntatem uestram iuste quisque mirabitur; orantibusque uobis optatum Deus tribuet effectum.' Cf. Athanasius, Ἐπιστολή Preface 1 (ed. Bartelink, SC 400, p. 126), see n. 62.

[66] Evagrius, *Vita Antonii* 6 (7) (ed. Migne, PL 73.131A), 'Vnde nec temporum longitudine laborum merita pensabat, sed amore et famulatu spontaneo semper, tanquam in principiis constitutus, ad profectum diuini metus desiderium concitabat.'

change Evagrius made to Athanasius' sentence was significant. Instead of it being an aphorism Antony used to say, it became a statement of how Antony's understanding of Christianity was put into practice in his actions through his voluntary decision. Evagrius changed Athanasius' text to write of 'voluntary servitude' (*uoluntaria seruitus*) and 'freely chosen service' (*famulatus spontaneus*): in both statements, voluntariness was emphasised.

Immediately after the episode in which Jesus told Antony that he was waiting to see if Antony fought bravely against the devil, and that once Antony had proved his courage, Jesus would help him, Athanasius described how Antony: 'Was even more eager with regard to piety' and left his home to learn more.[67] Evagrius translated 'more eager' (προθυμότερος) as 'with a ready will' (*uoluntate prompta*), and significantly in the same sentence he introduced the idea of merit in association with this 'will': 'Because through his ready will he was growing in spiritual merits'.[68] Shortly afterwards, Antony told the devil that he would not impede Antony's 'will' (Athanasius' προθυμία was here translated by Evagrius as *uoluntas*).[69] Thus in Evagrius' version of the *Life of Antony*, Antony's virtue was portrayed as a function of his will.[70] Likewise, when Athanasius' Antony listed scorn for money among the qualities of a virtuous life, Evagrius accentuated the voluntariness of this virtue, rendering this as 'voluntary poverty'.[71]

It is also instructive to note the subtle changes Evagrius made to Athansius' statement that Christians should not listen to the devil when he quoted Scripture. Once again, Evagrius elucidated the process, adding detail. For example, he mentioned that the monks should follow Christ's example; and what Athanasius described as 'paying attention to' the devil, Evagrius glossed as 'giving consent to evil', which highlighted the human act of will in the process:

> 'So that, following His example, we should not give them our consent in anything, even if they should advise useful things, because it is in no way right to take advice about how to live from the devil, after the Lord has bestowed on us freedom and the life-giving precepts of the Scriptures'.[72]

---

[67] Athanasius, Ἐπιστολή 11.1 (ed. Bartelink, SC 400, p. 164), Ἔτι μᾶλλον προθυμότερος ἦν εἰς τὴν θεοσέβειαν.

[68] Evagrius, *Vita Antonii* 10 (11) (ed. Migne, PL 73.133A), 'Cum uoluntate prompta per merita religiosa succresceret'.

[69] Evagrius, *Vita Antonii* 10 (11) (ed. Migne, PL 73.133B), '"You will not impede my will"'; '"Non impedies uoluntatem meam"'. The anonymous translator used the phrase *prompta uoluntas*: see n. 44.

[70] Evagrius regularly described the monks' choice of life as determined by their will (*uoluntas*). For example, Evagrius, *Vita Antonii* 58 (91) (ed. Migne, PL 73.167A), '"Judge that religious zeal caught you up today, and let the strength of your will grow as if it had just begun"'; '"Hodie uos religiosum studium arripuisse arbitremini, et quasi coeptae uoluntatis fortitudo succrescet."'

[71] Athanasius, Ἐπιστολή 30.2 (ed. Bartelink, SC 400, p. 218), Τὸ ἀφιλάργυρον; Evagrius, *Vita Antonii* 17 (30) (ed. Migne, *PL* 73.141B), 'Voluntaria paupertas'.

[72] Evagrius, *Vita Antonii* 16 (26) (ed. Migne, PL 73.139B), '"Vt nos eius exemplo, etiamsi profutura suaderent, in nullo his commodaremus assensum, quia profecto non congruit nos post libertatem a Domino concessam, et Scripturarum praecepta uitalia, a diabolo uiuendi capere consilia"'. Cf. Athanasius, Ἐπιστολή 26.3–4 (ed. Bartelink, SC 400, p. 208), see n. 63.

Athanasius stated simply that Christians possessed 'freedom' (ἐλευθερία) from the Saviour; human freedom was simply stated as a fact. Evagrius first mentioned Christ's example as the proper model for the monks; and, second, he put the gift of freedom into the past tense (*libertas concessa*) as granted by Christ's advent and the Scriptures. In Evagrius' translation there was no sense that the freedom was regranted at any point, nor any mention of the Holy Spirit. The result was that Evagrius drew attention to Christ's example and to the freedom to be virtuous granted to mankind once and for all by Christ's incarnation. In this way he explicitly stated that the monks were already free, and had all the freedom required in order to reject evil and choose virtue.

Another passage relevant to the question of free will was one in which Athanasius referred to how demons fell from heaven. All three versions of the *Life of Antony* stated that demons were originally created good, because God could not create evil. Athanasius made no mention of what caused them to fall from the heavenly mind: "'Yet they themselves were also created good, but cast out of the heavenly wisdom, thereafter they roll around the earth'".[73] The Latin translations chose to emphasise the role of the will in the demons' fall. The anonymous translator made a rare alteration to Athanasius' text when he gave the additional information that this happened 'through their own will' (*uoluntate sua*).[74] Evagrius, meanwhile, made a particular point of stressing that their will was the cause of their fall:

> 'That perversity is a fault not of nature, but of the will (*uoluntatis*). In fact they were good, in so far as they were created by God, but they fell headlong from heaven to earth by their own judgement of mind (*ex proprio mentis arbitrio*)'.[75]

Evagrius contrasted 'nature' (*natura*) with 'will' (*uoluntas*), and his phrase 'their own judgement of mind' (*proprium mentis arbitrium*) intentionally brought the concept of free will into the foreground of the reader's mind. This passage addressed free will to do evil, and, as has been noted, for all three authors rejection of evil and choice of virtue were the same decision. In the later controversy about grace and free will all sides argued that humans acted badly of their own free will. Augustine asserted that God never caused men to fall to damnation, but Pelagius and others argued that by choosing to give the grace of salvation to some, the God of Augustine's approach to Christianity thereby at the same time chose not to give it to others. This was the logical problem they saw in a proposed distinction between free will to evil and free will to virtue, and consequently in a distinction

---

[73] Athanasius, Ἐπιστολή 22.2 (ed. Bartelink, SC 400, pp. 194–6), Ἀλλὰ καλοὶ μὲν γεγόνασι καὶ αὐτοί, ἐκπεσόντες δὲ ἀπὸ τῆς οὐρανίου φρονήσεως, καὶ λοιπὸν περὶ τὴν γῆν καλινδούμενοι.

[74] Anon. trans., *Vita Antonii* 22.2 (ed. Bartelink, p. 52), "'For they too were themselves created good, but through their own will falling from the heavenly mind and for the rest of time rolling on the earth'"; "'Nam et ipsi boni facti sunt, sed excidentes a mente caelesti, et de cetero in terra euoluti uoluntate sua'".

[75] Evagrius, *Vita Antonii* 15 (22) (ed. Migne, PL 73.137C), "'Peruersitas ista, non naturae, sed uoluntatis est uitium. Boni etenim, utpote a Deo conditi, ex proprio mentis arbitrio ad terras ruere de caelis'".

between single and dual predestination.[76] For the moment, however, it is simply worth noting that the Latin translations of Athanasius' text both departed from the original Greek in order to introduce the concept of the will into this passage.

Pelagius

This evidence shows that when he wrote that an individual's will determined his virtue, Pelagius was simply repeating ideas that were well established in ascetic paraenetic literature.[77]

A Third Doctrine Asserted by Pelagius: that God's Grace Was Received in Accord with Merit

Part of tenet 9 in the list of theses Augustine attributed to 'Pelagianism' condemned 'Pelagianism' for the statement: 'God's grace is given in accord with our merits.' The tenet embodied Augustine's focus on prevenient grace as the key aspect of God's grace, although at least seven different facets of God's grace were regularly referred to in Christian texts in this period. Augustine insisted that no kind of grace was given in accord with autonomous human merits. This is exemplified by his comment about Pelagius' trial at the synod of Diospolis:

> For among the other things that were raised as objections to him, this objection was also raised, namely that he said that the grace of God is given in accord with our merits. This is so foreign to catholic teaching and so inimical to the grace of Christ that if he had not condemned this objection raised against him, he would have come away condemned …. And they strive in every way they can to show that the grace of God is given in accord with our merits, that is, that grace is not grace.[78]

---

[76] See Chapter 1, n. 40.

[77] Pelagius, *Ad Demetriadem* 3 (ed. Greshake, p. 62), 'It was because God wished to bestow on the rational creature the gift of doing good of his own will and the power of free judgement, by implanting in man the possibility of choosing either alternative, that he made it his own decision to be what he wanted to be, so that capable of good and evil, he could by nature do either and bend his will in either direction'; 'Volens namque Deus rationabilem creaturam uoluntarii boni munere et liberi arbitrii potestate donare, utriusque partis possibilitatem homini inserendo, proprium eius fecit: esse, quod uelit, ut boni ac mali capax naturaliter utrumque posset et ad alterutrum uoluntatem deflecteret'; 8 (ed. Greshake, pp. 82–4), 'This is how we should understand the matter of the brothers Cain and Abel and of the twins Esau and Jacob also, and we have to know that the will is the sole cause when there are contrary merits in the same nature'; 'Hoc de Cain et Abel fratribus, hoc etiam de Esau et Iacob geminis intelligendum est, ac sciendum solam uoluntatem esse causam, cum in eadem natura merita aduersa sunt.'

[78] Augustine, *De gratia et libero arbitrio* 5.10–11 (ed. Chéné and Pintard, BA 24, pp. 114–16), 'Nam inter caetera quae illi obiecta sunt, et hoc obiectum est, quod diceret gratiam Dei secundum merita nostra dari: quod sic alienum est a catholica doctrina et inimicum gratiae Christi, ut nisi hoc obiectum sibi anathemasset, ipse inde anathematus exisset …. Omnino laborant, quantum possunt, ostendere gratiam Dei secundum merita nostra dari: hoc est, gratiam non esse gratiam.'

In AD 426 in his first letter to Abbot Valentinus of Hadrumetum, Augustine stated unequivocally that grace was not given in accord with merit:

> Let no one say that the grace of God was given to him because of the merits of his works, or because of the merits of his prayers, or because of the merits of his faith; and let it not be thought that what those heretics say is true, that God's grace is given in accord with our merits, which is completely and utterly false.[79]

In the same year in his second letter to Abbot Valentinus, Augustine specifically characterised the idea that grace was given in accord with merit as new. Referring to monks he had kept with him in order to instruct them, he stated:

> We have kept them a little longer in order that they might return to you better instructed against the new Pelagian heretics, into whose error one falls if one thinks that the grace of God, which alone sets a human being free through our Lord Jesus Christ, is given in accord with any human merits.[80]

As was observed in Chapter 1, the idea that grace was given in accord with merit was something that Pelagius taught. But was this a new teaching, original to Pelagius?

Athanasius

Athanasius' *Life of Antony* has a consistent and coherent message on this topic, constructed from the outset of the work. The account of Antony's youth and the beginning of his ascetic way of life centred on his battles with demons. Athanasius explicitly stated that God co-operated with Antony in Antony's struggles against the devil and the devil's minions: 'For the Lord was co-operating with him'.[81] In addition, the citation that followed emphasised this model of synergy, stating that this co-operation allowed the ascetic to remain humble, disavowing his own self-sufficiency in accordance with the biblical citation: *Yet not I, but the grace of God with me* [1 Cor. 15:10].[82] The preposition σὺν means 'together with', not 'in', and it refers back to the verb συνεργεῖν, meaning 'to work together with'. Shortly after Athanasius had established this model of co-operation in his narrative, a turning point came for Antony when he had a vision of light coming down through the roof of the tomb in which he was living. Antony asked who it was and why he had not helped him earlier. A voice replied that he had in fact been present earlier but had waited until Antony had shown his determination to resist the devil: '"Antony,

---

[79] Augustine, *Ep.* 214.4 (ed. Chéné and Pintard, BA 24, p. 56), 'Ne quisquam dicat meritis operum suorum, uel meritis orationum suarum, uel meritis fidei suae, sibi traditam Dei gratiam, et putetur uerum esse quod illi haeretici dicunt, gratiam Dei secundum merita nostra dari, quod omnino falsissimum est'.

[80] Augustine, *Ep.* 215.1 (ed. Chéné and Pintard, BA 24, p. 62), 'Quos ideo tenuimus aliquanto diutius, ut instructiores ad uos redirent aduersus nouos haereticos Pelagianos, in quorum errorem cadit, qui putat secundum aliqua merita humana dari gratiam Dei, quae sola hominem liberat per Dominum nostrum Iesum Christum.'

[81] Athanasius, Ἐπιστολή 5.7 (ed. Bartelink, SC 400, p. 144), Συνήργει γὰρ ὁ Κύριος αὐτῷ.

[82] Athanasius, Ἐπιστολή 5.7 (ed. Bartelink, SC 400, p. 146), Οὐκ ἐγὼ δέ, ἀλλ' ἡ χάρις τοῦ θεοῦ ἡ σὺν ἐμοί [1 Cor. 15:10].

I was there, but I was waiting to see you battle. And so, since you have stood your ground and have not been defeated, I will always help you and I will make you famous everywhere."'[83] The key word in this passage is 'since' (ἐπεὶ); Athanasius made God's help dependent on Antony's first having proved his determination to resist the devil, and, after seeing this proof, God would always help Antony. It is important to note that this help was *dependent on* and *subsequent to* Antony's virtue. This same sequence of dependence applied concerning Antony's fame later in his life. It is also important to note that Athanasius characterised this action by God as 'help' (ἀντίληψις or βοηθὸς), not causation.[84]

To convey this message more clearly still, Athanasius placed within Antony's teaching to the monks who sought his guidance this same model of co-operation subsequent to, and consequent on, individual virtue: '"Therefore, my children, let us hold to our asceticism and let us not neglect it. For in this we have also the Lord as our co-worker, as it is written: with all who choose the good *God co-operates for the good* [Rom. 8:28]."'[85] Athanasius thus stated clearly that God's help postdated an individual's choice to be virtuous. Different forms of the word 'choice' (προαίρεσις) occur in key moments in the text and contain a presumption of autonomous human decision-making. As yet this presumption of effective free will had not been queried.

Athanasius was also explicit that grace was given to those who already believed; he did not suggest that grace caused faith. For example, the demons knew that God had given to believers the power to defeat demons: '"For they know the grace given by the Saviour to believers against them".'[86]

Athanasius' message stressed that gifts from God were given to those who were virtuous. For example, the person given the power to see further than the spirits had earned this gift through purifying his soul and returning it to its natural state.[87] The model Athanasius clearly and consistently set before the reader was of co-operation between God and the man seeking to be virtuous.[88] This is exemplified

---

[83] Athanasius, Ἐπιστολή 10.3 (ed. Bartelink, SC 400, p. 164), Ἀντώνιε, ὧδε ἤμην, ἀλλὰ περιέμενον ἰδεῖν τὸν σὸν ἀγωνισμόν. Ἐπεὶ οὖν ὑπέμεινας καὶ οὐχ ἡττήθης, ἔσομαί σοι ἀεὶ βοηθὸς καὶ ποιήσω σε ὀνομαστὸν πανταχοῦ γενέσθαι.

[84] Athanasius, Ἐπιστολή 10.1–3 (ed. Bartelink, SC 400, pp. 162–4).

[85] Athanasius, Ἐπιστολή 19.1 (ed. Bartelink, SC 400, p. 184), Ἐχώμεθα οὖν, τέκνα, τῆς ἀσκήσεως, καὶ μὴ ἀκηδιῶμεν. Ἔχομεν γὰρ ἐν τούτῳ καὶ τὸν Κύριον συνεργόν, ὡς γέγραπται· Παντὶ τῷ προαιρουμένῳ τὸ ἀγαθὸν συνεργεῖ ὁ θεὸς εἰς τὸ ἀγαθόν [Rom. 8:28].

[86] Athanasius, Ἐπιστολή 30.3 (ed. Bartelink, SC 400, p. 220), Ἴσασι γὰρ τὴν κατ' αὐτῶν δοθεῖσαν χάριν τοῖς πιστοῖς παρὰ τοῦ Σωτῆρος.

[87] See n. 9.

[88] See also Athanasius, Ἐπιστολή 35.4–5 (ed. Bartelink, SC 400, pp. 230–2), '"For it is possible and easy to discern the presence of evil and of good spirits when God gives this ability. For the vision enjoyed by the holy is undisturbed .... Peacefully and gently it becomes such that at once joy and exaltation and confidence exist in the soul. For the Lord is with them, who is our joy, and the power of God the Father"'; Καὶ γὰρ τὴν τῶν φαύλων καὶ τῶν ἀγαθῶν παρουσίαν εὐχερὲς καὶ δυνατόν ἐστι διαγνῶναι, τοῦ θεοῦ διδόντος οὕτως. Ἡ μὲν τῶν ἁγίων ὀπτασία οὐκ ἔστι τεταραγμένη .... Ἡσύχως δὲ καὶ πράως γίνεται οὕτως, ὡς εὐθὺς χαρὰν καὶ ἀγαλλίασιν γίνεσθαι καὶ θάρσος τῇ ψυχῇ. Ἔστι γὰρ μετ' αὐτῶν ὁ Κύριος, ὅς ἐστιν ἡμῶν μὲν χαρά, τοῦ δὲ θεοῦ πατρὸς ἡ δύναμις.

by Athanasius' depiction of miracles. Antony's teaching to his monks stressed that miracles (or signs) were the work of God. He contrasted the power to cast out demons with the monks' names being written in heaven, and explained that his name being written in heaven was an indicator of a monk's virtue, while power over demons was something that God achieved. The clear implication in the Greek text was that this was a distinction between, on the one hand (τὸ μὲν), something for which the monks were responsible and, on the other hand (τὸ δὲ), something for which they were not responsible and for which they could take no credit:

> 'For working miracles does not belong to us, but is the work of the Saviour. Indeed he said to the disciples: *Do not rejoice because demons are made subject to you, but because your names have been inscribed in the heavens* [Luke 10:20]. For on the one hand the fact that names are written in heaven is witness to our virtue and our life, but on the other hand casting out demons is the grace of the Saviour who has granted it.'[89]

Later in the same passage, Antony referred to a similar gift from God—the ability to distinguish between spirits—and he stated that moral virtue was required: '"For the Lord does not recognise the ways of the impious. But in general it is necessary to pray, as I have said, in order to receive the gift of discerning between spirits"'.[90] Thus, here again, virtue (in this case piety) preceded grace, and grace was specifically depicted as a gift of a special power from God to the virtuous. The same sequence of virtue first, and then a gift from God consequent on virtue, was described by Antony elsewhere with regard to the ability to perceive differences between spirits, with the conjunction ἵνα ('so that') indicating the causal dependence: '"And therefore there is need of much prayer and asceticism, so that a person, having received the gift of discernment between spirits from the Holy Spirit, will be able to know about them"'.[91] Discerning between spirits was a result of Antony's ascetic virtue.[92] Likewise, Christ worked through those who believed in him.[93]

---

[89] Athanasius, Ἐπιστολή 38.2–3 (ed. Bartelink, SC 400, p. 238), Τὸ γὰρ ποιεῖν σημεῖα οὐχ ἡμῶν, τοῦ δὲ Σωτῆρος ἐστὶ τὸ ἔργον. Τοῖς γοῦν μαθηταῖς ἔλεγεν· Μὴ χαίρετε, ὅτι τὰ δαιμόνια ὑμῖν ὑποτάσσεται, ἀλλ' ὅτι τὰ ὀνόματα ὑμῶν γέγραπται ἐν τοῖς οὐρανοῖς [Luke 10:20]. Τὸ μὲν γὰρ ἐν οὐρανῷ γεγράφθαι τὰ ὀνόματα, μαρτύριόν ἐστι τῆς ἡμῶν ἀρετῆς καὶ τοῦ βίου· τὸ δὲ ἐκβάλλειν δαίμονας, τοῦ δεδωκότος Σωτῆρός ἐστιν ἡ χάρις.

[90] Athanasius Ἐπιστολή 38.5 (ed. Bartelink, SC 400, p. 238), Οὐ γὰρ γινώσκει Κύριος τὰς ὁδοὺς τῶν ἀσεβῶν. Καθόλου δὲ εὔχεσθαι δεῖ, καθὰ προεῖπον, λαμβάνειν χάρισμα διακρίσεως πνευμάτων.

[91] Athanasius, Ἐπιστολή 22.3 (ed. Bartelink, SC 400, p. 196), Διὸ καὶ πολλῆς εὐχῆς καὶ ἀσκήσεώς ἐστι χρεία, ἵνα τις, λαβὼν διὰ τοῦ πνεύματος χάρισμα διακρίσεως πνευμάτων, γνῶναι δυνηθῇ τὰ κατ' αὐτούς.

[92] Athanasius, Ἐπιστολή 88.1 (ed. Bartelink, SC 400, p. 360), 'Moreover it was another major aspect of Antony's asceticism that, as I have said, he had the gift of discerning between spirits'; Καὶ γὰρ καὶ τοῦτο ἦν μέγα τῆς ἀσκήσεως Ἀντωνίου ὅτι, καθὰ προεῖπον, χάρισμα διακρίσεως πνευμάτων ἔχων.

[93] Athanasius, Ἐπιστολή 80.6 (ed. Bartelink, SC 400, p. 338), '"It is not us who does these things, but it is Christ who does these things through those who believe in Him. Therefore, do you believe also"'; Οὐκ ἐσμὲν ἡμεῖς οἱ ποιοῦντες, ἀλλ' ὁ Χριστός ἐστιν, ὁ διὰ τῶν εἰς αὐτὸν πιστευόντων ταῦτα ποιῶν. Πιστεύσατε οὖν καὶ ὑμεῖς.

Athanasius' Antony regularly acknowledged the help he received from God, which underlined the co-operative character of his victory over evil.[94] Whether in regard to demons or to healing he always attributed special abilities to God.[95] A distinction should be made between the author's co-operative model of the process at work in Antony's resisting evil, and the message Athanasius made Antony convey, which had to embody humility and self-deprecation as the proper attributes of an ascetic holy man. But Antony's words also made it clear that the gift of a special power was dependent on pre-existing virtue.

This same co-operative model was consistently presented with regard to Antony's healing: he prayed so that everyone could see that it was the Lord who achieved the healing:

> So Antony did not heal by giving orders, but by praying and calling on Christ so that it would be clear for all to see that it was not he who did it, but the Lord who through Antony showed his love for mankind and healed those who were suffering. By contrast only the prayer and the asceticism, for the sake of which he sat on the mountain, belonged to Antony.[96]

In this passage the δὲ pointed up the contrast between the two agents in the healing, suggesting that it was Antony's role to be virtuous and God's to heal. The efficacy of his prayer was implicitly attributed to his ascetic virtue. The critical point about the co-operative model was that it assigned a role in the process to Antony, and according to Athanasius that role was to be virtuous.

The anonymous translator

The anonymous translator conveyed exactly the same causal dependency of grace on moral goodness that Athanasius had portrayed: God's co-operation was subsequent to and dependent on Antony's virtue.[97]

---

[94] For example, he cited Ps. 118:7: *The Lord is my helper*, Athanasius, Ἐπιστολή 6.4 (ed. Bartelink, SC 400, p. 148).

[95] Athanasius, Ἐπιστολή 58.4 (ed. Bartelink, SC 400, p. 290), '"This success is not my doing, so that a person should go to me, insignificant man that I am; but the healing is the work of the Saviour, who works His mercy in every place on those who appeal to Him"'; Οὐ γὰρ ἐμόν ἐστι τοῦτο κατόρθωμα, ἵνα καὶ πρὸς ἐμὲ τὸν οἰκτρὸν ἄνθρωπον ἔλθῃ· ἀλλὰ τοῦ Σωτῆρός ἐστιν ἡ θεραπεία, τοῦ ποιοῦντος ἐν παντὶ τόπῳ τὸ ἔλεος αὐτοῦ τοῖς ἐπικαλουμένοις αὐτόν.

[96] Athanasius, Ἐπιστολή 84.1–2 (ed. Bartelink, SC 400, p. 352), Οὐ προστάττων γοῦν ἐθεράπευεν ὁ Ἀντώνιος, ἀλλ' εὐχόμενος καὶ τὸν Χριστὸν ὀνομάζων, ὡς πᾶσι φανερὸν γενέσθαι, ὅτι οὐκ ἦν αὐτὸς ὁ ποιῶν, ἀλλ' ὁ Κύριος ἦν, ὁ δι' Ἀντωνίου φιλανθρωπευόμενος καὶ θεραπεύων τοὺς πάσχοντας. Ἀντωνίου δὲ μόνον ἦν ἡ εὐχὴ καὶ ἡ ἄσκησις, ἧς ἕνεκεν ἐν τῷ ὄρει καθήμενος.

[97] Latin *ut* ('so that') expressed the causal dependence: Anon. trans., *Vita Antonii* 22.3 (ed. Bartelink, p. 52), 'For this reason there is need of both continual prayer and also ascetic endeavour is necessary, so that he who receives the gift of discerning spirits through the Holy Spirit, may know what is going on concerning the demons'; 'Vnde et orationis continuae opus est, et studium religionis necessarium est, ut qui per Spiritum accipiens donum discretionis spirituum scire possit quid agitur circa daemones'.

Evagrius

Evagrius popularised Athanasius' programme in the Latin West, but it was already fully constructed and coherent. Like Athanasius, Evagrius asserted that God's gifts were the direct result of human virtue. However, where Athanasius used the word 'virtue' (ἀρετή), Evagrius introduced the word 'merit' (plural *merita*, verb *mereri*), which made the causal connection between virtue and reward more explicit. Subsequently, the concept of merit became commonplace in the Latin West. It was conventional, for example, in Jerome's paraenesis, as will be seen in Chapter 3. In the *Life of Antony*, Jesus told Antony that 'because of' (ἐπει in Athanasius, *quia* in Evagrius) Antony's brave resistance to evil, he would help him in the future.[98] The repeated careful pairing of human effort and divine agency in Athanasius' narrative was replicated in Evagrius' version of the *Life of Antony*.[99] Each pairing reinforced the underlying principle that God helped the individual who chose to endeavour to achieve virtue.

Evagrius repeated certain terms to convey to the reader a more pointed message on particular subjects than was present in Athanasius' original *Life of Antony*. Merit was one of these. Right at the start of his version of the *Life of Antony*, Evagrius imported the word 'merits' (*merita*) into Athanasius' ascetic programme where no equivalent was present in the Greek original.[100] This was a pattern Evagrius

---

[98] Evagrius, *Vita Antonii* 9 (10) (ed. Migne, PL 73.132D), '"Because you have not ceased from fighting bravely, I will always help you"'; '"Quia dimicando uiriliter non cessisti, semper auxiliabor tibi"'.

[99] Evagrius, *Vita Antonii* 5 (7) (ed. Migne, PL 73.130B–D), 'But this was Antony's first victory against the devil, or rather it was the victory of the power of the Saviour in Antony: *Who condemned sin in the flesh, so that the justification of the law should be fulfilled in us, we who walk not according to the flesh but according to the spirit* [Rom. 8:4]. But this one triumph did not give Antony security, nor did the devil's powers, though broken once, fail completely. For he: *Roaring like a lion* [1 Pet. 5:8], was seeking an entrance through which he could break in; and Antony, having learnt from the discourse of the Scriptures that: *The snares of demons are many* [Eph. 6:11], kept safe his commitment by means of skilful effort, keeping in mind that although Satan had been defeated in the struggle of the flesh, he could mobilise more fiercely against Antony stratagems of new frauds. For this reason Antony subdued his body more and more, lest though the victor in some struggles he might be defeated in others [cf. 1 Cor. 9:27]. Organising his life therefore by a stricter rule, while everyone marvelled at the untiring dedication of this young man, he would bear the holy work patiently, because the dedication of voluntary servitude to the work of God over a long period of time had turned habit into nature for him'; 'Haec autem Antonii contra diabolum fuit prima uictoria, imo uirtus in Antonio Saluatoris: *Qui peccatum in carne condemnauit, ut iustificatio legis in nobis compleretur, qui non secundum carnem ambulamus, sed secundum spiritum* [Rom. 8:4]. Sed neque Antonio securitatem dedit hic unus triumphus, nec diabolo semel fractae defecere uires. Nam et iste: *Vt leo rugiens* [1 Pet. 5:8], quaerebat aditum per quem posset irrumpere; et ille Scripturarum doctus eloquio: *Multas esse daemonum captiones* [Eph. 6:11], solerti proposito labore seruabat; considerans quia posset Satanas in carnis colluctatione superatus, nouarum aduersus se artium machinas acrius commouere. Idcirco magis ac magis subiugabat corpus suum, ne uictor aliorum, in aliis uinceretur [cf. 1 Cor. 9:27]. Disponens igitur duriori se uitae lege constringere, cum omnes infatigabilem adolescentis mirarentur instantiam, sanctum toleranter ferebat laborem, quia uoluntariae seruitutis longum in Dei opere studium, consuetudinem in naturam uerterat.'

[100] Athanasius, Ἐπιστολή Preface 5 (ed. Bartelink, SC 400, p. 128), Athanasius concluded his preface by saying that his concern was for truth: 'So that neither should someone, having heard a great many things, disbelieve them, nor again should he, having learnt less than was necessary, think lightly of the man'; Ἵνα

repeated. Later, when Antony told the monks that miracles were God's work and not a matter of human agency, so they should not rejoice in defeating demons but in their names being written in heaven, Athanasius' Antony said: "'For names being written in heaven is witness to our virtue and our life'". Evagrius' Antony said: "'For the writing of names in the book of life is testimony to virtue and merit'".[101] Both authors explicitly contrasted this with the power to cast out spirits which was the Saviour's 'grace' (χάρις) or 'generous gift' (largitio). Thus virtue was stated by both writers to be achieved through human agency, but Evagrius introduced the word 'merits' in association with the word 'virtue'. Athanasius then went on to stress that God did not recognise the way of the impious, and to emphasise the need for prayer. Evagrius retained this advice but here introduced the word 'merit' a second time: "'Therefore let us pray fervently for this, so that we may merit to receive the gift of discerning spirits'".[102]

In Section 3 the use of the word 'grace' in the three versions of the *Life of Antony* is examined, but one usage belongs in this section also. Evagrius' seventh use of the word 'grace' (*gratia*) is significant for the argument of this book, and it occurred where neither Athanasius nor the unknown translator used the word. The story of Martinianus featured in all three versions of the *Life of Antony*: a military officer whose daughter was possessed by an evil spirit, Martinianus asked Antony to cure his daughter, and Antony advised him to pray, whereupon the girl was restored to health. In this episode, Athanasius repeated his earlier formula, stating that the Lord worked this healing through Antony, and he cited the first part of Matt. 7:7, which later became a proof-text for those who argued that human merit through endeavour was an essential part of the Christian message of salvation: 'And the Lord who said: *Ask, and it shall be given to you* [Matt. 7:7] worked many other things as well through Antony.'[103] The anonymous translator rendered

---

μήτε πλέον τις ἀκούσας ἀπιστήσῃ, μήτε πάλιν ἐλάττονα τοῦ δέοντος μαθών, καταφρονήσῃ τοῦ ἀνδρός. Evagrius also ended his preface by mentioning his concern for truth: Evagrius, *Vita Antonii* Preface (ed. Migne, PL 73.127), 'So that neither should someone hearing a great deal, not believe the piling-up of miracles, nor again should he, knowing less than Antony's merits, not think him worthy of a miracle though a man of such great reputation'; 'Vt neque plus aliquis audiens, miraculorum congestionem non credat, nec rursum meritis eius inferiora cognoscens, non putet dignum esse miraculo pro tanti nominis uiro.'

[101] Evagrius, *Vita Antonii* 19 (38) (ed. Migne, PL 73.143D), "'For to perform miracles is not a matter of our insignificant selves, but is a matter of the power of the Lord, who said to the disciples when they were boasting: *Do not rejoice because demons are subject to you, but because your names are written in heaven* [Luke 10:20]. For the writing of names in the book of life is testimony to virtue and merit; but the expulsion of Satan is a gift bestowed by the Saviour'"; "'Nam signa facere non est nostrae paruitatis, sed Domini potestatis, qui ad discipulos gloriantes in Euangelio ait: *Ne gaudeatis quia daemones uobis subiecti sunt, sed quod nomina uestra scripta sunt in caelis* [Luke 10.20]. Nominum enim in libro uitae conscriptio testimonium est uirtutis et meriti; expulsio autem Satanae largitio Saluatoris est.'" Cf. Athanasius, Ἐπιστολή 38.2–3 (ed. Bartelink, SC 400, p. 238), μαρτύριόν ἐστι τῆς ἡμῶν ἀρετῆς καὶ τοῦ βίου. See n. 89 for full text.

[102] Evagrius, *Vita Antonii* 19 (38) (ed. Migne, PL 73.144A), "'Hoc ergo magnopere postulemus, ut donum spirituum discernendorum mereamur accipere'".

[103] Athanasius, Ἐπιστολή 48.3 (ed. Bartelink, SC 400, p. 264), Πολλά τε καὶ ἄλλα δι' αὐτοῦ πεποίηκεν ὁ Κύριος, ὁ λέγων: Αἰτεῖτε, καὶ δοθήσεται ὑμῖν [Matt. 7:7].

Athanasius without alteration. Evagrius, on the other hand, reworked and extended this sentence so as to state explicitly that grace was given in reward for merit:

> The Lord also worked many other miracles through him, and deservedly so; he who promised in the Gospel: *Ask, and it shall be given to you* [Matt. 7:7] did not deny his power to the man He found who merited to receive his grace.[104]

Evagrius used two words here to make it clear that Antony merited this grace— 'deservedly' (*merito*) and 'deserved' (*mereretur*)—neither of which were in Athanasius, and he specifically introduced into the narrative the word 'grace'. Pelagius cannot therefore be said to have invented the idea that grace could be merited, and if Pelagius was condemned for this, then Evagrius of Antioch should be condemned also.

In his ch. 88, Athanasius described Antony's gift of discernment between spirits and how he helped others in their struggles with demons. A comparison of Athanasius' text with Evagrius' at this point shows that Evagrius expanded Athanasius' narrative in this section and added the concept of merit here too. Where Athanasius wrote that it was an element in Antony's asceticism that he had the gift of discerning spirits, Evagrius explicitly credited Antony's ability to discern between spirits (elsewhere described as grace) to the 'merits of his life' (*uitae merita*).[105]

In the paragraphs following Antony's death, Evagrius made further significant additions to the Greek text: he added the word '*merits*' three times. First, after following Athanasius in observing that: 'This was the end of Antony's life', Evagrius added words that were not in Athanasius' text: 'These were his principal merits'.[106] He added the word *merita* a second time when he explained why Antony's body remained unchanged after his death: 'Because of his merits'.[107] Athanasius gave no explanation. In the very final section of the review of Antony's life, Evagrius then added a third use of the word *merita*. Where Athanasius wrote that the Lord made a reclusive ascetic such as Antony famous as a result of his virtue and because of the usefulness of his virtue to others, Evagrius wrote that the Lord made ascetics famous: 'So that both they themselves might benefit

---

[104] Evagrius, *Vita Antonii* 24 (48) (ed. Migne, PL 73.148A), 'Multa et alia mirabilia per illum Dominus operatus est, et merito; qui enim promisit in Euangelio: *Petite, et dabitur uobis* [Matt. 7:7], inuento qui eius gratiam mereretur accipere, suam potentiam non negauit.'

[105] Evagrius, *Vita Antonii* 55 (88) (ed. Migne, PL 73.165C), 'For Antony knew under what misfortune each person was labouring, and perceiving the difference between spirits as a result of the merits of his life, he would apply a cure for each disease according to the wounds present'; 'Sciebat enim quo quisque laboraret incommodo, et ex uitae meritis discretionem spirituum agnoscens, adhibebat morborum, prout erant uulnera, sanitatem.' Cf. Athanasius, Ἐπιστολή 88.1 (ed. Bartelink, SC 400, p. 360), 'Moreover it was another major aspect of Antony's asceticism that, as I have said, he had the gift of discerning between spirits'; Καὶ γὰρ καὶ τοῦτο ἦν μέγα τῆς ἀσκήσεως Ἀντωνίου ὅτι, καθὰ προεῖπον, χάρισμα διακρίσεως πνευμάτων ἔχων.

[106] Evagrius, *Vita Antonii* 60 (93) (ed. Migne, PL 73.168A), 'Hic Antonio uitae terminus fuit, ista principia meritorum'.

[107] Evagrius, *Vita Antonii* 60 (93) (ed. Migne, PL 73.168B), 'Meritorum gratia'.

from praise of their merits and also others might be inspired by their example.'[108] So where Athanasius referred to 'virtue' (ἀρετή), Evagrius referred to 'merits' (*merita*). This was a significant semantic shift because merit contained, in addition to a quality of moral goodness, the notion of something due as a reward, the idea of causal entailment.

Evagrius made another significant addition during this discussion of why God made Antony famous. One of the key points of debate in the controversy over free will concerned whether or not biblical references to predestination could be explained by reference to God's foreknowledge of autonomous human actions. These would be actions that were carried out by humans who, when they made their choices, possessed effective free will to both moral goodness and evil. In close apposition to the references to Antony's merits just discussed, Evagrius added another line that was not in Athanasius' Greek text, asking to whom his fame should be attributed if not to Christ: 'Who, foreseeing Antony's devotion to his majesty, revealed this man who was hidden almost in another world ... as he had promised he would at the beginning.'[109] The word 'foreseeing' (*praeuidens*) here is significant because it refers to God's foreknowledge of Antony's autonomous action. Evagrius deliberately chose to add this explicit reference to the contemporary debate and to make his position known: he supported the argument for human free will, and, for him, reference to God's foreknowledge was the means to preserve this free will in the Christian account of salvation. The treatment of this topic by the writer known as Ambrosiaster, discussed in Chapter 3, shows that this subject was being debated in Latin Christian texts in the 370s.

It is important to note the conjunction of these ideas in Evagrius' version of this final summary of Antony's life. It is in this same section that alongside the reference to God's foreknowledge of Antony's devotion, Evagrius placed his third mention of 'merits' where Athanasius had mentioned 'virtue' (ἀρετή). Here too he twice mentioned example, bringing to the reader's attention the power of good example to engender virtue, and making explicit what was implicit in Athanasius' text. Athanasius wrote of the usefulness of Antony's life to others; Evagrius used the word 'example' (*exemplum*) to bring to the fore the process at work. This same passage also featured a direct causal equation between virtue and reward, as Athanasius (and, following him, Evagrius) advised that the *Life of Antony* should be read aloud to let Christians and monks know that those who served the Lord would be welcomed into heaven:

> And so read this book to the brothers with great attentiveness, so that when they learn about the faithful life of these outstanding Christians and monks they may know that

---

[108] Evagrius, *Vita Antonii* 62 (94) (ed. Migne, PL 73.168C), 'Vt et ipsi fruantur laude meritorum, et caeteri eorum prouocentur exemplis.'

[109] Evagrius, *Vita Antonii* 61 (93) (ed. Migne, PL 73.168B), 'Qui deuotos eius animos erga suam praeuidens maiestatem, hominem alio pene orbe celatum ... ut in exordio promiserat, demonstrauit.' It is noteworthy also that Evagrius highlighted how God kept his promise, thereby underlining the security of the causal entailment between virtue and reward.

our Saviour Jesus Christ glorifies those who glorify Him, and grants not only the kingdom of heaven to those who serve Him, but also the nobility of fame to those who in this life desire to lie hidden in remote mountains areas; clearly, they do this both so that they themselves might benefit from praise of their merits, and also so that others might be spurred on by their examples.[110]

Finally, Evagrius changed Athanasius' account of why God spread awareness of Antony's life. Athanasius wrote: 'So that in this way those hearing it may know that the commandments can be fulfilled successfully and so that they may take up zeal for the path of virtue.'[111] Evagrius added mention of how example, persuasion and imitation created virtue, and highlighted how virtue came from within:

So that through the examples of holy people it should be taught that virtue was possible and was not external to human nature; and so that every good man might be persuaded to imitate the blessed life by the fruit of his labour.[112]

The review of Antony's life is therefore an example of the internal strength of the programme set out. All its elements were linked together to create a coherent message. Evagrius' text shows that he advocated this Athanasian programme of the goodness of contemporary human nature, human free will, and a co-operative model for the relationship between man and God. His additional references to merits, to God's foreknowledge of autonomous human virtue, to example and to imitation all reinforced this scheme.

The significance of this evidence is that the only tenet attributed to 'Pelagianism' that can be found in Pelagius' writings is the idea that God's grace was given in accord with merit, and this was clearly and repeatedly stated by Evagrius of Antioch in a work that has never been labelled heretical.

Pelagius

As discussed in Chapter 1, Pelagius stated that grace was given in accord with merit.[113]

---

[110] Evagrius, *Vita Antonii* 62 (94) (ed. Migne, PL 73.168C), 'Hunc itaque fratribus librum magnopere perlegere curate, ut, agnita fideli uita sublimium Christianorum et monachorum, sciant quod Saluator noster Iesus Christus glorificantes se glorificat, et seruientibus sibimet, non tantum regna caelorum, sed etiam hic in ipsis montium secretis latere cupientibus, famae tribuit nobilitatem; scilicet, ut et ipsi fruantur laude meritorum, et caeteri eorum prouocentur exemplis.' This is an example of Evagrius' changing Athanasius' ἀρετή to *merita*, and he also changed Athanasius' ὠφέλεια ('benefit') to *exemplum* ('example'), prefiguring the stress laid on the power of example by later writers of Latin ascetic paraenesis.

[111] Athanasius, Ἐπιστολή 93.6 (ed. Bartelink, SC 400, pp. 374–6), Ἵνα καὶ οὕτως οἱ ἀκούοντες γινώσκωσι δυνατὰς εἶναι τὰς ἐντολὰς εἰς τὸ κατορθοῦν καὶ ζῆλον τῆς ἐπ' ἀρετὴν ὁδοῦ λανθάνωσιν.

[112] Evagrius, *Vita Antonii* 61 (93) (ed. Migne, PL 73.168C), 'Vt uirtus possibilis nec extra humanam esse naturam sanctorum doceatur exemplis, et ad beatae uitae imitationem, ex fructu laboris optimus quisque impellatur.'

[113] See Chapter 1, n. 41.

Other Ideas for which 'Pelagianism' Was Criticised by its Opponents

A direct causal relationship between an individual's virtue on earth and his reward for this virtue in the afterlife

Athanasius

An essential assumption of the ascetic movement, which had gone unquestioned before study of the Pauline Epistles came into vogue in the Latin West in the second half of the 4th century, was that there was a direct correlation between ascetic effort in this life and reward from God in the next. This secure and transparent causal relationship between effort and reward was the basis on which asceticism operated and was its primary motivation. This assumption was ubiquitous in Athanasius' *Life of Antony*. For example, he talked of the despair of demons when they found monks focused on their rewards to come.[114] Confident reference to 'good things to come' appears to have been unproblematic for Athanasius.[115] Although he warned against thinking that special powers should be expected in payment for ascetic effort, he assumed that asceticism equated to future entry into heaven:

> 'And so whenever we continue with asceticism for all our eighty or even a hundred years, we will not rule for a period equal to a hundred years, but rather in place of the hundred years we will rule for eternity. And after we have battled on earth, we will not inherit on earth, but rather we have our promises in heaven. When we have laid down this corruptible body, we receive in return an incorruptible one.'[116]

Athanasius used a verb in the future tense to describe the monks' salvation ('we will rule'), and a verb in the present tense ('we have') to assert that once they had battled against evil on earth, the monks possessed their promises in heaven. The grammatical construction of ἵνα plus a subjunctive ('so that') expressing causal entailment was repeatedly placed as a link between effort and salvation in

---

[114] Athanasius, Ἐπιστολή 42.7 (ed. Bartelink, SC 400, p. 250), '"If they find us rejoicing in the Lord and thinking about the good things to come"'; Ἐὰν δὲ χαίροντας ἡμᾶς εὕρωσιν ἐν Κυρίῳ καὶ λογιζομένους περὶ τῶν μελλόντων ἀγαθῶν.

[115] Athanasius, Ἐπιστολή 14.7 (ed. Bartelink, SC 400, p. 174), 'Conversing and calling to mind the good things to come'; Διαλεγόμενος δὲ καὶ μνημονεύων περὶ τῶν μελλόντων ἀγαθῶν. 66.8 (ed. Bartelink, SC 400, p. 310), 'They would learn that the fruit of asceticism was good'; Μανθάνουσι τῆς ἀσκήσεως εἶναι καρπὸν ἀγαθόν.

[116] Athanasius, Ἐπιστολή 16.7–8 (ed. Bartelink, SC 400, p. 180), Ὅταν τοίνυν πάντα τὰ ὀγδοήκοντα ἔτη ἢ καὶ ἑκατὸν διαμείνωμεν ἐν τῇ ἀσκήσει, οὐκ ἴσα τοῖς ἑκατὸν ἔτεσι βασιλεύσομεν, ἀλλ' ἀντὶ τῶν ἑκατὸν αἰῶνας αἰώνων βασιλεύσομεν. Καὶ ἐπὶ γῆς ἀγωνισάμενοι, οὐκ ἐν γῆ κληρονομοῦμεν, ἀλλ' ἐν οὐρανοῖς ἔχομεν τὰς ἐπαγγελίας. Πάλιν δὲ φθαρτὸν ἀποθέμενοι τὸ σῶμα, ἄφθαρτον ἀπολαμβάνομεν αὐτό.

Athanasius' narrative.[117] This aspect of God's grace, the grace of salvation, was presented unequivocally as dependent on effort. With no mention of God's prior causation of a monk's perseverance in virtue through the operation of prevenient grace, the causal equation of autonomous human effort on earth and divine reward in heaven was uninterrupted and secure. Athanasius presented this simple entailment as a given when Antony advised the monks not to become disheartened because of the demons' attacks: "'But rather let us take heart and rejoice always as ones who are saved.'"[118]

In his final words of advice to the monks, Antony made explicit once more the direct causal relationship between their ascetic effort and the reward they would receive, with the causal entailment again expressed in the word ἵνα ('so that'). He advised them always to hasten to join themselves first to the Lord, and then to the saints: "'So that after death they will receive you into the eternal realms as friends and people familiar to them.'"[119] Antony discussed his reception into heaven as a future fact.[120] This idea of a direct causal relationship between human effort and divine reward depended for its efficacy on a presumption of human free will. Thus a nexus of several ideas that were commonplace in contemporary Christian teaching were fundamentally at variance with the notion of a grace that was always prevenient to human effort.

Aside from such overt statements of a transparent causal relationship between effort and reward, three aspects of Athanasius' teaching in his *Life of Antony* asserted the principle that effort was directly causally related to reward. First, his use of reward and investment language, which suggested a direct causal link between effort and salvation. Second, his references to personal choice; although not frequent, these were clear and significant. And third, his ubiquitous stress on individual personal effort in achieving virtue, which he then linked to attainment of salvation in an overt causal entailment.

The language of reward and investment

Christian ascetic paraenesis took its cue from the many biblical passages that employed the language of financial investment and return. Athanasius asserted that the promise of eternal life was something a Christian bought for himself: "'And while everything in the world is purchased at a fair price, and a person exchanges one thing for another of equal value, by contrast the promise of eternal

---

[117] For example, Athanasius, Ἐπιστολή 17.3 (ed. Bartelink, SC 400, pp. 180–2); 17.6 (ed. Bartelink, *SC* 400, p. 182).

[118] Athanasius, Ἐπιστολή 42.3 (ed. Bartelink, SC 400, p. 248), Θαρρῶμεν δὲ μᾶλλον καὶ χαίρωμεν ἀεὶ ὡς σῳζόμενοι.

[119] Athanasius, Ἐπιστολή 91.5 (ed. Bartelink, SC 400, p. 368), Ἵνα μετὰ θάνατον ὑμᾶς εἰς τὰς αἰωνίους σκηνάς, ὡς φίλους καὶ γνωρίμους, δέξωνται.

[120] Athanasius, Ἐπιστολή 91.8 (ed. Bartelink, SC 400, p. 370), talking about his body after his death, Antony said: "'For at the resurrection of the dead I will receive it uncorrupted from the Saviour'"; Ἐγὼ γὰρ ἐν τῇ ἀναστάσει τῶν νεκρῶν ἀπολήψομαι παρὰ τοῦ Σωτῆρος ἄφθαρτον αὐτό.

life is sold cheaply.'"[121] He used the vocabulary of profit to underline this seamless equation between the expenditure of effort on earth and reward in heaven:

> 'Just as if someone thinks lightly of a single bronze drachma so that he may gain a profit of a hundred gold drachmas, in the same way he who is lord of all the earth and renounces it all, gives up a little thing and receives a hundred times as much.'[122]

A little later in the same passage, Athanasius repeated the language of profit to argue for the rejection of material possessions. The idea that the monks would see a return was again expressed in the conjunction 'so that' (ἵνα):

> 'And so why do we not abandon them for the sake of virtue, so that we also may inherit a kingdom? For this reason, let none of us take up enthusiasm for possessions. For what profit is there in possessing these things which we do not take with us?'[123]

The anonymous translator

Because he rendered Athanasius' text into Latin very closely, the anonymous translator canvassed in equally clear terms the same direct entailment between the achievement of Christian virtue in this life and reward in the next as Athanasius promoted. Antony reminded the monks of the good things that would come, and how every individual determined his own fate on the Day of Judgement.[124] He described the monks as courageous against the demons because they were

---

[121] Athanasius, Ἐπιστολή 16.5 (ed. Bartelink, SC 400, p. 178), Καὶ πᾶν μὲν πρᾶγμα ἐν τῷ κόσμῳ τοῦ ἀξίου πιπράσκεται, καὶ ἴσον ἴσῳ τις ἀντικαταλλάσσει, ἡ δὲ ἐπαγγελία τῆς αἰωνίου ζωῆς ὀλίγου τινὸς ἀγοράζεται.

[122] Athanasius, Ἐπιστολή 17.3 (ed. Bartelink, SC 400, pp. 180–2), Ὡς γὰρ εἴ τις καταφρονήσειε μιᾶς χαλκῆς δραχμῆς, ἵνα κερδήσῃ χρυσᾶς δραχμὰς ἑκατόν, οὕτως ὁ πάσης τῆς γῆς κύριος ὢν καὶ ἀποτασσόμενος αὐτῇ, ὀλίγον ἀφίησι καὶ ἑκατονταπλασίονα λαμβάνει.

[123] Athanasius, Ἐπιστολή 17.6 (ed. Bartelink, SC 400, p. 182), Διὰ τί οὖν μὴ δι' ἀρετὴν ἡμεῖς καταλιμπάνομεν, ἵνα καὶ βασιλείαν κληρονομήσωμεν; Διὰ τοῦτο μηδὲ τοῦ κτᾶσθαι τις ἡμῶν ἐπιθυμίαν λαμβανέτω. Τί γὰρ κέρδος ταῦτα κτᾶσθαι, ἃ μηδὲ αἴρομεν μεθ' ἑαυτῶν; Analogous to the language of financial investment in its presumption of a direct causal relationship between effort and reward was the vocabulary of athletic victory. The added element here was the competitive aspect implicit in such metaphors. In winning a race it would have been seen as unfair if an outside agency had interfered in the race to determine its outcome. Thus such language was also founded on the presumption of human free will. Athanasius used the metaphor of athletic competition when he described how Antony ignored gold left in his path: Athanasius, Ἐπιστολή 12.1 (ed. Bartelink, SC 400, p. 166), 'Whether it was the devil showing him this, or whether it was some higher power exercising the athlete and showing the devil that Antony was heedless of substantive wealth'; Εἴτε δὲ τοῦ ἐχθροῦ δείξαντος, εἴτε τινὸς κρείττονος δυνάμεως γυμναζούσης τὸν ἀθλητὴν καὶ δεικνυούσης τῷ διαβόλῳ, ὅτι μηδὲ τῶν ἀληθῶς φροντίζει χρημάτων.

[124] Bona superuentura: Anon. trans., Vita Antonii 14.7 (ed. Bartelink, p. 38), '[Antony] But speaking to them and causing them to recall the good things that would arrive'; '[Antonius] Loquens autem et memoriam faciens bonorum superuenturorum'; Anon. trans., Vita Antonii 33.6 (ed. Bartelink, p. 74), '"But every individual will be judged on these things, whether he has kept the faith and whether he has kept the commandments"'; '"Sed in his unusquisque habet iudicium, si fidem seruauit, si mandata custodiuit."'

thinking of the good things to come.[125] The fruit of asceticism was good.[126] And the causal equation between virtue and attainment of the kingdom of heaven was transparent and certain.[127] The language of investment and profit was also part of the anonymous translator's Latin lexicon of reward for effort expended.[128] Just as Athanasius had done, his Latin version of the *Life of Antony* talked of buying and selling access to the kingdom of heaven.[129]

Evagrius

The direct causal equation between ascetic effort and reward advertised by Athanasius was also a fundamental principle of Evagrius' text.[130] As in Athanasius' narrative, desire for such rewards was recommended as defensive armour against the temptations of the devil: '"But if we are eager for the Lord and a desire for future good things has set us aflame with passion … no demon will be able to approach in order to conquer us"'.[131] Evagrius slightly strengthened the autonomous responsibility of the monks in this process by adding to Athanasius' text the statement that the monks had to be eager.

Another small change which contributed to this sharpening of the message was Evagrius' introduction of the term 'rewards' (*praemia*) into the discourse. Where Athanasius wrote of how: 'Desire came into his mind for the heavenly things to

---

[125] *Bona futura*: Anon. trans., *Vita Antonii* 42.7 (ed. Bartelink, p. 88), '"[If the demons find us] thinking about the good things that are coming"'; '"Cogitantes nos de bonis futuris"'; 44.2 (ed. Bartelink, p. 92), 'And so there were dwelling-places of monks singing psalms in the mountains like tabernacles full of heavenly choirs because of the hope of good things to come'; 'Erant itaque mansiones monachorum in montibus uelut tabernacula plena choris diuinis psallentium propter spem bonorum futurorum'.

[126] Anon. trans., *Vita Antonii* 66.8 (ed. Bartelink, p. 130).

[127] Anon. trans., *Vita Antonii* 94.1 (ed. Bartelink, p. 176), the *Life of Antony* should be read so that monks would be sure of this causal entailment: 'And so read everything to the brothers, so that they may learn of what sort the life of a monk should be, and so that they should be persuaded that the Lord our Saviour Jesus Christ glorifies those who glorify Him and serve Him to the end, and not only introduces them into the kingdom of heaven, but also makes well-known and the subject of preaching those who are hidden away and who hasten to withdraw from society'; 'Ergo omnia fratribus quidem legite, ut discant qualis debet esse monachorum uita, ut et persuasi sunt quia Dominum et Saluatorem nostrum Iesum Christum clarificantes eum clarificare, et seruientes illi usque ad finem, non solum introducit in regno caelorum, sed et hic absconsos et festinantes secedere manifestos et praedicabiles facit'.

[128] Anon. trans., *Vita Antonii* 17.3 (ed. Bartelink, p. 42), '"For if someone despises one bronze drachma so that he can make a profit of a hundred gold drachmas, in the same way, if someone is lord of the whole earth and he renounces it, he gives up something small and gets a hundred times its value"'; '"Quomodo enim si quis contemnat unam drachmam aeraminis ut lucrum faciat centum drachmas auri, si quis totius terrae dominus est et renuntiauerit ei, modicum mittit, centum accipit."'

[129] Anon. trans., *Vita Antonii* 16.5 (ed. Bartelink, p. 40), '"And indeed in this world everything is sold for a price matching its worth and things of equal value are exchanged for things of equal value, but the promise of eternal life is bought for the tiniest price"'; '"Et omnis quidem res pretio condigno uenditur in hoc mundo et aequalia aequalibus mutantur, promissio uero uitae aeternae pretio minimissimo emitur."'

[130] Eg. *bona futura*: Evagrius, *Vita Antonii* 13 (14) (ed. Migne, PL 73.134C); *fructus laboris*: 39 (66) (ed. Migne, PL 73.156B); 22 (45) (ed. Migne, PL 73.146D), 'Antony, remembering the mansions set in heaven'; 'Antonius, mansionum in caelo positarum recordans'.

[131] Evagrius, *Vita Antonii* 20 (42) (ed. Migne, PL 73.145D), '"Si autem alacres fuerimus in Domino, et futurorum bonorum cupido nos succenderit … nullus daemonum ad expugnandum ualebit accedere"'.

come', Evagrius wrote: 'His mind blazing with eagerness for heavenly rewards'.[132] This modification in terminology put in place a development in meaning because it introduced a sense of something due, of virtue that would receive a return. 'Rewards' (*praemia*) as a translation of 'heavenly things to come', and 'merits' (*merita*) as a translation of 'virtue', were both terms that expressed a subtle shift in the discourse.

Evagrius sharpened the focus of other aspects of Athanasius' programme also. For example, he accentuated the language of investment. The section from ch. 16 to ch. 18 in Athanasius' text dealt with why a lifetime of effort was a small investment for an everlasting return in heaven. He used vocabulary taken from commerce five times in this section, whereas Evagrius condensed Athanasius' text and used eight words derived from trade, with the result that the message was more pointed.[133] Both writers also included comments about reciprocity in this section, and the overall impression conveyed was that gaining salvation could be likened to a commercial transaction.[134] Both writers also occasionally used verbs in the future tense, which underlined the impression of a guaranteed causal entailment.[135]

Another example of the way in which Evagrius strengthened and clarified some of the implications of Athanasius' programme is offered by the changes he made to Athanasius' account of Antony's final speech of advice to his monks. Athanasius stressed the need for individual effort as Antony twice told the monks they had to strive and be eager, and as has been seen, Athanasius also presented one clear statement of the certainty that the causal entailment of the monks' industry would be their attainment to salvation.[136] Evagrius meanwhile added a

---

[132] Athanasius, Ἐπιστολή 35.5 (ed. Bartelink, SC 400, p. 232), [Ψυχή] πόθος τῶν θείων καὶ τῶν μελλόντων αὐτῇ ἐπεισέρχεται. Cf. Evagrius, *Vita Antonii* 18 (35) (ed. Migne, PL 73.142D), 'Anima caelestium praemiorum auiditate flagrans'.

[133] Athanasius, Ἐπιστολή 16.5–17.6 (ed. Bartelink, SC 400, pp. 178–82): πιπράσκεται, ἀντικαταλλάσσει, ἀγοράζεται, κερδήσῃ, κέρδος; Evagrius, *Vita Antonii* 15 (16–17) (ed. Migne, PL 73.135A–136A): commutatione commercia; emente; uendit; pretio; compensare; praemiis: lucranda; lucretur.

[134] Evagrius, *Vita Antonii* 15 (17) (ed. Migne, PL 73.135C), '"And so if even renouncing the whole world, we cannot give anything in exchange which equals in value the heavenly dwellings, let everyone consider himself and he will immediately realise that having spurned a few acres and walls or a modest portion of gold, he ought not to feel proud of himself as if he had given up a great deal; nor should he become despondent as if he will receive a small return. For just as a person scorns one bronze drachma in order to procure a hundred gold drachmas, so even he who has abandoned the rule of the whole world will receive a hundred times as much in better rewards in the heavenly realm"'; '"Si ergo nec uniuerso orbi renuntiantes, dignum aliquid habitaculis possumus compensare caelestibus, se unusquisque consideret, et statim intelliget, paruis aruris et parietibus, uel modica auri portione contempta, nec gloriari se debere quasi magna dimiserit, nec taedere quasi parua sit recepturus. Vt enim contemnit aliquis unam aeream drachmam ad drachmas centum aureas conquirendas, ita etiam qui totius orbis dominium dereliquit, centuplum de melioribus praemiis in sublimi sede recipiet."'

[135] For example, Evagrius used the future tense, *recipiet*. See n. 134.

[136] Athanasius, Ἐπιστολή 91.2–5 (ed. Bartelink, SC 400, p. 368), '"Be zealous to preserve your own eagerness"'; Σπουδάσατε τηρεῖν τὴν προθυμίαν ἑαυτῶν. And: '"But instead be zealous always to bind yourselves fast chiefly to the Lord and then also to the saints, so that after death they may receive you into the eternal realms as friends and as people with whom they are familiar"'; Σπουδάζετε δὲ μᾶλλον καὶ ὑμεῖς ἀεὶ συνάπτειν ἑαυτούς, προηγουμένως μὲν τῷ Κυρίῳ, ἔπειτα δὲ τοῖς ἁγίοις, ἵνα μετὰ θάνατον ὑμᾶς εἰς τὰς αἰωνίους σκηνάς, ὡς φίλους καὶ γνωρίμους, δέξωνται.

second clear statement of this causal entailment, accentuating Athanasius' narrative on this point: "'Every day think over in your minds the hazardous nature of life, and the heavenly reward will be assigned to you without delay.'"[137] In this same passage, Evagrius reinforced the causal equation between Christian virtue and reward in heaven, mentioning 'reward' (*praemium*) with its inherent sense of repayment due, and naming the 'will' (*uoluntas*) as the determining factor in pursuit of this way of life.[138] Overall, Athanasius' message was conveyed more pointedly by Evagrius, and Evagrius directed the attention towards subtly different concepts through his choice of vocabulary. A similarly suggestive shift is revealed at the start of the *Life of Antony*, when Athanasius described the early development of monasticism in Egypt, and how those who wished 'to give heed to themselves' pursued asceticism away from their villages. The verb used by Athanasius was 'to give heed to oneself' (προσέχειν ἑαυτῷ); the anonymous translator used the words *sibi attendere* ('to give heed to oneself'); Evagrius phrased this as those who desired 'to benefit themselves' (*sibimetipsi prodesse*) in the service of Christ, which relocated the meaning to focus on the advantage that would accrue as a result of their effort.[139] By such shifts in sense and the accentuation of certain elements in the overall programme of ascetic paraenesis, Evagrius developed the terminology of the programme so that his text became the model from which Pelagius drew all the principles that appeared in his writings: 'will' (*uoluntas*), 'merit' (*merita*) and 'reward' (*praemium*).

In all three versions of the *Life of Antony* the direct causal relationship between human effort and divine reward was unquestioned, and it was their authors' main lever of persuasion in their sales pitch for ascetic Christianity. It was the unique selling point of asceticism.

Pelagius

A fundamental principle of Pelagius' teaching was that there was a secure and transparent causal entailment between righteousness on earth and reward in heaven. It was with this vision of future glory that he sought to motivate Demetrias to strive for virtue, advising her to keep it in mind at all times:

> Let these be the thoughts that revolve continually in the virgin's heart. To these let your effort be directed throughout the day, on these lay down your head to rest at night, for these let your soul awake again in the morning. No labour ought to seem too difficult, no time too long to wait, when the prize at stake is everlasting glory.[140]

---

[137] Evagrius, *Vita Antonii* 58 (91) (ed. Migne, PL 73.167A), "'Vitam quotidie ancipitem retractate, et caeleste uobis praemium sine cunctamine tribuetur.'"

[138] For the reference slightly earlier in the same passage to *uoluntas* as the determinant, see n. 70.

[139] Athanasius, Ἐπιστολή 3.2 (ed. Bartelink, SC 400, p. 136); Anon. trans., *Vita Antonii* 3.2 (ed. Bartelink, p. 10); Evagrius, *Vita Antonii* 3 (3) (ed. Migne, PL 73.128A).

[140] Pelagius, *Ad Demetriadem* 30 (ed. Greshake, p. 172), 'Haec iugiter uirginis corde uoluantur. In his totius diei uersetur labor, in his noctis somnus reponatur, in haec anima rursus euigilet. Nullus labor durus, nullum tempus longum uideri debet, quo gloria aeternitatis acquiritur.'

Perfection as a goal and the possibility of human sinlessness

Another criticism levelled at 'Pelagianism' was that it asserted the possibility of human sinlessness. According to the critique, this was not just an impossible or unlikely proposition but a sacrilegious one because it was arrogant and disrespectful to God. This was the accusation that underlay tenet 14 of the theses that Augustine attributed to 'Pelagianism': 'From Peter's statement: *We are sharers in the divine nature* [2 Pet. 1:4], it follows that the soul can be as sinless as God.' The charge that Pelagius preached that human sinlessness was achievable was sometimes modified to the charge that he preached that sinlessness could be achieved 'without God's help'.[141] This accusation was the central substantive allegation that Jerome made against Pelagius in his *Dialogue against the Pelagians* (*Dialogus aduersus Pelagianos*).[142] It was therefore an important indictment of 'Pelagianism' as it was characterised by its opponents.

In his *On the Deeds of Pelagius*, Augustine stated that it was acceptable, as the bishops concluded at Pelagius' trial at Diospolis, to say that a man could be: 'Without sin by God's help and grace'. Here, Augustine argued that what mattered was what was meant by grace. He was certain that his interpretation of grace as an absolute form of prevenient grace was the only interpretation possible for catholic Christians, and that the bishops at Diospolis must have understood it in this sense.[143] In his *On the Perfection of Human Righteousness*, Augustine wrote concerning Caelestius:

> For he has not dared to say that anyone, either he himself or someone else, is without sin, but has only answered that one can be, a point that we do not deny either. The question is when one can be and through whom one can be.[144]

Augustine then went on to associate Caelestius' statements with the suggestion that sinlessness was possible without God's help, and to make the assertion that sinlessness was only possible after death. He then drew a distinction between running perfectly and achieving perfection, in order to explain biblical references to perfect righteousness: 'That is, let as many of us as run perfectly bear in mind that we are not yet perfect, in order that we may be made perfect in that place toward which we are running perfectly [i.e. the kingdom of heaven

---

[141] Jerome discussed these two assertions: *Dialogus aduersus Pelagianos* 1.1 (ed. Moreschini, CCSL 80, pp. 6–7). He then used both these versions of the charge: Jerome, *Dialogus aduersus Pelagianos* 3.15–19 (ed. Moreschini, CCSL 80, pp. 118–23).

[142] Jerome, *Dialogus aduersus Pelagianos* 1.1–21 (ed. Moreschini, CCSL 80, pp. 6–27). Jerome developed an argument that there were two types of perfection, in order to explain biblical references to perfection: Jerome, *Dialogus aduersus Pelagianos* 1.15–19 (ed. Moreschini, CCSL 80, pp. 17–25). See Chapter 3 for a discussion of this.

[143] Augustine, *De gestis Pelagii* 6.16–11.26 (ed. Urba and Zycha, CSEL 42, pp. 68–80).

[144] Augustine, *De perfectione iustitiae hominis* 7.16 (ed. Urba and Zycha, CSEL 42, p. 14), 'Quia non est ausus dicere esse hominem sine peccato, uel aliquem uel se ipsum, sed tantummodo esse posse respondit, quod neque nos negamus. Quando autem possit et per quem possit, hoc quaeritur.'

after death]'.[145] So in writings criticising Pelagius, the grounds of the accusation against Pelagius shifted from condemnation of the statement that man could be sinless, to condemnation of the statement that man could be sinless without God's help, back to condemnation of the statement that man could be sinless.

The use of the word 'perfection' to express aspiration concerning imitation of Christ had not previously been scrutinised in a hostile manner, and such language was commonplace in ascetic literature. The Greek word τελειότης ('completeness', 'perfection') was rendered by Tertullian, writing in the early 3rd century AD, as *perfectio*. Subsequent Christian Latin writers followed Tertullian's usage. The Greek word τελειότης was used regularly without adverse comment. In practice it meant 'perfection' and retained little or no semantic connection to τέλος ('end' or 'goal'), even though etymologically it was linked to the idea of a 'goal'. The Latin *perfectio* had no such etymological link to the idea of something 'aimed at'; it emphatically designated something 'achieved' through its derivation from the passive past participle of 'to achieve' (*perficere*).[146]

The new element, introduced during the controversy over Pelagius' teaching, was the suggestion that reference to 'perfection' was sacrilegious. In his *On Nature and Grace* (*De natura et gratia*), Augustine side-stepped the question of righteousness and perfection even though it was one of the anathemata he attributed to 'Pelagianism'. He stated that he was not interested in the topic of perfection, and he glossed over any distinction between righteousness and perfection:

> As for those who are making progress in this way, I do not much care about where and when they may be made perfect by complete righteousness; but wherever and whenever they might be made perfect, I assert that they cannot be made perfect except by the grace of God through our Lord Jesus Christ.[147]

The conclusion of the Synod of Diospolis was that what was reprehensible was the statement that sinlessness could happen without God's grace and help.[148] The picture in *Life of Antony*, in which Antony was shown being helped by God, complied with the Diospolis proviso, but the synod's ruling did not stipulate the exact nature of the 'grace and help'. The nature of that grace was not spelt out at Diospolis to Augustine's satisfaction because it was not specified as prevenient grace.[149] Three years later in AD 418, Canons 7–9 of the Council of Carthage

---

[145] Augustine, *De perfectione iustitiae hominis* 8.19 (ed. Urba and Zycha, CSEL 42, p. 17), 'Id est: quotquot perfecte currimus, hoc sapiamus, quod nondum perfecti sumus, ut illic perficiamur quo perfecte adhuc currimus'. See also Orosius, *Liber apologeticus* 4 (ed. Zangemeister, CSEL 5, p. 608).

[146] The Greek text of Matt. 19:21: *If you would be perfect*, was Εἰ θέλεις τέλειος εἶναι, which Jerome rendered in his translation of the Gospel as: *Si uis perfectus esse*. For Jerome's interpretation of this passage in his *Commentary on Matthew*, see pp. 142–3.

[147] Augustine, *De natura et gratia* 68.82 (ed. Urba and Zycha, CSEL 60, p. 297), 'Sic autem proficientes ubi et quando plenissima iustitia perficiantur non nimis curo; ubicumque autem et quandocumque perfecti fuerint, non nisi gratia Dei per Iesum Christum Dominum nostrum perfici posse confirmo.'

[148] Augustine, *De gestis Pelagii* 6.16 (ed. Urba and Zycha, CSEL 42, pp. 68–9).

[149] Augustine, *De gestis Pelagii* 6.20–10.22 (ed. Urba and Zycha, CSEL 42, pp. 72–5).

anathematised the proposition that sinlessness was ever possible.[150] But what had been the position on sinlessness and perfection asserted in the three versions of the *Life of Antony*?

Athanasius

Athanasius' Antony said that it was possible to cease sinning:

> 'But let us have this observance also in order to be safe from sinning. Let us each note and record in writing the actions and the movements of our souls, as if we are going to declare them to each other. And be confident that purely through shame at their being known, we will cease from sinning and cease entirely from holding anything impure in our hearts.'[151]

Athanasius' statement that it was possible to return the soul to God in the state in which He had created it (already discussed) was also an assertion of the possibility of human sinlessness. Taking his cue from the biblical citation of Matt. 19:21–2, which launched Antony's ascetic career, the language of purity was common in Athanasius' narrative.[152] He described Antony's soul as pure.[153] When Antony experienced being carried up to heaven by angels, and demons accused Antony of sin, Athanasius implied that from the time when he became a monk onwards, Antony committed no sin, because when the demons demanded that he 'render an account', Athanasius wrote that they were unable to prove their accusations of sin.[154]

The anonymous translator

The anonymous translator altered nothing of Athanasius' text on this topic. Where Athanasius wrote that the disposition of Antony's soul was 'pure' (καθαρός), the anonymous translator rendered this as 'pure' and 'clean' (*purus* and *mundus*).[155] His Latin version rendered faithfully Antony's statement that if the monks all had to report their sins to each other, they would not sin.[156]

---

[150] *Concilium Carthaginense A. 418* (ed. Munier, CCSL 149, pp. 71–3 and pp. 76–7 for canons 7–9 in both the two recensions, one drawn from the *Collectio canonum Quesnelliana*, and the other the Gallican recension).

[151] Athanasius, Ἐπιστολή 55.9–10 (ed. Bartelink, SC 400, p. 284), Ἔστω δὲ καὶ αὕτη πρὸς ἀσφάλειαν τοῦ μὴ ἁμαρτάνειν παρατήρησις. Ἕκαστος τὰς πράξεις καὶ τὰ κινήματα τῆς ψυχῆς, ὡς μέλλοντες ἀλλήλοις ἀπαγγέλλειν, σημειώμεθα καὶ γράφωμεν. Καὶ θαρρεῖτε ὅτι, πάντως αἰσχυνόμενοι γνωσθῆναι, παυσόμεθα τοῦ ἁμαρτάνειν καὶ ὅλως τοῦ ἐνθυμεῖσθαί τι φαῦλον.

[152] Athanasius, Ἐπιστολή 67.5 (ed. Bartelink, SC 400, p. 312), Ἡ τῆς ψυχῆς καθαρότης.

[153] Athanasius, Ἐπιστολή 14.3 (ed. Bartelink, SC 400, p. 172), 'But as for the state of his soul, it was in a pure condition'; Τῆς δὲ ψυχῆς πάλιν καθαρὸν τὸ ἦθος.

[154] Athanasius, Ἐπιστολή 65.5 (ed. Bartelink, SC 400, p. 306), 'Then when they were accusing him and could not prove their accusations'; Τότε κατηγορούντων καὶ μὴ ἐλεγχόντων.

[155] Anon. trans., *Vita Antonii* 14.3 (ed. Bartelink, p. 36), 'They saw that the character of his soul was pure and clean'; 'Animi ipsius puros et mundos mores uidebant.' See also 67.5 (ed. Bartelink, p. 132), where the anonymous translator rendered Athanasius' 'the purity of his soul' (ἡ τῆς ψυχῆς καθαρότης, see above, n. 152) as: 'The purity of the character of his soul'; 'Animi ipsius morum ... puritas.'

[156] Anon. trans., *Vita Antonii* 55.9–12 (ed. Bartelink, pp. 112–14).

Evagrius

From the outset of his version of Athanasius' *Life of Antony*, Evagrius used variants of the word 'perfect' (*perfectus*) to establish the standard set by Antony and the standard to which monks should aspire: 'Indeed to know who Antony was offers the perfect path to virtue.'[157] Athanasius' text did not mention perfection at this point.[158] When Antony was briefly carried up to the heavens in spirit and demons tried to detain him, Evagrius inserted into his translation of the *Life of Antony* a statement not present in Athanasius' text: Athanasius merely commented that the demons could not prove their accusations and so could not detain Antony, but Evagrius noted in addition the specific cause of their failure, as the angels asked the demons why they were holding him back: 'When Antony had no faults.'[159]

Evagrius felt free to proclaim perfection as the goal of endeavour—'"In this life it is proper for you to imitate what is perfect"'—another reference to perfection or lack of sin that was not in Athanasius' original.[160] When Antony felt he had to reveal a vision to the monks, Athanasius asserted that Antony's conscience was clear that he was not motivated by a desire to boast. Evagrius meanwhile inserted a more positive statement about Antony: 'For his soul was pure in Christ'.[161] Thus Evagrius altered Athanasius' text to state explicitly that Antony achieved purity of soul, where Athanasius had left that conclusion implicit. This evidence suggests that Evagrius saw no harm in asserting Antony's perfection and stating that Antony was 'pure in spirit'. In fact he deliberately advertised Antony's sinlessness as an inspiration and model for others.

[157] Evagrius, *Vita Antonii* Preface (ed. Migne, PL 73.127), 'Perfecta est siquidem ad uirtutem uia, Antonium scire quis fuerit.'

[158] Athanasius, Ἐπιστολή Preface 3 (ed. Bartelink, SC 400, p. 126), 'For Antony's life is a sufficient model of asceticism for monks'; Ἔστι γὰρ μοναχοῖς ἱκανὸς χαρακτὴρ πρὸς ἄσκησιν ὁ Ἀντωνίου βίος.

[159] Evagrius, *Vita Antonii* 37 (65) (ed. Migne, PL 73.155B), 'Nullis existentibus in Antonio criminibus.' In the subsequent sentences *crimen* was glossed both as *peccatum* and as *delictum*: 'When the demons tried to go over his sins since the very beginning at his birth, the angels shut their slanderous mouths, saying that they should not recount his transgressions from his birth, which were now laid to rest through the goodness of Christ; but if they knew of anything from after the time when he became a monk and consecrated himself to God, they were allowed to bring those forward. Lying shamelessly, the demons accused him of many things; and since their lies lacked proofs, Antony's free ascent was opened up'; 'Illis uero ab exordio natiuitatis replicare peccata nitentibus, calumniosa angeli ora clauserunt, dicentes non debere eos a natiuitate eius delicta narrare, quae iam Christi essent bonitate sopita; si qua autem scirent ex eo tempore quo factus esset monachus, et Deo se consecrasset, licere proferri. Accusabant daemones multa procaciter mentientes; et cum deessent probamenta fallacibus, liber Antonio conscensus aperitur.'

[160] Evagrius, *Vita Antonii* 19 (38) (ed. Migne, PL 73.143D), '"In hac uita et imitari uos quae perfecta sunt conuenit"'. Cf. Athanasius, Ἐπιστολή 38.2 (ed. Bartelink, SC 400, p. 238), '"Let a person examine closely the asceticism of each, and either imitate it and strive for it, or criticise it"'; Ἑκάστου δὲ τὴν ἄσκησιν καταμανθανέτω τις, καὶ ἢ μιμείσθω καὶ ζηλούτω, ἢ διορθούσθω.

[161] Evagrius, *Vita Antonii* 39 (66) (ed. Migne, PL 73.156B), 'Nor did he want to conceal anything from his spiritual sons for his soul was pure in Christ'; 'Nec spirituales filios pura in Christo anima occultare quidquam uolebat'. Cf. Athanasius, Ἐπιστολή 66.8 (ed. Bartelink, SC 400, p. 310).

Pelagius

Pelagius both argued that there had been men of perfect righteousness in the Old Testament as part of his proof that human nature was inherently good and also held up before Demetrias the goal of perfection.[162] If Pelagius was indicted for using the word 'perfection' (*perfectio*) to describe the aim of ascetic endeavour, then the same charge must also be made against Evagrius of Antioch. Just as Athanasius and Evagrius wrote of Antony's pure conscience, Pelagius advised Demetrias that where sinners feared the Lord's coming, she could look forward to it because her conscience was pure.[163] In the context, surrounded by descriptions of experiences on the Day of Judgement, this remark functioned not as flattery but as a warning.

God listens to the prayers of the righteous so that their prayers are more efficacious than the prayers of people who are not righteous

A teaching attributed to 'Pelagianism' that was criticised by its opponents was the suggestion that God listened to the prayers of the righteous more favourably than he did to the prayers of sinners. This was not one of the fourteen tenets, nor did it underlie any tenet, but it embodied and furthered the charge of arrogance laid against 'Pelagianism'. It was presented as an entailment of the idea that grace was merited, and the unwarranted inference was drawn from Pelagius' writings that he suggested that some of his addressees were perfect, which was then stigmatised as arrogance. The suggestion that Pelagius told some of his correspondents that they were righteous or perfect was reading into his writings something that was not there. An example of this critique is the hostile interpretation disseminated by Pelagius' opponents of the widow's prayer in *On the Christian Life*. The prayer was not in fact a suggested prayer for the widow to whom the letter was addressed; it was a hypothetical scenario proposed as a motivational tool in order to encourage her to strive for righteousness by reminding her of how effective

---

[162] In his *Letter to Demetrias*, Pelagius set out the biblical references to the righteousness of figures such as Abel (described as 'righteous', *iustus*), and then referred to how Christ set out the grounds of Abel's 'perfection' (*perfectio*): Pelagius, *Ad Demetriadem* 5 (ed. Greshake, p. 70), 'The Lord himself, recalling this righteous man in the Gospel, briefly expounded his perfection'; 'Quem iustum in Euangelio Dominus ipse commemorans breuiter perfectionem eius exposuit.' Holding up the goal of perfection to Demetrias: Pelagius, *Ad Demetriadem* 17 (ed. Greshake, pp. 116–18), with reference to God's injunction to man not to sin, 'The Scripture continues: *So that you are blameless and simple* [Phil. 2:15], in reference to complete moral perfection .... Therefore direct the gaze of your mind now to complete moral perfection'; 'Sequitur: *Vt sitis irreprehensibiles et simplices* [Phil. 2:15] ad omnem morum perfectionem .... Nunc ergo ad omnem perfectionem morum aciem mentis intende'; 8 (ed. Greshake, p. 86), 'So that I might lay before you a more level path to perfect righteousness'; 'Vt tibi planiorem uiam ad perfectam iustitiam sterneremus'; 5 (ed. Greshake, p. 74), 'Joseph, loyal servant of the Lord and perfect from childhood, through his tribulations is shown to be more righteous '; 'Ioseph, fidelis Domini famulus et perfectus a puero, tribulationibus magis iustus ostenditur.'
[163] Pelagius, *Ad Demetriadem* 30 (ed. Greshake, p. 170).

she would be if she could pray as a righteous person.[164] The accusation made by critics of Pelagius was that this prayer was gross flattery of the widow because it suggested that she possessed perfect righteousness, and it exemplified the arrogance of Pelagius in suggesting that anyone could address God with such confidence in their own righteousness.[165] This misreading of the passage was used to support the characterisation of 'Pelagianism' as arrogant, even though it was not, and is not, clear that Pelagius wrote *On the Christian Life*.

Athanasius

Athanasius portrayed Antony as someone to whose prayers God listened. He immediately followed this assertion with the statement that Antony did not let this make him arrogant:

> He empathised with those who were suffering and he prayed with them. Often and for many people, the Lord heard him. And neither when Antony was heard did he boast, nor when he was not heard, did he grumble.[166]

With reference to Antony's ability to heal, although Athanasius emphasised that it was not Antony who achieved healing but Christ working through him, at the same time the model he consistently depicted was of Antony's prayers being effective because of his virtue.[167]

The anonymous translator

The anonymous translator did not alter Athanasius' text.

Evagrius

Once again, Evagrius made explicit what had been implicit in Athanasius' text. He stated explicitly that God answered Antony's prayers because of his virtue, and added the word 'merit': 'Antony merely prayed and the Lord granted everything as a reward for the merits of his life.'[168]

---

[164] Anon., *De uita christiana* 11.1–2 (ed. Migne, PL 50.396B–C).

[165] Augustine, *De gestis Pelagii* 6.16–17 (ed. Urba and Zycha, CSEL 42, pp. 68–9), discussing the letter Augustine referred to: 'Those reprehensible writings written to the widow which were said to have been written by Pelagius'; 'Ea quae ad uiduam reprehensibilia scripta dicebantur Pelagium scripsisse'; Jerome, *Dialogus aduersus pelagianos* 3.14–16 (ed. Moreschini, CCSL 80, pp. 116–20).

[166] Athanasius, Ἐπιστολή 56.1 (ed. Bartelink, SC 400, p. 286), Πολλάκις τε ἐν πολλοῖς ἐπήκουεν ὁ Κύριος αὐτοῦ. Καὶ οὔτε ἐπακουόμενος ἐκαυχᾶτο οὔτε μὴ ἐπακουόμενος ἐγόγγυζεν.

[167] Athanasius, Ἐπιστολή 84.2 (ed. Bartelink, SC 400, p. 352), see n. 96.

[168] Evagrius, *Vita Antonii* 52 (84) (ed. Migne, PL 73.164A), 'Antonius tantum orabat, et ob uitae eius merita cuncta Dominus largiebatur.'

Pelagius

In *On Virginity*, Pelagius asserted this same idea when he told his addressee: 'God listens to holy lips, and quickly assents to those prayers which an unstained tongue speaks.'[169] However, as has just been seen, Evagrius had already stated that Antony's merits caused his prayers to be answered, and Pelagius did not invent a new doctrine when he repeated this idea. When Evagrius made the assertion, it was acceptable within Christian teaching and no one remarked on it because it had a clear scriptural basis [1 Pet. 3:12, Ps. 34:15]. But once the myth of 'Pelagianism' had been invented and characterised as arrogant, hostile interpreters of Pelagius' writings, and writings that his opponents associated with Pelagius, now read the same statement that Evagrius had made forty years previously as displaying arrogance.

That virtue could be achieved easily

Although not one of the tenets attributed to 'Pelagianism' in synodal anathemata, the suggestion that virtue could be achieved easily was another criticism Augustine levelled at Pelagius by means of which Augustine characterised Pelagius' teaching as arrogant.[170] Augustine objected that Pelagius had afterwards added the word 'easily' (*facile*) to his account of his answers at Diospolis, when the word 'easily' was not included in the original question put to Pelagius by the synod, and Augustine characterised use of the adverb as a controversial point:

> For those who raised the objection had by some negligence omitted a word which is the subject of considerable controversy. For they set down that he said: 'Man can be without sin, if he wants, and he can obey the commandments, if he wants': no mention was made of *easiness*. Moreover, in response he stated: 'We said that human beings can be without sin, if they want, and can keep the commandments of God, if they want'. He did not say that they can 'easily keep', but only that they can 'keep' the commandments.[171]

---

[169] Pelagius, *De uirginitate* 10.1 (ed. Halm, CSEL 1, p. 238), 'Labia sancta exaudit Deus et ipsis annuit cito precibus, quas lingua inmaculata pronuntiat.'

[170] Augustine, *De gestis Pelagii* 30.55 (ed. Urba and Zycha, CSEL 42, p. 109), 'A letter of fleshly windiness and pride flies about … saying that fourteen Eastern bishops have approved the statement that a man can not only be without sin and keep the commandments of God, but also that he can keep them easily, making no mention of God's help, but saying only: "If he wants". Thus God's grace, on behalf of which a battle was being fought most fiercely, was passed over in silence, so that in this letter there is found only human arrogance deceiving itself as if it had triumphed'; 'Epistola carnalis uentositatis et elationis uolat … ut quattuordecim episcopis orientalibus placuisse dicatur non solum posse esse hominem sine peccato et Dei mandata custodire, sed et facile custodire nec nominato Deo iuuante, sed tantum "si uelit": ut uidelicet tacita, pro qua uehementissime pugnabatur, diuina gratia restet, ut sola in epistola legatur infelix et se ipsam decipiens uelut uictrix humana superbia'. Orosius repeated this critique: *Liber apologeticus* 11 (ed. Zangemeister, CSEL 5, pp. 617–9).

[171] Augustine, *De gestis Pelagii* 30.54 (ed. Urba and Zycha, CSEL 42, p. 107), 'Nam et illi qui obiecerunt, nescio qua incuria, minus posuerunt uerbum, de quo non parua est controuersia. Posuerunt enim eum dixisse: "Posse hominem, si uelit, esse sine peccato, et Dei mandata custodire, si uelit": de

Athanasius

Athanasius stated several times that the achievement of righteousness was easy.[172] Antony specifically argued that the path of righteousness: 'Is not a difficult thing', and: 'Is an easy thing'.[173] He also portrayed the suggestion that it was difficult as the argument of the devil, deliberately aimed at deceiving Antony into giving up his ascetic efforts.[174]

The anonymous translator

The anonymous translator was faithful to Athanasius' message on this, stating three times that virtue was easily achieved.[175] He relayed the contrast that Athanasius drew between man's innate goodness and something that came from outside a person, a contrast designed to emphasise that since virtue was innate to man, it was therefore not difficult to achieve.[176] A rare change to Athanasius' text came when the anonymous translator altered Antony's advice to the monks to keep in mind the acts of the saints in order to train their own souls to imitate the saints' zeal. At this point the translator added two comments of his own. First, he said that they should remember the saints: '"In order to be inspired with zeal for leading your souls into the sight of God."' Second, he added the observation that this would be easy: '"But you can complete this easily if you remember God's commandments."'[177] Thus the anonymous translator added a reminder of the goal they were achieving for themselves, and inserted his own third affirmation of the easiness of leading their souls into God's sight.

---

facilitate nihil est dictum. Deinde ipse respondens ait: "Posse quidem hominem esse sine peccato, et Dei mandata custodire, si uelit, diximus". Neque ipse dixit "facile custodire", sed tantummodo "custodire."'

[172] Athanasius, Ἐπιστολή 7.5 (ed. Bartelink, SC 400, p. 150), others were amazed at Antony's asceticism: 'But he bore the effort quite easily'; Αὐτὸς δὲ ῥᾷον τὸν πόνον ἔφερεν.

[173] Athanasius, Ἐπιστολή 20.8 (ed. Bartelink, SC 400, p. 190), Οὐκ ἔστι δυσχερὲς τὸ πρᾶγμα. Athanasius, Ἐπιστολή 20.3 (ed. Bartelink, SC 400, p. 188), Εὔκολόν ἐστι τὸ πρᾶγμα.

[174] Athanasius, Ἐπιστολή 5.2 (ed. Bartelink, SC 400, p. 142).

[175] Anon. trans., *Vita Antonii* 20.3 (ed. Bartelink, p. 48), '"This is an easy thing when we want it"'; '"Facile est res ista cum uoluerimus"'; 7.5 (ed. Bartelink, p. 22): here the editor added the word 'facile', which seemed to be required for sense and by its presence in the Greek original, but was not present in the only surviving witness to this version of the *Life of Antony*. See n. 177 for the third use of 'facile'. See also 20.8 (ed. Bartelink, p. 48), '"And so it is not a difficult thing"'; '"Itaque non est res difficilis."'

[176] Anon. trans., *Vita Antonii* 20.9 (ed. Bartelink, pp. 48–50), '"If, however, we had to seek sacred virtue from outside ourselves, it would truly be a difficult thing"'; '"Si autem extrinsecus adquirenda erat nobis uirtus deifica, difficile uere esset res."'

[177] Anon. trans., *Vita Antonii* 55.4 (ed. Bartelink, p. 110), '"Mementote actuum sanctorum ut zelum accipiatis ad dirigendum animum uestrum in conspectu Dei. Facile autem hoc perficere potestis, si mandatorum Dei memoriam habueritis."' Cf. Athanasius, Ἐπιστολή 55.3 (ed. Bartelink, SC 400, p. 282), describing how to all the monks who came to him, Antony continuously gave this instruction: 'To learn by heart the commands in the Scriptures, and to call to mind the actions of the saints so as to train their soul according to the saints' zeal, as it remembers the commandments'; Ἀποστηθίζειν τὰ ἐν ταῖς γραφαῖς παραγγέλματα, καὶ μνημονεύειν τῶν πράξεων τῶν ἁγίων πρὸς τὸ τῷ ζήλῳ τούτων ῥυθμίζεσθαι τὴν ψυχὴν ὑπομιμνησκομένην ἐκ τῶν ἐντολῶν.

Evagrius

In contrast to Athanasius, Evagrius did not use the word 'easy' in Antony's long speech on the goodness of human nature. Elsewhere, however, he added something not in Athanasius' original when he reported that: '[Antony] also used to say that the path to virtue was a wide one, if individual monks would either observe what they themselves did or report all the thoughts of their minds to the brothers.'[178] This implied that it was possible for many to take the path of virtue, and therefore that it was not a difficult path accessible only to a few. This opinion was located within his argument that contemporary human nature was innately inclined to goodness, and that shame and conscience were aspects of this natural inclination to virtue.

Pelagius

In his *Letter to Demetrias*, Pelagius argued that zeal and application would make the: 'Light and sweet yoke of Christ, sweeter and lighter'.[179] Conversely, in *Letter to Celantia* he described the path of chastity as difficult.[180]

This evidence suggests that statements about the easiness of adhering to Christ's injunctions were not uncommon in ascetic paraenesis that had been in circulation for decades when Augustine characterised this idea as part of a 'new heresy'. Criticism of Pelagius for using such language (in Pelagius' case far more guardedly than Athanasius had done) should be levelled at Athanasius also.

Christianity advocated the abandonment of property because it taught that rich people could not enter the kingdom of heaven

Athanasius, the anonymous Latin translation, Evagrius and Pelagius

Tenet 7 in Augustine's list attributed this view to 'Pelagianism'. All three versions of the *Life of Antony* proposed Antony as a model of Christian virtue, and an important aspect of this virtue was that he rejected property ownership. His lack of interest in material possessions was regularly proposed as a virtue in all three versions of the *Life of Antony*. Athanasius' Antony told the monks that an upright life and faith in God were a defence against demons, and he listed the elements of their way of life which the demons feared, of which 'not being attached to money' (τὸ ἀφιλάργυρον) was one. In Evagrius' list this was subtly altered to make explicit the elements in the ascetic programme. This item appeared as 'voluntary poverty'

---

[178] Evagrius, *Vita Antonii* 28 (55) (ed. Migne, PL 73.151C), 'Necnon dicebat magnam esse ad uirtutem uiam, si singuli uel obseruarent quod gererent, uel uniuersas mentium cogitationes fratribus referrent.'
[179] Pelagius, *Ad Demetriadem* 13 (ed. Greshake, p. 102), 'If you wish to make the light and sweet yoke of Christ, sweeter and lighter for yourself'; 'Si leue ac suaue Christi iugum suauius tibi leuiusque uis facere'.
[180] Pelagius, *Ad Celantiam* 31 (ed. Hilberg, CSEL 56, p. 355), 'And the path of chastity is arduous'; 'Arduumque est iter castitatis'.

(*uoluntaria paupertas*), so that an attitude of mind became a material condition. This was another of the marginal changes which in combination made Evagrius' version of the ascetic project more programmatic.

This definition of Christian virtue as requiring disdain for material wealth cannot be directly equated to a doctrine that rich people would not be able to enter heaven. To read such a doctrine into the *Life of Antony* would be to falsely attribute a teaching to it. Yet in their promotion of the rejection of material possessions the three versions of the *Life of Antony* presented a more radical picture of Christian virtue than Pelagius did in his letters to Demetrias and Celantia, in neither of which did he suggest that his addressee should give away her property. Pelagius told both these women from wealthy families that they could hope to enter the kingdom of heaven. His strategy to counter excessive materialism was instead to redefine wealth in spiritual terms in order to foster spiritual values in place of materialistic ones.

The accusation of arrogance

As noted in Chapter 1, a key aspect of the caricature of Pelagius' teaching created by proponents of the triune was the claim that it was arrogant. Both Augustine and Jerome linked this arrogance to Phariseeic self-righteousness, implicitly associating Pelagius with the toxicity of the Pharissees as agitators for Jesus' death.[181]

Athanasius

As has been shown, Antony was made the embodiment of the human will to pursue virtue. As Christian literary discourse was increasingly permeated by ascetic values, the effect of this was to put human intention at the forefront of the reading Christian's attention. If the human spirit was going to play such a prominent role in the Christian message of salvation, it had to be presented as part of a characterisation of the human–divine dynamic as one of co-operation, and there had to be continuous stringent warnings against the danger of arrogance in overstepping the appropriate balance in this relationship. This co-operative model was presented fully formed in the three versions of the *Life of Antony*—that is to say, a preventative strategy was already in place to deal with the potential pitfall of arrogance. Athanasius' *Life of Antony* was interspersed with regular admonition to avoid arrogance. A potential cause of arrogance might have been the special powers attributed to Antony, and Athanasius was well aware of this risk. His two tactics to prevent arrogance were, first, to affirm on every occasion that it was God who worked healings through Antony and, second, always to describe the power as a gift, because this maintained God's omnipotence and established a requirement

---

[181] Augustine, *De peccatorum meritis* 2.5.6 (ed. Urba and Zycha, CSEL 60, p. 76); Jerome, *Dialogus aduersus pelagianos* 3.14–16 (ed. Moreschini, CCSL 80, pp. 116–20).

for gratitude. The concepts of 'grace' (χάρις) and 'gift' or 'favour' (χάρισμα) were used to instil mandatory gratitude. In the three versions of Antony's life, 'grace' (χάρις, *gratia*) played this essential role in the preventative strategy. The danger of arrogance had therefore already been identified and provided for by those who advertised this approach to Christianity, and it was the idea of a 'gift' ('grace'), that they used to prevent arrogance. Every time Athanasius credited Antony with some special ability, he at the same time pointed out God's agency and referred to the power as a gift, consistently removing any opportunity for arrogance.[182]

Antony always thought in advance about how to forestall pride:

> When he saw himself importuned by many people and not permitted to withdraw on retreat according to his purpose as he wished, taking care lest because of the things that the Lord did through him either he himself might become proud, or someone else might think him better than he was, he thought about this in advance, and hastened to go up to the upper Thebaid.[183]

Athanasius' choice of words emphasised how Antony forestalled any chance of arrogance in himself or an inflated opinion of him in others: 'he took care' (εὐλαβηθείς) and 'he thought about it in advance' (ἐσκέψατο). This mirrors the author's own actions in the composition of his narrative: at every turn he forestalled any opportunity for pride. Every time Antony defeated the devil, Athanasius depicted Antony attributing his success to the Lord.[184] All miracles were expressly stated to have been achieved by God, not Antony.[185] Antony himself stressed the need to avoid arrogance.[186] Athanasius' Antony advised the monks to scrutinise their own actions for sin and he expressly prohibited pride in the eventuality that they could find no sin in themselves: '"If he has not sinned, let him not boast, but let him persevere in virtue and not slacken off, and let him not condemn his

---

[182] For example, Athanasius, Ἐπιστολή 56.1–2 (ed. Bartelink, SC 400, pp. 286–8), concerning how when the sick came to Antony, he prayed with them: 'And often and for many the Lord used to hear Antony. And when Antony was heard, he did not boast, nor did he grumble when he was not heard, but he himself always thanked the Lord, and encouraged those who were ill to be patient and to know that healing is not in Antony's power or the power of any human, but God alone achieves it, when and upon whom He wishes .... And those who were healed learned to give thanks not to Antony but to God alone'; Πολλάκις τε ἐν πολλοῖς ἐπήκουεν ὁ Κύριος αὐτοῦ. Καὶ οὔτε ἐπακουόμενος ἐκαυχᾶτο οὔτε μὴ ἐπακουόμενος ἐγόγγυζεν, ἀλλ' ἀεὶ μὲν αὐτὸς ηὐχαρίστει τῷ Κυρίῳ, τοὺς δὲ πάσχοντας παρεκάλει μακροθυμεῖν καὶ εἰδέναι, ὅτι οὔτε αὐτοῦ οὔθ' ὅλως ἀνθρώπων ἐστὶν ἡ θεραπεία, ἀλλὰ μόνου τοῦ θεοῦ τοῦ ποιοῦντος, ὅτε θέλει, καὶ οἷς βούλεται .... Καὶ οἱ θεραπευόμενοι δὲ ἐδιδάσκοντο μὴ Ἀντωνίῳ εὐχαριστεῖν, ἀλλὰ μόνῳ τῷ Κυρίῳ.

[183] Athanasius, Ἐπιστολή 49.1 (ed. Bartelink, SC 400, p. 266), Ὡς δὲ εἶδεν ἑαυτὸν ὀχλούμενον ὑπὸ πολλῶν καὶ μὴ ἀφιέμενον κατὰ γνώμην ἀναχωρεῖν ὡς βούλεται, εὐλαβηθεὶς μὴ ἐξ ὧν ὁ Κύριος ποιεῖ δι' αὐτοῦ, ἢ αὐτὸς ἐπαρθῇ ἢ ἄλλος τις ὑπὲρ ὅ ἐστι λογίσηται περὶ αὐτοῦ, ἐσκέψατο καὶ ὥρμησεν ἀνελθεῖν εἰς τὴν ἄνω Θηβαΐδα.

[184] For example, Athanasius, Ἐπιστολή 40.6 (ed. Bartelink, SC 400, p. 244); 80.6 (ed. Bartelink, SC 400, p. 338).

[185] Athanasius, Ἐπιστολή 38.2 (ed. Bartelink, SC 400, p. 238); 48.3 (ed. Bartelink, SC 400, p. 264); 84.1 (ed. Bartelink, SC 400, p. 352).

[186] Athanasius, Ἐπιστολή 55.3 (ed. Bartelink, SC 400, p. 282), Antony's instruction to the monks was: 'To flee self-conceit'; Φεύγειν τε κενοδοξίαν.

neighbour nor pronounce himself righteous"'.[187] Antony was portrayed as a model of humility, for example in his relations with those in clerical orders.[188]

The anonymous translator

The earlier Latin version of the *Life of Antony* translated Athanasius' strictures against arrogance faithfully without alteration.[189]

Evagrius

Evagrius accepted unreservedly Athanasius' stress on the need to avoid arrogance as an essential part of the theological programme of asceticism. On some occasions, Evagrius relayed Athanasius' strictures on this subject without changing them.[190] On four occasions, however, when Athanasius censured arrogance, Evagrius conveyed this advice but also added to it. The first occasion came when Antony told the monks that it was Christ who healed and not Antony (in ch. 80 of Athanasius' text), and here Evagrius made an important addition. The healing occurred in the context of persuading pagans that the Christian God was superior to their own gods, so that the implication in all three versions was that the pagans could choose to believe, which presupposed free will. Evagrius added a description of the healing as the gift of God, but also as 'merited', alongside a condemnation of arrogance concerning rhetorical skill which by analogy worked as a condemnation of arrogance of any sort, including in relation to gifts from God:

> For they were amazed and terrified by the man to whom, in addition to such intelligence, the divine gift of miracles flowed in abundance. But Antony attributed everything to Christ who heals, and answered: 'Do not think that I have given these people health, Christ works these miracles through his servants. You believe also, and you will see that faith devoted to God, and not the swollen pride of empty rhetoric, may merit such miracles.'[191]

Thus where Athanasius' Antony simply stated that Christ healed through those who believed in him, Evagrius' Antony explicitly asserted that healing was a gift that was the result of merit, and in the same sentence he condemned pride.

---

[187] Athanasius, Ἐπιστολή 55.7 (ed. Bartelink, SC 400, p. 284), Εἰ δὲ μὴ ἥμαρτεν, μὴ καυχάσθω, ἀλλ' ἐπιμενέτω τῷ καλῷ καὶ μὴ ἀμελείτω μηδὲ κατακρινέτω τὸν πλησίον μηδὲ δικαιούτω ἑαυτόν.

[188] Athanasius, Ἐπιστολή 67.1 (ed. Bartelink, SC 400, p. 310).

[189] Anon. trans., *Vita Antonii* 17.1 (ed. Bartelink, p. 42); 44.1 (ed. Bartelink, p. 90); 58.4 (ed. Bartelink, p. 116); 66.7 (ed. Bartelink, p. 130); 84.1 (ed. Bartelink, pp. 158–60).

[190] For example, when Athanasius stressed that healing was the action of God working through Antony, Evagrius' text reflected Athanasius' exactly: Athanasius, Ἐπιστολή 56.1–2 (ed. Bartelink, SC 400, pp. 286–8), see n. 182; cf. Evagrius, *Vita Antonii* 28 (56) (ed. Migne, PL 73.151D–152A).

[191] Evagrius, *Vita Antonii* 49 (80) (ed. Migne, PL 73.161D–162A), 'Expauerunt enim stupentes hominem, cui post tantum ingenium afflueret signorum diuina largitio. At ille uniuersa Christo qui curat ascribens, usus est affatu reciproco, et ait: "Nolite me putare his sanitatem dedisse, Christus per seruos suos facit ista miracula. Credite et uos, et uidebitis quia deuota Deo fides, non eloquentiae uanus tumor talia signa mereatur."'

Evagrius made the same addition to Athanasius' next prohibition against arrogance. In ch. 83 and ch. 84, Athanasius embarked on a long refutation of the idea that miracles were the work of humans. Evagrius added two rhetorical questions to make the refutation more effective, and once more added the idea that such healings were gifts that were the result of merit.[192] A third occasion when Evagrius augmented Athanasius' injunctions against arrogance came when Evagrius inserted an extra sentence warning of hell.[193] This accentuated the consequences of breaking Athanasius' ban on self-righteousness, strengthening the prohibition.

In a fourth instance, where Athanasius endorsed humility and by implication condemned arrogance in a passage in which he described how Antony showed great deference to all ecclesiastics, Evagrius added to this passage also to stress condemnation of pride.[194] The small changes he made were not due to Evagrius' greater literary awareness as much as to his desire to bring to the fore certain elements of Athanasius' programme in such a way that no one could mistake the point he was making. Clearly Athanasius was concerned that his programme ran the risk of arrogance. Evagrius was equally aware of this risk and sought to establish his preventative measures even more emphatically in the minds of his readers. One of the ways that Evagrius did this was through adding mention of heaven and hell, warning of the consequences of the monks' choices in order to sharpen the persuasive edge of his narrative.

[192] Evagrius, *Vita Antonii* 52 (83–4) (ed. Migne, PL 73.163D–164A), 'Was it by the authority of his own power that Antony used to heal? Did he judge that what he had done was the result of his own capability? The demons and illnesses ceased as a result of his prayers, not his commands, and everything was always accomplished by calling on the name of Christ, our God .... Antony just used to pray, and the Lord granted everything because of the merits of Antony's life'; 'Nunquid suae uirtutis imperio curabat Antonius? Nunquid suae possibilitatis arbitrabatur esse quod fecerat? Orationibus, non praeceptis daemones morbique cesserunt, et ad Christi Dei nostri nominationem semper uniuersa perfecta sunt .... Antonius tantum orabat, et ob uitae eius merita cuncta Dominus largiebatur' (final sentence cited earlier at n. 168).

[193] Evagrius, *Vita Antonii* 28 (55) (ed. Migne, PL 73.151B), 'Many are the ways (as the Bible says) that seem just to men but they end with a view into the depths of hell [cf. Prov. 14:12 and 16:25]; often we cannot see our own sins, often we are deceived in our account of our actions; the judgement of God who sees everything is a different thing, God who judges not on the basis of a superficial view of bodies but according to the hidden recesses of minds'; 'Multas esse (ut scriptum est) uias quae uidentur hominibus iustae, sed fines earum ad profundum respicere inferni [cf. Prov. 14:12 and 16:25]; saepe nostra non posse nos intelligere peccata, saepe falli in ratione gestorum; aliud esse Dei cuncta cernentis iudicium, qui non ex superficie corporum, sed ex mentium iudicat arcanis.'

[194] Evagrius, *Vita Antonii* 39 (67) (ed. Migne, PL 73.156A–B), in this one chapter: first, where Athanasius wrote that Antony did not willingly reveal a vision he had seen to the monks, but did not state the reason why Antony was unwilling, Evagrius added the detail that Antony did this to avoid boasting: 'But he did not tell the brothers what had been revealed to him in order to avoid boasting'; 'Neque uero id, quod sibi reuelatum fuerat, causa iactantiae fratribus indicabat'; second, where Athanasius stated that Antony was forbearing and humble, Evagrius made this statement more dramatic: 'He was never provoked by sudden anger to shatter his patient attitude, nor did he elevate humility into pride'; 'Nunquam ille aut ira subita concitatus patientiam rupit, aut humilitatem erexit in gloriam'; third, where Athanasius stated that Antony deferred to all ecclesiastics, Evagrius added that in his relations with bishops and presbyters Antony behaved: 'As if he was their pupil in humility'; 'Quasi humilitatis discipulus'.

The argument that the doctrine of effective free will was inherently arrogant, and therefore it was not a caricature of Pelagius' position to characterise it as such, is vitiated by this embedded programmatic concern to maintain gratitude to God for his gifts. The unremitting stress that Athanasius and Evagrius placed on the need for humility suggests that arrogance was not a necessary corollary of the argument for effective free will. Pelagius' advice repeated their insistence on the need for humility.[195]

Section 2: Reference to Original Sin, Prevenient Grace, or Predestination, or the Characterisation of Man's Nature as Sinful and Man's Will as Weak and in Need of External Assistance in Order to Choose Virtue

Absence of the doctrine of original sin

The three versions of the Life of Antony

Athanasius' theology did not simply omit mention of original sin; it ruled out its possibility. There was no mention of a change in the state of human nature. Speaking to his monks in his own day, Antony asserted that their human nature was inherently inclined to moral goodness. Indeed, Athanasius stated emphatically that the soul was untainted by sin, as if to counter any suggestion that this might be possible. Both the anonymous translator and Evagrius expounded this same anthropology.

Absence of mention of God's grace as causing human virtue

Athanasius and the anonymous translator

There is a complete absence of any suggestion that 'grace' (χάρις, *gratia*) caused virtue in the three versions of the *Life of Antony*. None of these texts mentioned grace as a cause or inspiration of right action. Nowhere was there any mention of receiving virtue, and none of the three texts suggested asking God to give virtue. There was, however, regular advice to ask God for help to resist evil.

Athanasius stated that faith was given to man by God through Jesus Christ. The implication of this was that the Christian faith was given to mankind generally through Christ's advent, and not that specific individuals received their faith from

---

[195] Pelagius, *Ad Celantiam* 20 (ed. Hilberg, CSEL 56, pp. 346–7): see Chapter 1, n. 72.

God.[196] Furthermore, Athanasius was writing in the context of persuading pagans to convert, an activity that presupposed their effective free will. By contrast, Augustine argued that access to salvation was determined not by effective free will causing merit but by God's prevenient grace, which also caused faith itself.[197]

Evagrius

Writing about the powerlessness of the devil being proved by the fact that the devil had to ask God for permission to tempt Job, Athanasius had Antony conclude: "'So that this also shows that the enemy should instead be despised, because although he desired it, he did not have power against even one just man. For if he had had the power, he would not have asked'".[198] Evagrius, by contrast, although in the surrounding sentences he followed Athanasius' original closely, did not refer to 'a just man' but expanded the meaning of that phrase in terms of its consequences in a way that clearly omitted reference to grace in the process of reaching heaven. Referring to anyone who asks how the devil had the power to destroy Job's family and possessions, he wrote:

> 'He who makes this objection, let him hear the contrary argument: it was not the devil who was able to do this, but the Lord, by whom power over us is granted in two directions, either to glory if we are approved of, or to punishment if we transgress. What is more, let him note from this example that the devil was not able to do anything even against one man, if he had not received power from the Lord. For no one asks someone else for something which is in his own power.'[199]

---

[196] Athanasius, Ἐπιστολή 78.1 (ed. Bartelink, SC 400, pp. 332–4), '"Accordingly we Christians do not hold mystery to be in the wisdom of Greek reasoning, but in the power of a faith that has been supplied to us by God through Jesus Christ"'; Ἡμεῖς τοίνυν οἱ χριστιανοὶ οὐκ ἐν σοφίᾳ λόγων Ἑλληνικῶν ἔχομεν τὸ μυστήριον, ἀλλ' ἐν δυνάμει πίστεως ἐπιχορηγουμένης ἡμῖν διὰ Ἰησοῦ Χριστοῦ παρὰ τοῦ θεοῦ.

[197] In his letter to Sixtus of AD 418, Augustine argued that the merits for which salvation was given were themselves given, hence the grace of eternal life was given to prevenient grace: Augustine, *Ep.* 194.5.19 (ed. Goldbacher, CSEL 57, pp. 190–1), 'Eternal life, which will certainly be had in the end without end, is given in return for preceding merits, yet because those same merits to which it is given in return, were not produced by us through our own abilities but were produced in us by grace, it is also itself called grace, for no other reason than that it is given gratuitously; and not because it is not given for merits, but because even the very merits to which it is given were given to us. But where we find eternal life is also called grace, we have in the words of the same magnificent defender of grace the apostle Paul: *The wages of sin are death*, he says, *but the grace of God is eternal life in Jesus Christ our Lord* [Rom. 6:23]'; 'Aeterna uita, quae utique in fine sine fine habebitur, et ideo meritis praecedentibus redditur, tamen, quia eadem merita quibus redditur, non a nobis facta sunt per nostram sufficientiam, sed in nobis facta per gratiam, etiam ipsa gratia nuncupatur, non ob aliud nisi quia gratis datur; nec ideo quia non meritis datur, sed quia data sunt et ipsa merita quibus datur. Vbi autem inuenimus etiam uitam aeternam gratiam nuncupari, habemus apud eundem gratiae magnificum defensorem apostolum Paulum: *Stipendium,* inquit, *peccati mors; gratia autem Dei uita aeterna in Christo Iesu Domino nostro* [Rom. 6:23].'

[198] Athanasius, Ἐπιστολή 29.3 (ed. Bartelink, SC 400, p. 216), Ὥστε καὶ ἐκ τούτου μᾶλλον καταγνωστέος ἐστὶν ὁ ἐχθρὸς ὅτι, καίτοι θέλων, οὐδὲ καθ' ἑνὸς ἴσχυσεν ἀνθρώπου δικαίου. Εἰ γὰρ ἴσχυσεν, οὐκ ἂν ἤτησεν.

[199] Evagrius, *Vita Antonii* 17 (29) (ed. Migne, PL 73.141A), '"Qui hoc opponit, audiat e diuerso: non diabolum potuisse hoc, sed Dominum, a quo potestas aduersum nos dupliciter datur, uel ad gloriam, si

Evagrius therefore went out of his way to expand the notion of a 'just man' to focus on the human choice to be just or wicked and its consequences. In his statement of the options: 'Glory if we are approved of, punishment if we transgress', Evagrius encapsulated the view that man had free will to choose. Being just meant precisely this choice, and the consequences of the choice were brought into the foreground because they were a more pointed incentive than a simple adjective attributing righteousness. In this way Evagrius again brought out the detail underlying Athanasius' programme in order to make it explicit; the ascetic model Evagrius presented was highly incentivised.[200] This was a constant subtle process of clarification and explanation of the principles underlying the ascetic project for Christianity. Evagrius' text presented the implications of this approach to Christianity as relevant to everyone, since the choice Evagrius presented applied to all Christians, not just monks.

Evagrius made a similar subtle change when he translated Antony's advice that each person was judged on whether or not he had kept the faith and fulfilled the commandments. As already noted, Evagrius' expansion of this brought out the individual's agency in the result in the verb with reflexive pronoun ('prepares for himself', *sibi praeparat*).[201] In both texts this simple equation left no room for grace; but whereas Athanasius took it for granted that the individual possessed moral autonomy, Evagrius' statement specifically excluded any external agency in the attainment of salvation.

Another addition to Athanasius' text which made explicit the absence of a role for prevenient grace as a cause of moral virtue came when Antony spoke of the need to pay attention to the body: '"So that [the soul] should not be dragged down by the pleasures of the body, but instead the body should be its servant.'"[202] Evagrius expanded this to add a statement that made explicit the soul's power over its own body, and its resulting responsibility for the body and for its own condition. He also added a statement that made a man responsible for his own salvation, asserting man's ability to achieve perfection. This personal responsibility was again expressed through a reflexive pronoun. Evagrius strengthened the idea that the soul could control the body:

---

probamur, uel ad poenam, si delinquimus. Quin potius ex hoc animaduertat, ne contra unum quidem hominem diabolum quidquam potuisse, si non potestatem accepisset a Domino. Nullus enim quod suae ditionis est ab alio deprecatur.'"

[200] Evagrius made small changes to Athanasius' text in order to heighten the drama of Athanasius' warning about the Day of Judgement (and used the word *incentiua* of the lusts of the flesh): Evagrius, *Vita Antonii* 15 (19) (ed. Migne, PL 73.136B–C), '"Keeping before our eyes always the coming of the final retribution, because a greater fear of judgement and a terrible dread of punishment destroy the incentives of the lustful flesh and hold back the soul as it rushes, as it were, over a precipice'"; '"Ante oculos semper habentes ultimae retributionis aduentum, quia maior formido iudicii et poenarum timor horridus, simul et lubricae carnis incentiua dissoluit, et ruentem animam quasi ex aliqua rupe sustentat.'" Cf. Athanasius, Ἐπιστολή 19.5 (ed. Bartelink, SC 400, p. 186).

[201] See n. 50.

[202] Athanasius, Ἐπιστολή 45.6 (ed. Bartelink, SC 400, p. 258), Ἵνα μὴ αὕτη καθέλκηται ὑπὸ τῶν ἡδονῶν τοῦ σώματος, ἀλλὰ μᾶλλον τὸ σῶμα παρ' αὐτῆς δουλαγωγῆται.

> All the effort of the soul should be directed to preventing the soul from being overcome by bodily vices and pushed into the eternal darkness of hell; instead, laying claim to the control over the flesh granted to it, the soul should raise up its dwelling-place to the third heaven, like the apostle Paul [2 Cor. 12:2].[203]

In this account of salvation there was no room for divine agency as a causal factor in salvation. This sentence expanded and clarified Evagrius' earlier additional words, 'prepares for himself' (*sibi praeparat*). In this sentence, when he referred to the soul's having been 'granted control over the flesh' (*indultum sibi in carne imperium*), Evagrius asserted the view that the soul did have power over the body and ruled out any other agency in the attainment of salvation, and he cited Paul [2 Cor. 12:2] perhaps to answer the apostle's comments elsewhere in which Paul suggested that he lacked control over his own body.[204] Whereas in Athanasius' text there was simply an absence of mention of God's prevenient grace as an agent in human virtue, in his version of the *Life of Antony*, Evagrius specifically ruled out any extra-human agency in determining salvation.

Pelagius

Pelagius, by contrast, mentioned grace regularly in relation to righteousness, urging that Christians were particularly able to be morally upright because in addition to Christ's example and Scripture, they were also assisted in achieving righteousness by the help of divine grace and the Holy Spirit.[205]

Section 3: Use of the Word χάρις ('Grace') and Its Latin Equivalent, *Gratia*

The use of the word 'grace' (χάρις, *gratia*) is similar in all three versions of the *Life of Antony*. The question at issue is whether the term 'grace' in these narratives ever referred to something that could be identified as prevenient grace—that is, the prior inspiration of the Holy Spirit causing a human to act virtuously.

χάρις in Athanasius' *Life of Antony*

Excluding its use as a preposition, Athanasius used the word 'grace' (χάρις) eight times in his *Life of Antony*. Of these, the first was in the citation of 1 Cor. 15:10: *Yet not I, but the grace of God with me* (a Pauline reference cited by Augustine

---

[203] Evagrius, *Vita Antonii* 22 (45) (ed. Migne, PL 73.147A), 'Omne studium animae conferendum, ne uitiis superata corporeis, ad aeternas inferni tenebras truderetur; quinimo indultum sibi in carne imperium uindicans, domicilium suum, ut apostolus Paulus [2 Cor. 12:2], ad tertium caelum subleuaret.'

[204] For example, Rom. 7:14–25.

[205] Pelagius, *Ad Demetriadem* 3 (ed. Greshake, p. 66), 'Who are also assisted by the help of divine grace'; 'Qui diuinae quoque gratiae iuuantur auxilio.' See also Chapter 1, n. 34–8.

to support his account of prevenient grace). As already discussed, the passage in which Athanasius used this citation highlighted co-operation between God and man using the verb 'to work together' (συνεργεῖν), and this context suggests how the citation should be read. There are seven further instances of Athanasius' use of the word χάρις, and these offer evidence about what he understood by the term and what he thought was the cause of grace. In addition, Athanasius used the word χάρισμα five times; in three of these uses, χάρισμα stood alone, but in two of them it was used in close apposition to χάρις in a way that suggests that the words were synonymous in Athanasius' usage.

Of the seven relevant uses of the word χάρις by Athanasius, five referred to a special power given to Antony. The first occurred when after describing special abilities Antony possessed, including how God healed through Antony, Athanasius followed these statements by saying that in addition God gave Antony 'grace in speaking'.[206] Here χάρις was a God-given special power to speak well, a gift, and the τε ('and') suggests that it was a further gift; this implied that the healing should be viewed as a gift also, and Athanasius emphasised God's agency by making God the subject of the verbs 'to heal' (θεραπεύειν) and 'to cleanse' (καθαρίζειν). In terms of the cause of this gift, the context was the discussion of Antony's special virtue gained through ascetic endeavour, so that his powers were presented as resulting from his virtue.

The second use of χάρις does not fit the pattern of the others. I shall discuss it after the five uses that are similar.

The third use appears in the context of a power given to believers to tread on snakes and scorpions. Antony told the monks to fear only God and not to pay attention to demons:

> 'But the more they do these things, the more let us intensify our asceticism against them. For an upright life and belief in God are powerful armour against them. For they certainly fear the fasting of ascetics, their vigils, their prayers, their gentleness, their calm, their lack of interest in money, their unconcern for fame, their humility, their care for the poor, their almsgiving, their patience, and most of all their piety toward Christ. For this is the reason that they do everything so that they should not be trodden underfoot. For they know the grace given to believers by the Saviour, when he said: *See I have given you authority to tread on snakes and scorpions, and over all the power of the enemy* [Luke 10:19]'.[207]

---

[206] Athanasius, Ἐπιστολή 14.6 (ed. Bartelink, SC 400, p. 174), 'He gave Antony grace in speaking'; Χάριν τε ἐν τῷ λαλεῖν ἐδίδου τῷ Ἀντωνίῳ.

[207] Athanasius, Ἐπιστολή 30.1–3 (ed. Bartelink, SC 400, pp. 218–20), Ἀλλὰ καὶ μᾶλλον ὅσῳ ταῦτα ποιοῦσιν, ἐπιτείνωμεν ἡμεῖς τὴν ἄσκησιν κατ' αὐτῶν. Μέγα γὰρ ὅπλον ἐστὶ κατ' αὐτῶν βίος ὀρθὸς καὶ ἡ πρὸς θεὸν πίστις. Φοβοῦνται γοῦν τῶν ἀσκητῶν τὴν νηστείαν, τὴν ἀγρυπνίαν, τὰς εὐχάς, τὸ πρᾶον, τὸ ἥσυχον, τὸ ἀφιλάργυρον, τὸ ἀκενόδοξον, τὴν ταπεινοφροσύνην, τὸ φιλόπτωχον, τὰς ἐλεημοσύνας, τὸ ἀόργητον, καὶ προηγουμένως τὴν εἰς τὸν Χριστὸν εὐσέβειαν. Διὰ τοῦτο γὰρ καὶ πάντα ποιοῦσιν, ἵνα μὴ ἔχωσι τοὺς πατοῦντας αὐτούς. Ἴσασι γὰρ τὴν κατ' αὐτῶν δοθεῖσαν χάριν τοῖς πιστοῖς παρὰ τοῦ Σωτῆρος, λέγοντος αὐτοῦ· Ἰδοὺ δέδωκα ὑμῖν ἐξουσίαν πατεῖν ἐπάνω ὄφεων καὶ σκορπίων, καὶ ἐπὶ πᾶσαν τὴν δύναμιν τοῦ ἐχθροῦ [Luke 10:19].

The context was clearly one of Christian virtue when Antony talked of the power that believers had over demons: χάρις was again a gift of a special power given to those who already believed and who were virtuous. It is clear that it was not their faith that was given to believers but a special power, because it was additionally glossed in the biblical citation as a 'power' or 'authority' (ἐξουσία) given by God. When Athanasius described virtue and Christian faith as armour against the demons, this statement worked both to encourage Christians to virtue and to persuade pagans to convert to Christianity, showing that Athanasius saw virtue and faith as deriving from human choice, hence his effort to persuade. At the same time he was clear that the only power capable of defeating the demons was God, and therefore any human who was able to withstand demons was only able to do so in so far as he partook of God's power through faith in Christ.

In Athanasius' fourth use of the term, χάρις was again the gift from the Saviour of a special power to drive out demons: "'But driving out demons is the grace of the Saviour who has given it.'"[208] In this passage the word χάρισμα occurred as well and appears to be a synonym for χάρις since it was used shortly afterwards to describe a second God-given special power: 'The gift of discernment of spirits' (χάρισμα διακρίσεως πνεύματων).[209] This same ability to discern between good and evil spirits was elsewhere described by the word χάρις alone, confirming that Athanasius used χάρις and χάρισμα interchangeably as words to describe a God-given special power.[210] In this passage a contrast was drawn between the sign of a virtuous life (the writing of one's name in heaven), for which man had responsibility, and a gift from the Saviour. Athanasius immediately added that those who became arrogant because of such powers were impious, and God would not respond to them. Thus Athanasius here depicted a process of co-operation, in which the virtuous man prayed and God gave a special power; and he warned against the arrogance of a lack of humble gratitude in acknowledgment of God's gift.

Another facet of Athanasius' use of the word χάρις appears in his use of it to describe the appearance of Antony's face: 'In addition his face had great grace (χάρις).'[211] Here grace was a special quality. In the next line, Athanasius referred to an effect of this quality with the word χάρισμα:

---

[208] Athanasius, Ἐπιστολή 38.3 (ed. Bartelink, SC 400, p. 238), Τὸ δὲ ἐκβάλλειν δαίμονας, τοῦ δεδωκότος Σωτῆρός ἐστιν ἡ χάρις.

[209] Athanasius, Ἐπιστολή 38.5 (ed. Bartelink, SC 400, p. 238), "'But in sum it is necessary to pray, as I said, to receive the gift of discerning spirits'"; Καθόλου δὲ εὔχεσθαι δεῖ, καθὰ προεῖπον, λαμβάνειν χάρισμα διακρίσεως πνευμάτων. χάρισμα occurs with exactly the same meaning of a special gift, again of discerning spirits, at 88.1 (ed. Bartelink, SC 400, p. 360).

[210] Athanasius, Ἐπιστολή 44.1 (ed. Bartelink, SC 400, p. 254), 'Everyone was persuaded to despise the demons' plots, wondering at the grace given to Antony by the Lord for discerning spirits'; Πάντες τε ἐπείθοντο καταφρονεῖν τῆς δαιμονικῆς ἐπιβουλῆς, θαυμάζοντες τὴν δοθεῖσαν παρὰ τοῦ Κυρίου χάριν τῷ Ἀντωνίῳ εἰς τὴν διάκρισιν τῶν πνευμάτων.

[211] Athanasius, Ἐπιστολή 67.4 (ed. Bartelink, SC 400, p. 312), Καὶ μὴν καὶ τὸ πρόσωπον αὐτοῦ χάριν εἶχε πολλήν.

And he also had this unusual gift (χάρισμα) from the Saviour. For if Antony was among a multitude of monks, and someone wished to see him and had not seen his face before, making for Antony straightaway, he ignored the others and ran up to him as if drawn by his eyes.[212]

In this passage, χάρις and χάρισμα again appear to be synonymous, both meaning a gift from God of a special quality or power. Athanasius then explained exactly how Antony's face obtained its special grace, and left the reader in no doubt that it was Antony's virtue that was the origin of this grace, so that it was not an entirely 'free' gift from God unrelated to Antony's actions but was the result of Antony's ascetic endeavour:

> But he did not differ from others in his height or in his girth, but by the state of his morals and the purity of his soul. For because his soul was untroubled, his external appearance was also undisturbed; so that because of the joy of his soul his face was smiling also, and from the movements of his body the state of his soul could be perceived and apprehended, as it is written: *When the heart is glad the face is cheerful, but when the heart is sad, the face is sullen* [Prov. 15:13].[213]

Here χάρις and χάρισμα were explicitly portrayed as gifts from God given as a result of Antony's virtue, which throughout the *Life of Antony* was attributed to Antony's effort.

In another passage, Athanasius used the word χάρισμα to describe a gift from God and immediately explained this phenomenon with a scriptural citation, saying that God instructed the holy person:

> Again he had this gift (χάρισμα) also: when he was sitting alone on the mountain, if ever he was at a loss about something he was pondering, as he prayed it would be revealed to him by divine providence. For as it is written, the blessed man was *instructed by God* [cf. Isa. 54:13, John 6:45, 1 Thess. 4:9].[214]

In this context also, therefore, the narrative presented a co-operative process in which the gift of a special power from God was directly related to Antony's virtue. The gift was a response to prayer, but Athanasius used a citation to point to Antony's virtue as the cause of his receiving the gift.

---

[212] Athanasius, Ἐπιστολή 67.4 (ed. Bartelink, SC 400, p. 312), Καὶ παράδοξον εἶχε δὲ καὶ τοῦτο τὸ χάρισμα παρὰ τοῦ Σωτῆρος. Εἰ γὰρ μετὰ τοῦ πλήθους τῶν μοναχῶν παρῆν, καὶ τοῦτον ἰδεῖν τις ἐβούλετο μὴ πρότερον γινώσκων, προσελθὼν εὐθύς, τοὺς μὲν ἄλλους ὑπερέβαινεν, πρὸς αὐτὸν δὲ ἔτρεχεν, ὡς ὑπὸ τῶν ὄψεων αὐτοῦ ἑλκόμενος.

[213] Athanasius, Ἐπιστολή 67.5–6 (ed. Bartelink, SC 400, p. 312), Οὐχ ὕψει δέ, οὐδὲ τῷ πλάτει διέφερε τῶν ἄλλων, ἀλλὰ τῇ τῶν ἠθῶν καταστάσει καὶ τῇ τῆς ψυχῆς καθαρότητι. Ἀθορύβου γὰρ οὔσης τῆς ψυχῆς, ἀταράχους εἶχε καὶ τὰς ἔξωθεν αἰσθήσεις· ὡς ἀπὸ τῆς χαρᾶς τῆς ψυχῆς ἱλαρὸν ἔχειν καὶ τὸ πρόσωπον, καὶ ἀπὸ τῶν τοῦ σώματος κινημάτων αἰσθέσθαι καὶ νοεῖν τὴν τῆς ψυχῆς κατάστασιν κατὰ τὸ γεγραμμένον· Καρδίας εὐφραινομένης πρόσωπον θάλλει· ἐν δὲ λύπαις οὔσης σκυθρωπάζει [Prov. 15:13].

[214] Athanasius, Ἐπιστολή 66.1–2 (ed. Bartelink, SC 400, p. 308), Εἶχε δὲ καὶ τοῦτο πάλιν χάρισμα. Ἐν γὰρ τῷ ὄρει κατὰ μόνας καθήμενος, εἴ ποτέ τι πρὸς ἑαυτὸν ζητῶν ἠπόρει, τοῦτο αὐτῷ παρὰ τῆς προνοίας εὐχομένῳ ἀπεκαλύπτετο. Καὶ ἦν, κατὰ τὸ γεγραμμένον, θεοδίδακτος γενόμενος ὁ μακάριος [cf. Isa. 54:13; John 6:45; 1 Thess. 4:9].

There are two uses of the word χάρις in the *Life of Antony* that do not fit this precise meaning of the gift of a special quality or power that was given because of Antony's virtue. On an occasion when Antony was encouraging the monks not to be afraid of illusions created by demons, he made the general observation that it was God who ensured that the demons' machinations came to nothing: "'For through the grace of the Lord all their pursuits come to nothing.'"[215] This was a gift or favour given by God to mankind universally; the term offered a generalised way to express thanks to God for his care for humanity. The second less frequent usage came when Athanasius described how the devil spoke to Antony and bemoaned how he was being driven out by the growing number of Christians and monks. Here too, χάρις referred to a generalised gift and favour to mankind, explained as Christ's coming in Antony's words to the devil:

> 'Then, wondering at the grace (χάρις) of the Lord, I said to him: "Though you always lie and never speak the truth, nevertheless even though you do not want to, you have spoken this truth now. For when Christ came he made you weak"'.[216]

In both these usages, χάρις referred to a universal kindness towards mankind for which gratitude was appropriate in return. There was no sense that this was earned by human virtue; it was here a free gift, evidence of God's love for mankind.

In summary, four of the seven uses of χάρις in Athanasius' narrative referred to a gift from God of a special power, bestowed on Antony because of his virtue—for example, the power to heal, exorcise or discern between good and wicked spirits. One usage referred to a preternatural quality of appearance given to Antony by God as a result of his ascetic virtue. Two referred to a general gift bestowed on mankind which was not earned and which was the result of God's love for mankind. Thus there were two main usages of the word 'grace' within Athanasius' narrative: an *ad hominem* gift given to virtue, and a universal gift unrelated to virtue. It is also clear from Athanasius' text that, although in the majority of cases Athanasius made it clear that grace resulted from Antony's virtue (although he did not use the words 'merit' or 'earn'), he was aware that this causal relationship between ascetic effort and grace might become a source of arrogance, and he worked hard to forestall such an outcome.

Taking the narrative as a whole, Athanansius explained that it was the Christian faith brought to mankind that allowed Christians to defeat the demons, and he described how χάρις was given to believers. So the overall picture presented by Athanasius showed the free gift of Christ's coming and the Christian faith that resulted, working in partnership with individuals who chose to believe and to strive for virtue; such individuals might then be found worthy of receiving from God the

---

[215] Athanasius, Ἐπιστολή 24.9 (ed. Bartelink, SC 400, p. 204), Πάντα γὰρ αὐτῶν διὰ τὴν τοῦ Κυρίου χάριν εἰς οὐδέν ἐστι τὰ ἐπιτηδεύματα.

[216] Athanasius, Ἐπιστολή 41.5 (ed. Bartelink, SC 400, p. 246), Τότε θαυμάσας ἐγὼ τοῦ Κυρίου τὴν χάριν, εἶπον πρὸς αὐτόν· Ἀεὶ ψεύστης ὢν καὶ μηδέποτε λέγων ἀλήθειαν, ὅμως τοῦτο νῦν, καὶ μὴ θέλων, εἴρηκας ἀληθές· ὁ γὰρ Χριστὸς ἐλθὼν ἀσθενῆ σε πεποίηκε.

special personal gift of the ability to defeat demons. Thus in Athanasius' text, after the general gift of Christ's coming, the decision to believe lay with humans. His text was also aimed at persuading pagans to adopt Christianity, and the necessary presumption underlying this attempt at persuasion was that this choice lay with the individual. So in Athanasius' representation of Christianity, an individual chose faith and chose to exert effort to complete that faith in virtue, and this effort might result in receiving special powers.

The model advertised in Athanasius' *Life of Antony* was that the more complete a Christian's virtue, the greater the gifts conferred on him by God: χάρις was given to the virtuous believer. The advantages of Christian faith were advertised primarily as serenity and joy in this life, and heaven in the next. Overall there was slightly less frequent emphasis on rewards in the next life than there was in the ascetic paraenesis of Evagrius, Jerome or Pelagius.

Gratia in the anonymous translation of Athanasius' *Life of Antony*

The anonymous translator's use of the word *gratia* tracked Athanasius' use of χάρις closely. His first use of *gratia* was as a translation of 'agreeableness' (τὸ χαρίεν) in a list of human good qualities of character, and this use can be set aside as not relevant to the theological meaning of the word.[217] Following Athanasius' Greek text, the citation of 1 Cor. 15:10 was situated within a context of co-operation between man and God, so that it expressed the desire to attribute an action to God that nevertheless required both parties to participate.[218] After this, the anonymous translator used the word *gratia* a further eight times, one more than Athanasius because on one of the occasions when Athanasius used χάρισμα the anonymous translator rendered this as *gratia*. On the other four occasions when Athanasius used χάρισμα, the anonymous translator used the word *donum* to render χάρισμα into Latin. The fact that he used *gratia* to translate one occurence of χάρισμα, with reference to the gift of distinguishing between spirits, suggests that he believed that for Athanasius the two words were synonymous. Thus while Athanasius referred to this special power of distinguishing between spirits with the word χάρισμα three times and the word χάρις once, his anonymous translator used the word *gratia* twice and the word *donum* twice. In addition, when Athanasius paired the two in the passage describing the grace of Antony's facial appearance and the gift of his being immediately recognisable even to those who had never seen him before, the anonymous translator likewise used *gratia* for the first usage

---

[217] Anon. trans., *Vita Antonii* 4.1 (ed. Bartelink, p. 12).
[218] Anon. trans., *Vita Antonii* 5.7 (ed. Bartelink, p. 18), 'The Lord who took on flesh for our sake and who also gave the body victory against the devil, co-operated with him in such a way that individuals contending in this way might say: *Yet not I, but the grace of God that is with me* [1 Cor. 15:10]'; 'Cooperabatur ei Dominus qui carnem indutus est propter nos, qui et corpori dedit uictoriam aduersus diabolum, ita ut singuli taliter certantium dicerent: *Non ego autem, sed gratia Dei qui mecum est* [1 Cor. 15:10].'

and *donum* for the second, supporting the view that he understood the two words to mean the same thing in this context.

As Athanasius had done, the anonymous translator described Antony's ability to speak persuasively as 'grace' (*gratia*).[219] Just as in the Greek original, Antony's persuasive power was presented as being in addition to the healing and driving out spirits carried out by God through him, implying that these abilities too might be described as 'grace'. Just as in Athanasius' narrative, the gift of persuasive speech was set within a context of Antony's virtue, and thus with an implicit but not explicit causal link between these two things. The 'power' (*potestas*) to tread serpents underfoot was similarly cited in the context of the statement that the Christian virtue of the monks was their best defence against demons, and that the power to defeat demons was a grace given to the faithful.[220]

Where Athanasius distinguished between the writing of their names in heaven and the gift of driving out spirits to differentiate between something which directly reflected an individual's virtue and something for which only God should be credited, the anonymous translator translated 'virtue' (ἀρετή) as 'sacred virtue' (*uirtus deifica*), and where Athanasius paired χάρις and χάρισμα respectively as the gifts of driving out demons and discerning between spirits, the anonymous translator used the word *gratia* for both special powers.[221]

The next question is whether the anonymous translator altered anything in Athanasius' account of what caused or triggered the special gifts given, or changed anything in the two uses of χάρις by Athanasius to denote a generalised, untriggered, 'free' grace. In explaining the origin of the grace visible in Antony's face, the anonymous translator used the word 'to show' or 'declare' (*indicare*) to say that Antony's moral and spiritual purity and stability declared who he was, but the monks being drawn to Antony was also described as a 'gift' (*donum*).[222] This causal link between his virtue and the special quality was perhaps made slightly more explicit by the anonymous translator than it had been by Athanasius, through the use of the verb 'to show' (*indicare*); but as in the Greek text, in the anonymous translation something that was depicted in the narrative as the result of effort on Antony's part was denoted as *gratia* and *donum*, both words meaning in their contexts a 'gift' from God. In the two cases of a generalised grace that was not

---

[219] Anon. trans., *Vita Antonii* 14.6 (ed. Bartelink, p. 38).

[220] Anon. trans., *Vita Antonii* 30.3 (ed. Bartelink, p. 68).

[221] Anon. trans., *Vita Antonii* 38.3–5 (ed. Bartelink, pp. 80–2).

[222] Anon. trans., *Vita Antonii* 67.4–5 (ed. Bartelink, p. 132), 'For his face too had great grace. He also possessed this exceptional gift from the Saviour: for if he was with a multitude of monks, and someone who had never seen him before wanted to see him, passing by the others he would run straight up to Antony, drawn by his face and his appearance. Not because he was taller or broader than the others, but the seriousness, stability, and purity of his morals declared him'; 'Nam et facies eius magnam gratiam habuit. Habuit et hoc praeclarum donum a Saluatore: si enim et cum multitudine monachorum esset, et aliquis uidere illum uolebat de his qui aliquando non uiderunt illum, statim ceteros pertransiens ad illum currebat a facie et uisu illius tractus. Non quia excelsior erat aut latior a ceteris, sed hoc indicabat animi ipsius morum grauitas et stabilitas et puritas.' Cf. Athanasius, Ἐπιστολή 67.4–5 (ed. Bartelink, SC 400, p. 312): see n. 211–13.

related to an individual but given to mankind, the anonymous translator changed nothing of Athanasius' account, using *gratia* to translate χάρις.[223]

Gratia in Evagrius of Antioch's version of Athanasius' *Life of Antony*

There are ten uses of the noun 'grace' in Evagrius' *Life of Antony*. The first came when, as the anonymous translator had done, Evagrius used the word *gratia* in his translation of the passage in which Athanasius described how Antony sought to imitate the virtues of older monks. Athanasius did not mention χάρις in this passage but referred to 'agreeableness' (τὸ χαρίεν). The unknown translator used *gratia* here to mean the quality of agreeableness, but Evagrius used *gratia* in the plural to mean 'gifts' in association with the adjective *proprius* (meaning 'personal' or 'special', and having a sense that ties it to the individual). The context shows that he meant by it the 'gift' of a good quality of character more in the sense of someone being 'gifted':

> He obeyed all those whom he visited in his enthusiasm to learn, and would drink in the personal gifts (*gratiae*) of each of them; he would strive after the self-control of this one, the cheerfulness of another; he would emulate the gentleness of this one, the vigils of that one, and the application in reading of another; he would admire one who fasted, another who slept on the ground; he would praise the patience of one and the compassion of another. He kept in mind also the love that they all showed one another, and he would return to his own dwelling-place refreshed by all the aspects of their virtues. There, thinking over all these things to himself, he would strive to imitate all their good qualities in himself.[224]

The semantic denotation of *gratia* in this context is clarified by the fact that Evagrius glossed these qualities as 'virtues' and used the verbs 'to strive after' (*sectari*), 'to emulate' (*aemulari*) and 'to strive' (*niti*) to describe how Antony achieved them for himself. Thus they were gifts, but not ones given to Antony by

---

[223] Anon. trans., *Vita Antonii* 24.9 (ed. Bartelink, p. 58), "'[The demons] For all their strivings came to nothing because of the Lord's grace'"; "'Omnes enim eorum adfectiones propter Domini gratiam ad nihilum deductae sunt.'" The second generalised sense usage was emended away to non-existence by Bartelink in his edition: Anon. trans., *Vita Antonii* 41.5 (ed. Bartelink, p. 86); Bartelink gave: "'Tunc ego Christi gratias [agens] admiratus sum, et dixi ad eum ...'". However, comparison with the Greek makes it more likely that the corrupt manuscript reading of: 'Tunc ego Christi gratias dixit admiratus sum et dixi ad eum' should instead be emended to: 'Tunc ego Christi gratiam admiratus sum et dixi ad eum' because of the translator's usual habit of translating the Greek literally, and because of the likelihood that first 'dixit' was the result of dittography from the 'dixi' a few words further on in the text.

[224] Evagrius, *Vita Antonii* 3 (4) (ed. Migne, PL 73.128C–129A), 'Omnibus, ad quos studio discendi pergebat, obediens, proprias singulorum gratias hauriebat: huius continentiam, iucunditatem illius sectabatur; istius lenitatem, illius uigilantiam, alterius legendi aemulabatur industriam; istum ieiunantem, illum humi quiescentem mirabatur; alterius patientiam, alterius mansuetudinem praedicabat. Omnium quoque uicariam erga se retinens caritatem, atque uniuersis uirtutum partibus irrigatus, ad sedem propriam regrediebatur. Ibi secum uniuersa pertractans, omnium in se bona nitebatur exprimere.'

someone else; they were qualities of character that Antony was shown creating in himself.

Evagrius' second use of the term 'grace' came when he followed Athanasius in his citation of 1 Cor. 15:10 as a statement of co-operation between man and God. Like Athanasius, Evagrius set the citation within a context of a personal duel between a young man and the devil.[225] The author stated that Antony defeated the devil:

> [The devil] who considered that he could be like God, was now being tricked by a young man as if he were the most wretched creature; and he who vented his rage against flesh and blood was defeated by a man of flesh and blood.[226]

This defeat of evil was then explained as the result of the joint action of Antony and God, but only after the picture of Antony's agency, a young man apparently fighting alone against the devil, had been established. The message for Christians was that when they were struggling against sin and thought they were alone, in fact God was watching over them and would help them. Where Athanasius asserted co-operation using the verb 'to work together' (συνεργεῖν), Evagrius used the word 'to help' (adiuuare):

> For the Lord used to help his servant, the Lord who, taking on bodily form for our sake, granted the body victory against the devil, so that for those individuals struggling in this way, it would be possible to cite the Apostolic words: Yet not I, but the grace of God that is with me [1 Cor. 15:10].[227]

This citation was therefore not presented by Evagrius as an affirmation of grace being responsible for virtue in man but as a comforting statement that man was never alone in striving for virtue and could rely on the help of God, and also as an expression of humility and gratitude. Just as Athanasius' use of the citation should be, Evagrius' interpretation of this citation should be read in the context of the rest of his narrative, and through the lens of what Christ subsequently said to Antony when he asked where Christ had been:

---

[225] This duel was established through repeated opposition between *ille* and *hic*, and by the use of vocabulary of military conflict, such as 'weapons' (*arma*), 'to fight' (*dimicare*) and 'to fortify' (*uallare*).

[226] Evagrius, *Vita Antonii* 4 (5) (ed. Migne, PL 73.129D), '[Diabolum] qui enim similem se Deo fieri posse existimabat, nunc ab adolescente ut miserrimus deludebatur; et qui contra carnem et sanguinem saeuiebat, ab homine qui carnem portabat elisus est.'

[227] Evagrius, *Vita Antonii* 4 (5) (ed. Migne, PL 73.129D–130A), 'Adiuuabat enim seruum suum Dominus, qui nostri gratia carnem suscipiens, uictoriam corpori contra diabolum largitus est, ut, singulis ita certantibus, apostolicum liceret proferre sermonem: *Non autem ego, sed gratia Dei quae mecum est* [1 Cor. 15:10].' Cf. Athanasius, Ἐπιστολή 5.7 (ed. Bartelink, SC 400, pp. 144–6), 'For the Lord was co-operating with him, who took on bodily form for our sake and gave to the body victory over the devil, so that each person struggling against the devil in this way might say: *Yet not I, but the grace of the Lord with me* [1 Cor. 15:10]'; Συνήργει γὰρ ὁ Κύριος αὐτῷ, ὁ σάρκα δι' ἡμᾶς φορέσας καὶ τῷ σώματι δοὺς τὴν κατὰ τοῦ διαβόλου νίκην, ὥστε τῶν οὕτως ἀγωνιζομένων ἕκαστον λέγειν· Οὐκ ἐγὼ δέ, ἀλλ' ἡ χάρις τοῦ θεοῦ ἡ σὺν ἐμοί [1 Cor. 15:10].

'Where were you, good Jesus? Where were you? Why were you not at hand from the start to heal my wounds?' And a voice came to him saying: 'Antony, I was here, but I was waiting to watch your struggle. Now however, because you have not ceased from contending bravely, I will always help you, and I will make your name known all over the world.'[228]

As with Athanasius, Evagrius' use of the term 'grace' has to be understood in the context of his overall characterisation of the relationship between man and God.

Evagrius' third and fourth uses of the word 'grace' came in the passage in which Athanasius described how God gave to Antony the 'grace' (χάρις) of persuasive speech. Evagrius used the word *gratia* twice, but neither use referred to the ability to speak persuasively. Athanasius described Antony's unchanged appearance when he emerged from his isolation, and Evagrius described this as the 'grace of his face' (*oris gratia*). Athanasius stated that God healed the bodies of many through Antony and freed many from demons. Evagrius phrased this as: 'Everyone was amazed at the grace of his face and the dignified bearing of his body .... And so the grace of God freed many from evil spirits and various illnesses through Antony.'[229] Thus Evagrius transposed *gratia* from the grace of speech to the grace of Antony's appearance and the grace of God driving out evil spirits through Antony. The first of these aspects of grace was a special quality created through Antony's asceticism, and the second was God's power working through Antony. There is no substantive difference in the meaning of the two writers concerning whose was the agency in the healing and driving out of spirits. It may be noteworthy that Evagrius chose to use the word *gratia* twice, to describe the healing as well as Antony's preternatural appearance, but as Athanansius had done, Evagrius attributed the healing to God's agency in order to forestall the potential for human arrogance, a recurring theme in Athanasius' work and that of both his interpreters. As Athanansius had done, Evagrius set these two uses of the word *gratia* in the context of Antony's virtue. In all three versions of the *Life of Antony* it was made clear that these things happened because of Antony's virtue; grace did not cause his virtue. Nevertheless, with regard to the healing and persuasive speech, two parallel forms of causal agency were portrayed in operation at the same time, insofar as Antony could not have achieved these special powers by himself, but his virtue was a necessary precondition for their occurrence and was his contribution to their creation.

The first generalised use of the word χάρις in Athanasius' *Life of Antony* was omitted by Evagrius. Athanasius' Antony observed that the demons' machinations came to nothing through the grace of the Lord. This passage does not appear in

---

[228] Evagrius, *Vita Antonii* 9 (10) (ed. Migne, PL 73.132D), '"Vbi eras, bone Iesu? Vbi eras? Quare non a principio affuisti, ut sanares uulnera mea?" Et uox ad eum facta est, dicens: "Antoni, hic eram, sed expectabam uidere certamen tuum. Nunc autem, quia dimicando uiriliter non cessisti, semper auxiliabor tibi, et faciam te in omni orbe nominari."'

[229] Evagrius, *Vita Antonii* 13 (14) (ed. Migne, PL 73.134B–C), 'Obstupuerunt uniuersi et oris gratiam et corporis dignitatem .... Plurimos igitur ab immundis spiritibus et infirmitatibus uariis Dei gratia per Antonium liberauit.'

Evagrius' narrative. Likewise the next two uses of χάρις in Athanasius' text were omitted by Evagrius, making a run of three that are missing in Evagrius' *Life of Antony*. The second use omitted referred to the power given to believers to tread on snakes and scorpions. The third referred to the power to drive out demons.[230] The second generalised use of the word χάρις in Athanasius' *Life of Antony* was, however, retained by Evagrius. He kept the story of the devil bemoaning his weakness in the face of Christianity and asking Antony for respite from attack, and Antony's amazement at this admission of weakness: "'Then I marvelled with joy at God's grace'" (Evagrius' fifth use of the term). Antony's reply to the devil attributed to Jesus responsibility for this gift to mankind: "'For truly Jesus has utterly destroyed your powers'".[231] In this context, *gratia* meant a generalised 'free' gift that referred to Christ's coming, and the gift of Christianity given to all mankind and unrelated to any human activity, as it did in Athanasius' text.

In Evagrius' sixth use, the word *gratia* meant a special power to distinguish between spirits, and in this usage he translated Athanasius verbatim.[232] Evagrius' seventh use of the word 'grace' occurred during the story of the healing of Martinianus' daughter, already discussed; it is significant because Evagrius used the word 'grace' where it was not present in Athanasius' text and stated explicitly that God's grace was merited.

As has been noted, Athanasius used the word χάρις, and shortly afterwards χάρισμα as a gloss on χάρις, when he related how Antony's face had great grace, and Antony received the additional gift of being instantly recognisable even to monks who had never seen him before. These were both stated to be gifts from the Saviour, but once again Athanasius also made it clear that these 'gifts' were connected to Antony's virtue; it was as if Antony's eyes drew monks to him, and this was a result of his purity of soul. Thus in Athanasius' account, two agents were at work in creating this special quality: Antony in some sense caused it, but it was also described as a gift given by the Saviour. The anonymous translator rendered Athanasius faithfully without amendment, using the words *gratia* and *donum* respectively for χάρις and χάρισμα in this passage. Evagrius, however, altered Athanasius' text slightly. The χάρις of Antony's face he rendered as *gratia*, and the χάρισμα of being recognisable he translated as a 'gift' (*munus*), but he omitted Athanasius' explanation that Antony did not stand out for his height or girth, and went straight from the monks running up to Antony, to the reason why they recognised Antony:

---

[230] Athanasius, Ἐπιστολή 30.3 (ed. Bartelink, SC 400, p. 220); Athanasius, Ἐπιστολή 38.3 (ed. Bartelink, SC 400, p. 238): see n. 207–8.

[231] Evagrius, *Vita Antonii* 20 (41) (ed. Migne, PL 73.145B–C), "'Tunc ego Dei gratiam cum alacritate miratus .... Vere enim Iesus tuas funditus subruit uires'".

[232] Evagrius, *Vita Antonii* 20 (44) (ed. Migne, PL 73.146B), 'They marvelled at such a great grace of discerning between spirits in Antony, which he had received when the Lord granted it to him'; 'Mirabantur in Antonio tantam gratiam spirituum discernendorum, quam Domino tribuente perceperat'; cf. Athanasius, Ἐπιστολή 44.1 (ed. Bartelink, SC 400, p. 254), Θαυμάζοντες τὴν δοθεῖσαν παρὰ τοῦ Κυρίου χάριν τῷ Ἀντωνίῳ εἰς τὴν διάκρισιν τῶν πνευμάτων.

> But he had great grace in his face and he had received from the Saviour this gift
> (*munus*) also: if someone who did not know him wanted to see him amidst a crowd
> of monks, with nothing pointing him to Antony, passing by the others, he would run
> up to Antony; he would both recognise the purity of his mind from his face, and he
> would see the grace of his holy mind through the mirror of his body.[233]

Thus Evagrius introduced an additional (second) use of the word *gratia* into the
passage, and it described something ('a holy mind', *mens sancta*) that Evagrius
had consistently depicted Antony as striving to achieve within himself. Thus this
quality was denoted with a word that elsewhere in the narrative meant 'gift', while
at the same time the quality was throughout the text portrayed as something that
Antony brought about in himself. This suggests that Evagrius chose to represent
a type of dual causality similar to the one Athanasius had pictured, but he emphasised more explicitly than Athanasius that this was how grace operated in man: he
highlighted the co-operative character of the way grace operated even more than
Athanasius had done. When this passage is read in the light of the earlier explicit
statement that Antony merited the grace he received, it can only be understood as
intentionally reinforcing that same message.

Evagrius' tenth and final use of the word *gratia* is interesting because it does
not occur in Athanasius' text or in the anonymous translation, and it is a specific
meaning of the word *gratia* unrelated to religious belief. Athanasius described
how judges came to Antony for advice and he advised them to prize justice above
all else, warning them that as they judged so they would themselves be judged.
The anonymous translator made a faithful translation of the Greek. By contrast,
Evagrius' Antony did not tell the judges to prefer justice to all else; Evagrius modified the sentence, and had Antony advise the judges to put fear of God before
'hatred and favour' (*odium et gratia*). This illustrates the fact that in Latin *gratia*
had an alternative negative meaning as 'special favour', in the sense of corruption
in relation to magistrates and officials, and unfairness, as noted in Chapter 1.[234]
Later on, opponents of predestination would argue that a special grace bestowed
in advance on a select few was unjust and contradicted the message of God's
universal salvific will, and they tried to link this meaning of *gratia* as corruption
to the concept of *gratia praeueniens* as God's prevenient gift of love of virtue
given to a preordained limited number of people (the elect). How significant was
Evagrius' use of the term *gratia* here? On the one hand, it might seem unlikely that
in the 370s AD Evagrius was pointing out the fact that *gratia* was potentially unfair
unless it was either universal or anchored firmly to merit. On the other hand, he
used the term here precisely in a discussion of justice and the Day of Judgement,

---

[233] Evagrius, *Vita Antonii* 40 (67) (ed. Migne, PL 73.156C), 'Habebat autem et in uultu magnam
gratiam et admirabile a Saluatore etiam hoc munus acceperat: si quis enim ignarus eius inter multitudinem monachorum eum uidere desiderasset, nullo indicante, caeteris praetermissis, ad Antonium
currebat; et animae puritatem agnoscebat ex uultu, et per speculum corporis gratiam sanctae mentis
intuebatur.'

[234] See Chapter 1, n. 33. I am indebted to Kate Cooper for pointing out to me the relevance of this usage
of *gratia* in the context of the controversy.

and throughout his version of the *Life of Antony* he emphasised how grace was earned as well as being a gift from God, for which an individual should always thank God.

Four conclusions emerge from this evidence. First, in all three versions of the *Life of Antony* χάρις/*gratia* was not antecedent to autonomous human virtue; it was a gift from God to the already virtuous individual. Second, χάρις/*gratia* was not prevenient grace but was instead either a gift of a special power or quality by God to a virtuous individual, or an unearned universal gift to mankind. Third, its function in all three texts was to forestall self-righteousness and arrogance. Fourth, Evagrius stated explicitly that God's grace was given in accord with merit.

Section 4: A Supposed Hallmark Idea Associated with 'Pelagianism' by Scholars

Stress on the need to obey God's commands as a hallmark of 'Pelagianism'

This is not a tenet attributed to 'Pelagianism' by its opponents in the 5th century, but scholarly accounts of Pelagius' teaching regularly cite stress on the need for all Christians to obey God's commands as a hallmark of 'Pelagianism'.[235] Applied to all Christians, this standard for attainment of salvation is often presented as exceptional and novel, and as a defining characteristic of 'Pelagianism'.

---

[235] P. Brown, 'Pelagius and his Supporters: Aims and Environment', *Journal of Theological Studies* 19 (1968), pp. 102–3: 'The most marked feature of the Pelagian movement is far from being its individualism: it is its insistence that the full code of Christian behaviour, the Christian *Lex*, should be imposed, in all its rigours, on every baptised member of the Catholic Church .... This insistence meant, in practice, that the standards of perfection, evolved in the past generation by the leading representatives of the ascetic movement, will be prescribed as the basis of the morality of the average Christian: the stream of perfectionism which, in a Jerome, a Paulinus, an Augustine, had flowered in a concentrated jet, will be widened, by Pelagius and his followers, into a flood, into whose icy puritanism they would immerse the whole Christian community. The exposure of the whole community to ideals held to be binding, previously, only on the few is the hallmark of Pelagian literature'. Judged by Brown's analysis, Evagrius wrote 'Pelagian' literature. Solignac likewise characterised what he called a 'movement' by its strict apostolic demands: 'The literature of the movement clearly gets its bearings from the radical demands of the Gospel' ('La littérature du mouvement s'oriente nettement vers les exigences radicales de l'évangile'): F. G. Nuvolone and A. Solignac, 'Pélage et Pélagianisme', in *Dictionnaire de spiritualité, ascetique, mystique, doctrine et histoire*, 17 vols (Paris, 1932–95), vol. 12.2, col. 2933. See also: De Bruyn, *Pelagius's Commentary*, p. 24.

Athanasius and the anonymous translator

Emphasis on the need to obey God's commands because that would determine every Christian's fate on Judgement Day was clear in Athanasius' text, written in the 360s.[236] Antony's advice to the monks to consider themselves God's slaves epitomises his strictness about adherence to Christ's injunctions.[237] The anonymous translator made no alteration to Athanasius' words on this topic.

Evagrius

Evagrius retained Athanasius' strictures on the need to fulfil all of God's commandments, and he added further insistence on this requirement.[238] When Antony advised the monks to consider themselves God's slaves, Evagrius added further comment:

> 'It is fitting for us also to obey the divine commands in the same way, knowing that this even-handed judge will judge each person as he finds him [cf. Ezek. 33:20] .... For this reason the continuous rigour of our way of life must be maintained'.[239]

In Antony's final speech of advice to the monks, Athanasius had him tell the monks to bind themselves fast principally to the Lord, and then to the saints, so that they would gain salvation; Evagrius added the instruction: "'But instead be anxious in this, that you should keep the Lord's commands'".[240] These additions are easy to overlook because they do not change the principles of the programme advanced; rather, they serve to underline its component elements. It is important

---

[236] Athanasius, Ἐπιστολή 33.6 (ed. Bartelink, SC 400, p. 228), see n. 50.

[237] Athanasius, Ἐπιστολή 18.2 (ed. Bartelink, SC 400, p. 184), "'In the same way we too should persevere in our asceticism every day, knowing that if ever we should be negligent for one day, he will not yield to us because of the time that has passed, but will be angry with us for the negligence'"; Οὕτω καὶ ἡμεῖς καθ' ἡμέραν ἐπιμείνωμεν τῇ ἀσκήσει, εἰδότες ὅτι, ἐὰν μίαν ἡμέραν ἀμελήσωμεν, οὐ διὰ τὸν παρελθόντα χρόνον ἡμῖν συγχωρήσει, ἀλλὰ διὰ τὴν ἀμέλειαν ἀγανακτήσει καθ' ἡμῶν.

[238] For example, describing Antony's knowledge of Scripture, Evagrius added the information that he kept all God's commandments where it was not present in the Greek text: Evagrius, *Vita Antonii* 3 (3) (ed. Migne, PL 73.128C), 'Keeping all of the Lord's commands'; 'Vniuersa Domini praecepta custodiens'. Cf. Athanasius, Ἐπιστολή 3.7 (ed. Bartelink, SC 400, p. 138).

[239] Evagrius, *Vita Antonii* 15 (18) (ed. Migne, PL 73.136A), "'Sic et nos diuinis congruit parere praeceptis, scientes quod aequus ille retributor, in quo quemque inuenerit, in eo sit iudicaturus [cf Ezek. 33:20] .... Idcirco tenendus est continuus instituti rigor'"; cf. Athanasius, Ἐπιστολή 18.2 (ed. Bartelink, SC 400, p. 184), see n. 237.

[240] Evagrius, *Vita Antonii* 58 (91) (ed. Migne, PL 73.167B), "'In hoc autem magis estote solliciti, ut Domini praecepta seruetis'"; cf. Athanasius, Ἐπιστολή 91.5 (ed. Bartelink, SC 400, p. 368). At another point again, Evagrius added to Athanasius' text his own assertion of the need to obey all God's commands twice in close succession. When Athanasius wrote that all would be judged on whether or not they kept the commandments, Evagrius highlighted the agency of the individual in determining his own salvation as already noted, but he also added two further references to obedience to God's commands that were not in Athanasius' text: Evagrius, *Vita Antonii* 17 (33) (ed. Migne, PL 73.142B), "'Obeying the Lord's injunctions .... To fulfil what is commanded'"; "'Praeceptis Domini obediens .... Implere quae iussa sunt'"; cf. Athanasius, Ἐπιστολή 33.6–34.1 (ed. Bartelink, SC 400, pp. 226–8).

to note also that Evagrius' version of the *Life of Antony* addressed all Christians, not just monks: "'Now Christians and monks should take care lest through their idleness they give strength to the demons.'"[241]

Pelagius

Some forty or fifty years after Athanasius wrote his *Life of Antony*, obedience to scriptural precept was central to Pelagius' advice to his correspondents.[242] In the same way as the three writers who produced versions of the *Life of Antony* had done, Pelagius asserted that Judgement Day was the reason for this obedience.[243]

Athanasius and Evagrius were clear that God's judgement applied to all human beings; this was the reason they proposed for becoming an ascetic. The evidence presented in this chapter suggests that Evagrius had already enlarged the remit of ascetic values to encompass all Christians.[244] Pelagius did not alter this message in any way. The difference lies in our perception, which is influenced by the fact that texts survive that show that Christians living in an urban environment sought advice from Pelagius about how to live according to ascetic values. This change arose because such values became fashionable among Christians generally. The question of whether obedience to scriptural precept required withdrawal from society was one that would have to be resolved when the ascetic movement caught on among a wider section of the Christian community (at the same time as Christianity itself was adopted by a growing number people). This question was raised by the success of the ascetic movement; it was not something triggered by Pelagius. It was not an alleged 'Pelagian' movement that suggested that all Christians should obey God's commandments; it was adherents of the ascetic movement who promoted this agenda. 'Pelagianism' was invented to stand for this approach to a wider question facing Christianity, as the implications of ascetic entryism began to be felt. This does not mean that 'Pelagianism' existed.

[241] Evagrius, *Vita Antonii* 20 (42) (ed. Migne, PL 73.145C–D), "'Iam curae Christianorum et monachorum sit ne per eorum inertiam uires daemonibus praebeantur.'"

[242] Pelagius, *Ad Demetriadem* 16 (ed. Greshake, p. 112), 'For we ought not to select some of God's commandments, as if to suit our own will, but we should fulfil all of them without exception'; 'Non enim quasi ad arbitrium nostrum quaedam ex mandatis Dei debemus eligere, sed generaliter uniuersa complere.'

[243] Pelagius, *Ad Celantiam* 9 (ed. Hilberg, CSEL 56, p. 336), 'We who confess with the most pure faith that every man must appear before the tribunal of Christ: *So that each one may receive good or evil according to what he has done in the body* [2 Cor. 5:10]'; 'Nos uero, qui purissima confitemur fide omnem hominem manifestandum esse ante tribunal Christi: *Vt recipiat unusquisque propria corporis prout gessit, siue bonum siue malum* [2 Cor. 5:10]'; see also Pelagius, *Ad Demetriadem* 30 (ed. Greshake, p. 170).

[244] See n. 241.

Section 5: The Overall Message Conveyed by the Three Versions of the *Life of Antony*

A hymn to individual effort

The three versions of the Life of Antony

Athanasius' *Life of Antony* was a hymn to individual moral endeavour and agency. Much text has been quoted, but in fact the whole of the *Life* was a tissue of ascetic paraenesis predicated on the idea that God would reward autonomous human effort to achieve righteousness. Every page tells the same story. Athanasius employed a consistent vocabulary to promote effort: 'zeal' (σπουδή), 'to be earnest' (σπουδάζειν), 'eagerness' (προθυμία), 'to be concerned about' (ἐνθυμεῖσθαι), 'to become accustomed' (in the sense of 'to train', ἐθίζειν), 'choice' (προαιρέσις) and 'resolve' (πρόθεσις), are a few examples. Athanasius' text was also a blueprint for co-operation between the human and the divine. These two aspects of the Christian message as reported by Athanasius contrasted starkly with the unpredictability, incommunicability and distance of pagan gods. They were a unique selling point of this account of Christianity, which proposed that Christians could be sure that moral goodness would be rewarded in the next life in a transparent retributive system. This offered ultimate justice as some compensation for the injustices and mixed moral messages of outcomes in the present life. The model of co-operation offered a distinctive collegiate relationship with the divine. It could be said that these ideas were in some respects an attempt to bring the divine under human control. But they also presented an ordered, confident account of man's place in the universe that was attractive because it offered a clear contrast with the randomness of paganism. The nub of the decision that would inevitably have to be taken was whether this constituted a true reflection of Christ's message, or hubris. Athanasius was very aware of the potential charge of the Christian equivalent of hubris; he repeatedly stressed the need for humility and acknowledged that man endeavoured and man requested help, while God controlled. Evagrius likewise focused on these key messages that God would reward virtue, and that the relationship between man and God was one of co-operation in which God had ultimate control of all reward, but he also clarified and incentivised the programme he was advertising.

The function of the co-operative model in the ascetic programme

Athanasius

Athanasius' model of co-operation between man and God was driven by two purposes. First, it prevented the argument for free will appearing to lack a need for God at all, so the model of co-operation preserved God's omnipotence and maintained human dependency on God, as well as a humble, grateful attitude on the part of man towards God. Second, it provided comfort to humans because it proclaimed the help they could hope for from God. Although pursuit of virtue was sometimes described as 'easy' in the text, this was contradicted by the message of the text as a whole, since the vocabulary used to refer to ascetic endeavour was always that of struggle and warfare, suggestive of difficulty; because of this, the prospect of help was key to encouraging Christians to attempt to follow scriptural injunctions. An example of this link between the co-operative model and the solace of divine help comes on one of the many occasions when Antony advised the monks not to fear the demons' attacks:

> 'And let us consider in our souls that the Lord is with us, who puts them to flight and renders them without effect. And let us have in mind and always be conscious that since the Lord is with us, our enemies will not do anything to us.'[245]

Athanasius' model of co-operation was also part of his account of the goodness of contemporary human nature and his characterisation of God's favour as something for which humans strove, and so it has already been discussed under those headings because these ideas are closely intertwined in his text, but a list of explicit references to and depictions of co-operation and help is given here also.[246] This idea of help, embedded in the model of co-operation, was all-pervasive in Athanasius' text; first, because his text was the story of one man's struggle to achieve virtue, which was depicted as a fight against evil; and second, because Athanasius presented a considered theological programme with an integrated anthropology and soteriology. His programme combined a positive anthropology with a soteriology that gave effective free will to man and at the same time preserved God's omnipotence and man's humility. The care with which Athanasius explicitly paired human effort and divine agency testifies to his having been acutely aware of the risk of human self-sufficiency and arrogance that might result from a doctrine of complete human autonomy. He presented a carefully crafted human autonomy that was nevertheless entirely dependent on God and in need of God's help at all times. This was Athanasius' project throughout the *Life* and a theme so constant that its implication might be overlooked. Athanasius' descriptions of Antony's struggles with the devil always conveyed this message: 'But Antony was encouraged by the Saviour and he persisted, unhurt by his [the devil's] wickedness and varied cunning.'[247] In this sentence, Antony's persistence (διαμένων) was set alongside God's help (παρεκαλεῖτο παρὰ τοῦ Σωτῆρος), and this pattern was repeated throughout the

---

[245] Athanasius, Ἐπιστολή 42.4 (ed. Bartelink, SC 400, p. 248), Καὶ λογιζώμεθα τῇ ψυχῇ ὅτι Κύριος μεθ' ἡμῶν ἐστιν, ὁ τροπώσας καὶ καταργήσας αὐτούς. Καὶ διανοώμεθα δὲ καὶ ἐνθυμώμεθα ἀεὶ ὅτι, ὄντος τοῦ Κυρίου μεθ' ἡμῶν, οὐδὲν ἡμῖν οἱ ἐχθροὶ ποιήσουσιν.

[246] Athanasius, Ἐπιστολή 5.7 (ed. Bartelink, SC 400, p. 144); 6.4 (ed. Bartelink, SC 400, p. 148); 10.1–3 (ed. Bartelink, SC 400, pp. 162–4); 19.1 (ed. Bartelink, SC 400, p. 184); 34.1 (ed. Bartelink, SC 400, p. 228); 52.1 (ed. Bartelink, SC 400, p. 274); 54.4 (ed. Bartelink, SC 400, p. 280); 84.1–2 (ed. Bartelink, SC 400, p. 352).

[247] Athanasius, Ἐπιστολή 52.1 (ed. Bartelink, SC 400, pp. 274–6), Ὁ δὲ Ἀντώνιος παρεκαλεῖτο παρὰ τοῦ Σωτῆρος, ἀβλαβὴς διαμένων ἀπὸ τῆς ἐκείνου πανουργίας καὶ τῆς ποικίλης μεθοδείας.

Life. Chapter 7 is a good example of this pattern because it is dedicated to merging the two potentially divergent principles of human autonomy and human dependency on God:

> This was Antony's first victory over the devil; or rather this also was the success of the Saviour in Antony, the Saviour: *Who condemned sin in the flesh, so that the justification of the law should be fulfilled in us, we who walk not according to the flesh but according to the spirit* [Rom. 8:3–4]. But Antony was not careless in future nor did he have an inflated opinion of himself, nor did the devil stop laying his snares because he had been defeated. For he prowled around anew like a lion, seeking some pretext against Antony. But Antony, having learnt from the Scriptures that: *The snares of the enemy are many* [cf. Eph. 6:11], yearned intensely for asceticism, reckoning that if the devil did not have enough strength to deceive Antony's heart with pleasures of the flesh, he would no doubt try to set traps by other methods; for the devil loves sin. And so Antony wore out his body and forced it to servitude more and more, lest having: *Conquered in some struggles he should be defeated in others* [cf. 1 Cor. 9:27]. Accordingly he wanted to accustom himself to harsher training regimes. And many people were amazed, but he bore the effort quite easily. For the eagerness of his spirit, maintained over a long period of time, produced in him a virtuous habit, so that deriving also a small impetus from others, he showed himself full of zeal in this thing.[248]

At the start of this passage, Athanasius asserted that this could be described as Antony's victory, but more correctly it should be understood as Christ's victory. He then detailed at length Antony's effort and his rejection of self-satisfied complacency. This constant pairing of human effort and God's agency sought to create a coherent fusion of the two and to forestall human self-sufficiency. This programme had already been created and disseminated, and its potential flaws had already been addressed, fifty years before Pelagius began to write.

The model of co-operation between man and God was something for which Pelagius was criticised by Jerome, after Jerome's volte-face on his understanding of the soteriology of Christianity.[249] It was, however, at the heart of the programme disseminated in ascetic paraenesis, which was what Pelagius wrote, and it was perhaps the underlying target of the accusation of arrogance. But in ascetic

---

[248] Athanasius, Ἐπιστολή 7.1–5 (ed. Bartelink, SC 400, p. 150), Τοῦτο πρῶτον ἆθλον Ἀντωνίου γέγονε κατὰ τοῦ διαβόλου· μᾶλλον δὲ τοῦ Σωτῆρος καὶ τοῦτο γέγονεν ἐν Ἀντωνίῳ τὸ κατόρθωμα· Τοῦ τὴν ἁμαρτίαν κατακρίναντος ἐν τῇ σαρκί, ἵνα τὸ δικαίωμα τοῦ νόμου πληρωθῇ ἐν ἡμῖν, τοῖς μὴ κατὰ σάρκα περιπατοῦσιν, ἀλλὰ κατὰ πνεῦμα [Rom. 8:3–4]. Ἀλλ' οὔτε Ἀντώνιος, ὡς ὑποπεσόντος τοῦ δαίμονος, ἠμέλει λοιπὸν καὶ κατεφρόνει ἑαυτοῦ, οὔτε ὁ ἐχθρός, ὡς ἡττηθείς, ἐπαύετο τοῦ ἐνεδρεύειν. Περιήρχετο γὰρ πάλιν ὡς λέων, ζητῶν τινα πρόφασιν κατ' αὐτοῦ. Ὁ δὲ Ἀντώνιος, μαθὼν ἐκ τῶν γραφῶν πολλὰς εἶναι τὰς μεθοδείας τοῦ ἐχθροῦ, συντόνως ἐκέχρητο τῇ ἀσκήσει, λογιζόμενος ὅτι, εἰ καὶ μὴ ἴσχυσε τὴν καρδίαν ἐν ἡδονῇ σώματος ἀπατῆσαι, πειράσει πάντως δι' ἑτέρας ἐνεδρεῦσαι μεθόδου· ἔστι γὰρ φιλαμαρτήμων ὁ δαίμων. Μᾶλλον οὖν καὶ μᾶλλον ὑπεπίαζε τὸ σῶμα καὶ ἐδουλαγώγει μήπως, ἐν ἄλλοις νικήσας, ἐν ἄλλοις ὑποσυρῇ [cf. 1 Cor. 9:27]. Βουλεύεται τοίνυν σκληροτέραις ἀγωγαῖς ἑαυτὸν ἐθίζειν. Καὶ πολλοὶ μὲν ἐθαύμαζον, αὐτὸς δὲ ῥᾷον τὸν πόνον ἔφερεν. Ἡ γὰρ προθυμία τῆς ψυχῆς, πολὺν χρόνον ἐμμείνασα, ἕξιν ἀγαθὴν ἐνειργάζετο ἐν αὐτῷ, ὥστε καὶ μικρὰν πρόφασιν λαμβάνοντα παρ' ἑτέρων, πολλὴν εἰς τοῦτο τὴν σπουδὴν ἐνδείκνυσθαι.

[249] For Jerome's condemnation of *cooperatores Christi*, see Chapter 3, n. 220.

paraenesis it was part of the strategy aimed at preventing arrogance, along with stress on avoiding any sense of self-sufficiency, on gifts from God and on the need to credit God with any powers received, which ran concurrently with the message of individual effort. To suggest that this programme was not thought through or that it necessarily left the door open to arrogance is to fail to pay attention to the careful deliberation that had gone into crafting the programme proposed. However, for proponents of original sin, prevenient grace, and predestination interpreted as preordainment, God's omnipotence was paramount and his control absolute.

The anonymous translation

The anonymous translator rendered the whole of Athanasius' programme into Latin with its vocabulary of co-operation ('to co-operate', *cooperari*), 'assistance' (*opitulatio*), Christ as 'helper' (*auxiliator*) and 'the Lord our co-worker' (*Dominus cooperarius*).[250] In addition, just as in Athanasius' text, the process of co-operation was depicted in action even when the word itself did not appear.[251]

Evagrius

Evagrius adopted in its entirety Athanasius' programme of a positive anthropology and co-operation between humans and God in the achievement of salvation. He popularised among a Latin readership Athanasius' model of paired divine and human agency in human rejection of evil and achievement of virtue.[252] As has been seen, he also added phrases and extended passages to bring this programme into sharper focus. Evagrius' changes are noteworthy but they did not alter the fundamentals of the theological programme set out by Athanasius.[253] His additions reinforced the link between the anthropology and the soteriology of the programme.

When Athanasius wrote of the need to maintain an unwavering commitment to ascetic endeavour: 'For we also have the Lord as our co-worker in this', Evagrius translated συνεργός as *auxiliator* and in the biblical citation the verb συνέργειν was translated as *cooperari*, familiarising a Latin audience with the vocabulary of this approach to Christianity.[254] Athanasius' insistence on constant personal

---

[250] *Cooperari*: Anon. trans., *Vita Antonii* 5.7 (ed. Bartelink, p. 18); *auxiliator*: 6.4 (ed. Bartelink, p. 20); *opitulari, opitulatio, auxiliator*: 10.1–3 (ed. Bartelink, p. 30); *Dominus cooperarius*: 19.1 (ed. Bartelink, p. 46); 34.1 (ed. Bartelink, p. 74).

[251] For example, Anon. trans., *Vita Antonii* 84.1–2 (ed. Bartelink, pp. 158–60).

[252] Evagrius, *Vita Antonii* 25 (52) (ed. Migne, PL 73.149D), 'And with the Saviour's help Antony persevered, safe from all the traps'; 'Et ille Saluatoris auxilio ab uniuersis tutus perseuerabat insidiis.'

[253] For example, in the passage in which Athanasius cited 1 Cor. 15:10 as proof of God's co-operation with man within the context of Antony's duel with the devil, Evagrius added the fact that during the struggle Antony kept his purity of mind intact: Evagrius, *Vita Antonii* 4 (5) (ed. Migne, PL 73.129D), '[Antony] He, thinking about the eternal torments of future judgement, preserved the purity of his mind untainted throughout the temptations'; '[Antonius] Hic aeterna futuri iudicii tormenta considerans, illaesam animae puritatem per tentamenta seruabat.'

[254] Athanasius, Ἐπιστολή 19.1 (ed. Bartelink, SC 400, p. 184); Evagrius, *Vita Antonii* 15 (19) (ed. Migne, PL 73.136A).

effort was rendered into Latin, and Evagrius added greater stress to certain elements of this model.[255] A key phrase added to the narrative by Evagrius came when Athanasius stated that each individual controlled his fate on Judgement Day according to whether or not he had truly kept the commandments. At this point, Evagrius added that the ascetic pursued this way of life: "'So that obeying the Lord's commandments, he might begin to be the Lord's friend rather than his servant.'"[256] This phrase exemplified the confident character of the relationship between the human and the divine in the Greek original and made it more explicit.[257] With his comment, Evagrius was suggesting a paradigm for the relationship between God and man in which the model of co-operation was viewed positively as confidence, in contrast to a paradigm that focused on subjection and fear of overstepping the bounds of subservience. Just as in Athanasius' text, this characterisation of the divine–human relationship as collegial was hedged about with strictures about obedience, praying for help and not presuming on the basis of effort expended.[258] Like Athanasius, Evagrius clearly believed that he could only dare such a confident account of man when it was circumscribed by injunctions to humility.

On one occasion, when Athanasius had Antony advise the monks not to be afraid and to have courage because the Lord was with them, Evagrius summarised Antony's advice and restated it from a slightly different perspective. Rather than stressing fear and its opposite, courage, and repeating that the Lord was with them, Evagrius stressed that an individual was responsible for the state of his thoughts, giving demons an entrance if these thoughts were wicked or fearful. Evagrius also had Antony address this instruction to all Christians and not just monks, and he introduced the word 'idleness' (*inertia*) to highlight the fault of not striving.[259] Where Athanasius wrote of 'cowardice' (δειλία), Evagrius wrote of 'idleness', and

---

[255] For example, it seems that he may have added a phrase to Athanasius' original in the second half of this sentence: "'It is the command of the divine voice that we guard our spirit with unceasing vigilance, and guide it through to success with every care and effort'": Evagrius, *Vita Antonii* 15 (21) (ed. Migne, PL 73.137B), 'Diuinae uocis praeceptum est ut iugi custodia tueamur animam nostram et ad profectum cum omni cautela et industria perducamus'. In Rosweyde's text of Evagrius' *Life of Antony* in PL 73, and in Pascal Bertrand's unpublished PhD edition, the words *et ad profectum cum omni cautela et industria perducamus*, which are an additional phrase not found in Athanasius' original, are omitted from the main text. However, they are included in Montfaucon's edition, reprinted in PG 26 (ed. Migne, PG 26.873–6), and as Bertrand noted in his app. crit., they are in an important witness of the text (identified with the siglum P4 by Bertrand).

[256] Evagrius, *Vita Antonii* 17 (34) (ed. Migne, PL 73.142B), "'Vt praeceptis Domini obediens, amicus esse incipiat de seruo.'"

[257] Cf. Athanasius, Ἐπιστολή 34 (ed. Bartelink, SC 400, p. 228).

[258] Evagrius, *Vita Antonii* 17 (34) (ed. Migne, PL 73.142B–C), "'We must not worry about knowing what is coming, but about fulfilling what has been commanded; nor should we demand this reward for our good way of life, when we should rather beg for victory against the devil from the Lord our helper'"; "'Curandum est non praescire quae ueniunt, sed implere quae iussa sunt; nec institutionibus bonis hanc flagitare mercedem, cum magis debeamus uictoriam contra diabolum ab auxiliatore Domino postulare.'"

[259] See n. 241.

he repeated that word elsewhere.[260] So Evagrius widened the target audience for his paraenesis to embrace all Christians, and he added the idea that effort was an obligation for Christians rather than a vocation. This surely was an early example of the idea that all Christians were obliged to strive to obey Christ's injunctions, which was later restated, in a more assertive manner, as the distinction between true Christians and those who were Christians in name only.

In their printed editions, the two Latin translations share an epilogue that is identical (aside from minor variants in inflections), and which was not present in Athanasius' text, since it reflects on the process of translation into Latin. It is not possible to know whether this epilogue originated with the anonymous translator or with Evagrius, because the anonymous translation survives in a *codex unicus* so there is no other manuscript with which to compare this sole witness, which dates from the 10th or 11th century. In this Latin epilogue is another clear affirmation of a synergistic relationship between man and God: 'May the Almighty God who co-operated with this great man to produce such things also cooperate with us to imitate him'.[261]

Pelagius

As noted already, Pelagius referred to God's help for man, and suggested a model of co-operation in the attainment of salvation, sometimes expressed using the idea of consent.[262] The idea that man could be confident of divine help and confident in his relationship with God was present in Pelagius' paraenesis also.[263] The transparency of God's justice and a confident relationship with God were thus elements of the ascetic programme that Pelagius shared with Athanasius and Evagrius. In the second decade of the 5th century, this confidence would come to be stigmatised as arrogance. Yet strictures against arrogance and about the need for humility were abundant in Pelagius' writings.[264]

Pelagius' opponents labelled him the originator of the collegial approach to man's relationship with God promoted by Athanasius and Evagrius, and criticised

---

[260] Evagrius, *Vita Antonii* 15 (19) (ed. Migne, PL 73.136A–B), '"But in order to stamp on idleness let us reflect upon the Apostle's words when he testifies that he dies each day [1 Cor. 15:31]"'; '"Ad inertiam autem calcandam, Apostoli praecepta replicemus, quibus se mori quotidie testabatur [1 Cor. 15:31]"'.

[261] Anon. trans., *Vita Antonii* Epilogus 2 (ed. Bartelink, p. 178) and Evagrius, *Vita Antonii* Epilogus (ed. Migne, PL 73.169), 'May the Almighty God who co-operated with this great man to produce such things also co-operate with us to imitate him'; 'Deus autem omnipotens, qui tanto uiro cooperatus est ad facienda talia, et nobis cooperetur ad imitandum ipsum'.

[262] See Chapter 1, n. 34–9.

[263] For example, Pelagius, *De uirginitate* 10.2 (ed. Halm, CSEL 1, p. 239), where Pelagius advised the young woman for whom he wrote *On Virginity* that if she maintained her vocation and followed Christ's injunctions, she should: 'Look forward with every confidence to receiving the palm of virginity'; 'Cum omni fiducia palmam uirginitatis exspecta.'

[264] See Chapter 1, n. 72. Further examples of condemnation of arrogance and insistence on the need for humility are: Pelagius, *Ad Demetriadem* 21 (ed. Greshake, p. 136); *Ad Celantiam* 19 (ed. Hilberg, CSEL 56, p. 346); *De diuina lege* 6.3 (ed. Migne, PL 30.112A).

Pelagius for its supposed arrogance. Once again, however, it turns out to have been an idea freely expressed in ascetic literature that had been in circulation for decades when Pelagius himself started to write. *Cooperor* was a word that Augustine used occasionally but which was adopted as the verb of choice for anti-predestinarians in southern Gaul, such as Faustus of Riez, to explain that both human initiative and divine grace were required to achieve salvation.[265]

The ambition of asceticism

Athanasius, the anonymous translation, Evagrius of Antioch and Pelagius

Athanasius stated that God made Antony's fame spread in order that Antony would be a model for others to imitate and an inspiration to others, showing them that virtue was achievable: 'So that in this way also those who hear about him may know that it is possible to carry out the commandments successfully, and so that they take up zeal for the path of virtue.'[266] The anonymous translator simply relayed Athanasius' words.[267] Evagrius, however, made a point of repeating the idea that virtue 'was not something external to human nature' (*nec extra humanam esse naturam*), and he also added reference to people of high social rank ('all the best people', *optimus quisque*):

> So that they might learn that virtue is possible and not beyond the bounds of human nature, and so that all the best people might thus be impelled by the fruits of his labour to imitate his blessed life.[268]

Here, in the comment Evagrius added to Athanasius' text, is evidence of the development within the ascetic movement of an ambitious social aim. Asceticism was now being orientated not just towards those who withdrew from society into the desert but at everyone, including those at the top of the social hierarchy. This was the notion that an ascetic approach to Christianity was appropriate for all Christians whatever their rank, expressed at least thirty years before Pelagius started to write. Athanasius concentrated his focus on monks but included 'all

---

[265] Faustus, *De gratia* 1.10 (ed. Engelbrecht, CSEL 21, p. 33), 'He promised the kingdom of heaven to those who serve him through the duties of laborious service with the co-operation of grace'; 'Per laboriosae seruitutis officia, gratia cooperante, seruantibus regnum caeleste promisit'; 1.14 (ed. Engelbrecht, CSEL 21, p. 46), 'Without the co-operation of the human will, grace is of no benefit'; 'Sine cooperatione uoluntatis humanae, gratiam nil prodesse'.

[266] Athanasius, Ἐπιστολή 93.6 (ed. Bartelink, SC 400, pp. 374–6), Ἵνα καὶ οὕτως οἱ ἀκούοντες γινώσκωσι δυνατὰς εἶναι τὰς ἐντολὰς εἰς τὸ κατορθοῦν καὶ ζῆλον τῆς ἐπ' ἀρετὴν ὁδοῦ λαμβάνωσιν.

[267] Anon. trans., *Vita Antonii* 93.6 (ed. Bartelink, p. 176), 'Vt sic audientes sciant quanta possunt mandata, et scientes dirigant se, et zelum habeant uiae uirtutis deificae.'

[268] Evagrius, *Vita Antonii* 61 (93) (ed. Migne, PL 73.168C), 'Vt uirtus possibilis nec extra humanam esse naturam sanctorum doceatur exemplis, et ad beatae uitae imitationem, ex fructu laboris optimus quisque impellatur.'

Christians';[269] Evagrius, meanwhile, developed an ambitious inclusive remit for asceticism, pointing out that the social elite were also included in the obligations involved in this account of Christianity.

Pelagius too aimed his ascetic paraenesis at all Christians, including those of high social rank, urging abandonment of the trappings of worldly status, and he proposed a new form of nobility, a spiritual one, to replace the old. But this same discussion was being conducted in the 4th century. Precisely this question of the message and ambition of Christianity was being explored and contested in the *Life of Antony* and its translations. In the 4th-century stage of the development of the ascetic movement, evident in Athanasius' work but more so in that of Evagrius of Antioch, the ambition to disseminate the message that all Christians should question themselves as to how far they imitated Christ was acceptable. In the light of this textual evidence, the idea that Christians were not already, at the end of the 4th century, well aware of these two possible route maps for Christianity is not sustainable.

Conclusion on the three versions of the Life of Antony

This evidence suggests that all the key tenets that appear in Pelagius' writings were actively advertised by these proponents of the ascetic ethos long before Pelagius began to write. Athanasius' text stressed that man's nature was inherently good, that each individual was an autonomous agent in achieving his own virtue, that virtue came from within an individual, that it was possible to obey God's commandments successfully, that righteousness was not difficult to achieve, and that dedication and the habit it instilled were the means by which to achieve it. Athanasius did not perceive a need to defend free will to virtue; he took it for granted. This shows how widespread was the assumption of effective free will.

Evagrius of Antioch drew out and made explicit the implications of Athanasius' programme. To Athanasius' model he added explicit stress on the will as the determining factor in virtuous action, on Antony's sinlessness after he became a monk, on the invalidity of excusing sin on the basis that man's nature was inherently sinful, on perfection as Antony's goal, and on a transparent entailment between effort and salvation expressed through the concepts of merit and reward. Within this account of Christianity, Evagrius brought to the fore first, the detail of the process, such as the role of the will, and second, the consequences, with more frequent mention of the results of virtue or vice in terms of heaven or hell. Evagrius advertised this programme to all Christians, advocating that they should seek to imitate Antony's pursuit of perfection. He made explicit what Athanasius had sometimes left implicit, and through numerous subtle alterations he incentivised the message

---

[269] Athanasius, Ἐπιστολή 23.1 (ed. Bartelink, SC 400, p. 198), "'And so whenever the demons saw all Christians, but particularly monks, enjoying working and making progress, first they endeavoured and tried to set obstacles in their way'"; Οὗτοι μὲν οὖν, ἐὰν ἴδωσι καὶ πάντας μὲν χριστιανούς, μάλιστα δὲ μοναχούς, φιλοπονοῦντας καὶ προκόπτοντας, πρῶτον μὲν ἐπιχειροῦσι καὶ πειράζουσιν ἐχόμενα τρίβου τιθέναι σκάνδαλα.

of asceticism so that his version of the *Life of Antony* was a more focused act of marketing aimed at a wider target audience. The many small changes Evagrius made to Athanasius' *Life of Antony* created a text that communicated its message more effectively, and contained important Latin terminological developments from the Greek vocabulary (such as introducing the terms 'merit' and 'reward'), which ushered in conceptual developments. Perhaps the most important of these was the paradigm of confident collegiality in man's relationship with God. The difference in Evagrius' text comprised an accumulation of marginal gains that created a highly influential model for a Christian life.

All three versions of the *Life of Antony* asserted a reliable and transparent causal link between virtue and reward, and nowhere was there any suggestion that Antony's piety was given to him. None of the three versions mentioned grace as a cause of right action or even as a contributory factor in it. In all three, grace was understood as a specific gift of a special power or quality to an already virtuous individual. On two occasions it referred to a general unearned gift to humanity, either the gift of Christ's advent and the Christian faith this brought, or the gift of Christ's victory over the devil. The three versions of the *Life of Antony* therefore suggest that Pelagius' paraenetic method and message were already established features of the ascetic movement when Pelagius began to write.

Both anthropologies, negative and positive, had been present in Christian literature prior to the controversy in the 5th century. The creation of what would be claimed to be dogma in this area established original sin as perceived orthodoxy, even though original sin was not part of any creed, nor was it asserted by the decision of an ecumenical council.[270] The controversy forced Christians in the West to choose to reject or accept the doctrine of original sin, where previously no such choice had been required. To argue that Pelagius' choice to reject it was a 'new idea' is wrong both because a positive account of the innate goodness of human nature had a long history in Christian teaching prior to Pelagius' defence of this principle, and because rejection or acceptance had not been mandatory before. It was the requirement to choose between competing anthropologies that was new, not the idea that human nature as created in God's image was fundamentally good, which was a standard and previously unexceptional idea in Christian discourse.

This positive account of contemporary human nature was widely canvassed in Christian ascetic paraenesis, so that it cannot be said that Pelagius invented the idea. These texts have never been labelled heretical. This leaves the options either that they should be relabelled as heretical, or that Pelagius should be reclassified as orthodox in contemporary terms. Athanasius and Evagrius of Antioch cannot be described as 'Pelagian' without anachronism, and if the attempt were made to describe them as in some way 'pre-Pelagian', such a descriptor would be false in four respects: first, in that the concept of 'Pelagianism' necessarily

---

[270] For an opaque indictment of Pelagius and Caelestius for denying the doctrine of original sin characterised as accepted dogma and self-evident truth, see Honorius, *Constitutio prima Honorii Imperatoris ad Palladium* (ed. Migne, PL 48.379A–386A).

suggests that these ideas had some special link to Pelagius; second, in that use of the term would be anachronistic; third, in that these ideas were in fact unexceptional when they were advanced and in no way heterodox; and fourth, in that such a descriptor would obscure the actual process that took place in the condemnation of Pelagius, which was that dogma was created on these topics in the early 5th century to the extent that original sin and prevenient grace came to be perceived as elements within 'official' orthodoxy in some (but not all) ecclesiastical statements of doctrine. The compelling overall reason for rejecting some notion of 'pre-Pelagian' doctrine is that it is historically accurate to acknowledge that the ascetic movement was founded on, and had long proposed, the ideas that Pelagius later defended when they were called into question. The idea of original sin may also have had precursors in Christian writing, but its installation as a required element for orthodoxy was a development of the early 5th century.

It is absolutely legitimate to argue that Christian doctrine developed to note that merit was itself given by God, as Augustine proposed. But it is not possible to argue that Pelagius invented new doctrines when he wrote that contemporary human nature was inclined to goodness, that humans possessed effective free will and that grace was given in accord with merit. The evidence of the three versions of the *Life of Antony* shows that such views were widely held and transmitted in Christian ascetic paraenesis in Greek and Latin at least forty years before Pelagius began to write. It is therefore not historically accurate to attach Pelagius' name to these ideas.

The process that occurred when the idea that grace was given in accord with merit was declared anathema in several African councils should therefore be seen as a new development in Christian doctrine; as synodal rulings on a matter that had not previously been the subject of synodal *acta*, legislating for a set of doctrines that were contrary to views that were widely held in contemporary Christianity. The method used was to anathematise objections to the triune of original sin, absolute prevenient grace, and predestination interpreted as preordainment, with the anathemata carrying the concomitant implication that the triune already constituted orthodoxy. Several other ideas, which were not the two fundamental tenets that Pelagius asserted and which were susceptible to condemnation as heterodox, were added to the list of anathemata in order to bring into disrepute those who denied the triune.

It is worth noting that in his *Confessions*, Augustine recorded the influence that the Latin translation of Athanasius' *Life of Antony* had on him.[271] Nowhere did he condemn Athanasius or his translator for their positive statement of the inherent goodness of human nature or for their stress on the individual's ability

---

[271] Augustine struck by Antony's example after hearing about him: *Confessiones* 8.6.14–8.19 (ed. Verheijen and Skutella, CCSL 27, pp. 121–6); Augustine influenced by the example of Antony hearing the biblical verse Matt. 9:21 and taking it as a sign: *Confessiones* 8.12.29 (ed. Verheijen and Skutella, CCSL 27, p. 131); Augustine considered becoming a hermit: *Confessiones* 10.43.70 (ed. Verheijen and Skutella, CCSL 27, p. 193).

to achieve virtue by his own efforts. Augustine subsequently condemned Pelagius for expressing these same ideas when, as a result of his own study of the Bible, Augustine's account of Christianity developed a different anthropology and soteriology.

Reading the different versions of the *Life of Antony* in the light of Pelagius' letters, it is impossible not to conclude that Athanasius' programme was exactly what Pelagius later taught. The same is even more true for Evagrius, whose text advertised still more of the elements that later comprised Pelagius' writings, and who stated them in a form more precisely the same as the form they took in Pelagius' works. All the teaching, all the concepts and all the terminology that Pelagius used were already published and widely disseminated in the three versions of the *Life of Antony*. It is impossible not to view Pelagius' writings as deeply derivative of Athanasius of Alexandria and Evagrius of Antioch.

3

Pelagius did not Invent Anything: All the Teachings in His Writings Had Already Been Widely Disseminated in Ascetic Paraenesis

Part II

The Doctrinal Assumptions in Jerome's Letters and Exegesis, and the Change in His Doctrinal Position

Jerome's letters and exegesis articulated the same set of doctrinal assumptions as appear in the *Life of Antony*, particularly in Evagrius of Antioch's version of the *Life*, which developed and made explicit some of the implications of Athanasius' original. These are the same ideas that also appear in Pelagius' surviving writings, because they were fundamental to ascetic paraenesis. Like the three versions of the *Life of Antony*, the evidence of Jerome's writings suggests that Pelagius explicitly defended these principles but did not introduce any new doctrine. The evidence presented in this chapter will show that Jerome either explicitly asserted or implicitly assumed effective free will in the achievement of human virtue. Indeed, before he became aware of the danger to himself contained in the accusation of heresy levelled at Pelagius, Jerome had previously been less willing to compromise in his promotion of the pursuit of perfect imitation of Christ than Pelagius was. For example, he can be linked more closely than Pelagius to tenet 7 of the accusations made against Pelagius, the idea that the rich could not enter the kingdom of heaven. Some time between AD 410 and 413–14, however, Jerome attempted to change his position concerning effective free will and attacked Pelagius for making statements that he himself had made as late as AD 410.

Section 1: Ideas for which Pelagius was Criticised

The Two Key Doctrines Asserted by Pelagius: the Innate Goodness of Human Nature Even after Adam's Sin, and Man's Effective Free Will

1. The innate goodness of human nature and the achievability of goodness by means of willing

Jerome wrote of the retained goodness of human nature even after the Fall of Man, and referred to 'the good of nature'. He also specifically denied that human nature was inclined to evil. In his *Commentary on Ecclesiastes* written in around AD 388–9, he asserted that God created human nature such that it could avoid evil. Jerome did not refer to Adam or to a changed human condition after Adam's expulsion from Eden, but instead to 'we', suggesting that he considered contemporary humans to be able to avoid evil:

> So as not to appear to condemn the common nature of humanity, and to make God the author of evil in creating beings of a kind unable to avoid evil, he distinctly guards against this by saying that we were created good by God, but because we are left to our free will, we slip toward what is morally inferior by our own fault.[1]

This passage highlights the close link between the idea that human nature was good and the principle of effective human free will.

In his *Commentary on Matthew*, written in AD 398, Jerome interpreted a passage in Jesus' explanation of the parable of the sower as intended to refute the idea that human nature was inclined to sin:

> Matt. 13:15: *For the heart of this people has been hardened, and with ears they have heard with difficulty, and they have closed their* eyes …. And lest perhaps we should think that the hardness of heart and the difficulty of the ears are by nature and not voluntary, he attaches the blame to their will and says: *They have closed their eyes lest at any time they might see with their eyes and hear with their ears and understand in their heart and be converted, and I would heal them.* They do hear, then, in parables and in a riddle, these people who with closed eyes are unwilling to discern the truth.[2]

---

[1] Jerome, *In Ecclesiasten*, on Eccles. 7:28–30 (ed. Adriaen, CCSL 72, p. 312), 'Ne uideretur communem hominum damnare naturam, et Deum auctorem facere mali, dum talium conditor est, qui malum uitare non possint, argute praecauit, et ait bonos nos a Deo creatos; sed quia libero sumus arbitrio derelicti, uitio nostro ad peiora labi'.

[2] Jerome, *In euangelium Matthaei* 2, on Matt. 13:15 (ed. Bonnard, SC 242, p. 268), '*Incrassatum est*, inquit, *cor populi huius, et auribus* suis *grauiter audierunt*; ac ne forte arbitremur crassitudinem cordis et grauitatem aurium naturae esse, non uoluntatis, subiungit culpam arbitrii et dicit: *Oculos suos*

Here Jerome stated explicitly that we should not think that their sin happened as a result of their nature. A little earlier, commenting on Matt. 13:12, Jerome again referred to 'the good of nature' that gave the Jews some virtue despite their unwillingness to believe Christ's message.[3] This supports the interpretation of this present passage as specifically rejecting the notion that human nature was inclined to sin by means of asserting the voluntariness of human action. The vocabulary of this passage uses all the terminology that would later become controversial: 'will' (*uoluntas*), 'judgement' (*arbitrium*) and 'the good of nature' (*bonum naturae*). For Jerome, the cause of the sin lay in their 'not wanting' (or 'not willing', *nolunt*) what was virtuous. Once again these two ideas—the goodness of human nature and effective free will—were closely linked. In this passage written in AD 398, Jerome paired them so closely as to bind them together inextricably, mirroring the relationship of mutual dependence between the idea of original sin and that of an absolutist account of prevenient grace with its entailment of predestination interpreted as preordainment.

Commenting on Matt. 25:26–9, Jerome referred to the good of nature several times and asserted that the Lord recognised the goodness even of pagans, because a natural law of goodness existed in all humans, and he cited the virtue of non-Christians as evidence of the goodness of human nature:

> We understand that the Lord accepts the good life even of the Gentiles and philosophers. He regards those who behave justly one way, and those who behave unjustly in another way. Those who neglect the written law will be condemned in comparison with the one who serves the natural law .... Many are wise by nature and have an acute natural intelligence. But if they become negligent and corrupt the good of nature by idleness, in comparison with him who a little more tardily through his effort and industry compensated for what he had less of, they lose the good of nature, and the reward that had been promised to them they will see pass to others.[4]

Pelagius was later condemned for arguing that the existence of good pagan philosophers proved that human nature was inclined to goodness through a natural law written in human hearts.[5]

In his *Commentary on Isaiah* of AD 410, Jerome again denied that human nature was inclined to sin. Discussing the Babylonians and Isa. 47:12–15, he wrote:

---

clauserunt ne quando oculis uideant et auribus audiant et corde intellegant et conuertantur et sanem eos. In parabolis ergo audiunt et in aenigmate, qui clausis oculis nolunt cernere uerum.'

[3] Jerome, *In euangelium Matthaei* 2, on Matt. 13:12 (ed. Bonnard, SC 242, pp. 266–8).

[4] Jerome, *In euangelium Matthaei* 4, on Matt. 25:26–9 (ed. Bonnard, SC 259, pp. 226–8), 'Intellegimus etiam gentilium et philosophorum bonam uitam recipere Dominum et aliter habere eos qui iuste, aliter qui iniuste agant et ad comparationem eius qui naturali legi seruiat, condemnari eos qui scriptam legem neglegant .... Multi cum sapientes sint naturaliter et habeant acumen ingenii, si fuerint neglegentes et desidia bonum naturae corruperint, ad comparationem eius qui paululum tardior labore et industria compensauit quod minus habuit, perdunt bonum naturae, et praemium quod eis fuerat repromissum uident transire ad alios.'

[5] Pelagius, *Ad Demetriadem* 3–8 (ed. Greshake, pp. 64–84).

Let us ask those who assert that there are different kinds of natures whether Babylon had an evil or a good nature. If they say evil, which will undoubtedly be their response, how is it that they are being summoned to repentance and it is said to her: *Sit pierced with remorse, go into darkness, O daughter of the Chaldaeans* [Isa. 47:5]? And what is more, why is it said next, after the listing of her sins and wicked deeds: *You have coals of fire, you shall sit upon them; these shall be your help*? And what does it mean when the same Septuagint adds: *You have laboured with change from youth*? What is this '*change*'? Surely it is that from good into evil. From this it is clear that those who are good by nature become evil by their own will. After all he goes on to say: *A man has wandered into himself*, not by means of his nature, but by the choice of his mind.[6]

In asserting that the Babylonians were capable of change and repentance, Jerome insisted that their nature was good originally, and he used the vocabulary of the 'will' (*uoluntas*) and 'judgement of the mind' (*arbitrium mentis*) to explain their change from goodness to sin. This underscores again how closely linked were the two doctrines of the goodness of human nature and free will. Furthermore, in order to preserve the permanent possibility of repentance and thus God's fairness, Jerome asserted that the Babylonians became evil by their own choice, with the implicit assumption that they could have chosen virtue at any point. In his *Commentary on Isaiah*, Jerome repeatedly stated that nothing in their nature made men choose sin: '*Their ways are crooked* [Prov. 2:15] not by nature but by their own will. For whatever is crooked and bent is twisted into perverseness from being straight.'[7]

This evidence shows that Jerome interpreted Scripture so as to deny that human nature was inclined to sin, and that he did this in order to preserve effective free will in man.

2. The will, habit and effort as the causes of human goodness

In his *Commentary on Isaiah* of AD 410, Jerome explained that virtue was created in humans by a combination of the goodness of human nature and learning; he made no mention of grace:

---

[6] Jerome, *In Esaiam* 13.13, on Isa. 47:12–15 (ed. Gryson et al., pp. 1403–4), 'Interrogemus eos qui diuersas asserunt esse naturas utrum Babylon malae naturae sit, an bonae? Si malae dixerint, quod eos responsuros esse non dubium est, quomodo prouocatur ad paenitentiam, et dicitur ei: *Sede compuncta, intra in tenebras, filia Chaldaeorum*. Ac deinceps post enumerationem peccatorum et criminum: *Habes carbones ignis, sedebis super eos; hi erunt tibi in adiutorio*? Et quid sibi uelit quod infertur iuxta eosdem Septuaginta: *Laborasti in commutatione ab adulescentia*? Quae sit ista commutatio? Vtique de bono in malum. Ex quo perspicuum est natura bonos uoluntate malos fieri. Denique infertur: *Homo in semetipso errauit*, non natura, sed mentis arbitrio.'

[7] Jerome, *In Esaiam* 16.28, on Isa. 59:6b–8 (ed. Gryson et al., p. 1701), '*Viae eorum peruersae* [Prov. 2:15], non natura, sed propria uoluntate. Quidquid enim peruertitur atque curuatur, de recto torquetur in prauum.'

Learn to do good [Isa. 1:17]. Virtue therefore must be learned, nor is the good of nature sufficient on its own to create justice, unless a person is educated in the corresponding disciplines .... *No one who fails to learn justice on the earth will do the truth* [Isa. 26:10]. Justice therefore must be learned.[8]

Human nature was good but required training for the achievement of virtue: 'We must have our inclinations trained to distinguish good and evil'.[9] In his *Letter to Rusticus* of AD 412, Jerome advised him that habit would enable him to avoid sin: 'What was first compulsory, by habit gradually becoming ingrained, you will begin to wish for, and your labour will delight you, who will forget your prior way of life.'[10]

3. Free will

In around AD 383, while in Rome, Jerome composed a letter for Pope Damasus, who had asked for an explanation of the parable of the Prodigal Son. Jerome explained the words *And he divided to them his substance* [Luke 15:12] in this way:

That is, he gave them free will, he gave them the choice of their own mind, so that each might live not according to God's command, but to please himself; that is, not out of necessity but by their will, in order that virtue might have its place, so that on the model of God we have been permitted to do as we wish, differing in this from other living things. Hence both a just punishment is repaid to sinners and a reward is repaid to saints or the righteous.[11]

In this letter, Jerome glossed 'free will' (*liberum arbitrium*) as 'will'/'desire'/ 'choice' of 'their own mind' (*mentis propriae uoluntas*), suggesting that he saw these two things as synonymous. His repetition of the word *uoluntas* in the phrase *ex uoluntate* (which usually means 'of his own free will') supports this understanding of Jerome's use of the term *uoluntas* in this passage. It seems that *uoluntas* is best translated here as 'will' or 'choice' because it seems clear that Jerome was referring to the concept of free will, and his repeated reference to this

---

[8] Jerome, *In Esaiam* 1.23, on Isa. 1:17 (ed. Gryson et al., p. 169), '*Discite benefacere.* Virtus ergo discenda est nec naturae tantum bonum sufficit ad iustitiam, nisi quis erudiatur congruis disciplinis .... *Omnis qui non didicerit iustitiam super terram ueritatem non faciet* [Isa. 26:10]. Discenda est ergo iustitia'.

[9] Jerome, *In Esaiam* 15.18, on Isa. 56:1 (ed. Gryson et al., p. 1590), 'Exercitatos sensus ad discretionem boni ac mali habere debemus'.

[10] Jerome, *Ep.* 125.16 (ed. Hilberg, CSEL 56, p. 136), 'Inolescente paulatim consuetudine, quod primum cogebaris, uelle incipies et delectabit te labor tuus oblitusque praeteritorum'; cf. Pelagius, *Ad Demetriadem* 13 (ed. Greshake, pp. 102–4).

[11] Jerome, *Ep.* 21.6 (ed. Hilberg, CSEL 54, p. 118), 'Id est, dedit liberum arbitrium, dedit mentis propriae uoluntatem, ut uiueret unusquisque non ex imperio Dei, sed ex obsequio suo, id est non ex necessitate, sed ex uoluntate, ut uirtus haberet locum, ut a ceteris animantibus distaremus, dum ad exemplum Dei permissum est nobis facere quod uelimus. Vnde et in peccatores aequum iudicium et in sanctos aut in iustos praemium retribuetur.'

concept, in varied terminology, suggests that he was stressing its role because he thought it important.[12]

As it had been in the writings of Athanasius and Evagrius of Antioch, for Jerome, free will was dual and was the foundation of virtue; and reward for virtue was secure and direct in a transparent retributive process. In the same letter, Jerome restated this principle of dual free will as a fact: 'It is only God on whom sin does not fall; the rest, since they have free will, because man too was made in the image and likeness of God, can turn their will in either direction.'[13]

In his *Commentary on Philemon*, written in around AD 387, Jerome answered the question of why God did not create man incapable of sin. His main argument was that voluntariness was an essential element in virtue:

> For nothing can be called 'good' except what is voluntary …. The question posed earlier is therefore resolved as follows: God could have made man good without a role for man's will (*uoluntas*). But if He had done this, moral goodness would not have been freely willed but would have been done out of necessity. But what is good by necessity is not good, and by another classification is censured as evil. Therefore leaving us to our own personal judgement, He instead made us in His own image and likeness.[14]

[12] The Latin word *uoluntas* in the singular had a range of possible meanings, including 'will', 'choice', 'wish', 'desire' and 'inclination' (in the plural *uoluntates* usually meant 'desires'). Thus *uoluntas* could refer to a decision-making faculty ('the will'), to a contingent quality of emotion ('desire') or to a specific decision ('choice'). In Jerome's usage he occasionally used *uoluntas* as a synonym for *arbitrium* in the phrase *liberum arbitrium* ('free will') as in this letter to Damasus. This may sometimes have been for reasons of stylistic variation, but his use of the word *uoluntas* suggests the lack of a developed psychological analysis of human agency. Nevertheless, when Jerome used the phrase *liberum arbitrium* or the word *uoluntas*, it seems that he was referring to the seat of agency in man, even if he had not defined or differentiated between the different impulses or processes that lay behind human decision-making. His use of the phrase *liberum arbitrium* clearly shows that for him it denoted the philosophical concept of free will as a principle. Given this, and the fact that *uoluntas* could have different possible meanings, I have translated *uoluntas* as seemed appropriate to Jerome's overall point on each occasion, but its semantic range should be borne in mind. For a discussion of Augustine's conception of the will, see J. M. Rist, *Augustine. Ancient Thought Baptized* (Cambridge, 1994), pp. 179–88; and J. M. Rist, *Augustine Deformed. Love, Sin and Freedom in the Western Moral Tradition* (Cambridge, 2014), pp. 28–83.

[13] Jerome, *Ep.* 21.40.3 (ed. Hilberg, CSEL 54, pp. 139–40), 'Solus Deus est, in quo peccatum non cadit; cetera, cum sint liberi arbitrii, iuxta quod et homo ad imaginem et similitudinem Dei factus est, in utramque partem possunt suam flectere uoluntatem.' Jerome here equated *arbitrium* ('judgement'), used in the phrase *liberum arbitrium* ('free will'), with *uoluntas* ('will', 'desire', 'choice'), suggesting that he understood them as synonyms here.

[14] Jerome, *In epistolam ad Philemonem*, on Phil. 14 (ed. Bucchi, CCSL 77C, p. 97), 'Nihil quippe bonum dici potest, nisi quod ultroneum est …. Superior ergo quaestio ita soluitur: potuit Deus hominem sine uoluntate eius facere bonum; porro si hoc fecisset, non erat bonum uoluntarium, sed necessitatis. Quod autem necessitate bonum est, non est bonum, et alio genere malum arguitur. Igitur, proprio arbitrio nos relinquens, magis ad suam imaginem et similitudinem fecit.' For Jerome it was axiomatic that virtue was determined by will and intentionality: *Commentarii ad Ephesios* 1, on Eph. 1:4 (ed. Migne, PL 26.447C–D), 'Holiness is connected with the will and zeal …. But a person is "holy" who is full of virtues'; 'Sanctitas uoluntate et studio comparatur …. Sanctus autem is qui uirtutibus plenus sit'.

Jerome wrote his commentaries on the four Pauline Epistles—Galatians, Ephesians, Titus and Philemon—in around AD 387. In this exegesis he explicitly stated the case for effective free will. The importance he attributed to the principle of free will in Christianity is shown by his correction of a reading in Latin manuscripts of Gal. 5:8, which might have attributed human judgements to God's causal agency:

> But the meaning cannot stand thus, such that those he had just reprimanded for not obeying the truth, thereby showing that obedience or disobedience has been left to their judgement, he would now assert conversely regarding them that their belief and obedience were not so much in the power of the called as *in the power of the one doing the calling*. Therefore the better reading that is more faithful [to the Greek] is: *That belief of yours does not come from the one who has called you*. The work of God is of course one thing, the work of men another: God's work is to call, and men's work is either to believe or not to believe. And wherever else in Scripture the notion of free will (*liberum arbitrium*) is upheld, as here: *If you are willing and listen to me* [Isa. 1:19]; and again: *And now, O Israel, what does the Lord your God ask of you?* [Deut. 10:12], and it is most forcefully affirmed in the passage under discussion. But some less sophisticated folk have expunged the word 'not' and have made this verse mean the opposite of what the Apostle intended, thinking that they are giving honour to God by conceding to Him power over our belief (*persuasio*) also. Neither God not the devil is the reason why we incline either toward good or toward evil, because our *belief comes not from the one who has called* us but from us, who either give our consent to, or do not give our consent to, the one who calls.[15]

This passage of exegesis specifically refuted the possibility that Gal. 5:8 implied any diminution of human moral autonomy, and made exactly the same case for effective free will as Pelagius articulated twenty-five years later.

Jerome's commentaries on Galatians, Ephesians, Titus and Philemon are important evidence because in them he discussed several Pauline passages that Augustine used in support of his account of prevenient grace and predestination as preordainment. One of these was about conflict between the spirit and the flesh, at Gal. 5:17: *So that you do not do what you want*:

> The soul stands in the middle of this struggle; it has in its power to will or not to will good and evil, but does not possess this willing and being unwilling forever, because it can happen that the soul will consent to the flesh and do the works of the

---

[15] Jerome, *In epistolam ad Galatas* 3, on Gal. 5:8 (ed. Raspanti, CCSL 77A, pp. 161–2), 'Sed nec sic potest stare sensus, ut quos modo accusauerat quare non oboedierint ueritati, ostendens in eorum arbitrio positum uel oboedire uel non oboedire, nunc econtrario adserat *persuasionem* et oboedientiam eorum non tam ex ipsis esse qui uocentur, quam *ex eo qui uocet*. Melius igitur et uerius sic legitur: *persuasio uestra non est ex eo qui uocauit uos*. Aliud quippe Dei opus est, aliud hominum: Dei opus est uocare, hominum uel credere uel non credere. Et sicubi alibi de Scripturis liberum hominis adfirmatur arbitrium ut ibi: *Si uolueritis et audieritis me* [Isa. 1:19]; et iterum: *Et nunc Israel, quid petit a te Dominus Deus tuus* [Deut. 10:12], et ex hoc loco uel maxime comprobatur. Verum simpliciores quique putantes se deferre Deo, ut *persuasio* quoque nostra in eius sit potestate, abstulerunt partem orationis *non* et sensum contrarium Apostolo reddiderunt. Siue ergo in bonam, siue in malam partem, nec Deus nec diabolus in causa est, quia *persuasio* nostra *non est ex eo qui uocauit* nos, sed ex nobis qui uel consentimus uel non consentimus uocanti.'

flesh; conversely, tormenting itself by means of penitence, it may be joined with the *Spirit* and carry out works of the Spirit .... Paul does not do away with our free will by which we assent either to the *flesh* or to the *Spirit*; rather, he points out that what we do is not our own work, but the work itself is attributed to either the *flesh* or the *Spirit*.[16]

Jerome did not read this sentence as saying that we are unable to do what our will prompts; instead he interpreted it as saying that we give our consent either to evil or to good, and as a result of our choice our works are classified as either of the flesh or of the Spirit.

In his *Commentary on Ephesians*, he went out of his way to make it clear that the process of coming to faith was internal to the individual: 'Those whom he had called holy, he also called the faithful, because faith derives from the judgement of our own mind; but sanctification is sometimes received as a result of the generosity of the one doing the sanctifying, without the involvement of our will.'[17] Jerome highlighted man's control over his faith by contrasting it with God's gift of sanctification which did not involve man's 'will' (*uoluntas*), suggesting that faith was controlled by the will; whereas sanctification came from God, given to those who had already chosen to believe.

His translation work gave Jerome a sensitivity to different possible meanings of the Bible's words. In his commentaries he considered carefully possible interpretations of passages, and offered alternative explanations of phrases. The one constant, however, was that throughout his exegesis he worked tirelessly to preserve effective human free will.[18] Another passage later used by Augustine to

---

[16] Jerome, *In epistolam ad Galatas* 3, on Gal. 5:17 (ed. Raspanti, CCSL 77A, p. 179), 'Inter hoc iurgium media anima consistit habens quidem in sua potestate bonum et malum, uelle uel nolle, sed non habens hoc ipsum uelle ac nolle perpetuum, quia fieri potest ut cum *carni* consenserit et opera eius fecerit, rursum per paenitentiam se remordens, *Spiritui* copuletur et opera eius efficiat .... Non quo proprium nobis tulerit arbitrium quo uel *carni* uel *Spiritui* adsentiamur, sed quia quod facimus non est nostrum proprie sed opus ipsum uel *carni*, uel *Spiritui* deputatur.' As discussed in Chapter 2, n. 41, in translating I have opted for 'free will' to translate *liberum arbitrium*, because historically discussion of this topic in English has used the phrase 'free will' to translate *liberum arbitrium*, even though 'judgement' is the more correct translation of *arbitrium*, and *uoluntas* in the singular most often means 'will', 'desire' or 'choice'. Jerome, however, varied his phrasing. In my view, in Jerome's usage, *proprium arbitrium* ('own personal judgement') referred to the same concept as *liberum arbitrium*, since Jerome used *proprium arbitrium* to make the same point as he made when using *liberum arbitrium*: that it was down to each individual as to what they decided—that is, the phrase denoted where control of a decision lay.

[17] Jerome, *Commentarii ad Ephesios* 1, on Eph. 1:1 (ed. Migne, PL 26.444A–B), 'Eos quos sanctos dixerat, uocauit et fideles, quia fides ex mentis propriae descendit arbitrio; sanctificatio uero ex sanctificantis interdum, absque uoluntate nostra, sumimur largitate.' Despite his constant stress on effective human free will, Jerome perhaps took the same position that Cassian took in his *Conference* 13, allowing for the action of both divine grace and human free will in man, both together and separately. Here perhaps Jerome used a distinction between *fides* and *sanctificatio* to allow for both causal agencies in human virtue.

[18] Jerome, *Commentarii ad Ephesios* 1, on Eph. 1:22–3 (ed. Migne, PL 26.462B–C), commenting on *And he subjected all things to his feet*, Jerome wrote that this *either* referred to God's foreknowledge of the end of days: 'Or, certainly, if it is to be understood of the past, we ought to take it in the sense that

assert the agency of prevenient grace was Eph. 2:8–9: *For you have been saved by grace by means of faith, and this is not from yourselves for it is the gift of God, not from works, so that no one may glory*. Jerome's interpretation of this passage preserved dual free will:

> It is not that human free will (*liberum arbitrium*) is removed, and in accordance with what the Apostle says to the Romans: *It is not of him who runs, nor of him who wills, but of God who shows mercy* [Rom. 9:16]; but rather freedom of the will (*libertas arbitrii*) itself has God as its author, and all things are referred to God's kindness, since it is He himself who has permitted us even to will the good.[19]

The interpretation of grace used by Jerome to reconcile Paul's statement with effective free will was that grace here referred to the grace of creation, one aspect of which was that God made humans with free will. Jerome confirmed that he understood grace in this passage to refer to the grace of creation, including the gift of free will, in the sentences that immediately followed:

> He has related the reasons why we have been saved by grace through faith, and this itself is not from ourselves but is from the gift of God, when he says: *For we are what he has made*. That means that the fact that we live, breathe, understand, and can believe comes from Him, because He is our creator.[20]

Jerome understood free will as inherently effective, or dual. The notion of free will to sin only does not appear in his writings: the freedom was always binary. The problem with an interpretation of predestination as God's own action in preordaining, rather than his foreknowledge of autonomous human action, was the 'implied reprobation of the non-elect'; that is, God's action in some cases implied his inaction in others.[21] This is the question concerning 'single' free will (to sin only), which is inherent in the notion of single predestination, which Augustine asserted. Jerome, however, described free will as inherently binary. Contrasting

---

even those things which have not been subjected to Him by their choice may be subject by the condition of their nature, for example, demons, Jews, and Gentiles. For they do not serve Christ nor have they been subjected to his feet and yet, because they were created by Him to be good, they have been placed under his authority without their willing it, even if they fight against Him by the choice of their free will'; 'Aut certe si de praeterito sentiendum est, sic debemus accipere, quod etiam ea quae non sunt ei uoluntate subiecta, naturae conditione deseruiant, uerbi causa, daemones, Iudaei, atque Gentiles. Non enim seruiunt Christo nec subiecti sunt pedibus eius, et tamen quia ab eo in bonam partem creati sunt, subditi sunt potestati eius inuiti, tametsi aduersum eum repugnent liberi arbitrii uoluntate.' Thus as a way to reconcile God's omnipotence with human free will, Jerome here implicitly referred to the 'grace of creation', which he also referred to explicitly later in the commentary.

[19] Jerome, *Commentarii ad Ephesios* 1, on Eph. 2:8–9 (ed. Migne, PL 26.470B), 'Non quod liberum homini tollatur arbitrium, et secundum illud Apostoli ad Romanos: *Non sit currentis neque uolentis, sed miserentis Dei* [Rom. 9:16]; uerum quod arbitrii ipsa libertas Deum habeat auctorem, et ad illius beneficium cuncta referantur, cum etiam bonum nos uelle ipse permiserit.'

[20] Jerome, *Commentarii ad Ephesios* 1, on Eph. 2:10 (ed. Migne, PL 26.470B–C), 'Reddidit causas quare gratia saluati sumus per fidem, et hoc ipsum non ex nobis, sed ex munere Dei, dicens: *Ipsius enim factura sumus,* hoc est, quod uiuimus, quod spiramus, quod intelligimus, et credere possumus, ipsius est, quia ipse conditor noster est.'

[21] T. Scheck, *St Jerome. Commentary on Isaiah* (New York, 2015), p. 45.

Paul's advice to the sinful Corinthians with his advice to the virtuous Ephesians, Jerome wrote:

> Each of us has the power of free will to follow either the Corinthians or the Ephesians, and to be saved either by the servitude of the Corinthians or by the freedom of the Ephesians .... Let us therefore strive with all our strength to emulate the Ephesians rather than the Corinthians.[22]

Freely chosen effort to be virtuous was the bedrock of the brand of Christianity Jerome advertised, as it had been for Athanasius and Evagrius of Antioch.

As well as arguing that effective free will was necessary in order to preserve God's justice, Jerome frequently argued that it was necessary so that man could not complain that he had been created inclined to sin and unable to be virtuous. In his *Commentary on Ecclesiastes* of AD 388–9, Jerome's explanation of evil was that through it man learnt lessons, and God had therefore made the world full of opposites:

> This is God's doing, so that there should be scope for wisdom in choosing the good and avoiding the bad, and so that free will (*liberum arbitrium*) should be left to man, so that he should not say that he has been brought into existence by God as senseless or stupid; but God made different things so that man could not complain of his own condition.[23]

This argument that it was essential that man had free will in order that he should not be able to complain of his own condition was also propounded by Evagrius of Antioch, and was later repeated by Pelagius.[24]

Jerome was aware that biblical material on the subject of free will might convey mixed messages. In his *Against Jovinian* of around AD 393, he strung together biblical quotations to create a long passage in which he stated that effective free will existed, and then followed this by quoting Rom. 9:16:

> And truly the unrighteousness of God would be great if He merely punished sin, and did not acknowledge good works. 'I have so spoken', says the Apostle, 'to withdraw you from your sins, and to make you more careful through fear of despair. *But, beloved, I trust in better things and things closer to salvation from you. For God's justice does not forget good works and the service that you have shown and do show to the Saints for His name's sake, and remember sins only* [Heb. 6:9–10]'. The apostle James also, knowing that the baptised can be tempted, and fall of their own free will, says: *Blessed is the man who endures temptation; such a one has stood the test and will receive the crown of life* [Jas. 1:12] which the Lord promised to

---

[22] Jerome, *Commentarii ad Ephesios* 3, on Eph. 5:24 (ed. Migne, PL 26.531D–532A), 'Habet unusquisque arbitrii liberam potestatem, uel Corinthios sequi uel Ephesios, et saluari aut seruitute Corinthii, aut Ephesii libertate .... Vnde omni labore nitendum ut magis Ephesios quam Corinthios aemulemur'.

[23] Jerome, *In Ecclesiasten*, on Eccles. 7:15 (ed. Adriaen, CCSL 72, pp. 306–7), 'Hoc autem fecit Deus, ut habeat locum sapientia et in eligendo bono et uitando malo, liberum homini relinquatur arbitrium, ne se dicat insensibilem, et stolidum a Deo esse generatum; sed eum ideo fecisse diuersa, ut homo queri de sua conditione non posset.'

[24] For Evagrius, see Chapter 2, n. 15; Pelagius, *Ad Demetriadem* 3 (ed. Greshake, p. 64).

those who love him. And lest we might think that we too are tempted by God, as it is written in Genesis Abraham was, he says: *Let no man say when he is tempted, I am tempted by God, for God cannot be tempted by evil and He Himself tempts no one. But each man is tempted by his own desire, having been lured and enticed by it. From that point the lust, when it has conceived, gives birth to sin; and that sin, when it is fully grown, gives birth to death* [Jas. 1:13–15]. God created us with free will, and we are not dragged by necessity either to virtue or to vice. Otherwise, where there is necessity, there is no crown. In the same way with good works God brings them to perfection for: *It is not of him who wills, nor of him who runs, but of God who shows mercy* [Rom. 9:16] and gives us help, so that we may be able to reach the goal.[25]

In this passage, Jerome made it clear that the reason for the necessity of effective free will was that this preserved God's justice, and he went out of his way to state explicitly that God would reward good works. The exact way in which God 'brought good works to perfection' and the nature of God's 'help' were not yet problematical in AD 393, and Jerome could simply state that both things were true. This passage replicated the care with which Athanasius, and following him Evagrius of Antioch, paired human initiative with divine help to present a model of co-operation between man and God.

Jerome wrote his *Commentary on Matthew* in two weeks in March of AD 398. The fact that it was written in haste arguably makes it good evidence for the ideas that Jerome considered to be the acknowledged and settled principles of Christian teaching. Effective free will was clearly in this category. Jerome particularly highlighted man's freedom to both virtue and vice, contrasting the law of the Old Testament, which judged actions, with the New Testament, which judged willingness:

> In the law works are demanded in which he who does them will live; in the Gospel willingness (*uoluntas*) is sought which, even if it does not have the effectual achievement, nevertheless does not lose its reward. The Gospel commands things that we are able to do, for example, that we should not lust. This lies in our judgement (*arbitrium*).[26]

---

[25] Jerome, *Aduersus Iouinianum* 2.3 (ed. Migne, PL 23.286B–287A), 'Et reuera grandis iniustitia Dei, si tantum peccata puniret, et bona opera non susciperet. "Ita locutus sum", inquit Apostolus, "ut uos a peccatis retraherem, et desperationis metu facerem cautiores. *Caeterum confido de uobis, dilectissimi, meliora et uiciniora saluti. Neque enim iustitiae Dei est, ut obliuiscatur bonorum operum, et ministerii quod propter nomen eius exhibuistis, et exhibetis in sanctos, et tantum meminerit peccatorum* [Heb. 6:9–10]. Sed et apostolus Iacobus sciens baptizatos posse tentari, et propria corruere uoluntate: *Beatus,* ait, *uir qui suffert tentationem, quia cum probatus fuerit, accipiet coronam uitae, quam repromisit Deus diligentibus se* [Jas. 1:12]. Ac ne putaremus secundum illud Geneseos, ubi scribitur Abraham a Deo fuisse tentatum, nos quoque tentari a Deo: *Nemo,* inquit, *cum tentatur, dicat, quoniam a Deo tentor. Deus enim intentator malorum est, ipse autem neminem tentat. Vnusquisque uero tentatur a concupiscentia sua abstractus et illectus. Dehinc concupiscentia cum conceperit, parit peccatum; peccatum autem cum consummatum fuerit, generat mortem* [Jas. 1:13–15]. Liberi arbitrii nos condidit Deus, nec ad uirtutes, nec ad uitia necessitate trahimur. Alioquin ubi necessitas, nec corona est. Sicut in bonis operibus perfector est Deus, *non est enim uolentis, neque currentis, sed miserentis* et adiuuantis *Dei* [Rom. 9:16], ut peruenire ualeamus ad calcem'.

[26] Jerome, *In euangelium Matthaei* 2, on Matt. 11:30 (ed. Bonnard, SC 242, p. 234), 'In lege opera requiruntur quae qui fecerit uiuet in eis; in Euangelio uoluntas quaeritur quae si etiam effectum non

Just two sentences earlier in the same passage, Jerome referred to 'the grace of the Gospel'. Had he wanted to mention grace as an agent in the process of willing and choosing virtue over sin, he surely would have done so, since the word and concept were in his mind as he composed this passage.

He also proclaimed free will to virtue in his comments on the episode when Jesus was told that his mother and brothers were waiting outside. Jerome wrote that the inner meaning was that Jesus was instructing the nations, and that his mother and brothers represented the Jewish people: 'Whenever they ask and seek and send a messenger, they receive the response that they have free will (*liberum arbitrium*). They can enter if they are willing to believe.'[27] This is an explicit statement of free will to believe—that is, free will to virtue.

When Jerome explained Jesus' statement: *Every plant that my heavenly Father has not planted will be uprooted* [Matt. 15:13], he emphasised the co-operative character of human and divine relations, and he cited Jeremiah:

> In another place he says: *We are God's co-workers* [1 Cor. 3:9]. But if we are God's co-workers, then while Paul plants and Apollos waters, God is planting and watering along with his workers .... But let them hear the following from Jeremiah: *I have planted you as a true vineyard; why did you turn into the bitterness of a foreign vine?* [Jer. 2:21] God planted it indeed, and no one can uproot his planting. But because that planting depends on the volition of its own will, no other can uproot it unless it bestows its assent.[28]

Jerome's use of the phrase 'volition of its own will' (*uoluntas proprii arbitrii*) shows that in AD 398 he was entirely unafraid to use the explicit terminology of effective free will. For him the essence of free will was that it could move in either direction to choose virtue or vice, and he saw no possibility of free will to sin only. This is clear in his interpretation of the parable about the householder who leased out his vineyard. In this parable, God was the householder: 'But He [God] seemed to go away from the vineyard so that He might leave the vine-dressers free will with regard to labouring.'[29] In practice in this story, free will was free will to sin, but Jerome went out of his way to show that God's foreknowledge of the outcome did not mean that dual human free will was not still vital. He explained that God

---

habuerit, tamen praemium non amittit. Euangelium ea praecipit quae possumus: ne scilicet concupiscamus, hoc in arbitrio nostro est'.

[27] Jerome, *In euangelium Matthaei* 2, on Matt. 12:49 (ed. Bonnard, SC 242, p. 262), 'Cumque rogauerint et quaesierint et nuntium miserint, responsum accipiunt liberi eos esse arbitrii et intrare posse, si uellent et ipsi credere'.

[28] Jerome, *In euangelium Matthaei* 2, on Matt. 15:13 (ed. Bonnard, SC 242, p. 326), 'Et in alio loco: *Cooperatores Dei sumus* [1 Cor. 3:9]. Si autem cooperatores, igitur et plantante Paulo et rigante Apollo Deus cum operatoribus suis plantat et rigat .... Sed audiant illud Hieremiae: *Ego uos plantaui uineam ueram, quomodo uersi estis in amaritudinem uitis alienae?* [Jer. 2:21] Plantauit quidem Deus, et nemo potest eradicare plantationem eius. Sed quoniam ista plantatio in uoluntate proprii arbitrii est, nullus alius eam eradicare poterit nisi ipsa tribuerit adsensum.'

[29] Jerome, *Commentarii in euangelium Matthaei* 3, on Matt. 21:33 (ed. Bonnard, SC 259, p. 130), 'Sed abire uidetur a uinea, ut uinitoribus liberum operandi arbitrium derelinquat.'

sent servants frequently: 'So that he might provoke the evil tenants to penitence', and for Jerome it was not problematical that God should will something that would not come to pass: 'For what would the householder not know, since in this passage he represents God the Father? But God is always said to be uncertain so that free will (*libera uoluntas*) in man may be preserved.'[30] In the same year, in his *Letter to Pammachius*, Jerome again drew attention to 'will' (*uoluntas*) and 'judgement' (*arbitrium*) as the effective causes of virtue and its reward.[31] His explanation of these passages makes it clear that, for him, effective free will was a critical element in the Christian message of salvation.

The hardening of Pharoah's heart and predestination

Two biblical episodes in particular became the focus of the debate over the nature of predestination: the stories of Jacob and Esau and the hardening of Pharoah's heart. Because predestination and prevenient grace were, as Augustine said, two parts of the same process, these episodes touched directly on the free will debate, which was itself tied to to the anthropology of Christianity because it involved the question of whether or not man's nature was such that he was able to make an autonomous choice to be virtuous without God's prior causation.[32]

In his *Commentary on Eccclesiastes* of AD 388–9, Jerome explained the biblical assertion that God hardened Pharaoh's heart using an analogy with the different effects of the sun's heat which he borrowed from Origen's interpretation of the hardening of Pharaoh's heart:

> On this subject we must take evidence from Psalm 17 where God is addressed: *With the pure you will be pure, and with the crooked you will be perverse* [Ps. 17:27], as in Leviticus: *If they walk contrary to me, I too will walk contrary to them in my fury* [Lev. 26:27–8]. That will also be able to explain why God hardened Pharaoh's heart: just as one and the same working of the sun liquefies wax and dries mud, the wax liquefying and the mud drying according to their own nature, so the single working

---

[30] Jerome, *Commentarii in euangelium Matthaei* 3, on Matt. 21:36–7 (ed. Bonnard, SC 259, p. 132), 'Frequentius miserit ut malos colonos ad paenitentiam prouocaret .... Quid enim nesciat paterfamilias, qui hoc loco Deus pater intellegitur? Sed semper ambigere dicitur Deus ut libera uoluntas homini reseruetur.'

[31] Jerome, *Ep.* 66.8.1–2 (ed. Hilberg, CSEL 54, p. 656), 'Great enterprises are always left to the judgement of those who hear of them .... *If you wish to be perfect* [Matt. 19:21]: no necessity is laid upon you, so that your will may obtain its reward'; 'Semper grandia in audientium ponuntur arbitrio .... *Si uis perfectus esse* [Matt. 19.21]: non tibi inponitur necessitas, ut uoluntas praemium consequatur.' In the same letter, Jerome used the metaphor of a chariot race with Jesus the charioteer to describe how Paula, Eustochium, Paulina and Pammachius strove using their mind and will to attain salvation: 66.2.2 (ed. Hilberg, CSEL 54, p. 649), 'With an unlike course but with a like mind they strain to reach the prize; the horses are of different colour, but they share the same will and drag the same yoke of the chariot, not waiting for the blows of the whip, but eager at the exhortations of his [sc. Jesus'] voice'; 'Inpari cursu, pari animo ad palmam tenditur, discolores equi, sed uoluntate concordes unum aurigae iugum trahunt, non expectantes flagelli uerbera, sed ad uocis hortamenta feruentes.'

[32] For Augustine's statement that prevenient grace and predestination were two parts of the same process, see Chapter 1, n. 42.

of God in the signs of Egypt softened the heart of the believers and hardened the unbelievers. They, through their hard-hearted impenitence, were: *Storing up wrath for themselves on the day of wrath* [Rom. 2:5] from the miracles which they did not believe, despite seeing them happen.[33]

Also in his *Commentary on Ecclesiastes*, Jerome referred implicitly to Rom. 9:20 and explained that it did not mean that human decisions were predetermined:

> Some think that this passage at that point means that God already knows the name of all those who will exist and are to be clothed in a human body; and that man cannot answer back to his maker about why he was made this way or that. For the more we seek, the more our vanity and superfluous words are displayed; and it is not that free will (*liberum arbitrium*) is removed by God's foreknowledge, but that there is an antecedent cause for each and every thing being as it is.[34]

In the light of the previous passage in his exegesis, 'antecedent cause' must refer to autonomous human action. This reading of biblical references to the hardening of Pharoah's heart led Jerome to choose to refer to God's 'foreknowledge' (*praescientia*) rather than his 'predestination' (*praedestinatio*). In the same commentary, he explained how sin caused anxiety in the sinner, and how God was not the cause of this distress. This passage too should be referred back to his explanation of the hardening of Pharaoh's heart and confirms that Jerome's view was that man brought about his own punishment, which was not caused by divine predestination of human decisions.[35]

In around AD 406 in his *Commentary on Malachi*, Jerome discussed Paul's reading of the story of Jacob and Esau at Rom. 9:11–13. Jerome's 'spiritual interpretation' affirmed dual free will:

---

[33] Jerome, *In Ecclesiasten*, on Eccles. 7:14 (ed. Adriaen, CCSL 72, pp. 305–6), 'Sumendum est in hoc loco testimonium de septimo decimo psalmo, in quo ad Dominum dicitur: *Cum sancto sanctus eris et cum peruerso peruerteris* [Ps. 17:27]. Et dicendum sanctum Dominum esse cum eo, qui sanctus est et peruerti apud eum, qui sua uoluntate fuerit ante peruersus. Iuxta illud quoque, quod in Leuitico scriptum est: *Si ambulauerint ad me peruersi et ego ambulabo ad eos in furore meo peruersus* [Lev. 26:27–8]. Quod quidem et illud poterit exponere, quare indurauerit Deus cor Pharaonis. Quomodo enim una atque eadem solis operatio liquefacit ceram et siccat lutum, et pro substantia sua et liquescit cera, et siccatur lutum; sic una Dei in Aegypto signorum operatio molliebat cor credentium et incredulos indurabat, qui iuxta duritiam suam, et impaenitens cor: *Thesaurizabant sibi iram in die irae* [Rom. 2:5] ex his mirabilibus, quae cum uiderent fieri, non credebant.'

[34] Jerome, *In Ecclesiasten*, on Eccles. 6:10 (ed. Adriaen, CCSL 72, p. 300), 'Nonnulli illud in hoc loco significari putant, quod omnium, qui futuri sunt, et hominum corpore circumdandi, iam Deus uocabulum nouerit; nec possit homo respondere contra artificem suum, quare ita uel ita factus sit. Quanto enim amplius quaesierimus, tanto magis ostendi uanitatem nostram et uerba superflua; et non ex praescientia Dei liberum tolli arbitrium, sed causas ante praecedere, quare unumquodque sic factum sit.'

[35] Jerome, *In Ecclesiasten*, on Eccles. 2:24–6 (ed. Adriaen, CCSL 72, p. 272), 'It is not to be wondered at that he said: *To the sinner he has given anxiety*, etc; this is to be referred to the sense that I have repeatedly discussed: the reason anxiety or distress has been given to him is that he was a sinner, and the cause of the distress is not God, but the man who, of his own volition, sinned beforehand'; 'Nec mirandum, quod dixerit: *Peccatori dedit sollicitudinem,* et cetera. Ad illum enim sensum de quo saepe tractaui, hoc referendum est: Propterea datam ei esse sollicitudinem siue distentionem, quia peccator fuerit, et non esse causam distentionis in Deo, sed in illo qui sponte sua ante peccauerit.'

And the Lord replies that Esau and Jacob were produced from one stock, which is to say: vices and virtues proceed from the one source, the heart, while we go in either direction as we wish because of our free will; but earlier vices are born during infancy, childhood, and youth, which the stronger age that follows reproaches and overthrows. The older brother is rough and bloodthirsty for hunting [cf. Gen. 25:27], he delights in forests and wild beasts. The younger brother is gentle and simple, and dwells at home innocently .... Moreover God's love and hatred is born either from His foreknowledge of future events, or from their works; besides we know that God loves everything, nor does he hate anything that he has created; but he protects with his love in particular those who are the enemies of sins and who fight against sins. And conversely he hates those who wish to rebuild what God has destroyed.[36]

Jerome's interpretation of the meaning of the Jacob and Esau story rejected any notion of predestination as being God's preordaining of events. Instead his explanation of the story was that it propounded effective human free will ('we go in either direction as we wish', *in utramque partem ut uolumus declinamus*).

Jerome wrote his *Letter to Hedibia* (*Letter* 120) in around AD 406–7, and in it he answered 12 questions Hedibia had put to him. Her tenth question asked for an explanation of Rom. 9:14–29, and in response Jerome gave his longest account of the question of human free will and the related issues of the stories of the hardening of Pharaoh's heart, and of Jacob and Esau. It is important to study Jerome's explanation of the passage in detail because of the date when it was composed, and because of its fullness. With regard to the date, it is clear from what Jerome wrote that he was aware of the sensitivity of this question. He described Paul's letter to the Romans as difficult and mysterious, and mentioned a commentary he had read that made Paul's response to his own question entangle the matter more rather than resolve it. In a reference to the idea of reincarnation, he asserted that the desire to preserve God's justice led some into heresy through the suggestion that preceding causes led to God's choice to love Jacob and hate Esau; he himself, however, only wanted to express the consensus view: 'But nothing pleases me except what the Church states and what we are not afraid to say in public in church'.[37] With this comment Jerome showed, first, that he felt a need for caution in interpreting this

---

[36] Jerome, *In Malachiam*, on Mal. 1: 2–5 (ed. Adriaen, CCSL 76A, pp. 905–6), 'Dominusque respondit, Esau et Iacob de una stirpe generatos, hoc est uitia atque uirtutes ex uno cordis fonte procedere; dum ex arbitrii libertate in utramque partem ut uolumus, declinamus; sed priora nascuntur uitia per infantiam, pueritiam, iuuentutem, quae postea aetas firmior corripit atque supplantat. Maior frater hispidus est et sanguinarius uenationibus [cf. Gen. 25:27], siluis et bestiis delectatur. Minor leuis et simplex, et innocenter habitans domum .... Porro dilectio et odium Dei uel ex praescientia nascitur futurorum, uel ex operibus; alioquin nouimus quod omnia Deus diligat, nec quicquam eorum oderit quae creauit; sed proprie eos suae uindicet caritati, qui uitiorum hostes sunt et rebelles. Et econtrario illos odit, qui a Deo destructa cupiunt rursum exstruere.'

[37] Jerome, *Ep.* 120.10.2 (ed. Hilberg, CSEL 55, p. 500), 'Nobis autem nihil placet, nisi quod ecclesiasticum est et publice in ecclesia dicere non timemus'. In his *Letter* 124 *To Avitus*, Jerome explained how in order to preserve God's justice, Origen hypothesised that 'preceding causes' for God's love of Jacob and hatred of Esau lay in their actions in previous lives. Jerome translated Origen's *On First Principles*, and borrowed from Origen frequently.

subject and, second, that he believed that what he went on to expound was the Church's view and represented the mainstream.

Jerome's interpretation was that this passage in Romans was, in fact, an assertion of effective free will in humans. According to him, Paul raised an objection in order to then counter it:

> In his usual way, he proposes a question that comes in from the flank, and discusses it, and when he has resolved it, he returns to the point with which he began the discussion. If Esau and Jacob were not yet born and had not done anything either good or evil such that they either deserved well of God or offended him, and their election and rejection shows not the merits of individuals but the will of the one choosing and rejecting, what then shall we say? Is God unjust? .... If we interpret this, says the Apostle, as saying that God does whatever he wants and either chooses someone or condemns him without merit and works: *Then it is not of him who wills nor of him who runs, but of God who shows mercy* [Rom. 9:16], especially when in the same Scripture the same God says to Pharaoh: *I have raised you up for the very purpose of showing my power in you, so that my name may be proclaimed in all the earth* [Rom. 9:17, cf. Exod. 9:16]. But if this is so, and if God shows mercy to Israel and hardens Pharaoh's heart as he pleases, therefore it is in vain that He complains and blames us for not doing what is good or for doing evil, when it lies in His power and will, without reference to good or bad human actions, either to select someone or to cast him aside, especially when human weakness is unable to resist His will. This strong argument, woven from Scriptural authority and almost insoluble, the Apostle resolves in a brief sentence: *O man, who are you to answer back to God?* [Rom. 9:20]. And this is the meaning: the fact that you answer back to God and accuse Him and make such a search through the Scriptures so that you can speak against God and search for grounds to accuse His will, shows that you have free will and you do what you want, either to be quiet or to speak. For if you think that you were created by God in the likeness of a clay vase and cannot resist His will, consider this, a clay vase does not say to the potter: *Why did you make me like this?* [Rom. 9:20] For a potter has the power to make from the same clay and: *From the same lump of clay one vase for honorable use but another for discredit* [Rom. 9:21]. But God made all men with the same condition and he gave them freedom of the will so that each person might do what he wants, whether good or bad; but he gave this power to all mankind to such an extent that the impious speaker argues against his Creator and scrutinises the reasons for his Creator's will.[38]

---

[38] Jerome, *Ep.* 120.10.6–11 (ed. Hilberg, CSEL 55, pp. 502–3), 'Venientem e latere quaestionem more suo proponit et disserit, et hac soluta reuertitur ad id, de quo coeperat disputare. Si Esau et Iacob necdum nati erant, nec aliquid egerant boni aut mali, ut uel promererentur Deum uel offenderent; et electio eorum atque abiectio non merita singulorum, sed uoluntatem eligentis et abicientis ostendit, quid ergo dicimus? Iniquus est Deus? .... Si hoc, inquit, recipimus, ut faciat Deus quodcumque uoluerit, et absque merito et operibus uel eligat aliquem uel condemnet: *Ergo non est uolentis neque currentis, sed miserentis Dei* [Rom. 9:16], maxime cum eadem Scriptura, hoc est idem Deus loquatur ad Pharaonem: *In hoc ipsum excitaui te, ut ostendam in te uirtutem meam, et adnuntietur nomen meum in uniuersa terra* [Rom. 9:17, cf. Exod. 9:16]. Si hoc ita est, et pro uoluntate sua miseretur Israheli et indurat Pharaonem, ergo frustra queritur atque causatur nos uel bona non fecisse, uel fecisse mala, cum in potestate illius sit et uoluntate, absque bonis et malis operibus, uel eligere aliquem uel abicere, praesertim cum uoluntati illius humana fragilitas resistere nequeat. Quam ualidam quaestionem Scripturarum ratione contextam, et paene insolubilem, breui Apostolus sermone dissoluit, dicens: *O homo! Tu quis es qui respondeas*

So, according to Jerome, Paul's answer to his own question was that the fact that man answered God back and accused Him of injustice showed that God gave man the free will to be able to show impiety by answering Him back, and Paul's intention in the passage was to reject the idea that man was moulded by God as a potter shapes clay. Jerome explained that Paul said that God's patience hardened Pharaoh's heart. God allowed Pharaoh free will, and Pharaoh chose to abuse His forebearance. This passage therefore showed how particularly just God was:

> If God's patience, says the Apostle, hardened Pharoah's heart and God's patience put off punishment of Israel for a long time so that he might more justly condemn those whom he had sustained for a long time, God's patience and infinite mercy should not be criticised, but the stubbornness of those who abused the benevolence of God for their own destruction should be criticised.[39]

Jerome then used once again Origen's interpretation of the hardening of Pharaoh's heart to explain it by analogy with the twofold effects of the sun: hardening mud and melting wax. God's forbearance caused men who were good to love God more, and men who were bad to be stubborn. Jerome concluded that man had free will and that God's justice was transparent:

> He does not save randomly and without true discernment, but on the basis of preceding causes, namely because some did not receive the son of God, and others of their own free will wanted to receive him.[40] But this vessel of mercy represents not only the Gentiles but also those of the Jewish people who wanted to believe, and one people of believers was created; from which fact it is demonstrated that it is not races that are chosen, but the wills of men.[41]

In his final paragraphs on the question, Jerome repeated a further three times his assertion that the will to believe was the effective agent of salvation or punishment,

---

Deo? [Rom. 9:20]. Et est sensus: ex eo quod respondes Deo et calumniam facis et de Scripturis tanta perquiris, ut loquaris contra Deum et iustitiam uoluntatis eius inquiras, ostendis te liberi arbitrii, et facere quod uis, uel tacere uel loqui. Si enim in similitudinem uasis fictilis te a Deo creatum putas, et illius non posse resistere uoluntati, hoc considera: quia uas fictile non dicit figulo: *Quare me sic fecisti?* [Rom. 9:20] Figulus enim habet potestatem de eodem luto et: *De eadem massa, aliud uas facere in honorem, aliud uero in contumeliam* [Rom. 9:21]. Deus autem aequali cunctos sorte generauit, et dedit arbitrii libertatem, ut faciat unusquisque quod uult, siue bonum siue malum. In tantum autem dedit omnibus potestatem, ut uox impia disputet contra Creatorem suum, et causas uoluntatis illius perscrutetur.'

[39] Jerome, *Ep.* 120.10.12 (ed. Hilberg, CSEL 55, p. 504), 'Si, inquit, patientia Dei indurauit Pharaonem et multo tempore poenas distulit Israhelis, ut iustius condemnaret, quos tanto tempore sustinuerat, non Dei accusanda patientia est et infinita clementia, sed eorum duritia, qui bonitatem Dei in perditionem suam abusi sunt.'

[40] That is, 'preceding causes' that were not reincarnation but were instead autonomous human decisions.

[41] Jerome, *Ep.* 120.10.13–14 (ed. Hilberg, CSEL 55, p. 504), 'Non saluat inrationabiliter et absque iudicii ueritate, sed causis praecedentibus, quia alii non susceperunt Filium Dei, alii recipere sua sponte uoluerunt. Haec autem uasa misericordiae non solum populus gentium est, sed et hi qui ex Iudaeis credere uoluerunt, et unus credentium effectus est populus. Ex quo ostenditur non gentes eligi, sed hominum uoluntates'.

referring to 'those who wanted to believe'. He ended with an injunction to be silent and not to disturb God with this question. Clearly, he thought his explanation of Rom. 9—namely, that Paul's letter asserted effective human free will—should be the end of the matter. So instead of using this passage to argue that God controlled man, Jerome interpreted it as showing that He did not control man. And he considered this interpretation to be mainstream: the sort of thing he would not be afraid to say in public in church; it was *ecclesiasticus*.

In the same letter to Hedibia, in answer to another of her questions, Jerome repeated his assertion of effective free will. Dealing with the question of how there could still be people who did not believe after all Paul's work, Jerome replied that this happened because of human free will:

> Because men are left to their own judgement, for they do not do good by necessity but voluntarily, so that those who believe may receive a crown and the unbelievers are delivered up to punishments. Therefore sometimes the aroma that we spread, though intrinsically good, is transformed into either life or death, depending on the virtue or the vice of those who receive or reject the Gospel.[42]

For Jerome, the story of the hardening of Pharoah's heart could not signify that God caused Pharoah's stubbornness. Thomas Scheck referred to Jerome's 'strong defence of the freedom of the human will in the process of salvation and damnation', and identified Jerome's position as 'reminiscent of Origen and the Greek theological tradition'.[43] Commenting on Isa. 63:17: *O Lord, why do you make us stray from your ways, and harden our heart so that we do not fear you?*, Jerome explained that God did not actually harden any human heart but his patience made it seem that He did so, because he stayed His hand from punishment; those uttering this prayer: 'Refer to God what is their own fault.'[44] As Scheck noted, Jerome always read divine foreknowledge as foreknowledge of autonomous human action, not as a causal agency founded on divine predetermination of events.[45]

---

[42] Jerome, *Ep.* 120.11.10 (ed. Hilberg, CSEL 55, p. 509), 'Quia homines suo arbitrio derelicti sunt, neque enim bonum necessitate faciunt sed uoluntate, ut credentes coronam accipiant, increduli suppliciis mancipentur. Ideo odor noster, qui per se bonus est, uirtute eorum et uitio, qui suscipiunt siue non suscipiunt, in uitam transit aut mortem.'

[43] Scheck, *St Jerome, Commentary on Isaiah*, pp. 41–2.

[44] Jerome, *In Esaiam* 17.32, on Isa. 63:17–9 (ed. Gryson et al., p. 1798), 'It is not that God is the cause of human straying and obstinacy, but that his patience, which waits for our salvation, while he does not correct those who transgress, appears to be the cause of error and obstinacy'; 'Non quo Deus erroris causa sit et duritiae, sed quo illius patientia, nostram exspectantis salutem, dum non corripit delinquentes, causa erroris duritiaeque uideatur'; 'Suam culpam referre in Deum.'

[45] For example, Jerome, *In Esaiam* 5.74, on Isa. 16:13 (ed. Gryson et al., p. 597), 'It is not that the foreknowledge of God offered the cause of the devastation, but that the coming devastation was foreknown by the majesty of God'; 'Non quo praescientia Dei causam uastitatis attulerit, sed quo futura uastitas Dei maiestati praenota sit.'

Jerome's Commentary on Isaiah

Jerome's *Commentary on Isaiah* is a storehouse of explicit stress on effective human free will. He published the *Commentary* in AD 410, just a few years before he attempted to alter his position, so it is important evidence for the 'before' stage prior to his apparent switch to a different perspective. In Book 1 of his commentary concerning Isa. 1:19–20: *If you are willing and obedient, you shall eat the good of the land; but if you refuse and rebel, you shall be devoured by the sword*, he wrote: 'He preserves free will, so that for either direction taken, not derived from a prior judgement made by God, but derived from the merits of individual people, there should be either punishment or reward.'[46] This is a clear statement of free will to virtue as well as sin, and an assertion that the reason this principle was essential to Christianity was because it preserved the justice of the Christian system.[47] In this passage, Jerome clearly rejected predestination as preordaining (*non ex praeiudicio Dei*) and asserted that 'merit' determined 'reward' (*merita* and *praemium*).

In his frequent references to human free will, Jerome regularly specifically appended the assertion that free will was dual—that is, to good as well as evil. Speaking initially in the persona of God about how some of the Jewish people did not acknowledge Christ, he wrote:

> 'This is why I was unable to hold on to your adulterous mother any longer, but permitted her to go away willingly'. For each one is sold to his own sins, so long as we are left to our own judgement and we are led by our own will either to good or to evil.[48]

Jerome went on to quote from the Pauline Epistles; it seems that he did not see anything in them to contradict his teaching on free will when he wrote his *Commentary on Isaiah*. According to him, humans were always able to choose virtue through the exercise of their own free will:

> This must be said, that evils need to be turned into goods, and virtues should be born from vices .... What the Gospel says: *A good tree cannot make bad fruit* [Matt. 7:18] does not refer to the peculiar property of its nature, as the heretics want, but to the choice of the mind. After all, he adds: *Either make a tree good, and its fruit is good* [Matt. 12:33]. From this it is very clear that it is by one's own will (*propria uoluntas*) that each person makes his own soul a good or an evil tree, whose fruit are different.[49]

---

[46] Jerome, *In Esaiam* 1.26, on Isa. 1:19–20 (ed. Gryson et al., p. 171), 'Liberum seruat arbitrium, ut in utramque partem non ex praeiudicio Dei, sed ex meritis singulorum uel poena uel praemium sit.'

[47] Jerome considered justice the cardinal virtue: Jerome, *In Esaiam* 15.18, on Isa. 56:1 (ed. Gryson et al., p. 1591), 'Under the name of justice every area of morality appears to me to be signified; for the one who does a single justice is shown to have fulfilled all the virtues'; 'In nomine iustitiae omnis moralis mihi uideatur significari locus, quod qui unam iustitiam fecerit, cunctas uirtutes implesse doceatur'.

[48] Jerome, *In Esaiam* 13.26, on Isa. 50:1 (ed. Gryson et al., p. 1444), '"Vnde adulteram matrem uestram ultra tenere non potui, sed uolentem abire permisi". Quod autem peccatis suis unusquisque uendatur, dum proprio arbitrio derelicti nostra uoluntate uel ad bonum, uel ad malum ducimur'.

[49] Jerome, *In Esaiam* 15.17, on Isa. 55:12–13 (ed. Gryson et al., pp. 1588–9), 'Hoc dicendum est, quod mala uertantur in bona, et pro uitiis nascantur uirtutes .... Ergo illud quod in Euangelio dicitur: *Non potest arbor bona facere fructus malos* [Luke 6:43, Matt. 7:18], nequaquam refertur ad naturae

For Jerome, free will was inherently binary; it could not function in one direction only.[50] When he discussed Jerusalem (here representing for him the Jewish people), he emphasised that the option to act virtuously was always present; the Jewish nation could have chosen to recognise Jesus:

> You bowed down by your own will …. Let this be said in accordance with the history that Jerusalem, if she should be willing to be lifted and to arise, she will in no way drink the cup of the fury of the Lord …. Here one should equally take note that they did not bow it down by force, so that what had formerly been raised erect was made to stoop toward the earth, but they left it to its own judgement, but that soul by its own will laid down its neck.[51]

The only potential problem Jerome saw in his assertion of human dual free will lay in how it could be reconciled with the omnipotence of God, since it meant that God willed something that did not come about because humans disobeyed his commands. Jerome wrote in the person of Jesus questioning God about this:

> 'How is it Father, that you have been glorified in me, one who has *laboured in vain*, and who was unable to call the majority of the Jewish people back to you?' But all this is said in order that man's free will (*liberum arbitrium*) may be demonstrated. For it is God's to call, and ours to believe; and God is not immediately powerless, if we ourselves do not believe, but he leaves his power to our judgement so that our will justly obtains its reward.[52]

This stated the whole of Pelagius' argument for free will: that humans had dual free will, that this was necessary in order to preserve God's justice, that it did not diminish God's omnipotence, and that the process of achieving virtue was a co-operative one in which both God and man were agents. Jerome used the same

---

proprietatem, ut haeretici uolunt, sed ad mentis arbitrium. Denique infertur: *Aut facite arborem bonam et fructus eius bonos* [Matt. 12:33]. Ex quo perspicuum est unumquemque propria uoluntate facere animam suam bonam uel malam arborem, cuius fructus uarii sunt.'

[50] Other examples of his assertion of dual free will are Jerome, *Ep* 49.21.4 (ed. Hilberg, CSEL 54, p. 387), 'It lies in our judgement whether we follow either Lazarus or the rich man'; 'In nostro arbitrio est uel Lazarum sequi uel diuitem'; Jerome, *In Esaiam* 16.4, on Isa. 57:6 (ed. Gryson et al., p. 1633), writing of those who worshipped false gods in the time of Moses: 'They did this by their own will, because to choose good or evil lies in our judgement'; 'Hoc fecerunt propria uoluntate, quia in nostro consistit arbitrio bonum malumue eligere.' Jerome repeated the phrase 'free will is left to man' ('liberum homini relinquatur arbitrium') twice in his *Commentary on Ecclesiastes*: Jerome, *In Ecclesiasten*, on Eccles. 4:9–12 (ed. Adriaen, CCSL 72, p. 287); on Eccles. 7:15 (ed. Adriaen, CCSL 72, p. 306), see n. 23.

[51] Jerome, *In Esaiam* 14.14, on Isa. 51:21–3 (ed. Gryson et al., pp. 1488–9), 'Voluntate propria incuruata es …. Hoc iuxta historiam dictum sit, quod Hierusalem, si eleuari uoluerit atque consurgere, nequaquam bibat calicem furoris Domini …. In quo pariter adnotandum quod non eam incuruauerint nec uim fecerint, ut prius erecta inclinaretur in terram, sed proprio arbitrio dereliquerint, illa autem uoluntate sua posuerit ceruices'.

[52] Jerome, *In Esaiam* 13.19, on Isa. 49:1–4 (ed. Gryson et al., p. 1420), '"Quomodo in me glorificatus es, pater, qui *in uacuum laboraui*, et magnam partem populi Iudaeorum ad te reuocare non potui?" Haec autem uniuersa dicuntur, ut liberum hominis monstretur arbitrium; Dei enim uocare est, et nostrum credere. Nec statim si nos non credimus, impossibilis Deus est, sed potentiam suam nostro arbitrio derelinquit, ut iuste uoluntas praemium consequatur.' Jerome argued that Isaiah's words should be understood as Christ speaking.

terminology as Pelagius later did: 'free will' (*liberum arbitrium*), 'will' (*uoluntas*) and 'reward' (*praemium*). Since human dual free will did not diminish God's omnipotence, it was therefore not a disrepectful or arrogant attitude to Him to assert that God gave man free will. Jerome was uncompromising in his argument that God willed that everyone should believe:

> This therefore was the Father's will, that the wicked vinedressers should have received the Son who had been sent and should have rendered the fruit of the vine-yard, who instead killed him.[53]

Jerome repeated his statement of the universality of God's salvific will later in his *Commentary on Isaiah* when he directly asked the question why, if God wanted all men to be saved, were some people not saved:

> Why are many not saved? .... A clear reason is supplied: *But they did not believe, and they provoked his Holy Spirit* .... Consequently, God willed to save those who desire salvation, and he summoned them to salvation, so that their will would have its reward; but they refused to believe .... And he is not immediately at fault if the majority refused to believe, but the will of the one who came was that everyone should believe and be saved.[54]

Thus the transparency of the justice of the Christian God and the permanence of the invitation to come to God, perceived as an integral part of the justice of the Christian God, were explicitly canvassed by Jerome in AD 410.

Furthermore, concerning this same passage in Isaiah, Jerome explained Paul's comment at Eph. 2:8: *For by grace you have been saved through faith, and this is not your own doing; it is the gift of God*, cited by Augustine to argue that God brought about all virtue in man, as referring instead to Jesus' advent which brought the possibility of salvation to those who chose of their own free will to believe. God wanted to save his people:

> *Not by angels* and prophets and other holy men, but He himself came down to the lost sheep of the house of Israel [cf. Matt. 15:24] .... Therefore, not as an *ambassador*, nor as an *angel, but he himself saved* those who have received salvation, not by the merit of works, but by the love of God. *For God so loved the world that he gave his only begotten Son, that everyone who believes in him may not perish, but may have eternal life* [John 3:16].[55]

---

[53] Jerome, *In Esaiam* 13.20, on Isa. 49:5–6 (ed. Gryson et al., p. 1422), 'Haec igitur uoluntas Patris fuit, ut pessimi uinitores missum susciperent Filium, et fructus uineae redderent, qui interfecerunt eum'.

[54] Jerome, *In Esaiam* 17.29, on Isa. 63:8–10 (ed. Gryson et al., p. 1790), '"Quare multi non sunt saluati?" .... Infertur causa perspicua: *Ipsi autem non crediderunt et exacerbauerunt Spiritum Sanctum eius* .... Voluit itaque Deus saluare cupientes, et prouocauit ad salutem, ut uoluntas haberet praemium; sed illi credere noluerunt .... Nec statim in culpa est, si plures credere noluerunt, sed uoluntas uenientis haec fuit, ut omnes crederent et saluarentur.'

[55] Jerome, *In Esaiam* 17.29, on Isa. 63:8–10 (ed. Gryson et al., pp. 1789–90), '*Non per angelos* et prophetas et alios sanctos uiros saluare uoluit populum suum, uerum ipse descendit ad oues perditas domus Israhel [cf. Matt. 15:24] .... Nequaquam igitur ut *legatus*, nec ut *angelus*, sed ipse saluauit eos qui receperunt salutem, non operum merito, sed caritate Dei. *Sic enim dilexit Deus mundum, ut Filium suum unigenitum daret, ut omnis qui crediderit in eum non pereat, sed habeat uitam aeternam* [John 3:16].'

Jerome's explanation of the phrase 'not by the merit of works' was that this referred to the fact that humanity in general did not deserve the gift of Christ's advent. He did not read it as saying that individual people did not have their own merits, and possessed only merits created in them by God; nor that man did not have the strength of will to choose virtue unaided and that God's grace was prevenient and caused all human virtue. In Jerome's analysis the grace of salvation was offered to all by Christ's coming, and God willed all to take it up; nevertheless, some people chose not to take up the gift offered. By contrast, in Augustine's analysis, God exercised all control, and determined who was saved and who was not; God was responsible, not man. Ultimately the argument was about where control lay. The evidence of Jerome's *Commentary on Isaiah* shows clearly on which side of this argument Jerome stood in AD 410. It is not relevant to the argument of this book either whether Jerome was engaged in anti-gnostic polemic in his *Commentary on Isaiah* or whether he was recycling Origen's exegesis; the relevant point is that this position concerning free will was accepted among Christian commentators and was not something that Pelagius invented.

Jerome's Commentary on Ezekiel

Jerome wrote his *Commentary on Ezekiel* during a period of four years between AD 410 and 414. He composed book one in AD 410, and in it he once again asserted dual human free will and a synergist account of the relationship between man and God:

> And to the open mouth God grants food, so that the beginnings of the will should lie within us and we should obtain the perfection of blessedness from the Lord: *For it is not of him who wills nor of him who runs, but of God who has mercy* [Rom. 9:16]; nevertheless it lies in our judgement both to will and to run.[56]

Jerome wrote Book 4 of the same commentary after the winter of AD 411, by which time Pelagius had been in Palestine for some months. In that book, Jerome repeated his assertion of human dual free will and his synergist position in his explanation of Ezek. 16:14: *Your fame spread among the nations on account of your beauty, for it was perfect because of my splendour that I had bestowed on you, says the Lord God*:

> *Unless the Lord watches over the city, in vain he keeps watch who guards the city* [Ps. 127:1]; *for he who plants and waters is nothing but only the Lord who grants growth* [cf. 1 Cor. 3:7]; because: *It is not of him who wills nor of him who runs, but of God who shows mercy* [Rom. 9:16]; so that, after we have done everything, we should say: *We are worthless slaves; we have done only what we ought to have done* [Luke 17:10]; this is not said such that as a result of God's beneficence man's free

---

[56] Jerome, *In Hiezechielem* 1, on Ezek. 3:2–3 (ed. Glorie, CCSL 75, p. 31), 'Et aperto ore Dominus largitus est cibos, ut initia uoluntatis in nobis sint, et perfectionem beatitudinis a Domino consequamur: *Non est enim uolentis neque currentis, sed miserentis est Dei* [Rom. 9:16]; attamen et uelle et currere nostri arbitrii est.'

will (*liberum arbitrium*) is removed, but such that man's freedom itself should have the Lord as its helper.[57]

It is interesting that Jerome went out of his way here to take into account again Rom. 9:16 and citations that might be read as stressing God's control of human outcomes; once again, however, his interpretation asserted human free will and co-operation between man and God. It may be that this represents a stage at which Jerome had become aware of criticism of emphasis on human free will, and his response was to acknowledge this critique and to reassert his synergist position.

Book 10 of Jerome's *Commentary on Ezekiel* was written between AD 412 and AD 413.[58] In his interpretation of Ezek. 33:1–9 about the watchman who failed to warn his people, he emphatically asserted human dual free will, and he described the process whereby a person chose to act well or badly as entirely internal to the human mind:

> From which we learn that a man, even though he is unjust and impious, can be saved from his impiety if he hears the teacher's words and does penance; likewise we learn that a teacher suffers judgement if he is unwilling to teach, either because of fear of judgement or because he despairs of the sinner, while he is guilty of the blood of the sinner who could have been saved and snatched from death if he had not perished because of the silence of the teacher; and in both of these persons free will is preserved since it lies both in the will of the teacher as to whether he is silent or speaks, and also it lies in the judgement of the hearer as to whether he hears and acts and is saved, or despises to hear and perishes as a result of his own contempt. Nor does it immediately follow that because the prophet prophesies, what he prophesies should come about. For he does not prophesy in order that it should happen, but so that it should not happen; nor because God speaks is it necessary that what he threatens will come to be; but he threatens so that he who is threatened should be converted to penitence, and so that what will happen if the words of God are despised should not in fact come about. We can explain this passage in three ways .... Or indeed as referring to the spirit of the believer which entrusts to its mind and rational faculty command over the people and the mob of its own thoughts, in order that it should not act on all the impulses of its thoughts, but should judge between them and discern which should be pursued and which should be shunned.[59]

---

[57] Jerome, *In Hiezechielem* 4, on Ezek. 16:14 (ed. Glorie, CCSL 75, p. 180), '*Nisi Dominus custodierit ciuitatem, in uanum uigilauit qui custodit eam* [Ps. 127:1]; *qui plantat enim et qui rigat, nihil est, nisi Dominus dederit incrementum* [cf. 1 Cor. 3:7], quia: *Non est uolentis neque currentis, sed miserentis Dei* [Rom. 9:16], ut, postquam omnia fecerimus, dicamus: *Serui inutiles sumus; quae debuimus facere, fecimus* [Luke 17:10]; non quo ex beneficentia Dei liberum hominis tollatur arbitrium, sed quo ipsa libertas Dominum debeat habere adiutorem.'

[58] J. N. D. Kelly, *Jerome: His Life, Writings, and Controversies* (London, 1975), pp. 304–8.

[59] Jerome, *In Hiezechielem* 10, on Ezek. 33:1–9 (ed. Glorie, CCSL 75, p. 468), 'Ex quibus discimus: posse hominem, quamuis iniquum et impium, si magistri uerba audierit et egerit paenitentiam, a sua impietate saluari; nec minus magistrum subire discrimen si docere noluerit, uel timore discriminis uel desperatione peccantis, dum reus est sanguinis eius qui liberari potuit et de morte erui, nisi magistri silentio concidisset; et in utroque liberum seruari arbitrium, dum et in magistri uoluntate est uel tacere uel loqui, et in auditoris arbitrio uel audire et facere atque saluari, uel contemnere et proprio perire contemptu. Nec statim sequitur ut, quia propheta praedicit, ueniat quod praedixit. Non enim praedicit ut ueniat, sed ne ueniat; nec quia Deus loquitur, necesse est fieri quod minatur; sed ideo comminatur,

In the exegesis that followed, Jerome widened the meaning of 'teacher' (*magister*) to include all prophets, bishops and presbyters, decrying those who failed to warn their people even if the people did not act on the warnings, and he concluded that: 'Everyone is judged on the basis of his own mind and duty'.[60] This shows how justice was the founding principle of Jerome's Christianity. It is clear from this passage in Book 10 that as late as AD 412 or 413, he was still saying what he had been saying since the 380s. He was still emphasising human dual free will, and he characterised moral action as the internal rational mind of man choosing between impulses and thoughts. Nowhere in this passage did Jerome mention God's grace as an external agent in this internal process, nor did he suggest that Christians should ask in their prayers to be made virtuous.

This evidence shows that Jerome picked up where Evagrius of Antioch had left off in increasingly presenting the idea of free will as central to the Christian message of salvation. Where it was occasionally referred to in Evagrius' *Life of Antony*, Jerome regularly adduced human free will to virtue as well as vice, making no distinction between these two, as a central concept in Christian teaching. For Jerome, effective free will was axiomatic. It was something that he specifically stressed in exactly the same terms as those that Pelagius later used.

Because he had propounded effective free will throughout his career, Jerome was unable consistently to maintain the new position he tried to adopt when he was faced with the threat of an accusation of heresy posed by the campaign against Pelagius. For example, he ended the preface of his *Dialogue against the Pelagians*, written in AD 415, with a statement of free will: 'I do not want to learn faithlessness through fear when Christ has left the true faith up to my own will.'[61] It is interesting that Jerome used the word 'fear', because by doing so he unconsciously revealed how accusations of heresy created a climate of fear.

A Third Doctrine Asserted by Pelagius: That God's Grace Was Received in Accord with Merit

In his *Commentary on Titus* of around AD 387, Jerome discussed grace. He referred to 'the perfect' as if they existed in fact, and he used the language of commerce to

---

ut conuertatur ad paenitentiam cui minatur, et non fiat quod futurum est si uerba Domini contemnantur. Possumus autem tripliciter locum istum disserere …. Vel certe anima credentis quae mentem atque rationem praeponit populo ac turbae cogitationum suarum, ut non omnia cogitationum incentiua suscipiat, sed iudicet atque discernat quae sectanda sibi quaeue fugienda sint.'

[60] Jerome, *In Hiezechielem* 10, on Ezek. 33:1–9 (ed. Glorie, CCSL 75, p. 469), 'Vnusquisque enim ex suo animo atque officio iudicatur'.

[61] Jerome, *Dialogus aduersus pelagianos* Preface 2 (ed. Moreschini, CCSL 80, p. 5), 'Nolo timore perfidiam discere, cum ueram fidem meae Christus reliquerit uoluntati.'

suggest that grace was something an individual sought, found and bought through effort expended:

> Noah, a just man, who alone was saved from the world's shipwreck, is not said to have found in the sight of God many graces, but one grace. And Moses said to the Lord: *If I have found grace before you* [Exod. 33:13]; and wherever else grace is recorded in the person of the saints: *Seek and you will find* [Matt. 7:7] that they did not find graces, but grace. That merchant from the Gospel who had many pearls, in the end found one precious one, which alone from among many pearls he bought. For it belongs to the perfect to buy one pearl and one treasure by means of all their pearls and by trading all their other possessions. But it belongs to beginners and to those who are still en route not yet to have only one, but to have many.[62]

If grace was something that an individual had to seek in order to find it, then it could not be something that a person received without initiative or effort on his own part. Grace for Jerome was something you put in effort to acquire; it was bought with work. He considered it appropriate to use the simile of the merchant and the language of commerce with regard to acquiring grace.

In his *Commentary on Ecclesiastes* written in AD 388–9, Jerome very deliberately explained that God gave gifts to those who deserved them, using the verb 'to merit' (*mereri*). He specifically highlighted the chronological sequence in which autonomous human choice of virtue preceded God's gifts:

> But it is quite right that God gives wisdom, understanding and happiness to the man who is good: for unless a man has been good and has previously corrected his moral behaviour through his own will, he does not deserve wisdom, understanding and happiness, according to what is said elsewhere: *Sow for yourselves in justice, reap in enjoyment of life, light the light of knowledge for yourselves* [Hos. 10:12]. Clearly the sowing of justice must come first.[63]

---

[62] Jerome, *In epistolam ad Titum* 1:1b–4 (ed. Bucchi, CCSL 77C, p. 12), 'Noe, uir iustus et naufrago solus orbe seruatus, non dicitur plures gratias, sed unam gratiam inuenisse in conspectu Dei; et Moyses ad Dominum: *Si inueni*, inquit, *gratiam apud te* [Exod. 33:13]; et sicubi alibi in persona sanctorum gratia posita est: *Quaere et reperies* [Matt. 7:7], non eos gratias inuenisse, sed gratiam. Mercator ille de Euangelio qui plures habuit margaritas, ad extremum unam pretiosam repperit quam de multis margaritis solam coemit. Perfectorum quippe est unam margaritam et unum thesaurum omnibus margaritis et totius substantiae suae emere commercio; incipientium uero et adhuc in itinere positorum, necdum unam et solam habere, sed plures.'

[63] Jerome, *In Ecclesiasten*, on Eccles. 2:24–6 (ed. Adriaen, CCSL 72, p. 272), 'Pulchre autem homini bono Deus dat sapientiam et scientiam et laetitiam: nisi enim bonus fuerit, et mores suos proprio arbitrio ante correxerit, sapientiam, et scientiam, et laetitiam non meretur, secundum illud quod alibi dicitur: *Seminate uobis in iustitia, uindemiate in fructu uitae, illuminate uobis lumen scientiae* [Hos. 10:12]. Seminanda quippe ante iustitia'. In their note to their translation of this passage, Goodrich and Miller acknowledge that Jerome's position was similar to the one later expounded by Pelagius, and they note the chronological anteriority of Jerome's exegesis: 'Although the *Commentary* predated the Pelagian controversy, this idea that the desire to improve oneself originates in a person's will rather than in God's grace has Pelagian overtones'. This comment does not confront the question this passage raises about the anachronistic nature of the term 'Pelagian' in such a context, or the fact that what they describe as 'Pelagian overtones' in Jerome's exegesis does not accurately describe the similarity, since Jerome's position was not merely similar to, but was exactly the same as, the one that Pelagius subsequently expressed; J. Goodrich and J. D. Miller, *St Jerome. Commentary on Ecclesiastes*, The Works of the Fathers in Translation 66 (New York, 2012), p. 182.

Jerome then repeated this idea.[64]

Jean-Louis Gourdain is the most recent scholar to argue that a series of homilies on Mark should be attributed to Jerome. He dated them to between AD 397 and AD 402, and suggested they were given in Bethlehem, where Jerome regularly delivered homilies on Sundays to a multilingual audience.[65] In his *Homily* 6 on Mark 9:1–8, Jerome explicitly asserted that grace was merited:

> But when six days have passed, he who is Peter, that is, he who has received his name from Christ the Rock, will merit to see the kingdom of God. For in the same way that we are called Christians from Christ, Peter was named from the rock, that is πέτρινος. And so if one of us is πέτρινος and has such faith that the Church of Christ may be built upon him; if one of us is like James and John, blood-brothers not as much as they were spiritual brothers; if one of us is Jacob πτερνιστήρ, that is *supplanter*, and John, meaning *grace of the Lord*, for when we have supplanted our adversaries, then we will merit the grace of Christ; if one of us has more sublime teachings and a more excellent understanding, and merits to be called Son of Thunder: it is necessary that such a person be led by Jesus to the mountain.[66]

Gourdain argued that in his homilies, Jerome was careful to expound a theology that was perfectly orthodox.[67] Gourdain also suggested that in these sermons, Jerome appeared as: 'A sort of witness to the common theological usage of his epoch, which he forcefully recalled to refute all heresies'.[68] Jerome clearly did not believe that the concept of meriting grace was doctrinally questionable; he was happy to assert that virtue merited grace in a sermon in church.

In his *Letter to Furia*, written in around AD 395–6, Jerome stated that Anna 'earned spiritual grace'.[69] The principle of merit was ingrained in his understanding

---

[64] Jerome, *In Ecclesiasten*, on Eccles. 2:24–6 (ed. Adriaen, CCSL 72, p. 272), 'And so, just as God has given wisdom and the other things to the man who is good before him, in the same way, abandoning the sinner to his free will, he has made him gather riches'; 'Vt ergo bono coram se dedit Deus sapientiam et cetera, sic peccatorem suo arbitrio derelinquens, fecit congregare diuitias'.

[65] J.-L. Gourdain, *Jérôme. Homélies sur Marc*, Sources Chrétiennes 494 (Paris, 2005), pp. 9–21.

[66] Jerome, *Tractatus* 6, on Mark 9:2 (ed. Gourdain, SC 494, p. 158), 'Cum autem pertransierint sex dies, qui fuerit Petrus, hoc est, qui ut Petrus a Petra Christo nomen acceperit, regnum uidere merebitur. Quomodo enim a Christo dicimur Christiani, ita a Petra dictus est Petrus, hoc est πέτρινος. Si quis ergo de nobis fuerit πέτρινος, et talem, hoc est, eam fidem habuerit, ut super illum aedificetur Ecclesia Christi: si quis fuerit ut Iacobus et Iohannes, fratres non tantum sanguine quantum spiritu: si quis fuerit Iacobus πτερνιστήρ, id est *subplantator*, et Iohannes, id est, *gratia Domini* – cum enim subplantauerimus aduersarios nostros, tunc merebimur gratiam Christi – si quis habuerit sublimiora dogmata et intellegentiam excellentiorem, et meruerit uocari filius tonitrui, necesse est ut ab Iesu ducatur in montem.'

[67] Gourdain, *Jérôme*, p. 44.

[68] Gourdain, *Jérôme*, p. 46: 'Jérôme, dans ses homélies, apparaît donc comme une sorte de témoin de la vulgate théologique de son époque, qu'il rappelle avec force contre toutes les hérésies.'

[69] Jerome, *Ep.* 54.16.1 (ed. Hilberg, CSEL 54, p. 483), 'And so because from her youth up to the age of 84 years she had borne the burden of widowhood, and would not depart from God's temple, devoting herself to fastings and prayers night and day, for this reason she merited spiritual grace, and was called "Daughter of the face of God"'; 'Quia ergo ab adulescentia usque ad octoginta quattuor annos uiduitatis onus sustinuerat et non recedebat de templo Dei diebus ac noctibus insistens ieiuniis et obsecrationibus, idcirco meruit gratiam spiritalem et nuncupatur "Filia uultus Dei"'.

of Christianity: the grace of salvation was merited.[70] He regularly depicted virtuous people receiving grace; and also individuals causing themselves to be distant from God's grace.[71]

In his *Commentary on Matthew* of AD 398, interpretating Matt. 20:23, Jerome asserted that merit earned salvation:

> This should be understood in the following manner: the kingdom of heaven does not belong to the one giving but to the one receiving: *For God is not a respecter of persons* [Acts 10:34, Rom. 2:11]; but whoever behaves in such a way that he becomes worthy of the kingdom of heaven will receive what has been prepared, not for particular persons but for a particular kind of life. And so, if you merit to attain to the kingdom of heaven, which my Father has prepared for the triumphant victors, you too will receive it.[72]

---

[70] Jerome, *Ep.* 21.7.2 (ed. Hilberg, CSEL 54, p. 118), 'He says to those who prefer their own boasting and do not merit to be with the Lord: *Depart from me, I do not know you, you who work iniquity* [Matt. 7:23]'; 'Ad eos qui sui iactantiam praeferunt et esse cum Domino non merentur, dicit: *Discedite a me, non noui uos, qui operamini iniquitatem* [Matt. 7:23].'

[71] A virtuous person receiving grace: Jerome, *In Esaiam* 7.11, on Isa. 19:1 (ed. Gryson et al., p. 796), 'We should know that this means that the prophet received spiritual grace from the Lord so that he recognised the mysteries of Egypt'; 'Hoc scire debemus accepisse prophetam a Domino gratiam spiritalem, ut Aegypti sacramenta cognosceret'. A person causing himself to be distant from God's grace: Jerome, *Ep.* 21.28.3 (ed. Hilberg, CSEL 54, p. 130), concerning the prodigal son's older brother: 'Sweating from his labour over earthly things, far from the grace of the Holy Spirit'; 'In terrenis operibus labore desudans, longe a gratia Spiritus Sancti'.

[72] Jerome, *In euangelium Matthaei* 3, on Matt. 20:23 (ed. Bonnard, SC 259, p. 94), 'Sic intellegendum: regnum caelorum non est dantis sed accipientis: *Non est enim personarum acceptio apud Deum* [Acts 10:34, Rom. 2:11], sed quicumque talem se praebuerit ut regno caelorum dignus fiat, hic accipiet quod non personae sed uitae paratum est; si itaque tales estis qui consequamini regnum caelorum quod Pater meus triumphantibus et uictoribus praeparauit, uos quoque accipietis illud.' Later in the same commentary, Jerome again asserted at length that merit earned the grace of salvation when he interpreted the parable of the guest at the wedding feast who was not wearing the appropriate wedding clothes: Jerome, *In euangelium Matthaei* 3, on Matt. 22:11–12 (ed. Bonnard, SC 259, pp. 142–4), 'When the king came to see those who were reclining at his feast (that is to say, when on the day of judgement he visits the guests resting, as it were, in his faith, and discerns the merits of each one), he finds one who was not clothed in a wedding garment. That one represents all who are associated with evil. But the wedding garments are the Lord's commands and the works that are fulfilled from the law and the Gospel, and they form the clothing of the new man. If, therefore, at the time of judgement anyone is found with the name of Christian who does not have wedding clothes, that is, the garment of the heavenly man from above, but has a polluted garment, that is, the skin of the old man, he is immediately accused …. At that time there will be no room for impudence nor the capability for denying'; 'Cum uenisset rex ut uideret discumbentes in conuiuio suo (hoc est, in sua quasi fide requiescentes ut in die iudicii uisitaret conuiuas, et discerneret merita singulorum) inuenit unum qui ueste indutus non erat nuptiali. Vnus iste omnes qui sociati sunt malitia intelleguntur. Vestes autem nuptiales praecepta sunt Domini et opera quae complentur ex lege et euangelio, nouique hominis efficiunt uestimentum. Si quis igitur in tempore iudicii inuentus fuerit sub nomine christiano non habere uestimentum nuptiale, hoc est uestem supercaelestis hominis, sed uestem pollutam, id est ueteris hominis exuuias, hic statim corripitur …. In tempore enim illo non erit locus inpudentiae nec negandi facultas'.

Jerome then explained that Jesus refrained from naming those who would reach the kingdom of heaven so that no one felt excluded.[73] The disheartening effect of the doctrine of absolute prevenient grace and predestination interpreted as preordainment was a practical objection to it, and Jerome was clearly aware of this problem.

In his *Commentary on Isaiah* of AD 410, Jerome stated explicitly that grace was merited:

> Let the most depraved heresy hear that he *has become* the Lord for those who are saved and those for whom he was not the Lord before. Consequently we should understand creation and *becoming* in the Scriptures not always as the establishment of those things that did not exist before but occasionally as grace for those who merited that he become their God.[74]

Later in the same commentary he repeated that grace was merited. He interpreted Isa. 44:6–20 as referring to the time after Christ's advent, and stated that the Holy Spirit was given to those who already believed, with merit determining who received it:

> This is said after the preaching of the apostles, the calling of the Gentiles, the coming of the Saviour, and the outpouring of the Holy Spirit whom he promised to give to all believers. At that time, according to the variety of merits, one will say: 'I am the Lord's', another will call on the name of Jacob, another will write with his own hand that he is the Lord's [cf. Isa. 44:5].[75]

Later again in the same commentary, Jerome stated that grace was merited a third time: 'Blessed is the one who has such great virtue and merit that he may be called an ornament of the Church! Now I think that various spiritual graces are being signified'.[76] Grace here was either a quality of virtue or was given to virtue, and was in the plural, so it could not have been prevenient grace that he had in mind.

This evidence shows that, like his friend Evagrius of Antioch, Jerome wrote that God's grace was given in accord with merit. His free use of the language of merit with regard to grace suggests that he thought it unproblematical. Even after he had started to express his views more cautiously, Jerome could not prevent himself

---

[73] Jerome, *In euangelium Matthaei* 3, on Matt. 20:23 (ed. Bonnard, SC 259, p. 94), 'The reason he does not name those who are to sit in the kingdom of heaven is to prevent others from thinking that they have been excluded, because only a few have been named'; 'Ideo enim sedentium in regno caelorum uocabula non dicuntur ne paucis nominatis ceteri putarentur exclusi.'

[74] Jerome, *In Esaiam* 4.19, on Isa. 12:1–2 (ed. Gryson et al., p. 456), 'Audiat sceleratissima haeresis factum Dominum his qui saluantur et quorum prius Dominus non erat, ut creationem in Scripturis atque facturam non semper conditionem eorum quae non erant, sed interdum gratiam in eos qui meruerint sibi Deum fieri intellegamus.'

[75] Jerome, *In Esaiam* 12.18, on Isa. 44:6–20 (ed. Gryson et al., p. 1352), 'Post praedicationem apostolorum, uocationem gentium, saluatoris aduentum et effusionem Spiritus Sancti, quem cunctis credentibus daturum se esse promisit, quando pro uarietate meritorum alius dicet "Domini ego sum", alius uocabit in nomine Iacob, alius scribet manu sua esse se Domini [cf. Isa. 44:5]'.

[76] Jerome, *In Esaiam* 13.23, on Isa. 49:14–21 (ed. Gryson et al., p. 1435), 'Felix qui tanti meriti est tantaeque uirtutis, ut ornamentum dicatur Ecclesiae! Puto autem diuersas significari gratias spiritales'.

from referring to merit. In his *Commentary on Jeremiah*, begun in AD 414–15, he described how Elisha merited to receive the Holy Spirit.[77] His assertions that grace was merited contradicted Augustine's account of prevenient grace. Augustine stated: '[God] does not act in response to our merit, but he himself causes our merit. For God's grace would not be grace at all, unless it was gratuitous in every respect.'[78]

Other Ideas for which 'Pelagianism' Was Criticised by Its Opponents

A direct causal relationship between an individual's virtue on earth and his reward for this virtue in the afterlife

Commenting on Ephesians in around AD 387, Jerome asserted that reward depended directly on freely willed virtue. At the end of days all would believe in God, some willingly, others by necessity:

> We also now see fulfilled in part that the reward of him who follows God willingly is one thing, and that of him who follows by necessity is another .... Christ will only be preached as long as he knows (both he who hopes and he who hopes previously), that different rewards will be received based on the difference of their hope.[79]

In this exegesis the fact that someone had prior belief and freely chosen hope determined the reward he would receive. The causal entailment between autonomous human virtue and reward from God was advertised as transparent and guaranteed.

In AD 398 in his *Commentary on Matthew*, Jerome again asserted the direct causal entailment between righteousness in this life and reward in the next that was the cornerstone of his Christianity, using the language of God's 'owing' (*debere*) reward. Discussing the three types of eunuch, he wrote:

> There is a third kind: *Who have made themselves eunuchs for the kingdom of heaven* and who, though they could be men, become eunuchs for Christ. To these a reward

---

[77] Jerome, *In Hieremiam* 6.35.3, on Jer. 32:12 (ed. Reiter, CCSL 74, p. 332), 'Elijah's servant, Elisha, so pleased God that after his teacher was taken up to heaven, he even merited to receive a double spirit [2 Kings 2:9–11, 15]'; 'Heliseus, minister Heliae, in tantum placuit Deo ut post translationem magistri etiam duplicem spiritum mereretur accipere.'

[78] Augustine, *De gratia Christi et de peccato originali* 2.24.28 (ed. Urba and Zycha, CSEL 42, p. 187), '[Deus] non merita sequens, sed etiam ipsa merita faciens. Non enim Dei gratia gratia erit ullo modo, nisi gratuita fuerit omni modo.'

[79] Jerome, *Commentarii ad Ephesios* 1, on Eph. 1:12 (ed. Migne, PL 26.456A), 'Nunc ex parte uidemus expleri, quia alia sit merces eius, qui uoluntate sequatur Deum, alia qui necessitate .... Tantum Christus annuntietur dummodo sciat, et sperans et ante sperans, quod pro diuersitate spei diuersa sint praemia recepturi.'

is promised, but to the former types, to whom there is compulsion to chastity, not the will for it, nothing is owed at all.[80]

Also in AD 398, Jerome wrote a letter of ascetic exhortation to the Roman senator Pammachius, in which he advertised the same direct causal relationship between ascetic effort in this life and reward in the next.[81] He quoted Cyprian as having made the same correlation between righteousness and reward.[82] In his *Commentary on Isaiah* of AD 410, Jerome interpreted Isa. 1:17–18a, which follows a string of commands to behave virtuously, as confirming the principle of reward for virtue: "'When you have done this", [the Lord] says: "*Accuse me*, if I do not pay back the rewards I have promised."'[83] Reward for virtue was axiomatic for Jerome, who insistently advertised its transparency.[84] Both Jerome and Pelagius used the citation about the many mansions in the Father's house to explain how different levels of merit would receive different rewards in heaven.[85]

The language of reward and investment

Reward for effort was a working assumption of Jerome's promotion of asceticism. In AD 384 he began his *Letter to Eustochium* by advertising the legitimacy of expecting a return on effort expended by advising her to ask: 'What payment (*merces*) do I receive in return for this?'[86] He twice used the word 'payment' (*merces*) to suggest a commercial transaction. He finished on the same note, advising Eustochium to focus her thoughts on the rewards to come: 'It is a great effort, to be as the martyrs, to be as the apostles, to be as Christ is, but the reward (*praemium*) is great.'[87] Referring

---

[80] Jerome, *In euangelium Matthaei* 3, on Matt. 19:12 (ed. Bonnard, SC 259, p. 72), 'Tertii sunt: *Qui se ipsos castrauerunt propter regnum caelorum* et qui cum possint esse uiri, propter Christum eunuchi fiunt. Istis promittitur praemium, superioribus autem quibus castimoniae necessitas non uoluntas est, nihil omnino debetur.' Jerome asserted this causal entailment again later in the commentary: Jerome, *In euangelium Matthaei* 3, on Matt. 19:29–30 (ed. Bonnard, SC 259, p. 82), 'Therefore, those who for the sake of faith in Christ and the proclamation of the Gospel have despised all affections and wealth and the pleasures of the world: *Will receive a hundredfold and will possess eternal life*'; 'Qui ergo propter fidem Christi et praedicationem euangelii omnes affectus contempserint atque diuitias et saeculi uoluptates, isti: *Centuplum recipient et uitam aeternam possidebunt.*'

[81] Jerome, *Ep.* 66.5.3 (ed. Hilberg, CSEL 54, p. 653), 'Bestower of gifts on the poor, his soul made white by his efforts on behalf of the needy, in this way he hurries to heaven'; 'Munerarius pauperum, egentium candidatus sic festinat ad caelum.'

[82] Jerome, *Ep.* 66.5.4 (ed. Hilberg, CSEL 54, p. 653), 'The blessed Cyprian sets out in a long work how great the power is of mercy and what rewards it is destined to be given'; 'Quantas uirtutes habeat misericordia et quibus donanda sit praemiis, et beatus Cyprianus grandi uolumine exsequitur'.

[83] Jerome, *In Esaiam* 1.24, on Isa. 1:17–18a (ed. Gryson et al., p. 170), '"Cum autem", inquit, "haec feceritis, *arguite me* si non reddidero praemia quae pollicitus sum."'

[84] Jerome, *In Esaiam* 10.2, on Isa. 30:27–9 (ed. Gryson et al., p. 1108), 'Rewards were promised to the good and the obedient'; 'Bonis et oboedientibus praemia repromissa sunt'.

[85] Jerome, *Dialogus aduersus pelagianos* 1.17 (ed. Moreschini, CCSL 80, p. 22); Pelagius, *Ad Demetriadem* 17 (ed. Greshake, p. 118).

[86] Jerome, *Ep.* 22.1.4 (ed. Hilberg, CSEL 54, p. 145), 'Quid pro hoc mercedis accipio?'

[87] Jerome, *Ep.* 22.38.6 (ed. Hilberg, CSEL 54, p. 204), 'Grandis labor, sed grande praemium, esse quod martyras, esse quod apostolos, esse quod Christus est.' Cf. Pelagius, *Ad Demetriadem* 28 (ed.

to Matt. 7:7: *Ask, and it will be given to you; seek and you will find; knock and the door will be opened to you*, Jerome stressed initiative and effort: 'Unless you knock with urgency, you will not receive the sacramental bread.'[88] Matt. 7:7 subsequently became a proof-text for those who opposed predestination interpreted as preordainment, and for their argument that God and man co-operated.[89]

In his letter to Hedibia of around AD 406–7, Jerome again advertised the return that ascetic virtue would accrue, and canvassed a reliable, transparent entailment between virtue and reward as a fundamental of the Christian message:

> The apostles say that they have abandoned all their possessions and boldly request a reward for this virtue from Jesus Christ. The Lord replies to them: *Everyone who has abandoned his home, or his brothers, or his sisters, or his father, or his mother, or his wife, or his children, or his lands, for my name's sake, will receive a hundredfold and will possess eternal life* [Matt. 19:29]. O what blessedness to receive great things for small things, eternal things in return for brief things, things that will live forever for things that will die, and to have the Lord as your debtor![90]

For Jerome, free will was a prerequisite for reward, and he described this reward using words which had commercial connotations (*merces* meaning 'payment' and *debitor* meaning 'debtor'). Writing a letter of paraenesis to Rusticus in AD 412, his comparison of Rusticus to a merchant taking risks in order to acquire wealth emphasised that this was an investment in which Rusticus could expect to see a return on his outlay: 'What should Christ's merchant do who sells everything in

---

Greshake, pp. 162–4), 'It is a great effort. But think of what is promised .... Consider, I beg you, the magnitude of your reward'; 'Grandis labor est. Sed respice quod promissum est .... Considera quaeso, magnitudinem praemii tui'.

[88] Jerome, *Ep.* 22.40.5 (ed. Hilberg, CSEL 54, pp. 208–9), 'Nisi pulsaueris inportune, panem non accipies sacramenti.' Jerome told Eustochium to picture herself greeted by her bridegroom Christ in heaven, and he again used the word *merces* to suggest that this reward was something bought: Jerome, *Ep.* 22.41.1–5 (ed. Hilberg, CSEL 54, pp. 209–10), 'Leave for a while your body and your present labour, and picture before your eyes your payment .... Cross over to paradise in your mind'; 'Egredere quaeso paulisper e corpore et praesentis laboris ante oculos tuos pinge mercedem .... Ad paradisum mente transgredere'. Another example of his use of the term *merces* came in his *Commentary on Ephesians*: Jerome, *Commentarii ad Ephesios* 3, on Eph. 5:25 (ed. Migne, PL 26.532D) concerning sexual self-denial in marriage: 'Men should recognise that this has been left to their judgement so that there may be reward for abstinence from pleasures'; 'Hoc in hominibus sciant arbitrio derelictum, ut merces esset ex abstinentia uoluptatum.'

[89] Faustus, *De gratia* 2.10 (ed. Engelbrecht, CSEL 21, p. 87); Vincent of Lérins, *Commonitorium* 26.8–9 (ed. Demeulenaere, CCSL 64, p. 185); Cassian, *Conlatio* 13.9.1 (ed. Kreuz and Petschenig, CSEL 13, p. 372); it was cited five times in the *Praedestinatus*: Anon., *Praedestinatus* Praefatio 1 (ed. Gori, CCSL 25B, p. 8); 3.8 (ed. Gori, CCSL 25B, p. 74); 3.13 (ed. Gori, CCSL 25B, p. 88); 3.22 (ed. Gori, CCSL 25B, p. 105); 3.28 (ed. Gori, CCSL 25B, pp. 112–13).

[90] Jerome, *Ep.* 120.1.10–11 (ed. Hilberg, CSEL 55, p. 477), 'Dicunt Apostoli se omnia, quae sua fuerint dimisisse et mercedem pro hac uirtute audacter exposcunt. Quibus respondit Dominus: *Omnis, qui relinquit domum uel fratres aut sorores aut patrem aut matrem aut uxorem aut filios aut agros propter nomen meum, centuplum accipiet et uitam aeternam possidebit* [Matt. 19:29]. O quanta beatitudo, pro paruis magna recipere, aeterna pro breuibus, pro morituris semper uiuentia, et habere Dominum debitorem!'

order that he may acquire: *The most precious pearl* [cf. Matt. 13:45–6], who with all his possessions buys one field in which he may find a treasury?'[91]

Perfection as a goal and the possibility of human sinlessness

In his *Commentary on Matthew* of AD 398, Jerome explicitly advertised perfection as the proper goal of Christians. In one passage he combined eight key aspects of his ascetic brand of Christianity: the possibility of achieving perfection, criticism of those who were Christians in name only, a demanding standard laid on all Christians and not just monks, the requirement to abandon all property in order to be a true Christian, the assertion of a direct causal entailment between virtue and reward, the individual's control over his own salvation, human dual free will, and a confident relationship between man and God:

> It is in our power whether we want to be perfect. Yet whoever wants to be perfect ought to sell what he has and sell not merely a part of it, as Ananias and Sapphira did, but sell everything. And when he has sold it he must give everything to the poor. In this way he prepares for himself a treasure in the kingdom of heaven. Nor is this sufficient for perfection unless after wealth has been despised, one follows the Saviour. That is to say, when evils have been forsaken, one must do good things. For a wallet is more easily despised than the will. Many who abandon wealth do not follow the Lord. But he follows the Lord who is his imitator and walks in his footsteps. For: *Whoever claims to believe in Christ ought to walk just as he walked* [1 John 2:6] …. *Then Peter responded and said to him: 'Behold, we have left everything and have followed you; what then will there be for us?* This is great confidence. Peter was a fisherman … and yet he speaks confidently: '*We have left everything*'. And because it is not sufficient merely '*to leave*', he adds what is perfect: '*And we have followed you*'. We have done what you ordered; what will you give us therefore in reward?[92]

All of these eight ideas have been seen as diagnostic of Pelagius' teaching, yet Jerome had already proclaimed them in AD 398. His phrase 'he prepares for

---

[91] Jerome, *Ep.* 125.4 (ed. Hilberg, CSEL 56, p. 122), 'Quid Christi negotiatori faciendum est, qui uenditis omnibus quaerit: *Pretiosissimum margaritum* [cf. Matt. 13:45–6], qui totis substantiae suae opibus emit agrum, in quo repperiat thesaurum?'

[92] Jerome, *In euangelium Matthaei* 3, on Matt. 19:21–7 (ed. Bonnard, SC 259, pp. 78–82), 'In potestate nostra est utrum uelimus esse perfecti. Tamen quicumque perfectus esse uoluerit debet uendere quae habet et non ex parte uendere sicut Ananias fecit et Saphira, sed totum uendere et cum uendiderit dare omne pauperibus et sic sibi praeparare thesaurum in regno caelorum. Nec hoc ad perfectionem sufficit nisi post contemptas diuitias Saluatorem sequatur, id est relictis malis faciat bona. Facilius enim sacculus contemnitur quam uoluntas. Multi diuitias relinquentes Dominum non sequuntur. Sequitur autem Dominum qui imitator eius est et per uestigia illius graditur. *Qui* enim *dicit se in Christo credere debet quomodo ille ambulauit et ipse ambulare* …. *Tunc respondens Petrus dixit ei: "Ecce nos reliquimus omnia et secuti sumus te; quid ergo erit nobis?"* Grandis fiducia. Petrus piscator erat … et tamen loquitur confidenter: *Reliquimus omnia*. Et quia non sufficit tantum relinquere iungit quod perfectum est: *Et secuti sumus te*. Fecimus quod iussisti; quid igitur nobis dabis praemii?'

himself' exactly replicated the words Evagrius had Antony say about each person's path to salvation.[93]

In his *Commentary on Ephesians* of AD 387, Jerome referred to perfection as if it was a real possibility.[94] In his *Against Jovinian* of around AD 393, he used the word 'perfection' to describe what Christian behaviour should be.[95] And in his *Letter to Pammachius* of AD 398, he again canvassed the possibility of perfection:

> To be a perfect and complete man (*perfectus et consummatus uir*) it is not enough to despise wealth or to squander or fling away one's money .... It is not enough for you to despise wealth, unless you follow Christ. But he follows Christ who casts aside sins and is a companion of the virtues.[96]

Jerome repeatedly advertised perfection as Pammachius' goal, citing Matt. 19:21: *If you want to be perfect* four times within a few sentences. His wording suggested that perfection was the only worthwhile goal and, by the time of his fourth repetition of the citation, that it was a real possibility.[97]

In fact throughout his career Jerome continuously recommended to his correspondents that they should aim for perfection, and regularly slipped into phraseology that suggested that perfection was possible in this life. A prime example of this slippage was his *Letter* 120 to Hedibia, written in around AD 406–7. In it he answered the question of the aristocratic woman from Gaul: 'How can anyone be perfect?' In 1,243 words, Jerome advertised perfection as the goal of a serious Christian:

> So I too will reply to you with the words of our Lord: *If you wish to be perfect* [Matt. 19:21] and to carry your cross and to follow the Lord our Saviour and imitate Peter who said: *Behold, we have left everything and we have followed you* [Mark 10:28, Luke 18:28], go and give away everything you have and give to the poor and follow the Saviour .... And *if you wish to be perfect*, he lays no yoke of necessity upon you, but grants free will to your power. Do you wish to be perfect and raise yourself to the highest rank? Do what the apostles did, sell everything you have and give it to the poor and follow the Saviour; naked and alone follow naked virtue only. Do you not want to be perfect, but instead to hold the second rank of virtue? Abandon everything

---

[93] See Chapter 2, n. 50.

[94] Jerome, *Commentarii ad Ephesios* 1, on Eph. 1:14 (ed. Migne, PL 26.457C), 'A person may be holy and perfect, and thought worthy of blessedness by all'; 'Sanctus sit aliquis atque perfectus, et omnium iudicio beatitudine dignus putetur'; on Eph. 1:22–3 (ed. Migne, PL 26.464A), 'It is difficult for all the virtues to be present equally even in holy and perfect men'; 'Difficile est etiam in sanctis uiris atque perfectis omnes pariter esse uirtutes.'

[95] Jerome, *Aduersus Iouinianum* 1.13 (ed. Migne, PL 23.232A), '*Depart from evil*, he says, *and do good* [Ps. 36:27]. We abandon the former, we pursue the latter. In one lies the beginning, in the other lies perfection'; '*Declina*, inquit, *a malo, et fac bonum* [Ps. 36:27]. Illud declinamus, hoc sequimur. In altero initium, in altero perfectio est.'

[96] Jerome, *Ep.* 66.8.3–4 (ed. Hilberg, CSEL 54, pp. 657–8), 'Non est satis perfecto et consummato uiro opes contemnere, pecuniam dissipare et proicere .... Tibi non sufficit opes contemnere, nisi Christum sequaris. Christum autem sequitur, qui peccata dimittit et uirtutum comes est'; *Ep.* 66.12.1 (ed. Hilberg, CSEL 54, p. 662), 'Imiteris filium hominis'; 'You should imitate the son of man'.

[97] Jerome, *Ep.* 66.8.1–2 (ed. Hilberg, CSEL 54, p. 656); the fourth citation: '*Si ergo uis esse perfectus*'.

you have, give it to your children, give it to your relations. No one will rebuke you if you pursue an inferior rank, as long as you know that she who chooses the first rank is justly considered senior to you .... For the rest we are allowed free choice whether to give or not to give, although for the person who desires to be perfect, his present poverty must be compensated for by future riches.[98]

Hedibia asked Jerome explicitly: 'How can anyone be perfect?' Jerome's answer was a description of how to be perfect, not a denial that it was possible.[99]

In his *Letter to Rusticus* of AD 412, Jerome stated that Rusticus' goal should be perfection: *To be without spot or wrinkle* [Eph. 5:27], and to be a new man, reborn in Christ.[100] In his *Letter to Demetrias* written in AD 413–14, Jerome advocated a pursuit of perfection that was predicated on the assumption of effective free will. These two ideas were closely linked:

> It is the summit of complete and apostolic virtue to sell all one has and distribute it to the poor, and thus light and unencumbered, to fly up to the heavens with Christ. To us, no—to you, a careful stewardship is entrusted, although in such matters free will is left to every individual, whatever their age. *If you wish*, he says, *to be perfect* [Matt. 19:21]: 'I do not compel you, I do not command you, but I set the palm before you, I show you the prize; it is for you to choose whether you will enter the arena and win the crown.'[101]

---

[98] Jerome, *Ep.* 120.1.2–15 (ed. Hilberg, CSEL 55, pp. 474–9), 'Itaque et ego tibi Domini nostri respondebo sermonibus: *Si uis esse perfecta,* et tollere crucem tuam et sequi Dominum Saluatorem, et imitari Petrum dicentem: *Ecce nos omnia nostra dimisimus, et secuti sumus te* [Mark 10:28, Luke 18:28], uade et uende omnia tua quae habes, et da pauperibus et sequere Saluatorem .... Et *si uis esse perfecta*, non tibi iugum necessitatis inponit, sed potestati tuae liberum concedit arbitrium. Vis esse perfecta, et in primo stare fastigio dignitatis? Fac quod fecerunt apostoli, uende omnia quae habes, et da pauperibus et sequere Saluatorem, et nudam, solamque uirtutem, nuda sequaris et sola. Non uis esse perfecta, sed secundum gradum tenere uirtutis? Dimitte omnia tua quae habes, da filiis, da propinquis. Nemo te reprehendit si inferiora secteris, dummodo illam scias tibi iure praelatam, quae elegerit prima .... Alioquin licet libere uel dare uel non dare, quamquam ei, qui cupiat esse perfectus, praesens paupertas futuris diuitiis conpensanda sit.'

[99] See n. 62 for another illustration of how Jerome used the language of perfection in a casual and unconcerned manner in his exegesis.

[100] Jerome, *Ep.* 125.20 (ed. Hilberg, CSEL 56, pp. 140–1), 'So that I may free my young man from lascivious itching in both tongue and ears, so that I may produce him, reborn in Christ: *Without spot or wrinkle* [Eph. 5:27], as a chaste virgin, and holy as much in mind as in body'; 'Vt adulescentem meum et linguae et aurium prurigine liberem, ut renatum in Christo: *Sine ruga et macula* [Eph. 5:27] quasi pudicam uirginem exhibeam sanctamque tam mente quam corpore'. Cf. Pelagius, *Ad Demetriadem* 17 (ed. Greshake, p. 116), '*So that you are blameless and innocent* [Phil. 2:15] refers to the fully perfect life .... *So that you are without blemish.* For it is not becoming that the stain of sin should be found in the children of God, who is himself the fount of righteousness'; '*Vt sitis irreprehensibiles et simplices* [Phil. 2:15] ad omnem morum perfectionem .... *Vt immaculati simus.* Neque enim conuenit in filiis Dei, qui fons ipse iustitiae est, peccati maculam reperiri'; Pelagius, *De uirginitate* 11.3 (ed. Halm, CSEL 1, p. 241), 'It is proper for all who have been cleansed by the sanctification of the spiritual water to lead a spotless life, so that they may be able to be brought into the heart of the Church, which is described as: *Without spot or wrinkle* [Eph. 5:27] or anything of that kind'; 'Omnes quicumque spiritualis lauacri sanctificatione purgantur, inmaculatam decurrere conueniat uitam, ut Ecclesiae, quae: *Sine macula, sine ruga* [Eph. 5:27], sine aliquo eiusmodi esse describitur, possint uisceribus intimari'.

[101] Jerome, *Ep.* 130.14.2 (ed. Hilberg, CSEL 56, p. 193), 'Apostolici fastigii est, perfectaeque uirtutis,

Furthermore, Jerome preached the ideal of perfection both of individuals and of the Church. In his *Commentary on Ephesians*, writing in the context of discussion of marriage as a bar to perfection, he wrote of Christ creating a Church that was perfect:

> The Church of Christ is: *Glorious, not having spot or wrinkle or any such thing* [Eph. 5:27]. One therefore who is a sinner and stained with any filth cannot be declared to belong to the Church of Christ nor be said to be subject to Christ. It is possible, however, that as the Church which first had wrinkle and spot has afterwards been restored in its youth and purity, so also a sinner may run to the physician, for: *The healthy have no need of a physician, but those who are sick* [Luke 5:31], and his wounds may be healed and he may become a member of the Church which is the body of Christ.[102]

In this same passage of exegesis, Jerome implied that a virtuous Christian should avoid trade and marriage. Although he was careful not to condemn marriage outright, the implication was that it was of a lower status than chastity.[103] On this point he stood close to the ideas expressed in the Caspari Corpus letter *On Chastity* (*De castitate*).

Just as in Evagrius' *Life of Antony*, the evidence of Jerome's writings suggests that exhortation to perfection was common in ascetic literature in Latin. The demanding standard of the rejection of sin, imitation of Christ and pursuit of perfection that Jerome advocated in his paraenesis was later made a ground for criticism of Pelagius when a hostile inference was drawn from his presentation of the same ideas that Jerome had earlier expressed, and then attributed to him as something he wrote. From the proposition put forward by Pelagius that a Christian ought to abandon sin and ought to imitate Christ was drawn the inference that

---

uendere omnia et pauperibus distribuere, et sic leuem atque expeditum cum Christo ad caelestia subuolare. Nobis, immo tibi, diligens credita est dispensatio, quamquam in hoc omni aetati, omnique personae, libertas arbitrii derelicta sit. *Si uis,* inquit, *esse perfectus* [Matt. 19:21]: "Non cogo, non impero, sed propono palmam, ostendo praemia; tuum est eligere, si uolueris in agone atque certamine coronari."'

[102] Jerome, *Commentarii ad Ephesios* 3, on Eph. 5:24 (ed. Migne, PL 26.531B–C), 'Ecclesia Christi: *Gloriosa est, non habens maculam neque rugam* [Eph. 5:27], aut quid istiusmodi. Qui ergo peccator est, et aliqua sorde maculatus, de Ecclesia Christi non potest appellari, nec Christo subiectus dici. Possibile autem est, ut quomodo Ecclesia quae prius rugam habuerat et maculam, in iuuentutem et munditiam postea restituta est, ita et peccator currat ad medicum, quia: *Non habent opus sani medico* [Luke 5:31], sed male habentes, et curentur uulnera ipsius, et fiat de Ecclesia quae corpus est Christi.'

[103] Jerome, *Commentarii ad Ephesios* 3, on Eph. 5:24 (ed. Migne, PL 26.532A), 'Woe, the Saviour says, *to those who are pregnant and giving suck on that day* [Matt. 24:19], that is the day of judgement. These are especially the works of marriage in the proper sense. Let us, therefore, strive with all our strength to emulate the Ephesians rather than the Corinthians. And let us not be caught in the flood, as it were, while buying and selling, marrying and joining in marriage, but with our loins girded let us hold our lamps in our hands [Luke 17:26–8; 12:35]'; '*Vae,* inquit Salvator, *praegnantibus et lactantibus in die illa* [Matt. 24:19], hoc est, iudicii, quae utique proprie opera nuptiarum sunt. Vnde omni labore nitendum, ut magis Ephesios quam Corinthios aemulemur; nec deprehendamur quasi in diluuio ementes, et uendentes, nubentes et matrimonio copulati, sed accinctis lumbis lucernas teneamus in manibus [Luke 17:26–8; 12:35].' Cf. Anon., *De castitate* (ed. Hammam, PLS 1.1465–505).

sinlessness was possible, and that inference was attributed to Pelagius as an assertion that he made.[104] It is deeply ironic that Jerome attacked Pelagius on the grounds that Pelagius suggested that sinlessness was possible, since Jerome had himself earlier proposed this very same argument in the same terms in many of his letters. In reality, the language of perfection was the common currency of the ascetic movement and Pelagius' use of it was nothing new. Jerome regularly cited Matt. 19:21: *If you wish to be perfect* in his ascetic paraenesis, not least because his correspondents often wrote to him about how best to live the ascetic life.[105] Such language had not previously been considered problematic because it had been taken as expressing an aspiration to live as Christ had lived. Jerome was more guilty of casual use of the language of perfection, which slipped into language suggesting that it was achievable in this life, than Pelagius.

After a career spent canvassing perfection, in his *Commentary on Jeremiah*, begun in AD 414–15, Jerome repositioned himself to fit in with what he perceived to be the new orthodoxy:

> It is obvious that one does not reach perfection while on the road, but at the end of the road and in the mansion prepared for the saints in heaven …. In vain therefore a new heresy, that has arisen from an old one, supposes that perfect victory happens here, where there is struggle, combat and an uncertain end in the future.[106]

God listens to the prayers of the righteous so that their prayers are more efficacious than the prayers of people who are not righteous

In his *Commentary on Matthew*, Jerome made it clear that the efficacy of prayer depended on the virtue of the one praying: 'Whenever we do not receive, it is not a question of the inability of the giver, but the fault lies with those who are praying.'[107] That the prayers of the virtuous were more effective than those of sinners was an idea he actively canvassed.[108] In his *Commentary on Isaiah* he cited

---

[104] Pelagius held up the goal of perfection as an inspiration for his addressees just as Jerome did: Pelagius, *Ad Demetriadem* 10 (ed. Greshake, p. 96), 'Let your perfect rank be followed by perfection in life'; 'Perfectum gradum uitae perfectio subsequatur.'

[105] He used it in his *Aduersus Iouinianum* (five times), in his *Tractatus lix in psalmos*, and he used the exact phrase or variants of it in his *Letters* 14, 58, 60, 79 and 118 (in addition to *Letters* 66, 120 and 130 discussed here).

[106] Jerome, *In Hieremiam* 1.17.3, on Jer. 2:6 (ed. Reiter, CCSL 74, p. 15), 'Ex quo perspicuum est non esse in uia perfectionem, sed in fine uiae et in mansione, quae sanctis in caelestibus praeparatur …. Frustra igitur noua ex ueteri heresis suspicatur hic perfectam esse uictoriam, ubi pugna est atque certamen et incertus exitus futurorum.' Jerome made frequent references to heresy and 'the new heresy' in his *Commentary on Jeremiah*, so it seems he was thinking about what he understood as 'Pelagianism' a good deal, such as on Jer. 2:35–6 (ed. Reiter, CCSL 74, p. 29).

[107] Jerome, *In euangelium Matthaei* 3, on Matt. 17:19–20 (ed. Bonnard, SC 259, p. 40), 'Ergo quotiens non accipimus, non praestantis est inpossibilitas sed culpa precantium.'

[108] Jerome, *In Danielem* 1, on Dan. 4:24 (ed. Glorie, CCSL 75A, p. 816), 'And yet the sentence of God was changed in response to the prayers of Hezekiah and the city of Nineveh, not because of the ineffectualness of the judgement itself but because of the conversion of those who merited pardon. Moreover in

Ps. 34 in support of this argument: 'And the Lord will answer him: *For the eyes of the Lord are upon the just, and his ears are open to their prayer* [Ps. 34:15].'[109]

That virtue could be achieved easily

Just as Athanasius' Antony taught his disciples, so Jerome suggested to Eustochium that her asceticism would become easy: 'Let us too love Christ, let us always seek his embraces, and everything difficult will seem easy.'[110] Jerome referred to God's: 'Light yoke, that is, the easy precepts of his commandments'.[111]

Christianity advocated the abandonment of property because it taught that rich people could not enter the kingdom of heaven

In AD 384, Jerome advised Eustochium against retaining property.[112] In AD 398, in his *Commentary on Matthew*, his reading of Matt. 19:21–3 was that the rich could enter the kingdom of heaven only if they ceased being rich: 'Therefore they will not enter as long as they are rich'. Abandoning wealth was difficult but not impossible, and Jerome repeated his exhortation to give away all property.[113] He

---

Jeremiah God states that He threatens evil for the nation, but if it does that which is good, He will alter His threats to bestow mercy. Again, He affirms that He makes promises to the man who does good; and if the same man thereafter works evil, He says that He changes His decision, not with regard to the men themselves, but with regard to their works which have then changed in character. For God is not angry with men but with their sins'; 'Et tamen, ad preces et Ezechiae et Niniue, Dei sententia commutata est, non uanitate iudicii, sed eorum conuersione qui meruere indulgentiam; alioquin et Hieremiae loquitur Deus: se mala minari super gentem et, si bona fecerit, minas clementia commutare: rursum bona agenti se asserit polliceri et, si mala fecerit, dicit se suam mutare sententiam, non in homines sed in opera quae mutata sunt – neque enim Deus hominibus sed uitiis irascitur'.

[109] Jerome, *In Esaiam* 14.18, on Isa. 52:7–8 (ed. Gryson et al., p. 1504), 'Et Dominus respondebit ei: *Oculi enim Domini super iustos, et aures illius in precem eorum* [Ps. 34:15].'

[110] Jerome, *Ep.* 22.40.1–2 (ed. Hilberg, CSEL 54, p. 207), 'Amemus et nos Christum, semper eius quaeramus amplexus, et facile uidebitur omne difficile.'

[111] Jerome, *Ep.* 21.20 (ed. Hilberg, CSEL 54, p. 126), 'Iugum suum leue, id est mandatorum suorum facilia praecepta'.

[112] Jerome, *Ep.* 22.31.1 (ed. Hilberg, CSEL 54, p. 191), 'You must also avoid the evil of avarice, not merely to the extent that you do not seize what belongs to others, for this public laws punish too, but so that you do not keep your property, which is now not your own'; 'Auaritiae quoque tibi uitandum est malum, non quo aliena non adpetas, hoc enim et publicae leges puniunt, sed quo tua, quae sunt aliena, non serues.'

[113] Jerome, *In euangelium Matthaei* 3, on Matt. 19:21–3 (ed. Bonnard, SC 259, pp. 78–80), 'Whoever wants to be perfect ought to sell what he has and sell not merely a part of it, as Ananias and Sapphira did, but sell everything .... How did the rich men Abraham, Isaac and Jacob enter the kingdom of heaven, and in the Gospel, how is it that Matthew and Zacchaeus are commended by the Lord's testimony when they abandoned their wealth? Well, one should consider that at the time when they entered, they had ceased being rich. Therefore, as long as they are rich, they will not enter. And yet, since riches are despised with difficulty he did not say: "It is impossible for the rich to enter the kingdom of heaven", but: "It is *difficult*". Where difficulty is recorded he is not alleging impossibility, but pointing out rarity'; 'Quicumque perfectus esse uoluerit debet uendere quae habet et non ex parte uendere sicut

bundled together commerce and crime, and condemned all activities involving money.[114] As already seen, in AD 406–7 in answer to Hedibia's question 'How can anyone be perfect?', Jerome made it clear that giving away all her property would bring Hedibia a special reward, but he went on to indict all wealth as derived from injustice:

> *Make friends for yourself from the injustice of riches* [mammon] *who may receive you into the eternal dwelling-places* [Luke 16:9]. And it was well said: *From the injustice*; for all riches derive from injustice, and unless one man loses another cannot gain. For this reason the vulgar saying seems to me to be very true: 'The rich man is either unjust, or the heir of an unjust person.'[115]

If she wanted to enter heaven, Hedibia had to abandon her wealth:

> He did not say it was impossible, but difficult, although the example given was of something impossible: *It is easier for a camel to pass through the eye of a needle than for a rich man to enter the kingdom of heaven* [Matt. 19:24, Mark 10:25]. But this is not so much difficult as impossible; for it could never happen that a camel could pass through the eye of a needle. And so will a rich person never be able to enter the kingdom of heaven? But a camel is crooked and curved and weighed down with a heavy burden; and therefore we also, when we enter on bad paths and abandon the right way and are loaded down with worldly riches or with the weight of our sins, are unable to enter the kingdom of God. Whereas if we lay down our excessively heavy burden and take for ourselves the wings of a dove, we will fly away, and we will find rest.[116]

Ananias fecit et Saphira, sed totum uendere …. Quomodo Abraham, Isaac et Iacob diuites intrauerunt in regna caelorum, et in euangelio Matheus et Zacheus diuitiis derelictis Domini testimonio praedicantur? Sed considerandum quod eo tempore quo intrauerunt diuites esse desierant. Tamdiu ergo non intrabunt quamdiu diuites fuerint. Et tamen quia difficulter diuitiae contemnuntur non dixit: "Impossibile est diuites intrare in regna caelorum", sed: "*Difficile*". Vbi difficile ponitur non impossibilitas praetenditur, sed raritas demonstratur.'

[114] Jerome, *In euangelium Matthaei* 3, on Matt. 18:15–17 (ed. Bonnard, SC 259, p. 58), 'But when it is said: *Let him be to you as a pagan and a tax-collector*, it is shown that the one who has the name of believer but who does the work of unbelievers is more accursed than those who are openly Gentiles. For they are called "tax-collectors" in a tropological sense, referring to those who pursue worldly gain and collect taxes by means of business, fraud, theft, crimes, and perjury'; 'Quando autem dicitur: *Sit tibi sicut ethnicus et publicanus*, ostenditur maioris esse detestationis qui sub nomine fidelis agat opera infidelium quam hi qui aperte gentiles sunt. Publicani enim uocantur secundum tropologiam qui saeculi sectantur lucra et exigunt uectigalia per negotiationes et fraudes et furta, scelera atque periuria.'

[115] Jerome, *Ep.* 120.1.7 (ed. Hilberg, CSEL 55, p. 476), 'Fac tibi amicos de iniquo mamona: *Qui te recipiant in aeterna tabernacula* [Luke 16:9]. Pulchreque dixit *de iniquo*; omnes enim diuitiae de iniquitate descendunt, et nisi alter perdiderit, alter non potest inuenire. Vnde illa uulgata sententia mihi uidetur esse uerissima: "Diues aut iniquus, aut iniqui heres."'

[116] Jerome, *Ep.* 120.1.8–9 (ed. Hilberg, CSEL 55, pp. 476–7), 'Non dixit inpossibile, sed difficile, licet exemplum posuerit inpossibilitatis: *Facilius camelus per foramen acus transire poterit, quam diues in regna caelorum* [Matt. 19:24, Mark 10:25]. Hoc autem non tam difficile est, quam inpossibile; numquam enim fieri potest, ut camelus transeat per foramen acus. Numquam igitur diues intrare poterit regna caelorum? Sed camelus tortuosus et curuus est, et graui sarcina praegrauatur; et nos ergo, quando prauas ingredimur semitas, et rectam uiam dimittimus, et oneramur mundi diuitiis siue pondere delictorum, regnum Dei ingredi non ualemus. Quod si deponamus grauissimam sarcinam, et adsumamus nobis pennas columbae, uolabimus et requiescimus'.

In this letter, Jerome asserted that all wealth was gained through injustice and that the rich could not enter heaven without giving up their wealth. In AD 410 in his *Commentary on Isaiah*, he repeated that all wealth derived from injustice: 'For money is not accumulated by one person except by means of another person's loss and harm.'[117]

In his *Letter to Rusticus* of AD 412, Jerome's final words called on Rusticus to give all his property to the poor. In his calls to abandon wealth, he always paired it with the 'rewards' (*praemia*) it would win, proposing a direct entailment between ascetic effort and reward in the next life:

> If you have property, sell it and give it to the poor; if you do not have any, you are free of a great burden; naked, follow a naked Christ. It is a hard task, heavy, and difficult, but the rewards are great.[118]

As has been seen, Matt. 19:21 was frequently cited by Jerome in his letters of exhortation; it was a favourite citation of all exponents of asceticism. That this was a common idea among those pursuing asceticism in the late 4th and early 5th centuries is shown by the examples of Melania the Younger and her husband Pinianus, who sold their estates to pursue an ascetic life in the Holy Land in AD 407 or 408; Julian of Aeclanum, who also sold his estates; and Jerome's eulogy of Paula for repudiating her family wealth for the sake of apostolic poverty.[119] These cases suggest that asceticism became in vogue for some patrician Christians in the early 5th century. This was a fashion, not a doctrine attributable to Pelagius. Whether or not Jerome contributed to the growth of this trend, in his statements that all wealth derived from injustice he stood closer than Pelagius did to the attitude towards wealth taken by the anonymous author of the Capari Corpus letter *On Riches* (*De diuitiis*).[120] If we are looking for the writer who influenced the anonymous author of *On Riches*, we should look to Jerome rather than Pelagius as the source of his ideas. The author of *On Riches* did not write anything that Jerome had not already propounded.

In his *Dialogue against the Pelagians* of AD 415, Jerome tried to adapt the interpretations he had previously propounded so as to avoid the accusation of

---

[117] Jerome, *In Esaiam* 10.12, on Isa. 33:13–19 (ed. Gryson et al., p. 1147), 'Nisi enim alterius damno et malo pecuniae alteri non coaceruantur.'

[118] Jerome, *Ep.* 125.20.5 (ed. Hilberg, CSEL 56, p. 142), 'Si habes substantiam, uende et da pauperibus, si non habes, grandi onere liberatus es; nudum Christum nudus sequere. Durum, grande, difficile, sed magna sunt praemia.' Jerome made this same entailment between virtue and reward in his *Letter to Demetrias*, see n. 101.

[119] Jerome, *Ep.* 108.5.1 (ed. Hilberg, CSEL 55, p. 310).

[120] Anon., *De diuitiis* 12.2 (ed. Hamman, PLS 1.1401), 'Remove the rich man, and you will not find the poor man. Let no one have more than he needs, and all will have as much as they need. The rich few are the cause of the many poor'; 'Tolle diuitem et pauperem non inuenies. Nemo plus quam necessarium est possideat, et quantum necessarium est omnes habebunt. Pauci enim diuites pauperum sunt causa multorum'; 7.5 (ed. Hamman, PLS 1.1388), 'So are riches sinful? Well, I do not say that they are sinful in themselves, but I do think that for the most part they are the result of sin'; 'Ergo diuitiae iniquitates sunt? Non dico quod ipsae iniquitates sunt, sed existimo quod uel maxime ex iniquitate descendunt.'

heresy made against Pelagius. But he was unable consistently to abandon the principles he had canvassed throughout his career, and, while attacking Pelagius for preaching sinlessness, he repeated his assertion that a rich man could not enter the kingdom of heaven, and finished by giving his usual advice that Christians should abandon their property and pursue perfection. Citing Christ about the camel and the eye of the needle, Jerome wrote:

> For in this statement no reference was made to what was possible, but rather one impossibility was compared to another impossibility. For just as a camel cannot pass through the eye of a needle, so also a rich man will not enter the kingdom of heaven .... Do not cite Abraham and the other rich men who entered the kingdom of heaven, for they ceased to be rich men because they used their wealth to do good; in fact since they were rich men not for themselves but for others, they should be referred to as stewards of God rather than as rich men. But we should strive for the perfection of the Gospel in which it is commanded: *If you would be perfect, go, sell all you have, and give to the poor, and come, follow me* [Matt. 19:21].[121]

Jerome then finished with a statement that the will determined whether or not an individual achieved perfection: '*If you would be perfect* is addressed to him who could not be perfect, or rather, who was unwilling to be perfect and for this reason could not be.'[122] This shows how difficult he found it to abandon his former principles, which resurfaced at intervals even in a dialogue intended to refute the purported tenets of what its opponents called the heresy of 'Pelagianism'. In his *Dialogue against the Pelagians*, Jerome ended by asserting the positions he had set out to refute.

Pelagius

The idea that a Christian ought to give away all his property and embrace apostolic poverty was promoted by Jerome. It has been associated with Pelagius despite the fact that renunciation of property was not something that Pelagius advised. Pelagius argued that earthly rank had no value and redefined status as spiritual; spiritual riches were the only form of wealth worth having. But Pelagius left each reader to assess the implications of this argument for his own situation, and did not take the step of asserting that wealth had to be given away.[123]

---

[121] Jerome, *Dialogus aduersus pelagianos* 1.10 (ed. Moreschini, CCSL 80, p. 13), 'In hoc enim non quo fieri possit, dictum est, sed impossibile impossibili comparatum: quomodo enim camelus non potest intrare per foramen acus, ita et diues non ingredietur regna caelorum. Aut si potueris ostendere quod diues ingrediatur regna caelorum, sequetur ut et camelus intret per foramen acus. Nec mihi Abraham et ceteros, quos in ueteri Testamento diuites legimus, exempla proponas, qui diuites ingressi sunt regna caelorum, cum tamen ipsis diuitiis ad bona abutentes opera, diuites esse desierint, immo non sibi, sed aliis diuites fuerint et dispensatores magis Dei quam diuites appellandi sint. Sed nobis euangelica perfectio requirenda est, in qua praecipitur: *Si uis perfectus esse, uade, uende omnia tua quae habes et da pauperibus, et ueni, sequere me* [Matt. 19:21].'

[122] Jerome, *Dialogus aduersus pelagianos* 1.11 (ed. Moreschini, CCSL 80, p. 13), '*Si uis esse perfectus ei dicitur qui non potuit, immo noluit et idcirco non potuit.*'

[123] Pelagius, *Ad Demetriadem* 22 (ed. Greshake, pp. 136–8).

The accusation of arrogance

Jerome propounded as established doctrine the idea of degrees of chastity, with virginity the first in status and reward, continence the second in rank and marriage the third.[124] On the basis of this ranking system, in AD 384, Jerome encouraged Eustochium to see herself as better than married women: 'Learn in this respect a holy arrogance (*superbia sancta*), know that you are better than them.'[125]

Jerome used a misreading of *On the Christian Life* to criticise Pelagius for engendering arrogance by flattering his correspondents, but he himself had praised the virtue of members of his circle of correspondents, many of whom were actual or potential patrons, because this was the customary literary trope in addressing patrons.[126] Although he criticised Pelagius on the basis of a misreading that attributed arrogance to the widow's prayer in *On the Christian Life*, in around AD 387, Jerome wrote: 'If our conscience does not rebuke us and we have the confidence of piety before the Lord, we will pray with our spirit and we will pray with our mind'.[127] In the same passage of exegesis he asserted that control over his belief and moral purity lay with each individual.[128]

Selling asceticism on the basis of exclusivity

According to Jerome, what made Eustochium higher in status as a Christian was the closeness of her imitation of Christ.[129] He advertised the exclusive status this would confer: 'That is shared with many, but this is shared with only a few.'[130] Writing to Pammachius in AD 398, Jerome again advertised perfection on the basis

---

[124] Jerome, *Ep.* 22.15.2 (ed. Hilberg, CSEL 54, p. 163), Jerome referred to: 'The second rank of chastity'; 'Secundus pudicitiae gradus'; and: 'The lesser reward of continence'; 'Minor continentiae merces'.

[125] Jerome, *Ep.* 22.16.1 (ed. Hilberg, CSEL 54, p. 163), 'Disce in hac parte superbiam sanctam, scito te illis esse meliorem.'

[126] Jerome referred to the 'holiness' (*sanctitas*) of Paula, Paulina and Eustochium: Jerome, *Ep.* 66.2.2 (ed. Hilberg, CSEL 54, p. 649); he wrote of the 'miracle of Demetrias': Jerome, *Ep.* 130.2.2 (ed. Hilberg, CSEL 56, p. 176), 'What merit I consider her to possess, or rather the miracle of our virgin'; 'Quantum sit apud me meritum, immo miraculum uirginis nostrae'.

[127] Jerome, *In epistulam ad Titum* 1, on Titus 1:15 (ed. Bucchi, CCSL 77C, p. 36), 'Si conscientia nostra nos non reprehenderit et habuerimus fiduciam pietatis ad Dominum, orabimus spiritu, orabimus et mente'.

[128] Jerome, *In epistulam ad Titum* 1, on Titus 1:15 (ed. Bucchi, CCSL 77C, p. 36), Jerome interpreted the regulations of the law concerning food as a metaphor for belief in Christ and moral purity: 'And so, to eat either pure or impure things lies with us. For if we are pure, for us the created thing is pure. But if on the other hand we are impure and unbelieving, everything becomes common to us, either through the heresy inhabiting our hearts or through the consciousness of transgression'; 'In nobis itaque est uel munda comedere uel immunda. Si enim mundi sumus, munda nobis est creatura. Sin autem immundi et infideles, fiunt nobis uniuersa communia, siue per inhabitantem in cordibus nostris haeresim, siue per conscientiam delictorum.'

[129] Jerome, *Ep.* 22.17.3 (ed. Hilberg, CSEL 54, p. 165), 'You follow in Christ's tracks'; 'Tu Christi comitata uestigiis'.

[130] Jerome, *Ep.* 22.23.1 (ed. Hilberg, CSEL 54, p. 175), 'Illud commune cum pluribus, hoc cum paucis.'

of its exclusivity and the special status it conferred: 'The most distinguished privilege loses its prestige when lavished on a crowd'.[131] Pre-eminence was still the goal, just of a different type from secular social status.[132] In AD 413–14, Pelagius also used the argument from exclusivity to sell asceticism to Demetrias, following in the footsteps Jerome had laid down thirty years before.[133]

Section 2: Reference to Original Sin, Prevenient Grace, or Predestination, or the Characterisation of Man's Nature as Sinful and Man's Will as Weak and in Need of External Assistance in Order to Choose Virtue

Absence of the doctrine of original sin

In around AD 387, Jerome was clear that infants had no sin: 'Children indeed are unstained because they have committed no sin in their entire body.'[134] In Book 4 of his *Commentary on Ezekiel*, written after the winter of AD 411, he still held this view, since he stated in passing that the infant spirit did not have any sin: 'What we said about Jerusalem, we should take to refer to our spirit, which as long as it is established in infancy, lacks sin'.[135]

In his *Commentary on Isaiah* of AD 410, Jerome's interpretation of Isa. 43:27: *Your first father sinned* as referring to the fathers and ancestors of the Jewish people is significant. Writing in the persona of God, Jerome explained:

> And so that you may know that I show mercy to you not because of your merit but for the sake of my mercy, I will repeat from your fathers and your ancestors, so that you may understand that you have been born from sinners: *Your first father sinned* in the wilderness. That is to say, the whole people of Israel, or the author of your race, Abraham, is convicted of having sinned, at that time when the Lord promised the

---

[131] Jerome, *Ep.* 66.7.2 (ed. Hilberg, CSEL 54, p. 655), 'Quamuis clarus honor uilescit in turba'.

[132] Jerome, *Ep.* 66.8.3 (ed. Hilberg, CSEL 54, p. 657), 'The disciple of Christ ought to excel more than the disciple of worldy affairs'; 'Plus debet Christi discipulus praestare quam mundi'.

[133] Pelagius, *Ad Demetriadem* 1 (ed. Greshake, p. 56), 'She is not content with this common, mediocre kind of life, and finds herself to be easily capable of being cheapened by association with the majority. She seeks something new and unusual, she demands something special and singular'; 'Contenta non est communi hoc mediocrique genere uiuendi et quod facile ipsa multorum societate uilescat. Nouum aliquid et inusitatum requirit, praecipuum ac singulare quiddam flagitat'.

[134] Jerome, *Commentarii ad Ephesios* 1, on Eph. 1:4 (ed. Migne, PL 26.447C), 'Paruuli quippe immaculati sunt, quia integro corpore nullum fecere peccatum'.

[135] Jerome, *In Hiezechielem* 4, on Ezek. 16:8a (ed. Glorie, CCSL 75, p. 168), 'Quod de Hierusalem diximus, referamus ad animam nostram, quae quamdiu in infantia constituta est, peccato caret'.

promised land to his seed, and he answered: *How shall I know that I shall possess it?* [Gen. 15:8][136]

If Jerome had believed that humans inherited original sin from Adam, he would surely have explained Isa. 43:27 by reference to it. The fact that he did not read 'your first father' as a reference to Adam suggests that original sin was not a doctrine that Jerome taught. Instead, in interpreting this passage, he explained that God was saying: '*And I will not remember your sins* any longer, which I will forgive you in baptism if you are willing to believe.'[137] Thus Jerome interpreted this passage as demonstrating man's free will to goodness (here to believe in Christ), which he expressed through words he put into God's mouth: 'if you are willing to believe'. In Jerome's Christianity, God's forgiveness was causally dependent on autonomous human decisions.

When Jerome commented on Isa. 14:19–20, he explained the term 'evil seed' (used in reference to Babylon) in such a way as to exclude the possibility that human nature was inclined to sin: 'Not that the seed itself is bad in and of itself, for God made all things good, but from those who are evil by their own will, bad seed has arisen, which happens by their will, not by their nature.'[138] Likewise he explained that the phrase 'sons of perdition' in Isaiah did not refer to an evil nature, because Gospel parables like that of the lost sheep declared that sinners could repent: 'And so those who are now called sons of perdition, or of iniquity and wickedness, abandoned God through their own fault and from being the Lord's sons, began to be sons of perdition'.[139] Even at the end of his life when he adjusted his position in response to the doctrinal battle over the anthropology of Christianity, Jerome was aware of the implications of a negative anthropology and rejected them: 'But you will never hear from me that human nature is evil'.[140]

Absence of mention of God's grace as causing human virtue

In his *Letter to Eustochium* of AD 384, Jerome did not advise her to ask God for virtue or to attribute her virtue to God. Nowhere in his letter did he mention grace in

---

[136] Jerome, *In Esaiam* 12.16, on Isa. 43:25–8 (ed. Gryson et al., pp. 1345–6), 'Et ut scias me misereri tui non ob meritum tuum, sed propter meam clementiam, a patribus tuis repetam atque maioribus, ut intellegas te de peccatoribus esse generatum: *Pater tuus primus peccauit* in solitudine. Omnis uidelicet populus Israhel siue auctor generis tui Abraham peccasse conuincitur, quando Domino terram repromissionis semini illius pollicente, respondit: *In quo sciam quia possidebo eam?* [Gen.15:8].'

[137] Jerome, *In Esaiam* 12.16, on Isa. 43:25–8 (ed. Gryson et al., p. 1345), '*Et peccatorum tuorum ultra non recordabor*, quae tibi, si credere uolueris, in baptismate dimissurus sum.'

[138] Jerome, *In Esaiam* 6.30, on Isa. 14:20c–22 (ed. Gryson et al., p. 737), 'Non quo ipsum semen per se malum sit – Deus enim omnia fecit bona – sed ab his qui sua uoluntate sunt pessimi, semen ortum sit malum, quod uoluntate fit, non natura.'

[139] Jerome, *In Esaiam* 16.3, on Isa. 57.4b–5 (ed. Gryson et al., p. 1631), 'Ergo isti qui nunc appellantur filii perditionis siue iniquitatis ac sceleris, proprio uitio dereliquerunt Deum et de filiis Domini filii perditionis esse coeperunt'.

[140] Jerome, *Ep.* 133.9.2 (ed. Hilberg, CSEL 56, p. 254), 'A me numquam audies malam esse naturam'.

the process of achieving either righteousness or salvation. Likewise, twenty-eight years later there was no reference to grace anywhere in Jerome's *Letter to Rusticus* of AD 412, nor were there any of the verbal formulae that Augustine required concerning goodness being given to man, nor any mention of the action of the Holy Spirit in causing goodness within an individual.

The fact that Jerome never suggested that God's grace had a causal agency in human virtue is exemplified by a passage in his *Commentary on Ecclesiastes* of AD 388–9. As Evagrius of Antioch had done and as Pelagius was later to do, Jerome argued that humans tried to find excuses for their sin, and he advised Paula and Eustochium that they should remember that God was present at every action. This discussion of God's presence was the perfect occasion to mention His inspiration to virtue through His presence. But Jerome used the fact of God's presence to argue for human free will, and to make the point that what God was watching was their autonomous decisions:

> In the unreality, cloud, and darkness in which we live, we can find many things that seem plausible to us and seem to excuse our sins. For this reason I warn you that the one thing you must avoid is to suppose that God is not there; but instead you should fear Him and know that He is beside you, present at your every action; and that you are endowed with free will and are doing what you are doing of your own volition, not under compulsion.[141]

Jerome used the words 'free will' (*liberum arbitrium*) here, and nowhere mentioned grace or the inspiration of the Holy Spirit as playing a part in their decisions. Jerome's God was watching, but not intervening.

In his *Commentary on Matthew* of AD 398, Jerome explicitly rejected an interpretation of Matt. 19:11: *Not all receive these words, but those to whom it is given,* as meaning that God caused virtue:

> Let no one think that by these words he is introducing the doctrine of fate or chance and is saying that they are virgins to whom it is given by God, or whom some sort of chance led to this state. On the contrary, it is given to those who ask, who have willed it, who have expended effort to receive it. For to everyone who asks, it will be given; and the one who seeks will find; and to the one who knocks, it will be opened [cf. Matt. 7:8, Luke 11:10].[142]

---

[141] Jerome, *In Ecclesiasten*, on Eccles. 5:6 (ed. Adriaen, CCSL 72, p. 293), 'In somno uitae istius et imagine umbra nube qua uiuimus, multa possumus inuenire quae nobis uerisimilia uideantur et nostra excusare peccata. Propterea admoneo, ut id solum caueas, ne putes absentem Deum sed eum timeas, et scias cunctis operibus tuis adesse praesentem; teque liberi arbitrii conditum non cogi, sed uelle quod facias.'

[142] Jerome, *In euangelium Matthaei* 3, on Matt. 19:11 (ed. Bonnard, SC 259, p. 72), 'Nemo putet sub hoc uerbo uel fatum uel fortunam introduci, quod hi sint uirgines quibus a Deo datum sit aut quos quidam ad hoc casus adduxerit, sed his datum est qui petierunt, qui uoluerunt, qui ut acciperent laborauerunt. Omni enim petenti dabitur et quaerens inueniet et pulsanti aperietur [cf. Matt. 7:8, Luke 11:10].' Augustine's interpretation of Christianity took the opposite view on the causation of virginity; Augustine advised Demetrias' mother, Juliana, that God gave Demetrias this virtue: Augustine, *Ep.* 188.2.5–6 (ed. Goldbacher, CSEL 57, pp. 123–4).

In his *Letter to Demetrias*, Jerome wrote of the example Christ gave Christians in a way similar to Pelagius, suggesting that Christ's example contributed to the creation of virtue.[143]

Pelagius

In contrast to the absence of mention of grace in Jerome's letter of ascetic exhortation to Eustochium, thirty years later when Pelagius wrote to Demetrias, he explicitly noted the help of divine grace. He mentioned the assistance of grace six times, and in addition referred to the help of the Holy Spirit against the snares of the devil. In *On Virginity*, Pelagius mentioned the role of grace nine times and referred to those who had been chosen by the Holy Spirit to live more perfect lives. In *On the Divine Law*, Pelagius mentioned grace ten times and referred to Paul as inspired by the Holy Spirit.

Predestination

In his *Commentary on Ephesians* of around AD 387, Jerome discussed the issue of predestination and specifically interpreted it so as to keep human free will intact:

> Eph. 1:11: *Of Him who brings all things to pass according to the counsel of His will.* We must give attention to the fact also that προορισμός and πρόθεσις, that is predestination and purpose, are placed together, according to which God works all things according to the counsel of His will. It is not that all things that come about in this world are accomplished by the will and counsel of God, otherwise evil things too could be imputed to God, but that everything which He does He does by His counsel and will since, of course, they are also full of the reason and power of the maker .... *No one*, however, *can resist Him* [Ps. 75:8] but He does everything which He wills. Moreoever He wills that all those things which are full of reason and counsel: *Be saved and come to the knowledge of the truth* [1 Tim. 2:4]. But because no one is saved except by his own will, for we have free will, He wants us to want what is good, so that when we have willed it, He himself may also wish to fulfil His counsel in us.[144]

---

[143] Jerome, *Ep.* 130.10.2 (ed. Hilberg, CSEL 56, p. 190), 'The saviour of the human race, who has left to us the example of his virtues and his way of life'; 'Saluator generis humani, qui uirtutum et conuersationis suae nobis reliquit exemplum'.

[144] Jerome, *Commentarii ad Ephesios* 1, on Eph. 1:11 (ed. Migne, PL 26.455A–B), 'Considerandum quod et hic προορισμός et πρόθεσις, id est, *praedestinatio* et *propositum,* simul posita sint, iuxta quae operatur omnia Deus secundum consilium uoluntatis suae. Non quo omnia quae in mundo fiant, Dei uoluntate et consilio peragantur: alioquin et mala Deo poterunt imputari; sed quo uniuersa quae facit, consilio faciat et uoluntate, quod scilicet et ratione plena sint et potestate facientis. Nos homines pleraque uolumus facere consilio: sed nequaquam uoluntatem sequitur effectus. Illi autem nullus resistere potest, quin omnia quae uoluerit, faciat. Vult autem ea quaecumque sunt plena rationis atque consilii, *uult saluari omnes, et in agnitionem ueritatis uenire* [1 Tim. 2:4]. Sed, quia nullus absque propria uoluntate saluatur (liberi enim arbitrii sumus), uult nos bonum uelle, ut cum uoluerimus, uelit in nobis et ipse suum implere consilium.'

This passage suggests that Jerome was aware of difficulty surrounding the interpretation of God's omnipotence in relation to human free will. Already he saw the potential for contradiction between predestination, defined as the preordaining of decisions, and human free will; and the allied potential for contradiction between God's omnipotence and the principle of 1 Tim. 2:4: *God who wants all men to be saved*. But Jerome consistently explained predestination as foreknowledge:

> The fact that he has declared that we were chosen before the creation of the world: *That we should be holy and unstained before him*, that is, before God, pertains to God's foreknowledge, for whom: *All future things have already been done* [Eccles. 3:15] and: *All things are known before they come to pass* [Dan. 13:42].[145]

Jerome composed Book 1 of his *Commentary on Ezekiel* in AD 410, and in it he made a pointed denial of the interpretation of predestination that limited effective free will. Instead he propounded the explanation of predestination that it was divine foreknowledge of autonomous human decisions:

> But God says these things with a state of mind that is undecided, so that these words should demonstrate man's free will, lest foreknowledge of good or bad in the future might make unchangeable what God knows will happen: for it is not necessary that, because He knows what is going to happen, we must do what he knows in advance; but what we are going to do by our own will, He knows will happen, through His divine nature.[146]

In Jerome's account, God's 'state of mind' (*affectus*) was described as 'undecided' (*ambigens*) and waiting on man's autonomous freely willed choices. It is noticeable that in this passage he did not use the word 'predestination' and opted instead for 'foreknowledge'.

Section 3: Use of the Word 'Grace' (*Gratia*)

Grace in Jerome

An exhaustive survey of Jerome's use of the word 'grace' is beyond the scope of this book, but the following uses are illustrative of the understanding of divine grace articulated by him in his writings.

---

[145] Jerome, *Commentarii ad Ephesios* 1, on Eph. 1:4 (ed. Migne, PL 26.446C), 'Quod autem electos nos: *Vt essemus sancti et immaculati coram ipso*, hoc est, Deo, ante fabricam mundi testatus est, ad praescientiam Dei pertinet, cui: *Omnia futura iam facta sunt* [Eccles. 3:15], et: *Antequam fiant uniuersa sunt nota* [Dan. 13:42].'

[146] Jerome, *In Hiezechielem* 1, on Ezek. 2:4–5 (ed. Glorie, CCSL 75, p. 28), 'Loquitur autem haec Deus ambigentis affectu, ut liberum hominis monstrent arbitrium, ne praescientia futurorum mali uel boni immutabile faciat quod Deus futurum nouerit: non enim quia ille uentura cognoscit, necesse est nos facere quod ille praesciuit, sed quod nos propria sumus uoluntate facturi, ille nouit futurum quasi Deus.'

Jerome understood the word *gratia* to encompass several different gifts given by God to humanity. In his *Commentary on Ephesians*, he explained Paul's opening phrase: '*Grace to you and peace from God our Father.* The grace of the Father would consist in the fact that He considered it worthy to send the Son for our salvation'.[147] Here, therefore, Jerome explained that this use of the word 'grace' referred to Christ's incarnation. This was the aspect of grace to which Jerome referred most often. He also referred to the grace of baptism.[148] In addition, he referred to the grace of the Holy Spirit: 'What flesh and blood was not able to reveal the grace of the Holy Spirit has revealed .... Here too by another interpretation it is demonstrated that Christ was revealed to him as the Son of God, not through the teaching of the Pharisees, but by the grace of God.'[149] Jerome also referred to the grace of the Gospel; and to the grace of the laying on of hands by a priest.[150]

For Jerome it was the grace of Christ's incarnation and cleansing of man's sins that was unmerited, and he paired this aspect of grace with human dual free will. Thus in his *Commentary on Isaiah*, Jerome wrote that Isaiah's lips were cleansed by 'the grace of the Lord', but Isaiah's will was part of the process by which virtue came to exist in him:

> But the Lord does not say whom he is instructing to go, but offers the hearers a choice, so that the will may obtain a reward. And it was not rashly and by the arrogance of his own conscience that the prophet promises that he will go, but with confidence, since his lips have been purged, his iniquity has been removed, and his sin has been cleansed .... Isaiah offers himself for ministry not on the basis of his own merit, but by the grace of the Lord by which he was purged.[151]

In this passage, grace was the cleansing of sin, and the purging of Isaiah's lips was analogous to baptism after Christ's advent. The unearned aspect of grace was the gift of Christ's advent which brought salvation to man, and the individual's will was the determinant of whether or not he received this salvation offered to all. Jerome then asserted dual free will as the explanation why some were not in

---

[147] Jerome, *Commentarii ad Ephesios*, on Eph. 1:1 (ed. Migne, PL 26.444C), 'Gratia Patris in eo sit, quod Filium pro salute nostra dignatus est mittere'.

[148] Jerome, *Ep.* 69.6.9 (ed. Hilberg, CSEL 54, p. 692), 'Micah prophesied about the grace of baptism'; 'Micheas de gratia baptismi uaticinatur'.

[149] Jerome, *In euangelium Matthaei* 3, on Matt. 16:17 (ed. Bonnard, SC 259, pp. 14–16), 'Quod caro et sanguis reuelare non potuit, Spiritus Sancti gratia reuelatum est .... Hic quoque sub alio sensu demonstretur quod ei non per doctrinam Pharisaeorum sed per Dei gratiam Christus Dei filius reuelatus sit.'

[150] Jerome, *In euangelium Matthaei* 3, on Matt. 20:1–2 (ed. Bonnard, SC 259, p. 88), 'The grace ... of the Gospel'; 'Euangelii ... gratia.' Jerome, *Ep.* 53.3.3 (ed. Hilberg, CSEL 54, p. 447), 'So that he should not neglect the grace that was given to him in the laying-on of hands of the presbyter'; 'Ne neglegat gratiam, quae data est ei per inpositionem manus presbyterii.'

[151] Jerome, *In Esaiam* 3.8, on Isa. 6:8 (ed. Gryson et al., pp. 321–2), 'Propterea autem non dicit Dominus quem ire praecipiat, sed proponit audientibus optionem, ut uoluntas praemium consequatur. Et propheta non temeritate et arrogantia propriae conscientiae se ire promittit, sed fiducia, quoniam purgata sunt labia eius et ablata iniquitas mundatumque peccatum .... Esaias non sui merito, sed Domini gratia qua purgatus est, offert se ad ministerium'.

fact saved.[152] Jerome repeatedly characterised grace as Christ's incarnation and teaching, and paired it with effective human free will:

> Those who are willing to believe shall be redeemed by no means with silver and *money*, but with the precious blood of Christ [cf. 1 Pet. 1:18–19], so that they may hear through the apostles: *Grace to you and peace* [Eph. 1:12]. For we have been reconciled to God not because of our merits, but because of the grace and faith of Christ [cf. 2 Cor. 5:18–20].[153]

Confirmation that Jerome did not interpret this grace as prevenient grace comes in the sentences that follow this passage, in which he first asserted that the human body is not damned by nature, and then stated that humans earned salvation through merit.[154]

Jerome regularly referred to the grace of Christ's advent as unmerited.[155] When he contrasted grace with works, it was always this generalised grace that could not be merited.[156] Specific gifts of grace, by contrast, were given to the virtuous and to those who were already believers. In his *Commentary on Titus*, written in around AD 387, Jerome discussed the use of the word 'grace' at Titus 2:11–14:

> *For the grace of God our Saviour has dawned upon all men.* For there is no differ-ence between free and slave, Greek and barbarian, circumcised and uncircumcised, woman and man, but we are all one in Christ. We are all called to the kingdom of God, we are all to be reconciled to our Father after stumbling, not through our merits but through the grace of the Saviour. This is either because Christ himself is the grace, living and subsisting from God the Father, or because this is the grace of Christ, God and Saviour; and we are saved not by our merit according to what

---

[152] See n. 52.

[153] Jerome, *In Esaiam* 14.16, on Isa. 52:2–3 (ed. Gryson et al., pp. 1494–5), 'Redimentur autem qui uoluerint credere, nequaquam argento et *pecunia*, sed pretioso Christi sanguine, ut audiant per apos-tolos: *Gratia uobis et pax*. Non enim ob merita, sed ob gratiam et fidem Christi Deo reconciliati sumus.'

[154] Jerome, *In Esaiam* 14.16, on Isa. 52:2–3 (ed. Gryson et al., pp. 1495–6), 'Not that the flesh, whose creator is God, is damned by nature, and in which many have pleased God and reign with Christ, but that the works of the flesh should be rejected .... Instead may we merit to hear with the bride: *How beautiful are your cheeks, as a turtledove's* [S. of S. 1:9]'; 'Non quo carnis natura damnetur, cuius conditor Deus est, et in qua plurimi placuerunt Deo regnantque cum Christo, sed quo opera carnis repudientur .... Sed cum sponsa mereamur audire: *Quam pulchrae sunt genae tuae sicut turturis* [S. of S. 1:9]'.

[155] Jerome, *In Esaiam* 18.7, on Isa. 65:8 (ed. Gryson et al., pp. 1838–9), 'It should be known that in Hebrew, for heat, *thoda* is written, which means *grace*, which of course refers to the fact that Israel is saved by the grace of God, and not by the merit of their own works'; 'Et tamen sciendum in hebraico pro calore scriptum esse THODA, quod interpretatur "gratia", quod scilicet gratia Dei, et non merito operum suorum, saluatus sit Israhel.' Christ's advent unmerited: 16.31, on Isa. 59:15c–18 (ed. Gryson et al., p. 1709), 'So that those who have willed to be converted from error are saved not by their own merit, but by the mercy of God'; 'Vt qui uoluerint ab errore conuerti, non suo merito, sed Dei clementia conseruentur.'

[156] Jerome, *Commentarii ad Ephesios* 1, on Eph. 2:5 (ed. Migne, PL 26.468B), '*You have been saved by grace.* If the sufferings of this time are not worthy of the future glory which will be revealed in us [cf. Rom. 8:18], we have been saved by grace rather than by work. For we can give nothing back to the Lord for all the things which he has given us'; '*Gratia saluati estis.* Si non sunt dignae passiones huius temporis ad futuram gloriam quae reuelabitur in nobis [cf. Rom. 8:18], gratia magis sumus quam opere saluati. Nihil enim possumus Domino retribuere pro omnibus quae retribuit nobis.'

is said in another place: *You will save them for nothing* [Ps. 56:7]. This grace, then: *Has dawned on all men to teach us to renounce impiety and worldly desires, to live chastely and justly and piously in this world.*[157]

Jerome here asserted once again the universality of God's salvific will, and characterised grace as universal and as referring to Christ's incarnation and teaching.

In his *Letter to Hedibia* of AD 406–7, he referred to the 'different graces of the Holy Spirit', and then glossed grace as a special ability given to the apostles through the Holy Spirit.[158] This use of the word 'grace' recalls its meaning when it described the special powers granted to Antony. Just as in the *Life of Antony*, in this usage by Jerome, grace was a special ability conferred on a virtuous person. This was also his view in his *Commentary on Ephesians*, in which he stated that:

---

[157] Jerome, *In epistolam ad Titum* 2, on Titus 2:11–14 (ed. Bucchi, CCSL 77C, pp. 52–3), '*Illuxit enim gratia Dei Saluatoris omnibus hominibus*. Non est enim aliqua differentia liberi et serui, Graeci et Barbari, circumcisi et habentis praeputium, mulieris et uiri, sed cuncti in Christo unum sumus, uniuersi ad Dei regnum uocamur, omnes post offensam Patri nostro reconciliandi sumus non per merita nostra, sed per gratiam Saluatoris. Vel quod Dei Patris uiuens et subsistens gratia ipse sit Christus, uel quod Christi Dei Saluatoris haec sit gratia, et non nostro merito saluati sumus, secundum illud quod in alio loco dicitur: *Pro nihilo saluabis eos* [Ps. 56:7]. Quae *gratia omnibus hominibus* ideo *illuxit*, ut *erudiret nos, abnegantes impietatem et saecularia desideria, pudice et iuste et pie uiuere in hoc saeculo.*'

[158] Jerome, *Ep.* 120.9.1–7 (ed. Hilberg CSEL 55, pp. 492–5), '*How does the Saviour according to John breathe the Holy Spirit into his apostles and according to Luke say that he will send it to them after his ascension?* The solution to this question is very easy, if we are acquainted with the diverse graces of the Holy Spirit according to the teaching of the apostle Paul. For he writes in the first letter to the Corinthians: *Now there are varieties of gifts but the same Spirit; and there are varieties of ministries, but the same Lord; and there are varieties of activities, but the same God activates all of them in everyone. To each is given the manifestation of the Spirit as it is useful* [1 Cor. 12:4–7] .... And so on the first day of his resurrection they received the grace of the Holy Spirit by which they might dismiss sins and baptise and make sons of God and bestow the spirit of adoption on believers .... But on the day of Pentecost more was promised to them, that they would be baptised in the Holy Spirit and would be clothed in the power by which they would preach the Gospel of Christ to all the peoples .... So that they would possess the ability to work with powers and the grace of healing and they would receive the different languages so that they would preach to many peoples .... For he who was going to preach to many peoples had received the grace of many languages .... But the word *effusio* (*pouring forth*) signifies the bestowing of grace and means the very thing that the Lord promised: *But you will be baptised with the Holy Spirit not many days from now* [Acts 1:5]'; '*Quomodo Saluator secundum Iohannem insufflat Spiritum Sanctum apostolis et secundum Lucam post ascensionem missurum esse se dicit?* Huius quaestionis perfacilis solutio est, si docente apostolo Paulo Spiritus Sancti diuersas gratias nouerimus. Scribit enim in prima ad Corinthios: *Diuisiones donorum sunt, idem uero Spiritus; et diuisiones ministeriorum, idem autem Dominus; et diuisiones operationum et idem Deus, qui operatur omnia in omnibus. Vnicuique autem datur manifestatio Spiritus ad id quod expedit* [1 Cor. 12:4–7] .... Primo igitur die resurrectionis eius acceperunt Spiritus Sancti gratiam, qua peccata dimitterent et baptizarent et filios Dei facerent, et spiritum adoptionis credentibus largirentur .... Die autem Pentecostes eis amplius repromissum est, ut baptizarentur Spiritu Sancto et induerentur uirtutem, qua Christi euangelium cunctis gentibus praedicarent ... ut haberent operationem uirtutum et gratiam sanitatum et praedicationi multis gentibus acciperent genera linguarum .... Qui enim multis gentibus adnuntiaturus erat, multarum linguarum acceperat gratiam .... Verbum autem effusionis significat gratiae largitatem et id ipsum sonat, quod Dominus repromisit: *Vos autem baptizabimini Spiritu Sancto non post multos hos dies* [Acts 1:5].'

'Grace is given to believers "according to measure"', and he explained this citation as referring to special gifts.[159]

In his *Commentary on Joel* of AD 406, Jerome described the different types of
grace conferred by the Holy Spirit, and in this usage the term 'grace' meant the gift
of a special power. He also related the receiving of grace to merit, and referred to
the grace of faith and of salvation:

> But nor will everyone who receives the Holy Spirit at once possess also spiritual
> grace, but through the pouring out of the Holy Spirit, each will attain to different
> graces. Some receive prophecy, as sons and daughters who are of greater merit;
> others receive dreams, as old men already of advanced age; others receive visions,
> as young men who have conquered evil; but slaves and serving girls, who already
> have the spirit of fear and not the spirit of love because: *Perfect love casts out fear*
> [1 John 4:18], will not possess prophecy, or dreams, or visions, but content through
> the pouring forth of the Holy Spirit, they will possess only the grace of faith and the
> grace of salvation.[160]

Here, 'grace' for Jerome equated to 'gift', and denoted the many varied gifts given
by God.

In his *Letter* 122 to Rusticus of around AD 407, Jerome interpreted Ps. 30:7:
*By your favour, O Lord, you had established me as a strong mountain; you hid
your face and I was dismayed*, as showing how grace was conferred after virtue
had been chosen by an individual: '"When I forsook the foulness of my faults for
the beauty of virtue, God strengthened my weakness with his grace"'.[161] In this
explanation, Jerome made a point of asserting that an individual's decision to be

---

[159] Jerome, *Commentarii ad Ephesios* 2, on Eph. 4:8 (ed. Migne, PL 26.497D–498A), 'Because he
had said above: *But to each of us grace has been given according to the measure of the gift of Christ*,
so that he might confirm that these very gifts, which he enumerates a little later when he says: *And he
gave some as apostles, and some as prophets, others as evangelists, others as pastors and teachers*
etc., have been given by the Saviour, by adding the testimony of the sixty-seventh Psalm, so that we
might know that these are the spoils distributed to mankind which Christ merited as victor, because:
Ascending on high he led captivity captive'; 'Quia supra dixerat: *Vnicuique autem nostrum data est
gratia secundum mensuram donationis Christi*, ut confirmaret haec ipsa dona, quae post paululum
quoque enumerat, dicens: *Et ipse dedit quosdam quidem apostolos, quosdam autem prophetas, alios
euangelistas, alios pastores et magistros*, et reliqua, a Saluatore esse donata, testimonium de sexa-
gesimo septimo psalmo assumpsit, ut sciamus illas esse manubias hominibus distributas, quas Christus
uictor emeruit: *Ascendens quippe in altum, captiuam duxit captiuitatem*'; on Eph. 1:17 (ed. Migne, PL
26.458D), Jerome also stated: '[God] gives the spirit of wisdom and of revelation to those who believe
in his Son, so that they become wise'; '[Deus] dat credentibus in Filium suum spiritum sapientiae et
reuelationis, ut sapientes fiant'.
[160] Jerome, *In Ioelem* 2, on Joel 2:28–32 (ed. Adriaen, CCSL 76, pp. 194–5), 'Neque uero omnis qui
acceperit Spiritum Sanctum, statim habebit et gratiam spiritalem, sed per effusionem Spiritus Sancti
diuersas gratias consequetur. Alii prophetiam, ut filii et filiae qui maioris sunt meriti; alii somnia, ut
senes iam prouectioris aetatis; alii uisiones, ut iuuenes qui uicerunt malignum; serui uero et ancillae qui
adhuc spiritum timoris habent, et non dilectionis, quia: *Perfecta dilectio foras mittit timorem* [1 John
4:18], non habebunt prophetiam, non somnia, non uisiones, sed Spiritus Sancti effusione contenti, fidei
tantum et salutis gratiam possidebunt.'
[161] Jerome, *Ep.* 122.1.10 (ed. Hilberg, CSEL 56, p. 59), '"Postquam enim foeditatem delictorum
meorum uirtutum decore mutaui, infirmitatem meam tua gratia roborasti"'.

just was chronologically prior to, and was followed by, God's helping him in that choice through the gift of his grace. Jerome made this assertion in the context of stressing God's universal salvific will, which meant that no one should ever despair, and denying that any individual's fate was preordained:

> Lest the mind should despair through disbelief in the promise of good things, and the soul once destined (*destinatus*) for perdition should fail to apply a cure to its wound because it thinks it cannot be cured.[162]

In his *Letter to Hedibia*, Jerome again characterised the process of coming to believe as internal to the individual: 'The aroma of the knowledge of God is being spread among the Gentiles, and the silent thought comes into their minds that if the Gospel were not true, no one would defend it with his blood.'[163] Jerome did not suggest that grace caused belief; he stated explicitly that God saved those who were willing to believe in him through the humility and incarnation of Christ, and made no mention of prevenient grace.[164] In the same letter he also described how the 'graces' of the Holy Spirit were put to good or bad use by man, when he discussed what 'spirit' (*spiritus*) meant at 1 Thess. 5:23: *May your spirit and soul and body be kept sound and blameless at the coming of our Lord Jesus Christ*:

> But I think (as I said earlier) that *spirit* in the present passage, which is preserved intact with the soul and the body, is not the substance of the Holy Spirit, which is imperishable, but is His graces and gifts that we receive, which are either kindled or extinguished in us, according to our virtue or our vice.[165]

It was fundamental to Augustine's account of prevenient grace that it could not be resisted, because it was an expression of God's omnipotence. Jerome, however, wrote of plural 'graces', paired them with 'gifts' and held that man controlled whether he accepted or rejected these graces. Likewise in his *Commentary on Ephesians*, commenting on Paul's reference to: *The wealth of his grace which has abounded in us* [Eph. 1:7–8], Jerome asserted that God's grace was accepted by the virtuous and rejected by others.[166]

---

[162] Jerome, *Ep.* 122.1.9 (ed. Hilberg, CSEL 56, p. 59), 'Ne mens incredula bonorum repromissione desperet et semel perditioni animus destinatus non adhibeat uulneri curationem, quod nequaquam aestimat posse curari.'

[163] Jerome, *Ep.* 120.11.9 (ed. Hilberg, CSEL 55, p. 509), 'Odor notitiae Dei disseminatur in gentes, et subit tacita cogitatio quod nisi uerum esset Euangelium, numquam sanguine defenderetur.'

[164] Jerome, *Ep.* 120.10.14 (ed. Hilberg, CSEL 55, p. 505), 'So that by means of the humility and incarnation of Christ, he would save those who were willing to believe in him'; 'Vt humilitate et incarnatione Christi eos saluos faceret, qui in eum credere uoluissent.'

[165] Jerome, *Ep.* 120.12.11 (ed. Hilberg, CSEL 55, pp. 514–15), 'Nos autem in praesenti loco, ut supra diximus, spiritum, qui cum anima et corpore integer conseruatur, non substantiam Spiritus Sancti, quae non potest interire, sed gratias eius donationesque accipimus, quae nostra uel uirtute uel uitio et accenduntur et extinguntur in nobis.'

[166] Jerome, *Commentarii ad Ephesios* 1, on Eph. 1:7–8 (ed. Migne, PL 26.452A), 'He does not make this wealth of graces in himself to be vain, who as far as human frailty is able, labours, strives and vigorously exerts himself, and says with the Apostle: *His grace was not in vain in me* [1 Cor. 15:10]. But in that person who is unmindful of the magnitude of the favour, the rich grace of God will degenerate,

From this brief survey of Jerome's use of the word 'grace', it is clear that what he did not refer to was 'prevenient grace' (*gratia praeueniens*), as Augustine characterised it.

Section 4: Supposed Hallmark Ideas Associated with 'Pelagianism' by Scholars

Stress on the need to obey God's commands as a hallmark of 'Pelagianism'

Stress on the need to obey God's commands has been seen as a hallmark of 'Pelagianism', but it was a core element of Jerome's paraenesis; he urged a demanding standard of imitation of Christ as much as any ascetic propagandist.[167] Following the Lord was: 'A thing proper to apostles and believers.'[168] Jerome equated being a Christian with keeping Christ's commandments.[169] The smallest deviation from God's commands rendered obedience worthless.[170] For example, the prodigal son's older brother was not righteous because he did not keep God's commandments.[171]

The distinction between those who are true Christians and those who are Christians in name only

The distinction between real Christian virtue and pretence of it has been regarded as one of the hallmarks of Pelagius' teaching, and was seen as such by Augustine, who made ironic reference to it, but it was equally a feature of Jerome's writings.[172]

---

and the opulent largesse will be reduced to poverty'; 'Has diuitias gratiarum ille in se non facit uacuas, qui quantum ualet humana fragilitas, nititur, laborat, atque contendit, et cum Apostolo loquitur: *Gratia eius in me non fuit uacua* [1 Cor. 15:10]. Qui uero beneficii magnitudinem non recordans, ad deteriora delabitur, in isto diues gratia Dei, et opulenta largitio paupertate tenuatur.'

[167] See n. 102.

[168] Jerome, *In euangelium Matthaei* 3, on Matt. 19:28 (ed. Bonnard, SC 259, p. 82), '[Dixit] *Qui secuti estis me*, quod proprie apostolorum est atque credentium.'

[169] Jerome, *Ep.* 7.6.2 (ed. Hilberg, CSEL 54, p. 30), 'You confess Christ every day, while you keep his commandments'; 'Cotidie Christum confiteamini, dum eius praecepta seruatis'.

[170] Jerome, *In euangelium Matthaei* 1, on Matt. 5:19 (ed. Bonnard, SC 242, p. 112), concerning the Pharisees: 'Their teaching among the people is of no benefit to them if they destroy even a little bit from what was commanded in the law .... Nor is it advantageous to teach a righteousness that the smallest fault destroys'; 'Non eis prosit doctrina in populis, si uel parum quod in lege praeceptum est destruant .... Nec prosit docere iustitiam quam minima culpa destruit'.

[171] Jerome, *Ep.* 21.34.7 (ed. Hilberg, CSEL 54, p. 134), 'He did not walk according to the judgements of God and did not carry out His commands'; 'In Dei iudiciis non ambulauit et eius mandata non fecit.'

[172] Augustine, *De gratia Christi et de peccato originali* 1.10.11 (ed. Urba and Zycha, CSEL 42,

The distinction between being a Christian in fact and not just in name only was a rhetorical trope in his literary output.[173] Concerning the gospel of Matthew, he wrote: 'It is shown that the one who has the name of believer but does the works of unbelievers is more detestable than those who are openly pagan'.[174] In his advice to Rusticus, Jerome repeatedly stressed the distinction between real asceticism and the mere pretence of it, and he urged him to avoid being an ascetic 'in name only' (*solo nomine*):

> I emphasise these points so that I may free my young man from the itching of tongue and ears, so that I may present him reborn in Christ *without spot or wrinkle* [cf. Eph. 5:27] like a chaste virgin, holy as much in mind as in body, so that he should not glory in possession of the name only.[175]

This was a theme in Jerome's letter.[176] If stressing this distinction was a hallmark of 'Pelagianism', then Jerome should be classified as 'Pelagian'. In reality, however, the distinction between the true Christian and someone Christian in name only is not diagnostic of Pelagius' writings because it was a rhetorical trope of ascetic literature. Jerome used it regularly: 'But now under the title of religion people occupy themselves with unjust profits, and the good reputation of the name Christian more often carries out fraud than suffers it.'[177] Commenting on Titus 1:16: *They confess to know God, but by their deeds they deny him*, Jerome made rhetorical play with the disparity between professed faith and the reality of

---

p. 135), 'Pelagius ought to confess this grace if he wants not just to be called a Christian but truly to be a Christian'; 'Hanc debet Pelagius gratiam confiteri, si uult non solum uocari, uerum etiam esse christianus.'

[173] For example, he used it in his discussion of the parable of the guest at a wedding feast not clothed in wedding garments, see n. 72; see also Jerome, *In euangelium Matthaei* 1, on Matt. 5:19 (ed. Bonnard, SC 242, p. 112), 'And blessedness is perfected which realises in actions what it teaches in words'; 'Beatitudoque perfecta sit quae sermone docueris opere complere.'

[174] Jerome, *In euangelium Matthaei* 3, on Matt. 18:15–17 (ed. Bonnard, SC 259, p. 58), 'Ostenditur maioris esse detestationis qui sub nomine fidelis agat opera infidelium quam hi qui aperte gentiles sunt.'

[175] Jerome, *Ep.* 125.20.1 (ed. Hilberg, CSEL 56, pp. 140–1), 'Haec expressius loquor, ut adulescentem meum et linguae et aurium prurigine liberem, ut renatum in Christo *sine ruga et macula* [cf. Eph. 5:27] quasi pudicam uirginem exhibeam sanctamque tam mente quam corpore, ne solo nomine glorietur'.

[176] Jerome, *Ep.* 125.7.1 (ed. Hilberg, CSEL 56, p. 124), 'But if for your part you desire to be a monk and not just seem one'; 'Tu uero, si monachus esse uis, non uideri'; 125.16.1 (ed. Hilberg, CSEL 56, pp. 134–5), 'I have seen some who, after renouncing the world, while they changed their clothes and made a verbal profession, in fact changed nothing of their former way of life'; 'Vidi ego quosdam, qui, postquam renuntiauere saeculo, uestimentis dumtaxat et uocis professione, non rebus, nihil de pristina conuersatione mutarunt.' Jerome made the same point to Eustochium: Jerome, *Ep.* 22.15.1 (ed. Hilberg, CSEL 54, p. 162), 'And so when these have been cast out and banished, who do not want to be virgins, but want to seem to be virgins'; 'Explosis igitur et exterminatis his, quae nolunt esse uirgines, sed uideri'.

[177] Jerome, *Ep.* 125.16.4 (ed. Hilberg, CSEL 56, p. 136), 'Nunc autem sub religionis titulo exercentur iniusta conpendia et honor nominis Christiani fraudem magis facit quam patitur.' Other examples are *Commentarii ad Ephesios* 1, on Eph. 1:6 (ed. Migne, PL 26.450B), 'Everyone loves Christ, in so far as he signifies diverse virtues, although many cannot prove by their deeds that they love him'; 'Christum, secundum id quod diuersas uirtutes sonat, omnes diligunt, licet plures factis non possint probare quod diligunt'; *Ep.* 45.4.2 (ed. Hilberg, CSEL 54, p. 326); *Ep.* 13.3 (ed. Hilberg, CSEL 54, p. 43).

behaviour, citing Isa. 29:31: *This people honours me with their lips, but their heart is far from me*, and he developed the idea to comment: 'But see the Apostle asserts that God is denied when all actions are done that are evil.'[178] The disparity was a topos of Christian paraenesis because it was a biblical topos. Since it was also a useful rhetorical contrast between words and deeds, it featured in much ascetic advice. As Pelagius did later, Jerome taught that Christian faith had to mark a profound change in behaviour: 'He who ... wants to follow the Saviour, who says: *Whoever wants to come after me, let him deny himself* [Matt. 16:24, Luke 9:23], having stripped off the old man with his works, and having put on the new, will follow his God.'[179]

Section 5: The Overall Message Conveyed by Jerome

A hymn to individual effort

Just as in Athanasius' programme, and Evagrius of Antioch's development of it, individual initiative and effort were the touchstones of the Christianity that Jerome propounded.[180] Even when trying to refute Pelagius, Jerome retained the principle of 'effort' (*labor*).[181]

The function of the co-operative model in the ascetic programme

Jerome canvassed the same co-operative, or synergistic, relationship between man and God that his friend Evagrius of Antioch had promoted, similarly arguing that a Christian could become God's friend rather than his slave.[182] As already noted,

---

[178] Jerome, *In epistulam ad Titum* 1, on Titus 1:16 (ed. Bucchi, CCSL 77C, p. 37), 'Sed ecce Apostolus omnibus quae peruersa sunt factis Deum adserit denegari.'

[179] Jerome, *In epistulam ad Titum* 1, on Titus 1:16 (ed. Bucchi, CCSL 77C, p. 37), 'Qui ... sequi uoluerit Saluatorem loquentem: *Quicumque uult uenire post me, abneget seipsum* [Matt. 16:24, Luke 9:23], exutus ueterem hominem cum operibus eius et indutus nouum, sequetur Deum suum.' See also n. 72 for another reference to the 'new man', in Jerome's exegesis on the parable of the wedding guest not wearing wedding clothes.

[180] Jerome eulogised Paula for her efforts: Jerome, *Ep.* 45.3.2 (ed. Hilberg, CSEL 54, p. 325). Jerome likewise extolled his own labour: *Ep.* 22.7 (ed. Hilberg, CSEL 54, pp. 152–4) and that of the coenobitic monks he described to Eustochium: *Ep.* 22.35 (ed. Hilberg, CSEL 54, pp. 197–200).

[181] Jerome, *Dialogus aduersus pelagianos* 3.6 (ed. Moreschini, CCSL 80, p. 104), Atticus (Jerome) '[God crowns] our will which offered all it could, our effort which strove so that it might achieve it, and our humility, which always looked to God's help'; '[Deus coronat] uoluntatem nostram, quae obtulit omne quod potuit, et laborem, quo contendit ut faceret, et humilitatem, quae semper respexit ad auxilium Dei.'

[182] Jerome, *In epistulam ad Galatas* 3, on Gal. 5:13b–14 (ed. Raspanti, CCSL 77A, p. 175), 'By no means is he called a slave, but instead a friend'; 'Nequaquam seruus, sed amicus uocatur'.

in his *Commentary on Matthew*, he declared that God and man worked together.[183] This is also clear in his *Commentary on Ecclesiastes*, where he argued that in facing temptation to sin it was better for a Christian to have Christ as his co-worker and thus to be in a partnership working together to defeat the devil:

> Obviously the reward of fellowship is demonstrated at once in the actual value of companionship. For if one falls, Christ will lift his partner .... And if the devil, stronger in overcoming resistance, stands against a man, the man will stand and Christ too will stand up for his man, for his companion; not because the power of Christ alone is weak against the devil, but because man's will is left free, and when we strive, Christ himself is stronger in waging war.[184]

In this passage, Jerome asserted human 'free will' (*liberum arbitrium*), stressed the need for effort (using a compound of a verb he favoured: 'to strive', *niti*), and presented a picture of man and Christ co-operating in a confident account of the relationship between man and God. Once again the language of commercial investment was used ('payment', *merces*). Jerome's characterisation of man's relationship to Christ with words such as *contubernium* ('fellowship', often used of soldiers in the sense of 'occupying a tent together'), *particeps* ('comrade', 'sharer', 'partner'), *homo suus* ('his man') and *sodalis* ('comrade', 'colleague') deliberately creates a military metaphor of fellow soldiers and partnership. This was the same account of Christianity as Athanasius and Evagrius of Antioch had propounded. At times, Jerome proposed a relationship of friendship between man and God, in which man could be a confident partner, recalling Evagrius' characterisation of man's relationship with God.[185] The function of this synergistic model was the same for Jerome as it had been for Athanasius and Evagrius, since Jerome's ascetic Christianity was modelled on their programme.

The ambition of asceticism

The ambition of the ascetic project that Jerome canvassed picked up where Evagrius left off, in that all Christians were included in the remit of the programme. In practice, since patrons able to provide either financial resources or career-building

---

[183] See n. 28.

[184] Jerome, *In Ecclesiasten*, on Eccles. 4:9–12 (ed. Adriaen, CCSL 72, p. 287), 'Merces quippe contubernii statim in ipsa societatis utilitate monstratur. Si enim ceciderit unus, erigit Christus participem suum .... Et si aduersum hominem robustior in expugnando diabolus astiterit, stabit homo, stabit et Christus pro homine suo, pro sodali suo. Non quod solius Christi aduersus diabolum uirtus infirma sit, sed quod liberum homini relinquatur arbitrium et adnitentibus nobis, ipse in proeliando fortior fiat.'

[185] Jerome, *In Esaiam* 12.21, on Isa. 45:1–7 (ed. Gryson et al., p. 1364), Cyrus saw the Jews as: 'God's close friends, as it were'; 'Iudeos quasi Dei familiares'; 15.6, on Isa. 54:9–10 (ed. Gryson et al., p. 1548), 'God's friendship'; 'Amicitia Dei'; Jerome, *In euangelium Matthaei* 3, on Matt. 19:27 (ed. Bonnard, SC 259, p. 80), 'This is great confidence .... [Peter] speaks confidently'; 'Grandis fiducia .... Loquitur confidenter'.

influence were only to be found among the social elite, Jerome's letters of advice and interpretation of Scripture were often addressed to Christians of patrician rank.

Section 6: The Shift in Jerome's Position

Jerome wrote two works intended to refute Pelagius: his *Letter* 133 *To Ctesiphon* of AD 414, and his *Dialogue against the Pelagians* of AD 415. His central concern lay in not being accused of heresy himself. His career was driven by the need to construct authority through a claim to expertise in asceticism and Scripture. A label of heresy was calamitous to any claim to authority. The problem Jerome faced after the arrival with him in Palestine of Orosius in AD 415, bringing letters and a dossier from Augustine, was that there was no difference between the position he had himself consistently articulated for the previous thirty years since around AD 384 and what Pelagius wrote from around AD 404 onwards.[186] Jerome therefore had to manufacture criticism of Pelagius. He did not do this by asserting the doctrines that were at issue—that is original sin, prevenient grace, and predestination interpreted as preordainment. Instead, in his *Letter to Ctesiphon* and his *Dialogue against the Pelagians*, Jerome attacked Pelagius for two things that Pelagius did not assert: first, that Pelagius taught that sinlessness was possible in this life; and, second, that Pelagius denied God's grace. These were both unwarranted inferences read from Pelagius' ascetic paraenesis with hostile intent, used to attribute to Pelagius' writings doctrines that were not there, to which Jerome was himself more vulnerable than Pelagius.

Fear of an accusation of heresy

Jerome's *Letter to Ctesiphon* reveals that in AD 414 he felt himself under attack for his views.[187] Crucially, his *Dialogue against the Pelagians* shows that he faced precisely the criticism that he had written the same things as Pelagius: 'If anyone cries aloud that false charges are being brought against him and boasts that he is in

---

[186] *Contra* Kelly, *Jerome*, pp. 311–12: 'From the start Jerome found certain features of Pelagius's programme objectionable, particularly his exaltation of free will and his doctrine of the possibility of living without sin in this life'. The evidence presented in this chapter suggests that this is not correct.

[187] Jerome, *Ep.* 133.12.1 (ed. Hilberg, CSEL 56, pp. 258–9), 'From my youth up until now I have written various little works and I have always tried to teach my hearers the doctrine that I had been taught publicly in church .... I challenge my opponents thoroughly to sift all my past writings and if they should find anything faulty in my little intellect, to bring it into the open. Either my works will be found good and I shall confute their false charges; or they will be found reprehensible and I will confess my error'; 'Multi anni sunt, quod ab adulescentia usque ad hanc aetatem diuersa scripsi opuscula, semperque habui studium audientibus loqui, quod publice in ecclesia didiceram .... Prouoco aduersarios, ut omnes retro chartulas discutiant, et si quid in meo ingeniolo uitii reppererint, proferant in medium. Aut enim bona erunt, et contradicam eorum calumniae aut reprehensibilia et confitebor errorem'.

agreement with our views'.[188] This critique put Jerome under pressure. His interpretation of Rom. 9:16 in his *Letter to Hedibia* was that Paul raised the possibility that God controlled man as a potter controls clay in order to reject it.[189] This interpretation was singled out and condemned by Augustine as 'Pelagian' heresy.[190]

An episode in Jerome's relationship with Augustine from ten years earlier throws light on Jerome's stance. In AD 403, he wrote to Augustine complaining that a letter by Augustine critical of Jerome's writings was circulating in Italy when it should have been sent to Jerome first. Jerome had read the letter and suggested that Augustine was 'showing off his erudition' in order to augment his own reputation, and he was critical of Augustine's work: 'I considered some of the statements in it to be heretical'.[191] In addition, he told Augustine he had not read his works, of which he possessed only two, with attention: 'Were I willing to examine them closely, I could show that they are at variance, I will not say with me, who am of no significance, but with the interpretations of earlier Greek writers.'[192] It is important to consider the subsequent letters from Jerome to Augustine about this matter, and to compare the change in tone between Jerome's next to Augustine, *Letter* 112 written in around AD 404, and his *Letter* 115 to Augustine, written either later in AD 404 or in 405. *Letter* 112 was a typical Hieronymian combination of aggression and defensiveness: in one sentence Jerome combined fear of Augustine stirring up his congregation against him with scathing attack.[193] The key points to take from *Letter* 112 are, first, the fear and threat that riddle the letter. Jerome

---

[188] Jerome, *Dialogus aduersus pelagianos* Preface 2 (ed. Moreschini, CCSL 80, p. 5), 'Si quis autem falso se infamari clamitat et gloriatur nostra sentire'.

[189] See n. 38.

[190] Augustine, *De gestis Pelagii* 16.39 (ed. Urba and Zycha, CSEL 42, p. 95), writing about Pelagius' *Commentary on the Pauline Epistles*: 'He must either deny that this perverse interpretation is his own, where he wanted it to be understood that the Apostle had not held this view but rather had rejected it, or he must not hesitate to change and correct it'; 'Oportet ut illam expositionem peruersam, ubi hoc non sensisse apostolum, sed potius redarguisse intellegi uoluit, aut suam neget aut corrigere atque emendare non dubitet.'

[191] Jerome, *Ep.* 105.2.2 (ed. Hilberg, CSEL 55, p. 243), 'Quaedam in illa heretica iudicarem'; 105.3.2 (ed. Hilberg, CSEL 55, p. 244), 'But if you wish either to show off or to practise your doctrine'; 'Sin autem tuam uis uel ostentare uel exercere doctrinam'.

[192] Jerome, *Ep.* 105.5.2 (ed. Hilberg, CSEL 55, p. 246), 'Quos si uellem discutere, non dicam a me, qui nihil sum, sed a ueterum Graecorum docerem interpretationibus discrepare.'

[193] Jerome, *Ep.* 112.18.2 (ed. Hilberg, CSEL 55, p. 388), 'Nor should you incite the little crowd of uneducated people against me who revere you as a bishop and receive you with the honour due to a priest as you declaim in church, but have little respect for me, at the end of my life and almost decrepit, living hidden in a monastery in the countryside; and may you find for yourself people you may teach or criticise. For the sound of your voice barely reaches us, separated from you by such a distance of sea and lands'; 'Neque mihi inperitorum plebeculam concites, qui te uenerantur ut episcopum et in ecclesia declamantem sacerdotii honore suscipiunt, me autem aetatis ultimae et paene decrepitum ac monasterii et ruris secreta sectantem parui pendunt, et quaeras tibi, quos doceas siue reprehendas. Ad nos enim tantis maris atque terrarum a te diuisos spatiis uix uocis tuae sonus peruenit'. Jerome responded to Augustine's criticism with barbed haughtiness: Jerome, *Ep.* 112.19.1 (ed. Hilberg, CSEL 55, p. 389), 'With respect, I would say that you appear to me not to understand what you have asked'; 'Pace tua dixerim, uideris mihi non intellegere quod quaesisti.'

read Augustine's 'questions' (*quaestiones*) as 'criticism' (*reprehensio*), and his language throughout was of battle and warfare. He raised the spectre of an accusation of heresy where Augustine had not done so, and got his attack in first by suggesting that Augustine was introducing heresy into the Church.[194] This was a symptom of Jerome's lifelong fear of losing his authority as an exegete through an accusation of heresy.[195] The second key point is that he presented the dispute as a conflict between tradition and innovation, with Jerome basing his interpretations on the long tradition of the Greek Fathers and Augustine introducing novelty. Jerome argued precisely that Augustine was an innovator and was not following tradition: 'And so you ... thought up a new argument'.[196] Throughout, he contrasted his learned seclusion in his monastery with Augustine's public recognition, and ended with this same picture of disparity: 'You are a young man firmly established at the pinnacle of episcopal dignity; teach your people and enrich the Roman storehouses with the fruits of the new Africa. It is enough for me to whisper to some reader or listener in an impoverished corner of a monastery.'[197] In these last words of the letter the subtext of novelty versus innovation was underlined in the phrase 'new Africa' (*nouis Africa*).

The third point to take from *Letter* 112 is that although it was about Jerome's discussion in his *Commentary on Galatians* of Paul's critique of Peter for sanctioning Jewish rituals, Jerome's treatment raised some issues close to the debate about original sin, prevenient grace, and predestination interpreted as preordainment, since he referred to grace as the gift of Christ's advent and its effects.[198] He also referred tangentially to God's universal salvific will and the fact that human nature was not 'unclean', albeit in reference to Gentiles as well as Jews being called to the faith and to ritual pollution, and not original sin: 'It is shown that no

---

[194] Jerome, *Ep.* 112.13 (ed. Hilberg, CSEL 55, pp. 381–2).

[195] Jerome had experienced a catastrophic loss of reputation before, along with the failure of his hopes of an episcopacy, when he was forced to leave Rome following the death of Paula's daughter Blesilla. He had worked hard to rebuild a career. On the growing intolerance in theological controversy from the time of Constantine I onwards, see G. Bonner, '*Dic Christi Veritas Ubi nunc Habitas*: Ideas of Schism and Heresy in the Post-Nicene Age', in *The Limits of Ancient Christianity*, ed. W. E. Klingshirn and M. Vessey (Ann Arbor, MI, 1999), p. 65.

[196] Jerome, *Ep.* 112.5.1 (ed. Hilberg, CSEL 55, p. 372), 'Tu igitur ... nouum argumentum repperisti'. Jerome also pointed out that no one else had propounded Augustine's interpretation: 6.2 (ed. Hilberg, CSEL 55, p. 373), 'You will have to bring forward at least one person who supports the truth of your opinion'; 'Tu ueritatis tuae saltem unum adstipulatorem proferre debebis.'

[197] Jerome, *Ep.* 112.22.4 (ed. Hilberg, CSEL 55, p. 393), 'Tu, qui iuuenis es et in pontificali culmine constitutus, doceto populos et nouis Africae frugibus Romana tecta locupleta. Mihi sufficit cum auditore uel lectore pauperculo in angulo monasterii susurrare.'

[198] Jerome, *Ep.* 112.14.3 (ed. Hilberg, CSEL 55, p. 383), '*Grace and truth were created through Jesus Christ* [John 1:17]. Instead of the grace of the law, which came first, we have received the permanent grace of the Gospel'; '*Gratia et ueritas per Iesum Christum facta est* [John 1:17]. Pro legis gratia, quae praeteriit, gratiam euangelii accepimus permanentem'. Jerome here referred to the generalised grace of Christ's incarnation, which was his usual understanding of the word 'grace'; *gratia permanens euangelii* was not *gratia praeueniens*.

man is polluted by nature, but all are called equally to the Gospel of Christ.'[199] By AD 404, Jerome might well have come across Augustine's *Confessions*, and it is perhaps not credible that he would have been unaware that fundamental elements in his own understanding of Christianity diverged from Augustine's account of Christianity.

The contrast between *Letter* 112 and *Letter* 115 is striking. The second was a short apology for the first. Its tone was conciliatory and deferential. Jerome's last words are the critical evidence: 'Please let us play on the field of Scripture without hurting each other.'[200] He was now afraid of being hurt by Augustine. At some point in the interval between writing these two letters, Jerome decided to defer to Augustine. Some ten years later when the question of an absolutist account of prevenient grace and predestination interpreted as preordainment came to a head, Jerome's decision about which side he would be on had already been taken. Where Pelagius was prepared to argue against the triune of original sin, prevenient grace, and predestination interpreted as preordainment, Jerome had long before taken the decision not to defend his account of Christianity.

Did Jerome change his position?

The evidence of his writings suggests that Jerome attempted to shift his position some time between AD 410 and 414.[201] It is interesting to see how he articulated his altered position. A text that shows signs of a change in Jerome's exegesis is his *Commentary on Ezekiel*, written between AD 410 and 414, and so potentially offering a 'before' and 'after' perspective on the change in his awareness of his vulnerability in the controversy. As already shown, Jerome continued to assert effective free will throughout this commentary.[202] It was with regard to the language of perfection that he sought to realign his position.

According to the chronology offered by François Glorie, Jerome began his *Commentary on Ezekiel* in AD 410 but quickly stopped after events left him unable to continue. Books 1–3 were completed by AD 411; Books 4–6 by the autumn of AD 412; books seven and eight were in AD 412–13; and Books 9–11 by the middle of AD 413. Book 12 was started in AD 414, but Jerome interrupted his work on it to write to Demetrias, after which he finished it and then completed Books 13 and 14 before the end of AD 414.[203] Thus Books 13 and 14 postdated his *Letter*

---

[199] Jerome, *Ep.* 112.7.1–2 (ed. Hilberg, CSEL 55, p. 373), 'Ostenditur nullum hominem secundum naturam esse pollutum, sed aequaliter omnes ad Christi euangelium prouocari.'

[200] Jerome, *Ep.* 115.3 (ed. Hilberg, CSEL 55, p. 397), 'In scripturarum, si placet, campo sine nostro inuicem dolore ludamus.'

[201] G. Martinetto, 'Les Premières Réactions Antiaugustinienne de Pélage', *Revue des Études Augustiniennes* 18 (1971), p. 117.

[202] See pp. 132–4.

[203] F. Glorie, *Sancti Hieronymi presbyteri Opera. Commentariorum in Hiezechielem libri XIV*, Corpus Christianorum Series Latina 75 (Turnhout, 1964), pp. vii–viii.

to Demetrias.[204] It has been shown convincingly that there are verbal parallels between Jerome's *Letter to Demetrias* and Pelagius'. The consensus is that Jerome echoed Pelagius, not vice versa.[205] If this is true, then it means that Jerome was well aware of the substance of Pelagius' position when he composed the last two books of his *Commentary on Ezekiel*.

In Book 1, written in AD 410, Jerome paired Rom. 9:16 with the idea that humans chose whether to act sinfully or virtuously: 'Nevertheless it lies in our judgement both to will and to run' ('attamen et uelle et currere nostri arbitrii est').[206] In his *Letter to Demetrias* of AD 414, he changed his wording of this same combination of Rom. 9:16 with the idea that humans chose whether to be virtuous or sinful. Writing to Demetrias he omitted the word 'judgement' (*arbitrium*), and qualified his observation: 'And yet it is ours to will and not to will; and this very thing that is ours, without the mercy of God is not ours.'[207] This might suggest that by this point Jerome was aware of argument about a possible opposition between grace and free will, and he may have omitted the word 'judgement' (*arbitrium*) for fear of being identified as on the free will side of the controversy. A clear reference to the controversy about interpretation of the word grace came in the sentence that preceded his reworking of the pairing of ideas that he had earlier employed in his *Commentary on Ezekiel*: 'Now where there is grace this is not given in return for works but is the free gift of the giver, so that the Apostle's words are fulfilled: *It is not of him who wills, nor of him who runs, but of God who has mercy* [Rom. 9:16].'[208] By the time he wrote to Demetrias, Jerome was aware of Augustine's criticism that Pelagius failed to acknowledge the gratuity of grace. This statement may therefore represent Jerome making sure that he could not be accused of that sin of omission. This statement to Demetrias went some way to complying with Augustine's teaching that both free will and prevenient grace existed and that the gratuity of grace should be consistently affirmed in a verbal formula designed to preserve humility, and was therefore perhaps an attempt by Jerome to acknowledge Augustine's account of grace, although he presented the resulting situation as a paradox.[209] However, Jerome's statement did not strictly acknowledge the

---

[204] Kelly, *Jerome*, p. 306, n. 55, noted that Jerome mentioned in section 2 of his *Ep.* 130 that he was writing his commentary on Ezekiel's vision of the restored temple when he received the invitation to write a letter of advice to Demetrias.

[205] G. De Plinval, *Essai sur Le Style et La Langue de Pélage suivi du traité inédit De induratione cordis Pharaonis* (Fribourg, 1947), p. 246, n. 1; Kelly, *Jerome*, p. 313, n. 19; A. Cain, *The Letters of Jerome: Asceticism, Biblical Exegesis, and the Construction of Authority in Late Antiquity* (Oxford, 2009), pp. 163–5.

[206] See n. 56.

[207] Jerome, *Ep.* 130.12.3 (ed. Hilberg, CSEL 56, p. 192), 'Et tamen uelle et nolle nostrum est; ipsum quoque, quod nostrum est, sine Dei miseratione non nostrum est.'

[208] Jerome, *Ep.* 130.12.3 (ed. Hilberg, CSEL 56, p. 192), 'Vbi autem gratia, non operum retributio, sed donantis est largitas, ut inpleatur dictum Apostoli: *Non est uolentis, neque currentis, sed miserentis Dei* [Rom. 9:16].'

[209] Augustine recognised this paradox in his letter to Abbot Valentinus of Hadrumetum, in which he wrote that God's commands to us to be virtuous proved that we have free will, and scriptural

prevenient action of grace as Augustine required. It was the only concession he made to Augustine's argument for grace in his letter to Demetrias, and he did not discuss which of the many possible aspects of grace he was referring to in this statement, so that there is no proof that he was referring to prevenient grace. In all his previous exegesis, when Jerome stressed that salvation was not given on the basis of merit, he was referring to the fact that Christ's incarnation and the remission of sins it brought were not the result of human merit.

Later, in his *Letter to Demetrias*, Jerome advised her to avoid heresy. He did not name a heresy, but in his letter to Ctesiphon of AD 414 he concluded that 'Pelagianism' was another outbreak of Origenism. Since in his letter to Demetrias he also referred to discussion of the origin of the soul, God's justice and the fate of infants, he was probably making a veiled allusion to what he understood to be 'Pelagianism'.[210] The evidence suggests that Jerome was aware that Demetrias had received Pelagius' letter and was cautious about what he wrote to her on the topics raised in the controversy about original sin, prevenient grace, and predestination interpreted as preordainment.

Jerome's first overt attack on Pelagius came in his *Letter 133 To Ctesiphon* of AD 414, so this work offers a secure *terminus ante quem* for the change in his exegesis. Book 14 of the *Commentary on Ezekiel* offers evidence concerning how Jerome managed this manvoevure in presentational terms, because, while he continued to assert effective free will, in Book 14 he discussed the idea of perfection at length. As has been shown, although he chose the accusation of teaching perfectibility as one of the two grounds that he advanced for condemning Pelagius, Jerome was himself far more vulnerable to this charge than Pelagius was. For this reason, too, his discussion of perfection in Book 14 is particularly interesting. It may be that he was influenced by Pelagius' advice to Demetrias against thinking that perfection was possible in this life, since, as Pelagius had done, Jerome cited Phil. 3:13–14:

> And when the people of the land come before the Lord at the appointed festivals whoever enters by the north gate to worship shall go out by the south gate; and whoever enters by the south gate shall go out by the north gate: they shall not return by way of the gate by which they entered, but shall go out from that region: which is commanded not only of those who were leaving Sodom and to whom it was said: And do not look back [Gen. 19:17], nor only of those who put their hands to the plough, so that they should not look back at the things that are behind their back, but it is commanded also of those who are established in the house of the Lord, lest they should look back and: Be turned back to the weak and beggary elemental spirits

---

commands to us to ask God for virtue showed that God causes virtue: Augustine *Ep.* 214.7 (ed. Chéné and Pintard, BA 24, p. 58), 'Where you think that you do not understand, believe for the time being the words of God that there exist both man's free will and the grace of God, without the help of which free will can neither turn toward God nor make progress toward God'; 'Vbi sentitis non uos intellegere, interim credite diuinis eloquiis quia et liberum hominis est arbitrium et gratia Dei, sine cuius adiutorio liberum arbitrium nec conuerti potest ad Deum, nec proficere in Deum'.

[210] Jerome, *Ep.* 130.16.3–4 (ed. Hilberg, CSEL 56, pp. 196–7).

[Gal. 4:9], and lest just starting out in the Spirit they are destroyed by the flesh; but rather so that from spiritual things too they should progress to greater things and so that they should say with the Apostle: *Forgetting what lies behind, and straining forward to what lies ahead* [Phil. 3:13], so that by no means should they know in part and prophesy in part, but so that they should reach perfection, relative to that perfection, however, which human nature can attain, so that we might understand that Gospel saying: *And you also, when you have done all that you were ordered to do, say: 'We are worthless slaves; we have done only what we ought to have done'* [Luke 17:10]. Whence in the same letter the Apostle also speaks about two sorts of perfection; for he writes as one who is *imperfect: Not because I have already obtained this and because I am already perfect; but I pursue it, if I can make it my own, because Jesus Christ has made me his own* [Phil. 3:12]. And immediately he speaks as one who is perfect: *But this one thing I do, forgetting what lies behind and straining forward to what lies ahead, I press on according to my resolution to the prize of the heavenly calling. Therefore as many of us as are perfect, we know this thing* [Phil. 3:13–15] – for how can this sentence stand such that someone who had said: *Not because I have already obtained this and because I am already perfect* might dare to say: *Therefore as many of us as are perfect, we know this thing*? From this it is evident that every human and all of creation, although it may have reached perfection, is nevertheless in need of God's mercy, and possesses complete perfection as a result of grace, and not as a result of merit.[211]

In this exegesis, Jerome took care to nuance his statements about perfection where he had not done so before. He suggested that there are 'two sorts of perfection' (literally 'two perfections', *duae perfectiones*), 'perfection' and 'complete perfection' (*perfectio* and *plena perfectio*), and he concluded with a statement that

---

[211] Jerome, *In Hiezechielem* 14, on Ezek. 46:8–11 (ed. Glorie, CCSL 75, pp. 695–6), '*Et cum intrabit populus terrae in conspectu Domini in sollemnitatibus, qui ingreditur per portam aquilonis ut adoret, egrediatur per uiam portae meridianae; et qui ingreditur per uiam portae meridianae, egrediatur per uiam portae aquilonis: non reuertetur per uiam portae per quam ingressus est, sed e regione illius egredietur* – quod non solum his praecipitur qui egrediuntur de Sodomis et dicitur eis: *Nec respicias retrorsum* [Gen.19:17], neque illis qui manum mittunt ad aratrum, ut non respiciant ea quae post tergum sunt, sed in domo quoque Domini constitutis iubetur ne post terga respiciant et: *Reuertantur ad egena et infirma elementa* [Gal. 4:9], et incipientes spiritu, carne consumentur; sed ut de spiritalibus quoque ad maiora procedant et dicant cum Apostolo: *Praeteritorum obliuiscens, et in priora me extendens* [Phil. 3:13], ut nequaquam ex parte cognoscant et ex parte prophetent, sed ueniant ad perfectum: iuxta eam tamen perfectionem quam potest capere humana natura, ut intellegamus illud Euangelicum: *Et uos, cum omnia feceritis, dicite: "Serui inutiles sumus: quod debuimus facere, fecimus"* [Luke 17:10]. Vnde et Apostolus in eadem epistola de duabus loquitur perfectionibus: quasi *imperfectus enim scribit: Non quia iam accepi, et quia iam perfectus sum; persequor autem, si apprehendam in quo et comprehensus sum a Christo* [Phil. 3:12]. Statimque quasi perfectus loquitur: *Vnum autem: posteriorum obliuiscens, ad ea quae in priora sunt me extendens, iuxta propositum persequor ad brauium supernae uocationis. Quotquot ergo perfecti, hoc sapimus* [Phil. 3:13–15] – quomodo enim potest stare sententia, ut qui dixerat: *Non quia iam accepi aut quia iam perfectus sum*, audeat dicere: *Quotquot ergo perfecti, hoc sapimus*? Ex quo perspicuum est omnem hominem et uniuersam creaturam, quamuis ad perfectionem uenerit, tamen indigere misericordia Dei et plenam perfectionem ex gratia, non ex merito possidere.' *In his edition at this point, Glorie gave 'perfect' (*perfectus*) not 'imperfect' (*imperfectus*), and in his app. crit. to line 560 on p. 696 he noted the emendation by Hrabanus Maurus and Vallarsi to *imperfectus*. I concur with Maurus and Vallarsi that *imperfectus* is vital to the point that Jerome is making in this passage; without it the sentence does not make sense.

showed that he was now aware of Augustine's argumentation when he wrote that every human was in need of God's mercy and: 'Possesses complete perfection as a result of grace, not as a result of merit'. It is interesting that at this point Jerome explored how apparently contradictory biblical use of the vocabulary of perfection should be reconciled. This was not a line of enquiry that he had pursued before. His primary need, however, was to justify his own written output of the previous thirty years, in which he had advocated pursuit of perfection without mention of divine grace, and which made him vulnerable to the same charge that he was levelling at Pelagius. Jerome repeated his idea of two perfections in his *Dialogue against the Pelagians* in the following year, and yet in this work he ended by endorsing the principle of merit in the economy of salvation:

> Are we to think ... that he who laboured more abundantly than all of them does not have greater merit? *In my Father's house there are many mansions* [John 14:2], because merits are also different. *Star differs from star in glory* [1 Cor. 15:41], and in the one body of the Church there are different members .... *Strive for the greater gifts* [1 Cor. 12:31], so that we may merit greater rewards for our faith and industry than the rest of the annointed, and be better than those who, in comparison with us, are placed in the second or third rank.[212]

It is noteworthy that in Book 14 of his *Commentary on Ezekiel*, Jerome ended his interpretation of Ezek. 46:9 by referring to salvation being merited.[213] He also followed this with an assertion of human free will set within a discussion of sacrifices:

> But there will not be a fixed number concerning lambs, nor will the judgement of the will be disregarded, but he who uses his mental strength and his good conscience so that he offers as much as he can rather than as much as he wants, and: *In addition a hin of olive oil for each ephah* [Ezek. 46:5] so that similar things are annointed and a lamp is lit in the sight of the Lord, and *he who uses it might be able to say: *But I am like a fruitful olive tree in the house of the Lord* [Ps. 52:8].[214]

---

[212] Jerome, *Dialogus aduersus pelagianos* 1.17 (ed. Moreschini, CCSL 80, pp. 22–3), 'Putamusne ... non plus habere meritorum eum, qui plus omnibus laborauit? *Multae mansiones apud Patrem* [John 14:2], quia et merita diuersa. *Stella a stella differt in gloria* [1 Cor. 15:41] et in uno Ecclesiae corpore membra diuersa sunt .... *Aemulamini dona maiora* [1 Cor. 12:31], ut fide et industria plus ceteris charismatibus habere mereamur melioresque simus his, qui comparatione nostri in secundo uel tertio gradu positi sunt.'

[213] Jerome, *In Hiezechielem* 14, on Ezek. 46:1–7 (ed. Glorie, CCSL 75, p. 694), 'And six unblemished lambs and rams and the other things which are offered on the Sabbath, so that we may obtain eternal salvation and may merit to hear: *Well done, good slave; because you have been faithful in a few things, I will put you in charge of many things: enter into the salvation of your Lord* [Matt. 25:21]'; 'Et agni sex et aries immaculati et cetera quae offeruntur in sabbatis, ut aeternam requiem consequamur, et mereamur audire: *Euge, serue bone, quia in paucis fidelis fuisti, super multa te constituam: intra in requiem Domini tui* [Matt. 25:21]'.

[214] Jerome, *In Hiezechielem* 14, on Ezek. 46:8–11 (ed. Glorie, CCSL 75, p. 697), 'In agnis uero non erit certus numerus, nec uoluntati dimissum arbitrium sed uiribus quis utetur et bono conscientiae, ut quantum potest non quantum uult offerat; et super omnia olei "hin" per "oephi" singula, ut ungatur simila et lucerna accendatur in conspectu Domini, et qui eo *utitur possit dicere: *Ego autem sicut oliua fructifera in domo Domini* [Ps. 52:8].' *In his app. crit. to line 609, Glorie gave *utuntur possint* in the

It seems clear that Jerome did not at this stage abandon the linked concepts of merit and effective free will in his account of the Christian message ('nor will the judgement of the will be disregarded', *nec uoluntati dimissum arbitrium*). In this passage there was no mention of divine grace causing or helping this personal effort to be virtuous. Jerome had simply nuanced his interpretation of biblical references to perfection so as to allow him to criticise Pelagius for preaching sinlessness, and so as to evade condemnation himself on this front. In his *Commentary on Ezekiel* he achieved this by verbal acknowledgement of the role of grace, as Augustine stipulated, without using the precise phrase 'prevenient grace' (*gratia praeueniens*). Jerome chose to attack Pelagius on the grounds of Pelagius' preaching the possibility of sinlessness, rather than on the grounds of his defence of effective free will and the goodness of human nature, because Jerome could not yet bring himself to abandon effective free will, despite his fear of being accused of heresy.

An uncomfortable combination

In his *Commentary on Jeremiah*, begun in AD 414–15, Jerome tried to combine his commitment to effective free will with deferral to the aspect of grace stressed by Augustine, but the result was not entirely comfortable, or clear in its import: 'For although we return to the Lord by our own will, nevertheless we will not be able to be saved unless he draws us and by his aid strengthens our desire.'[215] In passing he cited Luke 20:13: *I will send my son; perhaps they will respect him*, and commented that this was said: 'So that through the ambiguity of the statement and the sense of doubt in the words, man's free will is demonstrated.'[216] At the same time Jerome questioned what he now characterised as overemphasis on the human will: 'Where are those who say that by our will we can be made free from all sin?'[217] He described stress on the will as a 'new' phenomenon: 'Let these new preachers be ashamed who say that each person is governed by their own will'.[218] Without mentioning Pelagius by name, he regularly attacked a 'most arrogant heresy'.[219] Where before Jerome

---

main text in his edition here, and noted the emendation by Hrabanus Maurus and Vallarsi to *utitur possit*. I concur with Maurus and Vallarsi that *qui eo utitur possit* is the preferable reading because it refers back to *uiribus quis utetur* earlier.

[215] Jerome, *In Hieremiam* 1.63.3, on Jer. 3:21–2 (ed. Reiter, CCSL 74, p. 38), 'Quamuis enim propria uoluntate ad Dominum reuertamur, tamen, nisi ille nos traxerit et cupiditatem nostram suo roborauerit praesidio, salui esse non poterimus.'

[216] Jerome, *In Hieremiam* 1.94.2, on Jer. 5:4–5a (ed. Reiter, CCSL 74, p. 53), 'Vt ex ambiguitate sententiae et suspensione uerborum liberum hominis monstretur arbitrium.'

[217] Jerome, *In Hieremiam* 2.51.2, on Jer. 8:6 (ed. Reiter, CCSL 74, p. 87), 'Vbi sunt, qui in nostra esse dicunt positum uoluntate omni carere peccato?'

[218] Jerome, *In Hieremiam* 2.96, on Jer. 10:23 (ed. Reiter, CCSL 74, p. 110), 'Erubescant noui praedicatores, qui aiunt unumquemque suo arbitrio regi'.

[219] Jerome, *In Hieremiam* 4, Preface 6 (ed. Reiter, CCSL 74, p. 175), 'Superbissima heresis'; 4.60.3–6, on Jer. 23:28–9 (ed. Reiter, CCSL 74, pp. 226–7); 6.46, on Jer. 32:34 (ed. Reiter, CCSL 74, p. 343), 'New doctrine is fabricated and ... worshipped in secret'; 'Nouum dogma construitur et ... adoratur in abscondito'.

had championed a synergistic account of the relationship between man and God in the human attainment of salvation, in his *Commentary on Jeremiah* he rejected this interpretation of Christianity and labelled those who advocated a co-operative model heretics and idolaters.[220] Where Jerome had spent a lifetime expounding the universality of God's salvific will, in the passage that followed this rejection of the co-operative model, he proposed the notion of the elect.[221]

But the combination Jerome tried to effect was unconvincing. At one moment he expounded a negative anthropology, importing into his exegesis on Jeremiah the same Pauline passages that Augustine used to support the idea of original sin; while at another he denied that man was inclined to evil: 'Whatever is learned does not come from nature but from effort and a person's own will, which by an excessive habit and love of sinning, can to some extent be changed into a sinful nature.'[222] In this same passage he suggested that it was God who changed a sinner into a good person, explaining Jeremiah's simile of the leopard's spots:

> But what is impossible for people is possible for God, even if the Ethiopian and the leopard appear unable to change their nature, he who works in the Ethiopian and the leopard is able to do so .... *What do you have that you have not received?* [1 Cor. 4:7] .... In all these things the virtue comes from Christ, not from those who would boast in their virtues.[223]

Yet in another passage of exegesis he concurrently propounded effective free will, writing about the potter shaping a lump of clay:

> The Lord says to the prophet: 'If a potter has the ability to make something again out of the same clay that has been spoiled, can I not also do this with you who, insofar as

---

[220] Jerome, *In Hieremiam* 2.88, on Jer. 10:11 (ed. Reiter, CCSL 74, p. 105), Jerome asserted that heretics twisted Scripture in order to fashion false idols and false gods, presenting themselves as gods, in a passage that seems to be aimed at Pelagius, at the end of which he concluded: 'This should be said to false gods that have been put together by craftsmanship – for they did not make the heavens and earth – those who are "co-operators with Christ", who are called "gods" and "lords", fashion these things for the most part out of ecclesiastical teaching'; 'Falsis dis et, qui artificio reconpositi sunt, ista dicenda sunt – illi enim nec caelos fecere nec terram – quaeque cooperatores Christi, qui dei uocantur et domini, per doctrinam ecclesiasticam magna ex parte fabricantur.'

[221] Jerome, *In Hieremiam* 2.89.7, on Jer. 10:12–16 (ed. Reiter, CCSL 74, p. 107), 'Heresy prevails for a time, in order to make clear who are the elect, and so that the elect may be proven true'; 'Ad tempus ualet heresis, ut electi quique manifesti fiant et probati sint'.

[222] Jerome, *In Hieremiam* 3.15.2, on Jer. 13:12–14 (ed. Reiter, CCSL 74, p. 129), '*For nothing good dwells in my flesh* [Rom. 7:18], and again: *For I do not do the good that I want, but the evil I do not want is what I do* [Rom. 7:19], and then: *Wretched man that I am! Who will deliver me from this body of death?* [Rom. 7:24]'; '*Non enim habitat in carne mea bonum* [Rom. 7:18], et iterum: *Non enim, quod uolo bonum, hoc facio, sed, quod nolo malum, hoc operor* [Rom. 7:19], ac deinde: *Miser ego homo, quis me liberabit de corpore mortis huius?* [Rom. 7:24].' Jerome, *In Hieremiam* 3.22.2, on Jer. 13:23 (ed. Reiter, CCSL 74, p. 134), 'Quicquid enim discitur, non naturae est, sed studii et propriae uoluntatis, quae nimia consuetudine et amore peccandi quodammodo in naturam uertitur.'

[223] Jerome, *In Hieremiam* 3.22.2–3, on Jer. 13:23 (ed. Reiter, CCSL 74, pp. 134–5), 'Sed hoc, quod hominibus inpossibile est, Deo possibile est, ut nequaquam Aethiops et pardus suam uideantur mutare naturam, sed ille, qui in Aethiope operatur et pardo .... *Quid habes, quod non accepisti* [1 Cor. 4:7] .... In omnibus his Christi uirtus sit, non eorum, qui in suis uirtutibus gloriantur.'

it depends on you, seem to be lost?' And in order to indicate freedom of the will, he says that he announced evil to one nation or kingdom and good to another, but what he predicted might not come about; instead the opposite might occur, so that both good shall come to evil people if they repent, and evil to good people, if after the promises made to them they are converted to sins. And we say this not because God is ignorant of what a certain nation or kingdom is going to do, but because God gives a person over to his own will, in order that he may receive either reward or punishment according to his merit. Yet that does not immediately mean that what happens will be entirely due to human effort, but to the grace of God who generously bestows all things; for the freedom of the will should be maintained in such a way that the grace of the generous bestower excels in all things.[224]

Jerome's final line in the passage above was his attempt to reconcile his lifelong devotion to effective free will with what he perceived to be the new orthodoxy.[225] He concluded with a non sequitur that summed up his predicament: 'Where is the power of free will or the judgement of our own will without the grace of God?'[226]

Within a single passage of exegesis, at one moment Jerome sought to preserve effective free will and explicitly rejected an account of predestination that made it anything more than God's foreknowledge of autonomous human decisions, and at the next moment he asserted the need to attribute all virtue to God and tried to take a swipe at concern for works:

[Jeremiah] says: *Perhaps they will listen and turn.* The word expressing uncertainty, *perhaps*, cannot be reflective of the Lord's majesty, but rather is said for the sake of our mental disposition, in order to preserve human free will; lest because of God's foreknowledge, the human will should be compelled as if by necessity either to do anything or not to do anything. For it is not because God knows that something will happen that it therefore happens; rather because it is going to happen God knows

---

[224] Jerome, *In Hieremiam* 4.2.5–7, on Jer. 18:1–10 (ed. Reiter, CCSL 74, p. 177), 'Dominus ad prophetam: "Si figulus", ait, "hanc habet potestatem, ut ex eodem luto rursum faciat, quod fuerit dissipatum, ego in uobis, qui, quantum in uobis est, perisse uidemini, hoc facere non potero?" Et ut liberum significaret arbitrium, dicit se et mala annuntiare genti et regno illi uel illi et rursum bona; nec tamen hoc euenire, quod ipse praedixerit, sed e contrario fieri, ut et bona malis eueniant, si egerint paenitentiam, et bonis mala, si post repromissiones fuerint ad peccata conuersi. Et hoc dicimus, non quo ignoret Deus hoc uel illud gentem aut regnum esse facturum, sed quod dimittat hominem uoluntati suae, ut uel praemia uel poenas suo merito recipiat. Nec statim totum erit hominis, quod eueniet, sed eius gratiae, qui cuncta largitus est; ita enim libertas arbitrii reseruanda est, ut in omnibus excellat gratia largitoris'.
[225] Compare Jerome's final line here: 'The freedom of the will should be maintained in such a way that the grace of the generous bestower excels in all things', with Pelagius' in his *Statement of Faith*: 'We confess free will in such a way that we always have need of God's grace': see Chapter 1, n. 38.
[226] Jerome, *In Hieremiam* 4.3.4, on Jer. 18:11–13 (ed. Reiter, CCSL 74, p. 178), 'Vbi est ergo absque gratia Dei liberi arbitrii potestas et propriae iudicium uoluntatis?' Jerome could not totally abandon the idea that grace was given to the virtuous: Jerome, *In Hieremiam* 6.32.3–4, on Jer. 32:6–7 (ed. Reiter, CCSL 74, p. 329), 'And so first we merit the peace of God, and after peace, grace is born to us, which is not by the will of the one who possesses it, but by the will of the one who gives it. *The grace of God* offers the right of purchase to him who converses in *lofty things*, so that although he might appear to be exalted, nevertheless he needs God's grace'; 'Primum ergo pacem meremur Dei et post pacem nobis gratia nascitur, quae non in possidentis, sed in donantis arbitrio est. Defert autem emtionem "gratia Dei" illi, qui in "sublimibus" conlocatus est, ut, quamuis uideatur excelsus, tamen gratia Dei indigeat.'

about it, since he knows the future .... Therefore it has been put into our power either to do things or not to do them – in such a way however, that we should ascribe to God's grace whatever good work that we intend, strive after, or accomplish; *For it is God*, as the Apostle says, who has granted us: *Both to will and to complete* [Phil. 2:13]. But if it is sufficient for a person to walk just once in the law that was given to us through Moses, as the foolish heresy supposes, then why did he add: *So that you might listen to the words of my servants the prophets?*[227]

Where before his position had been clear, in his *Commentary on Jeremiah* it was opaque: 'He gives free will in such a way that nevertheless the fear itself, which is given to us, remains by the grace of the giver.'[228] The transparency of God's justice, until now the cornerstone of Jerome's Christianity, was shattered: 'Sometimes, because God's wisdom is beyond measure, his judgements may appear unjust'.[229] The fact that Jerome was unable to articulate coherently the doctrines of original sin, prevenient grace, and predestination interpreted as preordainment is important evidence of how entrenched the principle of effective free will had been, and was still, in his conception of Christianity.

Jerome's *Dialogue against the Pelagians* was likewise an uncomfortable attempt to put clear water between himself and Pelagius.[230] The attempt hinged on a passage in which Jerome stated his synergistic position and had Critobulus (Pelagius) reject this co-operative model:

> Atticus (Jerome): 'Therefore, as I said, do I not need to ask God for help for every action I perform, since this help has been placed, once and for all, in my own judgement?'
>
> Critobulus (Pelagius): 'If he co-operates with me in everything I do, an act is not mine, but His who helps me, or rather His who operates in me, especially since I can accomplish nothing without Him.'[231]

---

[227] Jerome, *In Hieremiam* 5.36.5–37.2, on Jer. 26:1–6 (ed. Reiter, CCSL 74, pp. 253–4), '*Forsitan, inquit, audiant et conuertantur*. Verbum ambiguum "forsitan" maiestati Domini non potest conuenire, sed nostro loquitur affectu, ut liberum homini seruetur arbitrium, ne ex praescientia eius quasi necessitate uel facere quid uel non facere cogatur; non enim ex eo, quod Deus scit futurum aliquid, idcirco futurum est; sed quia futurum est, Deus nouit quasi praescius futurorum .... In nostra est ergo positum potestate uel facere quid uel non facere, ita dumtaxat, ut, quicquid boni operis uolumus, appetimus, explemus, ad Dei gratiam referamus, qui iuxta Apostolum dedit nobis: *Et uelle et perficere* [Phil. 2:13]. Sin autem sufficit semel ambulare in lege, quae nobis data est per Mosen, ut stulta heresis suspicatur, quomodo addidit: *Vt audiatis sermones seruorum meorum, prophetarum?*'

[228] Jerome, *In Hieremiam* 6.50.7, on Jer. 32:37–41 (ed. Reiter, CCSL 74, p. 346), 'Sic liberum donat arbitrium, ut tamen ipse timor, qui tribuitur, gratia permaneat largitoris.'

[229] Jerome, *In Hieremiam* 6.37.10, on Jer. 32:16–19 (ed. Reiter, CCSL 74, p. 335), 'Interdum pro nimia sapientia iudicia eius uideantur iniusta'.

[230] See T. Scheck, *St Jerome's Commentaries on Galatians, Titus and Philemon* (Notre Dame, IN, 2010), pp. 25–7, for observations made by earlier scholars that Jerome rejected predestination that diminished human autonomy, and for points at which Jerome asserted synergistic views.

[231] Jerome, *Dialogus aduersus pelagianos* 1.5 (ed. Moreschini, CCSL 80, p. 9), 'Atticus: "Ergo, ut dixi, non debeo a Deo per singula auxilium deprecari, quod semel meo datum est iudicio?" Critobulus: "Si in omnibus ille cooperatur, non est meum, sed eius qui adiuuat, immo qui in me operatur, praesertim cum absque eo facere nihil possim."'

Yet at the end of the same dialogue, Jerome restated his synergistic position and said that if Pelagius agreed with the co-operative model, then they held the same view, to which Pelagius replied that many of those who thought like him did indeed subscribe to the co-operative model:

> Critobulus (Pelagius): 'But there are many of us who would say that everything we do is done with the assistance of God.'

> Atticus (Jerome): 'He who says this has ceased to be one of you. And so, either you too say that, so that you may begin to be on our side, or if you do not say it, you will be an outsider along with these who do not profess our views.'[232]

The evidence that survives suggests that Pelagius was a synergist, but, in order to differentiate between himself and Pelagius, Jerome had to have Pelagius reject the co-operative model. This last passage suggests that Jerome did not even manage to do this successfully.[233] Meanwhile, his own clearly stated synergistic position was at variance with the doctrines of an absolute account of prevenient grace and predestination interpreted as preordainment.[234] Only in the final paragraphs of his *Dialogue against the Pelagians* did Jerome endorse positively any part of the triune by asserting original sin, though without using the precise phrase; and he ended by referring the task of refuting Pelagius onwards to Augustine, after which Atticus (Jerome) ended the discussion on grounds of length.

A more coherent statement of Jerome's altered presentation of his position on the question of original sin, prevenient grace, and predestination interpreted as preordainment is offered by his *Letter* 140 *To Cyprian*, dated by Vallarsi to AD 418. Here Jerome qualified his exegesis to fit in with Augustine's account of the operation of prevenient grace. His presentation of the relationship between man and God in his letter to Cyprian is very different from the approach he had declared was the Church's official position and *ecclesiasticus* in AD 410. Cyprian requested Jerome's interpretation of Ps. 90, and Jerome chose to work into his exegesis points relating to the controversy over grace and free will that were not self-evidently required by the contents of the psalm. Interpreting the first verse: *Lord you have been our dwelling-place in all generations*, Jerome wrote:

> Though he will narrate sad things and will shed tears over the human race, he begins from praise of God, so that whatever adversities man afterwards faces are seen to

---

[232] Jerome, *Dialogus aduersus pelagianos* 3.11 (ed. Moreschini, CCSL 80, p. 111), 'Critobulus: "Ceterum sunt plerique nostrorum, qui omnia quae agimus dicant fieri praesidio Dei." Atticus: "Qui hoc dicit, uester esse cessauit. Aut igitur et tu ista dicito, ut noster esse incipias, aut si non dicis, alienus eris cum his qui nostra non dicunt."'

[233] Elizabeth Clark pointed out that Jerome's *Dialogue against the Pelagians* reflected: 'Jerome's knowledge of the Palestinian councils that had approved Pelagius' teaching': Clark, *The Origenist Controversy*, p. 224. It may have been Jerome's knowledge of Pelagius' position that hampered his polemic against Pelagius; for the advantages for the moral entrepreneur seeking to create new rules of a lack of information about any actual person, see Chapter 6, p. 275.

[234] In the *Dialogue* Jerome also expressed a synergistic position at: *Dialogus aduersus pelagianos* 2.6 (ed. Moreschini, CCSL 80, p. 63); 3.1 (ed. Moreschini, CCSL 80, p. 98).

have happened not because of the harshness of the Creator but through the fault of
the one who was created. The man who endures a storm seeks the refuge of rock or
roof; the man whom an enemy pursues flees behind city-walls; the weary traveller
seeks the relief of shade as much from the sun as from dust; if a very savage beast
thirsts for a man's blood, that man desires to avoid the present danger however he
may: in the same way man too from the beginning of his creation has God as his
helper and, since it is through God's grace that he was created and it is through
God's mercy that he remains alive and lives, he can do no good action without God,
who granted free will in such a way that he would not deny his grace for individual
actions, lest free will should redound to the injury of the Creator and cause man to
be stubborn; man who was created free in such a way that he should know that he
is nothing without God. But that he says: *In all generations*, signifies all ages, both
before the law, and under the law, and under the grace of the Gospels. For this reason
too the Apostle says: *By grace you have been saved through faith, and this is not your
own doing; it is the gift of God* [Eph. 2:8]; and in the beginning of their salutations all
his epistles have not peace first and then grace, but rather grace first and then peace,
so that after our sins have been forgiven, we may obtain the peace of the Lord.[235]

In this exegesis, starting from the characterisation of the relationship between man
and God as one of co-operation (the synergistic position he shared with Athanasius
and Evagrius of Antioch), Jerome developed this to include statements prescribed
by Augustine to acknowledge the operation of prevenient grace, such as that: 'Man
can do no good action without God'. It is noteworthy that instead of saying that
human virtuous action was caused by God's prevenient grace, Jerome described
the situation by saying that God 'would not deny his grace' to humans who had
free will. This avoided the question of how it was logically possible to separate
God's gift of prevenient grace in some cases from his non-gift of it in others. The
idea that acknowledgement that grace was necessary 'for individual actions' was
a critical element in Augustine's condemnation of Pelagius, and it was picked up
by Jerome in this passage also.[236] As has been seen, Augustine wrote that this was

---

[235] Jerome, *Ep.* 140.5 (ed. Hilberg, CSEL 56, pp. 273–4), 'Narraturus autem tristia et genus deploraturus
humanum, a laudibus Dei incipit, ut quidquid postea homini accidit aduersorum, non Creatoris duritia,
sed eius qui creatus est culpa accidisse uideatur. Qui sustinet tempestatem, uel petrae uel tecti quaerit refu-
gium; quem hostis persequitur, ad muros urbium confugit; fessus uiator tam sole quam puluere umbrae
quaerit solacium; si saeuissima bestia hominis sanguinem sitiat, cupit utcumque potuerit praesens uitare
discrimen: ita et homo a principio conditionis suae Deo utitur adiutore et, cum illius sit gratiae, quod
creatus est, illius misericordiae quod subsistit et uiuit, nihil boni operis agere potest absque eo, qui ita
liberum concessit arbitrium, ut suam per singula opera gratiam non negaret, ne libertas arbitrii redundet
ad iniuriam conditoris, et ad eius contumaciam, qui ideo liber conditus est, ut absque Deo nihil esse se
nouerit. Quod autem dicit: *In generatione et generatione,* omnia significat tempora et ante legem et in
lege, et in Euangelii gratia. Vnde et Apostolus dicit: *Gratia salui facti estis per fidem, et hoc non ex uobis,
sed ex Dei dono* [Eph. 2:8], et omnes epistulae eius in salutationis principio, non prius pacem habent et
sic gratiam, sed ante gratiam et sic pacem, ut donatis nobis peccatis nostris pacem Domini consequamur.'
[236] Augustine, *De gestis Pelagii* 14.31 (ed. Urba and Zycha, CSEL 42, p. 86), 'The grace or help of
God is given for each single action, and it is something apart from free will or the law and teaching, and
through it we are ruled by God in each individual action when we act correctly'; 'Dei gratia uel adiutorium ad singulos actus datur excepto libero arbitrio uel lege atque doctrina, ac per hoc per singulos
actus a Deo regimur, quando recte agimus'.

the key element missing in Pelagius' writings, and when Melania the Younger, Pinianus and Albina wrote to Augustine, it seems that this was what they too understood to be the key point at issue, because they told Augustine that Pelagius had accepted and asserted this statement about grace being necessary 'every day for every individual action'.[237] This was the second critique of Pelagius that Jerome had made three years earlier in his *Dialogue against the Pelagians*, where 'denying grace' hinged on denying that it was needed for every single action.[238]

Jerome identified the root of Augustine's account of God's grace as residing in the need for humility before God, and so he stressed humility ('Man who was free such that he knew he was nothing without God'). More evidence that Jerome had adapted his exegesis to acknowledge Augustine's critique of effective free will comes in his condemnation of autonomous free will that might cause stubbornness. Where previously he had stated that the co-operative process was that God called and man chose to believe, so that man was responsible for the beginning of belief, here he cited Eph. 2:8 to suggest the opposite. Technically, of the various possible aspects of God's grace to which the word *gratia* could refer, all of Jerome's uses of the word in this letter could have been referring to grace that was not the prevenient grace that was the inspiration of the Holy Spirit which caused all human virtuous action. For example, the final use of the word 'grace' and its glossing as the forgiveness of sins could be vulnerable to the same charge that Augustine laid against Pelagius, that it was not clear which aspect of grace he was referring to when he wrote of humans needing God's grace. But the attitude of humility and man's worthlessness before God were in tune with Augustine's analysis of the relationship between man and God: the mood music in this letter reflected Augustine's account of the operation of God's prevenient grace.

Even in this letter to Cyprian, however, Jerome was unable to abandon the principle of merit and reward.[239] He combined it, however, with acknowledgement that God caused all human virtue: 'From which it is transparently evident also that holy and lofty virtues are always produced by the mercy of God', although he did not use the phrase 'prevenient grace'.[240] The final paragraph of his letter summed up the changed approach to free will he now expressed; where previously he had gone out of his way to propound and extol the principle of effective free will, he now stigmatised it and characterised both the assertion of free will, and also confidence, as evil and as things rejected by God:

---

[237] See Chapter 1, n. 37.

[238] Jerome, *Dialogus aduersus pelagianos* 1.4–5 (ed. Moreschini, CCSL 80, pp. 8–9).

[239] Jerome, *Ep.* 140.20.2 (ed. Hilberg, CSEL 56, p. 288), 'Whence the apostle John too writes to the infants, to the young men, to the fathers, corresponding to the merits of his children and the progress of their individual works'; 'Vnde et Iohannes apostolus secundum merita filiorum suorum profectusque operum singulorum scribit ad paruulos, scribit ad iuuenes, scribit ad patres'; 140.6.6 (ed. Hilberg, CSEL 56, pp. 275–6), 'But the spirit is *inhabited* and not *deserted* that merits God as its guest'; '*Habitata* est autem anima, non *deserta*, quae hospitem meretur Deum'.

[240] Jerome, *Ep.* 140.6.7 (ed. Hilberg, CSEL 56, p. 276), 'Ex quo liquido demonstratur sanctos quoque excelsasque uirtutes Dei semper misericordia procreari.'

Ps. 90:17: *And let the favour of the Lord our God be upon us and make secure for us the works of our hands and strengthen the works of our hands.* Septuagint: *And let the splendour of the Lord our God be upon us and direct for us the works of our hands and direct the works of our hands.* Where are they who, applauding themselves with the power of their free will, think they have obtained God's grace if they have the power of doing or not doing good or evil? See what the blessed Moses says here after the resurrection that he had requested: *Fill us in the morning with your mercy and we will both give praise and rejoice all our days*; by no means is he content at his own resurrection and his obtaining the rewards of eternal life, but he asks that the favour of the Lord his God should be upon those who are resurrected, and that it should shine in the spirits and hearts of the saints, and that God himself should direct the works of their hands and should make permanent and himself strengthen whatever goodness is seen in the saints. For just as the humility of one who begs merits rewards, in the same way the arrogance of one who is confident is deserted by God's help.[241]

In its references to begging and its characterisation of confidence as arrogance, the final sentence of this letter eerily echoes the observation made by the anonymous author of *The Predestined* (*Praedestinatus*) that what motivated adoption of the notion of predestination as preordainment was 'human fear or shame' (*timor humanus aut uerecundia*).[242] Begging by the powerless was now the properly subservient human relationship with God. Confidence was arrogance; powerless subjection was humility.

Conclusion on Jerome

For almost his whole career, until some time in around AD 414, Jerome continuously referred to effective free will in explicit and deliberate terms: assertions of 'free will' (*libertas arbitrii*), and phrases such as 'we have free will' (*liberi arbitrii sumus*) abound in his exegesis. Moreoever, he explicitly referred to free will to goodness, and asserted that without the quality of voluntariness, a virtuous act could have no moral value; virtue required effective free will. Jerome's conceptual framework and his terms of reference were the same as Pelagius': effective free will in humans, the goal of perfect imitation of Christ, a direct causal

---

[241] Jerome, *Ep.* 140.21 (ed. Hilberg, CSEL 56, pp. 288–9), 'Ps. 90:17: *Et sit decor Domini Dei nostri super nos, et opus manuum nostrarum fac stabile super nos et opus manuum nostrarum confirma.* Septuaginta: *Et sit splendor Domini Dei nostri super nos, et opera manuum nostrarum dirige super nos et opus manuum nostrarum dirige.* Vbi sunt, qui liberi arbitrii sibi potestate plaudentes in eo se putant Dei gratiam consecutos, si habeant potestatem faciendi uel non faciendi bona siue mala? Ecce hic beatus Moyses post resurrectionem quam postulauerat, dicens: *Imple nos matutina misericordia tua, et laudabimus et laetabimur in cunctis diebus nostris,* nequaquam surrexisse contentus est se et aeternae uitae praemia consecutum, sed postulat ut decor Domini Dei sui sit super eos, qui surrexerint, et splendeat in animabus cordibusque sanctorum et opera manuum eorum ipse dirigat, faciatque esse perpetua ipseque confirmet, quicquid in sanctis uidetur boni. Sicut enim humilitas deprecantis meretur praemia, ita superbia confidentis Dei auxilio deseretur.'

[242] Anon., *Praedestinatus* 3.2 (ed. Gori, CCSL 25B, p. 66), commenting on the predestinarians: 'So that human fear or shame should not make us their comrades'; 'Ne ergo participes nos eorum timor humanus aut uerecundia faceret'.

entailment between effort and reward, and a prize won by merit. In addition, Jerome propounded ideas that have been associated with Pelagius and character-ised as distinctively and diagnostically 'Pelagian', even though Pelagius did not himself advocate them, such as the idea that the rich could not enter the kingdom of heaven. Jerome stigmatised riches as inherently immoral and advised Christians to give away their property. He also implied that marriage was not virtuous, glossing it as an 'evil'.[243] On both these points, Jerome stood closer to the author(s) of the Caspari Corpus letters *On Chastity* and *On Riches* than Pelagius did. Jerome frequently used the biblical citation *God is no respecter of persons* [Acts 10:34, Rom. 2:11]. He also wrote of the disparity between true Christians and those who were Christian in name only, and contrasted such a nominal Christian with the Christian who was reborn as a new man and who lived according to Old and New Testament injunctions.

Jerome's Position as Cheerleader for Ascetic Entryism in the Latin West

In order to construct his authority as an expert on Christianity and so build a career, Jerome sought to make himself the chief salesman of asceticism in the Latin West. Before AD 383, Helvidius wrote against the perpetual virginity of Mary, a doctrine on which ascetics relied as proof of the superior status of virginity. Jerome replied to him and advertised this fact to Eustochium.[244] There was opposition to the intro-duction into Christianity of ascetic assumptions as norms, exemplified by Jovinian and Vigilantius, who raised objections to this ascetic entryism. In each case, Jerome was the advocate of asceticism who wrote replies to its critics.

Three conclusions flow from the above. First, Jerome was the leading Latin propagandist for the ascetic movement and its application to all Christians, not Pelagius. Jerome's panegyric for the coenobitic life in his letter to Eustochium was intended to establish his position as the leading proselytiser for asceticism in the Latin West.[245] He advocated a more demanding level of ascetic renuncia-tion than Pelagius, including the abandonment of all property.[246] He explicitly canvassed perfection as a goal. Second, all the ideas in Pelagius' writings were present in Jerome's works. Third, it seems possible that Jerome attacked Pelagius in order to defend himself from an accusation of heresy, since he had himself built his career on proposing either the same ascetic principles as Pelagius set out or more extreme versions of them. This left him more vulnerable to the charge of having propounded the theses alleged to constitute 'Pelagianism' than

---

[243] Jerome, *Ep*. 22.19.1–4 (ed. Hilberg, CSEL 54, pp. 168–9), 'I do not detract from marriage when I set virginity above it. No one compares an evil thing to a good thing …. So that you should know that virginity is natural, and marriage follows transgression'; 'Non est detrahere nuptiis, cum illis uirginitas antefertur. Nemo malum bono comparat …. Vt scias uirginitatem esse naturae, nuptias post delictum'. See also n. 103.

[244] Jerome, *Ep*. 22.22.1 (ed. Hilberg, CSEL 54, p. 174).

[245] Jerome, *Ep*. 22.35 (ed. Hilberg, CSEL 54, pp. 197–200).

[246] Jerome, *Ep*. 22.31 (ed. Hilberg, CSEL 54, pp. 191–2).

Pelagius himself was, because it was easier to read such unwarranted entailments into Jerome's ascetic paraenesis, since on several topics Jerome had taken more extreme positions than Pelagius. Jerome needed to put clear water between Pelagius and himself.[247]

It is important to note that Evagrius of Antioch was a friend and patron of Jerome. Jerome stayed with him, and when he went into the Syrian desert, he was in fact on Evagrius' estate, where Evagrius visited him regularly.[248] Yet in AD 415 in his *Dialogue against the Pelagians*, Jerome made the suggestion that sinlessness was achievable the mainstay of his accusation of heresy against Pelagius, despite the fact that his friend Evagrius had explicitly stated that Antony had no faults and had advocated pursuit of perfection.

These facts point to the conclusion that asceticism was a broad movement within which a range of positions were propounded by individuals. Pelagius in no way departed from its core assumptions, long canvassed by writers of the movement.

The evidence concerning Jerome's exegesis has been presented in chronological order to show how on each key issue his expression of his view was not an isolated incident, where he proposed this position just once or twice. These were the principles he consistently expressed across a literary career spanning thirty-five years. He attempted to modify them only from around AD 414 or 415 onwards, and then with difficulty and limited coherence. Under threat of an accusation of heresy because he had propounded the same ideas as Pelagius, Jerome sought to differentiate himself from Pelagius. In circumstances that were highly political, he caved in and attacked Pelagius even though it meant going against his lifelong principles that he had proclaimed in his writings for decades. Examination of Jerome's exegesis in depth reveals how difficult it was for him to accommodate his conception of Christianity to the new orthodoxy proposed by Augustine. Stephen Cooper has written about the 'variety of Christianity' set out by Marius Victorinus.[249] The late 4th and early 5th century was an era when individuals felt free to set out different accounts of Christianity, but this freedom to interpret Scripture became restricted as a result of fear engendered by successful indictments for heresy laid against some scriptural interpreters.

---

[247] In addition, there was Jerome's possible link to the Rufinus who wrote the *Liber de fide* in which it was argued that Adam was born mortal and would have died whether or not he had sinned.

[248] Cain, *The Letters of Jerome*, pp. 40–1. In a letter, Jerome spoke very highly of Evagrius: Jerome, *Ep.* 1.15.1 (ed. Hilberg, CSEL 54, p. 8), 'For now we come to the name of our friend Evagrius. I would be unwise if I were to judge that I could describe his labour on Christ's behalf; if I wanted to be quite silent about it, I should not be able to because my voice would burst out in joy'; 'Iam enim ad Euagrii nostri nomen aduenimus. Cuius ego pro Christo laborem si arbitrer a me dici posse, non sapiam, si penitus tacere uelim, uoce in gaudium erumpente non possim.'

[249] S. A. Cooper, *Metaphysics and Morals in Marius Victorinus' Commentary on the Letter to the Ephesians: a Contribution to the History of Neoplatonism and Christianity* (New York, 1995), p. 1.

Part III

Relevant Material in Selected other Christian Writings Circulating in the Late 4th and Early 5th Centuries

There were other Christian writers besides Athanasius, Evagrius of Antioch and Jerome who propounded effective free will, explained predestination as God's foreknowledge of autonomous human decisions and believed that human nature was inclined to goodness. Some examples are noted briefly below.

Ambrose

In his *On the Faith* (*De fide*) of AD 378, Ambrose explained predestination as God's foreknowledge of autonomous human decisions. Commenting on Matt. 20:23: *To sit at my right hand or left is not for me to grant; it is for those for whom it has been prepared by my Father,* he wrote:

> Then, referring to the Father, [Jesus] added: *For those for whom it has been prepared*, so that he might show that the Father also is not accustomed to pay heed to requests, but to merits, because: *God is not a respecter of persons* [Acts 10:34, Rom. 2:11]. For this reason the Apostle too said: *Those whom he foreknew and predestined* [Rom. 8:29]. For he did not predestine before he would have foreknown, but rather he has predestined the rewards of those people whose merits he foreknew.[250]

Augustine nevertheless reported that Ambrose's view of predestination was the same as his own.[251]

The Anonymous Author Known as Ambrosiaster

Three different versions of the *Commentary on the Pauline Epistles* written by the author known as Ambrosiaster survive. Stephen Cooper and David Hunter have jointly argued that the different recensions are the author's redactions of his own

---

[250] Ambrose, *De fide* 5.6.83 (ed. Faller, CSEL 78, pp. 246–7), 'Denique et ad patrem referens addidit: *Quibus paratum est*, ut ostenderet patrem quoque non petitionibus deferre solere, sed meritis, quia: *Deus personarum acceptor non est* [Acts 10:34, Rom. 2:11]. Vnde et apostolus ait: *Quos praesciuit et praedestinauit* [Rom. 8:29]. Non enim ante praedestinauit quam praesciret, sed quorum merita praesciuit, eorum praemia praedestinauit.'

[251] Augustine, *De dono perseuerantiae* 19.49 (ed. Chéné and Pintard, BA 24, pp. 722–4).

text, and they date the phases of composition from the 370s AD to AD 384.²⁵² All three versions of the commentary provide evidence that the author was concerned about how God's justice could be preserved alongside a process of predestination referred to in the Bible. The point is not whether the commentary composed by the anonymous author known as Ambrosiaster is doctrinally coherent but simply that it provides evidence for the ideas that were current in Christian literature in the late 4th century. These interpretations of Scripture were deemed acceptable at the time, and Ambrosiaster's commentary has not since been condemned as heretical.²⁵³

Predestination explained as foreknowledge

The author known as Ambrosiaster referred to the questions raised by Paul's statements about Jacob and Esau as a 'complaint' or 'accusation' (*querela*), and said that pagans interpreted Paul's statements as disproving Christianity's claim to present a just God.²⁵⁴ He interpreted Jacob and Esau as types who represented believers and non-believers.²⁵⁵ His explanation of the Jacob and Esau story was that this referred to God's foreknowledge. Ambrosiaster explained predestination as foreknowledge in an emphatic manner, using the word 'foreknowledge' or variants of it fifteen times in his comments on Rom. 9:11–16 to underline his argument that this was foreknowledge of autonomous human decisions.²⁵⁶ He repeated nine times that God was just.²⁵⁷ Reading Ambrosiaster's comments on Rom. 9:11–16, what come across strongly are his prioritising of justice, his overwhelming concern to interpret predestination as God's foreknowledge of autonomous human actions, his references to the 'will' (*uoluntas*) and the 'mind' (*mens*) of the individual as the factor determining God's responses, his references to merit, his suggestion that all nature is good and only the will creates evil, his concern that man should not be able to make excuses (the same argument that Evagrius, Jerome and Pelagius used), his reference to God's universal salvific will [1 Tim. 2:4], and the fact that in order to preserve God's justice he cited Acts 10:34, Rom. 2:11:*God is not a*

---

²⁵² There remains the possibility of later interpolations into these redactions.

²⁵³ See the appendix at the end of the book for a translation of Ambrosiaster's commentary on Rom. 9:11–16, given in full because it contains so many of the ideas for which Pelagius was later condemned. Ideally it should be read in full, rather than in selected excerpts. Of necessity, the text of this chapter contains only selected passages.

²⁵⁴ Ambrosiaster, *In epistolas Paulinas*, on Rom. 9:1–13 (ed. Vogels, CSEL 81/1, p. 317); all references and quotations are taken from the γ-text of Ambrosiaster's *Commentary on the Pauline Epistles*.

²⁵⁵ Ambrosiaster, *In epistolas Paulinas*, on Rom. 9:10 (ed. Vogels, CSEL 81/1, p. 311).

²⁵⁶ Ambrosiaster, *In epistolas Paulinas*, on Rom. 9:11–16 (ed. Vogels, CSEL 81/1, pp. 313–23). The evidence to support this argumentation can be found in the translation and text of Ambrosiaster, *In epistolas Paulinas*, on Rom. 9:11–16 in the appendix at the end of this chapter. The total of 15 uses of the word 'foreknowledge' includes only occurrences of the words *praescientia* and *praescius*, and omits the times he referred to God's knowing the future (*nouit/sciens futurum*, etc), of which there are several also. Ambrosiaster also propounded this argument that predestination was God's foreknowledge in his comments on Rom. 8:28–30 (ed. Vogels, CSEL 81/1, pp. 289–93).

²⁵⁷ Counting uses of the words 'justice' (*iustitia*), 'just' (*iustus*) and 'not unjustly' (*non iniuste*).

respecter of persons, to show that God did not have pre-selected favourites, just as Ambrose and Jerome did. Ambrosiaster then suggested that the complaint should cease because he had resolved the issue. He thus worked hard to interpret Paul's words to show that God's judgements were dependent on man's autonomous decisions:

> *For when they were not yet born nor had they done anything either good or bad, so that God's plan might continue according to his election, it was said not on the basis of works but on the basis of the calling, that the elder would serve the younger, as it is written: I loved Jacob, but Esau I hated* [Mal. 1:2–3]. That is in Malachi. Paul proclaims God's foreknowledge in these matters, because nothing else can happen other than what God knows will happen. For through his knowledge of what each of them will be in the future, he said: 'This one will be worthy, who will be the younger, and the one who will be older will be unworthy'. He chose one and rejected the other as a result of his foreknowledge. And God's plan continues with regard to the one he chose because nothing can happen except what God knows and has planned with regard to him, that he will be worthy of salvation; and concerning him whom God rejected, likewise God's plan continues, that he planned concerning him, because he will be unworthy. This God does as one who knows the future and not as a *respecter of persons* [Acts 10:34, Rom. 2:11], for he condemns no-one before they should sin, and he crowns no-one before they should conquer. This relates to the case of the Jews who defend their previous privilege as sons of Abraham.[258]

Ambrosiaster's explanation of Paul's meaning is at odds with Augustine's interpretation, in which prevenient grace was the cause of an individual's virtue and God's foreknowledge of an individual's free decision was not a viable escape route from that truth, as Augustine explained:

> But it is surprising to see the steep cliffs they hurl themselves over when they are trapped by these difficulties and fear the nets of truth. They say: 'He hated one and loved the other of those not yet born because he foresaw their future works'. Who would not be surprised that the Apostle lacked this very clever idea? .... Where now are the merits, where are the works either past or future, carried out or to be carried out, as if by the strength of free will? Did not the Apostle offer a clear statement concerning the excellence of gratuitous grace, that is, of true grace? .... Is it on

---

[258] Ambrosiaster, *In epistolas Paulinas*, on Rom. 9:11–13 (ed. Vogels, CSEL 81/1, p. 313), '*Nam cum nati nondum fuissent aut aliquid egissent bonum uel malum, ut secundum electionem propositum Dei permaneret, non ex operibus, sed ex uocatione dictum est, quia maior seruiet minori, sicut scriptum est: Iacob dilexi, Esau autem odio habui* [Mal. 1:2–3]. *Istud in Malachia habetur. Praescientiam Dei flagitat in his causis, quia non aliud potest euenire, quam nouit Deus futurum. Sciendo enim quid unusquisque illorum futurus esset dixit:* "Hic erit dignus, qui erit minor, et qui erit maior, indignus". *Vnum elegit praescientia et alterum spreuit. Et in illo quem elegit, propositum Dei manet, quia aliud non potest euenire quam scit et proposuit in illo, ut salute dignus sit; et in illo quem spernit, simili modo manet propositum, quod proposuit de illo, quia indignus erit. Hoc quasi praescius, non personarum acceptor* [Acts 10:34, Rom. 2:11], *nam neminem damnat, antequam peccet, et nullum coronat, antequam uincat. Hoc pertinet ad causam Iudaeorum, qui sibi praerogatiuam defendunt, quod filii sint Abrahae.*'

account of the future works of both of them which God foresaw? No, heaven forbid this also.[259]

It is noteworthy that in around AD 428–9, Prosper of Aquitaine wrote to Augustine saying that among earlier interpreters of Scripture the consensus understanding of predestination was that it was God's foreknowledge of autonomous human actions.[260]

Ambrosiaster on free will

Ambrosiaster wrote of free will as part of the process of coming to faith, and referred to a law of nature within man. Commenting on Rom. 6:17: *But thanks be to God that you, having once been slaves of sin, have become obedient from the heart to the form of teaching to which you were entrusted,* he wrote:

> Paul says that we have been made slaves of righteousness from our heart, not from the law; from our will, not from fear, so that our profession should be brought forth by the decision of our mind. For we have been brought to faith by nature not by law …. Hence Paul gives thanks to God because although we were slaves of sin, we listened from our heart, believing in Christ, so that we serve God not because of the law of Moses, but because of the law of nature.[261]

Ambrosiaster was unequivocal that belief was a matter of autonomous choice. In his exegesis, the human will determined belief:

> To believe or not to believe is a matter of will (*uoluntas*). No one can be forced toward what is not visible for all to see, but he is invited, because he is not coerced,

---

[259] Augustine, *Ep.* 194.8.35–9 (ed. Goldbacher, CSEL 57, pp. 204–7), 'Mirum est autem, cum his coartantur angustiis, in quanta se abrupta praecipitent metuentes retia ueritatis. "Ideo", inquiunt, "nondum natorum alium oderat, alium diligebat, quia eorum futura opera praeuidebat." Quis istum acutissimum sensum defuisse Apostolo non miretur? …. Vbi nunc merita, ubi opera uel praeterita uel futura tamquam liberi arbitrii uiribus adimpleta siue adimplenda? Nonne apertam protulit Apostolus de gratuitae gratiae, hoc est uerae gratiae commendatione sententiam? …. An propter opera quae futura praeuidebat amborum? Immo et hoc absit'.

[260] Prosper, *apud* Augustine, *Ep.* 225.8 (ed. Goldbacher, CSEL 57, p. 467), 'When the opinions of earlier teachers on this matter are reviewed, one and the same judgement is found in almost all of them, by which they have taken the plan and predestination of God as being based on his foreknowledge, so that God made some people vessels of honour and others vessels of reproach for this reason, namely, because he foresaw the end of each person and knew in advance how each would will and act in the future under the help of this grace'; 'Retractatis priorum de hac re opinionibus, paene omnium par inuenitur et una sententia, qua propositum et praedestinationem Dei secundum praescientiam recepe-runt, ut ob hoc Deus alios uasa honoris alios contumeliae fecerit, quia finem uniuscuiusque praeuiderit et, sub ipso gratiae adiutorio in qua futurus esset uoluntate et actione, praescierit.'

[261] Ambrosiaster, *In epistolas Paulinas*, on Rom. 6:17 (ed. Vogels, CSEL 81/1, pp. 205–7), concerning Paul: 'Dicit seruos nos factos iustitiae ex corde, non ex lege; ex uoluntate, non ex timore, ut professio nostra animi iudicio promatur. Per naturam enim inducti sumus ad fidem, non per legem …. Hinc gratias refert Domino, quia cum essemus serui peccati, obaudiuimus ex corde credentes in Christum, ut seruiremus Deo non per legem Moysi, sed per legem naturae.'

but persuaded. For this reason he obtains merit. For he believes what he does not see but hopes for.[262]

He described the process of coming to belief or not doing so as entirely internal to the human mind; each individual had to *persuade himself* to believe:

> Although the non-believer may seem to himself in no way guilty, because he was not able to deal with this thing in himself, nevertheless he is convicted by his reasoning, because he did not persuade himself that this thing is true, which he had seen confirmed by testimonies of powers and which he has seen many people accept.[263]

Ambrosiaster on grace

Interpreting Rom. 11:6: *But if it is by grace, it is no longer on the basis of works; otherwise grace would no longer be grace*, Ambrosiaster described two aspects of this unearned grace, both of which were a generalised grace given to all humanity. The first was God's forgiveness of mankind's sins, and the second was the aspect of God's kindness that sought to heal people; Ambrosiaster described grace as something offered.[264] God's grace did not control any individual since it could be rendered void.[265] Ambrosiaster consistently used the word 'grace' to refer to the universal gift of God's forgiveness of mankind's sins and Christ's advent.[266] He

---

[262] Ambrosiaster, *In epistolas Paulinas*, on Rom. 4:4 (ed. Vogels, CSEL 81/1, pp. 129–31), 'Credere autem et non credere uoluntatis est. Neque enim quis cogi potest ad id quod manifestum non est, sed inuitatur, quia non extorquetur, sed suadetur. Ideo ad meritum proficit. Credit enim quod non uidet, sed sperat.' The α-text of the commentary mentions 'consent', 'rewards' and Abraham, so that it resembles the language of Evagrius and Jerome even more closely: 'For this reason, consenting, he must obtain rewards, just as Abraham too believed what he did not see'; 'Quamobrem adsentiens praemiis adficiendus est, sicut {et} Abraham quod non uidit credidit.'

[263] Ambrosiaster, *In epistolas Paulinas*, on Rom. 2:16 (ed. Vogels, CSEL 81/1, p. 79), 'Quamuis enim sibi uideatur minime reus qui non credidit, quia apud se tractare istud non potuit, ratione tamen conuincitur, quia non sibi suasit uerum hoc esse, quod de uirtutum testimoniis uiderat firmari et multos sequi.'

[264] Ambrosiaster, *In epistolas Paulinas*, on Rom. 11:6 (ed. Vogels, CSEL 81/1, p. 365), '*But if it is by grace, then it is not on the basis of works*. It is clear that because grace is the gift of God, it is not a reward due for works, but is granted freely by reason of the mercy which intervenes. *Otherwise grace would not be grace*. It is true that if it is a reward it is not grace; but because it is not a reward, it is undoubtedly grace, since to grant pardon to sinners is nothing other than grace, granted to those who are not asking for it but offered to them so that they might believe. Grace therefore has two aspects to it, because it is a characteristic of God, who abounds in mercy, so that it also seeks out those whom it heals gratuitously'; '*Si autem gratia, iam non ex operibus*. Manifestum est, quia gratia donum Dei est, non debita merces operibus, sed gratuita ratione misericordia interueniente concessa. *Alioquin gratia iam non est gratia*. Verum est, quia si merces est, non est gratia; sed quia merces non est, sine dubio gratia est, quia ueniam peccantibus dare non est aliud quam gratia, et his qui non requirunt, sed offertur illis ut credant. Duplex ergo gratia est, quia hoc conpetit Deo, qui abundat misericordia, ut et requirat quos gratis curat.'

[265] Ambrosiaster, *In epistolas Paulinas*, on Rom. 9:4 (ed. Vogels, CSEL 81/1, p. 303), 'Once the adopted sons of God, they have made the affection and grace of God the Father ineffectual'; 'Olim filii adoptati affectum et gratiam Dei patris in irritum deduxerunt.'

[266] Ambrosiaster, *In epistolas Paulinas*, on Rom. 5:15–16 (ed. Vogels, CSEL 81/1, p. 181), 'The grace of God abounded in the descent of the Saviour, granting forgiveness to all, when they have been raised

described the action of grace as 'to goad' (*conpungere*), and 'to help' (*adiuuare*).[267] Faith was something to which Paul provoked people ('to provoke', *lacessere*) through his teaching and through example.[268] Ambrosiaster glossed the word 'grace' as Paul's teaching.[269]

Ambrosiaster consistently assumed that grace was something given to those who were worthy of receiving it, and that individuals controlled whether or not they were worthy. Just as Evagrius had done, Ambrosiaster used reflexive personal pronouns to make clear the individual's control over whether or not he received grace.[270] He stated explicitly that grace was merited. Commenting on Rom. 16:20, he said of Paul: 'The grace which he promised he will give them by coming to them, he now prays that they will have. For if they merit to receive that grace, then he is already with them in hope.'[271] Clearly for Ambrosiaster the concept of meriting grace was acceptable.

Ambrosiaster used the word 'grace' to refer to Christ's wiping away of mankind's sins and the resultant reconciliation between man and God.[272] He also used it to denote salvation in a context in which he at the same time asserted that

---

up to heaven in triumph .... But the grace of God in Christ has justified men not from one sin but from many sins, by giving them remission of sins'; 'Gratia Dei abundauit in descensu Saluatoris, omnibus dans indulgentiam, cum triumpho sublatis eis in caelum .... Gratia uero Dei per Christum non ex uno delicto, sed ex multis peccatis iustificauit homines, dando illis remissionem peccatorum.'

[267] Ambrosiaster, *In epistolas Paulinas*, on Rom. 8:30 (ed. Vogels, CSEL 81/1, p. 291), '*But those whom he has predestined, he has also called.* To call is to help someone who is considering faith or to goad whomever God might know will listen'; '*Quos autem praedestinauit, illos et uocauit.* Vocare est cogitantem de fide adiuuare aut conpungere eum, quem sciat audire.'

[268] Ambrosiaster, *In epistolas Paulinas*, on Rom. 1:13 (ed. Vogels, CSEL 81/1, p. 33), 'He provokes them to correct faith by the example of the other Gentiles'; 'Lacessit illos ad fidem rectam exemplo ceterarum gentium.'

[269] Ambrosiaster, *In epistolas Paulinas*, on Rom. 1:11–12 (ed. Vogels, CSEL 81/1, pp. 27–9), 'He wants to come to them quickly, so that drawing them out of that tradition, he might give them a spiritual gift, so that he might acquire them for God, making them partakers in spiritual grace .... So that the application of spiritual grace through the preaching of the Apostle might bring about this effect'; 'Se autem cupere citius uenire, ut ab hac illos traditione abstrahens spiritale eis traderet donum, ut adquireret illos Deo, participes hos faciens gratiae spiritalis .... Vt administratio gratiae spiritalis euangelizante Apostolo hunc praestaret effectum.'

[270] Ambrosiaster, *In epistolas Paulinas*, on Rom. 1:13 (ed. Vogels, CSEL 81/1, pp. 31–3), 'He encourages them to prepare themselves, so that hearing that a spiritual grace is to be given to them, they should make themselves worthy to receive it'; 'Hos ut se praeparent hortatur, ut audientes gratiam sibi spiritalem ministrandam ad excipiendam eam dignos se efficerent.'

[271] Ambrosiaster, *In epistolas Paulinas*, on Rom. 16:20 (ed. Vogels, CSEL 81/1, p. 491), 'Gratiam quam promisit illis in aduentu suo, iam optat esse cum illis. Si enim merentur accipere, iam cum illis est in spe.'

[272] Ambrosiaster, *In epistolas Paulinas*, on Rom. 5:1 (ed. Vogels, CSEL 81/1, p. 151), 'Faith makes us have peace with God, not the law. For this reconciles us to God when our sins have been removed, which had made us God's enemies. And because the Lord Jesus is the minister of this grace, it is through him that we have made peace with God'; 'Pacem cum Deo habere fides facit, non lex. Haec enim nos Deo reconciliat sublatis peccatis, quae nos Deo fecerant inimicos. Et quia Dominus Iesus huius gratiae minister est, per ipsum pacificati sumus Deo.'

this salvation lay in the control of the autonomous human will; grace was given to those who already believed:

> [Christ] *Through whom also we have access to this grace, in which we stand and rejoice in our hope of sharing the glory of God.* It is clear that through Christ we have access to the grace of God. For he is the arbitrator between God and men, who, raising us up with his teaching, made those of us who stand in his faith hope for the gift of God's grace. And as a result of this we stand, because before we were prone on the ground, but believing, we have been raised upright, rejoicing in the hope of the glory which he has promised to us.[273]

Ambrosiaster's interpretation of 1 Cor. 4:7: *What do you have that you have not received?* made no reference to grace or to being given virtue. He explained the passage as Paul referring to the fact that the Corinthians had not received anything good other than Paul's own teaching, in the context of argument about which teachers the Corinthians should accept.[274]

Ambrosiaster's account of human nature

Ambrosiaster asserted that there was a 'natural law' (*lex naturalis*) that guided man to correct belief. He characterised belief as something to which individuals came through their own choice.[275] This natural law played a part in coming to salvation.[276]

---

[273] Ambrosiaster, *In epistolas Paulinas*, on Rom. 5:2 (ed. Vogels, CSEL 81/1, p. 153), '*Per quem et accessum habemus ad gratiam istam, in qua stamus et gloriamur in spe gloriae Dei. Manifestum est per Christum nos aditum habere ad gratiam Dei. Ipse est enim arbiter Dei et hominum, qui nos doctrina sua erigens sperare fecit donum gratiae Dei stantes in fide eius. Et ideo stantes, quia prius iacuimus, credentes autem erecti sumus gloriantes in spe claritatis quam promisit nobis.*'

[274] Ambrosiaster, *In epistolas Paulinas*, on 1 Cor. 4:7 (ed. Vogels, CSEL 81/2, p. 45), '*For what do you have that you have not received?* He says that that man has not obtained anything good from anyone else beyond what he had received from the Apostle, and so it is pointless to complain. For what they possessed, they had received from the Apostle. The Apostle seems to speak to one man, because he is speaking to a part of the people'; '*Quid autem habes quod non accepisti? Nihil illum boni ultra dicit consecutum ab aliis quam ab eo acceperat, ideo frustra queri. Quod enim habebant, ab Apostolo acceperant. Ad unum autem uidetur loqui, quia ad partem plebis loquitur.*'

[275] Ambrosiaster, *In epistolas Paulinas*, on Rom. 2:15 (ed. Vogels, CSEL 81/1, p. 77), 'This has the same meaning, because when they believe through the guidance of nature, they show the work of the law not through the letter but through their conscience. For the work of the law is faith, which while it is revealed in the words of God, shows itself to be a law laid down for itself by natural judgement, since it goes beyond what the law commands so that it believes in Christ .... These people believe because of the inner witness of their conscience, because they know in their conscience that what they believe is right'; '*Idem sensus est, quia dum natura duce credunt, opus legis ostendunt, non per litteram, sed per conscientiam. Opus enim legis fides est, quam cum dictis Dei exhibet, naturali iudicio ostendit semetipsum esse sibi legem, quia quod mandat lex, ultro facit ut credat in Christum .... Teste interiori conscientia sua credunt, quia conscii sibi sunt conuenire sibi quod credunt*'.

[276] Ambrosiaster, *In epistolas Paulinas*, on Rom. 1:11 (ed. Vogels, CSEL 81/1, p. 29), 'Taking thought for human weakness God decreed that the human race was saved by faith alone along with the natural law'; '*Consulens Deus infirmitati humanae fide sola, addita lege naturali, hominum genus saluari decreuit.*'

It taught men not to do to others what they did not want to suffer themselves.[277] Ambrosiaster discussed at length how there were men before Moses: 'Who had not sinned in the likeness of Adam', and he cited Abraham as one such who was 'guided by nature'.[278] This was the same argument that Pelagius later expounded about the natural goodness of some Old Testament figures. Ambrosiaster differentiated between the death of the body and the death of the soul in order to assert that: 'And so, as I said earlier, death did not reign in everyone, but only in those who sinned in the same way as Adam sinned.'[279] He referred to 'nature' and the 'natural law' (*natura, lex naturalis*), where Pelagius later referred to 'the good of nature' (*bonum naturae*), but the argument that there had been 'righteous men' (*iusti*) before Moses and before Christ's advent was the same in both authors. As has been seen, Ambrosiaster described how Paul's preaching facilitated people's partaking in spiritual grace, and in the same sentence he used the language of perfection as a commonplace: 'So that they might be perfect (*perfecti*) in their faith and in their public display of it.'[280]

Ambrosiaster on merit and reward

Ambrosiaster used the language of 'merits' (*merita*) and 'rewards' (*praemia*) to sell his brand of Christianity to his readers just as freely as Evagrius and Jerome did. He advertised a direct equation between virtue and reward just as they had done.[281] He compared David and Saul in order to illustrate how their autonomous decisions determined their merit, which in turn determined God's judgement:

> [Saul] was furious because twice his prayers were not heard, since he was unworthy. But rather than persist with prayer so that he would have created merit in himself,

---

[277] Ambrosiaster, *In epistolas Paulinas*, on Rom. 5:13 (ed. Vogels, CSEL 81/1, p. 167).

[278] Ambrosiaster, *In epistolas Paulinas*, on Rom. 5:14 (ed. Vogels, CSEL 81/1, pp. 173–5), 'As for those in whom [death] did not reign because they did not sin in the likeness of the transgression of Adam, they were set aside in the hope that a saviour would come to free them, as is said of Abraham, because although he was in hell, yet he was kept separate by a long distance, in such a way that there was a huge gulf between the righteous and sinners .... Therefore how can it be said that death reigned in someone who guided by nature, kept what the law later commanded before the law itself came?'; 'In quos autem non regnauit, quia non peccauerunt in similitudinem praeuaricationis Adae, sub spe reseruati sunt aduentui saluatoris in libera, sicut legitur de Abraham, quia quamuis apud inferos fuerit, discretus tamen longo interuallo, ita ut chaos esset ingens inter iustos et peccatores .... Igitur qui ante legem hoc seruauit natura duce quod postea lex mandauit, numquid potest dici, quia mors regnauit in eum?'

[279] Ambrosiaster, *In epistolas Paulinas*, on Rom. 5:14 (ed. Vogels, CSEL 81/1, p. 179), 'Itaque non in omnes regnauit mors, sed in eos qui peccauerunt in similitudine praeuaricationis Adae, sicut supra memoraui.'

[280] Ambrosiaster, *In epistolas Paulinas*, on Rom. 1:11 (ed. Vogels, CSEL 81/1, p. 29), 'Vt in fide et professione sua essent perfecti.'

[281] Ambrosiaster, *In epistolas Paulinas*, on Rom. 5:3 (ed. Vogels, CSEL 81/1, p. 153), Ambrosiaster stated that virtue, in the form of steadfast hope: 'Has great merit with God'; 'Magnum meritum est apud Deum.'

through which he would have become worthy, instead impatient and indignant at God's judgement, he sought help from idols that he had previously condemned as worthless. See then how it is clear that the judgement of God's foreknowledge is just, even to those who do not want it.[282]

Ambrosiaster's interpretation of the simile of the potter shaping pots at Rom. 9:21 made God's justice paramount, and this justice referred back to God's foreknowledge of autonomous human decisions.[283]

   This is a very brief survey of the extent to which the author known as Ambrosiaster took the same interpretative standpoint as Pelagius did later. It serves to illustrate the typical content of 'vulgate' doctrine in circulation in the Latin West in the late 4th century. It also shows how far interpretation of the Bible was an unsupervised arena in which individuals were free to express themselves and to think creatively in writing. This presumption of free discussion was the norm inherited from classical traditions of philosophical enquiry and the rhetorical educational system.[284]

Apponius' *Commentary on the Song of Songs*

The editors of Apponius' *Commentary on the Song of Songs*, Bernard De Vregille and Louis Neyrand, dated the work to between AD 404 and 410.[285] The commentary is further evidence that the ideas and concepts Pelagius used were commonplaces of Christian ascetic writing. It further underlines the fact that Pelagius did not invent any doctrine but instead was representative of mainstream Christian thought in his era. Furthermore, Apponius was aware of controversy about grace and free will.[286] Despite this, he referred to the 'good of nature' (*bonum naturae*).[287] He also described the men of the Old Testament before Moses as 'perfect' (*perfecti*).[288] Apponius also suggested that human initiative played a part

---

[282] Ambrosiaster, *In epistolas Paulinas*, on Rom. 9:16 (ed. Vogels, CSEL 81/1, p. 323), '[Saul] furens, quia semel et iterum non sit auditus, cum esset indignus, nec in prece perstitit, ut meritum sibi faceret, per quod esset dignus, sed inpatiens et de Dei iudicio indignatus ab idolis, quae prius uelut nullius momenti damnauerat, auxilium requisiuit. Ecce iustum esse iudicium praescientiae Dei etiam nolentibus manifestum est.'

[283] Ambrosiaster, *In epistolas Paulinas*, on Rom. 9:21 (ed. Vogels, CSEL 81/1, p. 329), 'For as I said earlier, he knows who ought to be shown mercy'; 'Scit enim cuius debeat misereri, sicut supra memoraui.'

[284] Cameron, *Christianity and the Rhetoric of Empire*, p. 222.

[285] L. Neyrand and B. De Vregille, ed., *Apponii In Canticum Canticorum Expositio*, Corpus Christianorum Series Latina 19 (Turnhout, 1986), pp. CVIII–CX.

[286] Apponius, *In Canticum* 7.57, ll. 790–2 (ed. Neyrand and De Vregille, CCSL 19, p. 179).

[287] Apponius, *In Canticum* 4.45, ll. 575–6 (ed. Neyrand and De Vregille, CCSL 19, p. 110), concerning how the bride was the Church: 'Ready to confess the God of heaven through the good of nature'; 'Per bonum naturae ad confitendum Deo caeli paratam'.

[288] Apponius, *In Canticum* 8.53, ll. 774–80 (ed. Neyrand and De Vregille, CCSL 19, pp. 203–4), 'Which *columns*, however, so that a gateway to learning what is good might be revealed to us by very ancient

in coming to belief.[289] God gave man's nature, made in the image and likeness of God, a rational sense: 'Through which he may know to seek good and to reject evil'.[290] There are many points of contact between Pelagius' argumentation and the positions asserted in the *Commentary on the Song of Songs*. To cite just one example, Apponius stated that God set what he commanded within human power, so that his reward and punishment might be just. In the same passage he suggested that some had perfected God's will:

> That they are kindled by the love of the bridegroom is the characteristic gift of the Word of God, who perfects our steps so that we run, who illuminates our eyes so that we see, who opens our lips so that we speak, who casts out fear of present death by his visit, when his perfect love has been sent into our hearts; and all these things he has conferred on men by revealing himself like a lamp to this world. He has also placed what he has commanded within our power, so that by a just judgement he may bestow either the eternal joy of the kingdom of heaven on those who keep his commandments, or the eternal affliction of hell on those who despise them. So that, if what has been written has been hidden from us, we should enquire of those who have already perfected his will.[291]

On the basis of linguistic similarities, the editors of Apponius' *Commentary on the Song of Songs* suggested that Apponius was also the author of *On the Hardening of Pharoah's Heart* (*De induratione cordis pharaonis*), written before he composed the *Commentary on the Song of Songs*, although they stopped short of a

---

and perfect men, are praised as *built on golden bases*. Among these *bases*, in my view, were Abel, Seth, Enoch, Noah, Abraham, Isaac, Jacob, Joseph, Job, Elijah, Elisha, Daniel and men like them, who truly are understood as *golden* through the goodness of nature, and as stable *bases* through the level ground of humility'; 'Quae tamen *columnae*, ut nobis a uiris antiquissimis et perfectis discendi quae bona sunt aditus panderetur, *super bases aureas fundatae* laudantur. De quibus *basibus* opinor esse Abel, Seth, Enos, Noe, Abraham, Isaac, Iacob, Ioseph, Iob, Heliam, Heliseum, Danihelem eorumque consimiles, qui uere per bonum naturae *aureae*, per humilitatis planitiem stabilitae *bases* intelleguntur.'

[289] Apponius, *In Canticum* 12.48, ll. 723–6 (ed. Neyrand and De Vregille, CCSL 19, p. 289). Apponius' interpretation was that in the *Song* the breasts signified the apostles, who provided milk, representing the Word of God, to little souls, and he wrote of these souls: 'Which are gathered through good will (*uoluntas*), are created through believing, are nourished by teaching and are made the most beautiful offspring from the ineffable and indivisible marriage celebrated between the Word and the spirit of our Lord Jesus Christ'; 'Quae concipiuntur per bonam uoluntatem, generantur credendo, nutriuntur doctrina, et efficiuntur pulcherrima proles de ineffabili indiuisibilique coniugio inter Verbum et animam Domini nostri Iesu Christi celebrato.'

[290] Apponius, *In Canticum* 2.24, ll. 482–3 (ed. Neyrand and De Vregille, CCSL 19, p. 54), 'Per quem sciat appetere bonum et respuere malum'.

[291] Apponius, *In Canticum* 1.25, ll. 394–404 (ed. Neyrand and De Vregille, CCSL 19, pp. 17–18), 'Quod flamma amoris sponsi accenduntur, proprium donum gratiae uerbi Dei est, qui perficit gressus ad currendum, qui illuminat oculos ad uidendum, qui aperit labia ad loquendum, qui uisitatione sua praesentis mortis timorem, perfecta caritate intromissa cordi nostro, foras expellit; et haec omnia, ostendendo se ut lampadam huic mundo, hominibus contulit. Etiam quae praecepit, in nostra posuit potestate, ut iusto iudicio aut custodientibus regni caelorum perpetuum gaudium tribuat, aut contemnentibus aeternum luctum gehennae. Vt si absconsa sunt a nobis quae scripta sunt, quaeramus ab eis qui eius iam perfecerunt uoluntatem.'

categorical assertion of this.[292] They observed that Paulinus of Nola asked Jerome about the same questions as were addressed in *On the Hardening of Pharoah's Heart*, and, in reply, Jerome sent Paulinus his translation of Origen's *On First Principles* (*De principiis*). In highlighting how *On the Hardening of Pharoah's Heart* was requested by a priest and this request was supported by a layman of noble birth, De Vregille and Neyrand drew attention to the circle of Christians who were exploring interpretations of these biblical citations and who found this interpretation of Christianity acceptable.[293] Without following them in identifying Paulinus of Nola as the priest to whom *On the Hardening of Pharoah's Heart* was dedicated, it is nevertheless worth noting that Christians holding ecclesiastical office (including the otherwise unknown priest Armenius to whom Apponius' *Commentary on the Song of Songs* was addressed), and lay members of the Church, sympathised with Apponius' approach to Christianity.[294] Additionally, De Vregille and Neyrand described the inventive creativity of the *Commentary on the Song of Songs* and its engagement with philosophy. This underscores how different brands of Christianity were freely proposed in Christian literature at this time, when a plurality of discourses was the norm.[295] Overall, Apponius' *Commentary on the Song of Songs* illustrates once more how Pelagius' assertions of effective free will and the goodness of human nature were commonplaces of Christian discourse.

Conclusion to Chapters 2 and 3

After examining the doctrinal assumptions of ascetic literature prior to and contemporary with Pelagius' writings, the question that arises is which of the ideas expressed in Pelagius' works had not already been canvassed by other proponents of the ascetic movement? Was any part of Pelagius' approach to Christianity distinctive or new?[296] Far from his having created a new and heretical set of theses, it seems more accurate to suggest that he was drawn into the defence of widely held principles.

If we take the account of 'Pelagianism' usually employed by scholarship—that it was a stringent ascetic focus on imitation of Christ's way of life predicated on an explicit assertion of effective human free will—the questions to ask are these: do we not have to class Jerome as a 'Pelagian'? Do we not have to classify Athanasius and Evagrius of Antioch as 'Pelagian' for good measure? Judged according to the conventional scholarly narrative about 'Pelagianism', Athanasius and Evagrius were even more 'Pelagian' than Jerome because they asserted the inherent goodness of human nature in a more emphatic manner than Jerome did. Furthermore, Jerome was more 'Pelagian' than Pelagius because he told Eustochium to cultivate

---

[292] Neyrand and De Vregille, *Apponii in Canticum*, pp. xciv–cv.

[293] Anon., *De induratione cordis pharaonis* 1 (ed. De Plinval, p. 137).

[294] Neyrand and De Vregille, *Apponii in Canticum*, pp. civ–cx.

[295] Neyrand and De Vregille, *Apponii in Canticum*, pp. cxi–cxii.

[296] Torgny Bohlin argued that all the elements of Pelagius' teaching were drawn from Christian tradition: T. Bohlin, *Die Theologie des Pelagius und ihre Genesis*, transl. H. Buch (Uppsala, 1957), p. 109.

a holy arrogance, proclaimed that all wealth was the result of injustice, and referred to perfection as if it had been and could be achieved. On the criterion of whether or not reference was made to the role of grace, since he did not refer to prevenient grace, Jerome's letters again displayed either the same ideas or more extreme so-called 'Pelagian' tendencies than are found in Pelagius' surviving writings.

The implication of the evidence adduced in Chapters 2 and 3, however, is not in fact that Athanasius, Evagrius, Jerome or anyone else should be labelled 'Pelagian'. The implication is that the ideas found in Pelagius' writings were by the first decade of the 5th century longstanding *topoi* of ascetic literature. The ideas Pelagius propounded were anything but new. The change was that Pelagius now had to argue for and defend what had previously been widely accepted and unquestioned assumptions of the ascetic movement. This fact proves that the notion of 'Pelagianism' was a fiction. Its invention was a tactic designed to bring these assumptions into disrepute, as a distraction under cover of which a new interpretation of Christian anthropology and of a Christian's relationship with God could be covertly installed. Agreement that a positive anthropology and effective free will necessarily entailed arrogant blasphemy surreptitiously implied that the opposite position was pious humility and the truth, and thus silently endorsed it as orthodoxy.

In the years that had intervened between Jerome's letter to Eustochium of AD 384 and his and Pelagius' letters to Demetrias in AD 413–14, a profound change had occurred. Where before Jerome had been able to take for granted the doctrinal assumptions that underpinned asceticism, by the second decade of the 5th century these assumptions were being challenged, and God's grace could no longer be referred to in an imprecise way. Pelagius stressed the human will, first, because his task was one of moral exhortation and, second, because he believed that the doctrines of original sin, prevenient grace, and predestination interpreted as preordainment enfeebled or contradicted the role of free will to an extent that undermined the principles of personal responsibility and divine justice in the Christian message of salvation. Augustine considered these principles less important than the principles of God's omnipotence and man's humility. He objected that when Pelagius mentioned grace, it was not clear that the specific type of grace that Augustine understood to be crucial was being referred to:

> How therefore can Pelagius be believed to have truly acknowledged the grace of God … the grace that is neither nature along with free will, nor knowledge of the law, nor merely forgiveness of sins, but the grace which is necessary for each of our actions … when in his letter … he did not mention the grace of God, only by confessing and adding which he escaped the penalty of ecclesiastical condemnation?[297]

---

[297] Augustine, *De gestis Pelagii* 31.56 (ed. Urba and Zycha, CSEL 42, pp. 110–11), 'Quomodo igitur credi potest Pelagium … Dei gratiam, quae neque natura est cum libero arbitrio neque legis scientia neque tantum remissio peccatorum, sed ea quae in singulis nostris est actibus necessaria, ueraciter fuisse confessum … quando in epistola sua … gratiam Dei non posuit, quam confitendo et addendo poenam ecclesiasticae damnationis euasit?' Augustine referred to Pelagius' use of the word grace,

This interpretation of grace as prevenient potentially ruled out a truly co-operative model of the interaction of divine grace and human free will. Augustine's position was that it was this critical prevenient aspect of God's grace that Pelagius failed to acknowledge properly, and, by failing to acknowledge it, Pelagius denied its role. For Augustine the role of God's prevenient grace was pre-eminent and absolute, and its agency was, in the final analysis, the determining factor in the attainment of salvation, uncomfortable though that truth might be. For proponents of the absolute prevenience of God's grace, the issue was precisely the exclusivity and priority of the efficacy of their chosen cause of human goodness. But was Pelagius an adherent of a similarly exclusivist position with regard to free will? The evidence of his *On the Divine Law* and of his *On Free Will*, and his comments to Melania, Pinianus and Albina, together with his *Statement of Faith*, suggest that he was not. Cassian rejected the idea of the exclusive agency of either prevenient grace or human free will.[298] The evidence that survives suggests that Pelagius too adhered to a synergistic position.

In Chapters 2 and 3 I have set out the evidence that other Christian writers had already asserted everything that Pelagius taught. The ideas Pelagius expressed had already been widely canvassed in mainstream Christian literature that has never been labelled 'Pelagian'. This evidence supports the thesis that the assertion of prevenient grace and a predestination that was entirely unrelated to human action was something that had not previously been examined or legislated on among Christians. It also supports the thesis that when Pelagius wrote, at the end of the *Statement of Faith* that he sent to Pope Innocent I, that his understanding of the relationship between grace and free will was the interpretation of Christian Scripture that had been handed down within the catholic Church, and which he himself had been taught as accepted doctrine, he was telling the truth: 'This is the faith, most blessed father, which we learnt within the catholic Church, and which we have always held, and hold still.'[299]

---

in this case in reference to the ability to come to Christ, at *De gratia Christi et de peccato originali* 1.14.15 (ed. Urba and Zycha, CSEL 42, p. 138), 'Pelagius locates the ability to come in nature, or even, as he now begins to say, in that grace, of whatever kind he means by that, "By which", as he puts it, "the ability is helped"'; 'Venire posse in natura ponit Pelagius uel etiam, ut modo dicere coepit, in gratia, qualemlibet eam sentiat, "Qua ipsa", ut dicit, "possibilitas adiuuatur"'.

[298] Cassian, *Conlatio* 13.18.5 (ed. Kreuz and Petschenig, CSEL 13, p. 396), Cassian concluded that both prevenient grace and effective free will should be retained, but that how exactly God achieved their symbiosis could not be understood by anyone: 'For how God works all things in us and yet everything can be ascribed to free will, cannot be fully grasped by the mind of man'; 'Quemadmodum et Deus omnia operetur in nobis et totum libero adscribatur arbitrio, ad plenum humano sensu ac ratione non potest conprehendi.'

[299] Pelagius, *Libellus fidei* 14 (ed. Migne, PL 45.1718), 'Haec fides est, papa beatissime, quam in ecclesia catholica didicimus quamque semper tenuimus et tenemus.'

4

No Organised Movement Existed, and No Individual Held the Collection of Views Attributed to 'Pelagianism'

The argument of this chapter is, first, that no organised movement existed in which several individuals shared a programme of doctrines; and, second, that no one individual ever held the particular collection of tenets attributed to 'Pelagianism', which was a composite fiction invented for polemical purposes.

It has been acknowledged for many years now that 'Pelagianism' was not a coherent, centrally promulgated set of doctrines. Brynley Rees described it as a 'matrix' of individuals, with particular subgroups of ideas personal to each author, and consensus has fallen in behind this account of a phenomenon that has been seen as spinning out from Pelagius' activity.[1] Josef Lössl commented: 'Pelagius, Caelestius and Julian of Aeclanum stand for a range of positions'.[2] It has also regularly been acknowledged that contemporary heresiologues sought to identify an organised programme as a prerequisite for the expulsion of an interpretation of Scripture from the body of doctrine deemed acceptable within the catholic Church.[3] However, the difficulties raised by the variation in ideas within what has been characterised as one discrete historical movement vitiate the notion of a movement.[4] Some of the material that disproves the existence of

---

[1] Rees, *Pelagius* vol. II, pp. 20–5; J. R. Morris, 'Pelagian Literature', *Journal of Theological Studies* 16 (1965), p. 43; G. Bonner, 'Rufinus of Syria and African Pelagianism', *Augustinian Studies* 1 (1970), p. 31; M. Lamberigts, 'Le Mal et Le Péché. Pélage: La Réhabilitation d'un Hérétique', *Revue d'Histoire Ecclésiastique* 95 (2000), p. 106.

[2] J. Lössl, 'Augustine, "Pelagianism", Julian of Aeclanum, and Modern Scholarship', *Zeitschrift für Antikes Christentum* 11 (2007), p. 141.

[3] Nuvolone and Solignac, 'Pélage', col. 2924; M. R. Rackett, 'What's Wrong with Pelagianism? Augustine and Jerome on the Dangers of Pelagius and his Followers', *Augustinian Studies* 33:2 (2002), p. 223; Dominic Keech referred to 'Augustine's construction of Pelagianism', and Augustine's 'twenty-year construction of Pelagianism as an arch-heresy': D. Keech, *The Anti-Pelagian Christology of Augustine, 396–430* (Oxford, 2012), p. 5, pp. 36–7, p. 63.

[4] In relation to the Christian–pagan dichotomy, Éric Rebillard has stressed the importance of studying individuals and not reifying groups under the influence of polemical source texts: É. Rebillard, 'Late

a discrete movement is also relevant to the impossibility of defining the concept 'Pelagianism' and its fundamental conceptual incoherence, an argument that will be set out in Chapter 5; but the point made in that chapter is not the same as the one being made here. The present argument shows how the members of this alleged group did not agree with each other on the allegedly defining doctrines of 'Pelagianism'. Indeed, the positions expressed by members of this supposed 'movement' contradict each other.

Forging a link

What is the link between these fervent Christians writing ascetic paraenesis in the early 5th century? It was vital to their opponents that a link should be established between some of them, and that they should be isolated from other writers who propounded the same approach to Christianity. Scholars have taken their cue from Pelagius' opponents in seeing a link between certain ideas, or a link between texts in which certain ideas appear, or a link between writers who expressed these ideas, and thus they have envisaged a self-acknowledged movement. This has led to circular reasoning in which a text with no secure authorial attribution is ascribed to a name that can in some way be associated with 'Pelagianism' on the basis of perceived 'Pelagian' ideas within the text. This circular process has propped up the notion of a movement of linked individuals. An example of this is attribution to Caelestius of interpolations into Pelagius' *Commentary on the Pauline Epistles*.[5] The desire to attach a known name to an anonymous work is a powerful tendency in scholarship.[6] But the opposite possibility needs to be considered: what if many of what scholars imagine to be hallmark 'Pelagian' ideas, as a result of the presence of which scholars describe a work as 'Pelagian' and then seek an appropriately 'Pelagian' author for the work, were in fact the norms of Christian thought? Then we have no guide at all as to who the author of the work was, and the possibility of construction of a group slips away through scholarly fingers like sand.

This question of whether or not there was a link between such texts and their authors has been insufficiently examined. When subjected to scrutiny, it is clear that the ideas contained in the surviving texts that have over the centuries been associated with each other, and classed by scholars as 'Pelagian', are too divergent to constitute a coherent school or programme, so that the term 'Pelagianism' used as a referent for a movement or grouping does not in fact denote something

---

Antique Limits of Christianness: North Africa in the Age of Augustine', in *Group Identity and Religious Individuality in Late Antiquity*, ed. É. Rebillard and J. Rüpke (Washington, DC, 2015), pp. 293–4. I would suggest that the same applies in study of supposed heretical 'groups'.

[5] Frede suggested that their author was 'perhaps' Caelestius: *Kirchenschriftsteller: Verzeichnis und Sigel*, Vetus Latina. Die Reste der altlateinischen Bibel, 1.1, 3rd rev. edn (Freiburg, 1981), p. 375; De Bruyn, *Pelagius's Commentary*, p. 27.

[6] K. Cooper, 'An(n)ianus of Celeda and the Latin readers of John Chrysostom', in *Studia Patristica* 27, ed. E. A. Livingstone (Louvain, 1993), p. 255.

that actually existed. The evidence for this argument lies in examples of widely divergent standpoints on issues that are usually considered points of 'Pelagian' doctrine, drawn from texts that are generally labelled 'Pelagian'.

Variation in ideas: Marriage, celibacy and virginity

An example of a supposedly defining 'Pelagian' viewpoint relates to the relative merits of marriage, celibacy and virginity in relation to attaining salvation. Continence of some kind was a fundamental of an ascetic approach to Christianity, and on this key issue three distinct standpoints were asserted by authors labelled 'Pelagian'. The unknown author of *On Chastity* (*De castitate*) asserted that marriage was an impediment to righteousness; it prevented the fulfilment of God's commands.[7] Although Pelagius argued that virginity attained a particular merit above marriage, he did not see it as a fundamental of righteousness.[8] Julian of Aeclanum meanwhile held marriage in high regard, and criticised Augustine for the denigration of procreation and thereby marriage, which he argued was entailed by Augustine's theory of original sin.[9] Therefore, on this one topic, three different positions were expressed within what is usually identified as 'Pelagian' thought.[10] The question is whether, if the same situation applies on several important issues, it is accurate to use the referent 'Pelagianism' at all.

---

[7] Anon., *De castitate* 7.2 (ed. Hamman, PLS 1.1475).

[8] Pelagius, *Ad Demetriadem* 9–10 (ed. Greshake, pp. 90-2), 'Marriage is allowed, so is the use of meat and wine, but abstinence from all three is advised by more perfect counsel .... The Apostle says that he does not in fact have a commandment of the Lord concerning virgins but that he is merely giving advice .... I have stated this before, and I now repeat it again, that in the matter of righteousness we all have one obligation: virgin, widow, wife, the highest, middle and lower stations in life, we are all without exception ordered to fulfil the commandments, nor is a man released from the law if he proposes to do more than it commands'; 'Conceduntur quidem nuptiae, carnium usus ac uini, sed horum omnium abstinentia consilio perfectiore suadetur .... Apostolus de uirginibus praeceptum quidem se dicit Domini non habere, sed dat consilium .... Dixi, itemque nunc repeto: In causa iustitiae unum debemus omnes, uirgo, uidua, nupta, summus, medius et imus gradus aequaliter iubentur implere praecepta. Nec a lege soluitur, qui supra legem facere proponit'. See also *Ad Celantiam* 2 (ed. Hilberg, CSEL 56, pp. 330–1), in which both marriage and wealth were acceptable conditions for attainment of *iustitia*. See also Augustine: *De gestis Pelagii* 13.29 (ed. Urba and Zycha, CSEL 42, p. 83), preserving the proceedings of the synod of Diospolis, where Pelagius stated that virginity was not commanded. Augustine conflated Pelagius' and Caelestius' positions, disbelieved Pelagius and concluded that the judges were unaware of Pelagius' real views: 'With what meaning Pelagius or Caelestius might have said that, the judges were unaware'; 'Quo autem sensu illud Pelagius siue Caelestius dixerit, iudices nescierunt.'

[9] Julian of Aeclanum, *Ad Turbantium* 1, frags. 24–30 (ed. De Coninck, CCSL 88, pp. 346–8).

[10] Kate Cooper pointed out that it is not possible to take for granted that there was a 'characteristic Pelagian position on marriage': Cooper, 'An(n)ianus', pp. 253–4.

Variation in ideas: The rich will not enter the kingdom of heaven

A second example of an idea often taken as a defining tenet of 'Pelagianism' is the rejection of wealth as incompatible with Christian righteousness.[11] This was one of the theses listed by a layman from Syracuse called Hilary in a letter to Augustine of AD 414, warning him about the spread of certain ideas in Syracuse.[12] As seen in Chapter 1, the idea that the rich could not enter the kingdom of heaven was included in the lists of tenets attributed to 'Pelagianism' by Pelagius' opponents, and was part of the caricature that was 'Pelagianism', but was not something that Pelagius taught.

Proof that the rich man could almost never attain righteousness, and of the inherent sinfulness of great wealth, were themes of *On Riches* (*De diuitiis*), another of the six letters in the Caspari Corpus. The scholarly consensus has been that these letters were written by one or more unknown author(s) who have been described as 'Pelagian'. The letters have been associated with Sicily because of Hilary's letter to Augustine, which is seemingly confirmed by the fact that the author of another of the Caspari Corpus letters mentioned that he was writing from Sicily.[13] It was Augustine who linked ideas circulating on Sicily to Caelestius, without giving evidence for this connection; through his assertion of a close association between Caelestius and Pelagius, he then attributed this idea to Pelagius. Key to this last step was the link between Caelestius and Pelagius forged by Pelagius' opponents by means of their repeated assertion that Caelestius and Pelagius spoke with one voice in disseminating a shared programme. Augustine consistently referred to Caelestius as the pupil of Pelagius, and he placed Caelestius in Sicily, referring to 'his disciples in Sicily' (*discipuli eius in Sicilia*). This has contributed to the association of Caelestius (and through him Pelagius) with the six letters of the Caspari Corpus.[14] According to Jerome, these same ideas were circulating on

---

[11] Brown wrote of 'Pelagian ideas on wealth': P. Brown, *The Ransom of the Soul. Afterlife and Wealth in Early Western Christianity* (Cambridge, MA, 2015), p. 96; Schlatter took this as a defining tenet of 'Pelagianism': F. W. Schlatter, 'The Pelagianism of the *Opus Imperfectum in Matthaeum*', *Vigiliae Christianae* 41 (1987), p. 276; Rees referred to this idea as one of those that have 'the authentic stamp of Pelagianism': *Pelagius* vol. II, p. 174.

[12] Augustine, *Ep.* 156 (ed. Goldbacher, CSEL 44, pp. 448–9).

[13] Anon., *Honorificentiae tuae* 5.2 (ed. Hamman, PLS 1.1692–3), 'In this land of Sicily, I have found a woman of great nobility in men's eyes, but much more noble in God's, who long ago, spurning and despising all her possessions, dedicated herself wholly to God'; 'In Siciliensi terra feminam quandam clarissimam secundum hominem reperi, sed secundum Deum multo clariorem, quam iam diu, omnibus suis spretis atque contemtis, Deo se penitus dedicauit.'

[14] Augustine, *De gratia Christi et de peccato originali* 2.11.12 (ed. Urba and Zycha, CSEL 42, p. 174), 'In the doctrine of Caelestius, Pelagius' pupil'; 'In doctrina Caelestii discipuli Pelagii'; Augustine quoted the proceedings of the synod of Diospolis which referred to Augustine's own reference to Caelestius and 'his disciples in Sicily', which gave it the appearance of fact: '[The synod said] that the holy bishop Augustine replied to Hilary, writing a book against the disciples of Caelestius in Sicily with regard to the points submitted to him'; '[Synodus dixit] quoniam sanctus episcopus Augustinus aduersus discipulos eius in Sicilia respondit Hilario ad subiecta capitula scribens librum'. Augustine also linked Caelestius to views circulating in Sicily at *De perfectione iustitiae hominis* 1 (ed. Urba and Zycha, CSEL 42, pp. 3–4).

other islands in the Mediterranean also, which suggests that Caelestius was not in fact their author or disseminator, and they were instead a broad current of contemporary thought.[15]

There is agreement that the six Caspari Corpus letters were not written by Pelagius. Within them two links to Pelagius have been identified: first, that they quoted from Pelagius' *Commentary on the Pauline Epistles*; and, second, that they shared some ideas with Pelagius.[16] The first of these links assumes that possession of a commentary by Pelagius or similar to Pelagius' is proof of a link to Pelagius himself. Frede showed, however, that another Latin commentary on the Pauline Epistles (of unknown authorship) existed, in addition to Ambrosiaster's, on which Pelagius drew also.[17] The existence of this and the Ambrosiaster commentary suggest that commentaries on the Pauline Epistles were widely available. The first link also begs the question as to how far the commentary as printed in Alexander Souter's edition can be attributed to Pelagius, because it ignores the process of creating composite commentaries by borrowing from and reworking existing ones, a process which was ongoing in the late 4th century and continued throughout the Middle Ages. For example, Frede argued that Pelagius' *Commentary on the Pauline Epistles* was revised during the 5th century, before Cassiodorus' revision in the 6th century. Cross-pollination between recensions was ongoing because this was the nature of the genre. Pelagius drew on other commentaries, and other Christian writers drew on Pelagius' work.

The second proposed link between the Caspari Corpus letters and Pelagius, that of shared ideas, disappears if both Pelagius and the anonymous author(s) of the Caspari Corpus letters are reclassified as writers of the ascetic movement, in the same bracket as Jerome and Evagrius of Antioch. This is the critical problem with asserting a close link between the Caspari Corpus texts and Pelagius. It is reasonable to assert the loose association of a shared ascetic approach to Christianity, which entailed that they had some ideas in common, but no more than that. A key point to note here is that the Caspari Corpus letter *To an Older Friend* stated that he was staying with a noblewoman who had 'long ago' rejected riches.[18] Since the author gave no hint that his views had become controversial, the letter probably dates to before AD 418.[19] The renunciation of wealth in pursuit of apostolic poverty which this lady had adopted years before cannot be attributed to a new set of theses recently invented by Pelagius. Clearly it was part of a wider phenomenon, the ascetic movement, which had begun to arrive in Western Christian thought from its birthplace in the East many decades before AD 400. The change was

---

[15] Jerome, *In Hieremiam* 4, Preface 2 (ed. Reiter, CCSL 74, p. 174).

[16] For example, Anon., *De diuitiis* 11.6 (ed. Hamman, PLS 1.1399) shares phrases with Pelagius, *Expositio* on Rom. 16:23 (ed. Souter, p. 125). See also: R. F. Evans, *Four Letters of Pelagius* (London, 1968), pp. 25–6.

[17] Frede, *Ein neuer* I, pp. 196–205; Frede, *Kirchenschriftsteller*, p. 96.

[18] See n. 13. This letter is also known by its first words: *Honorificentiae tuae*.

[19] This contrasts with Anon., *De malis doctoribus* 1.1 (ed. Hamman, PLS 1.1418).

simply the popularity and currency of such ideas, their adoption by high-profile members of the social elite which brought them to wider attention and produced a literary footprint, and the fact that they were now being preached as relevant to all Christians because ascetics had ambitiously begun to extend the requirement for imitation of Christ to all Christians, not just a few. It was not the idea that was new but the traction it was getting among Christian congregations, as a result of ascetics advocating it and the examples of prominent members of society taking it up.[20] Rejection of riches was a trend among aspirant 'serious' wealthy Christians, not an idea that Pelagius either introduced or taught.[21]

No one has suggested that Melania and Pinianus were 'Pelagians' despite the fact that they did give away their wealth, albeit gradually. Yet the link between Melania and Pinianus and the idea reported by Hilary to Augustine, and which Augustine listed as a heretical tenet, is much stronger than the link between this idea and Pelagius. Contemporary ecclesiastics did not criticise Melania and Pinianus as disseminators of a dangerous idea, or Melania the Elder, who influenced her grand-daughter's decision to abandon her property.[22] The family were major landholders in North Africa and patrons of the Church there, and this perhaps put the couple beyond criticism. Rather than ecclesiastics, it was Pinianus' brother Valerius Severus who tried to forestall the effects of their sale of their property, and the nobility of Rome, who found Melania's ideas disturbing and tried to stop Melania from acting on her belief that Christian faith required imitation of Christ's poverty.[23]

What Melania's behaviour reveals, like that of the unnamed noble lady on Sicily, is that the idea that riches were an impediment to entry into heaven was current among ascetically minded Christians; and it was increasingly the case that serious Christians were ascetically minded. Marcella, Melania the Elder and Paula had displayed their rejection of riches from the 360s onwards. Melania the Elder left for the East to visit ascetic hermits in AD 372 and adopted a monastic lifestyle thereafter. Paula and Eustochium left Rome for Palestine to become ascetics in a monastic environment in around AD 385. Thus the suggestion that the idea that the rich could not get into heaven was the product of Pelagius' teaching is untenable. This idea that excessive wealth was a bar to

---

[20] Kate Cooper described the role and influence of patrician women in the development of Christianity in Rome: *Band of Angels: the Forgotten World of Early Christian Women* (London, 2014), pp. 191–228.

[21] See Chapter 1, pp. 8–10.

[22] For Melania the Elder holding estates on Sicily (and selling them): Palladius, Λαυσιακον 54.6 (ed. Bartelink, p. 248); for Melania the Elder influencing her grand-daughter: 54.4 (ed. Bartelink, pp. 246–8); 61 (ed. Bartelink, pp. 264–8). The author of *To an Older Friend* (*Honorificentiae tuae*) said he was staying in the household of an illustrious lady on Sicily, and Melania the Elder had held and her grand-daughter retained estates there. If the anonymous illustrious lady was neither Melania the Elder nor Melania the Younger, then three ascetic Christian noblewomen on Sicily begins to look like a network of aristocratic women which had nothing to do with Caelestius (or Pelagius).

[23] Gerontius, *Vita sanctae Melaniae* 9–12 (ed. Laurence, pp. 170–80); P. Brown, *Through the Eye of a Needle. Wealth, the Fall of Rome, and the Making of Christianity in the West, 350–55 AD* (Princeton, NJ, 2012), pp. 295–9.

entry into the kingdom of heaven was a feature of the ascetic movement and in vogue. It was an idea that had germinated decades before Pelagius began to write.[24] From the mid-380s it was Jerome who had done most to disseminate in the Latin West the ideal that Melania the Younger pursued. It was still being preached in the 430s in Hilary of Arles' *Life of St Honoratus*, in which Honoratus' Christian credentials were proved by the enthusiasm with which he abandoned his wealth.[25]

Contact with the East, where the ascetic movement had emerged decades earlier, is a more likely source of the enthusiasm for an ascetic approach to Christianity and specifically rejection of riches than Pelagius' influence. An example of this is the visit by Athanasius of Alexandria and the hermits Isidore and Ammon to Rome in AD 339, recorded by Palladius of Helenopolis.[26] Palladius reported that during this visit, Isidore became known to Roman senators and their wives, and that Isidore later made a second visit. Palladius noted that although Isidore was wealthy, he rejected riches and left nothing to his sisters. Palladius himself was also a point of contact between Eastern asceticism and Christians in Rome.[27] After John Chrysostom was banished from Constantinople in AD 404, Palladius travelled to Rome to raise support for Chrysostom. While in Italy, Palladius stayed with Melania the Younger and her husband Pinianus, and this reveals the networks of contacts between ascetic Christians that already existed in AD 404.[28] In around AD 419–20, Palladius wrote the *Lausiac History*, a manifesto for ascetic pursuit of apostolic poverty, for Lausus, chamberlain of the Imperial Court at Constantinople.[29] Palladius taught rejection of riches; Pelagius did not. Demetrios Katos wrote of Palladius' Origenism and argued that Palladius' views were founded on: 'a tradition that rested upon a robust optimism concerning human self-determination and free will'.[30] Furthermore, in his *Lausiac History*, Palladius suggested that certain monks had achieved perfection.[31] While Pelagius was condemned for heresy in AD 418, at almost the exactly same time, in AD 419–20, Palladius produced his *Lausiac History* for a man at the centre of power

[24] The idea retained currency after Pelagius' condemnation—for example, writing his *Life of Melania* in around AD 452, Gerontius quoted Matt. 19:21 to show what good Christians Melania and Pinianus were, just as Athanasius had done about Antony: Gerontius, *Vita sanctae Melaniae* 9.2 (ed. Laurence, p. 172).

[25] Hilary of Arles, *Sermo de uita Sancti Honorati* 5–11 (ed. Valentin, SC 235, pp. 78–100).

[26] Palladius, Λαυσιακον 1.4 (ed. Bartelink, p. 20). Palladius is also known as Palladius of Aspuna.

[27] Palladius was appointed to the see of Helenopolis by John Chrysostom. He knew Athanasius' *Life of Antony*: Palladius, Λαυσιακον 8.6 (ed. Bartelink, p. 44). Palladius stayed with Evagrius of Pontus for several years; and he supported John Chrysostom at the synod of the Oak in AD 403, for which he was exiled. Later he was appointed to the see of Aspuna.

[28] Palladius, Λαυσιακον 61.7 (ed. Bartelink, p. 268).

[29] Examples of Palladius' advocacy of rejection of riches: Palladius, Λαυσιακον 1.4 (ed. Bartelink, p. 20); 10.1–4 (ed. Bartelink, pp. 46–8); 14.1–3 (ed. Bartelink, pp. 58–60).

[30] D. S. Katos, *Palladius of Helenopolis: the Origenist Advocate*, Oxford Early Christian Studies (Oxford, 2011), p. 8.

[31] Palladius, Λαυσιακον 14.4 (ed. Bartelink, p. 60).

in the Eastern Empire, in which Palladius assumed or stated the anthropology and soteriology which Pelagius asserted, and in which Palladius came closer to the caricature 'Pelagianism' than Pelagius ever did. Peter Brown observed that Aemilius, Bishop of Beneventum and future father-in-law of Julian of Aeclanum, led the embassy to Constantinople to plead on Chrysostom's behalf. In addition, Brown noted that in AD 436, while she was in Constantinople, Melania the Younger stayed with Lausus, for whom Palladius wrote his apology for asceticism.[32] In sum, there were many advocates of ascetic values besides Pelagius. To suggest that he 'set in motion' an 'ascetical and theological movement' ignores the many other propagandists for asceticism who had been promoting it for decades before Pelagius began to write, and those who did so contemporaneously with Pelagius' career.[33] An alternative scenario can be presented, one in which a group of patricians disseminated an ascetic brand of Christianity in Rome, adopting Jerome and later Pelagius into their circles because it suited them. They funded the activities of their spiritual and scriptural advisers. These aristocratic Romans were the drivers of the ascetic brand at Rome. Attracted to Eastern asceticism, they chose it because it suited their aspirations, and moulded it to fit their own inclinations.

Augustine's reply to Melania the Younger, Pinianus and Albina in his *On the grace of Christ and on original sin* was all about showing that Pelagius taught the same thing as Caelestius, which suggests that the three patrician Romans wrote to Augustine to ask him to differentiate between Pelagius and Caelestius (and so drop the charges against Pelagius). It may be noteworthy in this regard that in the Greek version of the *Life of Melania the Younger* written by Melania's priest Gerontius, Melania's uncle Volusianus stated that free will was God's gift to man and was necessary for virtue and reward. This point is made only in the Greek text, and the Latin text omits it.[34] This evidence may suggest that Melania the Younger

---

[32] P. Brown, 'The Patrons of Pelagius: the Roman Aristocracy between East and West', *Journal of Theological Studies* 21 (1970), pp. 61–2; Katos described Palladius' *Lausiac History* as an apologia for the Origenists and their ascetic programme: *Palladius of Helenopolis*, p. 6.

[33] Quotations from Keech, *Anti-Pelagian Christology*, p. 40.

[34] Melania wanted her uncle Volusianus, who was dying, to be baptised, and considered asking the emperor to command him to be baptised, but Volusianus rejected external influence: Gerontius, Βίος τῆς ὁσίας Μελάνης 53 (ed. Gorce, SC 90, p. 232), 'But he, when he perceived that she was planning to refer the matter to the Emperors, was sore at heart, and said to her: "I entreat your holiness, do not take from me the gift of self-determination with which God has honoured us from the beginning. For I am ready and long to wash away the filth of my many errors, but if I should do this at the command of the Emperors, I would be found to have gained it as if under compulsion and I would lose the reward of my free choice'; Ὁ δὲ ὡς ᾔσθετο αὐτὴν βουλευομένην περὶ τούτου τοῖς βασιλεῦσιν ἀνενέγκαι, ἐν πολλῇ κατανύξει γενόμενος ἔφη πρὸς αὐτήν· Παρακαλῶ τὴν σὴν θεοσέβειαν, μὴ ἀφέλῃς ἀπ' ἐμοῦ τὸ τοῦ αὐτεξουσίου δῶρον, ᾧ ἡμᾶς ὁ Θεὸς ἐξ ἀρχῆς ἐτίμησεν· καὶ γὰρ ἑτοίμως ἔχω καὶ εὔχομαι ἀπολούσασθαι τὸν ῥύπον τῶν πολλῶν μου παραπτωμάτων, ἀλλ' ἐὰν κατὰ πρόσταξιν τῶν βασιλέων τοῦτο ποιήσω, εὑρίσκομαι ὡς κατὰ βίαν ἐπὶ τοῦτο ἐρχόμενος καὶ ἀπόλλω τὸν μισθὸν τῆς ἐμῆς προαιρέσεως. Cf. the Latin version: Gerontius, *Vita sanctae Melaniae* 53.6 (ed. Laurence, p. 258), 'And so when the blessed Melania was considering suggesting to the Emperor and his queen that they might command this to persuade him, he noticed this and said that he did not want it to be implied to anyone that he had obeyed her will and her very sweet words'; 'Cum ergo cogitaret beatissima suggerere Augusto et reginae ut

had some sympathy with the account of human nature and free will propounded by Athanasius, Evgarius of Antioch, Jerome, Pelagius and other proponents of ascetic Christianity.[35] The Greek *Life* certainly suggests once again that free will was uncontroversial in the East.

It is helpful to situate the Caspari Corpus letters and the claim for a linkage to Pelagius in their historical context. Educated Christians felt abundantly qualified and free to write in this period. They wrote many different types of text: commentary, both formal and also less structured, paraenetic literature, advice and argument. As Jerome put it: 'Everyone prattles on saying what he thinks'.[36] He knew that his correspondent Rusticus would write and urged him to defer publishing his thoughts.[37] The Consentius who was a correspondent of Augustine felt himself more than qualified to publish his views.[38] His letter reveals that publishing one's writings was perceived as a way to stake a claim to expertise, and almost as a requirement for proof of a person's educational status. Augustine made ironic comment on the intellectual ability of those preaching ascetic values.[39] In reality it was not their intellect he objected to but their intellectual freedom.

---

iuberent de hoc suadere ei, sentiens autem dixit ipse ne uellet hoc alicui insinuare quia ipse uoluntati eius et suauissimis eloquiis obaudisset.' The rest of Volusianus' answer does not appear in the Latin *Life*. The question of which *Life* was written first and whether both versions derived from an earlier 'primitive' *Life* does not alter this point, but for discussion of this question see: P. Laurence, *Gérontius. La Vie latine de Sainte Mélanie. Edition Critique, Traduction et Commentaire* (Jerusalem, 2002), pp. 116–34; E. Clark, *The Life of Melania the Younger. Introduction, Translation, and Commentary*, Studies in Women and Religion 14 (New York, 1984), pp. 4–24. Clark also pointed out that when he was Prefect of Rome, Volusianus was slow to prosecute so-called 'Pelagians': *Decretum Constantii Imperatoris* (ed. Migne, PL 45.1750).

[35] See the discussion in Clark, *The Life of Melania the Younger*, pp. 141–4.

[36] Jerome, *Dialogus aduersus pelagianos* Preface 2 (ed. Moreschini, CCSL 80, p. 5), 'Garrit unus-quisque quod sentit'.

[37] Jerome, *Ep.* 125.18 (ed. Hilberg, CSEL 56, p. 137), 'Do not leap swiftly into writing and be carried away by some mad fancy. Learn for a long time what you may teach'; 'Ne ad scribendum cito prosilias et leui ducaris insania. Multo tempore disce, quod doceas.'

[38] Consentius *apud* Augustine (in the additional letters of Augustine discovered by J. Divjak, usually identified with an asterisk beside the letter number), *Ep.* *12.15–16 (ed. Divjak, CSEL 88, pp. 79–80), 'But the habit of my madness compelled me to write I know not how many things .... Yet still burning with my usual passion for writing, we laboured to hammer out a fourth book .... We also added the most powerful argument upon which our laziness most relies, so that we might persuade ourselves most absurdly that we ought not to read all those things before we ourselves write something'; 'Scribere autem plurima nescio quae me insaniae meae compulit consuetudo .... Tamen solito ad scribendum furore succensi quartum fere iam librum cudere laboramus .... Adiecimus etiam fortis-simum quo desidia nostra plurimum nititur argumentum, ut nobis absurdissimum suaderemus nos illa omnia, priusquam ipsi aliquid conscribamus, legere non debere'; see also *12.3–5 (ed. Divjak, CSEL 88, pp. 71–3).

[39] Augustine, *Ep.* 186.11.37 (ed. Goldbacher, CSEL 57, p. 76), 'With such great intellects'; 'Cum tantis ingeniis'.

Variation in ideas: Adam would have died whether or not he had sinned

A third example of variation of ideas within 'Pelagianism' is presented 'by the question of why Adam died. As was seen in Chapter 1, Pelagius wrote that Adam died because of his disobedience.[40] According to Augustine, Caelestius argued that Adam would have died whether or not he had sinned.[41] This position was attributed to 'Pelagianism' and attacked by Augustine.[42] Subsequently it was widely understood to be a fundamental tenet of 'Pelagianism'.[43] This was despite the fact that it is directly refuted in two of Pelagius' works and he rejected the idea at the synod of Diospolis.[44] Brynley Rees pointed out that on this question of why Adam died, Pelagius took the same position as Augustine. Where Pelagius differed from Augustine was in that he did not hold Augustine's further doctrines concerning Adam: first, that Adam transmitted his sin to all posterity as original sin; and thereby, second, that 'sexual desire' (*concupiscentia*) was the method of transmission of that sin.[45] But Pelagius' position was not the same thing as saying that Adam was born mortal and would have died whether or not he had sinned. That Adam died because of his sin does not entail that he transmitted this sin to his descendants physically rather than through example. Likewise, not believing in original sin does not entail believing that Adam was born mortal. The anonymous *On the Christian Life* was explicit that Adam's descendants perished by following Adam's 'example' (*suo exemplo*).[46] Once again, this is not the same thing as saying that Adam was born mortal.

Augustine's record of the transcript of the exchanges between Paulinus of Milan and Caelestius at the Council of Carthage suggests that Caelestius had reservations about the doctrine of original sin, and that these focused on the means of transmission of this sin, the implications of the doctrine for unbaptised infants, and the question of whether or not this issue had been officially installed as dogma

---

[40] See pp. 3–4.

[41] Augustine, *De gestis Pelagii* 11.23 (ed. Urba and Zycha, CSEL 42, p. 76), 'These objections made to Pelagius follow, which are said to have been found in the teaching of his disciple Caelestius. "Adam was created mortal, who would have died whether or not he had sinned"'; 'Haec enim sequuntur obiecta Pelagio, quae in doctrina Caelestii discipuli eius referuntur inuenta. "Adam mortalem factum, qui siue peccaret siue non peccaret, moriturus esset."'

[42] Rees, *Pelagius* vol. II, pp. 147–8, n. 3.

[43] Faustus, *De gratia* 1.1 (ed. Engelbrecht, CSEL 21, pp. 9–11). Faustus was a not entirely unsympathetic critic of Pelagius: *De gratia* 1.2 (ed. Engelbrecht, CSEL 21, p. 14). He had lived through the controversy and may have known of Pelagius' writings before the AD 418 condemnation, since he was probably resident at Lérins from the second decade of the 5th century onwards. That Pelagius' writings were known in southern Gaul is shown by Sulpicius Severus' support for Pelagius, reported by Gennadius of Marseilles in his continuation of Jerome's *On Famous Men* (*De uiris illustribus*).

[44] Augustine, *De gestis Pelagii* 11.24 (ed. Urba and Zycha, CSEL 42, pp. 77–8).

[45] Rees, *Pelagius* vol. II, p. 95, n. 12.

[46] Anon., *De uita christiana* 13.2 (ed. Migne, PL 50.398A).

or was as yet a matter of personal conscience.[47] Caelestius' position may have been quite separate from Pelagius'.

A text that did state that Adam was born mortal was the *Book on the Faith by Rufinus, a Priest of the Province of Palestine* (*Rufini presbyteri prouinciae Palestinae liber de fide*).[48] This survives in a 6th- or 7th-century *codex unicus*, now in the National Library of Russia in St Petersburg, but thought to have perhaps originated at Corbie.[49] The only connection between this text and Pelagius is the testimony of Pelagius' opponents asserting such a link. Augustine listed the idea that Adam was created mortal and would have died whether or not he had sinned as one of the tenets that Pelagius taught; and while prosecuting Caelestius at the Council of Ephesus in AD 431, Marius Mercator asserted an association between Rufinus and 'Pelagianism' on the basis of a tenuous link exercised with considerable selectivity. He did so on the grounds that Caelestius had expressed doubt about the transmission of original sin, and had said that he had been present at a discussion group at which a Rufinus had rejected the idea of the transmission of original sin. Once again it was Pelagius' opponents, whose aim it was to identify a group and label it, who established the link between the rejection of original sin and the statement that Adam was born mortal. But rejection of original sin does not equate to the view that Adam was born mortal and would have died whether or not he had sinned. The Rufinus who wrote *Book on the Faith* may have held both these views, but he may have been unique in doing so.

Rufinus the Syrian

To evaluate the validity of the link created by Pelagius' opponents between Rufinus the Syrian and Pelagius, it is necessary to examine the evidence concerning this name and persona. There are four potentially relevant extant uses of the name Rufinus in association with Palestine (who is not Rufinus of Aquileia), and this person (or persons) flits through sources from this period. First, there is the Rufinus mentioned in the explicit of the 6th- or 7th-century manuscript of the *Book on the Faith* which contained the statement that Adam was born mortal. Second, in Augustine's *On the Grace of Christ and Original Sin* are excerpts from the proceedings of the Council of Carthage which contain a mention of a Rufinus who was a guest at Pammachius' house in Rome, and was named by Caelestius as

---

[47] Augustine, *De gratia Christi et de peccato originali* 2.3.3–4 (ed. Urba and Zycha, CSEL 42, pp. 168–9), for the first part of which see n. 50. Also, in a book said to have been written by Caelestius, cited in the proceedings concerning Caelestius at Rome, Caelestius stated that he rejected original sin (but did not state that he thought Adam was born mortal): Augustine, *De gratia Christi et de peccato originali* 2.5.5–6.6 (ed. Urba and Zycha, CSEL 42, pp. 169–70).

[48] Rufinus, *Liber de fide* 29–30 (ed. Miller, pp. 94–6); for the explicit, see M. Miller, ed. and transl., *Rufini Presbyteri Liber De Fide. A Critical Text and Translation with Introduction and Commentary* (Washington, DC, 1964), p. 36, n. 2: 'Explicit Rufini presbyteri prouinciae Palestinae liber de fide, translatus de Graeco in Latinum sermonem.'

[49] Miller, *Rufini*, pp. 1–7.

someone who had rejected the notion of the transmission of original sin.[50] Third, there is the Rufinus whom Jerome mentioned in a letter to Rufinus of Aquileia as a priest whom Jerome sent to Rome and other places in Italy on various missions.[51] Several scholars have argued that the combined evidence of this letter and Jerome's *Against Rufinus* (Rufinus of Aquileia was the target of this work) is that this presbyter Rufinus had stayed in Jerome's monastery, and that he was someone Jerome entrusted with his personal communications.[52] They have taken this Rufinus to be the author of the *Book on the Faith*.[53] Fourth, there is 'Rufinus, once of the Syrian nation' (*Rufinus quondam natione Syrus*), cited by Marius Mercator as author of a *Book on the Faith*, and as the real originator of 'Pelagianism' through his deception of Pelagius, to whom Rufinus allegedly taught his heretical ideas.[54]

There has been discussion about whether all four occurrences of this name refer to the same person. The problem scholars have pondered is how this Rufinus kept so low a profile in the controversy if this was the case. Some have concluded that he disappeared from the scene early on because he was never mentioned by Jerome or Augustine during the course of the controversy.[55] Gerald Bonner took the view that all of the above mentions of Rufinus referred to one and the same person. He suggested an early date for the *Book on the Faith* (around AD 400), and referring to Rufinus' 'inactivity during the Pelagian controversy' he conjectured that Rufinus died early on.[56] TeSelle also took the several mentions of Rufinus to refer to one person, and wondered how Jerome could send to Italy someone who became key to the movement, yet could himself later attack 'Pelagianism' so vehemently.[57] He noted in addition the incongruity that Jerome's enemies never threw the fact in his face. TeSelle suggested that they simply did not make the

---

[50] Augustine, *De gratia Christi et de peccato originali* 2.3.3 (ed. Urba and Zycha, CSEL 42, p. 168), where Augustine apparently quoted from the minutes of the Council of Carthage at which Caelestius was tried for heresy: 'Caelestius said: "I said that I was in doubt about the transmission of the sin, but in such a way that I will agree with one to whom God has given the grace of knowledge, for I have heard differing things from those who have been made priests in the catholic Church". The deacon Paulinus said: "Tell us their names." Caelestius said: "The holy priest Rufinus who stayed with the holy Pammachius in Rome: I heard him saying that the transmission of sin did not exist"'; 'Caelestius dixit: "Dixi de traduce peccati dubium me esse, ita tamen, ut cui donauit Deus gratiam peritiae consentiam, quia diuersa ab eis audiui, qui utique in Ecclesia catholica constituti sunt presbyteri". Paulinus diaconus dixit: "Dic nobis nomina ipsorum." Caelestius dixit: "Sanctus presbyter Rufinus Romae qui mansit cum sancto Pammachio; ego audiui illum dicentem, quia tradux peccati non sit."'
[51] Jerome, *Ep.* 81.2 (ed. Hilberg, CSEL 55, p. 107).
[52] Jerome, *Contra Rufinum* 3.24 (ed. Lardet, CCSL 79, p. 96), 'Rufinus presbyter'.
[53] Altaner, 'Der *Liber de fide*: ein Werk des Pelagianers Rufinus des "Syrers"', *Theologische Quartalschrift* 130 (1950), pp. 438–40; Bonner, *Augustine and Modern Research*, pp. 19–22; Keech referred to 'Jerome's presence behind the *Liber de fide*': Keech, *Anti-Pelagian Christology*, p. 63.
[54] Marius Mercator, *Commonitorium aduersum haeresim Pelagii et Caelestii* 1 (ed. Schwartz, *ACO* 1.5.3, p. 5).
[55] Rees, *Pelagius* vol. II, p. 21.
[56] Bonner, 'Rufinus', pp. 38–40.
[57] E. TeSelle, 'Rufinus the Syrian, Caelestius, Pelagius: Explorations in the Prehistory of the Pelagian Controversy', *Augustinian Studies* 3 (1972), pp. 62–5, p. 94.

link.[58] Perhaps a more salient question is why Caelestius and this meeting were held up as indictments against Pelagius yet no smear was attached to Pammachius or Jerome. Pammachius' rank and his death in AD 410 would have prevented this. A contributory factor as to why Jerome was not accused of having harboured the Rufinus who wrote a *Book on the Faith* is perhaps that this might have associated the Furii name with the accusation of heresy, through Jerome's patrons and fellow ascetics in Palestine, Paula and Eustochium, at a time when all parties in the controversy were still hoping for the support of powerful patrician families in Rome to influence the eventual papal judgement on the anthropology and soteriology of Christianity, when it came. Jerome referred to the financial support of such families.[59] Augustine's reply to Juliana, mother of Demetrias, reveals that Juliana had sent him a stern repudiation of his suggestion that her family, the Anicii, had any association with heresy.[60]

The only link between Pelagius and the author of the *Book on the Faith* was the meeting of a Christian discussion group in Rome in the house of the senator Pammachius, at which a Rufinus who questioned the transmission of original sin, and thereby original sin itself, was present alongside Caelestius, Pammachius (presumably) and an unknown number of others. Caelestius undoubtedly queried the idea of original sin since he said at the Council of Carthage that he believed that the transmission of original sin was not a matter of Church dogma. He was perhaps trying to draw Jerome, via his messenger and colleague Rufinus, as well as Pammachius and therefore also his wife, Paulina, into the argument on the side of those who questioned whether original sin was part of Church dogma, presumably seeking to adduce these individuals as authoritative allies.[61] Because Pelagius' opponents insisted that Pelagius and Caelestius spoke with one voice and characterised Caelestius as Pelagius' 'pupil', they linked Pelagius to the discussion group via Caelestius, and thence to the ideas in the *Book on the Faith* via this discussion group. Yet if connection to Rufinus the Syrian is a link, and if the author of the *Book on the Faith* was a monk of Jerome's monastery, then Jerome was more closely associated with the *Book on the Faith* than Pelagius was.

Scholars have assumed a close connection between Pelagius and Caelestius because Pelagius' opponents asserted such a connection, but there is no independent evidence for this, and since no works by Caelestius survive (other than selected possible quotations preserved in the writings of his opponents), the matter is unverifiable. Acquaintance based on a shared enthusiasm for an ascetic approach to Christianity is not the same thing as joint creation of a programme of doctrinal

---

[58] TeSelle, 'Rufinus', p. 63.
[59] Jerome, *Ep.* 133.13.3 (ed. Hilberg, CSEL 56, p. 260). 'Those who supply money to men of this kind'; 'Qui huiusce modi hominibus opes suggerunt'.
[60] Augustine, *Ep.* 188.1.3 (ed. Goldbacher, CSEL 57, p. 121).
[61] Altaner, 'Der *Liber de fide*', p. 435.

theses.[62] A number of known individuals in Rome shared this enthusiasm for an ascetic approach to Christianity, including Pammachius, the Sixtus who became Pope Sixtus III, and Sixtus' deacon Leo, who was a friend of Cassian and became Pope Leo I. There must have been many more whose names have not come down to us. Until the controversy about original sin, prevenient grace, and predestination interpreted as preordainment, the ideas of effective free will, merit and man's capacity for autonomous virtue had underpinned the argument for asceticism in Christian literature, and were widely held.

Éric Rebillard has argued cogently for using rigorous source critical skills to study individuals and avoid reifying groups under the influence of polemical source texts.[63] He has also drawn attention to the intermittent nature of religious allegiances, and how individuals dipped in and out of a range of identities—identities which are presented as monolithic and mutually exclusive in Christian source texts.[64] All these texts were promoting their own agendas, often using binary oppositions as a rhetorical tool. Keeping these principles of source criticism in mind, it is worth considering as an example a piece of textual evidence that might initially seem to suggest a link between Caelestius and Pelagius, contained in the letter from Pope Zosimus to the African bishops informing them that Caelestius and Pelagius had been acquitted of heresy by a council in Rome. In this letter, Zosimus told the African bishops that a council had heard Caelestius in person, and had received documents from Pelagius. There had been a public reading of Pelagius' defence documents: 'Indeed everything they contained matched and was shaped by the same understanding and views as Caelestius had earlier brought forward.'[65] At this point, in September of AD 417, there may have been some similarity in their defences since they were defending themselves against the same charges. That still does not make them colleagues or a group, nor does it make either of them anything more than one of many proponents of an ascetic approach to Christianity. Furthermore, as will be discussed in Chapter 6, the comparative evidence presented by Lester Kurtz suggests that once accused of heresy, individuals often made contact with others facing the same charges. As Karen King pointed out, heresiological discourse generated divisions where there were none before.[66] In contrast with the idea that 'Pelagianism' was a divisive force in Roman politics, as suggested by Peter Brown, it was instead the accusation of heresy that

[62] Frede used the word 'friend' to describe Caelestius' relationship with Pelagius, showing how the account disseminated by Pelagius' opponents has determined scholarly analysis of events: Frede, *Kirchenschriftsteller* (1981), p. 231.

[63] É. Rebillard and J. Rüpke, 'Introduction. Groups, Individuals and Religious Identity', in *Group Identity and Religious Individuality in Late Antiquity*, ed. É. Rebillard and J. Rüpke (Washington, DC, 2015); Rebillard, 'Late Antique Limits'.

[64] É. Rebillard, *Christians and Their Many Identities in Late Antiquity, North Africa, 200–450 CE* (Ithaca, NY, 2012).

[65] Zosimus, *Ep. Posteaquam a nobis* 3 (ed. Günther, CSEL 35, p. 103), 'Omnia quidem paria et eodem sensu sententiisque formata, quae Caelestius ante protulerat, continebant.'

[66] King, 'Social and Theological Effects'.

was a divisive force, inventing a separate group where none existed, and characterising it as a dangerous enemy. Sometimes this process then generated an actual division, which followed on from the perception of division.[67]

Rather than the story of Rufinus the Syrian 'infecting' Pelagius and Caelestius with 'Pelagianism', proposed by Pelagius' opponent Marius Mercator, a more likely hypothesis is that Caelestius deliberately sought to make his prosecutors at the Council of Carthage aware of the powerful family in Rome associated with free denial of original sin, and to associate Jerome with the same position. This might have contributed to Jerome's later desire to distance himself from 'Pelagianism'.[68] He had to prove himself whiter than white to avoid contamination following Caelestius' incrimination of him at Carthage, and after a text written by his monastic colleague Rufinus became controversial and a charge of heresy was at stake. In sum, on this tenet also, there were closer associations linking Jerome with it than there were to link Pelagius with it, and there was no shared set of doctrines. All that existed was the ascetic movement, which inspired a huge, uncontrolled and varied literary output.

A further point that vitiates the idea of a movement is the fact that, as already noted, when Jerome wrote to Augustine to congratulate him following the AD 418 condemnations, he applauded him for the suppression of the 'Caelestian heresy'.[69] After Melania the Younger and her husband and mother had visited Pelagius and subsequently written to Augustine on his behalf, it seems that Jerome felt the need to dissociate himself from Pelagius' condemnation. Thus he put on record a letter to Augustine that identified Augustine and his fellow African bishops as the sole agents of Pelagius' condemnation by congratulating them on their achievement, and characterising himself as someone who could take no credit for it. His choice of terminology drew an implicit distinction between Pelagius' position and Caelestius'.

---

[67] For 'Pelagianism' as a divisive force, see Brown, 'Pelagius'.

[68] It might also explain Jerome's comment in a letter to Apronius about the destruction of his monastery: Jerome, *Ep.* 139.2 (ed. Hilberg, CSEL 56, p. 267), 'Although in part we deserve God's displeasure, who support the Lord's enemies'; 'Licet ex parte Dei mereamur offensam, qui inimicos Domini fouemus [fouerimus]', and associated *app. crit.* Hilberg here used the present tense indicative *fouemus* ('we support'), which occurred in four of the 11 witnesses he used for his edition, but he did not publish an account of his editorial decisions, so he did not explain why he rejected *fouerimus*, which appears in seven of the 11 witnesses he used. This was presumably because the present indicative would perhaps be the obvious choice grammatically. It is possible, however, that *fouerimus* was intended as a subjunctive perfect (arguably the *lectio difficilior*), giving the meaning 'Although in part we deserved God's displeasure, who have supported the Lord's enemies'. This might refer to the whole Christian community, or it might be an acknowledgement that Rufinus the Syrian, author of a *Book on the Faith*, had indeed been a member of Jerome's monastic community. If the latter, then this would be a further reason why Jerome needed to put as much distance as possible between himself and Pelagius, once he had been warned about Rufinus' *Book on the Faith* and the link made between that and the invention 'Pelagianism'.

[69] Jerome, *Ep.* 143.1.2 (ed. Hilberg, CSEL 56, pp. 292–3): see Chapter 1, n. 63.

There is in fact nothing, outside the writings of Pelagius' opponents, to link Pelagius to Rufinus of Syria's *Book on the Faith*. There is a link between the *Book on the Faith* and Caelestius, in that Caelestius had met a Rufinus who questioned the transmission of original sin and Caelestius himself did so also, but questioning or rejecting the transmission of original sin does not equate to asserting that Adam was born mortal and would have died whether or not he had sinned. And if attendance at the discussion group at Pammachius' house was sufficient to establish a link between Caelestius and Rufinus, then Pammachius was part of that group too. Attendance at this meeting does not, in fact, entail adherence to a shared programme of doctrines. If it did then Pammachius and, through him, his wife, Paulina, his sisters-in-law Blesilla, Rufina and Eustochium, and his mother-in-law, Paula, were presumably part of this group also; and Jerome was part of this family's circle in Palestine, as he had been in Rome.

Carefully selected targets

Did any individual hold the assemblage of tenets that Augustine identified as comprising 'Pelagianism'? The evidence for Pelagius is a clear 'no'. For other known figures in the story, the answer is either also 'no' or their writings do not survive for us to know. Hearsay evidence about what Pelagius taught as reported by his opponents is inadmissible. The example of Sulpicius Severus instils caution about accepting the hearsay report of opponents about a writer's doctrine. Gennadius of Marseilles recorded that Sulpicius sympathised with the approach to Christianity defended by Pelagius, yet his works have never been associated with heresy, highlighting how political factors determined the selection of targets for condemnation.[70]

A self-acknowledged group?

It might be countered that there is evidence that some individuals formed a self-acknowledged group and that they perceived a link between themselves. In his letter to Evangelus prefacing his translation of Chrysostom's homilies on Paul, Anianus of Celeda referred to the 'books of our people' in the context of endorsement of effective free will in opposition to a position attributed to Augustine. Praising Chrysostom's homilies on Paul, Anianus characterised them as opposing Augustine's position:

> For what great consolation arises for us, when we see that truth being asserted by such a learned and such an illustrious teacher of the East, which the Traducianist attacks in us. Which truth certainly the blessed John, as in all his books, so here also guards, fortified from every side, arms it, and kindles it, so that he seems not so much to have informed his contemporary pupils, as to have prepared in advance aids for

---

[70] Gennadius, *De uiris illustribus* 19 (ed. Richardson, p. 69); Peter Brown's assessment that Sulpicius' 'own writings betray no tendency towards Pelagius' doctrine' is an example of uncritical acceptance of the account of Pelagius' doctrine created by Pelagius' opponents: Brown, 'The Patrons', p. 60.

us, to defend against an assault on the true faith. For how much does that man rise up against necessity, how much does he rise up on behalf of free will? How, everywhere in agreement with the books of our people does he, when the right of the will has been protected, commend the help of divine grace? How, against the darkness of all vices, and as a mirror of every virtue, does he set up in opposition the most splendid vessel of election?[71]

Three links are revealed by this preface. First, in the letter, Anianus explicitly aligned himself with a theological position that defended free will, denied original sin and opposed Augustine's position. Second, Anianus addressed the prefatory letter to his translations of Chrysostom's homilies on Matthew to Orontius, who was one of the eighteen Italian bishops who, along with Julian of Aeclanum, resigned their sees in opposition to Zosimus' *Epistola tractoria* of AD 418 excommunicating Pelagius and Caelestius. Third, two letters survive from Patriarch Nestorius of Constantinople to Pope Celestine which mention Orontius being in Constantinople with Julian of Aeclanum, and their complaining of their being persecuted for their views.[72] Jerome linked Anianus with Pelagius.[73] The irreducible minimum seems to be that there was at least indirect contact between Anianus and Julian.

At first sight this might appear to be prime evidence against an argument put forward in this chapter that there was no organised group with a doctrinal programme. This assessment, however, would be wrong for four reasons. First, the fourteen tenets account of 'Pelagianism' cannot be linked with any of these individuals, so there is no link between them and the caricature which was designed to discredit the two doctrines that Pelagius defended. Second, if they are perceived to be a group on the basis of an account of 'Pelagianism' that defines it as the doctrines of effective free will and the goodness of human nature, then this falls prey to the critique put forward in Chapters 2 and 3—namely, that on this account of 'Pelagianism', Athanasius, Evagrius of Antioch, Jerome and others have to be described as 'Pelagian' also, and this cannot be so because of its obvious anachronism. This also obscures the historical process that took place in the attempt to install the doctrines of original sin, prevenient grace, and predestination interpreted as preordainment as dogma in an area previously outside official doctrinal prescription. Third, Anianus' prefatory letter dates from after the condemnations of AD 418; it is *ex post facto*. The evidence that will be adduced in Chapter 6 and

---

[71] Anianus of Celeda, *Ep. praefixa homiliis de laudibus Pauli* (ed. Migne, PL 48.629C–630A), 'Quantum enim nobis consolationis exoritur, cum cernimus tam erudito, tamque illustri Orientis magistro eam, quam in nobis Traducianus oppugnat, astrui ueritatem? Quam certe beatus Ioannes, ut in omnibus libris suis, ita hic quoque ab omni munitam latere custodit, armat, accendit, ut uideatur non tam praesentes informasse discipulos, quam nobis contra uerae fidei oppugnationem auxilia praeparasse. Quantus enim ille aduersus necessitatem, quantus pro libero surgit arbitrio? Quam nostrorum libris ubique concinens, uoluntatis iure seruato, diuinae gratiae praesidia commendat? Quam contra omnium uitiorum tenebras, quam pro cunctarum speculo uirtutum splendidissimum uas electionis opponit?' *Traducianist* (*Traducianus*) refers to someone proposing the transmission of original sin (*tradux peccati*), ie. Augustine.
[72] Nestorius, *Epp.* 1 and 2 (ed. Schwartz, *ACO* 1.2.3–4, pp. 12–15).
[73] Jerome, *Ep.* 143.2 (ed. Hilberg, CSEL 56, p. 293).

the case studies cited there suggest that after a campaign against individuals who are not linked to each other has begun, in the face of condemnation they may contact each other (as Julian of Aeclanum contacted his fellow Italian bishops). Thus the attempt to excommunicate individuals who are not in contact with one another causes a group to form, as those attacked are forced to contact others in order to co-ordinate a defence against their condemnation. Fourth, the notion of an organised group propounding new doctrines (spread by proponents of the triune) obscures the historical truth, which is that the movement of which these individuals were members was the ascetic movement, whose breadth and lack of organisation means that it cannot accurately be described as a group. The account disseminated by Pelagius' opponents has led scholars to focus on a small number of known names, rather than seeing the wider panorama and recognising that effective free will and the goodness of human nature were longstanding assumptions shared by ascetic Christians.

Gerald Bonner's suggestion that it is valid to identify a group because of a shared rejection of the idea of original sin, even if they were not a group until after the condemnation of AD 418, would still misrepresent what actually happened. The process that occurred was the installation of dogma in an area where none had existed previously. Effective free will and the goodness of human nature had been widely held assumptions within Christian literature which had not been queried up to this point. Athanasius of Alexandria, Evagrius of Antioch and Palladius of Helenopolis expressed the confident anthropology that they took to be fundamental to the Christian message. The reality was that disagreement developed between proponents of two different anthropologies, both of which could be supported by scriptural citations. No one had to be a member of a group, or influenced by anyone else, in order to have reservations about the idea of original sin, or to hold that God's universal salvific will was fundamental to the moral basis of Christianity, and that an interpretation of predestination as preordainment to salvation of a closed number of elect was incompatible with this principle. These were judgements that Christians could make independently. None of the above means that 'Pelagianism' existed. There was no newly invented heresy; the alleged programme was a synthetic construct put together to bring the arguments for the goodness of human nature and effective free will into disrepute, so as to enable the opposing positions to be installed as orthodoxy. As such, the process was standard rhetorical practice in which misrepresentation was the norm. To use modern parlance, it was spin.

Conclusion

The goal of perfect—in the sense of complete—imitation of Christ's way of life was a core principle of the ascetic movement. Many ascetic writers, including Evagrius of Antioch, Jerome and Palladius of Helenopolis, wrote of this sort of perfection as if it was achievable in this life. Rufinus the Syrian argued that Adam was born mortal and would have died whether or not he had sinned. Jerome wrote that wealth was achieved through injustice and that the rich could not enter the kingdom of heaven. He also claimed that marriage was inferior to virginity. Anonymous writers of the ascetic movement suggested likewise that the rich could not enter heaven, that wealth was achieved through injustice and that virginity was necessary for righteousness. God's foreknowledge of autonomous human decisions was the mainstream interpretation of the biblical concept of predestination, propounded, for example, by Ambrose and also the commentator known as Ambrosiaster. No organised self-identifying group can accurately be identified among these authors.[74] These writers were independent voices within the unorganised ascetic movement, at a time when ascetic values had taken over the centre ground of Christian belief and most Christians subscribed to them.

A different model

The model inherent in the notion of 'Pelagianism' is incorrect. It is not enough to acknowledge merely that individuals pursued their own agenda within a 'matrix', because the idea of a positive anthropology and a soteriology that included effective free will did not spin out from Pelagius, or any one person. The evidence presented in this chapter suggests that the only grouping that really existed was the ascetic movement, within which there were a multitude of different combinations of views. These emerged as the natural product of a society in which rhetorical education trained individuals to express themselves freely in writing, and intellectual cultural norms required literary activity and publication, which conferred authority.

An accurate historical analysis of the period is one which points out that individuals felt themselves free to express in writing their own interpretations of Scripture. The discussion group at Pammachius' house exemplifies this habit of intellectual freedom, as does Volusianus' letter to Augustine describing a discussion group whose topics of enquiry ranged across rhetoric, philosophy and Christian doctrine.[75] The questions about the truth of the virgin birth raised at

---

[74] For the tendency among historians still to reify groups and treat them as internally homogeneous, even when they accept that binary oppositions in textual sources are rhetorical tools, see Rebillard and Rüpke, 'Introduction', p. 5.

[75] Augustine, *Ep.* 135 (ed. Goldbacher, CSEL 44, pp. 89–91), 'We were present at certain gatherings of friends, and many views were expressed there in accord with our various talents and interests. The topic was nonetheless the rhetorical distribution of parts in a discourse .... Then the talk turned to philosophy, with which you are familiar and which you yourself had been accustomed to cultivate as esoteric in the manner of Aristotle. We were also asking about the achievement of the teacher from the Lyceum, about the multiple and prolonged doubt of the Academy .... While our conversation delayed over these ideas, one from among the many present asked: "And who is perfectly imbued with the wisdom of Christianity who can resolve certain ambiguous points on which I am stuck and strengthen my hesitant assent with true or probable grounds for belief?" We were stunned and silent. Then he suddenly burst forth with this: "I wonder whether the Lord and ruler of the world filled the body of an inviolate woman?"'; 'Quibusdam amicorum conuentibus aderamus, frequentes proferebantur illic pro ingeniis studiisque sententiae. Erat tamen sermo rhetorica partitio .... Tunc ad familiarem tuam philosophiam sermo deflectit, quam ipse Aristoteleo more tamquam esotericam fouere consueueras. Quaerebamus, et quid egerit praeceptor ex Lycio, quid Academiae multiplex et continuata cunctatio .... Dum in his confabulatio nostra remoratur, unus e multis: "Et quis", inquit, "est sapientia ad perfectum

the meeting Volusianus recorded could have been construed as heresy, but they were not. It should be noted that Volusianus was the son of Melania the Elder and the uncle of Melania the Younger. Nor should we fasten onto the meetings at Pammachius' house as the crucible for the formation of a set of ideas. Such discussion groups were going on across the empire. Robert Markus pointed out that in the later 4th century there were more highly educated Christians in the Church than there had ever been before, bringing with them habits inculcated by their education in rhetoric.[76] These new generations of Christians expected to be able to respond freely and personally to Scripture. They included the professors of rhetoric Marius Victorinus and Augustine.

If we think of two differing processes from the field of physical science, it might help to illustrate the way in which the model inherent in 'Pelagianism' is misleading. The analogy of virtual particles which occur randomly in an environment that supports their existence is a more accurate model for what occurred than a Big Bang model where everything spun outwards from one event. The environment congenial to the development of fervent ascetic paraenesis that presupposed a positive anthropology and a soteriology in which man had autonomy included (at a minimum) the following elements. First, the growth of asceticism within Christianity, which can accurately be called a movement, though an unorganised one. The principles underlying ascetic endeavour were set out by Athanasius of Alexandria: the goodness of human nature and effective free will, and the presumption of a transparent system of merit and reward.[77] That these ideas were widespread before Pelagius began to write has been shown in Chapters 2 and 3, and the same movement is also visible in Sulpicius Severus' *Life of Martin of Tours*; in Rutilius Namatianus' description of ascetics on the island of Capraria (who must already have been living there for several years before he saw them in AD 417) in his *Concerning His Return Home* (*De reditu suo*); and in the story of Honoratus, Bishop of Arles, who dedicated himself to asceticism in around AD 400 and set off for the East with his brother, founding Lérins a few years later.[78] A second element that made the environment congenial to the composition of ascetic paraenetic

---

Christianitatis inbutus, qui ambigua, in quibus haereo, possit aperire dubiosque adsensus meos uera uel uerisimili credulitate firmare?" Stupemus tacentes. Tunc in haec sponte prorumpit: "Miror utrum mundi Dominus et rector intemeratae feminae corpus impleuerit?"' For a discussion of this correspondence between Volusianus and Augustine, see É. Rebillard, 'Augustin et le rituel épistolaire de l'élite sociale et culturelle de son temps: Éléments pour une analyse processuelle des relations de l'évêque et de la cité dans l'Antiquité tardive', in *L'évêque dans la cité du IVe au Ve siècle: image et autorité*, ed. É. Rebillard and C. Sotinel (Rome, 2010), pp. 131–4; and Rebillard, *Christians and Their Many Identities*, pp. 81–2.

[76] R. A. Markus, 'Social and Historical Setting', in *The Cambridge History of Early Christian Literature*, ed. F. Young, L. Ayres and A. Louth (Cambridge, 2004), p. 412.

[77] See Markus' wide-ranging discussions of the ascetic movement and the reasons behind its rise, including: 'Social and historical setting', pp. 408–9; 'Between Marrou and Brown', pp. 8–11; *The End of Ancient Christianity* (Cambridge, 1990), pp. 34–43, 63–83, 157–79, 199–208, 213–14.

[78] Rutilius Namatianus, *De reditu suo* ll. 439–52 (ed. Doblhofer, p. 120); Hilary of Arles, *Sermo de uita Sancti Honorati* 11–15 (ed. Valentin, SC 235, pp. 96–110).

literature, with its underlying principles, was the existing cultural context in which Stoic ideals favoured ascetic values, and philosophical ideals privileged unconcern for wealth and worldly status. A third factor was Theodosius I's legislation that made Christianity the official religion of the empire in the 380s and 390s AD. A fourth element in the environment that produced this fervent ascetic literature was the traditional rhetorical system of education which put a premium on self-expression and demonstration of literary expertise through publication. A fifth was the fact that there were many areas of Christian thought which dogma did not cover, and for which there was no formula for orthodoxy, which may have encouraged intellectual enquiry. A sixth factor was that Scripture provided authority for both anthropologies, for both interpretations of predestination, and for many different conceptions of grace. Christianity's sacred writings required and invited interpretation, and prompted enquiry. All the foregoing might perhaps be summed up as the ascetic movement met classical culture. A final element that came into play later, from the second decade of the 5th century onwards, was the loss of cultural confidence triggered by Roman military defeat at the hands of barbarian invaders. Its effects are impossible to quantify, but it may have fed into a rejection of traditional social aspirations and a flight to alternative sources of validation.

Jerome did a great deal to create an environment congenial to an asceticism founded on the principles of effective free will and merit. But even if he was closer to being a progenitor of support for the two doctrines at issue, to describe Jerome as 'Pelagian' or his teaching as heretical would again be to employ a flawed model, since he was only one of several writers who built a career on bringing Christian literature from the Greek East to a Latin audience. An accurate historical model is one in which an individualistic tradition of freedom of thought and publication coincided with a powerful current running in the direction of asceticism, together with the cultural factors noted above.

5

Systemic Problems of Definition and Classification

After the initial enthusiasm, which began in the late 19th century, for finding and claiming a large number of works for Pelagius or so-called 'Pelagians', systemic problems regarding definition and classification have emerged. It has proved impossible either to define 'Pelagianism' or to establish a means by which to classify a text as 'Pelagian'. The argument of this chapter is that these systemic problems reveal the incoherence of the concept of 'Pelagianism'. By a definition I mean identification of its defining principle(s) or its constituent tenets. If the concept of 'Pelagianism' is not susceptible of definition, it should be questioned whether it has any coherence at all. The classification of texts as 'Pelagian' is logically conjoined to the question of definition, and is the practical application of the concept of 'Pelagianism'. If the descriptor 'Pelagian' is found to be indeterminate then this confirms the incoherence of the concept of 'Pelagianism'.

The evidence to support this argument consists of a survey of scholarship attempting to do each of these two things.[1] First, attempts to define 'Pelagianism' will be reviewed. Second, it will be shown that ascetic literature expressing the same principles that Pelagius expressed, which has no authorial attribution attached to it, has proved impossible to categorise. To illustrate the difficulty scholars have had in classifying texts, two test cases will be presented. By examining the anonymous letter *To a Mistress of a Household* (*Ad quandam matronam*) and an anonymous homily (known by its opening words *Ammoneo te*), it will be demonstrated once again that the anthropology and soteriology expressed in Pelagius' writings were the working assumptions of the ascetic movement, and that there are no diagnostic features that differentiate Pelagius' writings from other ascetic paraenesis. When faced with an anonymous text, if scholars are unable to determine whether to classify it as 'ascetic' literature or as 'Pelagian' literature, this suggests that the classification 'Pelagian' has no value.

---

[1] I shall discuss selected scholarly assessments to illustrate my point.

The danger of circularity in the use of the terms 'Pelagian' and 'Pelagianism' has practical effects. Texts have been attributed to Pelagius on the basis of their containing ideas that have been assumed to be 'Pelagian' without any questioning as to what constitutes a 'Pelagian' doctrine; witness the list of works under Pelagius' name in *Clavis Patrum Latinorum*, several of which could not possibly have been written by Pelagius because, for example, they contain the statement that the addressee would be given their goodness by God. Likewise, some scholars have classified a text as 'Pelagian' and used that classification to draw conclusions about who might be the author of that text, or to construct links between individuals. If we want to assess how much so-called 'Pelagian' material was transmitted from late antiquity to the print era, consideration of the range of potential candidates for inclusion under the label 'Pelagian' leads to the realisation that for many texts it is not easy to decide whether they should be classed as 'Pelagian' or simply as ascetic literature. If the term is to have any value there need to be criteria by which to classify a text as 'Pelagian'. Yet, as the evidence in this chapter will show, it turns out to be impossible to achieve a set of criteria unless one accepts uncritically the list of tenets offered by Pelagius' opponents as constituting 'Pelagianism', and by this criterion Pelagius' own works do not pass the test for being 'Pelagian'. These difficulties raise doubts about the validity of the terms 'Pelagian' and 'Pelagianism'.

This practical aspect of the incoherence of the concept of 'Pelagianism' becomes critical when one turns to manuscripts; the vast number of anonymous and pseudonymous texts making the same case that Pelagius made, and the scale of their transmission, makes this a pressing issue. If one does not look at manuscripts, it might be possible to ignore the problem; if one studies manuscripts, this question about the validity of the classification 'Pelagian' needs answering.

The Problem of Definition

Attempts to define the constituent tenets of 'Pelagianism' have failed. They have failed because 'Pelagianism' was a fabrication. The controversy during which the term emerged was many-headed in terms of authors and ideas, and both the unity of the programme 'Pelagianism' and its differentiation from the ascetic movement were a mirage of ideological manipulation. Unable to define 'Pelagianism', scholars have found it more productive to describe the controversy, and have suggested that it centred on some core idea such as the retention of effective free will or the rejection of original sin.

Previous attempts at definition

Gerald Bonner's distinction between the theological label and the historical movement was driven in part by the problem that he identified with the definition of 'Pelagianism'. On the historical side, he described 'Pelagianism' as 'an ascetic movement', but he did not consider how it might be differentiated from the ascetic movement in general. On the doctrinal side he suggested that the tenet that linked the various positions expressed in surviving texts was the rejection of the concept of original sin.[2] Georges De Plinval argued that a defining tenet of Pelagius' teaching was his insistence on a role for responsibility and merit in the Christian message of salvation. De Plinval identified 'the idea of liberty' as 'the core of Pelagius' doctrine', and he characterised that liberty as responsibility; he also regarded an eschatological mindset as a fundamental of Pelagius' thought.[3]

The bipartite article by Flavio Nuvolone and Aimé Solignac for *Dictionnaire de Spiritualité* demonstrated the different requirements, on the one hand, of a definition and, on the other, of guidelines for the classification of texts.[4] It had two sections: Nuvolone wrote about the authors of 'Pelagian' material and texts, and Solignac about the movement and its doctrine, thus separating the issues of classification and definition. They both occasionally referred to 'Pelagianism' in quotation marks, suggesting doubt about the term as a referent, but both described it as a 'movement'. In the second part of the article, Solignac offered a description of the doctrine of 'Pelagianism', setting out the teaching under four subheadings: anthropology and theology, ecclesiology, eschatology and ascetic programme. Solignac then described the position of Pelagius, as far as it could be reconstructed, on those subjects.[5] This was therefore a description, not a definition. Solignac identified its

---

[2] G. Bonner, 'Pelagianism Reconsidered', in *Studia Patristica* 27, ed. E. A. Livingstone (Louvain, 1993), p. 237, repr. in Bonner's *Church and Faith in the Patristic Tradition* (Aldershot, 1996), no. V. James Wetzel also identified the shared element as objection to original sin: 'Pelagianism refers to a loose confederation of theologies taking their name, but not necessarily their inspiration, from the British moralist, Pelagius. Those named for him are more or less united in their dislike of Augustine's doctrine of original sin': J. Wetzel, 'Snares of Truth. Augustine on Free Will and Predestination', in *Augustine and His Critics*, ed. R. Dodaro and G. Lawless (London, 2000), p. 126.

[3] G. De Plinval, 'L'heure est-elle venue de redécouvrir Pélage?', *Revue des Études Augustiniennes* 19 (1973), pp. 158–62: 'What is the core of the doctrine? Assuredly it is the idea of Liberty'; 'Quel est le fond de la doctrine? C'est assurément l'idée de Liberté'; 'Pelagius' Liberty is essentially a *responsibility* .... The notion of the *rewards* ... which occupy such an important position in Pelagius' eschatological vision'; 'La Liberté de Pélage est essentiellement une *responsabilité* .... La notion des *praemia* ... qui occupent une place si considérable dans la vision eschatologique de Pélage'. In the article, De Plinval acknowledged that the experience of political history in his own lifetime (meaning the Second World War) had shaped his interpretation of Pelagius' teaching and what he picked out from Pelagius' writings as valuable.

[4] Nuvolone and Solignac, 'Pélage', cols. 2889–942.

[5] Nuvolone and Solignac, 'Pélage', cols. 2926–36.

anthropology (based on the biblical doctrine of man created in the image of God) as 'the fundamental principle of Pelagian doctrine'.[6]

John Ferguson offered a description of the ideas he found in Pelagius' works, but, since he took it that the letters in the Caspari Corpus were written by Pelagius, his description was not based on sound foundations. He argued that Pelagius was a reformer, not concerned primarily with 'abstract problems of theology, but with Christian living'.[7] This underestimate of Pelagius' interest in Christian doctrine, perhaps motivated by a desire to rescue him from beneath the weight of Augustine's reputation for theological analysis, allowed Ferguson to avoid defining Pelagius' theology by suggesting that he did not have one.[8] Having stressed that Pelagius' purpose was paraenetic rather than doctrinal, Ferguson did find the 'apogee of Pelagius' outlook' in the principle of love, but he did not identify this as a defining principle of Pelagius' works.[9]

Robert Evans abjured description and found the 'central and organising principle' of Pelagius' theology in his 'conception of the nature and obligations of man'.[10] Evans' analysis was that this was the 'centre of gravity' of Pelagius' theology, which determined all of Pelagius' teachings. For him, Pelagius' teachings on freedom and grace were 'part of a larger theological scheme'. While Evans rejected Ferguson's suggestion that Pelagius had no theology, both scholars broke away from looking only at the the concerns of the controversy and read Pelagius' works in their own terms. They did not define Pelagius with reference only to the issues raised in the controversy; indeed, Ferguson drew an implicit distinction between Pelagius' teaching, on the one hand, and the concerns of 'Pelagianism', which emerged from the controversy, on the other.[11]

In 1972, Gisbert Greshake offered a description of aspects of Pelagius' thought concerning grace. He located the most important aspect of Pelagius' theology not in a conception of grace as human nature endowed with effective free will but in the enthusiasm of the monastic culture in the East.[12] This was a description that sought to find the differentiating characteristic in Pelagius' theology, and which highlighted the preaching and evangelising character of Pelagius' thought.[13] Greshake's insight about the influence of Eastern asceticism on Pelagius' theology was valuable, but he did not question the concept of 'Pelagianism' itself. He saw

[6] Nuvolone and Solignac, 'Pélage', col. 2926, '"The power and quality of human nature": this is the fundamental principle of Pelagian doctrine'; '"La force et la qualité de la nature humaine": tel est le principe fondamental de la doctrine pélagienne.'

[7] J. Ferguson, *Pelagius* (Cambridge, 1956), p. 159.

[8] Ferguson referred to Pelagius' message being buried 'in the ashes of obloquy which were heaped upon him': Ferguson, *Pelagius*, p. 146.

[9] Ferguson, *Pelagius*, p. 143.

[10] Evans, *Pelagius*, p. 92.

[11] Ferguson, *Pelagius*, pp. 144–58.

[12] G. Greshake, *Gnade als konkrete Freiheit. Eine Untersuchung zur Gnadenlehre des Pelagius* (Mainz, 1972), pp. 307–8.

[13] Greshake, *Gnade*, p. 54.

a phenomenon spinning out from Pelagius, and referred to Pelagius' 'followers' and 'pupils'.[14]

In a survey of the state of research on Pelagius, Otto Wermelinger argued that Pelagius' theology could not be recovered while Augustine's polemical construction of it was still accepted as fact.[15] He saw Pelagius' theology as deriving from a theological situation in Rome and the reception of the ascetic movement there, and he noted 'the diversity among so-called Pelagian works' as ascetic tendencies became more strict.[16] Although Wermelinger mentioned elements within Pelagius' theology, he focused on texts and attribution and did not seek to define 'Pelagianism'. He took it that 'Pelagian' was a valid classification and used Greshake's *pelagisch/pelagianisch* distinction.[17] In his review of texts, when attributing texts to authors, Wermelinger did not break out of the inherited paradigm, sticking with the usual suspects already identified as 'Pelagian'. Despite his statement that understanding Pelagius' theology required rejection of Augustine's invented programme, he did not question the idea of a coherent differentiable movement, only the particular theological content that Augustine attributed to it. Thus Wermelinger did not question the coherence of the concept of 'Pelagianism', which he took for granted existed as something discrete from the ascetic movement, despite the fact that he acknowledged that 'Pelagianism' arose within a long discussion about the ascetic lifestyle.[18] He described 'Pelagianism' in broad terms as a reaction against those who were careless about their Christianity, but did not question the notion of diagnostic tenets that could allow a text to be classified as 'Pelagian', since this idea was the basis of his review of texts and attribution of them to names linked to 'Pelagianism' by Pelagius' opponents. Wermelinger regularly referred to 'Pelagians' as a class of people that existed, with the implication that they could be differentiated from ascetically minded Christians.[19]

Andreas Kessler argued for moving away from a definition based on the internal doctrinal content of texts, which seemed too varied, to what he called 'an historical definition', which first and foremost consisted in details of historical circumstance and amounted to a description.[20] Writing in 2015 Gisbert Greshake noted an initial variety of loosely connected beliefs within what he termed 'so-called Pelagianism'. He identified the 'centre of Pelagius' thought' as 'nature as grace', and set out the ideas he found in Pelagius' *Letter to Demetrias* in order to support his identification of a 'spiritual theology' in Pelagius' letter. Greshake referred to 'so-called' Pelagianism', and used quotation marks when referring to

---

[14] Greshake, *Gnade*, pp. 38–9.

[15] Wermelinger, 'Neuere', pp. 189–91.

[16] Wermelinger, 'Neuere', p. 217.

[17] Greshake, *Gnade*, pp. 38–42.

[18] Wermelinger, 'Neuere', p. 190.

[19] For example, Wermelinger, 'Neuere', p. 215, 'A British Pelagian'; 'Einem britischen Pelagianer'.

[20] A. Kessler, *Reichtumskritik und Pelagianismus. Die pelagianische Diatribe de diuitiis*: *Situierung, Lesetext, Übersetzung, Kommentar*, Paradosis 43, Beiträge zur Geschichte der altchristlichen Literatur und Theologie (Fribourg, 1999), pp. 4–24.

a 'group', thereby seeming to call into question the reality of such a group.[21] Thus he seemed to be moving away from the idea that 'Pelagianism' existed, but he did not confront the issue, and his primary concern was to characterise and explain the 'theology' he found in Pelagius' *Letter to Demetrias*.

In sum, no consensus has emerged on a definition of 'Pelagianism', or on a fundamental principle. The lack of consensus on a defining principle matters less than the fact that none of the descriptions offered can differentiate this alleged discrete movement from the wider ascetic movement. Each of the descriptions proposed could apply equally well to the ascetic movement in general.

Some models proposed

The matrix model

As observed in Chapter 4, Brynley Rees described 'Pelagianism' as a 'matrix' of individuals. This analysis that refers to 'Pelagianism' as a matrix leaves three issues unresolved. First, it gives no help in achieving a definition of 'Pelagianism'. Second, it offers no practical guidance about how to classify a text as 'Pelagian'. Third, it only considers a few individuals over a limited timespan, and omits to address the fact that there were certain concerns that writers expressed for more than a century after the official condemnation of the caricature 'Pelagianism' in AD 418.[22] These included concerns about the need to retain the universality of God's salvific will and an interpretation of predestination that removed this principle of universality. The notion of a matrix is an example of the shift to offering a descriptive model, rather than a definition and criteria for classification, which is a way to evade the problems of definition and classification. It may look like a helpful escape route, the better to describe an historical situation, but it merely allows assumptions to remain unchallenged.

The reaction model

Another model that has been used to describe 'Pelagianism' (rather than define it) is the reaction model. In this account of 'Pelagianism', disparate expressions of anxiety about the need to retain the universality of God's salvific will and about the doctrine of predestination as preordainment, which continued to be

---

[21] G. Greshake, *Pelagius. Epistula ad Demetriadem. Brief an Demetrias. Einleitung, Edition und Übersetzung* (Freiburg, 2015), pp. 7–37.

[22] Honorius, *Constitutio prima Honorii* (ed. Migne, PL 48.380–6), Honorius' rescript cited only one theological tenet, the rejection of original sin: 'The error of primitive man ... has not come down to his descendants'; 'Primitiui hominis errorem ... delapsum ad posteros non fuisse'. The rescript then condemned other tenets that it did not name: '[He says] many other things also which speech rejects and the law opposes, which things it is extremely hateful to think of even in the arrangement of punishing them'; '[Dicit] alia quoque plurima, quae sermo respuit, et lex refutat, quae perexosum est recordari, etiam sub dispositione plectendi'; these *alia* the rescript did not list. The words used to characterise the rejected views were *a crafty mind* (*uersipellis ingenium*) and *trickery* (*uersutia*).

voiced throughout the 5th century, are argued to stand in some sort of relationship to each other. Nuvolone observed that the common ground between 'Pelagian' writers should not be reduced to 'an anti-Augustinian reaction'; but the reaction model has had some traction because one aspect of Pelagius' teaching was his rejection of the doctrine of the absolute prevenience of grace involved in predestination interpreted as preordainment, exemplified in the story that Augustine related of Pelagius' adverse response when he heard a recitation of Book 10 of *The Confessions* and the words: 'Give me what you command and command what you want.'[23] In addition, according to Pelagius' letter to Pope Innocent (in which he listed the works that proved that he acknowledged the role of grace), as early as AD 405–6 in a letter to Paulinus of Nola, Pelagius was already straining to give a place to grace in his teaching, and he later did so again in a letter to Bishop Constantius. This evidence suggests that he was indeed reacting to an account of the relative efficacy of grace and free will in which one specific aspect of grace was given absolute priority over any other agency in humans.[24] Pelagius also argued to Pope Innocent that he was forced to write his recent *On Free Will* (*De libero arbitrio*) in order to defend free will (and that in that work also he had professed both free will and grace).[25] So Pelagius' own characterisation of the situation was that he was reacting to an attack on something which he felt obliged

---

[23] Nuvolone and Solignac, 'Pélage', col. 2889: 'Une réaction antiaugustinienne'. Augustine, *Confessiones* 10.29.40 (ed. Verheijen and Skutella, CCSL 27, p. 176), 'Da quod iubes et iube quod uis.' Augustine's account of the episode: Augustine, *De dono perseuerantiae* 20.53 (ed. Chéné and Pintard, BA 24, p. 730), 'These words of mine, when they were recounted by a certain brother and fellow bishop of mine at Rome while Pelagius was present, Pelagius was unable to bear, and speaking against them somewhat heatedly, he almost took the person who had recounted them to court'; 'Quae mea uerba Pelagius Romae, cum a quodam fratre et coepiscopo meo fuissent eo praesente commemorata, ferre non potuit, et contradicens aliquanto commotius, pene cum eo qui illa commemorauerat litigauit.'

[24] Pelagius, *Ep. ad Innocentium, apud* Augustine, *De gratia Christi et de peccato originali* 1.35.38 (ed. Urba and Zycha, CSEL 42, p. 154), '"Let them read," he says, "that letter which we wrote to the holy man bishop Paulinus almost twelve years ago, which in almost three hundred lines confesses nothing other than the grace and help of God and that we can do absolutely nothing good without God"'; '"Legant," inquit, "illam epistulam, quam ad sanctum uirum Paulinum episcopum ante duodecim fere annos scripsimus, quae trecentis forte uersibus nihil aliud quam Dei gratiam et auxilium confitetur nosque nihil omnino boni facere posse sine Deo."' Theodore De Bruyn suggested that Pelagius' original *Expositio*, written between AD 405 and 410, might have contained more references to the role of *gratia* and greater acknowledgement of God's role in good actions than are visible in the pseudo-Jerome versions of the *Expositio*, created by a reviser who not only added material but also cut out phrases to make the *Expositio* more strongly 'Pelagian'. This is shown by variants in the Karlsruhe manuscript of the *Expositio* that are not present in the Balliol witness (the only other 'uninterpolated' full witness). On balance, De Bruyn concluded that the Karlsruhe variants were probably Pelagius' words. If correct, this might suggest that Pelagius was responding to Augustine's writings from an early date: De Bruyn, *Pelagius's Commentary*, pp. 24–35. See also Martinetto, 'Les premières réactions', pp. 83–117. For a different view, see De Plinval, who argued that Pelagius' and Augustine's 'theories' were conceived independently: De Plinval, 'L'heure', p. 159.

[25] Pelagius, *Ep. ad Innocentium, apud* Augustine, *De gratia Christi et de peccato originali* 1.41.45 (ed. Urba and Zycha, CSEL 42, p. 158), '"Let them also read," he says, "my recent short work in defence of free will, which we were recently forced to produce"'; '"Legant," inquit, "etiam recens meum opusculum, quod pro libero nuper arbitrio edere compulsi sumus"'.

to defend. Furthermore, after the official condemnation of AD 418, the dominant link that can be traced between writers is opposition to the logically conjoined doctrines of an absolutist account of prevenient grace and predestination interpreted as preordainment.[26]

This paradigm, however, which posits a link between individuals based on reservations about the doctrines of prevenient grace and predestination interpreted as preordainment, fails on several counts. First, it fails to address the disparity between these two concerns and the fictional construct disseminated by Pelagius' opponents. Second, Pelagius was not the author of these reservations, which were a matter of individual conscience, as shown by the concerns voiced by Bishop Hilary of Arles and ecclesiastics in southern Gaul, as reported by Prosper of Aquitaine.[27] Third, it obscures the fact that a positive anthropology and a soteriology that encompassed effective free will were longstanding tenets of Christian belief, which did not emerge only when an alternative anthropology and soteriology were promoted. Thus the underlying flaw in the reaction model is that it obscures the truth that 'Pelagianism' was a fiction invented to facilitate the displacement of widely held principles. Fourth, the description of 'Pelagianism' as a reaction avoids having to specify any positive doctrinal elements, the presence of which is a necessary condition for the existence of a discrete doctrinal programme. Lack of differentiability is a major argument against the existence of a supposed doctrinal programme termed 'Pelagianism'; Pelagius' writings are not differentiable from other ascetic paraenesis in terms of doctrine. What caused the lack of differentiability was that there were indeed two positive tenets at stake, but the goodness of human nature and effective free will were established principles in Christianity that were not devised late in the 4th or early in the 5th century. Describing 'Pelagianism' as a reaction obscures this fact.

Objection to the doctrines of original sin, prevenient grace, and predestination interpreted as preordainment is not the same thing as 'Pelagianism' as it was created and characterised by Pelagius' opponents; and the existence of such objections does not mean that 'Pelagianism' existed. It means only that objections to these concepts were widespread among Christians. Like the matrix model, the reaction model misrepresents the situation.

The longevity of concerns: the concept of 'semi-Pelagianism'

In discussing the rejection of the twin doctrines of an absolutist account of prevenient grace and predestination interpreted as preordainment by the ecclesiastics of southern Gaul in the 5th century, the term 'semi-Pelagianism' has sometimes been employed to describe this rejection as a distinct theological position that

---

[26] On the link between prevenient grace and predestination interpreted as preordainment, see Wetzel, 'Snares', p. 125. For Augustine's own comment on the link, see Chapter 1, n. 42.

[27] Prosper *apud* Augustine, *Ep.* 225.2–6 (ed. Goldbacher, CSEL 57, pp. 455–64).

was, by the use of the term, characterised as a recurrence of 'Pelagian' thought.[28] The validity of this term has been questioned on the basis of its anachronism.[29] To describe Faustus of Riez as 'semi-Pelagian' is unhistorical because Faustus rejected the doctrines attributed to the caricature 'Pelagianism' disseminated by Pelagius' opponents. The tenets of the caricature having been selected so as to be unendorsable, they were widely rejected even by ecclesiastics who shared Pelagius' concerns about Augustine's account of predestination.[30] In order to stay in communion with the Church in Rome, ecclesiastics were forced to defer to the condemnations which installed the caricature as truth. Recognition that the term 'semi-Pelagian' was an anachronism coined in the 16th century does not, however, pinpoint the problem with it, which is that 'Pelagianism' itself was a fiction.

There was indeed a link between Faustus and Pelagius in that Faustus sought to retain an element of free will in the achievement of salvation, he rejected predestination interpreted as preordainment, and he sought to retain a confident, positive account of man. Despite deferring to the notion of original sin in order to show what he perceived to be the proper humility and remain within the Church, Faustus described man's nature as rational, in essence good and created in the image of God.[31] The problem with the term 'semi-Pelagian' is not that it acknowledges

---

[28] T. A. Smith, *De Gratia. Faustus of Riez's Treatise on Grace and Its Place in the History of Theology* (Notre Dame, IN, 1990), p. 230. A few scholars have used the term with a less specific denotation, such as Auguste Piédagnel, who attributed a 'semi-Pelagian' viewpoint to a translation of some Chrysostom sermons by Anianus of Celeda: A. Piédagnel, ed., *Panégyriques de S. Paul*, Sources Chrétiennes 300 (Paris, 1982), pp. 98–9, n. 5.

[29] C. Leyser, 'Semi-Pelagianism', in *Augustine through the Ages. An Encyclopedia*, ed. A. Fitzgerald (Grand Rapids, MI, 1999), p. 761. It was a term coined by Dominicans in polemical circumstances in order to smear their Jesuit opponents in 16th-century counter-Reformation debates about faith and works, by associating them with 'Pelagianism'. In her introduction to the book *Grace for Grace*, Rebecca Harden Weaver acknowledged problems with the term, but did not grasp the nettle of identifying the source of those problems: R. Harden Weaver, 'Introduction', in *Grace for Grace. The Debates after Augustine and Pelagius*, ed. A. Y. Hwang, B. J. Matz and A. Cassiday (Washington, DC, 2014), pp. xiv–xvii.

[30] Vincent of Lérins, *Commonitorium* 9.9 (ed. Demeulenaere, CCSL 64, p. 158), gave what appears to have been the official view on 'Pelagianism': 'I shudder to say them: its tenets are so presumptuous that to refute them, let alone to utter them, is almost impossible without incurring some sort of sin'; 'Horreo dicere: sunt enim tam superba, ut mihi non modo adfirmari sed ne refelli quidem sine aliquo piaculo posse uideantur.' Faustus of Riez likewise condemned 'Pelagianism': Faustus, *De gratia* 1.1–2 (ed. Engelbrecht, CSEL 21, pp. 6–14).

[31] Faustus, *De gratia* 2.9 (ed. Engelbrecht, CSEL 21, pp. 78–9), 'On this account is man said to be the image of God, because with kindness and deeming him worthy, truth ingrafted in man righteousness, reason ingrafted in him wisdom, and perpetuity ingrafted in him eternal life. It is because man was made in the image of God that he understands, that he knows what is right, and that he distinguishes between bad and good when his judgement examines a matter'; 'Imago ergo Dei homo dicitur, quia ei indulgenter ac dignanter inseruit ueritas iustitiam, ratio sapientiam, perennitas aeternitatem. De imagine Dei est quod intellegit, quod rectum sapit, quod inter malum et bonum iudicio examinante discriminat.' Cf. Pelagius, *Ad Demetriadem* 2 (ed. Greshake, pp. 60–2), 'Measure the good of human nature by reference to its creator, obviously God, who is said to have made all the works of the world and what is within the world good, and exceedingly good. How much more outstanding do you think he made man himself? .... He determines to fashion him in his own image and likeness .... He armed man on the inside with reason and wisdom, so that by his intellect and vigour of mind, by which man

similarities of thought between Pelagius and Faustus; the problem with it is that 'Pelagianism' was a construct designed to misrepresent. When the evidence is set out showing links between texts written across the length of the 4th, 5th and 6th centuries, it becomes apparent that the phenomenon cannot be narrowed down to something either that Pelagius started in the first decade of the 5th century, or that Pope Zosimus ended in AD 418. The matrix model, the reaction model and the idea of a short-lived historical movement associated with Pelagius fail to address this fact. Faustus of Riez's rejection of predestinarianism did not make him a 'Pelagian' or a 'semi-Pelagian'; it made him a Christian who expressed mainstream views which were retained by many Christians, despite their deferral to the condemnation of a non-existent caricature after the AD 418 condemnations.

The grounds of the debate shifted

It might be argued that 'Pelagianism' has never been precisely defined because it was never a static set of theses. On this account it could be described as an amorphous, shifting collection of ideas orbiting around a belief in man's responsibility for his actions. The grounds of the debate shifted as Augustine developed his ideas in response to what he perceived to be 'Pelagianism'.[32] For example, Augustine admitted that he was forced to redefine his ideas in the course of his opposition to Pelagius, and he described it as elucidating his thinking. However he portrayed it, the full consequences of his theory of prevenient grace appear more clearly in his later writings.[33] These works then triggered the refutation of predestination interpreted as preordainment by some ecclesiastics in southern Gaul. However, to explain the difficulty of defining 'Pelagianism' as caused by the grounds of the debate shifting is to focus on the trees and fail to see the wood. It acknowledges that the controversy mutated over time, but it does not deal with the fictitious character of the concept of 'Pelagianism'. Pelagius' opponents gave the concept a specific constituent set of doctrines. It was characterised as arrogant and it was

---

surpassed the other animals, he alone would recognise the creator of all things'; 'Humanae naturae bonum de eius auctore metire, Deo scilicet, qui cum uniuersa mundi et, quae intra mundum sunt, opera bona et ualde bona fecisse referatur. Quanto putas praestantiorem ipsum fecit hominem .... Ad imaginem et similitudinem suam facere disponit .... Intus armauit ratione scilicet atque prudentia, ut per intellectum uigoremque mentis, quo caeteris praestabat animalibus, factorem omnium solus agnosceret'.

[32] Rackett observed that the grounds of the debate shifted. He noted Gerald Bonner's distinction between the theological heresy and an historical movement, describing the theological programme as 'largely an Augustinian construct', but despite this and noting the variety of positions within what he called a 'movement', he did not question the validity of the concept of 'Pelagianism': Rackett, 'What's Wrong?', pp. 223–37.

[33] Augustine, *De dono perseuerantiae* 21.55 (ed. Chéné and Pintard, BA 24, p. 734), 'I think that I have set out how it is also the gift of God to persevere to the end, in such a way as I have either never before or almost never before so expressly and evidently maintained this point in writing, unless my memory deceives me'; 'Puto me ita posuisse donum Dei esse, etiam perseuerare usque in finem ut hoc antea, si me non fallit obliuio, tam expresse atque euidenter, uel nusquam, uel pene nusquam scripserim.'

attributed to the individual Pelagius. To acknowledge that there was a long debate about the relationship between divine grace and human free will is in no way to acknowledge that 'Pelagianism' existed.

Thus negative accounts of 'Pelagianism' that characterise it as a reaction misrepresent the historical reality. It should nevertheless perhaps be considered whether or not the term 'Pelagianism' is a useful referent for adherence to a positive belief in either man's inherent goodness or his free will, or both. Historically, this has not been what the term has denoted, but might it be useful now as a theological term to denote these positions? The answer is again 'no', first, because 'Pelagianism' inherently bears an historical association with Pelagius as author of these ideas, when clearly they were fundamental Christian principles that underpinned asceticism in particular; and, second, because of the inevitable association the term brings with it to the fourteen tenets and characterisation attributed to 'Pelagianism' by Pelagius' opponents. Pelagius was not the author of widespread misgivings about the triune, newly canvassed as dogma, of original sin, prevenient grace, and predestination interpreted as preordainment.

Circular reasoning

Scholars have been trapped in circular reasoning concerning 'Pelagianism'. When they have tried to pinpoint what Pelagius taught that made it distinctively 'Pelagian', searching for a core belief from which all else flowed, they have begun from the assumption that 'Pelagianism' existed as an historical reality as something separate from the ascetic movement. It is possible to do this if one considers only a restricted range of texts already labelled 'Pelagian', and seek to identify the ideas that they have in common. But if one considers ascetic texts not already associated with the label 'Pelagian', it is clear that Pelagius' writings are not differentiable from the mass of ascetic literature surviving in manuscripts. Consideration of other ascetic texts leads to breaking out of the circular reasoning that says that 'Pelagianism' existed, therefore Pelagius' writings and those of the people named by his opponents as 'Pelagians' must share distinctive ideas, so if a text contains these ideas, it must be 'Pelagian'. This circular reasoning has it that 'Pelagianism' can be identified in these shared ideas, even though the two ideas of the goodness of human nature and effective free will were not the tenets attributed to the caricature condemned as 'Pelagianism' in AD 418.

To escape this circular thought pattern it is necessary to look at a wider range of texts. Having looked at works composed before Pelagius began to write, and texts that can only be seen as independent of Pelagius' influence because they were composed in milieux in which his writings were unknown, anonymous texts will be considered to see how the label 'Pelagian' has been applied in practice. Away from theological theory, does the classification 'Pelagian' work in reality?

The Problem of Classification

Attempts to classify texts as 'Pelagian' 1: Use a contemporary list of tenets

Having noted the difficulties surrounding definition, it is instructive to consider the related question of classification of texts as 'Pelagian' or not 'Pelagian'. First, the history of attempts to classify texts as 'Pelagian' will be reviewed, and then two particular test cases examined.

Anonymous texts which bring with them no presumption concerning the author's standpoint offer revealing examples of what happens when an attempt is made to classify a text as 'Pelagian'. One such example of the systemic problems involved in trying to classify a text as 'Pelagian' is provided by Fredric Schlatter's work on the *Incomplete Commentary on Matthew* (*Opus imperfectum in Matthaeum*). Schlatter addressed the question of the criteria by which a text could be judged 'Pelagian' when he sought to show that this text was primarily 'Pelagian' rather than Arian. He took as representative tenets of 'Pelagianism' the theses listed by the Sicilian layman Hilary writing to Augustine in AD 414 from Syracuse.[34] Thus Schlatter chose a method by which to classify a text as 'Pelagian' that begged the question of whether 'Pelagianism' existed, either as a coherent programme or as something that should be associated in particular with Pelagius. This approach also begged the question of whether Pelagius' actual teaching was something doctrinally distinct from other paraenetic literature produced by the ascetic movement. The possibility that the ideas Schlatter used as diagnostic were in fact widespread among contemporary Christians and not markers of a link to Pelagius was not something that Schlatter considered. Nor did he examine Pelagius' own works to see if these ideas were contained within them. Thus Schlatter's argument was circular because he sought to classify the text as 'Pelagian' on the basis of his prior assumption that certain ideas were distinctively 'Pelagian'.

The difficulties raised by the variation in ideas within what has been characterised as one historical movement are also illustrated by Schlatter's work. In addition to deriving ideas from Hilary's letter, Schlatter also took ideas from a letter in the Caspari Corpus, *On Chastity*, and showed that they were expressed in the *Incomplete Commentary on Matthew*. He did not consider the fact that these ideas were most prominently disseminated by Jerome. The views presented in

---

[34] Augustine, *Ep.* 156 (ed. Goldbacher, CSEL 44, pp. 448–9). The ideas Hilary mentioned were 1. that human beings can be without sin and can easily keep God's commandments if they want to; 2. that an infant who is not baptised before it dies cannot deserve to perish because it was born without sin; 3. that a rich man cannot enter the kingdom of God unless he sells all his possessions, and that using his riches to observe the commandments cannot benefit him; 4. one should not swear oaths at all; 5. a question as to which Church has no wrinkle or spot, as Scripture says, the present Church or the Church to come? Some were saying that it was the present Church and that it could not be without sin. Schlatter, 'The Pelagianism', pp. 267–84.

On Chastity were not the same as Pelagius' teaching on the relative merits of marriage and celibacy, and had closer affinities with Jerome's teaching.[35] Thus in deciding what qualified a text to be 'Pelagian', Schlatter drew on a range of different ideas within a body of material which he grouped together on the basis of prior assumptions about what constituted 'Pelagianism'. However, he was seeking only to recategorise the *Incomplete Commentary on Matthew*, not to define the core tenets of 'Pelagianism', so for him the matter of identifying those tenets was not critical. He had only to show enough affinities between the *Incomplete Commentary on Matthew* and what he assumed were the contents of recognisably 'Pelagian' thought to make his case. But one of the ideas that he used to make his case—namely, that marriage was an impediment to righteousness—exemplifies the problem. As seen in Chapter 4, using this idea as a criterion by which to classify a text as 'Pelagian' assumes that 'Pelagianism' was a coherent programme, whereas in fact the variation in ideas within texts produced by this one alleged movement vitiates the idea of a programme and a discrete movement, and what we are left with is simply the ascetic movement, for which Pelagius was not responsible. Thus Schlatter's work demonstrates the problems inherent in attempting to categorise a text as 'Pelagian', and the circularity that attends such classification. Schlatter made assumptions about what constituted 'Pelagianism', and on finding such ideas in a text he labelled the text 'Pelagian', and then attributed it to a suitable name on the basis of that classification. He judged Anianus of Celeda suitable because Anianus was identified as a 'Pelagian' by Pelagius' opponents. Schlatter's work revealed that the method of taking a list of tenets and looking to see if they are present in a text does not work because of the fundamental incoherence of the notion of 'Pelagianism'.

Conclusion on the list of tenets method of classification: the case of the
Incomplete Commentary on Matthew

The number of surviving copies of the *Incomplete Commentary on Matthew* suggests that it was an influential work, and therefore classification of its doctrinal position has some importance. While Schlatter argued that it was fundamentally a 'Pelagian' work more than an Arian one, Franz Mali concluded that the author was not a 'Pelagian'.[36] He accepted the idea, however, that if a work exhibits a series of points of contact with 'Pelagian' teaching, then close contacts between the author and 'Pelagians' appear certain.[37] This assumption needs to be questioned. First,

---

[35] K. Cooper, *The Fall of the Roman Household* (Cambridge, 2007), pp. 169–70.
[36] F. Mali, *Das 'Opus imperfectum in Matthaeum' und sein Verhältnis zu den Matthäuskommentaren von Origenes und Hieronymus* (Innsbruck, 1991), p. 353, '*kein Pelagianer*'.
[37] Mali, *Das 'Opus'*, pp. 353–4, 'The author of the *Opus imperfectum* is no Pelagian, even if there are a number of points of contact with Pelagian teachings in the work which make the writer's close contacts with Pelagians seem assured'; 'Der Autor des OIM ist kein Pelagianer, auch wenn im Werk eine Reihe von Berührungspunkten mit pelagianischen Lehren zu finden sind, die enge Kontakte des Verfassers mit Pelagianern als gesichert erscheinen lassen'. Mali pointed out that although the *Opus imperfectum*

there is no necessity for any contact with Pelagius, or anyone who had known Pelagius, or for contact with the writings of any such, to enable the assertion of the principle of merit in the attainment of salvation and the consequent breaking of Augustine's rule that by definition grace had to be freely given, without any link to personal merit, in order for it to be grace. Joop Van Banning's suggestion that the author of the *Incomplete Commentary on Matthew* was an Arian bishop or priest, living in Illyricum, Dacia or Moesia, who was familiar with Constantinople, poses the same questions about the term 'Pelagian', and whether it is intended to denote someone who was aware of and had signed up to a programme (that is, had some link to an historical movement), or whether it refers to an approach to Christianity which presupposed the efficacy of merit in the economy of salvation and the need for imitation of Christ's way of life, or some more specific set of theses.[38] That is, whether 'Pelagian' refers to doctrine or to specific historical circumstances. And if all that exists in a text is the assumption of the efficacy of merit in the economy of salvation, then since this was a commonplace assumption of asceticism, all that its presence means is that the author subscribed to ascetic principles. Thus we come to the nub of the problem with classifying texts as 'Pelagian': Was anyone who preached ascetic practices on scriptural grounds a 'Pelagian'? If the *Incomplete Commentary on Matthew* is allowed into the corpus of 'Pelagian' texts, then there start to be a very large number of 'Pelagian' texts in circulation during the Middle Ages. But this would have occurred because the classification 'Pelagian' had been made very broad, categorising any text that proposed ascetic standards as 'Pelagian'. In Schlatter's analysis of the *Incomplete Commentary on Matthew*, the ascetic movement and 'Pelagianism' were equated. This illustrates how in practice the alleged discrete subgroup of 'Pelagian' texts is not in fact differentiable from other ascetic literature. What existed was a broad movement towards asceticism that became pervasive in Christianity, within which many different ideas gestated and surfaced, such as the idea that excessive wealth was un-Christian.

An unintended byproduct of Schlatter's work was to reveal once more how widespread such ideas were and how to try to categorise them as 'Pelagian' is to fail to see that these were not a newly invented programme of doctrines attributable to Pelagius, but rather the norms of ascetic Christianity, which became the dominant brand of Christianity during the second half of the 4th century and the 5th century.

---

contained statements that showed the influence of 'Pelagian' thinking, the work also included passages which asserted the opposite: Mali, *Das 'Opus'*, p. 354, n. 983. However, it should be noted that the possibility of interpolation during its transmission problematises discussion of the authorial viewpoint of the commentary, given that the genre was one open to alteration.

[38] J. Van Banning, ed., *Opus imperfectum in Matthaeum. Praefatio*, Corpus Christianorum Series Latina 87B (Turnhout, 1988), pp. V–VI.

Attempts to classify texts as 'Pelagian' 2: Create a list of 'Pelagian' texts

Approaching classification of texts as 'Pelagian' from the opposite direction to Schlatter, several lists of 'Pelagian' texts have been drawn up, and a review of the results reveals once more the unsustainability of the notion of 'Pelagianism'.

Nearly seventy years after Carl Paul Caspari first began the hunt for 'Pelagian' texts with his 1890 edition of the group of letters now commonly referred to as the Caspari Corpus, in 1958 Adalbert Hamman was obliged to make sense of the mass of texts that had been discovered and claimed for a variety of authors in order to create a supplement to the Patrologia Latina series. Hamman's method was to base his register of 'Pelagian' texts on the verdicts of other scholars.[39] He included anything that had been described in scholarship as 'Pelagian', with scholarly counter-claims where they existed, but with no further attempt at justification for inclusion in his list. Hamman's survey included the subgroups 'writings of doubtful belief' (*scripta dubiae fidei*) and 'other Pelagian writings' (*alia scripta pelagiana*), but he gave no reasons for the inclusion of texts under these headings, and among the texts he included are some that express views that ought theoretically to preclude their inclusion in a list of alleged 'Pelagian' texts.[40]

In reality, scholarly judgements on the classification of texts as 'Pelagian' have consistently been subjective. John Morris referred to the 'rich variety of Pelagian thought' as the concept of free will opened the doors to 'widely diverging social and religious philosophies'.[41] He stated that seventy 'Pelagian' texts survived, but his attention was in fact focused on a small group of texts and their authorial attribution. Morris was certain that he knew what 'a Pelagian document' looked like but gave no grounds for his certainty.[42] His interests lay in British history and in his vision of how one of Pelagius' supporters developed Pelagius' teaching into

---

[39] A. Hamman, ed., *Patrologia Latina Supplementum* 1 (Paris, 1958), cols. 1101–9.

[40] For example, [*CPL* 762] *Magnum cumulatur* (ed. Hamman, PLS 1.1694–8), listed by Hammam under 'Pelagian Writings' (*Scripta pelagiana*), which contains two short passages borrowed verbatim from Pelagius' *On the Divine Law*, but also four passages that suggest human helplessness in relation to moral decision-making. For example, concerning the devil: 'What are we to do except ask God's help against his attacks?'; 'Quid acturi sumus nisi Dei auxilium contra eius impetus postulemus?'; Concerning God: 'Imploring his help let us strive to keep his commandments as far as we are able'; 'Ipsius adiutorium inplorantes mandata eius in quantum possumus custodire studeamus'; 'Let us not be dejected nor sad, but rather, as I said, let us beseech Christ's help to enable us to repel the devil's temptations'; 'Non confundamur neque contristemur, sed sicut diximus, Christi auxilium ad repellendas diaboli temptationes inploremus'. The letter also quoted a signature biblical citation of Augustine's teaching: *No one comes to me unless the Father who sent me draws him* [John 6:44]. Taken together, these elements work against classification of the letter as expressing the approach to Christianity taken by Pelagius. Cf. Rees, *Pelagius* vol. II, pp. 326–7.

[41] Morris, 'Pelagian Literature', p. 27.

[42] Morris, 'Pelagian Literature', p. 32.

what Morris described as socialism.[43] Thus Morris did not deal with either issues of theology or practical issues of textual classification.

Another example of the subjectivity underlying classifications is the two-part article in *Dictionnaire de Spiritualité* already mentioned. In his section of the article on 'Pelagianism', Nuvolone directly faced the issue of how to identify the works produced by what he termed 'the Pelagian movement'.[44] This was more easily done for putative named authors, but, when it came to dealing with anonymous authors, Nuvolone further nuanced his terminology to describe the 'movement' as 'a theological situation', giving the impression that he was occasionally more comfortable describing 'Pelagianism' as a situation than as a programme of tenets; despite this he did not abandon the term 'movement'.[45]

Nevertheless, Nuvolone had to take some decisions. To explain the links between the texts in the Caspari Corpus and the works more certainly attributed to Pelagius, he referred to the author of the Caspari Corpus letters as a member of 'an identical movement', and he further elaborated: 'The assimilation of examples, of images and of arguments, drawing on ascetic literature, and the exchange of writings, can explain the connections between the two.'[46] According to Nuvolone, the texts in the Caspari Corpus seemed to lie within an inner circle.[47] Other works outside that close relationship were listed as 'of Pelagian inspiration', or 'attributable to the Pelagian trend', but the grounds for these assertions were not discussed systematically.[48] Some texts were 'close to the literature called Pelagian' because of their ascetic arguments and because they were anchored in the principle of an optimistic view of human capabilities.[49] A theme that has been viewed as a hallmark of Pelagius' teaching is that of the true Christian as opposed to the person who is Christian in name only, and Nuvolone equated this with the ascetic principle, which suggests that he did recognise the unity of these two things, even

[43] Morris, 'Pelagian Literature', pp. 50–60.
[44] Nuvolone referred to: *'Le mouvement "pélagien"'*: Nuvolone and Solignac, 'Pélage', col. 2889 and 2916. He also referred to 'le groupe de "pélagiens"' in reference to people in Britain, including Agricola and Severianus, to refute whom Germanus of Auxerre travelled to Britain: Nuvolone and Solignac, 'Pélage', col. 2912.
[45] Nuvolone and Solignac, 'Pélage', col. 2915, 'Pelagianism is indeed only the emergence of a complex theological situation, many of whose protagonists and writers will remain in darkness for good'; 'Le pélagianisme n'est en effet que l'émergence d'une situation théologique complexe, dont beaucoup d'acteurs et écrivains resteront définitivement dans l'ombre.' Nuvolone referred to the issue of 'les anonymes'.
[46] Nuvolone and Solignac, 'Pélage', col. 2915, 'Un mouvement identique'; 'L'osmose des exemples, des images et des arguments, relevant de la littérature ascétique, et l'échange des écrits peuvent expliquer les parentés entre les deux.'
[47] Nuvolone referred to 'l'intérieur du mouvement' in reference to *On Bad Teachers* (one of the Caspari Corpus letters): Nuvolone and Solignac, 'Pélage', col. 2916.
[48] Nuvolone and Solignac, 'Pélage', col. 2918, 'D'inspiration pélagienne'; 'Les compositions attribuables au courant pélagien'.
[49] Nuvolone and Solignac, 'Pélage', col. 2919, some texts: 'Se rapprochent de la littérature dite pélagienne par le biais des arguments ascétiques, s'ancre dans le principe d'une vue optimiste des possibilités humaines.'

if he did not deal with the incompatibility of this view with his simultaneous attempt to keep these two categories separate.[50] Sometimes Nuvolone gave his judgement on works without explanation. He noted that one text revealed a very positive role for grace but did not therefore exclude it from the list. Another 'is not particularly Pelagian'. He commented about yet another that 'its content is not Pelagian'.[51] In a further case, Nuvolone described a letter to a woman who was in danger of lapsing from her renunciation of the world, a letter essentially dealing with the subject of asceticism, as having principles close to the ascetic instruction of the 'Pelagian milieux' delivered to wealthy addressees, seemingly leaving it to the reader to decide whether or not that qualified the letter for inclusion under the heading 'Pelagian'. Finally, Nuvolone's reasons for including in his survey of 'Pelagian' texts a pseudo-Sulpician text, *To Claudia concerning the Last Judgement* (*Ad Claudiam de ultimo iudicio*), were, first, thematic because it dealt with the topics of the Day of Judgement, lust and riches; and, second, a question of literary technique, in this case the technique of putting fictional speeches into the mouths of biblical figures to remonstrate with the addressee. Nuvolone saw parallels to all these features in letters in the Caspari Corpus, and on this basis he judged *To Claudia concerning the Last Judgement* to be 'Pelagian'.

Another example of the intellectual incoherence of attempts to classify texts as 'Pelagian' rather than as ascetic literature is offered by the selection of texts made by Brynley Rees in his collection of 'Pelagian' letters. Rees never used quotation marks to refer to 'Pelagianism'; seemingly he never doubted that the term was an accurate and useful referent, even when he pointed out how far Augustine's characterisation of it was a fabrication created for polemical purposes.[52] Faced with the classification issue when deciding what texts to include in his translations of 'Pelagian' letters in his section entitled 'Miscellanea', Rees did offer some discussion of the grounds for classing a text as 'Pelagian', but his assessments were subjective and unsystematic, and he did not address the theoretical issue of definition lurking behind the difficulty of classification.[53] With a vagueness resembling Nuvolone's, Rees used such phrases as 'not markedly Pelagian', 'a touch of Pelagianism here and there' and 'not patently Pelagian, more the work of a sympathiser'. He approached the problem when he wrote of *To a Widow* (also known as *On the Preservation of Widowhood*, *De uiduitate seruanda*) that resemblances to the Caspari Corpus letters might be: 'Not so much characteristic of Pelagian teaching as commonplaces of contemporary writing on morality.'[54] Yet, on the whole, Rees seemed to identify strict asceticism as a defining trait of Pelagius'

---

[50] Nuvolone and Solignac, 'Pélage', col. 2919, 'A situation in which questions were being asked about the authentic Christian life, that is to say, the ascetic life'; 'Une situation de contestation de la vie authentiquement chrétienne, c'est-à-dire ascétique.'

[51] Nuvolone and Solignac, 'Pélage', col. 2920, 'N'est pas particulièrement pélagien'; 'Sa teneur n'est pas pélagienne.'

[52] Rees, *Pelagius* vol. I, pp. 89–91.

[53] Rees, *Pelagius* vol. II, pp. 301–44.

[54] Rees, *Pelagius* vol. II, p. 302.

teaching and a sufficient indicator of 'Pelagianism', and concluded that the author of *On the Preservation of Widowhood* was 'almost certainly Pelagian'.[55] Rees also gave as justification for including a letter the fact that it was: 'A typical example of the attitude of contemporary ascetics'.[56] His assumption begs the question of whether all ascetic literature was 'Pelagian' according to his definition. He did not consider the possibility that the reverse was the case: that what he identified as 'Pelagian' literature was simply ascetic literature. This was because despite glancing at the problem he sensed, Rees never gave serious consideration to how he could separate what he called 'Pelagian' literature from other ascetic writings. Nor did he give serious consideration to the possibility that on his understanding of 'Pelagianism', all Latin ascetic paraenetic literature qualified as 'Pelagian'. Furthermore, two of the letters which he included each contain, alongside their ascetic admonitions, several passages which endorse Augustine's account of prevenient grace.[57] Thus Rees did not deal with the incoherence of his grounds for classification of texts as 'Pelagian'.

Still another example of the unsustainability of the classification 'Pelagian' in practice is offered by the listings in *Clavis Patrum Latinorum*. References are made to scholarship, with notices of opinion concerning attributions, but there is no treatment of the issue of classification. A number of letters that have no link to Pelagius' teaching and contain statements that express Augustine's account of grace are included under the name of Pelagius himself.[58] There is a section entitled 'Doubtful and Spurious' (*dubia et spuria*), and 'To an Older Friend' (*Honorificentiae tuae*) is listed in a different section headed 'Pseudo-Jerome', although it is more usually classed as one of the Caspari Corpus letters along-side *To a Young Man* (*Humanae referunt litterae*) because the two travel together in the manuscript tradition. The result is confusion for anyone trying to grasp

---

[55] Rees, *Pelagius* vol. II, p. 302.

[56] Rees, *Pelagius* vol. II, p. 338.

[57] On *Magnum cumulatur*, see n. 40; [*CPL* 747] *Epistola ad uirginem deuotam* 2.4 (ed. Migne, PL 17.583C), '[God] who perhaps will see fit to hear our tears and our groans, so that he gives you the inclination to turn to him once again'; '[Deus] qui forte fletum nostrum et gemitum exaudire dignetur, ut det tibi animum conuertendi ad ipsum denuo'; 3.1 (ed. Migne, PL 17.583D), '*Pray to your Father* that he might give to you a good mind, and intellect, so that you know who to follow and who to avoid'; '*Ora Patrem tuum* ut det tibi mentem bonam, et intellectum, ut scias quos debeas sequi, et quos uitare'. This letter contains these acknowledgements of the role of prevenient grace, yet it has been classed as a 'Pelagian' text, showing the incoherence of the classification 'Pelagian'. Cf. Rees, *Pelagius* vol. II, pp. 338–44.

[58] *Magnum cumulatur*, see n. 40; *Epistola ad uirginem deuotam*, see n. 57; arguably also [*CPL* 743] *Epistola de uera paenitentia* (which appears under the title of *Ad quemdam qui in saeculo paenitebat* in Patrologia Latina), whose author seems to want to have both grace and free will in operation: *Epistola de uera paenitentia* 3 (ed. Migne, PL 30.243C), 'I call the man penitent, who beats his breast because he has done wrong, and asks the Lord so that he should not do again what he had admitted. I call the man penitent who does not go after his lusts, and prohibits himself from pursuing his own will'; 'Paenitentiam hominem dico, qui plangit quia fecit malum, et rogat Dominum, ut etiam non faciat quod admiserat. Paenitentem hominem dico, qui post concupiscentias suas non uadit, et a uoluntate sua se prohibet.'

what the term 'Pelagian' means, or the range and extent of the corpus of so-called 'Pelagian' material.

Andreas Kessler addressed the issues of definition and classification directly in the introduction to his edition of *On Riches* (*De diuitiis*). He identified the problems surrounding use of the term 'Pelagian' and noted the vagueness of the term.[59] He queried the use of a collective name, concluded that the term was useful and then argued that a set of criteria for the classification of 'Pelagian' writings was urgently needed.[60] He noted the assumption that the term 'Pelagian' has a definite meaning underlying lists of 'Pelagian' texts, despite the variety and contradictoriness among texts presented in such lists. Kessler's answer was to move from a definition based in the history of dogma to what he called an historical definition, although what he produced was not a definition but a detailed description. His approach proposed a number of different historical features as being elements that defined the phenomenon, but the result was essentially a summary of the history of the controversy, in which he picked out what he saw as its defining elements, such as its being embedded in the upper-class villa-based environment of Rome. The person of Pelagius and the character of Pelagius' activity were also defining elements for Kessler; a text had to have a direct point of contact with Pelagius' writings and the nature of Pelagius' characteristic activity for it to be considered 'Pelagian'. Instead of a definition, Kessler offered a very detailed set of criteria based on circumstances such as place, people and dates. He called these 'reference points for a definition'. His description of the key characteristics of Pelagius' activity contained some less convincing elements, such as place and audience, but also picked out as being definitive Pelagius' reforming purpose, his preaching and his intention to transform his hearers.[61]

Although Kessler correctly identified the problems with the descriptor 'Pelagian', there are four main faults with his attempt to solve these problems. First, to abandon a doctrinal definition of 'Pelagianism' is a mistake because this obscures what was going on in the controversy, which was a shift in Christian doctrine. The name Pelagius is known for reasons of doctrine, not because of details of circumstance. Second, Kessler did not consider the theological assumptions of the ascetic movement and their relationship to Pelagius' teaching, such as Jerome's proselytising for asceticism. Third, he failed to address important elements within the phenomenon, such as the long subsequent retention within Christian literature of the approach to Christianity expounded by Pelagius, including, for instance, a confident characterisation of the relationship between Creator and created being. And, fourth, Kessler did not consider the manuscript tradition and the range of surviving texts that express the same principles as are articulated in Pelagius' writings, including ones in which theological assumptions

---

[59] Kessler, *Reichtumskritik*, p. 4, 'Die "Diffusheit" des Begriffs Pelagianismus'; 'The vagueness of the concept of Pelagianism'.

[60] Kessler, *Reichtumskritik*, pp. 4–24.

[61] Kessler, *Reichtumskritik*, pp. 13–18.

are implicit. An example of the limitations of Kessler's approach is provided by a Reichenau homily fragment examined later in this chapter, which contained a message similar to Pelagius' in many ways, but whose author may have had no link to Pelagius in terms of historical circumstances.

Other scholars have identified the need for greater clarity about the classification of texts. Kate Cooper saw the need for an examination of the: 'Relationship of one treatise to another with a view to cataloguing a spectrum of theological and paraenetic stances', which would allow an understanding of the range of ideas held by those who 'rallied around Pelagius' and would contribute to resolving questions of authorial attribution.[62] In 2007, Josef Lössl at times used quotation marks in referring to 'Pelagianism' in an article that called into question the meaning and use of the term.[63] In summary, a defining principle and a list of constituent tenets have proved elusive, and scholars have begun to express concern about the paradigm.

Conclusion on attempts to create lists of 'Pelagian' texts

Attempts to create lists of 'Pelagian' texts have failed; they have created confusion rather than clarity. Their failure illustrates the systemic flaws in the notion of 'Pelagianism'. No one has tried to argue that the phenomenon identified by the term 'Pelagianism' should be restricted to texts written by Pelagius himself. Scholarship has seen 'Pelagianism' as a movement and 'Pelagian' as a distinct classification. This consensus that there were such things as diagnostically 'Pelagian' ideas has never been seriously questioned. In the latter part of the 20th century the preoccupation of scholarship moved from finding 'Pelagian' texts and questions of authorial attribution towards attempts to address the issue of what classified a text as 'Pelagian'. In his final article on the subject of Pelagius, De Plinval distinguished between four different things: 'Pelagianism' in the form in which it had been rejected by Church councils, which he referred to within inverted commas; the views of Caelestius; the views of Julian of Aeclanum; and the views of Pelagius. Yet even in his last word on the subject, De Plinval glossed over the problems involved in identifying Pelagius' canon. He referred to the possibility of presenting an account of Pelagius' thought: 'Such as it stands out in his *Commentary on the Pauline Epistles*, and in what remains to us of works of instruction (letters or treatises) which reflect his personal doctrine'.[64] But De Plinval attributed a larger number of texts to Pelagius than any other scholar. For example, he referred to Pelagius' having exalted grace in his *On Love* (*De amore*), a commentary on the *Song of Songs* that survives only in quotations that Bede made from it, and now held to be a translation or reworking by Julian of Aeclanum

---

[62] Cooper, 'An(n)ianus', p. 255; Gerald Bonner saw the need for a comparison of 'Pelagian' writers 'noting their similarities and disagreements', 'Pelagianism reconsidered', p. 237, n. 1.

[63] Lössl, 'Augustine, "Pelagianism"', p. 129, p. 142

[64] De Plinval, 'L'heure', p. 158, 'Telle qu'elle ressort de son *Commentaire sur les Épîtres de S. Paul* et de ce qui nous reste des oeuvres édifiantes (Lettres ou Traités) qui reflètent sa doctrine personelle'.

of Theodore of Mopsuestia's commentary on the *Song of Songs*. Although De Plinval sought to identify 'the true doctrine of Pelagius' from Pelagius' works, he did not sufficiently acknowledge the difficulty of establishing Pelagius' canon, on the basis of which he would reconstruct Pelagius' 'true doctrine', nor could he know the extent to which Souter's edition of Pelagius' *Commentary on the Pauline Epistles* would come into doubt as a reliable guide to Pelagius' original commentary. Crucially, De Plinval never considered the possibility that Pelagius' writings were not differentiable doctrinally from other ascetic paraenesis.

Gisbert Greshake drew a distinction between 'pelagisch' and 'pelagianisch' to denote the difference between Pelagius' own teaching and that of what he described as Pelagius' pupils or followers. He acknowledged difficulties over the attribution of texts, but he did not confront the fact that this attribution problem made it difficult to maintain his distinction in practice with regard to surviving texts.[65] More recently, Mathijs Lamberigts acknowledged that certain ideas had been 'designated as Pelagian' but could not be assumed to represent Pelagius' views. He did not address the possibility that the designation 'Pelagian' should cease to be used.[66] There has been insufficient discussion of the possibility of inclusion within the category 'Pelagian' of later texts such as *The Predestined* (*Praedestinatus*), the Reichenau homily fragment *Ammoneo te*, Gennadius' *Book of Ecclesiastical Dogmas* (*Liber ecclesiasticorum dogmatum*) and Faustus' *On the Grace of God and Free Will* (*De gratia Dei et libero arbitrio*).[67] Some of these have been cordoned off using the label 'semi-Pelagian', and although this term was coined in order to imply crypto-'Pelagianism', its use has meant that these texts have been largely excluded from discussion of Pelagius. This minimises the visibility of the extent to which Christians continued to adhere to the doctrines of the goodness of human nature and effective free will, and resisted the installation of a different anthropology and soteriology. It does this by segmenting opposition into two conflicts where in fact there was one long negotiation. The only distinction that can be drawn is between the period when the debate was open, before the AD 418 condemnation, and after it, when objection to the new doctrines was forced to become covert to a greater or lesser degree and ecclesiastics were obliged to defer to the official condemnation of the caricature 'Pelagianism'.

In these attempts at definition and classification, several questions have gone unconsidered, such as whether effective free will was a prevailing assumption of the ascetic movement, and whether the principle of merit and the injunction to imitate Christ and to obey God's commandments were fundamentals of the ascetic movement. If the defining tenet of 'Pelagianism' is reduced to the assertion of

---

[65] Greshake, *Gnade*, pp. 37–43.

[66] Lamberigts, 'Le Mal', pp. 97–101.

[67] M. Abel, 'Le "Praedestinatus" et le pélagianisme', *Recherches de Theologie ancienne et médiévale* 35 (1968), pp. 5–25; Smith, *De Gratia*; D. Ogliari, *Gratia et Certamen. The Relationship between Grace and Free Will in the Discussion of Augustine with the So-Called Semipelagians* (Louvain, 2003), pp. 429–36.

effective free will, it has to be acknowledged that this was the working assumption on which all ascetic literature was based prior to the controversy over original sin, prevenient grace, and predestination interpreted as preordainment, and to a great extent continued to be based after AD 418 also. At issue is whether it is accurate or possible to delimit a selection of ascetic texts with the label 'Pelagian', which both binds them together in a special way and separates them from other ascetic paraenesis.

Problems with the Paradigm: Anonymous Ascetic Texts that are Difficult to Classify

Anonymous texts from the 5th century test the viability of the classification 'Pelagian'. There are a number of anonymous ascetic texts that make no explicit doctrinal comment; for example, no overt defence of free will. Yet they share so many ideas with Pelagius' writings that scholars have been unable to resist classifying them in terms of some sort of relation to Pelagius. These texts illustrate the problem that has been caused by seeing Pelagius as separate from the ascetic movement and crediting him with undeserved importance as a progenitor of distinct new doctrines. Two examples will be considered here.

Test case 1: *To a Mistress of a Household (Ad quandam matronam)*

The Vienna/Milan letter fragment known by the generic title *To a Mistress of a Household (Ad quandam matronam)* exemplifies this problem of classification and raises pressing questions concerning the paradigm of 'Pelagianism'.[68] Its correspondences with letters unquestionably by Pelagius are so strong that if it is not regarded as having been written by him, then it is impossible to suggest that Pelagius was the originator of anything at all. And yet scholars have stopped short of ascribing it to Pelagius without facing the fact that if they do not, then the notion of 'Pelagianism' becomes meaningless and its incoherence is exposed. *To a Mistress of a Household* is therefore a textbook example of the problems involved in attempting to classify texts as 'Pelagian'.

---

[68] This letter is missing its beginning; Morin and Dold both edited the text on the basis of incorrect reconstructions of the original sequence of the folios (now held separately in Milan and Vienna). Editions by Duval and Frede rectified this problem: Y.-M. Duval, 'La Lettre de Direction (Acéphale) à une Mère de Famille du MS 954 de Vienne' (*CPL* 755). Edition des Divers Fragments dans leur Ordre Original', in *Valeurs dans le Stoïcisme. Du Portique à nos Jours. Textes rassemblés en hommage à Michel Spanneut*, ed. M. Soetard (Lille, 1993), pp. 203–43; H. J. Frede ed., [Anon., *Epistula ad quandam matronam christianam*] in *Vetus Latina. Die Reste der Altlateinischen Bibel* (Freiburg, 1996), pp. 35–76. Duval printed the text in shorter lines and divided it into more sections; I refer to the Duval edition because its format allows for more precise references.

To a Mistress of a Household is incomplete, but its fragmentary character does not make its classification different in kind from that of letters that are preserved in full. There is no sense in *To a Mistress of a Household* that its ideas are controversial, which suggests that it was composed before AD 418. It shares ideas, themes, phraseology and biblical citations with Pelagius' writings, particularly *Letter to Demetrias* and *Letter to Celantia*.[69] There is no doubt that these three letters convey the same message but, despite their strong similarity, no scholar has been willing to attribute the letter to Pelagius. This text was only reconstructed in the 1990s, by which time scholars had become cautious about attributing texts to him, perhaps wary of De Plinval's experience of having to retract ambitious claims for the scale of Pelagius' surviving canon. The unknowable element is whether there might have been something at the start of the letter that would have tied it in to Pelagius. In the surviving sections there is no explicit doctrinal statement about free will, and it is therefore a text that has all the doctrinal assumptions of ascetic paraenesis without argument for those assumptions. Because this text has close similarities to letters written by Pelagius, it focuses attention precisely on the question of whether this should be classed as an ascetic text, as a text by Pelagius or as a text by a 'Pelagian' writer, and what the difference between these categories might consist in.

The similarity between *To a Mistress of a Household* and the content of Pelagius' letters is clear to see. The author urged a demanding standard of obedience to God's commands based on imitation of Christ's way of life.[70] He characterised this life as preferring the 'narrow pathway' (*uia angusta*) to the 'broad pathway' (*uia spatiosa*), and as uncommon.[71] According to the author, man

---

[69] Frede, 'Epistula', pp. 71–6.

[70] Anon., *Ad quandam matronam* ll. 535–43 (ed. Duval, p. 241), 'For that reason I want you to understand that first of all you must abstain from all sin, then also you must pursue every work of righteousness and goodness, because it is not enough for anyone to be devoid of vices, unless he has filled himself with a succession of virtues: since it is necessary not just to avoid evil, but also to do good, as Scripture says: *Turn aside from evil and do good* [Ps. 34:14]'; 'Quapropter uolo, ut in primis ab omni peccato tibi intellegas abstinendum, deinde uniuersa iustitiae opera bonitatisque esse sectanda, quia non sufficit cuiquam uacuatum esse a uitiis, nisi se uirtutum successione compleuerit: quoniam non tantum declinare a malo, sed et bonum facere necesse est, scriptura dicente: *Declina a malo et fac bonum* [Ps. 34:14].' Also ll. 128–40 (ed. Duval, p. 221). Cf. Pelagius, *Ad Demetriadem* 15–16 (ed. Greshake, pp. 110-16); *Ad Celantiam* 4–6 (ed. Hilberg, CSEL 56, pp. 332–4).

[71] Anon., *Ad quandam matronam* ll. 414–25 (ed. Duval, p. 235), 'Surely what we trust that we will receive is not common or universal? Who would say such a thing, you will say, when it is certain that a heavenly reward is owed only to the righteous? Therefore, if what we hope for is not common, why do we want the way that we live to be common? For indeed Scripture says: *How broad and spacious is the way that leads to death, and there are many who enter it; how restricted and narrow is the way that leads to life, and few find it* [Matt. 7:13–14]'; 'Numquid commune uel omnium est, quod nos percepturos esse confidimus? Quis hoc dixerit, inquies, cum certum sit iustis tantum praemium celeste deberi? Ergo, si non commune est quod speramus, cur uolumus commune esse quod uiuimus? Dicit namque scriptura: *Quam lata et spatiosa est uia, quae ducit ad mortem, et multi sunt qui intrant per eam; quam arta et angusta uia est, quae ducit ad uitam et pauci sunt qui inueniunt eam* [Matt. 7:13–14]'. Cf. Pelagius, *Ad Demetriadem* 10 (ed. Greshake, p. 96); *Ad Celantiam* 10–11 (ed. Hilberg, CSEL 56, pp. 337–8).

possessed a natural instinct towards the good, of which Job was cited as an example.[72] He stated repeatedly that salvation was earned on the principle of merit and reward.[73] He asserted that Christ came in order to set an example, and also to wipe clean mankind's sins.[74] He affirmed the possibility of achieving salvation through the efforts of the mind alone.[75] Habit was stressed as the key that unlocked the ability to do what God commanded.[76] The author maintained that

---

[72] Anon., *Ad quandam matronam* ll. 270–5 (ed. Duval, p. 227), 'And so, imitate holy Job without any distinction between persons; Job of whom it is read that without the advice of the law, taught only by natural instinct, his blamelessness was such that he is taught not even to have harmed his slaves'; 'Imitare itaque sanctum Iob sine ulla personarum distinctione, qui, citra legis admonitionem, naturali tantum doctus instinctu, eius fuisse innocentiae legitur, ut ne seruulis quidem nocuisse doceatur'. Cf. Pelagius, *Ad Demetriadem* 6 (ed. Greshake, pp. 76–80); *Ad Celantiam* 7 (ed. Hilberg, CSEL 56, pp. 334–5).

[73] Anon., *Ad quandam matronam* ll. 394–414 (ed. Duval, pp. 233–5), 'It is also fitting for us to consider carefully the reward of our hope, so that the quality of our life is prepared also according to the quality of the hope itself. Certainly we hope that after death, after ashes and embers, we will be recreated not just in a pristine state, but in an even better condition .... Therefore, because it is for something genuine that we hope, the way that we live ought to be genuine. For how can it be that a merit that is not genuine and worthy receives a genuine reward? Furthermore, those things are without doubt great and divine with which we believe that we can be rewarded. Therefore we ought to live with great and divine endeavour, so that we may deserve to obtain great and divine things'; 'Spei quoque nostrae praemium diligenter considerare nos conuenit, ut secundum spei ipsius qualitatem uitae etiam qualitas praeparetur. Speramus certe nos post mortem, post cineres et fauillas, non in pristinum tantum, sed in multo etiam meliorem statum esse reparandos .... Ergo, quia in ueritate est quod speramus, in ueritate debet esse quod uiuimus. Nam qui fieri potest, ut uerum praemium non uerum dignumque meritum consequatur? Deinde, magna certe et diuina illa sunt, quibus munerari nos posse credimus. Magno ergo studio uiuere diuinoque debemus, ut magna consequi et diuina mereamur.' Also ll. 425–51 (ed. Duval, p. 235); ll. 225–34 (ed. Duval, p. 225); ll. 302–4 (ed. Duval, p. 229); ll. 530–5 (ed. Duval, pp. 239–41). Cf. Pelagius, *Ad Demetriadem* 17 (ed. Greshake, pp. 116-18); *Ad Celantiam* 2 (ed. Hilberg, CSEL 56, pp. 330–1).

[74] Anon., *Ad quandam matronam* ll. 311–19 (ed. Duval, p. 229), 'Be mindful that God and the son of God wanted to take up the humility of rank and to put on our human nature as a man, and to exist among us as if one of us primarily from this desire, that he might through himself provide an example for us of righteous and holy living, and that he might bring it about that we would escape from all the sins by which we were being held back and would devote ourselves only to virtues'; 'Memor esto Deum ac Dei filium hac maxime cura dignationis humilitatem uoluisse suscipere et hominem naturae nostrae induere, et inter nos ac si unus ex nobis existere, ut nobis iuste, sancte uiuendi per semet praeberet exemplum et ut nos ab omnibus uitiis, quibus detinebamur, eripere et uirtutibus tantum seruire perficeret'. Cf. Pelagius, *Ad Demetriadem* 8 (ed. Greshake, p. 86); *Ad Celantiam* 12 (ed. Hilberg, CSEL 56, pp. 338–9).

[75] Anon., *Ad quandam matronam* ll. 442–7 (ed. Duval, p. 235), 'That life is beyond what is human, as I would say it, which despises whatever human desire strives most to possess, and convinces itself that through the virtue of the mind alone it can suffice to gain a heavenly possession'; 'Supra hominem est, ut ita dixerim, uita illa, quae quidquid humana cupiditas pro magno nititur possidere contemnit et solam sibi per uirtutem animi caelestem possessionem sufficere posse persuadet.' Cf. Pelagius, *Ad Demetriadem* 2 (ed. Greshake, pp. 58–62); *Ad Celantiam* 22.2 (ed. Hilberg, CSEL 56, p. 348).

[76] Anon., *Ad quandam matronam* ll. 571–81 (ed. Duval, pp. 241–3), 'You ask this also, what thing chiefly might provide you with the easy ability to live righteously. Obviously the habit itself of acting righteously, which if it is continued uninterruptedly, will provide you with not only the ability, but also with the inclination. Which can easily be discerned even in things that require a great deal of effort and are more difficult, as they say someone said: "Such is the power of habit, that even hard work is

social status counted for nothing in the economy of salvation, where only spiritual status was efficacious, and further that the distinction between slave and free man did not exist before God.[77] Because of this he advised his addressee to behave towards household slaves as if she were their mother, an injunction strikingly similar to advice in *Letter to Celantia*.[78] *To a Mistress of a Household* contained a contrast between the true Christian and someone who was a Christian in name only.[79] Oaths were forbidden.[80] The Christian had a special dignity that came from

---

desired"'; 'Quaeris hoc quoque, quae tibi res potissimum benefaciendi possibilitatem pronam pariat. Ipsa scilicet benefaciendi consuetudo, quae tibi non possibilitatem solam, uerum etiam facilitatem, si fuerit continuata, praestabit. Quod etiam in rebus laboriosis ac difficilioribus facile dinoscitur, ut dixisse quendam ferant: "Tanta uis est consuetudinis, ut etiam labor desideretur."' Also ll. 545–70 (ed. Duval, p. 241). Cf. Pelagius, *Ad Demetriadem* 13 (ed. Greshake, pp. 102–4); *Ad Celantiam* 10 (ed. Hilberg, CSEL 56, p. 337).

[77] Anon., *Ad quandam matronam* ll. 260–70 (ed. Duval, p. 227), 'Remember the saying of the Apostle: *You masters also must do the same by them, giving up threats, knowing that both you and they have the same master in heaven* [Eph. 6:9], because the apostle wanted to show that no man is truly either the master or the slave of any other man, but all who would together have one and the same master, are instead fellow-slaves in relation to each other, by which means the Apostle might more easily make them more gentle, as towards men of the same status'; 'Memor esto dicentis Apostoli: *Et uos, domini, eadem facite illis, remittentes minas, scientes quia et uester et illorum dominus est in caelo* [Eph. 6:9], ostendere uolens nullum hominum alterius cuiuslibet hominis uere uel dominum esse uel seruum, sed omnes, qui in commune unum atque eundem dominum habeant, inter se potius esse conseruos, quo facilius eos erga eiusdem condicionis homines efficeret mitiores.' Also ll. 453–528 (ed. Duval, pp. 237–9). Cf. Pelagius, *Ad Demetriadem* 30 (ed. Greshake, pp. 166–8); *Ad Celantiam* 21 (ed. Hilberg, CSEL 56, p. 347).

[78] Anon., *Ad quandam matronam* ll. 255–60 (ed. Duval, pp. 227), 'Toward your slaves also it is appropriate for you to maintain not so much the sternness of a mistress as the affection of a mother, which is also why they are called mothers of the household. By this designation they are reminded that they ought to be mothers of their households rather than mistresses'; 'Circa seruulos quoque non tam dominae rigorem habere te conuenit quam matris affectum, unde et matresfamilias appellantur. Qua nuncupatione ammonentur familiae suae matres potius esse debere quam dominae.' Cf. Pelagius, *Ad Celantiam* 25 (ed. Hilberg, CSEL 56, p. 350), 'Rule and cherish your household in such a way that you wish to be seen as the mother more than the mistress of your household, from whose members gain respect by means of kindness rather than severity'; 'Familiam tuam ita rege et confoue, ut te matrem magis tuorum quam dominam uideri uelis, a quibus benignitate potius quam seueritate exige reuerentiam.'

[79] Anon., *Ad quandam matronam* ll. 353–65 (ed. Duval, p. 231), 'And so, as I have often said, if we do not want to be Christians in name only, we must flee from all evil, all ostentation, and all arrogance; and we must pursue Christ's goodness, we must pursue Christ's humility, we must pursue Christ's poverty. For nor did he descend unto the cross so that he might confer on us the bare name of Christianity, that is without virtues; but so that the action also should exist according to the quality of the name. What, I say, is a life that is common and miserable doing under such a holy name? What is a cruel and impious way of life doing under a word denoting piety?'; 'Fugienda itaque nobis est, ut saepius diximus, si non in solo nomine christiani esse uolumus, omnis malitia, omnis pompa, omnisque superbia; et sectanda Christi bonitas, sectanda humilitas, sectanda paupertas. Neque enim ille, ut nudum nobis, id est absque uirtutibus, christianitatis nomen conferret, ad crucem usque descendit; sed ut secundum qualitatem nominis etiam actus existeret. Quid, inquam, facit sub tam sancto nomine uita uulgaris et misera? Quid, sub pietatis uocabulo, conuersatio crudelis et impia?' In this section the author used the word *nomen* four times to emphasise his point. Also ll. 7–30 (ed. Duval, p. 215). Cf. Pelagius, *Ad Demetriadem* 23 (ed. Greshake, pp. 140–2); *Ad Celantiam* 8 (ed. Hilberg, CSEL 56, pp. 335–6).

[80] Anon., *Ad quandam matronam* ll. 287–91 (ed. Duval, p. 229), 'Refrain even from reasonable oaths, the frequent use of which can avoid perjury only with difficulty, recalling the Gospel statement of our

being a 'son of God'.[81] And no Christian should disparage others or listen to such disparagement.[82] Finally, a programme of prayer, fasting, reading and study of the Psalms was advocated.[83]

Bearing in mind these similarities between this letter fragment and in particular Pelagius' *Letter to Demetrias* and *Letter to Celantia*, the classification of this letter by scholars merits scrutiny. Germain Morin was the first to draw attention to the fragment in an article published in 1922.[84] He was only aware of the vellum leaves preserved in Vienna and some pages of transcription of leaves that had previously been there. He concluded that the fragment was drawn from two separate letters, which he described in the title of his article as two 'Pelagian fragments', and in his discussion as 'ascetic fragments'. Morin offered brief suggestions about their provenance as compositions and the approximate place to which they should be assigned within Christian literature. He considered it obvious that the Latinity of the fragment(s) placed them in the 5th century. He noted their similarity to Pelagius' letters to Demetrias and Celantia, and to *To Gregoria*, which Morin attributed to Arnobius Junior.[85] The reasons Morin advanced for linking the fragment(s) to Pelagius were, first, their focus on what he saw as the preferred themes of 'Pelagian' literature, which for Morin were discussion of what constituted a Christian life and the possibility of sinlessness; and, second, the characteristic traits that Morin identified in the fragment(s) which he saw also in the six

Lord, in which is contained: *But I say to you do not swear oaths at all* [Matt. 5:34]; 'A iusto etiam iuramento tempera, cuius assiduitas difficile potest uitare periurium, euangelicam Domini sententiam recolens, qua continetur: *Ego autem dico uobis non iurare in toto* [Matt. 5:34]'. Cf. Pelagius, *Ad Demetriadem* 19 (ed. Greshake, p. 12); *Ad Celantiam* 19 (ed. Hilberg, CSEL 56, p. 345).

[81] Anon., *Ad quandam matronam* ll. 180–6 (ed. Duval, p. 223), 'For it is inappropriate and quite unfitting for an honest mind to involve itself with empty chatter and delights, still less would I say for a Christian mind, which ought to conduct itself with greater honesty in proportion to how its origin, being of divine and not just human stock, gives it greater nobility'; 'Indecorum namque est honestae menti et satis incongruum, uanis se garrulitatibus oblectationibusque miscere, nedum dicam christianae, quae se tanto honestius agere debet, quanto amplius eam non humanae tantum sed diuinae stirpis origo nobilitat.' Also ll. 376–93 (ed. Duval, p. 233). Cf. Pelagius, *Ad Demetriadem* 19 (ed. Greshake, pp. 124–6); this idea does not appear in *Ad Celantiam*.

[82] Anon., *Ad quandam matronam* ll. 174–7 (ed. Duval, p. 223), 'But I want you to avoid most of all that vice with which in our time men and above all women are known to be afflicted, I mean disparagement of others'; 'Illud uero uel maxime uitium longius declinare te cupio, quo nostri temporis homines et potissimum feminae laborare noscuntur, obtrectationem dico'. Cf. Pelagius, *Ad Demetriadem* 19 (ed. Greshake, pp. 126–8); *Ad Celantiam* 16 (ed. Hilberg, CSEL 56, pp. 342–4).

[83] Anon., *Ad quandam matronam* ll. 83–6 (ed. Duval, p. 219), 'If you fast moderately, you will always be able also to pray, and to fast, and to practise abstinence, and to read, and to recite the Psalms'; 'Si moderate ieiunaueris, et orare et ieiunare et abstinere et legere poteris semper et psallere'. Cf. Pelagius, *Ad Demetriadem* 21–23 (ed. Greshake, pp. 134–42); *Ad Celantiam* 24 (ed. Hilberg, CSEL 56, p. 350).

[84] G. Morin, 'Fragments Pélagiens du Manuscrit 954 de Vienne', *Revue Bénédictine* 34 (1922), pp. 265–75.

[85] *To Gregoria* is usually dated to the fifth or sixth century and thought perhaps to be addressed to a woman in Constantinople: K. Cooper, *The Virgin and the Bride* (Cambridge, MA, 1996), p. 108. What may have lain behind Morin's suggestion was that *To Gregoria* reused several passages from Pelagius' *Letter to Demetrias* verbatim, borrowed by the author of *To Gregoria* without acknowledgement: M. Cozic, 'Présence de Pélage dans le *Liber ad Gregoriam* d'Arnobe le Jeune', *Revue d'Études augustiniennes et patristiques* 51 (2005), pp. 77–107.

letters of the Caspari Corpus. He had previously become convinced, first, that the six letters of the Caspari Corpus were by one author; and, second, that their author was the British bishop Fastidius mentioned by Gennadius of Marseilles. Morin noted also that the fragment(s) travelled alongside letters by Jerome, and that the Caspari Corpus letters were on some occasions transmitted under attributions to Jerome. Morin's interest in the fragment(s) focused on attribution and the figure of Fastidius, and not on the issue of classification.

In 1939, Alban Dold published an article about the Vienna letter fragment.[86] His interest in it was primarily palaeographical, but like Morin he too was interested in the authorship of the text, which he described as 'an ascetic letter'. He considered that biblical citations were the most useful diagnostic tool for attribution, and noted one in particular from Lev. 19:16–17, which was taken from a duplicated section of the original Leviticus, making it distinctive. This particular version of the Leviticus citation appeared in the fragment and in Pelagius' letters to Demetrias and Celantia. Dold stated that the author of the fragment had to be sought in the circle of Pelagius because its contents were taken straight from the 'Pelagian' thought world, and he cited three passages as examples that demonstrated this.[87] All three related to the issue of the possibility of achieving sinlessness, and the easiness of avoiding sin. He did not discuss other themes that were shared with Pelagius' letters. Dold expressed the wish that the questions surrounding: 'This ascetic literature, and especially the writings attributed to Pelagius and his circle', should be investigated in terms of both content and style.[88] Thus Dold acknowledged the existence of the

---

[86] A. Dold, 'Ein Aszetischer Brief aus dem 5. Jahrhundert im Codex Vindob. Lat. 54', *Revue Bénédictine* 51 (1939), pp. 122–38.

[87] Anon., *Ad quandam matronam* ll. 562–6 (ed. Duval, p. 241), 'If you always and studiously refuse to sin, as I would say it, one day you will not be able to either. For the course itself of your not sinning will somehow bring about the impossibility of doing wrong, if it is steered continually for a long time'; 'Si semper ac studiose peccare nolueris, ut ita dixerim, quandoque nec poteris. Ipse enim tibi non peccandi tenor quodammodo delinquendi impossibilitatem, si iugiter ac diu dirigatur, efficiet.' Second: Anon., *Ad quandam matronam* ll. 585–7 (ed. Duval, p. 243), 'Even if something good is difficult to achieve, yet it is easy to do it'; 'Et si bonum aliquod fieri difficile est, tamen esse perfacile est'; this quotation does not make a lot of sense taken out of context. The full passage refers to the power of habit: 'And so if a habit is maintained continually over a long period, through the ongoing use of that very habit, it will easily overcome every labour and difficulty, and will be among the first to complete that arduous journey as if it was over level ground and even ground that slopes downwards; because even if something good is difficult to achieve, yet it is easy to do it, in so far as everything may be laborious to a person as long as he is less accustomed to practising it, but when it becomes habit, exertion is transformed into ease and pleasure'; 'Haec igitur, si iugis ac diuturna seruetur, facile laborem omnem difficultatemque, ipso usu currente, transcendet et arduum illud in primis iter quasi planum ac decliue perficiet; quia et si bonum aliquod fieri difficile est, tamen esse perfacile est, eo quod omnis res tamdiu laboriosa cuiquam sit, quamdiu eam minus exercere consueuerit, at ubi in usum uenerit, facilitate labor ac delectatione mutatur.' And third: Anon., *Ad quandam matronam* ll. 567–70 (ed. Duval, p. 241), 'Whence someone put it elegantly: "He is happy who has so trained his mind that not only does he not want to sin, but he even cannot do so"'; 'Vnde eleganter quidam: "Beatus," inquit, "qui eo perduxerit animum suum, ut non solum nolit peccare sed etiam non possit."'

[88] Dold, 'Ein aszetischer', p. 138, 'Diese aszetischen Literatur, und besonders der Pelagius und seinem Kreis zugewiesenen Schriften'.

broad category of 'ascetic literature', of which the writings of Pelagius and those who held similar views represented a part.

In a brief note on Dold's article published in 1940, De Plinval noted the use in the fragment of a phrase that recurred in several other texts expressing an ascetic approach to Christianity which have been categorised as 'Pelagian'.[89] In 1989, Mirella Ferrari published an article about the contents of an envelope of vellum fragments in Milan's Biblioteca Ambrosiana. One was a bifolium that had been palimpsested and reused, and Ferrari realised that this derived from the same manuscript as the leaves that made up the Vienna fragment, allowing her to reconstruct the original order of the leaves.[90] She described the letter as 'Pelagian' (without use of inverted commas), citing similar passages in other 'Pelagian' letters in support of this classification.

In 1993, Yves-Marie Duval presented the first edition of the whole text in its correct original order. He made selective comments on the contents of the letter. For instance, he noted what he called 'its elitist character' with its encouragement of the addressee to achieve a spiritual nobility to match her social nobility, and its argument from fear of the shame of being of low status in the next life. According to Duval, the author did not argue for love of one's neighbour for its own sake but as a means by which to exercise one's virtue, and rather than stressing the need to request forgiveness of sins the author focused on the addressee striving not to have any sins. Prayer was advised, but without any stipulation of its content or purpose, thus the attitude motivating the prayer was not visibly one of praise or supplication.[91] Duval seemed implicitly to be addressing the accusation made

---

[89] Anon., *Ad quandam matronam* ll. 397–400 (ed. Duval, p. 233), 'Certainly we hope that after death, after ashes and embers, we will be restored not just to pristine condition, but to an even better state'; 'Speramus certe nos post mortem, post cineres et fauillas, non in pristinum tantum, sed in multo etiam meliorem statum esse reparandos'. This resembles Pelagius, *Ad Demetriadem* 28 (ed. Greshake, p. 164), 'After the departure of the spirit, after the destruction of the flesh, after embers and ash, virgin, you will be restored to a better state'; 'Post abscessum animae, post carnis interitum, post fauillas et cinerem in meliorem statum uirgo reparanda es.' De Plinval pointed out that it was also closely echoed in two letters in the Caspari Corpus: Anon., *De diuitiis* 13 (ed. Hamman, PLS 1.1402), 'You believe that, when you have died and been consumed in dust and embers, through the grace of resurrection you will be restored from the same ash of your body not just to a pristine state, but to a better state, namely one of immortality and incorruption'; 'Credis te, cum mortuus fueris et in puluerem fauillamque digestus, de eodem corporis tui cinere per resurrectionis gratiam non modo in pristinum, uerum in meliorem, immortalitatis scilicet et incorruptionis, statum esse reparandum'; and Anon., *De malis doctoribus* 11.2 (ed. Hamman, PLS 1.1436), 'Unhappy and miserable flesh that must soon be cultivated by worms and reduced to ash and embers'; 'Caro infelix et misera et mox exaranda uerminibus et in cinerem fauillamque redigenda': G. De Plinval, note under the title 'Belgique', *Revue d'Histoire Ecclésiastique* 26 (1940), p. 219.

[90] M. Ferrari, 'In margine ai codices latini antiquiores: spigolature ambrosiane del sec. VIII', in *Lateinische Kultur im VIII Jahrhundert. Traube-Gedenkschrift*, ed. A. Lehner and W. Berschin (St. Ottilien, 1989), pp. 60–8.

[91] Pelagius described the contents of prayer at *De uirginitate* 10 (ed. Halm, CSEL 1, p. 238), 'For it is shameful that those lips with which you confess God, make requests, bless, and praise God should be polluted by the filth of any sin'; 'Nefas est enim ut labia illa, quibus Deum confiteris, rogas, benedicis et laudas, alicuius polluantur sorde peccati.'

against Pelagius that he was insufficiently humble and encouraged an attitude of human self-sufficiency. Without acknowledging overtly that this was a criticism on which he was commenting, Duval identified how for the author of the letter the humility of Christ was embodied in man by the life of righteousness and avoidance of sin that he was advocating. Poverty, generosity of resources and spirit, and the rejection of pride created a humility that did its best to imitate Christ's humility. Thus an accusation that the letter did not stress requests for forgiveness of sins and thereby displayed arrogance would be a misrepresentation of the author's aim. This argumentation implied that Duval associated the letter with Pelagius.

Indeed, Duval seemed undecided about the term 'Pelagian'. He used it twice within inverted commas but then shortly afterwards without them as if he accepted it as a valid classification. Yet in his final sentence he seemed to back away again from using the term 'Pelagian'. He ended with a question which underlined his avoidance of the topic of attribution, as he wondered whether the author: 'Simply participated in a protest movement which one can see appearing at the end of the fourth century, or whether he was its initiator.'[92] Duval thus suggested that there was a movement differentiable from the ascetic movement, which he character-ised as one of protest. He raised the possibility that the letter might not have been written by Pelagius, but did not address the implication of this, which is that if this letter was not written by Pelagius, then Pelagius cannot be said to have initiated anything, or written anything in any way distinctive. If this letter fragment was not written by Pelagius then it is further evidence that many writers were producing ascetic paraenesis, and there are no diagnostic features that can be used to distin-guish Pelagius' writings from other ascetic literature. Duval's comments therefore typify the lack of clarity in scholarship about the classification 'Pelagian'.

Hermann Josef Frede produced an edition of *To a Mistress of a Household* as part of his series on texts which included Vetus Latina biblical citations.[93] Unlike previous scholars who had written about the fragment, Frede directly addressed the issue of the classification of the text and summarised previous attempts to establish categories within texts viewed as standing in some sort of relation to Pelagius. In his discussion, Frede did not look outside the traditional group of texts and authors labelled 'Pelagian'; he took it as read that there was such a thing as a 'Pelagian' text, and that this was a distinct group, separate from works such as the three versions of the *Life of Antony* or Jerome's paraenesis. Instead the problem that Frede examined was the distinction between texts written by Pelagius himself, and texts written by other 'Pelagians'. The question of attribution was his focus. Frede used Greshake's distinction between works termed *pelagisch* and those termed *pelagianisch*. He concluded that the contents of the letter showed that it was *pelagianisch*, and the evidence he adduced to support this link to Pelagius consisted of biblical citations.

---

[92] Duval, 'La lettre', p. 213. Duval wondered whether the author: 'Participe simplement à un mouve-ment de protestation que l'on voit apparaître à la fin du IVième siècle, ou s'il en est l'initiateur.'
[93] Frede, 'Epistula', pp. 35–76.

Without argumentation, Frede's subjective assessment was that stylistic comparison with *Letter to Demetrias* demanded a different author. Frede's second argument for two different authors related to content. First, the author of *To a Mistress of a Household* offered no introductory discussion of anthropology or salvation theory but launched straight into practical advice. Problems with this argument are that the start of the letter is missing and that *Letter to Demetrias* may be unsusual in this respect, since neither *Letter to Celantia* nor *On Virginity* contain an explicit discussion of doctrine either. Second, according to Frede, *To a Mistress of a Household* avoided radical statements and assertions that might incur an accusation of heresy, while at the same time it fully supported what Frede saw as Pelagius' distinctive approach to Christianity. But here again, Frede's prior assumptions about 'Pelagianism' determined his assessment; *Letter to Celantia* and *On Virginity* also lack statements that might be susceptible to a charge of heresy, but this may have been because when they were composed, effective free will was still part of the unquestioned mainstream approach to Christianity, and if *To a Mistress of a Household* was written at a time when the same applied, then the author was not 'avoiding' assertions that might incur a charge of heresy but simply working on the basis of principles that no one questioned, and which therefore did not need to be defended or even discussed. Frede did not question the idea that Pelagius had some sort of ownership over the ascetic agenda in the Latin West and that 'Pelagianism' existed.

At this point, Frede abruptly abandoned argumentation about attribution and made a general observation about study of Pelagius, saying that despite the assiduity with which it had been pursued, progress had not been made on attribution. Frede's assessment was that De Plinval's maximal attribution of works to Pelagius had met with strong opposition, and it had become clear that very few works by Pelagius himself now survived. For this reason, Frede argued, the distinction drawn by Greshake between works by Pelagius himself, and works by others who supported Pelagius' approach to Christianity was helpful, even though Greshake had decided to include in the classification *pelagisch* texts not written by Pelagius but composed by the first generation of writers who stood in a close relationship to him. Frede suggested that this compromise was indicative of the difficulty of the theoretical problem surrounding the concept of 'Pelagianism'. He noted that Wermelinger had formulated the criteria for distinction slightly differently, since he used *pelagisch* solely for works attributable to Pelagius himself, and *pelagianisch* for the works of pupils and sympathisers which contained 'radicalised' statements and views that aroused suspicion of heresy. While Greshake and Nuvolone had placed *To a Mistress of a Household* in the group of works that could with reasonable certainty be attributed to Pelagius himself, Frede concluded that the author of the letter should be sought not in Pelagius but in the circle of numerous but not yet identifiable 'Pelagians' of the first generation.

There are three problems with Frede's analysis. First, no one has offered a thorough analysis of the letter and assessed properly the evidence for authorship. Frede felt that style was an important factor, but made an entirely unargued subjective assessment about its style. Nor did he address the fact that *Letter to Demetrias* was perhaps atypical because it was written in such particular circumstances when Pelagius knew that it would be compared directly to advice to Demetrias from other leading exponents of Christian teaching, and believed that effective free will and the goodness of human nature needed to be defended. As a result, Pelagius may have made a special effort with his *Letter to Demetrias*, commensurate with the status of the family that requested it and the theological context. Thus comparison with *Letter to Demetrias* might not be helpful as a stylistic guide by which to establish the authorship of *To a Mistress of a Household*.

Second, although Frede acknowledged the problems of attribution within the group of 'Pelagian' texts, unlike Kessler, who glanced briefly at the possibility, he did not question whether 'Pelagian' was itself a useful and meaningful classification. He wrote of *To a Mistress of a Household* that it was: 'Certainly "Pelagian", but probably not by Pelagius'.[94] But the *pelagisch/pelagianisch* distinction suffers from the problems that derive from the fact that the notion of 'Pelagianism' is itself flawed; the idea that Pelagius founded something, or was the instigator of a distinctive approach to Christianity, is wrong on two counts. First, Pelagius was one of many writers active contemporaneously, and the concept of his pupils or sympathisers cannot be made to incorporate every writer who expressed the same views because there were so many, some producing texts when Pelagius was still in Britain. After Pelagius arrived in Rome, there were many ascetics writing who were independent of any influence by him, and Pelagius' leadership role was the invention of those in whose interests it was to be able to name a heresiarch.[95] The term *pelagianisch* implies both that this ascetic literature spun out from Pelagius, who was the lead voice in any grouping, and that the proposed grouping produced literature that was doctrinally distinct from other ascetic literature in circulation in the late 4th and early 5th centuries. Both these assumptions are false. Third, Frede thought that *To a Mistress of a Household* was not written by Pelagius; but if it was not, then the characterisation of Pelagius as a founder or leader of anything, or as having any distinctive features whatsoever, is unsustainable, because someone else was doing exactly the same thing, at exactly the same time, using the same set of arguments and biblical citations, addressing the same audience. So Frede's comments once again showed that scholarship has not addressed the incoherence of the notion of 'Pelagianism' and has been trapped in a circular argument. This anonymous text therefore illustrates how the concept of 'Pelagianism' does not withstand scrutiny.

---

[94] Frede, 'Epistula', pp. 75–6, 'Die sicher "pelagianisch", aber wohl nicht von Pelagius ist'.
[95] Examples of writers whose ascetic approach to Christianity cannot be attributed to the influence of Pelagius are Hilary of Arles and Sulpicius Severus.

Conclusion on To a Mistress of a Household

To a Mistress of a Household is, as has been shown, full of ideas from the ascetic movement that developed in the second half of the 4th century. Robert Markus argued that the ascetic agenda developed a reforming slant because of concerns that grew out of Christianity's change in status from persecuted minority to a position of wealth and prestige, problems such as that of career converts, and the accommodation within Christianity of much of pagan classical culture, which led some Christians to worry that their Christianity was not marking them out as sufficiently different from pagans.[96] These anxieties were not limited to Pelagius; they engendered concern among many Christians. The asceticism of Ambrose's sister and the circle around Marcella shows that fervent asceticism existed among patrician Roman women decades before Pelagius began to write. The patronage of such wealthy Roman ascetics facilitated both Jerome's and Pelagius' careers. It puts the cart before the horse to suggest that the approach to Christianity that Pelagius articulated in his letters to aristocratic Roman women was his own invention. It is more likely that he supplied his patrons with encouragement that spoke to the growing fashion and their own approach to Christianity. When ascetic doctrinal assumptions were subsequently challenged, Pelagius restated them. He cannot be credited with authorship of the principles that he propounded, which were already setting the agenda in the Christian community in Rome when he arrived probably some time around AD 380.

If someone other than Pelagius, such as Caelestius, Sixtus, Agricola, Severianus or Fastidius, to offer just some names known to us, was enthusiastically evangelising for asceticism in around AD 415 to the degree expressed in *To a Mistress of a Household*, then the concept of 'Pelagianism' is unhistorical, not least in the respect that Pelagius cannot accurately be described as its progenitor or leader.[97] If someone else wrote *To a Mistress of a Household*, then what existed were many Christians who shared a similar approach to Christianity, and no group can be defined by reference to Pelagius without historical misrepresentation.

---

[96] Pelagius, *Ad Celantiam* 8.2–9.1 (ed. Hilberg, CSEL 56, p. 336), 'For as faith ought, so life also ought to distinguish between the Christian and the pagan, and the different religion ought to show through different works .... Therefore let there be the greatest possible separation between us and them'; 'Inter Christianum enim atque gentilem cum fides tum debet etiam uita distinguere et diuersam religionem per diuersa opera monstrare .... Sit ergo inter nos atque illos maxima separatio'; Markus, 'Between Marrou and Brown', pp. 8–13.

[97] Prosper, *Chronicon* a. 429 (ed. Mommsen, MGH, Auctores Antiquissimi t. 9, p. 472), 'Agricola the Pelagian, son of Bishop Severianus the Pelagian, corrupted the churches of Britain with the influence of his own dogma'; 'Agricola Pelagianus, Seueriani episcopi Pelagiani filius, ecclesias Brittaniae dogmatis sui insinuatione corrumpit.' Gennadius of Marseilles reported on two works written by the British bishop Fastidius: see n. 106. Augustine's *Letters* 191 and 194 reveal that Sixtus (who became Pope Sixtus III) was a leading proponent of ascetic values: Augustine, *Ep*. 191 (ed. Goldbacher, CSEL 57, pp. 162–5); *Ep*. 194 (ed. Goldbacher, CSEL 57, pp. 176–214); and Basel, Universitätsbibliothek, Ms O.IV.18 (s. xii) has attributions of three of the Caspari Corpus letters to 'Syxtus episcopus martyrus', possibly a corruption of an original attribution to the Sixtus to whom Augustine wrote and who publicly renounced his support for Pelagius following Pelagius' condemnation in AD 418.

A more accurate account sees Pelagius as one voice amid a wave of ascetic enthusiasm that swept across the Western Empire in the late 4th and early 5th centuries. And if Pelagius was not proposing any arguments differentiable from the mass of ascetic literature being produced at that time, from Evagrius' *Life of Antony* to Jerome's letters, then the notion of 'Pelagianism' must be abandoned. The problem with the proposed distinction between *pelagisch* and *pelagianisch* is therefore that it is not possible to separate Pelagius from other ascetic propagandists, who may well have been writing works so similar to Pelagius' as to now be indistinguishable from them. How might one distinguish within these individuals between a writer who conveys the same message as Pelagius and another who develops his ideas further? Would it be possible to differentiate between an early letter by Caelestius, such as Gennadius reported were orthodox, and one by Sixtus, or some other young ascetic enthusiast from the same sort of educated background as the young monk Rusticus in Gaul for whom Jerome wrote ascetic paraenesis, such as the young Honoratus? It should be remembered that writing between AD 491 and AD 495, Gennadius of Marseilles described how Caelestius wrote three letters that Gennadius judged orthodox:

> Caelestius, before he got involved in the Pelagian dogma, while still a young man, wrote three letters in the form of little books to his parents from a monastery, letters that were morally upright and indispensable for every person who longs for God; since indeed what he said in them had nothing of the defect that afterwards appeared, but was entirely directed toward the encouragement of virtue.[98]

From Gennadius' report it can be deduced that these letters were still in circulation almost a hundred years later, since he only endorsed texts he had read himself. If these three texts were circulating as orthodox in southern Gaul in the 490s, the possibility cannot be dismissed that they may be extant now, but no one has identified them. The reason for this is that they would be indistinguishable from the mass of ascetic paraenesis that survives, in particular what Bernard Lambert described as the 'vast world' of texts currently classed as pseudo-Jerome.[99] It is important to remember that Caelestius wrote letters that Gennadius considered orthodox, and, since Caelestius was writing from a monastery, it is reasonable to assume that the letters, which Gennadius stated contained moral exhortation, were of an ascetic cast of mind.[100] The critical point is that, according to Gennadius,

---

[98] Gennadius, *De uiris inlustribus* 45 (ed. Richardson, pp. 77–8), 'Caelestius, antequam Pelagio concurreret, immo adhuc adulescens, scripsit ad parentes suos de monasterio epistulas in modum libellorum tres, omni Deum desideranti necessarias morales; siquidem in eis dictio nihil uitii postmodum proditi, sed totum ad uirtutis incitamentum tenuit.'

[99] B. Lambert, *Bibliotheca Hieronymiana Manuscripta*, 4 vols, Instrumenta Patristica IV (Steenbrugge, 1969–72), Préface, p. x. The number of texts in circulation during the Middle Ages that presupposed effective free will or were critical of the triune was very much greater than the selection examined in this book. Texts currently classed as 'pseudo-Jerome' are a rich source of such material. For discussion of just one example, see Elizabeth Clark's analysis of the text known as *The Dialogue between Jerome and Augustine on the Origin of the Soul*: Clark, *The Origenist Controversy*, p. 243.

[100] The biographical details in *Humanae referunt litterae* have been seen as precluding it from having been written by Caelestius because the author mentions his daughter, and Caelestius was described as a

Caelestius did this before he got involved in 'Pelagian' doctrine. We might adjust this to say that Caelestius did this before ascetic doctrinal assumptions came to be questioned during the controversy over the triune.

To a Mistress of a Household is therefore a test case because it raises questions surrounding the concept of 'Pelagianism': questions of attribution of texts; the question of what were the defining tenets of this notional 'Pelagian thought'; of whether these were distinct from the tide of ascetic fervour sweeping across the Western Empire at the time; and of whether Pelagius can correctly be considered the originator of any element of the array of ideas presented in surviving ascetic texts. None of the scholars who looked at *To a Mistress of a Household* were able to break out of the paradigm they inherited to see that 'Pelagianism' was a fiction from the start, invented for polemical purposes.

To a Mistress of a Household, Letter to Celantia, On Virginity and *Letter to Demetrias* are therefore examples of texts that show that where Evagrius had led with his version of the *Life of Antony*, where Jerome and Marcella and her circle had led also, others followed, as ascetics looked to widen their call to encompass civic society—that is, society in an urban situation, not withdrawn into isolation away from the secular world. It is possible to say that these texts were motivated by a similar enthusiasm for asceticism, but that is not to say either that 'Pelagianism' existed in the form that its opponents characterised it, or that it existed as a new and distinct doctrinal programme, or that Pelagius was an innovator. It is to say that the ascetic movement became strong and active, that it contained a number of people who were inspired by ascetic ideals to preach ascetic values as relevant to all Christians, and crucially that, having been trained in rhetoric, as a matter of course they expressed themselves in writing in order to do this, and to achieve social status or gain employment.

In this regard the context should also be borne in mind. The moral and intellectual battle between Christianity and paganism was in full swing during this same period from the second half of the 4th century to the first decades of the 5th. In this struggle, Christians based their case on their moral superiority. This claim to the moral high ground was a driver of ascetic paraenesis, which had one eye on pagans at the same time as it exhorted Christians.[101]

Test case 2: the Reichenau homily fragment, *Ammoneo te*

The anonymous fragment known as *Ammoneo te* ('I advise you') offers another test case for the viability of the category 'Pelagian'. In a Reichenau manuscript from the 8th or 9th century, Germain Morin found 430 lines of a homily that

---

eunuch by Marius Mercator, although this may have been simple disparagement. More problematically the author of *Humanae referunt litterae* mentioned that he was writing from the estate of a religious noblewoman on Sicily, not a monastery.

[101] Athanasius, Ἐπιστολή 72–80 (ed. Bartelink, SC 400, pp. 320–40).

contained several of the ideas asserted by Pelagius and other ideas shared with the six letters in the Caspari Corpus.[102] Morin identified it as a 'Pelagian' text because of its ascetic demands.[103] *Ammoneo te* is a call to ascetic dedication that specifically precludes civic life. It is an important piece of evidence that reveals the metamorphosis of the ascetic movement in the West. This had looked towards the civic milieu for a while, but subsequently refocused on withdrawal from urban life into isolation, and evolved into the monastic movement in the West.[104] The homily was addressed to young men who would normally expect to pursue a high-status secular career, and its aim was to seduce them away from the secular world into ascetic monastic dedication. *Ammoneo te* exemplifies the flaws in the concept of 'Pelagianism' as something distinct from the ascetic movement, which was a broad impulse towards imitation of Christ's way of life and renunciation of material goals. The similarities between this text and Pelagius' teachings are clear in terms of shared ideas, but that is only because they were all expressions of the ascetic impulse, not because the text has any link either to Pelagius or to the caricature that is 'Pelagianism'.

Morin's interest in the text

Morin's interest in the fragment was primarily that it was quoted in abridged form in a homily that was in his view produced by Caesarius of Arles, and had as its title *Excerpt from the Letter of Holy Fatalis concerning the Christian Life* (*Excarpsum de epistola sancti Fatali de uita christianorum*). Morin found this homily in a collection of sermons in a Vatican manuscript.[105] He included the collection in his edition of the homilies of Caesarius of Arles. For Morin this text resolved the issue of Gennadius' account of a British bishop called Fastidius who: 'Wrote to a certain Fatalis a book on the Christian life, and another concerning the preservation of widowhood, with sound doctrine worthy of God.'[106] Because of the title of the homily in the Vatican manuscript, Morin proposed that *Ammoneo te* was Fastidius' book *On the Christian Life*, as described by Gennadius. Furthermore,

---

[102] Karlsruhe, Badische Landesbibliothek, Aug. 221 (s. viii–ix), fols. 103–7. G. Morin, ed., '*Fastidius ad Fatalem? Pages Inédites du Cinquième Siècle D'Après le Manuscrit CCXXI de Reichenau*', *Revue Bénédictine* 46 (1934), pp. 3–17. Rees titled this text '*To Fatalis(?)*': Rees, *Pelagius* vol. II, pp. 306–13.
[103] Rees also commented on its 'abundance of Pelagian themes' and agreed that it was 'full of Pelagian echoes', but did not register its importance because his attention, like Morin's, was focused on questions of authorship. He did, however, note the strangeness of the possibility that Caesarius of Arles should have reused such material: Rees, *Pelagius* vol. II, pp. 306–7.
[104] I have used the earlier edition by Morin (in his article '*Fastidius ad Fatalem?*') for references because the Patrologia Latina Supplementum 1 edition is based on it, and Morin's edition has line numbers which allow more precise references.
[105] Rome, Biblioteca Apostolica Vaticana, Palatina Lat. 216 (s. viii–ix), fols. 100–4.
[106] Gennadius, *De uiris inlustribus* 57 (ed. Richardson, p. 81), 'Fastidius, Britannorum episcopus, scripsit ad Fatalem quendam de uita christiana librum, et alium de uiduitate seruanda, sana et Deo digna doctrina.' Morin dismissed as scribal error the problematical case endings in the title in the Vatican manuscript, with Fatalis in the genitive as the author of the letter rather than in the accusative as the recipient of the letter.

Caesarius' repackaged version of the homily in the Vatican manuscript also contained at its end seven lines taken from one of the Caspari Corpus letters, *To an Older Friend* (*Honorificentiae tuae*). This led Morin to conclude that, since the six Caspari Corpus letters were 'clearly' by the same author, and since Caesarius was 'probably' drawing from a book of works by the same author, the Caspari Corpus letters and the Reichenau homily were all by Fastidius, and the other work attributed by Gennadius to Fastidius, *On the Preservation of Widowhood* (*De uiduitate seruanda*), was the letter commonly known as *On the Christian life* (*De uita christiana*), which Morin considered to be clearly also by the same author as the Caspari Corpus letters. Thus eight works could now be attributed to Fastidius. There are problems with Morin's argument.[107] Furthermore, because of his focus on Fastidius, he missed the real interest of *Ammoneo te* and its reuse in the Caesarius of Arles homily collection preserved in the Vatican manuscript.

---

[107] Problems with Morin's argument are that Fatalis was a common name and it cannot be assumed that the two uses of the name adduced by Morin (in the title of the sermon in the Vatican manuscript Caesarius homily collection and in Gennadius' report of Fastidius) referred to the same person. Furthermore, although they contain some similar ideas, it has not been proved that the Caspari Corpus letters were all written by the same author. For example, at the very least it is possible that *Humanae referunt litterae* and *Honorificentiae tuae* were written by one author and the other four letters were written by a second. The manuscript transmission offers limited support for this possibility in so far as the first two are transmitted together in two manuscripts (Munich, Königlichen Bibliothek, Cod. Lat. 6299, s. viii–ix, and Salzburg, Bibliothek des Benedictinerstifts Sanct Peter zu Salzburg, Cod. a.VII.5, s. ix–x) while the other four are transmitted in a Vatican manuscript (Rome, Biblioteca Apostolica Vaticana, Palatina Lat. 3834, s. ix–x) of which three appear also in a Basel manuscript (Basel, Universitätsbibliotek, Ms O.IV.18, s. xii). The flaw in this otherwise neat division is that in the Vatican manuscript, *De possibilitate non peccandi* contains *Humanae referunt litterae* as part of its text. Another problem with Morin's argument is that several letters survive that could be Fastidius' *On Preserving Widowhood*, and there is no necessity to identify the text currently known as *On the Christian Life* as the letter by Fastidius titled *On Preserving Widowhood* mentioned by Gennadius. Furthermore, Gennadius described Fastidius' works as containing 'doctrine that is healthful and worthy of God' (*sana et Deo digna doctrina*), but Gennadius rejected the official presentation of Pelagius' and Caelestius' teaching, and it may be unlikely that he would have accepted as sound and worthy of God the widow's prayer in *On the Christian Life* to which Augustine and Jerome objected. Another problem is that this prayer and the letter *On the Christian Life* that contained it were quoted at the Synod of Diospolis in AD 415, so there may also be a chronological problem with suggesting that Fastidius composed it, given that Gennadius' entry concerning Fastidius suggests that he wrote in the 420s, although Gennadius' sequence in his entries does not offer an exact chronology. More importantly, the style of *Ammoneo te* is different from that of the Caspari Corpus letters, in that it is an oratorical work, not a literary one (Rees noted the difference in style, and agreed with De Plinval in judging the homily 'of small literary value', Rees, *Pelagius* vol. II, p. 306). It was intended to be heard as a sermon, not read, and is composed predominantly of short rhetorical questions; the author of *Ammoneo te* was a skilled preacher in Latin: Anon., *Ammoneo te* ll. 225–6 (ed. Morin, p. 10), 'Where are you going, you who say that you will return, and when will you do so?'; 'Quo uadis, qui dicis te quandoque rediturum?' Also, it was a call to monastic life in abandonment of secular life, not to a fully Christian life within the civic context, as the other letters in the Caspari Corpus were. These are some of the problems with Morin's thesis. The mangled case endings in the title in the Vatican manuscript do not point in any particular direction. If it had read *sancti Fatalis* it would suggest Fatalis was the author, but if Fatalis was its recipient, as suggested by Gennadius' record of Fastidius' composition, it should have read *sancto Fatali* or *ad sanctum Fatalem*, but such corruptions are common.

Ammoneo te *as evidence of developments within the ascetic movement*

The Reichenau fragment *Ammoneo te* is an example of developments within the ascetic movement as it redirected its focus away from calling for asceticism for all Christians, including those living within the civic sphere, and turned in on itself to call for isolation in order to pursue a fully Christian way of life. It shares many ideas with the ascetic writings of Evagrius of Antioch, Jerome and the Caspari writer(s), but whereas these authors reflect a trajectory of thought that started from monks in the desert in isolation and then turned its paraenetic aim to face outwards, directing it towards Christians in the secular world, *Ammoneo te* shows the retreat from this ambitious aim, back towards isolation.

The text was aimed at recruiting young men to the monastic life. Central ideas propounded in the text were: the need to be a Christian in action as well as name (repeated many times).[108] A fully Christian life was something uncommon.[109] Worldly possessions were not true possessions because they could be lost.[110] Excessive wealth derived from theft.[111] Celibacy was the mark of a Christian, while marriage prevented one from being pleasing to God.[112] Family attachments

---

[108] Anon., *Ammoneo te* ll. 66–7 (ed. Morin, p. 6), 'If we follow Christ, it ought to show in our actions'; 'Si Christum sequimur, debet in actibus apparere'; ll. 73–7 (ed. Morin, p. 7), 'I do not want that you should glory in the false title of Christian, I do not want that you be seduced by a pretence of faith and not true righteousness. The kingdom of God does not lie in a name, but in virtue'; 'Nolo falso Christianitatis nomine glorieris, nolo fide ficta et non uera iustitia seducaris. Regnum Dei non est in nomine, sed in uirtute'; also ll. 106–7 (ed. Morin, p. 7); ll. 141–3 (ed. Morin, p. 8); ll. 174–83 (ed. Morin, p. 9). Cf. Pelagius, *Ad Demetriadem* 23 (ed. Greshake, p. 142), '[God] who commands that his law not only be known but also be fulfilled. For it is of no benefit to have learnt what should be done, and not do it'; '[Deus] qui legem suam non solum sciri, sed etiam impleri iubet. Nihil enim prodest facienda didicisse, et non facere'; Anon., *De uita christiana* 1 (ed. Migne, PL 50.385A–B); 6 (ed. Migne, PL 50.398B–D).

[109] Anon., *Ammoneo te* ll. 82–3 (ed. Morin, p. 7), 'If what we seek is uncommon, then the way we live ought to be uncommon'; 'Si non est uulgare quod quaerimus, non debet uulgare esse quod uiuimus.' Cf. Pelagius, *Ad Demetriadem* 1 (ed. Greshake, p. 56), see Chapter 3, n. 133.

[110] Anon., *Ammoneo te* ll. 52–3 (ed. Morin, p. 6), 'Therefore a thing is not mine unless it is mine always'; 'Igitur meum non est, nisi quod mecum semper esse potuerit.' Cf. Pelagius, *Ad Demetriadem* 10 (ed. Greshake, p. 98), concerning spiritual riches, 'But these are under your control and are truly yours, because they do not come from outside you, but are created in the heart itself'; 'Haec uero in potestate tua sunt et uere propria, quia non extrinsecus ueniunt, sed ipso corde generantur.'

[111] Anon., *Ammoneo te* ll. 363–5 (ed. Morin, p. 14), concerning the rich man, 'Everything which he has amassed or seized or plundered he will leave behind in this world'; 'Cuncta, quae aut adquisiuit, aut inuasit, aut rapuit, in hoc mundo reliquerit'. Cf. Anon., *De diuitiis* 7.2–5 (ed. Hamman, PLS 1.1387–8).

[112] Just as the author of *On Chastity* did, the author of the homily-fragment argued both from the misery that came with marriage in practice, and also from the heavenly reward that chastity (*castitas*) would achieve: Anon., *Ammoneo te* ll. 306–19 (ed. Morin, pp. 12–13), 'Modesty is safe from all these evils. For amidst these shipwrecks of troubles and calamities, chastity fully enjoys peaceful and pure security. It does not have the temporary pleasure of the body, which the Apostle nevertheless called a tribulation, but it possesses a perpetual dwelling-place in heaven. It does not possess what death may carry off in the end, but it has what eternal life may safeguard. It is not joyful with men in the secular world, but it will rejoice with the angels at the resurrection'; 'Pudicitia ab his omnibus malis tuta est. Nam inter ista molestiarum calamitatumque naufragia castitas quieta et pura securitate perfruitur. Non habet corporis temporalem delectationem, quam tamen tribulationem apostolus nominauit, sed

should be rejected.[113] Yet the homily author struck out on a more extreme path. He overturned the accepted social norms of Roman civic life, arguing both that they were pitfalls that brought only misery, and that they were inherently un-Christian and would lead to hell. He preached the abandonment of family and civil society as seductions of the devil.[114] The activities of a Roman citizen displeased God; and devotion to *res publica* displeased God.[115] All semblance of moderation had been dropped. The homily was an attempt to persuade young men to abandon their families, their career paths and the civic values on which the Roman Empire was founded, and to take up ascetic monasticism.

---

habet perpetuam in caelestibus mansionem. Non habet quod mors extrema auferat, sed habet quod uita aeterna custodiat. Non laetatur cum hominibus in saeculo, sed cum angelis in resurrectione gaudebit'; ll. 245–9 (ed. Morin, p. 11); ll. 282–302 (ed. Morin, p. 12). Cf. Anon., *De castitate* 4.13 (ed. Hamman, PLS 1.1472), 'These are the things therefore that I would bring forward to show the misfortunes of marriage, from all of which chastity is immune and free'; 'Haec idcirco protulerim, ut casus ostenderem nuptiarum, a quibus omnibus pudicitia inmunis et libera est.'

[113] Anon., *Ammoneo te* ll. 352–8 (ed. Morin, pp. 13–14), 'Duties are evil that carry out those activities which derive profit in the future from sinful actions; and while a man acquires what he may bequeathe to his descendants, he condemns himself to eternal poverty'; 'Mala officia sunt illarum rerum, quae inde fructum expectant, unde peccata conquirunt; et dum quisque lucratur quod posteris derelinquat, seipsum aeterna mendicitate condemnat.'

[114] Anon., *Ammoneo te* ll. 259–76 (ed. Morin, pp. 11–12), 'Now Christians leave their parents so that they may be close to Christ .... If we do these things, they say, what use was it to have learned to read and write? Who will inherit that family estate he is hoping for? Who will look after his mother? Who will rule the household? Who will defend the clients? Lastly, who will endure the abuse of friends and fellow-citizens? These are the principal false enticements against the true life: with these devices the serpent seduces so that he may deceive. He burdens a man with love of his mother and family inheritance, so that he may separate a man from his eternal inheritance and the family of God'; 'Nunc Christiani relinquunt parentes, ut adhaereant Christo .... Quid ergo, dicunt, si ista facimus, profuit litteras didicisse? Quis illius patrimonii, quod in spe est, heres existet? Quis matrem solabitur? Quis familiam reget? Quis clientes defensurus est? Quis postremo amicorum et ciuium obpropria tolerabit? Haec aduersus ueram uitam principalia falsa sunt blandimenta: his dolis draco seducit, ut fallat. Matris et familiae hereditatis curam ingerit, ut homo ab hereditate aeterna et Dei familia separetur'. Cf. Anon., *De castitate* 17 (ed. Hamman, PLS 1.1502), 'We ought not to place our parents before him who placed neither his parents nor indeed himself before us'; 'Non debemus ei nostros praeferre parentes, qui nec suos nobis, nec se ipsum quidem praetulit'.

[115] Anon., *Ammoneo te* ll. 322–9 (ed. Morin, p. 13), concerning chastity, 'It does not deem it worthy to possess an earthly ancestral inheritance, because it rejoices in the possession of paradise with secure expectation. It does not own a villa, but neither does it pay tribute. It lacks property, but it is not harassed by anxiety. He renders no service to Caesar, who expends his whole being on his Creator'; 'Non dignatur patrimonium terrenum possidere, quia paradisi possessione spe certa laetatur. Villam non habet, sed nec tributum reddet. Caret proprietate, sed sollicitudine non uexatur. Nihil praestat Caesari, qui se totum inpendit auctori.' Anon., *Ammoneo te* ll. 164–73 (ed. Morin, p. 9), 'I ask, if we always perform actions which belong to men, when shall we perform those which are of God? And if our speech and thought and actions are expended for the sake of what benefits our bodies, for the sake of greed for wealth, for the sake of the State, for the sake of payment of tribute, when will our soul sigh for heavenly things? And we too will say with the Jews: *We have no king but Caesar* [John 19:15]'; 'Rogo, si semper agimus quae hominum sunt, quando acturi sumus illa quae Dei sunt? Et si sermo noster et cogitatus et actus pro commodis carnis, pro auaritiae lucris, pro re publica, pro tributis expenditur, quando de caelestibus animus suspirabit? Et nos dicemus cum Iudaeis: *Nos regem non habemus nisi Caesarem* [John 19:15].'

The importance of Ammoneo te

It is clear what this author owed to texts produced by earlier propagandists of the ascetic movement, but also how he developed the ascetic message. This was militantly anti-civic asceticism.[116] He preached rejection of the previously accepted values of home, hearth and state. This process may have been boosted by the collapse of the Western Empire if the way of life underpinned by Roman civic administration was threatened. The homily hinted at this when it pointed to the uncertainty of life at the time.[117] *Ammoneo te* captures a moment in the evolution of the ascetic movement in the West, abandoning civic asceticism to become the monastic movement. Its terms of reference were thoroughly Roman, depicting civic life under the empire.[118] But its call to monastic withdrawal from civic life was a new mindset in the Western Empire, and may point to a transitional context during the disintegration of the Western Empire in which traditional secular careers, with their lifestyle based around villa estates with associated urban residences, were familiar concepts but no longer widely available.

The arguments in *Ammoneo te* have more points of contact with the advertising of the ascetic life on show in the three versions of the *Life of Antony*, Jerome's paraenesis, Gerontius' *Life of Melania the Younger* and Palladius' *Lausiac History* than they do with Pelagius' output. Yet *Ammoneo te* contains many ideas that would normally lead to its being classed 'Pelagian'; and it was joined together, apparently by Caesarius of Arles, with lines from one of the Caspari Corpus letters, which have been cornerstones of the notion of a 'Pelagian' text. Because it is anonymous and rarely considered, it comes with no prior assumptions attached and tests the classification 'Pelagian'. The homily featured no explicit doctrine at all; simply the call to asceticism. It assumed that special effort would lead to special reward. It is impossible to say if this was deliberate avoidance of what had become controversial. Its lack of an authorial attribution and of doctrinal comment makes this anonymous text another test case for the classification 'Pelagian'.

Many of the ideas expressed in *Ammoneo te* have been taken by scholars to be diagnostically 'Pelagian'. Both Morin and Rees classed it as 'Pelagian', but if Morin was right to place the sermon into his edition of Caesarius of Arles' homilies, then Caesarius thought that these ideas were acceptable and promoted them by repackaging them for wide distribution, along with lines from *To an Older*

---

[116] Anon., *Ammoneo te* l. 215 (ed. Morin, p. 10), 'Let piety summon you to service as a soldier'; 'Vocet te ad militiam pietas'. Cf. Sulpicius Severus, *Vita Martini* 1 (ed. Halm, CSEL 1, p. 111), 'Heavenly warfare'; 'Caelestis militia'; 4 (ed. Halm, CSEL 1, p. 114), 'I am Christ's soldier'; 'Christi ego miles sum.'

[117] Anon., *Ammoneo te* ll. 239–41 (ed. Morin, p. 11), 'I commit myself for the future, who am uncertain about tomorrow'; 'Futurum tempus exspondeo, qui de crastino sum incertus.'

[118] For example, the *forum, secretarium, uilla, res publica*: Anon., *Ammoneo te* ll. 141–3 (ed. Morin, p. 8), 'The body comes to God's house, but the spirit remains behind in the council-chamber, or in the law-courts, or among the disgraceful soothsayers'; 'Corpus ad domum Dei uenit, et animus in secretario aut in foro aut in turpibus sortelogis remansit.'

Friend.[119] *Ammoneo te* has been dated to the early 5th century because of its content, which suggests the urban Roman context already noted, but by Caesarius' time, at the start of the 6th century, in theory the defeat of 'Pelagianism' was well in the past for Christians. Yet Caesarius still had access to this material, and his use of it suggests that he saw it simply as useful paraenesis and not as 'Pelagian'. This supports the view that the classification 'Pelagian' is a fiction. In reality, such a discrete subgroup of ascetic texts cannot be differentiated from the mass of ascetic paraenetic literature.

Ammoneo te confirms the view that Pelagius was part of the ascetic movement that began in the East among hermits and monks withdrawn from society, that took root in the Western Empire as the preoccupation of a minority, some of whom were from the social elite and who dominate the historical record because of their writings, and then gradually became a broad-based movement of withdrawal from secular society in succeeding centuries. This phenomenon was much larger than Pelagius and he was by no means at any point its leading or its most extreme advocate.

To a Mistress of a Household and *Ammoneo te* argue for reclassification of Pelagius because it is impossible to categorise them. The fact that there are two categories that overlap to such an extent that they are interchangeable, and these texts could be classed either as ascetic literature or as 'Pelagian', raises doubts about whether there is a difference between these two categories. They show that Pelagius' ideas were the working assumptions of the ascetic movement, and *Ammoneo te* also shows the link between Pelagius' teaching and the growth of the monastic movement in the West, which again suggests that Pelagius' writings were simply products of the ascetic movement.

Conclusion on definition and classification: Fatal flaws in the concept of 'Pelagianism'

There has been insufficient critical study of the concept of 'Pelagianism'. The fact that scholars have been unable to define it or establish the content of the descriptor 'Pelagian' is one strand of evidence among the five put forward in this book, which together show that when it is subjected to scrutiny, the notion of 'Pelagianism' is unsustainable. It is not possible to define 'Pelagianism' by reference to the tenets attributed to it by Pelagius' opponents because neither Pelagius nor anyone else, nor any group, held this set of views. Nor is it possible to define it by reference to contemporary texts, since there is too much variation in ideas within the texts classed as 'Pelagian' for it to be one programme. There is no set of tenets that can be identified as actual elements shared repeatedly in contemporary texts that were not already being canvassed in the 370s AD. The views expressed by Pelagius with regard to human free will and man's goodness as made in the image of God were longstanding and widely asserted ones, frequently rehearsed

---

[119]   Caesarius of Arles, *Sermo* 20 (ed. Morin, CCSL 103, pp. 91–4).

in ascetic literature. Thus Pelagius' two positive assertions, the principles which he felt unable to abandon, do not serve to differentiate his writings from ascetic literature in general.

The statement that 'Pelagianism' never existed addresses the fictitious assemblage of doctrines packaged together in the 5th century. It addresses the tenets and character attributed to this concocted programme. It does not address a possible modern redefinition of what might now be argued to have existed in fact. It might be countered that perhaps 'Pelagianism' could be redefined as objection to the three interlinked doctrines of original sin, prevenient grace, and predestination interpreted as preordainment. But there are good reasons why we should not accept such a modern redefinition. If it is proposed that 'Pelagianism' be redefined solely as objection to this triune, then it would have to be acknowledged, first, that this standpoint cannot be associated with the fourteen tenets and the character of 'Pelagianism' as disseminated by Pelagius' opponents; and, second, that the Church before AD 418 was 'Pelagian' and after AD 418 remained largely 'Pelagian' for many centuries, since predestination as preordainment was not explicitly installed as orthodoxy during the Middle Ages.[120] The consequence of a definition of 'Pelagianism' as objection to the doctrines of original sin, prevenient grace, and predestination interpreted as preordainment would be that a great number of Christian writers would fall into the category 'Pelagian', and an even larger number of texts would come under this classification. But the term would be anachronistic, and tying the classification to the 5th-century writer Pelagius creates the impression that new doctrines were invented by Pelagius in the 5th century. Both of these impressions are false. Furthermore, the myth of 'Pelagianism' with its specific character of arrogance and stress on human self-sufficiency has been in place for so long that it has become embedded in Christian thought. The majority of surviving ascetic texts take for granted effective human free will and do not explicitly argue against the triune of doctrines elucidated by Augustine. If we used a modern definition, we would have to propose that the underlying principles of such texts were 'Pelagian', but it would be misleading to impose a controversial standpoint on authors who perhaps never examined these issues. This cannot be the marker of 'Pelagianism' because what is in fact visible in contemporary texts is a vast range of standpoints of which the shared element is their ascetic values based on imitation of Christ's way of life. It is this historical reality—namely, the lack of differentiability in Pelagius' views from other ascetic literature—that is the decisive argument against such a modern redefinition. The concept of 'Pelagianism' is invalid because it suppresses this historical truth. And such a redefinition cannot be identified using the term 'Pelagianism' because no one has ever followed through the consequences of redefining 'Pelagianism' in this way and gone on to classify Jerome, Evagrius of Antioch and Athanasius as 'Pelagians', since this is

---

[120] It was later endorsed by, for example, John Calvin; see Calvin, *Institutes of the Christian Religion* 3.21.5–22.11 (ed. McNeill, pp. 926–47).

so far from what is commonly understood by the term as to make it something else altogether. Finally, if Pelagius was in no way the author of these views, there is good reason not to attach his name to them. In all these ways, then, the term would be misleading and would obscure the historical truth.

Rather than a redefinition as objection to the doctrines of original sin, prevenient grace, and predestination interpreted as preordainment, a better solution to the problems with the concept of 'Pelagianism' is to acknowledge that 'Pelagianism' was a deliberately created myth, and to reclassify Pelagius and his writings as part of the ascetic movement. The fact that in the West the ascetic movement morphed into the monastic movement is one key reason why Pelagius' writings were staples of medieval monastic book collections. This does not mean that the entire Western monastic movement was 'Pelagian'; it means simply that one explanation for the wide circulation of Pelagius' writings (travelling under false attributions) is that Pelagius was part of the ascetic movement and thus his writings were part of the paraenetic literature that was foundational for the monastic movement in the West. As will be seen in Chapter 7, across Western Europe, medieval monks were strikingly unable to see a difference between Jerome's letters and Pelagius'.

6

The Invention of 'Pelagianism':
Motive and Means

Identification of a motive for the creation of the myth and the means by which it was established supports the thesis that the concept of 'Pelagianism' was deliberately invented. It makes it possible to see why and how the concept of 'Pelagianism' came into being when no such programme existed in reality. Understanding why 'Pelagianism' was invented addresses motive; uncovering how it was invented encompasses both the method used to construct and install the myth, and also how it came to be accepted, in the sense of why the myth was allowed to succeed and was not rejected as fiction. A credible motive has been proposed. It is the argument of this book that 'Pelagianism' was invented in order to bring into disrepute the two principles of the goodness of human nature and effective free will; and that this was achieved by making the name Pelagius toxic and tarring his teaching by association with self-evidently unacceptable propositions, thereby facilitating the installation of alternative theses as orthodox dogma. The goodness of human nature and effective free will were longstanding principles of Christian belief that had to be displaced if the doctrines of original sin, an absolutist account of prevenient grace, and predestination interpreted as preordainment were to be installed as orthodoxy.

The goodness of human nature and effective free will were not the tenets listed by Augustine as constituting Pelagius' teaching because it would have been impossible to condemn and proscribe these two principles. Pelagius' opponents could not fight the doctrinal battle on the real issues because it was unlikely that they would win that battle. As seen in Chapter 1, Augustine himself admitted twice in writing that it was possible that Pelagius did not hold, teach or write the tenets that he listed as the constituents of 'Pelagianism'. Furthermore, he acknowledged the difficulty of presenting his own interpretation of Scripture. Aware that prevenient grace and predestination conceived of as preordainment would be rejected by some Christians, Augustine discussed at length how to present the doctrines so as to downplay or conceal their true meaning.[1] In a piece of circular reasoning

---

[1] Augustine, *De dono perseuerantiae* 22.57–61 (ed. Chéné and Pintard, BA 24, pp. 740–8), 'However,

he argued that the very weakness that made humans unable to choose to act virtuously without the prior inspiration of the Holy Spirit also made them unable to deal with the truth of prevenient grace, predestination and original sin:

> 'And if you obey, but it is foreknown that you will be rejected, you will cease to obey.' This is, of course, very true; it is surely true, but most brutal, most inopportune and most inappropriate; not because the statement is false, but because it is not applied in a salutary manner to the frailty of human weakness.[2]

---

predestination ought not to be preached to the people in such a way that the multitude of those who are uneducated or who are slower to understand think that it is in some way refuted by being preached .... And the foreknowledge of God can perhaps be preached in another way so that one wards off human laziness .... Although these statements are true, one should nonetheless not state them in the hearing of many people so that this language is aimed at them and those words of these brothers, which you included in your letter and which I quoted above, are addressed to them: "The definite decision of God's will concerning predestination comes to this: Some of you, having received the will to obey, come from unbelief to faith." What need is there to say: "Some of you"? .... Nor is it at all necessary to say what follows, namely: "The rest of you who linger in the enjoyment of sins have not yet risen up because the help of merciful grace has not yet raised you up", though it could and ought to be expressed well and conveniently thus: "But if there are some of you who still linger in the enjoyment of sins that bring damnation, learn a very healthful discipline" .... For why is it not rather put this way: "And if any are not yet called, let us pray for them that they may be called" .... But if one wants to or it is necessary to say something about those who do not persevere, why does one not rather at least phrase it as I did a little before: first of all, let it not be said concerning those who are listening to us among the people of God, but to these people concerning others: That is, so that it is not said: "If any of you obey, but are predestined to be rejected", but: "If any obey", with the rest in the third person, not the second .... For what does the statement lose if it is phrased thus: "But if any obey, but are not predestined for his kingdom and glory, they last only for a time and will not remain up to the end in the same obedience"? Is the same thing not stated with greater truth and fittingness so that we do not seem to desire so great an evil for them, but to report concerning others something that our listeners hate?'; 'Quae tamen non ita populis praedicanda est, ut apud imperitam uel tardioris intelligentiae multitudinem redargui quodam modo ipsa sua praedicatione uideatur .... Et si quo alio modo Dei praescientia praedicari potest, ut hominis segnitia repellatur .... Quamuis ergo haec uera sint, non tamen isto modo dicenda sunt audientibus multis, ut sermo ad ipsos etiam conuertatur, eisque dicantur illa istorum uerba, quae uestris litteris indidistis, et quae superius interposui: "Ita se habet de praedestinatione definita sententia uoluntatis Dei, ut alii ex uobis de infidelitate, accepta obediendi uoluntate, ueneritis ad fidem." Quid opus est dici: "Alii ex uobis"? .... Nec illud quod sequitur est omnino dicendum, id est: "Caeteri uero qui in peccatorum delectatione remoramini, ideo nondum surrexistis, quia necdum uos adiutorium gratiae miserantis erexit"; cum bene et conuenienter dici possit et debeat: "Si qui autem adhuc in peccatorum damnabilium delectatione remoramini, apprehendite saluberrimam disciplinam" .... Cur enim non potius ita dicitur: "Et si qui sunt nondum uocati, pro eis ut uocentur oremus"? .... Sed si et de iis qui non perseuerant, aliquid placet dicere uel necesse est, cur non potius ita saltem dicitur, ut paulo ante a me dictum est: primum, ut non de ipsis qui in populo audiunt, hoc dicatur, sed de aliis ad ipsos: id est, ut non dicatur: "Si qui obeditis, si praedestinati estis reiiciendi", sed: "Si qui obediunt"; et caetera per uerbi personam tertiam, non per secundam? .... Quid enim sententiae deperit, si ita dicatur: "Si qui autem obediunt, sed in regnum eius et gloriam praedestinati non sunt, temporales sunt, nec usque in finem in eadem obedientia permanebunt"? Nonne et uerius eadem res et congruentius dicitur, ut non ipsis tantum malum tanquam optare uideamur, sed de aliis referre, quod oderint?'

[2] Augustine, *De dono perseuerantiae* 22.61 (ed. Chéné and Pintard, BA 24, pp. 746–8), '"Et si qui obeditis, si praesciti estis reiiciendi, obedire cessabitis." Nempe hoc uerissimum est: ita sane, sed improbissimum, importunissimum, incongruentissimum; non falso eloquio, sed non salubriter ualetudini humanae infirmitatis apposito.'

The fact that Pelagius was acquitted of heresy three times demonstrates the difficulty of achieving a condemnation of his position. Thus instead of indicting Pelagius for writing that human nature was innately good because made in God's image, an unwarranted entailment was read into his ascetic paraenesis with hostile intent and the thesis was attributed to Pelagius that man could be perfect in this life, a toxic surrogate for his actual assertion, which was that human nature was capable of goodness, and therefore God did not demand behaviour of which man was incapable and Christians should strive for imitation of Christ.

The importance of presentation

When Augustine warned Demetrias' mother Juliana about Pelagius' statement that Demetrias had her virtuous behaviour from herself and only from herself, he argued that this did not give a proper role to God's grace, which had in reality made Demetrias choose virtuous action, and thus Pelagius' statement was arrogant. To the patrician Juliana, Augustine did not phrase his objection to Pelagius' comment as being on the grounds that original sin made human nature too weak to be able to choose virtue. Elsewhere he wrote that a good will was created entirely by God, but writing to Juliana he finessed his presentation of his position; speaking of Paul's virtue he wrote: 'Or if it came to him on account of his own will to some small degree, it still did not come only from him.'[3] This formulation of his doctrine suggested that the will might play some part in good action. Of Demetrias' dedication he commented that it was a gift of God: 'Although one bestowed on someone who believes and wills it'.[4] This evidence suggests that in lobbying Juliana to end her support for Pelagius, Augustine nuanced his phraseology. Elsewhere, however, he was open about the triune of doctrines that he believed were true.[5] In terms of careful use of language, he could be as flexible

---

[3] Augustine, *Ep.* 188.2.8 (ed. Goldbacher, CSEL 57, p. 126), 'Aut si propter arbitrium proprium aliquantum et ex illo, non tamen non nisi ex illo'.

[4] Augustine, *Ep.* 188.2.6 (ed. Goldbacher, CSEL 57, p. 123), 'Quamuis credenti uolentique conlatum'.

[5] Augustine, *Ep.* 194.5.19 (ed. Goldbacher, CSEL 57, pp. 190–1), 'What merit, then, does a human being have before grace so that by merit he may receive grace, since only grace produces in us every good merit of ours and since, when God crowns our merits, he only crowns his own gifts? …. Whence also eternal life itself, which certainly will be had in the end without end, and for this reason is given for preceding merits, yet because the same merits to which it is given in return were not produced by us through our own ability, but were produced in us through grace, it is itself also called grace for no other reason that it is given gratuitously, not because it is not given to our merits but because the very merits to which it is given were themselves given to us'; 'Quod est ergo meritum hominis ante gratiam, quo merito percipiat gratiam, cum omne bonum meritum nostrum non in nobis faciat nisi gratia et, cum Deus coronat merita nostra, nihil aliud coronet quam munera sua? …. Vnde et ipsa aeterna uita, quae utique in fine sine fine habebitur et ideo meritis praecedentibus redditur, tamen, quia eadem merita, quibus redditur, non a nobis facta sunt per nostram sufficentiam, sed in nobis facta per gratiam, etiam ipsa gratia nuncupatur non ob aliud, nisi quia gratis datur, nec ideo, quia non meritis datur, sed quia data sunt et ipsa merita, quibus datur.' Regarding the hardening of Pharoah's heart: *Ep.* 194.3.14 (ed. Goldbacher, CSEL 57, p. 187), 'We look for what merits this hardening, and we find it. For the whole mass was condemned as punishment for sin, and God does not harden by imparting malice but by not imparting mercy. For those to whom mercy is not imparted are neither worthy nor do they merit it, and instead they deserve and merit that

with his vocabulary as he suggested Pelagius was. Sometimes he asserted that human free will did still exist without acknowledging the logical flaw in maintaining that effective free will existed alongside absolute prevenient grace and predestination interpreted as preordainment: 'Nor is anyone forced by the power of God against their will either to do evil or to do good, but when God abandons them they turn toward evil in accord with their merits, and when God helps them they are turned toward good without any merits.'[6] By definition, if God's decision determined man's behaviour, then man was not in control of his own behaviour. Elsewhere again, Augustine cited Rom. 8:14 to argue that the will was in fact driven and governed by the Holy Spirit, as already noted.[7] Augustine's nuanced formulation of his position to Juliana suggests that the motivation for the invention of 'Pelagianism' was awarenesss that the triune would be found unpalateable and would be rejected. In this negotiation, presentation was critical; in order to achieve condemnation of Pelagius, a bogus list of tenets was attributed to him and the debate was not conducted openly on the actual positions of either side.

Motive

In order to install doctrines

At the start of the 5th century there was no Christian dogma concerning original sin, prevenient grace or predestination.[8] 'Pelagianism' was invented to facilitate the adoption of these three interlinked doctrines which ran counter to assumptions that were widespread and had underpinned Christian asceticism in particular.[9]

---

he should not impart mercy. But we look for what merits mercy, and we do not find it, because there is nothing, so that grace is not done away with, if it is not given gratuitously but is given in return for merits'; 'Quaerimus enim meritum obdurationis et inuenimus. Merito namque peccati uniuersa massa damnata est nec obdurat Deus impertiendo malitiam sed non impertiendo misericordiam. Quibus enim non impertitur, nec digni sunt nec merentur ac potius, ut non impertiatur, hoc digni sunt hoc merentur. Quaerimus autem meritum misericordiae nec inuenimus, quia nullum est, ne gratia euacuetur, si non gratis donatur, sed meritis redditur.' The whole of Augustine's *Letter* 194 is a hymn to prevenient grace and predestination interpreted as preordainment, so selecting passages is problematic and cannot convey the explicitness and uncompromising assertiveness with which Augustine set out the triune in his letter to Sixtus. See also: Augustine, *De dono perseuerantiae* 22.58 (ed. Chéné and Pintard, BA 24, pp. 740–2); 18.47 (ed. Chéné and Pintard, BA 24, pp. 714–8); 24.66 (ed. Chéné and Pintard, BA 24, p. 758).
[6] Augustine, *Contra duas epistolas Pelagianorum* 1.18.36 (ed. Urba and Zycha, CSEL 60, p. 453), 'Nec ex Dei potentia uel in malum uel in bonum inuitum aliquem cogi, sed Deo deserente pro meritis ire in malum et Deo adiuuante sine meritis conuerti ad bonum.'
[7] See Chapter 1, n. 57.
[8] Rees, *Pelagius* vol. II, pp. 9–10.
[9] Lamberigts, 'Le Mal', pp. 105–6; Martinetto referred to 'the Augustinian "novelty"' ('la "nouveauté" augustinienne'): Martinetto, 'Les Premières réactions', p. 117; Bohlin, *Die Theologie des Pelagius*, p. 110; Markus referred to 'the newly forged Augustinian orthodoxy': Markus, 'Pelagianism', p. 199; Clark referred to Augustine's 'new predestinarian determinism': Clark, *The Origenist Controversy*, p. 240.

These three doctrines were explicitly or implicitly asserted by councils in Africa, and the dissent from them expressed in verdicts given by the councils of Jerusalem and Diospolis in the East set up a political tension concerning the authority of the councils in the respective areas. This threatened the cohesion of the Church at a time when political and military crises made unity desirable.[10] The Jerusalem and Diospolis decisions also threatened the authority of Augustine's writings. Jerome's literary output is now seen as self-promotion, as a means of staking his claim to authority on the basis of his expertise in asceticism and Scripture.[11] This same perspective should be borne in mind with regard to all Christian writers.

To understand the creation of the myth, the theological background is important, and in particular the flowering of Pauline exegesis in Latin in the second half of the 4th century. Marius Victorinus, a pagan professor of rhetoric and philosophy in Rome, became a Christian late in life and turned his skills of interpretation and exposition to the Pauline Epistles in the AD 360s to create the first Latin commentary on them. According to Stephen Cooper's analysis, Victorinus' anti-Judaising stance led him to take a negative view of the Jewish law, and to stress faith, using the phrase 'faith alone' (*sola fides*). Cooper observed that *sola fides* was a phrase 'largely absent from Greek commentaries on Paul', but was present in Victorinus and Ambrosiaster.[12] Other commentaries on the Pauline Epistles followed in swift succession: the commentary by the author named Ambrosiaster, an anonymous commentary identified by Frede, the commentaries on selected Pauline letters by Jerome and Augustine, and Pelagius'. The increased interest in and interpretation of Paul's letters brought previously unexplored issues to the fore. This was a process in which doctrine was being explored and shaped through exegesis. After a lifetime spent working in the classical philosophical tradition, Victorinus had no inhibitions about contributing his own interpretations of Scripture and steering discourse in a direction of his own choosing. Developing and articulating their own system was what philosophers did.

Up to this point the doctrines of effective free will and the goodness of human nature as created in God's image had been assumptions often implicit within Christian belief. An exception was Origen, who explicitly canvassed free will. Ascetic paraenesis such as Athanasius' also explicitly affirmed these two doctrines. Subsequently they were challenged, partly as a result of the growth in exegesis

---

[10] Augustine, *De gestis Pelagii* 11.25 (ed. Urba and Zycha, CSEL 42, p. 79), 'These are the tenets that certain people who think such things were trying to convince many of our brothers about, such that they were threatening them with regard to the Eastern churches that unless they held these tenets, they might be condemned by the judgement of those churches'; 'Haec sunt quae nonnullis fratribus quidam talia sentientes ita persuadere conabantur, ut de orientalibus comminarentur ecclesiis quod, nisi qui haec tenerent, earum possent iudicio condemnari.'

[11] Cain, *The Letters of Jerome*, pp. 33–42.

[12] S. A. Cooper, *Marius Victorinus' Commentary on Galatians*, Oxford Early Christian Studies (Oxford, 2005), p. 194.

on the Pauline Epistles.[13] At his trial in Carthage, Caelestius deliberately directed attention to the issue of what was settled dogma and what was a matter for discussion, and likewise in the defence that he presented in Rome, he pointedly noted that he was not the author of any doctrine:

> 'If some questions have arisen aside from the faith', he said, 'about which there is dispute between many people, I have not set this up with definitive authority like the author of some doctrine; but what I have taken from the source of the prophets and apostles, we offer to be tested by the judgement of your apostolic authority, so that if by chance the error of ignorance has deceived me, as happens to men, it may be corrected by your verdict.'[14]

Caelestius' explicit point was that these topics were disputed. His implicit point was that there had been no ecumenical council to produce a judgement on these questions, and no individual should claim far-reaching authority for doctrine he had created. Augustine argued that Caelestius' words were a ploy to absolve himself of responsibility for his writings, but Caelestius was making the same point that Pelagius made at the end of his *Statement of Faith*, and that Vincent of Lérins made in his *Commonitorium*: that a longstanding and widely held understanding of Scripture was being displaced. This was clearly the view taken by contemporary Christians who opposed some or all of the triune.[15]

Means I

The methodology of heresy accusations

In order to have a doctrine condemned as heresy and so achieve its exclusion from orthodox doctrine, it was crucial to give it a name, usually the name of a supposed progenitor.[16] Attaching a label to an interpretation of Christianity was an essential precursor to expelling it from the Church. Sociologists have studied why and how deviance is created, and the function of deviance within society.[17] The interpretative

---

[13] On Augustine's 'system' of doctrines first appearing, in the course of interpretation of Rom. 9:10–29, in his *Ad Simplicianum* (completed by AD 396): Martinetto, 'Les Premières réactions', p. 85; p. 116.

[14] Augustine, *De gratia Christi et de peccato originali* 2.23.26 (ed. Urba and Zycha, CSEL 42, p. 185), '"Si qua uero", inquit, "praeter fidem quaestiones natae sunt, de quibus esset inter plerosque contentio, non ego quasi auctor alicuius dogmatis definita hoc auctoritate statui, sed ea, quae de prophetarum et apostolorum fonte suscepi, uestri apostolatus offerimus probanda esse iudicio, ut, si forte ut hominibus quispiam ignorantiae error obrepsit, uestra sententia corrigatur."'

[15] Pelagius, *Libellus fidei* 14 (ed. Migne, PL 45.1718), see Chapter 3, n. 299; on Vincent of Lérins, see n. 44–6.

[16] On the importance of naming an alleged heresy, see Cameron, 'How to Read Heresiology', pp. 198–202.

[17] Jacques Berlinerblau argued for the need to use sociological theory in the study of heresy, noting how rarely scholarship on heresy had done so: J. Berlinerblau, 'Toward a Sociology of Heresy, Orthodoxy, and *Doxa*', *History of Religions* 40:4 (2001), pp. 327–51.

model of interactionist theory throws valuable light on heresiology in general, and on the invention of 'Pelagianism' in particular.[18] It points out repeated patterns of behaviour that explain how deviance is created, and it offers analyses of specific heresy accusations which are revealing with regard to 'Pelagianism'. From these a clear picture emerges of the motivations that determine the creation of deviance and the methods by which it is created.

Interactionist theory, also known as labelling theory

Symbolic interaction theory began the creation of 'labelling perspectives' and subsequently evolved in several directions.[19] Symbolic interaction theorists developed insights and sensitising concepts, and theories about the functions of deviance for society.[20] Frank Tannenbaum coined the term 'the dramatisation of evil' to describe the labelling process.[21] Howard Becker popularised what has now come to be known widely as labelling theory, himself arguing that the term was a misnomer. Instead he preferred to call it interactionist theory, and it is now often called interactionism. The principle elements of Becker's analysis were as follows. The creation of deviance begins not when a person is labelled deviant but earlier when social groups or moral crusaders create rules.[22] All deviance is created when rules are created by moral entrepreneurs.[23] Since this is the case, scholarship that does not examine the actions and motivations of rule-creators as well as those of deviants is incomplete. Interactionist theory insists on its universality; all rules are created, therefore all deviance is created by moral entrepreneurs, and this process is universal to all organisations, communities and areas of life. The label of deviance created by rules places the deviants in the position of outsiders from the main group. The creation of rules and thereby deviance is always a political process; deviance is the result of conflict between groups within a community, and creation of deviance is therefore always part of a struggle for power.[24]

According to interactionist theory, control of definitions is key in the conflict from which rules and deviance are created; the drama is one of accusation and definition. Interactionism notes the effect of created definitions: 'The difference

---

[18] Éric Rebillard has also used this analytical tool in a discussion of controversy over interpretation of the word grace: Rebillard, 'Sociologie'.

[19] Symbolic interaction theory was a term coined by Herbert Blumer in 1969, after much had already been published setting out interactionist approaches.

[20] R. L. Matsueda, 'The Natural History of Labeling Theory', in D. P. Farrington and J. Murray, ed., *Labeling Theory. Empirical Tests*, Advances in Criminological Theory 18 (New Brunswick, NJ, 2014), pp. 17–18.

[21] F. Tannenbaum, *Crime and the Community* (Boston, MA, 1938), pp. 19–20; Matsueda, 'The Natural History', p. 18.

[22] H. Becker, *Outsiders. Studies in the Sociology of Deviance* (New York, 1963), p. 9.

[23] Becker, *Outsiders*, p. 162, 'Rules are not made automatically .... The harm needs to be discovered and pointed out. People must be made to feel that something ought to be done about it.'

[24] E. M. Schur, *The Politics of Deviance, Stigma Contests and the Uses of Power* (Englewood Cliffs, NJ, 1980), pp. 3–29.

in definition, in the label applied to the act, makes a difference in what everyone does subsequently.'[25] Control based on the manipulation of definitions and labels is a disguised form of control.[26] Interactionist theory observes that those in power use definition and labelling to maintain their positions as superordinates. The factors which determine the success of rule-creators are economic and political power. Interactionists characterise the rule-making process as a: 'Drama of moral rhetoric and action in which imputations of deviance are made, accepted, rejected, and fought over.'[27] Access to channels of publicity is key to success: 'Deviance outcomes are profoundly influenced by techniques of persuasion and pressure. Propaganda is thus a key weapon in the deviantising process.'[28] For a rule to be installed successfully, a necessary part of the process is that someone has to be found breaking the rule and be convicted for breaking it.[29] The label of deviant is a 'master label', meaning that it eclipses all the other labels a person might have acquired before receiving the label of deviant. The deviant is depersonalised by the label, and is often subsequently perceived as having always been deviant.

How does interactionism relate to heresy?

The rigorous scrutiny of all the agents in the 'drama of evil' was the scholarly revision achieved by interactionist theory. In addition, observations made by inter-actionist theorists about the processes involved in the creation of rules and the behaviour of moral entrepreneurs are relevant to study of the controversy about original sin, prevenient grace, and predestination interpreted as preordainment because they offer a disinterested analysis of the concept of deviance produced in an entirely unrelated context which is of universal application, and which exactly describes the process visible in the condemnation of Pelagius. While some scholars have acknowledged the role of the rhetoric deployed by Pelagius' opponents in bringing about his condemnation, interactionist theory insists that the actions and motivations of the moral entrepreneur cannot be omitted in any account of deviance.[30] All parties in the drama of deviance must be examined and no one is exempted from scrutiny: 'No matter how respectable or highly placed.'[31]

---

[25] Becker, *Outsiders*, p. 180.

[26] Becker, *Outsiders*, p. 205.

[27] Becker continued: 'The chief effect of interactionist theory has been to focus attention on that drama as an object of study, and especially to focus on some relatively unstudied participants in it – those sufficiently powerful to make their imputations of deviance stick': Becker, *Outsiders*, p. 186.

[28] L. Pietersen, 'Despicable Deviants: Labelling Theory and the Polemic of the Pastorals', *Sociology of Religion* 58:4 (1997), p. 347.

[29] Becker, *Outsiders*, p. 163, 'Once a rule has come into existence, it must be applied to particular people before the abstract class of outsiders created by the rule can be peopled. Offenders must be discovered, identified, apprehended, and convicted.'

[30] Becker, *Outsiders*, p. 197, 'To be exempted from study means that one's claims, theories, and state-ments of fact are not subjected to critical scrutiny.'

[31] Becker, *Outsiders*, p. 207.

Interactionism in relation to the 5th-century controversy about original
sin, prevenient grace, and predestination interpreted as preordainment

'Moral entrepreneur' is a term which includes both rule-creators and rule-enforcers.
Becker's analysis of rule-enforcers was that they were particularly inclined to take
a pessimistic view of human nature and were sceptical of attempts to reform it. He
suggested that: 'One of the underlying reasons for the enforcer's pessimism about
human nature and the possibilities of reform is the fact that if human nature were
perfectible and people could be permanently reformed, his job would come to an
end'. It may be that an underlying issue between the two sides was that groups
of Christians pursuing the goal of perfect imitation of Christ's way of life would
be outside episcopal authority. The conflict could be seen as part of the perennial
battle for autonomy or control between monastic groups and the secular Church.[32]
In the 5th-century context of competition for authority within the Christian hierarchy, authority could be constructed through publishing and through publicly
visible defence of the Church against heresy. To maintain authority, a Christian
leader might feel obliged to keep publishing and to keep identifying heretics. This
competition for authority encompassed both clerical and lay Christians, since
aristocratic patronage funded lay advisers on Christianity on the model of pagan
philosophers maintained by wealthy households.[33] It should not be forgotten how
competitive the world of late antique Christianity was, and how far the Roman
educational system inculcated competition, with winners and losers at every
stage.[34]

Becker also observed that rule-creators are often moral crusaders. They bring
attention to their cause using publicity, organise support from disparate interest
groups and lobby legislators to write laws favourable to their cause. The moral
crusader believes that some absolute evil exists which must be eradicated from
society. As a result: 'Any means is justified to do away with it', and compromise
is not in his mindset.[35] This observation about unwillingness to compromise may

---

[32] An example of this conflict over authority is offered by the comment made by the Irish monastic
leader Columbanus to Gallic bishops about the relative spiritual virtue of his monastic community and
the bishops. He equated closeness of imitation of Christ with authority, since he was arguing that he
and his community should be left in peace by the bishops, which in practice meant being exempt from
episcopal authority: Columbanus, *Ep.* 2.8 (ed. Walker, p. 20).
[33] Jerome, *Ep.* 133.13.3 (ed. Hilberg, CSEL 56, p. 260), on the provision of money to Christian
advisers by wealthy households.
[34] Brent Shaw suggested that Augustine may have been seeking impact and relevance since his victory
over Donatism was of no interest outside Africa: 'If he wished ever to be known outside of his own
small world, as any American businessman would say, Augustine would have to reposition himself in
the marketplace. A battle against a Mediterranean-wide heresy would provide the grounds on which his
important ideas would finally receive a worthy audience .... The construction of the Pelagian heresy
involved a lot of hard uphill struggle and sweat, and the remorseless education of churchgoers': B. D.
Shaw, *Sacred Violence: African Christians and Sectarian Hatred in the Age of Augustine* (Cambridge,
2011), pp. 311–14.
[35] Becker, *Outsiders*, p. 148, 'He operates with an absolute ethic; what he sees is truly and totally
evil with no qualification'; see also R. A. Markus, *Saeculum: History and Society in the Theology of*

explain the disparity between Augustine's desire to retain Antoninus of Fussala within the Church as a bishop, but to exclude Pelagius.[36] An interactionist explanation of this might suggest that Augustine did not create the rules by which Antoninus was indicted, so he had no personal investment in seeing those rules enforced. A further point Becker made about moral crusaders was that the success of a crusade might leave the crusader without a vocation: 'Such a man, at loose ends, may generalise his interest and discover something new to view with alarm, a new evil about which something ought to be done. He becomes a professional discoverer of wrongs to be righted, of situations requiring new rules.'[37] Creating rules might become a habit that is difficult to give up.

Becker noted a tension between rule-creators and rule-enforcers. Rule-creators often want to see their rules enforced in every case, while rule-enforcers are more realistic since they have to be selective about which rule-breaker to punish because they cannot punish them all. In the case of Pelagius' teaching in the 5th century, Pelagius' opponents were in the position of being rule-creators, so that they were anxious to see their rules enforced. Becker characterised the attitude of the rule-enforcer, incapable of enforcing rules on everyone and therefore being selective in enforcement, as professional. Rule-enforcers responded to the pressures of their situation, and enforced rules and created outsiders in a selective way, often not enforcing the rules on those with power or money. In this respect, then, what has been seen as the moderate inclusiveness of Augustine's approach to Christianity might more accurately be seen as professional, as the attitude of a man dealing with congregations, who could not seek to impose all God's commands on all Christians. However, when it came to rules which he had himself played a part in creating, he had the absolute ethic of the moral crusader as rule-creator.

Thus the difference in approach was due to the different roles each side was carrying out: ascetic propagandists did not aspire to be rule-creators and were in no position to enforce their rigorous standards, which were inherently voluntary, while Augustine and the North African bishops were rule-creators on some points of doctrine. The point is that ascetic propagandists perceived themselves to have no personal involvement in the rules they propounded, nor any power of enforcement.[38] Writers of ascetic paraenesis did not envisage sanctions except after death,

---

St. Augustine (Cambridge, 1970), pp. 134–45.

[36] Antoninus of Fussala was a member of Augustine's monastic community at Hippo who was ordained bishop of Fussala and subsequently used his episcopacy to oppress the local community: Augustine, Ep. 209.4–9 (ed. Goldbacher, CSEL 57, pp. 349–52); Augustine, Ep. *20.8 (ed. Divjak, CSEL 88, pp. 98–9); Shaw, Sacred Violence, pp. 396–404.

[37] Becker, Outsiders, p. 153.

[38] Pelagius, De diuina lege 1.1 (ed. Migne, PL 30.105C), 'I would be trying to excuse my presumption if both the time and the cause, and at the same time love did not defend me, and if I were wanting to impart to your hearing now my own words rather than God's. On top of this is added the fact that my exhortation has good faith as a result of its simplicity'; 'Praesumptionem meam excusare conarer, si me non et tempus et causa, simulque tuerentur et charitas, et si nunc propria magis uerba quam diuina uellem tuis auribus intimare. Accedit insuper quod exhortatio nostra habet ex simplicitate fiduciam'. Pelagius did not perceive the rules he discussed to be his own, and he saw his activity as 'exhortation'.

and their only power lay in persuasion; hence their stress on the differing situation in the next life of the true Christian and the person who did not obey Scripture's injunctions. They preached and published, but it was all just paraenesis.

Controlling definitions

In the 5th century, Augustine cited Paul to argue that the purpose of heresy was the identification of the orthodox, and by implication the clarification of orthodoxy, which neatly placed the focus on the deviance and glossed over the process of conflict that produced the clarification.[39] Thus this 5th-century analysis suffers from the specific inadequacy that interactionist theory identifies—namely, that it omits from study the creators and enforcers of rules. The very search for a purpose for heresy serves to distract attention away from the process of rule creation. It suggests that heresy is and always has been objectively evil, and it hides the process of conflict through which orthodoxy was formulated, and thus suppresses notice of the opposing argument in the debate and acknowledgement of its potential validity. The rule-maker conflates his own activity with God's in order to cement the authority of the rules he creates. Thus Augustine characterised God's truth as objective fact that man discovered in, rather than constructed from, Scripture.[40]

This meta-issue of the process by which doctrine was created was recognised in the 5th century in the argument that arose about what was traditional and what was innovation in Christian dogma. In a great many of his works opposing 'Pelagianism', Augustine felt the need to argue that his views on this subject were traditional in Christian teaching, suggesting that he was aware of the critique of novelty levelled against him.[41] The argument that his own position represented tradition was the corollary of his presentation of 'Pelagianism' as a 'new heresy'.[42]

---

[39] Augustine, *De gratia Christi et de peccato originali* 2.22.25 (ed. Urba and Zycha, CSEL 42, p. 184), 'So that ... the uneducated may be instructed, and what the enemy plotted for the destruction of the Church may be turned to its benefit, in accord with the words of the Apostle: *It is necessary that there be heresies so that the tried and true persons in your midst may be revealed* [1 Cor. 11:19]'; 'Vt ... instruantur indocti atque ita in ecclesiae conuertatur utilitatem, quod est inimicus in perniciem machinatus iuxta illud Apostoli: *Oportet et haereses esse, ut probati manifesti fiant inter uos* [1 Cor. 11:19].'
[40] Augustine, *De natura et origine animae* 1.19.34 (ed. Urba and Zycha, CSEL 60, p. 334), 'If, however, they do not find the absolutely certain authority of God's words about this thing ...'; 'Si autem non inueniunt certissimam de hac re auctoritatem diuinorum eloquiorum ...'.
[41] Augustine, *De dono perseuerantiae* 19.48–50 (ed. Chéné and Pintard, BA 24, pp. 718–26); *De praedestinatione sanctorum* 14.27 (ed. Chéné and Pintard, BA 24, pp. 544–6).
[42] The link between these two things is clear in Augustine's argumentation: Augustine, *De nuptiis et concupiscentia* 2.12.25 (ed. Urba and Zycha, CSEL 42, p. 278), 'I did not invent original sin, which the catholic faith has believed in from long ago; but you who deny this are undoubtedly a new heretic'; 'Non ego finxi originale peccatum, quod catholica fides credit antiquitus; sed tu, qui hoc negas, sine dubio es nouus haereticus'; Augustine, *Contra Iulianum opus imperfectum* 1.9 (ed. Kalinka and Zelzer, CSEL 85/1, p. 10), 'The ancient catholic faith, that was preached by the most illustrious teachers who lived before us and which you have now begun to attack, shows that you are new heretics'; 'Nouos haereticos uos antiqua catholica fides, quam modo oppugnare coepistis, a praeclarissimis qui fuerunt ante nos doctoribus praedicata demonstrat.' Augustine insisted on the *newness* of the two doctrines of the goodness of human nature and effective free will: Augustine, *Sermo* 26.8 (ed. Lambot, CCSL 41,

Pelagius' opponents had to present 'Pelagianism' as novel doctrine in order to win the fight for possession of the label of tradition. It was key to their success in this that they should not be defined as the creators of new rules. Thus Augustine argued that original sin was part of traditional Church teaching.[43]

As well as both Pelagius and Caelestius raising the issue of what was traditional in Christian doctrine, in AD 434, Vincent of Lérins moved towards an attempt at meta-analysis in his essay attempting to establish a general rule by which orthodoxy might be judged. He went back to first principles concerning the identification of heretical ideas, and argued that the distinction between novelty and tradition offered the means to differentiate between heresy and orthodox doctrine, quoting both Pope Celestine and Pope Sixtus III in support of his argument.[44]

---

p. 352); *De nuptiis et concupiscentia* 1.20.22 (ed. Urba and Zycha, CSEL 42, p. 235); 1.35.40 (ed. Urba and Zycha, CSEL 42, p. 251); 2.2.3 (ed. Urba and Zycha, CSEL 42, p. 255); 2.33.55 (ed. Urba and Zycha, CSEL 42, p. 312); *De gratia Christi et de peccato originali* 2.13.14 (ed. Urba and Zycha, CSEL 42, p. 176); *Sermo* 348A/Dolbeau 30*.13 (3) (ed. Dolbeau, *Augustin et la prédication*, p. 265); *De dono perseuerantiae* 19.50 (ed. Chéné and Pintard, BA 24, p. 726); 23.63 (ed. Chéné and Pintard, BA 24, p. 750); 23.65 (ed. Chéné and Pintard, BA 24, p. 756); *Ep.* 193.1.1 (ed. Goldbacher, CSEL 57, p. 168); *Ep.* 214.3 (ed. Goldbacher, CSEL 57, p. 382); *Ep.* 215.1 (ed. Goldbacher, CSEL 57, p. 388); *Contra Iulianum* 3.1.4 (ed. Migne, PL 44.703); 6.8.22 (ed. Migne, PL 44.835); *Contra Iulianum opus imperfectum* 1.2 (ed. Kalinka and Zelzer, CSEL 85/1, p. 6); 1.6 (ed. Kalinka and Zelzer, CSEL 85/1, p. 9); 1.73 (ed. Kalinka and Zelzer, CSEL 85/1, p. 89); 1.95 (ed. Kalinka and Zelzer, CSEL 85/1, p. 110); 3.182 (ed. Kalinka and Zelzer, CSEL 85/1, p. 482); 4.50 (ed. Zelzer, CSEL 85/2, p. 56); 4.75 (ed. Zelzer, CSEL 85/2, p. 77); 4.134 (ed. Zelzer, CSEL 85/2, p. 161); 6.5 (ed. Zelzer, CSEL 85/2, p. 297). In his review of his own *De libero arbitrio* in his *Retractationes,* Augustine characterised the two doctrines defended by Pelagius as not yet existing when he wrote his own work concerning free will (but as discussed in this book they were in fact the norm in ascetic Christian discourse and it was Augustine's account of Christianity that developed and changed, as he himself said, while he was writing *Ad Simplicianum*): *Retractationes* 1.9.4 (ed. Mutzenbecher, CCSL 57, p. 26), 'Which we dealt with sufficiently in other short works of ours, refuting those enemies of this grace, the recent heretics; although in these books also, which were not at all written against them because they did not yet exist, but against the Manicheans'; 'Quod in aliis opusculis nostris satis egimus, istos inimicos huius gratiae nouos haereticos refellentes; quamuis et in his libris, qui non contra illos omnino, quippe illi nondum erant, sed contra Manicheos conscripti sunt'; *Retractationes* 2.33 (ed. Mutzenbecher, CCSL 57, pp. 116–17), 'A necessity also came about which forced me to write against the new Pelagian heresy .... They founded a new heresy'; 'Venit etiam necessitas quae me cogeret aduersus nouam Pelagianam heresim scribere .... Illi nouam haeresim condiderunt'; 1.10.2 (ed. Mutzenbecher, CCSL 57, p. 30); 2.22.2 (ed. Mutzenbecher, CCSL 57, p. 108); 2.36 (ed. Mutzenbecher, CCSL 57, p. 120). Norman Baynes noted the powerful authority of the past in the Hellenistic Age, and the effect of this legacy: N. H. Baynes, 'The Hellenistic Civilisation and East Rome', *Byzantine Studies and Other Essays* (London, 1955), p. 10; Alain Le Boulluec noted that a rhetorical contrast between orthodoxy characterised as ancient and heresy characterised as later and secondary had a long history in Christian writings: Le Boulluec, *La notion d'hérésie*, p. 548.

[43] Augustine, *De peccatorum meritis* 3.1.1–7.14 (ed. Urba and Zycha, CSEL 60, pp. 128–41).

[44] Vincent of Lérins, *Commonitorium* 32.4–5 (ed. Demeulenaere, CCSL 64, p. 193), 'But the holy Pope Celestine also wrote in the same manner and with the same opinion. In a letter which he addressed to the bishops of Gaul and in which he accused them of passive collaboration, because by their silence they were forsaking the old faith and permitting profane novelties to arise, he said: "Rightly we have to bear the responsibility if by our silence we encourage error. Therefore, let those of this kind be reproached. Let them not have free speech as they will". One may perhaps doubt who those might be whom he wishes to deprive of their free speech: whether they are the preachers of what is traditional,

Vincent suggested that doctrine should be judged according to the principles of 'universality, antiquity, and consent', and his formula was: 'What has been believed everywhere, always, and by all.'[45] Although he did not name Augustine, he criticised the idea of a special form of grace, and implicitly rejected the idea of predestination as preordainment; in this context he cited Celestine's condemnation of novelty in his *Apostolici uerba* of AD 431. For Vincent, novelty denoted the doctrines of prevenient grace and predestination interpreted as preordainment.[46] The anonymous author of *The Predestined* likewise argued that the process at work in the controversy was the introduction of new doctrine, and he described predestinarianism as a 'new invention'.[47]

---

or the inventors of novelties'; 'Sed et sanctus Papa Caelestinus pari modo eademque sententia. Ait enim in epistula quam Gallorum sacerdotibus misit, arguens eorum coniuentiam quod antiquam fidem silentio destituentes, "profanas nouitates" exsurgere paterentur: "Merito," inquit, "causa nos respicit, si silentio foueamus errorem. Ergo corripiantur huiusmodi; non sit his liberum habere pro uoluntate sermonem." Hic aliquis fortasse addubitet, quinam sint illi, quos habere prohibeat liberum pro uoluntate sermonem, uetustatis praedicatores an nouitatis adinuentores.'

[45] Vincent of Lérins, *Commonitorium* 2.5–6 (ed. Demeulenaere, CCSL 64, p. 149), 'Vniuersitas, antiquitas, consensio'; 'Quod ubique, quod semper, quod ab omnibus creditum est.'

[46] Vincent of Lérins, *Commonitorium* 26.6–9 (ed. Demeulenaere, CCSL 64, p. 185), 'But if you ask one of the heretics who is about to persuade you to such ideas: "What are the foundations of your ideas and teachings, according to which I have to give up the universal and traditional faith of the catholic Church?" he will immediately say: "*For it is written* [Matt. 4:6]". He will then present you with thousands of testimonies, examples and authorities – from the law, the Psalms, the Apostles, the Prophets – which in his new and wrong interpretation precipitate your unhappy soul from the catholic fortress into the abyss of heresy. Here are the promises by which the heretics usually mislead those who are wanting in foresight. They dare to promise in their teaching that in their Church – that is in their own small circle, is to be found a great and special and entirely personal form of divine grace; that it is divinely administered, without any labour, zeal, or effort on their part, to all persons belonging to their group, even if they do not ask or seek or knock. Thus borne up by angels' hands – that is, preserved by angelic protection, they can never *dash their foot against a stone* [Matt. 4:6, cf. Rom. 14:21], they can never be scandalized'; 'Ac si quis interroget quempiam haereticorum talia sibi persuadentem: "Vnde probas, unde doces quod ecclesiae catholicae uniuersalem et antiquam fidem dimittere debeam?" Statim ille: "*Scriptum est enim* [Matt. 4:6]". Et continuo mille testimonia, mille exempla, mille auctoritates parat, de lege, de Psalmis, de Apostolis, de Prophetis, quibus nouo et malo more interpretatis ex arce catholica in haereseos barathrum infelix anima praecipitetur. Iam uero illis, quae sequuntur, promissionibus miro modo incautos homines haeretici decipere consuerunt. Audent etenim polliceri et docere quod in ecclesia sua, id est, in communionis suae conuenticulo, magna et specialis ac plane personalis quaedam sit Dei gratia, adeo ut sine ullo labore, sine ullo studio, sine ulla industria, etiamsi nec petant nec quaerant nec pulsent, quicumque illi ad numerum suum pertinent, tamen ita diuinitus dispensentur, ut angelicis euecti manibus, id est, angelica protectione seruati, numquam possint *offendere ad lapidem pedem suum* [Matt. 4:6, cf. Rom. 14:21], id est, numquam scandalizari.' On almost every page of his text, Vincent condemned novelty and praised tradition. His formula of 'universality, antiquity, and consent' was, however, problematic given that Christian doctrine was constantly developing. He did allow for development but argued that it must come from within the core of Christianity, on the analogy of a body growing. His solution was to look at what had been agreed by church councils where large numbers of ecclesiastics had gathered. The threat came always from an individual teacher going his own way. Vincent's examples suggested a particular concern with Africa, and created a subtext which appears to aim its criticism at Augustine.

[47] Anon., *Praedestinatus* Preface 4 (ed. Gori, CCSL 25B, p. 10), 'Noua adinuentio'.

The problem with Vincent's rule was that the Bible offered a range of possible interpretations of many aspects of doctrine, and other Christian literature was equally a hat out of which many different positions could be pulled and brandished as authority, facts of which Vincent was well aware.[48] For his part, Augustine insisted that the meaning of Scripture was transparent and incontestable: 'We do not simply suppose that this is true on the basis of some human conjecture, but rather we discern that it is true by the absolutely clear authority of the divine Scriptures.'[49]

Controlling the grounds of the argument

Advocates of original sin sought to define the controversy as a choice between arrogance and humility, rather than between free will and the goodness of human nature on the one hand, and predestination interpreted as preordainment and original sin on the other. Characterising original sin as a traditional part of the furniture of Christian dogma, and thus beyond question, also removed it from the centre of the argument. To do this they characterised the argument for free will as an arrogant lack of humility before God and smeared Pelagius first with the suggestion that he denied grace and second by association with a selection of propositions with which he had no connection. The successful tactic was to centre the controversy on the denial of God's grace and on arrogance, rather than on original sin or effective free will. Discussion of grace itself and its many aspects was avoided through accusations of a blasphemous denial of God's grace, which supported the arrogance indictment. Through these tactics, Pelagius' opponents controlled the narrative.

'Pelagianism' was successfully characterised as a coherent programme, as newly emerged and as heresy, but this was the record written by those who were trying to get the ideas condemned. This message was relentlessly drummed home

---

[48] A fact addressed by Vincent of Lérins, *Commonitorium* 2.3–4 (ed. Demeulenaere, CCSL 64, pp. 148–9), 'Because of its very depth, holy Scripture is not universally accepted in one and the same sense, but the same text is interpreted differently by different people, so that almost as many opinions can seem to be elicited thence as there are men .... And so for this reason, because of such great distortions caused by such varied errors, it is very necessary that the line of prophetic and apostolic interpretation is laid out according to the rule of ecclesiastical and catholic meaning'; 'Scripturam sacram pro ipsa sui altitudine non uno eodemque sensu uniuersi accipiunt, sed eiusdem eloquia aliter atque aliter alius atque alius interpretatur, ut paene quot homines sunt, tot illinc sententiae erui posse uideantur .... Atque idcirco multum necesse est propter tantos tam uarii erroris anfractus, ut propheticae et apostolicae interpretationis linea secundum ecclesiastici et catholici sensus normam dirigatur.' On the belief held by some Christian writers active when Vincent was writing that there was just one correct interpretation of Scripture, see M. J. Pereira, 'Augustine, Pelagius, and the Southern Gallic Tradition', in *Grace for Grace. The Debates after Augustine and Pelagius*, ed. A. Y. Hwang, B. J. Matz and A. Cassiday (Washington, DC, 2014), pp. 181–2.

[49] Augustine, *Contra duas epistolas Pelagianorum* 1.20.38 (ed. Urba and Zych, CSEL 60, p. 454), 'Hoc uerum esse non coniectura suspicamur humana, sed euidentissima diuinarum scripturarum auctoritate dinoscimus.'

in Augustine's writings: he unremittingly referred to it as a 'new heresy'.[50] Reading Augustine, it is hard not to think in terms of 'Pelagianism'. The reader's mindset becomes locked into that model, which was the author's aim.

Political lobbying

Interactionist theory observes that there are always factions within a community and there is always a process of disagreement and manoevuring in the creation of rules. Lobbying of powerful individuals for support for their position by aspiring rule-creators in the controversy can therefore be understood as a recognised characteristic of the process of creating deviance. Power differentials determine who gets to make the rules. The support of patrician Romans and the Western emperor were critical factors in the achievement of Pelagius' condemnation, and evidence of lobbying to win either backing or at least non-participation in the conflict is visible in letters written by those who sought to bring about Pelagius' condemnation.[51] Influential supporters of asceticism who shared Pelagius' approach to Christianity were asked to withdraw their support from him. In this way, Pelagius was isolated from other members of the ascetic movement in Rome, who were at the same time made aware of the threat of an accusation of heresy against themselves if they continued to support him. For example, the priest Sixtus, later Pope Sixtus III, had to renounce his association with Pelagius publicly in Rome and sent the deacon, Leo (later Pope Leo I), with a private message to Augustine and Alypius to assure them of his recantation.[52]

As a description of the situation revealed in the textual evidence surviving from the years after AD 418, Becker's observations on the enforcement of rules are pertinent: 'The problem of rule enforcement becomes more complicated when the situation contains several competing groups. Accomodation and compromise are more difficult, because there are more interests to be served, and conflict is more likely to be open and unresolved. Under these circumstances, access to the channels of publicity becomes an important variable'.[53] The role of publicity in the controversy before AD 418 was crucial, and, with regard to the situation after AD 418, interactionism's analysis is an apt description of the pamphlet war visible in texts such as Cassian's *Thirteenth Conference*, Prosper of Aquitaine's *On Grace*

---

[50] See n. 42.

[51] For example, Augustine's letters to Sixtus: Augustine, *Ep.* 191 (ed. Goldbacher, CSEL 57, pp. 162–5); *Ep.* 194 (ed. Goldbacher, CSEL 57, pp. 176–214); his letter to Paulinus of Nola: Augustine, *Ep.* 186 (ed. Goldbacher, CSEL 57, pp. 45–80); his letter to Juliana Anicia, which also mentions an earlier letter he had sent her warning her against Pelagius: Augustine, *Ep.* 188 (ed. Goldbacher, CSEL 57, pp. 119–30). Pope Innocent I's letters preserved among the letters of Jerome show how lobbying letters had reached Innocent from both Jerome, and Eustochium and Paula, complaining that Jerome's monastery in Bethlehem had been attacked. Neither of their letters named the persons responsible: Innocent I, *apud* Jerome, *Ep.* 136 and *Ep.* 137 (ed. Hilberg, CSEL 56, pp. 263–5).

[52] Augustine, *Ep.* 191.1 (ed. Goldbacher, CSEL 57, pp. 163–4); *Ep.* 194.1.1 (ed. Goldbacher, CSEL 57, p. 176).

[53] Becker, *Outsiders*, p. 127.

and Free Will against the Conferencer, the anonymous *The Predestined* and the anonymous *Hypomnesticon*.

Mythical wrongdoers

Also of note in the context of the 5th-century controversy is the observation Becker made about mythical wrongdoers, and how a lack of detailed information (whether enforced or chosen) allows myths about deviance to flourish.[54] A rule-creator wanting to create a mythical deviant in order to secure conviction of an actual individual (essential to the process of creating a rule) might not want to have much information. The advantage to such a rule-creator would be that mythical constructs cannot defend themselves. The original convictions were a necessary part of the installation of the rules. Subsequently, the fact that the deviance was mythical meant that since no one actually was a 'Pelagian' according to the definition of 'Pelagianism' fabricated by its creators, there would never again need to be trials and convictions, but the ideas had been successfully stigmatised, defined as deviant and rendered incapable of ever being officially endorsed as orthodoxy.

Case studies of heresy accusations using the interactionist theoretical model

Sociological studies have explored the motives of rule-creators and how rule creation is a source of self-constructed authority. On this analysis, denouncers obtain authority through denouncing ceremonies, which degrade the status of the person labelled deviant. In addition, case studies of individual heresy accusations provide valuable comparanda.

Lloyd Pietersen argued that a text could perform the function of a status degradation ceremony by means of which previously respected members of a community were given master labels as deviants and were transformed into 'outsiders' from the community. His analysis of the polemic against heretics in the Pastoral Epistles was that through the degradation ceremony of the epistles, the heretics were assigned a master label as false teachers.[55] Pietersen's analysis points to one function of the writings against Pelagius produced by his opponents. Harold Garfinkel listed the elements of a denunciation ceremony, which included the fact that the denouncer had to highlight the core values of the audience and deliver the denunciation in the name of those core values. The denouncer had to be invested with the right to speak in the name of those core values and be seen as a supporter of them.[56] Authors of writings attacking Pelagius regularly laid claim to speaking

---

[54] Becker, *Outsiders*, p. 193.
[55] Pietersen, 'Despicable Deviants', pp. 346–50.
[56] H. Garfinkel, 'Conditions of Successful Degradation Ceremonies', *American Journal of Sociology* 61:5 (1956), pp. 420–4.

for the Church, and accused Pelagius of impiety and blasphemy.[57] The argument from tradition also fulfilled this feature of denunciation ceremonies: the claim to represent the Church and the argument for the traditional character of the doctrine advocated were often paired by the inventors of 'Pelagianism'.[58]

George Zito observed that the collective response invoked by the rule-creator was always proposed in the name of collective unity. He also noted that often the rule-creator inferred possible consequences of a statement, rather than adducing actual statements made by the accused. Thus the denouncer often inferred corollaries or consequences of a statement made by the denounced person, and the threat identified was often an implied threat rather than an actual one. Both of these observations hold true for attacks on Pelagius; entailments were read into his writings with hostile intent. Zito's analysis of opposition to Arianism proposed that although its concerns appeared to be purely metaphysical, in reality they were driven by considerations of power.[59] According to Zito, beneath the accusation of heresy: 'Lies that "will to power" by which groups seek to appropriate the world for their own purposes and gratification.'[60]

The Catholic modernist controversy

A case study that is particularly relevant to the myth of 'Pelagianism' is Lester Kurtz's examination of the modernist controversy in Roman Catholicism, that ran from the 1870s to the 1940s.[61] For Kurtz the heresy hunt was an anxiety-relieving ritual for institutional elites which facilitated their dominance within the institution. It relieved social and psychological tensions and focused anxiety on something that was controllable. It was also a source of strength because the heretic served as a symbolic focus, as the source of attacks by perceived subversive forces

---

[57] The claim to be speaking for the 'catholic' Church was pervasive. Some examples are: Augustine, *Ep.* 194.10.47 (ed. Goldbacher, CSEL 57, pp. 213–14); Jerome, *Ep.* 141 (ed. Hilberg, CSEL 56, pp. 290–1); Marius Mercator, *Commonitorium aduersum haeresim Pelagii et Caelestii* (ed. Schwartz, *ACO* 1.5.3, p. 7); Prosper, *Contra collatorem* 1.2 (ed. Migne, PL 51.216A–217B). Examples of the accusation of impiety or blasphemy are: Augustine, *Contra Iulianum opus imperfectum* 2.220 (ed. Kalinka and Zelzer, CSEL 85/1, p. 332); Jerome, *Dialogus aduersus pelagianos* 3.6 (ed. Moreschini, CCSL 80, p. 104); Prosper, *Contra collatorem* 3.1 (ed. Migne, PL 51.222A).

[58] Augustine, *Contra duas epistolas Pelagianorum* 1.23.41 (ed. Urba and Zycha, CSEL 60, p. 458), 'Just like other heretics, you also should be segregated from the Church of Christ, which has held this doctrine from of old'; 'De ecclesia Christi, quae hoc antiquitus tenet, oportet ut sicut alii heretici segregemini et uos.'

[59] G. Zito, 'Toward a Sociology of Heresy', *Sociological Analysis* 44 (1983), p. 127: 'By insisting that Jesus and God the father were of the same substance but somehow different from other men and women, the orthodox position was able to maintain a separation between man and God that assured a power position for the Roman elite. Friedrich Nietzsche (1949) would reassert the primitive Christian ideal some 1,600 years later: "Jesus said to his Jews, 'The Law? The Law was made for slaves. What do we sons of God have to do with the Law?'" The hidden implication in the Arian heresy is that sons of God, like God himself, cannot be bound by laws and therefore do not require any mediating structure (such as the Church) between themselves and God.'

[60] Zito, 'Toward a Sociology of Heresy', p. 130.

[61] L. Kurtz, 'The Politics of Heresy', *American Journal of Sociology* 88 (1983), pp. 1085–1115.

responsible for the Church's problems. For Kurtz, heresy was always socially constructed and the labelling of heresy was tied to self-interest and group interest; it was a matter of 'status politics'. Using Max Weber's model of 'elective affinities', he argued that identifying the motives of the rule-creators was essential in order to understand the nature of heresy. He also noted that periods of social conflict intensified the phenomenon of heresy accusation.[62] In Kurtz's analysis the parties define their religion in ways that serve their respective interests, and then give to their definitions 'an aura of objective truth and universality.'[63] Those in power: 'Begin to attach their interests to certain definitions of orthodoxy and become convinced that the belief system itself would be endangered if their definitions of orthodoxy were challenged.'[64] For Kurtz, in the modernist controversy what caused the identification of heresy was not an opposition between science and religion but the fact that the ecclesiastical hierarchy identified its interest with opposition to science. This triggered the identification of heresy. For Kurtz the modernist controversy was not about two different methods of seeking truth: 'The issue of modernism was, fundamentally, a conflict between ecclesiastical authority and the authority of scholars.'[65] Kurtz's analysis was that a struggle for authority lay at the core of every heresy accusation.[66]

Applied to the controversy about original sin, prevenient grace, and predestination interpreted as preordainment, this interpretative model suggests a new way of understanding the process of formation of Christian doctrine at this time. According to this view, Augustine was reacting to an educated elite lay and monastic interpretation of Scripture that adhered to ascetic principles and was independent of ecclesiastical authority. In his *Life of Antony*, Athanasius worked hard to prevent a lack of respect for ecclesiastical authority. This suggests that Athanasius the bishop was trying to forestall the danger inherent in the ascetic way of life that he was canvassing, which was that ultimately it might have no need of the Church. Each individual ascetic was making his own progress towards God and had his own relationship with Christ. As long as there were within the ascetic community those who could deliver the sacraments, the ascetic might have no need of a mediator between himself and God. Although Athanasius was careful to have Antony defer to ecclesiastics, there was almost no mention of Church sacraments in the text. Augustine's reasons for objecting to the torrent of independent interpretation of Scripture circulating in influential patrician circles may have been both personal and ecclesiastical in terms of his own status, both as an interpreter of Scripture and as a bishop. The writings produced by the ascetic movement were a

---

[62] Kurtz, 'The Politics of Heresy', p. 1095, 'The way in which belief systems are formulated and articulated is largely shaped and influenced not only by their actual content but also by the interests of the groups adhering to them, particularly in times of social conflict.'

[63] Kurtz, 'The Politics of Heresy', p. 1096.

[64] Kurtz, 'The Politics of Heresy', p. 1098.

[65] Kurtz, 'The Politics of Heresy', p. 1098.

[66] Kurtz, 'The Politics of Heresy', pp. 1102–3, 'The question of authority, as in all cases of heresy, was in the final analysis at the core of the controversy.'

threat to his own status as an elite interpreter of the Word of God, and he identified his own interpretation with defence of the Church. Ascetic propagandists aimed to illuminate the path to heaven and claimed both to show Christians the way to perfect imitation of Christ's way of life and to embody this way of life. If authority was seen to derive from advanced virtue on the apostolic model, bishops might be unable to lay claim to such virtue, so there was a potential for conflict over the authority conferred by perceived virtue.

In his analysis of the modernist controversy, Kurtz highlighted how there was no organised movement of modernists; there were a few relatively isolated scholars. These individuals only became more organised after the persecution instigated by the heresy hunt began. Furthermore, there were divergent approaches among the identified modernists, but they were bundled together into one movement by the anti-modernists, and divergent views were systematised into one alleged unified programme of belief.[67] Kurtz described the resulting alleged heresy as a 'caricature' of the modernist movement.[68] Through a series of publications, the anti-modernists constructed an image of the modernist movement as a heretical conspiracy, and a root cause of the conspiracy was said to be pride.[69] Kurtz also noted how the modernist controversy pushed both sides towards polarised positions. Finally, he highlighted how once the mechanism of control was set in motion, there was no room for compromise. Applied to the early 5th century, this might suggest that after the Council of Carthage in AD 411, which condemned Caelestius, Augustine and the African bishops were locked into a process that disincentivised compromise. The tactics of the anti-modernist campaign described by Kurtz were identical to those used against Pelagius. It is as if in their own heresy hunt the anti-modernists used a playbook drawn from the strategy that secured condemnation of Pelagius.

In the 5th century the contested definitions, in the form of the triune of doctrines of original sin, prevenient grace, and predestination interpreted as preordainment, were not installed as orthodoxy with equal degrees of success: original sin was installed as dogma, prevenient grace was partially installed, and the word 'predestination' largely fell out of use. The caricature of Pelagius' teaching, however, was a definition that was installed successfully. A fundamental of orthodox Christianity after AD 418 was that the caricature of Pelagius' teaching that had been created was fact. To differentiate themselves from the bad thing that was this arrogant, deceitful self-sufficiency, and so to avoid the label of heresy themselves, ecclesiastics had to pay lip service to condemnation of the caricature 'Pelagianism'. There was, however, a continuous fight back in the 5th century asserting alternative definitions, conducted through the pamphlet war already mentioned. A feature of a number of such texts is that their authors remained anonymous, suggesting anxiety about engaging openly in the struggle.

---

[67]   Kurtz, 'The Politics of Heresy', pp. 1104–8.
[68]   Kurtz, 'The Politics of Heresy', p. 1094.
[69]   Kurtz, 'The Politics of Heresy', p. 1104.

*Conclusion on the relevance of interactionist theory for the study
of Pelagius*

Labelling theory is now used principally by criminologists, but interactionist
theory is relevant to the study of heresy, offering a useful model, comparable
examples and a technical vocabulary to describe the process involved in the
identification and condemnation of heretics. On the interactionist interpretative
model, the creation of the myth of 'Pelagianism' was part of a conflict over definitions. 'Pelagianism' was invented in order to delegitimise consensus principles
concerning the anthropology and soteriology of Christianity by bringing those
ideas into disrepute. Interactionist theory views Augustine as a moral entrepreneur.
His sermons and other published writing attacking 'Pelagianism' were propaganda
aimed at achieving a status degradation ceremony which culminated in Honorius'
rescript condemning Pelagius and Zosimus' Papal letter of excommunication. This
process can best be understood as a power struggle between adherents of different
approaches to Christian anthropology and soteriology. Status and authority were
at issue, and they drove the heresy accusation.

Broad comparative studies of heresy

In 1934, Walter Bauer began the process of mapping how power determined the
content of orthodox dogma in Christianity.[70] John Henderson's 1998 survey of the
construction of orthodoxy and heresy in neo-Confucianism, Islam, Judaism and
early Christianity demonstrated the value of comparative data.[71] The weight of the
evidence he presented for the development of a body of belief through rejection
of heresy and the gradual narrowing and increased precision of the concept of
orthodoxy was conclusive; it was the demonstrable pattern of the 'dynamic character of orthodoxy' repeated across several religions that had evidential force.[72]
Henderson pointed out that timing appeared to have played a part in determining
which doctrines won out in Christianity, as well as the construction of authority,
particularly by the See of Rome.[73] An important conclusion he reached was that
heresies were often conservative positions unable to move with doctrine as it
developed and changed. A pattern Henderson identified that is pertinent to the
labelling of Pelagius as a heretic was that: 'Part of the genius of neo-orthodoxy, if

---

[70] W. Bauer, *Orthodoxy and Heresy in Earliest Christianity*, ed. and trans. R. A. Kraft and G. Krodel
(Philadelphia, PA, 1971), pp. 95–240. Two different responses to Bauer's thesis (among many) are
Le Boulluec, *La notion d'hérésie*, pp. 547–55; and R. Williams, 'Does It Make Sense to Speak of
pre-Nicene Orthodoxy?', in *The Making of Orthodoxy*, ed. R. Williams (Cambridge, 1989). See also
Iricinschi and Zellentin, 'Making Selves and Marking Others'.
[71] J. B. Henderson, *The Construction of Orthodoxy and Heresy: Neo-Confucian, Islamic, Jewish, and
Early Christian Patterns* (Albany, NY, 1998).
[72] Henderson, *The Construction of Orthodoxy*, p. 39.
[73] Henderson, *The Construction of Orthodoxy*, pp. 42–6.

not its main polemical strategy, is to conceal its newness.' This explained why the changing nature of orthodoxy: 'Often passes unnoticed'.[74]

Means II

Why did the myth gain traction?

Several factors contributed to the successful installation of the myth, notably the political and ecclesiastical context in the first half of the 5th century.

Context 1: a crisis for Christianity

The years after AD 410 were a time of perceived danger for Christianity because of the pagan accusation that the adoption of Christianity as the official religion of the empire caused the disaster of the sack of Rome. This event and its implications defined the terms of Christian discourse for years afterwards. Christians saw the danger to Christianity posed by the accusation that the abandonment of the old gods had led to the sack of Rome.[75] The letters of Ambrose of Milan and Symmachus setting out their arguments concerning the Altar of Victory in the Senate had been composed only thirty-six years before.[76] A rumour blamed the Anicii, the wealthiest Christian patricians in Rome, for the sack of the city, suggesting a backlash against Christians.[77] Markus pointed out that the concept of *tempora christiana*, according to which God's purpose was fulfilled through the Roman Empire, proclaimed by Christian commentators following Theodosius I's legislation making Christianity the empire's official religion, had to be abandoned so that the fall of the empire would not pull Christianity down with it.[78] Augustine's principal reason for writing *City of God* was to uncouple the destiny

---

[74] Henderson, *The Construction of Orthodoxy*, p. 39.

[75] Augustine, *De ciuitate Dei* 1.30–6 (ed. Dombart and Kalb, CCSL 47, pp. 30–4); Anon., *Honorificentiae tuae* 1.7 (ed. Hamman, PLS 1.1690), 'You will quote to me that popular saying: "Then the whole world is perishing". Whether the whole world merits perdition or not, why is it wonderful that that which has happened once should happen again? .... But I would not have you embrace that wicked and blasphemous solution invented by certain heathens, that God cares not for his own'; 'Dices mihi illam uulgi sententiam: "Ergo totus mundus perit." Si non totus perditionis merito continetur, aut si totus, quid mirum si quod iam factus est, fiat? .... Illam uero impiam et sacrilegam definitionem nec suspicari te cupio, qua paganorum quidam dicunt curam Deo non esse de suis.'

[76] Ambrose, *Epp.* 72 and 73 (ed. Zelzer, CSEL 82/3, pp. 11–53); Symmachus, *Relatio* 3 (ed. Seeck, MGH, Auctores Antiquissimi t. 6, pp. 280–3).

[77] Procopius, *De bello Vandalico* 1.2.27 (ed. Haury and Wirth, p. 315); R. W. Mathisen, '*Roma a Gothis Alarico duce capta est*. Ancient Accounts of the Sack of Rome in 410 CE', in *The Sack of Rome in 410 AD. The Event, Its Context and Its Impact. Proceedings of a Conference Held at the German Archaeological Institute at Rome, 04–06 November 2010*, ed. J. Lipps, C. Machado and P. von Rummel, Palilia 28 (Wiesbaden, 2013), p. 96.

[78] Markus, *Saeculum*, pp. 44–7.

of Christianity from the destiny of the Roman Empire. He reversed the previous Christian narrative enshrined in *tempora christiana* triumphalism by asserting that in fact no city or empire on earth could be integral to God's plan for mankind.

Part of the motivation for accepting the condemnation of 'Pelagianism' may have been the danger to Christianity posed by the disintegration of the Western Empire. In this political context, anxiety about hubris may have contributed to deference to the caricature; after AD 410, confidence was not an idea that would have resonated with Christian Romans.[79] It is possible that Pelagius was used as a scapegoat for the arrogance inherent in the idea of *tempora christiana*; the genuine arrogance of the *tempora christiana* triumphalism was transferred onto Pelagius and ritually expelled from Christianity. Markus suggested that Augustine began to retreat from triumphalism after about AD 405, and abandoned it completely after the sack of Rome in AD 410.[80] The western Emperor Honorius may also have been looking for a scapegoat. Manifestly unfitted to the demands of his position in the circumstances, the characterisation of humanity as weak, sinful and not in control of events had the advantage for Honorius of ensuring that he could evade blame for the disasters taking place. In these ways, therefore, the political and military context are part of the explanation of how the myth of 'Pelagianism' gained traction and was installed successfully. The myth was advantageous to several parties as a scapegoat by which to visibly and ritually expel arrogance, and may have satisfied a need felt by some people after the sack of Rome. By expelling 'Pelagianism', confidence, newly perceived as arrogance, was itself being symbolically expelled. The classical model underpinning this fear was hubris, the rule that when humans thought themselves self-sufficient, the gods would punish them.[81]

Markus noted the link that Augustine asserted between Donatism and 'Pelagianism'. Augustine compared the way both asserted that the Church should be: *Without spot or wrinkle* [Eph. 5:27].[82] He characterised Pelagius' teaching as

---

[79] Some ascetic texts suggested confidence. For example, Anon., *De castitate* 17.11 (ed. Hamman, PLS 1.1504), 'The chaste and temperate man carries the infinite assurance of his conscience, and defended by the authority of his chastity, he does everything without fear. In prayer he speaks as if present with our Lord, no rather, like a friend speaks to a friend, as Scripture says: *But I have called you friends* [John 15:15]'; 'Pudicus et abstinens infinitam conscientiae fiduciam gerit, et pudicitiae auctoritate defensus cuncta intrepidus exercet. In oratione quasi praesens cum Domino, immo quasi amicus cum amico loquitur, scriptura dicente: *Vos autem dixi amicos* [John 15:15]'. It was a misreading of the 'widow's prayer' in *De uita christiana* to suggest that it showed arrogance, since the author was making the point that the sinner could not pray with a clear conscience and so his prayers were unlikely to be heard, but the sentiment is similar in both passages, and the word *fiducia* in *De castitate* is paralleled by *fidus* in *De uita christiana*; Anon., *De uita christiana* 11.2 (ed. Migne, PL 50.396C), 'That man ought to have a good conscience and be sure and confident in his innocence, who holds out his hands to God'; 'Bene sibi ille conscius esse debet et certus, et suae innocentiae fidus, qui ad Deum manus extendit'.

[80] R. A. Markus, '"*Tempora Christiana*" Revisited', in *Augustine and his Critics*, ed. R. Dodaro and G. Lawless (London, 2000), p. 205; *Saeculum*, pp. 45–71.

[81] I take the Latin equivalents of hubris to be *elatio, superbia* and *arrogantia*.

[82] Markus, *The End*, pp. 51–2; Augustine, *De gestis Pelagii* 12.27–8 (ed. Urba and Zycha, CSEL 42, pp. 80–2).

being just as divisive as Donatism in its insistence on virtue. This too may have influenced Christians to accept the view that 'Pelagianism' posed a similar threat to the unity of the Church. In fact, Pelagius did not say that the Church was without spot or wrinkle, but that this was what God desired and should be the aim.[83] If an entailment was read into this paraenesis in a hostile manner, this had the potential to exclude average Christians, as Peter Brown suggested, by setting the bar for entrance into the Church at a high level.[84] In Brown's interpretation, one aspect of what was being fought over in the controversy was the choice between an inclusive interpretation of Christianity in which Christians were not required to meet exacting standards, and an exclusive interpretation of Christianity in which only those who exerted a great deal of effort could be Christians. Those who accepted the definitions proposed by Pelagius' opponents might have been alarmed by the divisive potential of the mythical movement.

Context 2: political crisis

On the basis of this analysis, some scholars have labelled Pelagius elitist, arguing that his paraenesis was designed for an aristocratic audience with the purpose of maintaining their position of social superiority.[85] That is indeed the characterisation of 'Pelagianism' promulgated in Honorius' rescript of AD 418, condemning Pelagius and Caelestius.[86] The author of the rescript named only the denial of original sin as a doctrinal fault in Pelagius and Caelestius, and suggested that they advocated an intellectual snobbery that despised what was common and, by implication, the commons: 'Having been entrusted to the wind of a new intellect, it reckons it a clear sign of common cheapness to think as everyone does, and reckons it the palm of singular wisdom to destroy what has been communally agreed.'[87] At a time of political crisis the 'Pelagianism' crafted by Pelagius' opponents was a discrete and divisive movement.

---

[83] Pelagius, *Ad Demetriadem* 24 (ed. Greshake, p. 146), concerning Christ's wish for the Church: 'Since he has made his universal Church to be *without spot or wrinkle* [Eph. 5:27], purified by washing with the water of salvation, he desires her to become more beautiful day by day, so that once cleansed of vices and sins, she may be forever adorned with the splendour of virtues'; 'Cum uniuersam Ecclesiam salutaris aquae lauacro purificatam *sine macula rugaque* [Eph. 5:27] reddiderit, quotidie cupit eam fieri pulchriorem, ut semel uitiis peccatisque mundata, semper ornetur decore uirtutum.'

[84] Brown, 'Pelagius', pp. 112–14.

[85] J.-M. Salamito, *Les virtuoses et la multitude: aspects sociaux de la controverse entre Augustin et les pélagiens* (Grenoble, 2005), passim. For example, pp. 103–4, references to 'the aristocratic character of pelagianism' (*la caractère aristocratique du pélagianisme*), 'this religious élitism' (*cet élitisme religieux*), and 'an élitist vision of Christianity' (*une vision élitiste du christianisme*); Kessler characterised Pelagius as addressing *der Oberschicht* (*the upper classes*): *Reichtumskritik*, p. 11.

[86] On the idea of 'popular belief' as a rhetorical tool with which to delegitimise an opponent, see É. Rebillard, '*Dogma Populare*. Popular Belief in the Controversy between Augustine and Julian of Eclanum', in Rebillard's *Transformations of Religious Practices in Late Antiquity* (Farnham, 2013), p. 211.

[87] Honorius, *Constitutio prima Honorii* (ed. Migne, PL 48.380A–381A), 'Dum noui acuminis commendata uento, insignem notam plebeiae aestimat uilitatis sentire cum cunctis, ac prudentiae singularis palmam communiter approbata destruere'.

This interpretation of the controversy is, however, based on Augustine's characterisation of Pelagius' teaching, and the controversy could be interpreted differently. The characterisation of Pelagius as an exclusivist intellectual snob in Honorius' rescript seems likely to have been a statement of the opposite of the truth.[88] Because Pelagius argued against the existence of any status other than a spiritual one, he may have offered encouragement to those not from the patrician class, and this argumentation may have been perceived as a threat to the social order.[89] The characterisation communicated in the rescript was aimed at neutralising support for Pelagius. The condemnation of Pelagius suppressed the ambitious desire to bring the Christian message to everyone. In a sense, his condemnation therefore consigned the mass of Christians to secondary status, and represented a failure of ambition: the members of the 'mass condemned to hell' (*massa damnata*) were abandoned to their fate.

Augustine himself wrote that as he developed his views he came to elucidate more clearly the logical conclusion of his understanding of prevenient grace, which was predestination as preordainment.[90] This account of predestination created an interpretation of Christianity that postponed exclusivity to the next life, because although sinners and virtuous alike could be members of the Church on earth, in the afterlife only a preordained group of unknown membership would reach salvation. Later objectors to the doctrine of predestination as preordainment centred their objection to it on the need to maintain the universality of God's salvific will in the Christian message. The fact that no one was excluded from God's salvific will and Christ's redemption of humanity was the cornerstone of Faustus of Riez's argument, and he explicitly contrasted his own inclusive account of Christ's

---

[88] Proof that Pelagius dismissed earthly wealth and status is offered by the fact that Jerome was forced to reverse his earlier position and argue for markers of social status, such as rich clothing, of which he had previously been a leading critic: Jerome, *Dialogus aduersus Pelagianos* 1.30 (ed. Moreschini, CCSL 80, pp. 38–9), 'Why, I ask you, is it repugnant to God if I have an elegant tunic, if the bishop, the priest, and the rest of the ecclesiastical order proceed to the performance of their sacrifices robed in white vestments? Clerics, beware; monks, beware; widows and virgins you are courting disaster, unless the public see you looking filthy and dressed in rags! I say nothing of the men of the world, on whom war is openly declared, and who are declared repugnant to God if they wear costly and elegant dress'; 'Quae sunt, rogo, inimicitiae contra Deum, si tunicam habuero mundiorem, si episcopus, presbyter, diaconus et reliquus ordo ecclesiasticus in administratione sacrificiorum candida ueste processerint? Cauete clerici, cauete monachi; uiduae et uirgines periclitamini, nisi sordidas uos atque pannosas uulgus aspexerit. Taceo de hominibus saeculi, quibus aperte bellum indicitur et inimicitiae contra Deum, si pretiosis atque nitentibus utantur exuuiis.' Cf. Jerome's earlier condemnation of fine dress, such as his recommendation to Rufinus, *Ep.* 125.7 (ed. Hilberg, CSEL 56, p. 124), 'Let your garments be squalid to show that your mind is white, your tunic cheap to prove that you despise the world'; 'Sordes uestium candidae mentis indicio sint, uilis tunica contemptum saeculi probet'; or his praise of Pammachius, Paula, and Eustochium for avoiding fine clothing: Jerome, *Ep.* 66.6 (ed. Hilberg, CSEL 54, p. 654), concerning Pammachius, 'That he should walk among the purple-clad senators clothed in black, gloomy garments'; 'Inter purpuras senatorum furua tunica pullatus incederet'; 13 (ed. Hilberg, CSEL 54, p. 664), concerning Paula and Eustochium, 'Now wearing soiled and gloomy clothes'; 'Nunc sordidatae et lugubres'.

[89] Pelagius, *Ad Celantiam* 21 (ed. Hilberg, CSEL 56, p. 347).

[90] Augustine, *De praedestinatione sanctorum* 3.7–4.8 (ed. Chéné and Pintard, BA 24, pp. 478–88).

salvific purpose with the exclusivity of predestinarianism.[91] The bigger picture is important here; these tensions were inherent within Christian Scripture. This was a systemic clash, not a matter of individuals.

So historical circumstance contributed to the success of the installation of the myth of 'Pelagianism'. Peter Brown argued that the effect of 'Pelagianism' within Christianity was potentially divisive. He pointed out that after AD 410 there was an urgent need for unity in Rome and in the Church as a whole.[92] The possibility that 'Pelagianism' was a fiction in a discourse of heresy that deliberately generated division was not something Brown considered. This historical context privileged unity over perceived disunity, making free debate less attractive.[93] Julian of Aeclanum sought discussion of the issues in a synod, but this request was rejected by Pope Boniface. The specific political circumstances of the barbarian invasion of Italy and the disintegration of the Western Empire may have changed perceptions and prioritised unity, and thus the political context was unfavourable to free debate about core principles.

Context 3: ecclesiastical politics

Ecclesiastical politics also contributed to the myth gaining currency. The North African Church was distinctive for its large number of bishops, and as bishop of Carthage, Cyprian had developed the use of councils in order to govern the sprawling ecclesiastical hierarchy in his region.[94] During his disagreement with Pope Stephen in the 250s AD, Cyprian articulated an argument for episcopal autonomy that rejected the authority of the Bishop of Rome. With this tradition in mind, it is possible that the need felt by some African bishops to assert the authority of the decisions reached in African councils became part of the motivation for obtaining a condemnation of Pelagius that would ratify their decisions as authoritative. In this way, political considerations entered into decisions about the formation of Christian doctrine, and a struggle for authority determined outcomes.

---

[91] Faustus, *De gratia* 1.3 (ed. Engelbrecht, CSEL 21, p. 14), 'We confess that the benefits of grace are extended to the whole human race'; 'In totum genus humanum gratiae beneficia fatemur extendi'; 1.9 (ed. Engelbrecht, CSEL 21, p. 30), 'Righteousness is therefore not a gift given individually, but a universal and public gift of God'; 'Iustitia ergo in homine non personale, sed generale et publicum Dei munus est'; 1.9 (ed. Engelbrecht, CSEL 21, p. 31), 'In the same way the helping hand of protection and assistance is not denied to anyone'; 'Ita omnibus praesidii et adiutorii dextera non negatur'; 1.16 (ed. Engelbrecht, CSEL 21, p. 49), 'But the same Apostle declares that Christ came for all universally .... We bear witness that our Lord the redeemer came bringing the assistance of universal mercy'; 'Pro uniuersis autem uenisse Christum idem Apostolus declarat .... Dominum redemptorem cum generalis misericordiae beneficio uenisse testamur'. *Generalis* and *uniuersalis* were words Faustus continually repeated.

[92] Brown, 'Pelagius', pp. 98–113. Brown's analysis was that the inherently centrifugal forces of a competitive elite were replaced by the centripetal force exerted by this need for unity and reconstruction.

[93] A fact that might support this suggestion is that there was civil disorder in Rome concerning the appointment of the next Pope after Zosimus' death in December of AD 418.

[94] K. Pennington, 'The Growth of Church Law', in *Cambridge History of Christianity II: Constantine to c. 600*, ed. A. Casiday and F. W. Norris (Cambridge, 2007), p. 389.

During the period when the African bishops rejected Pope Zosimus' decisions and requested that he should instead endorse the canons of their councils, Zosimus sought to assert the authority of the See of Rome over the African Church in another decision. This might suggest that he saw that papal authority was being tested. He upheld an appeal made to him by the African priest Apiarius in AD 417–18, which sought to set aside a decision made by an African council, and sent representatives to Carthage to investigate the case.[95] Zosimus tried to reject African conciliar decisions and interventions directed towards himself concerning Pelagius, and perhaps sought to assert papal primacy in relation to Apiarius' appeal in order to bolster the authority of his decision regarding Pelagius.[96]

Caroline Humfress has shown how the official legal post of *defensor ecclesiae* ('advocate for the Church') was created in AD 407 at the request of North African bishops, in the context of the legal cases held before imperial magistrates to settle the dispute between the Donatists and the catholics in North Africa. She detailed the number of forensic lawyers appointed as bishops by both sides. This legal expertise gave the African Church a distinctive character; it made it an efficient lobbying organisation, and may have helped to shape its legalistic approach to the enforcement of orthodoxy and the authority of its conciliar canons.[97]

Conclusion

The establishment of motive and means for the creation of the myth is an important element in the case for the non-existence of 'Pelagianism'. The motive for the invention of 'Pelagianism' was that some Christians wanted to expel the principles of the goodness of human nature and effective free will from official Christian orthodoxy and install other ideas in their place. The notion of 'Pelagianism' was designed to conceal the fact that this was the process that occurred; that what had been for Christians traditional, often unquestioned, ideas were chased out and replaced under threat of an accusation of heresy. An essential part of the expulsion process was the creation of a label for the ideas being expelled. To achieve this uprooting of longstanding assumptions it was necessary to characterise these views as novel and immoral. This was difficult with regard to the goodness of human nature and effective free will, which were ideas that were deeply entrenched in Greco-Roman culture, so supporters of the triune assembled a set of theses that could be condemned easily and labelled these with Pelagius' name,

---

[95] Pennington, 'The Growth of Church Law', p. 393; Shaw, *Sacred Violence*, pp. 404–7.

[96] Zosimus, *Epp.* 2, 3, and 12 (ed. Günther, CSEL 35/1, pp. 99–108, and pp. 11–17).

[97] C. Humfress, 'A New Legal Cosmos: Late Roman Lawyers and the Early Medieval Church', in *Late Antiquity. A Guide to the Postclassical World*, ed. G. W. Bowersock, P. Brown and O. Grabar (Cambridge, MA, 1999), pp. 561–73. For discussion of prosecution for wrong belief under Roman law in the post-Constantinian period, see C. Humfress, 'Roman Law. Forensic Argument and the Formation of Christian Orthodoxy (III–VI Centuries)', in *Orthodoxie Christianisme Histoire*, ed. S. Elm, É. Rebillard and A. Romano (Rome, 2000), pp. 125–47; and C. Humfress, 'Citizens and Heretics. Late Roman Lawyers on Christian Heresy', in *Heresy and Identity in Late Antiquity*, ed. E. Iricinschi and H. M. Zellentin (Tübingen, 2008), pp. 128–42.

because heresies had to have the name of an author attached, and Pelagius was an able writer and had raised objections to the triune. For these reasons, Pelagius was the target chosen as the straw man; and also because others were too embedded in the senatorial aristocracy and could not be isolated, such as Sixtus, Honoratus and Sulpicius Severus. Thus far motive.

The important contribution that interactionist theory makes to study of the concept of 'Pelagianism' is that it insists on scrutinising the role of moral entrepreneurs in the creation of deviance. Interactionism asserts that in every case deviance is created through a process of conflict. In addition to offering theoretical insights, interactionist theory always presupposed its practical application; it expressed criticism of many aspects of the labelling process, and sought to drive out damaging language that codified definitions which served the interests of those with power.

An interactionist analysis of the controversy might lead us to see it as an instance of the perennial conflict over the power to control, between ascetic Christians seeking imitation of Christ's way of life as near perfect as they could achieve in a situation of autonomy, and bishops wanting to extend their control over all Christians. The controversy would therefore be viewed as another battle for authority. Rather than characterising it, as Peter Brown did, as a clash between a perfectionist exclusive brand of Christianity and a moderate inclusive brand, in fact the motivation of the two sides would be, respectively, an individualistic desire for autonomy based on a person's own relationship with God, versus an episcopacy keen to maintain control over congregations through control of access to salvation, motivated by a desire for authority and power. If humans were weak-willed and unable to achieve imitation of Christ then they would need mediators to manage their relationship with God. Ascetics posed a potential challenge to episcopal authority because of their independent relationship with God, which gave them spiritual autonomy, and which might not require mediation.

What proponents of original sin, prevenient grace, and predestination interpreted as preordainment could not do was identify accurately the views to which they were opposed; they had to attack theses that could garner universal condemnation, to narrow their target to focus on one person, and to characterise that individual as un-Christian and immoral. They had to change the definitions accepted by powerful people. Interactionist analyses show that the means by which they invented 'Pelagianism' are universal to all heresy accusations. The reasons why the fiction gained credibility were specific to the 5th century and the situation in the Western Empire.

But the origin of belief in man's innate goodness and his free will in relation to salvation is not dateable to the 5th century, nor locateable to one milieu or one person. Such a view of man can be found in the Bible and also transcends the Bible. These ideas cannot be referred to using the term 'Pelagianism' because this implies a genesis for them in a specific time, milieu and person. Pelagius was not the author within Christianity of the ideas of the goodness of human nature and effective free will; he was not the author of this anthropology or this account of Christian salvation.

Because the toxic myth of 'Pelagianism' was successfully installed into dogma, the real issues at stake were not discussed openly. Ironically, whereas the mythical caricature 'Pelagianism' was successfully installed as fact, the doctrines whose installation the myth was intended to secure were not installed with equal success. One part of the rule-creation process was achieved fully—the control of definitions with regard to deviance. However, another part, the enforcement of the rules, was not fully pushed through because of continued reservations about the rules, the impossibility of enforcement, and the lack of an unequivocal formula for orthodoxy on the matter published by the highest ecclesiastical authorities (be it a papal decretal or a formula agreed at an ecumenical council).

'Pelagianism' was a myth deliberately created to camouflage the installation of the triune into Christian teaching and to establish it as orthodoxy. Only a major shock such as the barbarian invasions, the sack of Rome and the disintegration of the Western Empire made possible the seismic cultural shift represented by the installation of the ideas of original sin, prevenient grace, and predestination interpreted as preordainment as official orthodoxy. Their acceptance as official orthodoxy was facilitated by a catastrophic loss of confidence, and it rendered that loss of confidence chronic.

7

The Manuscript Evidence and its Implications

On the Christian Life is a piece of Latin ascetic paraenesis written before AD 415, when it was quoted at the synod of Diospolis by Pelagius' accusers as an example of his writing.[1] This suggests that they perceived it to be typical of Pelagius' approach to Christianity. According to Yves-Marie Duval, more than 320 manuscript copies of *On the Christian Life* survive, making it the second most copied work of the medieval period after biblical and liturgical texts, and Augustine's *City of God*.[2] In manuscripts the text travels pseudonymously, mostly under an attribution to Augustine. How could it happen that a work condemned by Augustine as an example of what he called the 'Pelagian' heresy could be the second most copied

---

[1] Augustine, *De gestis Pelagii* 6.16 (ed. Urba and Zycha, CSEL 42, p. 68). I do not believe that Pelagius wrote the text that commonly travels under the title *On the Christian Life* in manuscripts (incipit: *Ut ego peccator*), for the following reasons. First, it contains a somewhat emotive digression, arguably not entirely focused on the argument at hand (ch. 3.2–3); this does not seem to me to reflect Pelagius' practice in *Letter to Celantia*, *On Virginity*, *On the Divine Law* or *Letter to Demetrias*, all of which are tightly argued. Second, the author's advice lacked coherence, because he addressed his letter to a widow living in a secular, apparently urban, situation, but as the work progresses, for the reader it becomes clear that the asceticism propounded by him would only be possible in complete withdrawal from a secular social environment. Third, while I acknowledge Robert Evans' case, my view is that there were many men enthused by ascetic Christianity who expressed their enthusiasm in writing, and *On the Christian Life* could have been written by Caelestius, Fastidius, Sixtus, Agricola or some other writer whose name does not survive. Fourth, from Augustine's report of the Synod of Diospolis it appears that in front of a synod of bishops Pelagius said that he did not write it. Likewise Jerome also wrote that Pelagius denied being its author: Jerome, *Dialogus aduersus Pelagianos* 3.16 (ed. Moreschini, CSEL 80, p. 120). Fifth, *On the Christian Life* does not to my mind display the same tone of confident mastery of his subject as the four letters that can be attributed to Pelagius securely. I acknowledge that these reasons are subjective. *On the Christian Life* clearly shares ideas with Pelagius' letters. For the argument for Pelagius' authorship, see Evans, *Four Letters* and R. F. Evans, 'Pelagius' Veracity at the Synod of Diospolis', in *Studies in Medieval Culture*, ed. J. Sommerfeldt (Kalamazoo, MI, 1964), pp. 21–30.

[2] Y.-M. Duval, 'Sur quelques manuscrits du *De uita christiana* portant le nom de Pélage', *Latomus* 64 (2005), p. 132, n. 1.

work of patristic literature during the Middle Ages, and travel under the name of the person primarily responsible for Pelagius' excommunication as a heretic?

The scale of the transmission of Pelagius' writings raises questions about the official narrative concerning Pelagius. This chapter explores the questions posed by the large scale of the manuscript tradition of his works. As has been seen, Pelagius' writings were not the only texts in circulation that took the goodness of human nature and effective free will to be integral to the Christian faith. Consideration of the manuscript transmission of all the texts that did this would be too large a subject for the present argument. Discussion will therefore be restricted to consideration of the manuscript transmission of Pelagius' writings plus *On the Christian Life*, because these texts illustrate the point at hand.

The manuscript evidence: Scale of transmission

False attributions have led to miscataloguing in the past, with the result that numbers of manuscript copies of Pelagius' works increase as more copies are discovered, and all figures offered here are provisional and provide guides rather than definitive totals. Pelagius was only rediscovered as an author in the first decades of the 20th century, enabling cataloguers thenceforward to attribute texts to him. Catalogues created before this time misattribute his works, including, for example, catalogues for municipal libraries in France that date from the 19th century, and the catalogues of British manuscript collections created by Montague Rhodes James from the early 20th century. Unless such older catalogues list the first lines of the texts in a manuscript, the only way to differentiate between, for example, Jerome's letter to Demetrias and Pelagius', is to look at the manuscript itself.

Pelagius' works travelled predominantly under attributions to Jerome and Augustine, so the two main reference works for locating manuscript copies of Pelagius' writings are Bernard Lambert's *Bibliotheca Hieronymiana Manuscripta* and the Austrian Academy's *Die handschriftliche Überlieferung der Werke des heiligen Augustinus* (usually abbreviated to *HÜWA*). Adding to the provisional character of any numbers is the fact that the volume of *HÜWA* covering manuscript holdings in France has not yet been published. Finally, the digitisation of manuscripts is enabling ongoing identification of previously undiscovered copies of Pelagius' works.[3]

---

[3] All figures given here for numbers of surviving manuscript copies are drawn from these two reference works and exclude manuscripts containing excerpts from a text. Because the volumes for France in the *HÜWA* series have not yet been published, all the figures quoted here will increase when these volumes appear. The figure for Pelagius' *Letter to Demetrias* uses these reference works but also includes the manuscript witnesses not listed in these reference works which I have found, plus an additional witness noted by Gisbert Greshake. There is no doubt that more manuscript copies of Pelagius' works survive but are not currently identified because they have been catalogued under erroneous attributions.

Notwithstanding the limitations of some catalogues, the evidence of surviving manuscripts suggests that Pelagius' writings were staples of medieval monastic book collections. Together, Lambert's *Bibliotheca Hieronymiana* and *HÜWA* list 115 copies of Pelagius' *Letter to Demetrias*, one more was noted by Greshake, and I have located a further sixteen, making 132 so far identified. Some 148 copies of Jerome's letter to Demetrias survive. As it stands, Pelagius' *Statement of Faith* survives in more than 200 copies, and it contains at its end an explicit endorsement of the principle of free will. His *Letter to Celantia* survives in 86 copies, his *On Virginity* in 85, and his *On the Divine Law* in 25.[4] Comparanda are Augustine's *City of God* with 365 surviving manuscript witnesses, his *Confessions* with 251 and his *On Christian Discipline* with 282. Augustine's *On the Gift of Perseverance* comes in at 74 copies.

*The significance of the scale of the manuscript tradition of Pelagius'
works*

In the 17th century, the Jesuit scholar Jean Garnier noted with surprise the number of manuscript copies of Pelagius' *Statement of Faith* that survived, and he queried how this could have happened:

> It is amazing that for so many centuries the eyes of almost all men were so captivated, that they were not able to see sufficiently, or rather did not want to see, however much Augustine was accustomed to warn, that this statement of faith was either written by a heretic, or was at least deservedly suspect. It is to the particular credit of our age, that we do not rashly play with goods of this kind: although we ought to take care lest prudence, which flees the folly of credulity, should fall into an intolerant lust for passing judgement, and the virtual tyranny of proscribing books just because they might not be pleasing.[5]

Garnier side-stepped giving a direct answer to the possible implications of this scale of transmission. He had studied what he knew as the 'Pelagian heresy' in depth, writing seven dissertations about it. His comment suggests that he felt that there was a tension between the official account of doctrinal history, on the one hand, and, on the other, the scale of the survival of manuscripts containing what he described as heretical 'Pelagian' material.

---

[4] As explained in the introduction, I have not included Pelagius' *Commentary on the Pauline Epistles* in this study because the text in Souter's edition is uncertain. However, for information, it survives in at least thirteen manuscript copies plus fragments of two further witnesses, and in several recensions; excerpts from it appear in compilation commentaries as well as marginal glosses in copies of the Pauline Epistles: Souter, *Pelagius's Expositions*, pp. 201–343; pp. 61–3.

[5] Garnier, *Dissertatio 5, De libellos fidei scriptis ab auctoribus et praecipuis defensoribus haeresis pelagianae* (ed. Migne, PL 48.497A–B), 'Mirum tot saeculis captos fuisse ita omnium fere hominum oculos, ut uidere satis non potuerint, aut noluerint potius, quantumcumque moneret Augustinus, hanc fidei expositionem, uel ab haeretico factam, uel saltem merito suspectam. Nostrae aetatis laus quaedam est, eaque praecipua, non temere illudi eiusmodi mercibus: quamquam cauere oportet ne prudentia, quae credulitatis intemperiem effugit, incidat in intolerabilem iudicii ferendi libidinem, ac pene proscribendi libros, si modo non placeant, tyrannidem.'

The significance of the afterlife of Pelagius' writings in relation to the concept of 'Pelagianism' is best explained by analogy with a ship in a storm. The large scale of the manuscript tradition of his works is like a ship at sea holding its position just off some rocks, despite a gale blowing it towards the rocks. Someone on the shore might infer the presence of a cable to the seabed holding the ship in place without being able to see it, but only by examining the cable under the water would it be possible to see how the boat was staying put and avoiding shipwreck. Examination of the cable would provide primary evidence of how the ship was keeping clear of the rocks. In this analogy, the ship holding its position represents the scale of copying of Pelagius' writings throughout the Middle Ages. The large scale of the manuscript tradition of his works is analogous to the fact of the ship holding its position; the five strands of argument presented in Chapters 1–6 are the cable holding the ship in place. The arguments in the cable prove that 'Pelagianism' never existed. The fact that it did not exist then helps to explain aspects of the manuscript tradition. It is one factor, perhaps the most important, among many that contributed to the scale of transmission of Pelagius' writings.

Other factors also contributed to the scale of transmission, including rote-copying of letter collections; the difficulty of telling apart the opposing positions in the controversy given the proliferation of confusing language and the complexity of the issues; the difficulty in enforcing doctrinal orthodoxy in the early medieval period due to constraints on communication in fractured and shifting political conditions; the usefulness of Pelagius' letters for the Western monastic movement because of their promotion of ascetic values; the fact that, during the Renaissance, Jerome became the poster boy for humanism, and, since several of Pelagius' works travelled under Jerome's name, the large number of 15th-century witnesses of Pelagius' letters may say little about the reception of Pelagius and more about individuals wanting to associate themselves with humanism; the usefulness of Pelagius' writings as models of good Latin; and the strength and duration of opposition to the doctrines of prevenient grace and predestination interpreted as preordainment, including the view that the relationship between grace and free will was not an issue that threatened the Church.[6]

---

[6] Evidence of opposition is provided by Pope Boniface II's letter of AD 531 to Caesarius of Arles in which he replied to Caesarius' query about what to do about bishops who held that the beginning of faith derived from effective free will: *Concilium Arausicanum, Ep. Bonifatii II*, ll. 13–16 (ed. De Clercq, CCSL 148A, p. 66), 'For you indicate that several bishops of the Gauls, although they already concede that other good things originate from the grace of God, want just the faith by which we believe in Christ to be a matter of nature, not of grace; and they want it to be conferred on men descended of Adam (which it is an abomination to say), that they have remained in a state of free will, and that not even now is faith conferred on individuals by the generosity of divine mercy'; 'Indicas enim, quod aliqui episcopi Galliarum, cum cetera iam bona ex Dei acquieuerint gratia prouenire, fidem tantum, qua in Christo credimus, naturae esse uelint, non gratiae; et hominibus ex Adam, quod dici nefas est, in libero arbitrio remansisse, non etiam nunc in singulis misericordiae diuinae largitate conferri'. A century earlier Prosper of Aquitaine reported to Augustine that some Gallic ecclesiastics did not think the issue was vital for the Christian faith: Prosper, *apud* Augustine *Ep.* 225.8 (ed. Goldbacher, CSEL 57, p. 466), 'Many people do not think that the Christian faith is injured by this difference of opinion'; 'Plerique non putant Christianam fidem hac dissensione uiolari'.

The numbers of manuscript copies, therefore, do not provide straightforward evidence about the reception of Pelagius. It is other evidence in manuscripts that may have more profound implications and may lead towards further areas of study; the manuscript evidence points towards lines of enquiry. Rather than the scale of transmission, it is textual evidence that leads to the conclusion that Pelagius' writings have been misclassified. They have been classified as 'Pelagian', but that category never actually existed as a differentiable grouping. The scale of copying, therefore, does not prove that 'Pelagianism' did not exist. It is other features of the manuscript evidence that can only fully be explained by this fact; they offer supporting evidence. They suggest that the direction of causal entailment runs in one direction: the fact that 'Pelagianism' did not exist is one of the reasons why many copies of Pelagius' works were made. Readers could not see the difference between Pelagius' writings and the mass of other ascetic writings because there was no difference. His letters travelled under the name of Jerome because Pelagius said the same things as Jerome did. His works travelled freely because he expressed the same ideas as Athanasius of Alexandria, Evagrius of Antioch and many other writers of Christian ascetic literature whose works were likewise staples of monastic book collections.

So the scale of copying revealed in the manuscript evidence has restricted primary evidential value for the argument that 'Pelagianism' was a deliberately invented fiction. The scale of manuscript transmission is not, in fact, the real story; it is simply an effect of the real story, which is that 'Pelagianism' was a fiction. The status of the manuscript evidence is therefore subsidiary to this argument, and it is not presented here as a strand in the cable of argumentation to show that 'Pelagianism' was a myth. Instead it is presented as supporting circumstantial evidence. However, the scale of transmission of Pelagius' writings remains an unarguable fact that disproves any suggestion that his teaching was expelled from Christianity. It calls into question the concept of 'Pelagianism' with its penumbra of associated myths.

Put simply, it is not the manuscript transmission that proves that 'Pelagianism' is a myth; it is the fact that 'Pelagianism' is a myth that explains the manuscript transmission.

The manuscript evidence: Marginalia

Marginalia—that is, comments written in the margins of manuscript copies of Pelagius' works—as well as the absence of such marginal comment, are an aspect of manuscript transmission that offers evidence about the reception of Pelagius. Overall, the most striking aspect of the manuscript transmission of his writings is that where there was no identification by an external authority of a text as having been written by Pelagius, no one noticed that it was heterodox. This suggests that of itself the internal content of Pelagius' works did not prompt comment. The situation of Pelagius' *Letter to Demetrias* was unusual because from the 5th century onwards several external authorities identified it as by Pelagius, and their number only increased as the information was passed on by later commentators and marginal annotators, with Bede playing an important role in disseminating the view that it was composed by Julian of Aeclanum.[7] Marginal warnings beside copies of Pelagius' *Letter to Demetrias* are often derivative, repeating the wording of Bede's warning or of earlier annotators. By contrast, Pelagius' *Letter to Celantia*, *On Virginity* and *On the Divine Law* travelled without comment. It is noteworthy that two great editors of Jerome's letters, Guiges, fifth prior of Grand Chartreuse in the 12th century, and the Veronan scholar Domenico Vallarsi in the 18th century, both saw nothing 'Pelagian' in *Letter to Celantia*. Vallarsi quoted Guiges on the letter and acknowledged that, as Guiges had argued, it was not by Jerome.[8] He mentioned that Erasmus had attributed *Letter to Celantia* to Paulinus of Nola, but that a recent editor of Paulinus' works had rejected that suggestion on stylistic grounds. Vallarsi himself suggested that it was composed by Sulpicius Severus, and he gave his reasons:

> The elegance and gravitas of that author and of our author seem to be the same; the way they use the Scriptures is even the same, as far as we have been able to understand from a comparison of some of their citations; they are clearly of the same mind.[9]

On the Christian Life attracted only a handful of marginal comments, and these were based on the fact that external authorities identified Pelagius as its author.[10] Had there not been this external identification, it would perhaps have travelled as Augustine entirely unnoticed for 1500 years, just as the three letters by Pelagius already discussed travelled as Jerome.

Thus there appear to be two distinct types of transmission context for Pelagius' writings. The first is where an external authority has identified the work as so-called

---

[7] The following writers quoted from the letter and identified it as written by Pelagius or as 'Pelagian': in the 5th century Augustine and Orosius; in the 8th century Bede (who concluded that it had been composed by Julian of Aeclanum); in the 12th century William of Malmesbury and Guiges, fifth prior of Grand Chartreuse; and in the 14th century Giovanni d'Andrea and Henry of Kirkstede. Bede did not cite Augustine or Orosius on the letter, but instead mentioned Jerome's *Dialogue against the Pelagians* in relation to it. It is unclear whether Bede derived his view of the letter from reading Augustine or Orosius quoting it. He made his attribution in the Preface to his *Commentary on the Song of Songs* and through the dissemination of this work his attribution of the letter to Julian reached the Anglo-Saxon mission fields on the Continent, where it was influential and appears in the earliest surviving copy of Pelagius' *Letter to Demetrias*: Karlsruhe, Badische Landesbibliothek, Aug. Perg. 105, s. viii–ix, f. 15r, where some words in the original rubric have been palimpsested and the words 'Iuliani heretici … male sentiens de libero arbitrio' ('by Julian the heretic … thinking badly about free will') have been written over some of the original title. The manuscript is available to view online via the e-codices website.

[8] Vallarsi placed Pelagius' *Letter to Celantia* at the end of his first volume containing Jerome's genuine letters, under the title *Falsely Attributed (Falso adscriptae)*, but he did not relegate it to the *False writings (Scripta supposititia)* in volume 11 of his edition of Jerome's collected works, where he put Pelagius' *Letter to Demetrias*: D. Vallarsi, ed., *Sancti Eusebii Hieronymi Stridonensis presbyteri, Opera omnia*, 11 vols (Verona, 1734–42).

[9] Vallarsi, *Sancti Eusebii*, vol. 1, col. 1089–90, note *a*: 'Eadem isti atque auctori nostro scribendi elegantia et grauitas uidetur esse: eadem etiam Scripturarum expressio, quantum e locorum collatione aliquot potuimus intelligere: ingenium plane idem.'

[10] Duval, 'Sur quelques manuscrits', pp. 137–52.

'Pelagian'; the second is where no external authority has identified the work as 'Pelagian'. Rather than straight numbers of surviving copies, a more striking implication of the manuscript transmission of Pelagius' works is that without an external authority that asserted that they were heretical, no one noticed that they were heterodox.

The conclusion to be drawn from this must be that when Pelagius' writings were read without preconceived ideas associating them with his name and the label of heresy attached to it, they were seen simply as examples of late antique ascetic literature. Vallarsi's assessment in relation to Sulpicius Severus, expressed in the phrase 'clearly of the same mind' (*ingenium plane idem*), supports this conclusion.

Revealing marginalia

Evidence that some readers could not see a doctrinal difference between Pelagius' *Letter to Demetrias* and Jerome's is visible in a marginal comment in London, British Library, Royal 6.D.i. This is a 12th-century copy of a Jerome letter collection in which the two letters to Demetrias by Pelagius and Jerome travel side by side, with Pelagius' first. It is clear that this marginal comment was copied along with the main text from the exemplar because it has been misplaced and copied alongside the previous letter in the collection, *To the Virgins of Aemona*. It says:

> Read Augustine's letter to Demetrias' mother Juliana, and you will observe that this letter to Demetrias and the one that follows are not by Jerome, but by Pelagius. Which fact both the style and the faith of the author clearly show.[11]

Whoever composed this comment could see no doctrinal difference between Pelagius' letter to Demetrias and Jerome's. He thought both were suspect judged according to Augustine's critique in his letter to Juliana. This supports the evidence presented in Chapter 3 showing that Jerome consistently explicitly asserted the two principles that Pelagius defended: the goodness of human nature and effective free will.

---

[11] London, British Library, Royal 6.D.i, s. xii, f. 137r, marginal annotation: 'Lege epistolam Augustini ad Iulianam matrem Demetriadis, et animaduertes hanc epistolam ad Demetriadem et subsequentem non esse Ieronimi, sed Pelagii. Quod et stilus et fides auctoris apertius ostendunt.' How the misplacement of this annotation came about is explained by looking at other witnesses and the shift from a two-column format to a single-column format. The normal order in this particular Hieronymian letter collection is for *To the Virgins of Aemona* to be followed by the two letters to Demetrias, with Pelagius' first. Since Jerome's *To the Virgins of Aemona* is a very short work, it filled only the left-hand column of f. 98v of, for example, Hereford, Cathedral Library, P.VIII.5, s. xii, and in this manuscript, Pelagius' letter began at the top of the right-hand column on the same page. In a witness laid out like the Hereford copy in a two-column format, the most convenient space for a marginal comment is on the left hand-side of the page, alongside *To the Virgins of Aemona*. A similar positioning in an exemplar with a two-column format may explain the misplacement of the marginal warning in London, British Library, Royal 6.D.i, a manuscript written in single-column format in which the marginal comment was retained alongside *To the Virgins of Aemona*.

The bind

Evidence in marginalia suggests that as a result of the condemnation of the mythical construct 'Pelagianism', Christians in the West were trapped in a bind, boxed in by the installation of the caricature of 'Pelagianism' as orthodoxy. Some Christians wanted to endorse effective free will and man's innate goodness, but they could not be seen to approve of Pelagius' writings. The arguments presented in Pelagius' *Letter to Demetrias* could not be upheld as correct once they had been identified as having been written by Pelagius. So these Christians worked out flawed fixes in which they posited contradictory theses simultaneously, because it was unacceptable to say that Pelagius was right. Christians of this way of thinking therefore defended erroneous attributions because they needed to maintain that the letter was written by Jerome, an author not smeared with the label of 'Pelagianism', endorsement of whom did not court a charge of heresy.

This bind is visible in manuscript marginalia such as the one in Paris, Bibliothèque Nationale, Lat. 1885, s. xii. This manuscript contains a Hieronymian letter collection. Pelagius' *Letter to Demetrias* is attributed to Jerome in the rubric above the text. There is a marginal comment alongside the main text, but it is not possible to say whether the comment was written at the same time as the main text was transcribed. The script in the annotation can be dated to the 12th or 13th century. It reads:

> Note: this letter is said by many not to be by Jerome, but by someone else who was a Pelagian, in so far as it asserts too much the good of human nature and free will. But it certainly does not detract from the grace of God in any way. Consequently whoever wrote it, I know this one thing: when it is understood in a catholic way and examined faithfully, it will bring you great edification. That it should be by Jerome, its ardent discourse persuades me. For both the style and the flavour resemble the author.[12]

This annotator clearly knew the theological grounds for criticism of Pelagius' letter, which he said was because its argument for the goodness of human nature and effective free will was too strong. Nevertheless, he wanted to retain the letter as orthodox and put the onus on the reader to read it 'in a catholic way' (*catholice*) and 'faithfully' (*fideliter*). This supports the view that the caricature of Pelagius' teaching disseminated by his opponents was the product of drawing unwarranted inferences from his writings with hostile intent, and then asserting that these were doctrines in his writings, when in reality they were not there. An example of this process is inferring from the statement that Christians should aim for perfect imitation of Christ the statement that man can be perfect in this life, and then attributing

---

[12] Paris, Bibliothèque Nationale, Lat. 1885, s. xii, f. 103r, marginal annotation: 'Nota: a plerisque dicitur haec epistola non esse Ieronimi sed alicuius pelagianiste. Eo quod nimis bonum naturae et liberum praedicet arbitrium. Sed certe gratiae dei in nullo detrahit. Cuiuscumque ergo sit, unum hoc scio, catholice intellecta et fideliter disputata magnam tibi afferet edificationem. Vt sit Ieronimi suadet mihi concio uiua. Nam satis auctorem sapit et stilus atque saliua.'

this doctrine to Pelagius' writings and stigmatising him for arrogance on the basis of it. It is also clear how much this annotator wanted the letter to be by Jerome through his statement that the 'style and flavour' of the letter were Jerome's. The style certainly was not, but the annotator's perception was that the two letters had the same 'flavour' (*saliua*). This annotation therefore also supports the evidence set out in Chapter 3, which shows that Jerome had previously propounded all the teachings that Pelagius proposed. This annotator was forced to maintain the untruth that this letter was by Jerome in order to retain it as orthodox. He could not afford to be associated with the toxic brand Pelagius. The condemnation of a caricature of Pelagius' teaching in AD 418 stigmatised the two doctrines 'the good of human nature and free will' as evil. So it was not respectable to profess these two positions, or to say that this letter was good teaching once it was identified as by Pelagius.

Further evidence suggesting that Christians in the West were left in a bind by the installation of the myth of 'Pelagianism' is visible in a 13th-century Italian manuscript, Firenze, Biblioteca Medicea Laurenziana, San Croce Plut.15. Dex.13. This is another Hieronymian letter collection and contains both Pelagius' *Statement of Faith* and his *Letter to Demetrias*. It is arranged for glossing in that it has two columns on the outer edge of each folio. The inner of the two notes the content of the main text in detail, while the outer makes more general summaries of the argument. These glosses were written at the same time as the main text. For Pelagius' *Statement of Faith*, the heresies refuted in turn by him are listed in the inner column. At the point where Pelagius declared his belief in free will 'in such a way that we always have need of God's grace', the note in the inner column reads: 'Against Pelagius' (*Contra Pelagium*). The note in the outer column reads: 'Concerning the praising of free will.' Another longer note in the outside column reads: 'This is the faith of Jerome. Which the Church in no respect differs from.'[13] So the annotator was saying that this statement of faith was by Jerome, and that it refuted Pelagius; and that Pelagius' statement was the Church's position.

Taken on their own, these comments alongside Pelagius' *Statement of Faith* might suggest simply that this annotator was confused about what consti-tuted orthodoxy with regard to free will, or that his understanding of Pelagius' teaching was based on the caricature 'Pelagianism'. They would nevertheless again support, as the Paris and London annotations did, the evidence set out in Chapter 3, showing how Jerome propounded effective free will throughout his career. However, the same manuscript also contains a copy of Pelagius' *Letter to Demetrias*, accompanied by marginal comments written in the same hand as those alongside his *Statement of Faith*. The running notes in the margin next to *Letter to Demetrias* say what the subject of each section is, or give an overview of the argu-ment made, except for one. At the point where Pelagius tells Demetrias that no one

---

[13] Firenze, Biblioteca Medicea Laurenziana, San Croce Plut.15.Dex.13, s. xiii, f. 98r, marginal anno-tations: 'De libero arbitrio praedicatione'; 'Haec est fides quam tenuit Hieronymus. Quam in nullo ecclesia uariat.'

can achieve virtue for her, only she can do it and it does not come from anyone else (which was the sentence to which Augustine objected most in the letter because it made no mention of God's prevenient grace as the cause of Demetrias' goodness), a longer comment has been written at the base of the page in the same hand as the other annotations. It reads:

> *You have* both here and below: *But no one can bestow spiritual riches on you except you yourself,* and so on. *Which cannot exist unless they come from you.* In a letter to Juliana, mother of Demetrias, Augustine refutes these words, as they are understood that she was called in this way, such that free will can be sufficient in the same way that God's grace is sufficient. But it is not true that Jerome said those words to mean this, but rather he was intending to distinguish between natural or temporal goods and spiritual goods; saying that the first indeed is to be accounted as if to our effort, but the second cannot be obtained without our zeal and effort co-operating, unless it is understood to be given by the grace of God. Whence perhaps, although incautiously, these words were said; nevertheless it is clear from these and other places that Jerome has not differed from Augustine.[14]

Bearing in mind that in his *Letter to Demetrias* Pelagius' statement of the argument for the goodness of human nature and effective free will was comprehensive and clear, several things follow from this. If the annotator had read Augustine's letter to Juliana, then he knew that the author of the letter was Pelagius and not Jerome, but he still said that the author was Jerome.[15] This annotator wanted to retain the arguments set out by Pelagius as acceptable. Using a distinction between 'natural or temporal goods' and 'spiritual goods' (*bona naturalia uel temporalia* and *bona spiritualia*), developed long after the 5th-century controversy, he worked hard to interpret the letter in such a way that it was not condemned as heresy and did not conflict with Augustine. This marginal comment cannot be put down to confusion, and it suggests that the earlier comments alongside Pelagius' *Statement of Faith* should not be viewed as the products of confusion either. Together they show that Christians in the West were caught in a bind by the mythical 'Pelagianism' and the toxicity it attached to Pelagius' name.

Further evidence of this predicament comes in a long note, written in the 14th century, appended to a 12th-century Hieronymian letter collection in a manuscript in Oxford. Its author complained about the deliberate attribution of Pelagius' *Letter to Demetrias* to Jerome by those who wanted to retain the letter as orthodox.[16] By

---

[14] Firenze, Biblioteca Medicea Laurenziana, Ms San Croce Plut.15.Dex.13, s. xiii, f. 181v, marginal annotation: '*Habes* et hic et infra: *spirituales uero diuitias nullus tibi praeter te conferre poterit*, et infra. *Quae nisi ex te esse non possunt.* Haec uerba Augustinus epistola ad Iulianam matrem Demetriadis ut datur intelligi quod sic fuit uocata redarguit tamquam sicut gratia Dei sufficere liberum arbitrium possit. Sed non uere Ieronimus ad hoc uerba ista dixisse sed potius quod intendebat distinguere inter bona naturalia seu temporalia, et bona spiritualia. Prima etiam sicut nostro exercitio dari dicens; secunda uero non posse sine nostro studio et exercitio optineri cooperante nisi ut datur intelligi gratia dei. Vnde forte licet incaute dicta sunt. Patet tamen ex hiis et ex aliis locis Ieronimus non discordasse ab Augustino.'

[15] Augustine, *Ep.* 188 (ed. Goldbacher, CSEL 57, pp. 119–30).

[16] Anon., *Note* [on the authorship of Pelagius' *Ad Demetriadem*], Oxford, Bodleian Library, Ms Bodl. 365, f. 340r/v: 'Certain advocates of Pelagius do not cease from presenting many and indeed clear

the 14th century, confidence was acceptable again, and in Oxford a generation of scholars who took inspiration from William of Ockham began to endorse a more positive anthropology, together with some form of effective free will. It seems probable that it was in this context that scholars cited Pelagius' letter as a patristic authority in order to support their arguments. In Oxford, Thomas Bradwardine reacted against these lecturers.[17] But across Europe the mood music had changed and in Italy Giovanni Pico della Mirandola was able to find an audience for his confident praise of human nature.[18]

Marginalia cannot constitute proof that 'Pelagianism' was a myth. Instead they show that something is wrong; they point to problems with the paradigm. They lead the reader to consider the lack of differentiability in Pelagius' writings from other ascetic literature, and to return to the history of ascetic literature to compare his writings with ascetic paraenesis already in circulation when he began to write. They prompt reconsideration of first principles, and lead to a reconsideration of the basic building blocks of the concept of 'Pelagianism', such as definition and classification. Ultimately, they lead to asking whether the question of the anthropology and soteriology of Western Christianity was ever resolved definitively.

Conclusion

There are five strands in the case for the mythical character of what was called 'Pelagianism'. The first is the evidence that the ideas attributed to 'Pelagianism' by Pelagius' opponents were not in Pelagius' writings. The second strand is the fact that Pelagius did not write anything new. The third strand in the cable of evidence is the fact that there was no discrete, differentiable programme or movement that constituted 'Pelagianism'; there was simply the ascetic movement which inspired many writers. The fourth strand in the case for the non-existence of 'Pelagianism'

---

words from the letter, as they say, of the blessed Jerome to Demetrias concerning the institution of virginity, by adducing it against the help of grace and on behalf of the sufficiency of free will for any virtuous works. But these people, as they seem, neglecting the writings of the Fathers on this matter, embrace more fondly a Pelagian text than one by Augustine, a heretical text more fondly than a catholic one'; 'Quidam Pelagii aduocati non desinunt oblatere multa quidem et manifesta uerba epistulae, sicut dicunt, beati Ieronimi ad Demetriadem de institucione uirginis allegando contra adiutorium gratiae et pro sufficentia liberi arbitrii ad opera quaelibet uirtuosa. Sed hii, ut uiderentur, negligentes in hac perte [for *parte*] scripta maiorum, scripturam Pelagianam quam Augustinianam, scripturam hereticam quam catholicam, carius amplectuntur.'

[17] Bradwardine, *De causa Dei contra Pelagium*. For Bradwardine's dispute with *modern Pelagians* (*Pelagiani moderni*), see G. Leff, *Bradwardinė and the Pelagians*, Cambridge Studies in Medieval Life and Thought 5 (Cambridge, 1957), pp. 127–264; J.-F. Genest, *Prédétermination et liberté Créée à Oxford au XIVe siècle: Buckingham contre Bradwardine*, Études de Philosophie Médiévale 70 (Paris, 1992), pp. 17–116; H. A. Oberman, *Archbishop Thomas Bradwardine. A Fourteenth Century Augustinian. A Study of His Theology in Its Historical Context* (Utrecht, 1957), pp. 28–48. Gordon Leff and Jean-François Genest both suggested that the scholars at Oxford whom Bradwardine saw as defending Pelagius' ideas included Robert Holcot, Adam of Woodham and Thomas Buckingham: Leff, *Bradwardine*, pp. 138–9; Genest, *Prédétermination*, p. 18.

[18] Pico della Mirandola, *Oration on the Dignity of Man* (*De hominis dignitate*) 1–8 (ed. Borghesi, Papio, and Riva, pp. 108–12).

lies in the conceptual incoherence of 'Pelagianism'; there are no criteria by which a text can be classified as 'Pelagian' rather than 'ascetic'. The fifth and final strand of evidence lies in the identification of motive and means, which support the argument that 'Pelagianism' was a deliberately invented fiction.

One of these strands, namely the proof that everything Pelagius taught had already been advertised in Christian literature for at least thirty years before he began to write, explains the manuscript transmission of Pelagius' writings. This earlier literature was never labelled heretical and continued in wide circulation. Doctrinally, Pelagius' writings did not differ from these works. His ascetic paraenesis was the same as Athanasius', Evagrius of Antioch's, Jerome's and much other ascetic literature. This fact is one facet of the truth that 'Pelagianism' did not exist, and it helps to account for the magnitude of the manuscript tradition of Pelagius' works. It is the primary cause of the scale of transmission of his writings.

Even with the many factors that contributed to its scale, the manuscript transmission of Pelagius' works poses the question that troubled Garnier about how supposedly heretical material could have circulated so widely. The answer lies in the two transmission contexts. If there was no external authority that quoted from a text and named Pelagius as its author, the internal content of his writings did not attract attention.

Marginalia offer corroborative evidence to suggest, first, that Pelagius' writings were not differentiable from Jerome's; second, that 'Pelagianism' was a caricature of Pelagius' teaching and his writings were unrecognisable as the fiction described by his opponents; and, third, that the myth of 'Pelagianism' put Western Christians in a bind because the toxicity of Pelagius' name, created by the myth, meant it was impossible to endorse him or ideas in texts associated with him.

Further myths

The scale of copying of Pelagius' works falsifies three further myths concerning Pelagius: first, the myth that his teaching was outside mainstream Christian belief; second, that it was dangerous to the Christian faith; and, third, that the issue of the relationship between grace and free will was ever resolved. The large number of other texts in circulation asserting the position that Pelagius defended, besides his own writings, lends further support to the case against these myths.[19]

It is clear that the manuscript tradition of Pelagius' writings invalidates the official narrative suggesting that his teaching was expelled from Christianity in AD 418. On the second myth, that Pelagius' writings were dangerous to Christianity,

---

[19] Such works include, for example, a great deal of Jerome's exegesis and many of his letters; Athanasius' *Life of Antony* and the Latin versions of it; Cassian's *Thirteenth Conference*; Gennadius of Marseilles' *Liber ecclesiasticorum dogmatum*, in which his attempt to explain orthodoxy on grace and free will in ch. 20 (ed. Turner, p. 93), created confusion; the anonymous *Praedestinatus*; and Faustus of Riez's *De gratia Dei*. Still other works assumed effective free will and presented salvation as dependent on freely chosen virtue, without explicit assertion of these principles.

Augustine argued that a positive anthropology was dangerous to the faith.[20] Yet Christianity thrived during the Middle Ages, when Pelagius' writings circulated freely. The third ancillary myth suggests that this issue was resolved in Western Christianity. Yet what papal statements there were on the subject did not produce a transparent formula for orthodoxy. Pope Celestine's *Apostolici uerba* of AD 431 was interpreted by both sides in the continuing debate as supporting their own perspective.[21] And the dossier of documents that emerged from the Second Council of Orange between AD 529 and 531, which included a letter from Pope Boniface II endorsing the canons of the council, has likewise been interpreted differently.[22] If the meaning of these two papal communications on the topic had been unequivocal, divergent interpretations of them would not have been possible.

Furthermore, dissension kept recurring, such as in the controversy triggered by Gottschalk of Orbais in the 9th century, and during the counter-Reformation debates between the Dominicans and the Jesuits in the Congregation on the Help of Grace (*Congregatio de auxiliis gratiae*) that began at the end of the 16th century at the behest of Pope Clement VIII, and continued for nine years without reaching any conclusion, after which Pope Paul V ordered the two sides to stop condemning each other and await his decision. He never did produce a ruling. The grace and free will issue was not resolved because it is impossible to resolve; it is either a false opposition or it is determined by personal experience or priorities.

Taken as a whole, surviving manuscripts show that mixed messages were transmitted in Christian literature in the West; diverse interpretations of the position of free will in Christian teaching have been widely available within the Western

---

[20] Augustine, *De gestis Pelagii* 35.66 (ed. Urba and Zycha, CSEL 42, p. 122), 'The impious doctrines of this sort of people must be refuted by all catholic Christians, even by those who live far away from these lands, so that they may not be able to cause harm wherever they go'; 'Impia quippe dogmata huiusce modi hominum a quibuslibet catholicis, etiam qui ab illis terris longe absunt, redarguenda sunt, ne ubicumque nocere possint, quo peruenire potuerint'; Augustine, *De gratia Christi et de peccato originali* 2.23.26 (ed. Urba and Zycha, CSEL 42, p. 184), 'Astutely wishing to evade being hated as heretics, they claim that: "This question falls outside anything of danger to the faith", so that, if indeed they should be convicted of having overstepped the bounds in these questions, their error would be regarded as a matter for a civil and not a criminal case'; 'Volentes haereseos astute inuidiam declinare asserunt: "Istam praeter fidei periculum esse quaestionem", ut uidelicet, si in ea fuerint exorbitasse conuicti, non criminaliter, sed quasi ciuiliter errasse uideantur.'

[21] For differing interpretations of Celestine's *Apostolici uerba*: Vincent of Lérins, *Commonitorium* 32.4–7 (ed. Demeulenaere, CCSL 64, p. 193); Prosper, *Contra collatorem* 21.2 (ed. Migne, PL 51.271C–272A).

[22] *Concilium Arausicanum, canones* (ed. De Clerq, CCSL 148A, pp. 53–76). For the view that the Orange II dossier was not the same as Augustine's position, but was instead a moderate version of it: R. A. Markus, 'The Legacy of Pelagius: Orthodoxy, Heresy and Conciliation', in *The Making of Orthodoxy: Essays in Honour of Henry Chadwick*, ed. R. Williams (Cambridge, 1989), pp. 226–7; W. E. Klingshirn, *Caesarius of Arles: The Making of a Christian Community in Late Antique Gaul* (Cambridge, 1994), pp. 141–2; Leyser, 'Semi-Pelagianism', p. 765; R. H. Weaver, *Divine Grace and Human Agency. A Study of the Semi-Pelagian Controversy* (Macon, GA, 1996), pp. 225–32; Ogliari, *Gratia et Certamen*, pp. 435–6. For discussion of the view that Orange II promulgated Augustine's doctrine without alteration: Leff, *Bradwardine*, p. 152; T. O'Loughlin, 'Caesarius of Arles', in *Augustine through the Ages. An Encyclopedia*, ed. A. Fitzgerald (Grand Rapids, MI, 1999), pp. 115–16.

Christian Church continuously from the 5th century to the present. Two parallel anthropologies and soteriologies circulated concurrently in Christian literature, and this falsifies the myth that effective free will was ever outside mainstream Christian teaching. In reality, it was an assumption before Pelagius wrote and thereafter circulated in Christian literature in every subsequent century, not least through the survival of Pelagius' writings.

Conclusion

The argument

Proof that 'Pelagianism' never existed in reality and was a deliberately invented fiction lies in the following evidence. First, Pelagius did not teach the tenets attributed to him, and Augustine admitted that he did not care whether or not Pelagius taught the propositions alleged to constitute 'Pelagianism'. Second, the two principles Pelagius defended were the goodness of human nature and effective free will, and these were longstanding principles within Christian literature that were explicitly advocated from the 360s AD onwards in Greek and Latin Christian texts. Pelagius did not invent these ideas, so to attach his name to them is misleading. Third, there was no one individual who held the set of views attributed to the programme 'Pelagianism', nor was there a group of people who held these views. The variation in ideas among the authors corraled together and labelled 'Pelagian' shows that there was no group. The only movement was the ascetic movement, which was a broad current of thought in Christianity, from whose stream many, many voices arose and wrote about their conception of Christianity. Fourth, when subjected to scrutiny, the concept of 'Pelagianism' falls apart. It cannot be defined, nor is the classification 'Pelagian' workable in practice with regard to texts. The descriptor 'Pelagian' has no fixed meaning other than that the text is ascetic paraenesis. Texts labelled 'Pelagian' are more accurately described as ascetic literature. They were the product of the ascetic fervour that overtook Christianity and generated a range of ideas during a period of prolific Christian literary activity, when Christians felt free to express their thoughts about their faith in writing. Fifth, sociological analysis of how deviance is created and comparative studies of heresy accusations reveal that the invention of heresy in order to relocate orthodoxy was the norm in the development of religious doctrine. The tactics of reading hostile entailments into the statements of alleged heretics, and raising alarm by inventing an organised group that threatened the unity and safety of the community, were universal practices. A credible motive and means for the invention of the myth are available, as well as an explanation of why the myth gained traction.

Manuscript evidence supports this argument. Pelagius' works were staples of medieval monastic book collections. Their internal content did not attract attention as heterodox; only when there was an external authority that quoted a text and identified it as 'Pelagian' did anyone see that it was not orthodox. The disparity between the caricature of 'Pelagianism' and the actual content of Pelagius' writings contributed to readers' failure to see that they were heterodox. As a result, the arguments for the goodness of human nature and effective free will were continuously in circulation in Christian literature and widely available.

In the 5th century an attempt was made by assiduous activists to install a set of doctrines that represented change and were new for most Christians. In order to displace the mainstream consensus, they constructed the heresy 'Pelagianism' and achieved the condemnation of two individuals for an alleged association with it. The person who forced the issue of original sin as Church dogma was Augustine, supported by others and in particular by his fellow African bishops. Scholarship has not referred to a controversy about original sin, prevenient grace, and predestination interpreted as preordainment, or identified a group that agitated to promote this set of ideas, although a stronger case might be put forward for a unified programme cohering in these doctrines and for an organised movement working to install them, than can be put together with regard to 'Pelagianism'.

The bigger picture

The prime minister, Lord Salisbury, once instructed his parliamentary colleagues to: 'Use a large map' because a change in the scale of map studied brought a different perspective.[1] With regard to the 5th-century controversy about prevenient grace and effective free will, two conclusions result from looking at the bigger picture. First, debate as to whether human nature is inclined to goodness, sin or neither particularly is perennial; it is a feature of human existence, along with questions about whether man is autonomous or controlled by external forces. The double determination portrayed in the *Iliad* posed this eternal question: Did Hector go out to kill Patroclus because of his own human motivations or because Apollo told him to? Heraclitus' 'character is destiny' (ἦθος ἀνθρώπῳ δαίμων) was one perspective on the relationship between human free will and divine control.[2] Sophocles explored the issue in his plays about Oedipus, and Euripides' *Bacchae* also addressed this question. The second benefit of looking at the wider canvas is that it allows us to see which of the changes that occurred in late antiquity really mattered. The cultural norm changed from intellectual life that assumed a plurality of discourses to a monopoly on discourse in which officially a restricted set of

---

[1] Lord Salisbury, three times prime minister, advised using a large-scale map. By contrast, my point is that using a small-scale map in which a greater breadth of terrain is seen in one vista, rather than focusing only on one small area in detail, changes the perspective usefully.
[2] Heraclitus (attributed).

interpretations were acceptable, and views outside their range might be deemed blasphemous. Competition between religions was progressively shut down in favour of a monopoly held by a version of Christianity that delegitimised alternative discourses.[3] The habit of intellectual freedom ingrained by the rhetorical educational system of the classical world was lost. The idea of a monopoly on discourse was the change. The important point about Honorius' rescript was that the apparatus of the state was used to proscribe the idea of confidence in man; it asserted that it was illegal to expound a positive anthropology.

Christianity achieved its monopoly on discourse during late antiquity in part through the financial resources directed to it, and also in part through the mass of literature produced at this time that talked about Christianity with real enthusiasm: commentary, paraenesis, poetry, translations of Greek works, records of the sayings of the Desert Fathers, hagiography, and personal and public letters. This fertile literary environment reflected engagement with Christianity and its ideas. The ascetic movement was the primary driver of this cultural success, and Pelagius was one voice among many championing ascetic Christian ethics with enthusiasm.[4] At

---

[3] An example of this delegitimisation of alternative discourses is offered by Augustine's *City of God*. This delegitimisation excluded both other religions, because Christian Scripture was interpreted as the sole source of truth, and also selected interpretations of Scripture and Christianity deemed unacceptable. Some examples are Augustine, *De ciuitate Dei* 14.8 (ed. Dombart and Kalb, CCSL 48, p. 424), 'Those writers whose authority we cannot reject without sin'; 'Eos quorum auctoritati resultare fas non est'; 15.9 (ed. Dombart and Kalb, CCSL 48, p. 466), 'Nor must we for that reason question the reliability of the sacred record of history, whose narrative we disbelieve with impudence as great as the certainty with which we see its prophecies fulfilled'; 'Nec tamen ideo fides sacrae huic historiae deroganda est, cuius tanto inpudentius narrata non credimus, quanto impleri certius praenuntiata conspicimus'; 12.16 (ed. Dombart and Kalb, CCSL 48, p. 372), 'So that those who read this may see what dangers of certain questions they ought to refrain from tackling, and so that they should not judge themselves fit to deal with every question'; 'Vt qui haec legunt uideant a quibus quaestionum periculis debeant temperare, nec ad omnia se idoneos arbitrentur'; 12.18 (ed. Dombart and Kalb, CCSL 48, p. 374), 'We are forbidden to believe that God is in one condition when he is at rest and another when he is at work; because God's 'condition' must not be spoken of at all'; 'Nobis autem fas non est credere, aliter affici Deum cum uacat, aliter cum operatur; quia nec affici dicendus est'; 12.19 (ed. Dombart and Kalb, CCSL 48, p. 375), 'So that they should dare to say, and in so doing should submerge themselves in an abyss of deep blasphemy, that God does not know all numbers'; 'Vt dicere audeant atque huic se uoragini profundae inpietatis inmergant, quod non omnes numeros Deus nouerit'; 5.26 (ed. Dombart and Kalb, CCSL 47, p. 163), 'I received information that this reply had been written, but the authors were looking for the right time when they could publish it without danger to themselves. I warn them not to wish for something which is not for their own good'; 'Deinde ad me perlatum est, quod iam scripserint, sed tempus quaerant, quo sine periculo possint edere. Quos admoneo, non optent quod eis non expedit.' Éric Rebillard has written of the 'marketplace of religions in the late Roman Empire': Rebillard, *Christians and Their Many Identities*, p. 97. Writing about Eusebius' *Ecclesiastical History*, Doron Mendels regularly referred to the 'religious marketplace' in which Eusebius composed his history. His focus, however, was on media management, and he did not engage with the implications of scholarship that has demonstrated the constructed, relational and processual character of orthodoxy and heresy: Mendels, *The Media Revolution of Early Christianity* (Grand Rapids, MI, 1999).

[4] In the long term it was perhaps counterproductive to ban one of Christianity's most eloquent apologists. To use an analogy, it would be like a football team not playing its star striker. All teams need a defender who is an enforcer who stops players on the opposing side from playing effectively, but they also need strikers. Coercion might work for an era or two, but, in the long term, persuasion is the only

the same time, doctrine was being formed during this literary outpouring. Exegesis had no set format or methodology; it was putty in the writer's hands. Christianity was evolving fast during this period; it was working out its dogma and doctrine in a competitive market, in terms of belief systems in wider society outside the Church, and within the Church itself. Both the secular and ecclesiastical spheres were competitive publishing environments. Within the Church, literary output was driven by a competitive market in authority; authority translated into jobs, security and status. The many surviving letter collections of pagans and Christians reveal networks of patronage and influence, and their role in career preferment, and how this epistolary culture seamlessly became Christianised, a process visible in the correspondence of Ausonius. The formation of doctrine was thus also drawn into a competitive marketplace, and an issue of far-reaching impact was decided through personal literary activity. Yet at the root of the two different anthropologies and soteriologies were different conceptions of God, and therefore man's relationship to God. The triune of original sin, an absolutist account of prevenient grace, and predestination interpreted as preordainment represented not just a different brand of Christianity but a different conception of man and God. It is important to understand the way this change was brought about, how the attempt to change doctrine was only partially successful and the effects it had.

Terminology matters

The term 'Pelagianism' embodies and perpetuates untruths. Its use leads inevitably to the assumption that such a set of ideas did indeed exist within an individual or group. A shorthand theological label is misleading in the context of historical analysis if it refers to something that never existed, because it inherently conveys the notion that someone did hold this set of tenets. The suggestion that it would be possible to have a theological label for a set of ideas that no one has ever held and which carries with it no implication that anyone has ever held those views creates a hypothetical. In this context a hypothetical is not helpful. In the context of Pelagius it is not possible to separate history from theology so completely that the theological label does not colour historical analysis. The notion of 'Pelagianism' imports an erroneous model into discussion of the process that occurred during the controversy. If historical accuracy is the aim, the word 'Pelagianism' should not be used, either as a referent to an historical group or as a theological label, or as any other type of referent, because it is inherently misleading. The term should be abandoned altogether because it introduces a faulty paradigm into every sentence in which it is used.

---

lever. Any team should work hard to accomodate both types of player. Manuscript evidence shows that in practice this is what Christianity did.

A positive paradigm

Correct terminology is therefore important, and historically accurate terminology is available. Pelagius should be reclassified as an advocate of asceticism who wrote in Latin. This change is long overdue. In 1968 Robert Evans noted that scholarship was starting to identify 'lines of continuity' between Pelagius and earlier Christian writers, as well as writers contemporary with Pelagius.[5] This book brings that analysis to its conclusion in arguing that the term 'Pelagianism' should be abandoned. Instead of the 'Pelagian' controversy, it is possible to refer to the controversy about original sin, prevenient grace, and predestination interpreted as preordainment; or to the controversy about Christian anthropology and soteriology. Within the wide current of the ascetic movement, many ideas surfaced, some further from the consensus than others, but in this tide that swept through Christianity there was nothing original about Pelagius. The persuasive power of his writing was the only feature that differentiated him from other advocates of ascetic values; his paraenesis was effective.[6] Pelagius was one writer among many in the ascetic movement; this was the only movement of which he was a member, and it was in no way an organised phenomenon. Referring to asceticism and the ascetic movement avoids importing untruths into discussion.

Loss of confidence

Many analyses have sought to identify the differences between the classical and medieval eras, and what triggered these perceived changes. Different types of cause have been proposed, including economic, military, political, cultural and religious ones. While these all played a part, a critical factor was loss of confidence. The condemnation of Pelagius stigmatised confidence as arrogance. Fear entered the intellectual climate as Christians competed to express man's powerlessness before God in more and more servile terms, because that was perceived to be the correct pious humility. The loss of confidence enshrined in the installation of a negative account of man as orthodoxy was a seismic discontinuity.[7] The barbarian invasions, the defeat of Roman military forces, the sack of Rome and the disintegration of the Western Empire triggered a loss of cultural confidence, and simultaneously a negative account of man's capabilities was codified into Western Christian doctrine.[8] Orosius reported that Augustine rejected confidence: 'According to my

---

[5] Evans, *Pelagius*, p. 43.

[6] The fact that Pelagius' *Letter to Demetrias* was translated into vernacular European languages suggests that it was perceived to be useful.

[7] Assessing the impact of the condemnation of Origenism and 'Pelagianism', Clark concluded: 'Their condemnation made effective in the West the flourishing of a Christian theology whose central concerns were human sinfulness, not human potentiality; divine determination, not human freedom and responsibility; God's mystery, not God's justice': Clark, *The Origenist Controversy*, p. 250.

[8] For evidence that Roman citizens at the time saw the consequences of the barbarian invasions and the sack of Rome as cataclysmic, see Pelagius, *De diuina lege* 3.3 (ed. Migne, PL 30.108B), 'Considering the state of mortality with daily departures of men dying and the ruin of the whole world as it gradually

blessed father Augustine: "Confidence is characteristic of an insane person, not a sane one."'[9] *City of God* sought to enforce this negative account of man in its promulgation of the doctrine of original sin as piety. In his letter to Sixtus of AD 418, Augustine told him that he should coerce people into accepting original sin, prevenient grace, and predestination interpreted as preordainment, and that fear was salutary.[10] It is fundamentally unlikely, however, that this change was the product of one man's thought world and doctrinal analysis. Augustine was pushing at an open door, as others went along with this characterisation of man as sinful and weak. The anonymous author of *The Predestined* was right to see fear or human shame as underlying susceptibility to this ideology of weakness. Ranked by significance, this loss of confidence should sit near the top of a list of the differences between the classical and medieval worlds. Only in the Renaissance did a confident account of man become publicly acceptable again, and this coincided with the rediscovery of classical literature. Pelagius' works played an important role in preserving a confident account of man across the intervening centuries.

---

sinks through one defeat after another'; 'Mortalitatis statum, per quotidie morientium hominum exitus, et totius saeculi paulatim per detrimenta labentis ruinam considerans'; 9.2 (ed. Migne, PL 30.115B), 'But let not the day of vengeance and retribution find us idle, that day which is proved to be imminent and near at hand both by the ruins that clash together on all sides and by the witness of the Scriptures'; 'Non nos inertes uindictae dies et retributionis inueniat, qui imminens ac uicinus esse, et saeculi ruinis undique concurrentibus, et Scripturarum contestatione probatur'; Sulpicius Severus in his *Life of Martin* referred to panic in Tours when a rumour suggested the barbarians were going to attack: *Vita Martini* 18.1 (ed. Halm, CSEL 1, p. 127); Julian of Aeclanum, *Tractatus prophetarum Osee Iohel et Amos*, on Hosea 9:5–6 (ed. De Coninck, CCSL 88, pp. 186–7). For further references, see Thomas Smith's discussion of evidence for the impact of the barbarian invasions: Smith, *De Gratia*, pp. 22–6. For the view that the sack of Rome had little impact, see P. Van Nuffelen, 'Not Much Happened: 410 and All That', *Journal of Roman Studies* 105 (2015), pp. 322–9.

[9] Orosius, *Liber apologeticus* 31 (ed. Zangemeister, CSEL 5, p. 658), 'Iuxta sententiam enim beati patris mei Augustini: "Non est sani fiducia, sed insani."'

[10] Augustine, *Ep.* 191.2 (ed. Goldbacher, CSEL 57, pp. 164–5), 'So that not only should those be punished with salutary severity who dare to spread through their chatter that error so dangerous to the Christian name, but these also, on account of the weaker and simpler of the Lord's sheep, should be guarded against most diligently with pastoral vigilance, who do not cease to whisper it, although more cautiously and timidly …. Nor must those be neglected, who through fear suppress what they think into deep silence, and yet do not stop thinking that same perversity …. For even if they should not be terrified, they should nonetheless be taught, and in my view they can be taught more easily while fear of severity acts in them to help the teacher of truth, so that once they have come to understand and love his grace with the Lord's help they may also fight in words against what they now do not dare to say'; 'Vt non solum salubri seueritate plectantur, qui errorem illum Christiano infestissimum nomini audent garrire liberius, sed etiam hi diligentissime caueantur uigilantia pastorali propter infirmiores et simpliciores dominicas oues qui eum pressius quidem atque timidius sed tamen insusurrare non cessant …. Nec illi neglegendi sunt, qui usque ad profundum silentium supprimunt timore, quod sentiunt, sed tamen eandem peruersitatem sentire non desinunt …. Etsi enim terrendi non sunt, tamen docendi sunt et, quantum existimo, facilius possunt, dum in eis timor seueritatis doctorem adiuuat ueritatis, ut opitulante domino gratia eius intellecta atque dilecta etiam loquendo expugnent, quod iam loqui non audent'; *Ep.* 194.1.2 (ed. Goldbacher, CSEL 57, p. 178), 'Some must be restrained more harshly, some must be investigated more carefully'; 'Alii seuerius cohercendi, alii uigilantius uestigandi'.

Appendix

Translation of the γ-text of Ambrosiaster's *Commentary on the Pauline Epistles* on Rom. 9:11–16 (with some text omitted). Text taken from Ambrosiaster, *Commentarius in epistulas Pauli* (ed. Vogels, CSEL 81/1, pp. 313–21).

At one point I have added the α-text between asterisks because it contains a significant alternative interpretation.

'Rom. 9:11–13: *For when they were not yet born nor had they done anything either good or bad, so that God's plan might continue according to his election, it was said not on the basis of works but on the basis of the calling, that the elder would serve the younger, as it is written: I loved Jacob, but Esau I hated* [Mal. 1:2–3]. That is in Malachi. Paul proclaims God's foreknowledge in these matters because nothing else can happen other than what God knows will happen. For through his knowledge of what each of them will be in the future, he said: "This one will be worthy, who will be the younger, and the one who will be older will be unworthy." He chose one and rejected the other as a result of his foreknowledge. And God's plan continues with regard to the one he chose because nothing can happen except what He knows and has planned with regard to him, that he will be worthy of salvation. And concerning him whom God rejected, likewise God's plan continues, that he planned concerning him, because he will be unworthy. This God does as one who knows the future and not as a *respecter of persons* [Acts 10:34, Rom. 2:11], for he condemns no one before they should sin, and he crowns no one before they should conquer. This relates to the case of the Jews who defend their previous privilege as sons of Abraham.'

[The author then says that Paul was consoling himself about the fact that some Jews did not believe by reminding himself that God had foreseen that some would not believe.]

'And so he lessens his grief by finding that it was once predicted that they would not all believe, so that he should only grieve for these who through ill-will would not at all believe. Yet they are able to believe, which he shows through what he adds subsequently. However, the predicted unbelievers should not be greatly grieved over, because they have not been predestined to life; for the foreknowledge of God decreed long ago that they should not be saved. For who would mourn someone who is long previously considered dead? But when the gentiles appeared, who previously were without God, and accepted the salvation which the Jews lost, his grief was revived; but then once again it is calmed because they are the cause of their own damnation. And so, knowing in advance those people who will be of evil will, God did not have them in the roll of the good, although the Saviour said to the seventy-two disciples whom he chose as a second class, and who later abandoned him: *Your names are written in heaven* [Luke 10:20]. But this was on account of justice, because this is just, that each person should receive a response in accordance with merit; for because they were good, they were chosen for the ministry and their names were written in heaven for the sake of justice, as I said; but according to foreknowledge they were among the number of the wicked. For God judges according to justice, not according to foreknowledge. Thus he said to Moses: *If someone sins against me, I shall delete him from my book* [Exod. 32:33], so that according to the justice of the judge his name should be seen to be deleted at that time when he should sin, but according to foreknowledge his name was never in the Book of Life. For this reason the apostle John too says of such a person: *They went out from us, but they were not of us; for if they had been of us, they would have remained with us* [1 John 2:19]. There is no respect for persons in the foreknowledge of God. For the foreknowledge of God is the information by which he has it set out what the will of each person will be in the future, in which each individual will remain, and by which each person may be either damned or crowned. Accordingly those whom God knows will remain good, were often previously wicked, and those whom he knows will continue wicked to the end, were sometimes before that good. For this reason let the complaint cease, because: *God is not a respecter of persons* [Acts 10:34, Rom. 2:11]. For both Saul and Judas Iscariot had previously been good, with Scripture saying of Saul: *He was a good man and there was none better in Israel* [1 Sam. 9:2]; and of Judas Iscariot the apostle Peter says: *Who was allotted a share of this ministry in performing signs and wonders* [Acts 1:17], that is the ministry of apostleship. And so how could he have been allotted a share of the salvation mission, unless he had been good? For in the part allotted to him God's judgement was that he was worthy at that time when he was chosen, just like those seventy-two also, whom I mentioned earlier. It is for this reason whence Judas also after committing a crime of total wickedness, moved by penitence, ended his life with a noose.

γ-text: *For goodness cannot be utterly obliterated in any person; for neither can nature herself be changed, but the will is changed, not however in every respect because there remains in any nature what is witness to the Creator.*

α-text: *And why is it surprising that these men are said to have been good, when all nature is good and evil has no substance, but only sin, which arises from the will? But the will is led astray by error.*

Rom. 9:14: *And so what will we say? Is God unjust? By no means*. For because he loves one and hates the other, surely, he says, God is unjust? Clearly not, but rather he is just. For he knows what he might do and yet his judgement is not bound to be revised. This is what it says in the prophet Malachi, just as I said above: *Jacob I loved, but Esau I hated* [Mal. 1:2–3]. He says this now from judgement, but previously he said from foreknowledge that: *The elder will serve the younger*, just as also as a result of foreknowledge he judged that Pharoah would be condemned, because he knew that Pharoah would not reform; but he chose the apostle Paul who was persecuting him, undoubtedly because he knew in advance that he would be faithful in the future. And so, he anticipated Paul ahead of time, because Paul was necessary, and he condemned Pharoah ahead of his judgement that lay in the future, so that people would believe that he was going to pass judgement.

Rom. 9:15: *For he says to Moses: "I will have mercy on whom I will have mercy, and I will have compassion on whom I will have compassion"*. Therefore: *I will have mercy*, he says, *on whom I will have mercy*. That is: I will have mercy on the one whom I knew in advance that I would show mercy to, because I knew that he would convert and would remain with me. *And I will have compassion on whom I will have compassion*, that is: I will show compassion on the one whom I have known in advance would come back to me, after his error, with an upright heart. In other words, he will give to the one to whom it should be given, and he will not give to the one to whom it should not be given, so that he calls whoever he knows obeys, but he does not call whoever he knows in no way obeys. But to call is to goad someone to receive the faith.

Rom. 9:16: *And so it is not of him who wills nor of him who runs, but of God who has mercy*. This is rightly said, because the response to what is requested ought to lie not in the will of the one asking but in the decision of the one giving. For whether or not it should be given ought to be weighed in the judgement of the one doing the giving. For Saul, in his sinning, when he asked for forgiveness did not receive it, but on the other hand David, in his sinning and asking for himself to be pardoned, received forgiveness. Assuredly from this the verdict must follow concerning God when he gives and when he does not give, that he does not judge unjustly: *Who wants all men to be saved* [1 Tim. 2:4] while justice is maintained. For the inspector of hearts knows concerning the person making a request whether he is making it with the sort of mind that means he merits to receive his request. And although it is dangerous to try to understand God's judgement, yet for the sake of unbelievers, so that their minds might obtain healing and so that they should not think that God's judgement is unjust, saying: *He calls one and ignores the other* [Luke 17:34] judging on this basis that those who are to be condemned can be excused, let us prove this with deeds rather than words. For where there are examples of deeds done no one dares to complain or to offer any excuse.'

Latin text

'Rom. 9:11–13: *Nam cum nati nondum fuissent aut aliquid egissent bonum uel malum, ut secundum electionem propositum Dei permaneret, non ex operibus, sed ex uocatione dictum est, quia maior seruiet minori, sicut scriptum est: Iacob dilexi, Esau autem odio habui* [Mal. 1:2–3]. Istud in Malachia habetur. Praescientiam Dei flagitat in his causis, quia non aliud potest euenire, quam nouit Deus futurum. Sciendo enim quid unusquisque illorum futurus esset dixit: "Hic erit dignus, qui erit minor, et qui erit maior, indignus." Vnum elegit praescientia et alterum spreuit. Et in illo quem elegit, propositum Dei manet, quia aliud non potest euenire quam scit et proposuit in illo, ut salute dignus sit; et in illo quem spernit, simili modo manet propositum, quod proposuit de illo, quia indignus erit. Hoc quasi praescius, *non personarum acceptor* [Acts 10:34, Rom. 2:11], nam neminem damnat, antequam peccet, et nullum coronat, antequam uincat. Hoc pertinet ad causam Iudaeorum, qui sibi praerogatiuam defendunt, quod filii sint Abrahae …'.

[The author then says that Paul was consoling himself about the fact that some Jews did not believe by reminding himself that God had foreseen that some would not believe.]

'Minuit ergo dolorem suum inueniens olim praedictum, quod non essent omnes credituri, ut his solis doleat, qui per inuidiam minime crediderunt. Possunt tamen credere, quod ex subiectis ostendit. Incredulis tamen praedictis non ualde dolendum, quia non sunt praedestinati ad uitam; praescientia enim Dei olim istos non saluandos decreuit. Quis enim plangat eum, qui olim mortuus habetur? Sed subintrantibus gentibus, quae sine Deo prius erant, et salutem quam illi perdiderunt, accipientibus exsuscitatur dolor; sed iterum quia ipsi sibi perditionis causa sunt, sopitur. Praescius itaque Deus malae illos uoluntatis futuros, non habuit illos in numero bonorum, quamuis dicat Saluator illis septuaginta duobus discipulis, quos elegerat secunda classe, qui ab illo post recesserunt: *Nomina uestra scripta sunt in caelo* [Luke 10:20]. Sed hoc propter iustitiam, quia hoc est iustum, ut unicuique pro merito respondeatur; quia enim erant boni, electi sunt ad ministerium et erant scripta nomina illorum in caelo propter iustitiam, sicut dixi; secundum praescientiam uero in numero erant malorum. De iustitia enim Deus iudicat, non de praescientia. Vnde et Moysi dixit: *Si quis peccauerit ante me, deleam illum de libro meo* [Exod. 32:33], ut secundum iustitiam iudicis tunc uideatur deleri, cum peccat, iuxta praescientiam uero numquam in libro uitae fuisse. Hinc et apostolus Iohannes de huiusmodi ait: *Ex nobis exierunt, sed non fuerunt ex nobis; si enim fuissent ex nobis, permansissent utique nobiscum* [1 John 2:19]. Non est personarum acceptio in praescientia Dei. Praescientia enim Dei est, qua definitum habet, qualis uniuscuiusque futura uoluntas erit, in qua mansurus est, per quam aut damnetur aut coronetur. Denique quos scit in bono mansuros, frequenter ante sunt mali, et quos scit malos permansuros, aliquoties prius sunt boni. Vnde cessat querela, quia: *Deus personarum acceptor non est* [Acts 10:34, Rom. 2:11]. Nam et Saul et Iudas [Scarioth] ante fuerunt boni dicente Scriptura de Saule: *Erat uir bonus et non erat melior illo in filiis Istrahel* [1 Sam. 9:2]; et de Iuda Scarioth dicit apostolus Petrus:

Qui sortitus est sortem ministerii huius [*in signis et prodigiis faciendis*] [Acts 1:17], id est apostolatus. Igitur quomodo ministerium salutare sortiretur, nisi esset bonus? In sorte enim Dei iudicium fuit dignum illum fuisse tempore, quo electus est, sicut et illi septuaginta duo, quos supra memoraui. Hinc est unde et Iudas post scelus mali totius admissum paenitentia motus laqueo uitam finiuit.

γ-text: *Non enim potest penitus in aliquo omne bonum obliterari; nec enim natura ipsa potest inmutari, sed uoluntas, non in omnibus tamen causis, quia remanet in natura, quod testimonio sit Creatori.*

α-text: *Et quid mirum, quia dicuntur fuisse boni, cum omnis natura bona sit et malum nulla substantia, sed sola praeuaricatio, quae oritur de uoluntate? Voluntas autem trahitur de errore.*

Rom. 9:14: *Quid ergo dicemus? Numquid iniquitas apud Deum? Absit.* Quia enim unum diligit et alterum odit, numquid, ait, iniquus Deus est? Non plane, sed iustus. Scit enim quid faciat et nec retractandum est eius iudicium. Hoc in Malachia habetur propheta, sicut supra dictum est: *Iacob dilexi, Esau autem odio habui* [Mal. 1:2–3]. Hoc iam de iudicio dicit, nam prius de praescientia ait quia *maior seruiet minori,* sicut et de praescientia Faraonem damnandum censuit sciens non correcturum; apostolum uero Paulum persequentem elegit, praescius utique, quod futurus esset fidelis. Hunc ergo praeuenit ante tempus, quia necessarius erat, et Faraonem ante futurum iudicium damnauit, ut crederetur iudicaturus.

Rom. 9:15: *Moysi enim dicit: Miserebor cui misertus ero, et misericordiam praestabo, cui misericordiam praestitero.* Ergo *miserebor,* inquit, eius *cui misertus ero.* Hoc est: illius miserebor, cui praescius eram quod misericordiam daturus essem, sciens conuersurum illum et mansurum apud me. *Et misericordiam praestabo ei, cui misericordiam praestitero,* id est: misericordiam dabo, quem praescii post errorem recto corde regressurum ad me. Hoc est dare illi, cui dandum est, neque non dare illi, cui dandum non est, ut eum uocet, quem sciat obaudire, illum autem non uocet, quem sciat minime obaudire. Vocare autem conpungere est ad recipiendam fidem.

Rom. 9:16: *Igitur non uolentis neque currentis, sed miserentis est Dei.* Recte, quia non in uoluntate petentis, sed in dantis arbitrio debet esse, quod poscitur. An enim dandum sit, dantis debet iudicio pensitari. Nam Saul peccans, cum petisset ueniam, non accepit, at contra Dauid peccans et ignosci sibi postulans ueniam consecutus est. Ex hoc utique dantis Dei et non dantis iudicium sequendum est, quia non iniuste iudicat: *Qui omnes saluos uult* [1 Tim. 2:4] manente iustitia. Inspector enim cordis scit petentem, an hac mente poscat, ut mereatur accipere. Et quamuis periculosum sit iudicium Dei discernere, tamen propter diffidentes, ut mens eorum medelam consequi possit, ne putent iniustum iudicium Dei dicentes: *Vnum uocat, alterum neglegit* [Luke 17:34], sic arbitrantes excusari posse damnandos, rebus hoc potius probemus quam uerbis. Vbi enim rerum gestarum exempla sunt, nemo audet queri nec aliquam excusationem obtendere.'

Bibliography

Primary Sources

Adriaen, M., ed., *Sancti Hieronymi presbyteri Opera. Commentarius in Ecclesiasten*, Corpus Christianorum Series Latina 72 (Turnhout, 1959).

Adriaen, M., ed., *Sancti Hieronymi presbyteri Opera. Commentarius in Ioelem*, Corpus Christianorum Series Latina 76 (Turnhout, 1969).

Adriaen, M., ed., *Sancti Hieronymi presbyteri Opera. Commentarius in Malachiam*, Corpus Christianorum Series Latina 76A (Turnhout, 1970).

Bartelink, G. J. M., ed. and transl., [Ἐπιστολὴ πρὸς τοὺς ἐν τῇ ξένῃ μοναχοὺς περὶ τοῦ βίου τοῦ μακαρίου Ἀντωνίου τοῦ μεγάλου] in *Athanase D'Alexandrie. Vie D'Antoine*, Sources Chrétiennes 400 (Paris, 1994).

Bartelink, G. J. M., ed. and transl., [*Vita Antonii. Antica versione anonima latina*] in *Vita di Antonio*, Vite dei Santi 1 (Milan, 1974).

Bartelink, G. J. M., ed., *Palladio. La Storia Lausiaca*, Vite dei Santi 2 (Milan, 1974).

Bertrand, P., ed., *Die Evagriusübersetzung der Vita Antonii. Rezeption – Überlieferung – Edition, unter besonderer Berücksichtigung der Vitas Patrum-Tradition*, unpublished PhD thesis (University of Utrecht, 2006).

Bonnard, E., ed., *Saint Jérôme: Commentaire sur Saint Matthieu*, 2 vols, Sources Chrétiennes 242, 259 (Paris, 1977–9).

Borghesi, F., Papio, M. and Riva, M., ed. and transl., *Pico della Mirandola, Oration on the Dignity of Man. A New Translation and Commentary* (Cambridge, 2012).

Bucchi, F., ed., *Sancti Hieronymi presbyteri Opera. Commentarii in Epistulas Pauli Apostoli ad Titum et ad Philemonem*, Corpus Christianorum Series Latina 77C (Turnhout, 2003).

Caspari, C. P., ed., *Briefe, Abhandlungen, und Predigten aus den zwei letzten Jahrhunderten des kirchlichen Alterthums und dem Anfang des Mittelalters* (Christiania, 1890).

Chéné, J. and Pintard, J., ed. and transl., *Oeuvres de Saint Augustin. Aux Moines d'Adrumète et de Provence*, Bibliothèque Augustinienne 24 (Bruges, 1962).

Clark, E., ed. and transl., *The Life of Melania the Younger. Introduction, Translation, and Commentary*, Studies in Women and Religion 14 (New York, 1984).

Davidson, I. J., ed., *Ambrose, De officiis*, 2 vols, Oxford Early Christian Studies (Oxford, 2001).

De Clerq, C., ed., *Concilia Galliae A.511–A.695*, Corpus Christianorum Series Latina 148A (Turnhout, 1963).

De Coninck, L., ed., *Iuliani Aeclanensis. Expositio Libri Iob. Tractatus Prophetarum Osee, Iohel, et Amos*, Corpus Christianorum Series Latina 88 (Turnhout, 1977).

Demeulenaere, R., ed., *Vincentii Lerinensis Commonitorium Excerpta*, Corpus Christianorum Series Latina 64 (Turnhout, 1985).

De Plinval, G., ed., [Anon, *De induratione cordis pharaonis*] in De Plinval, G., *Essai sur Le Style et La Langue de Pélage suivi du traité inédit De induratione cordis Pharaonis* (Fribourg, 1947).

Divjak, J., ed., *Sancti Aureli Augustini Opera. Epistolae ex duobus codicibus nuper in lucem prolatae*, Corpus Scriptorum Ecclesiasticorum Latinorum 88 (Vienna, 1981).

Doblhofer, E., ed., *Rutilius Claudius Namatianus. 'De reditu suo' siue 'Iter Gallicum'*, 2 vols (Heidelberg, 1972–7).

Dolbeau, F., ed., *Augustin et la prédication en Afrique: recherches sur divers sermons authentiques, apocryphes ou anonymes*, Collection des Études Augustiniennes 179 (Paris, 2005).

Dombart, B. and Kalb, A., ed., *Sancti Aurelii Augustini, De ciuitate Dei libri XXII*, 2 vols, Corpus Christianorum Series Latina 47, 48 (Turnhout, 1955).

Duval, Y.-M., ed., 'La Lettre de Direction (Acéphale) à une Mère de Famille du MS 954 de Vienne (CPL 755). Edition des Divers Fragments dans leur Ordre Original', in *Valeurs dans le Stoïcisme. Du Portique à nos Jours. Textes rassemblés en hommage à Michel Spanneut*, ed. M. Soetard (Lille, 1993), pp. 201–43. [This is Duval's edition of *Ad quandam matronam christianam*].

Engelbrecht, A., ed., *Fausti Reiensis Opera*, Corpus Scriptorum Ecclesiasticorum Latinorum 21 (Vienna, 1891).

Faller, O., ed., *Sancti Ambrosii Opera. Pars 8. De fide*, Corpus Scriptorum Ecclesiasticorum Latinorum 78 (Vienna, 1962).

Faller, O. and Zelzer, M., ed., *Sancti Ambrosi Opera. Epistolae et Acta*, 4 vols, Corpus Scriptorum Ecclesiasticorum Latinorum 82 (Vienna, 1968–96).

Frede, H. J., ed., [Anon., *Epistula ad quandam matronam christianam*] in *Vetus Latina. Die Reste der Altlateinischen Bibel* (Freiburg, 1996), pp. 35–76.

Glorie, F., ed., *Eusebius 'Gallicanus' Collectio Homiliarum*, 3 vols, Corpus Christianorum Series Latina 101, 101A, 101B (Turnhout, 1970–1).

Glorie, F., ed., *Sancti Hieronymi presbyteri Opera. Commentariorum in Danielem libri III*, Corpus Christianorum Series Latina 75A (Turnhout, 1964).

Glorie, F., ed., *Sancti Hieronymi presbyteri Opera. Commentariorum in Hiezechielem libri XIV*, Corpus Christianorum Series Latina 75 (Turnhout, 1964).

Goldbacher, A., ed., *Sancti Aureli Augustini Hipponensis episcopi Epistulae*, 5 vols, Corpus Scriptorum Ecclesiasticorum Latinorum 34/1, 34/2, 44, 57, 58 (Vienna, 1895–1923).

Gorce, D., ed. and transl., *Vie de sainte Mélanie* (Βίος τῆς ὁσίας Μελάνης), Sources Chrétiennes 90 (Paris, 1962).

Gori, F., ed., *Praedestinatus*, Corpus Christianorum Series Latina 25B (Turnhout, 2000).

Gourdain, J.-L., ed., *Jérôme. Homélies sur Marc*, Sources Chrétiennes 494 (Paris, 2005).

Greshake, G., ed., *Pelagius. Epistula Ad Demetriadem. Brief an Demetrias. Einleitung, Edition und Übersetzung*, Fontes Christiani 65 (Freiburg, 2015).

Gryson, R., Deproost, P.-A., Gabriel, C., Bourgeois, H., Couelle, J., Coulie, J., Leclerq, V., Somers, V., Stanjek, H. and Crousse, E., ed., *Commentaires de Jérôme sur le prophète Isaïe*, 5 vols, Vetus Latina. Aus der Geschichte der lateinischen Bibel 23, 27, 30, 35, 36 (Freiburg, 1993–9).

Günther, O., ed., *Epistulae Imperatorum pontificum aliorum. Inde ab A.367 usque ad A.553 datae. Auellana quae dicitur collectio*, Pars I, *Ep.* 1–104, Corpus Scriptorum Ecclesiasticorum Latinorum 35 (Vienna, 1895).

Halm, C., ed., [Pelagius, *De uirginitate* in] *Sulpicii Seueri Opera*, Corpus Scriptorum Ecclesiasticorum Latinorum 1 (Vienna, 1866).

Hamman, A., ed., [Anon., *De castitate,* Anon., *De diuitiis,* Anon., *Honorificentiae tuae,* Anon., *Magnum cumulatur,* Anon., *De malis doctoribus*] in *Pelagius Britannus: operum recensio*, Patrologia Latina Supplementum 1 (Paris, 1958).

Haury, J. and Wirth, G., ed., *Procopii Caesariensis, Opera omnia,* 2 vols, Bibliotheca scriptorum Graecorum et Romanorum Teubneriana (Leipzig, 1962–3).

Hilberg, I., ed., *Sancti Eusebii Hieronymi Opera. Epistulae,* 3 vols, Corpus Scriptorum Ecclesiasticorum Latinorum 54, 55, 56, revised edn (Vienna, 1996).

Kalinka, E. and Zelzer, M., ed., *Sancti Aureli Augustini Opera. Contra Iulianum opus imperfectum,* 2 vols, Corpus Scriptorum Ecclesiasticorum Latinorum 85 (Vienna, 1974–2004).

Kessler, A., ed., *Reichtumskritik und Pelagianismus. Die pelagianische Diatribe de diuitiis: Situierung, Lesetext, Übersetzung, Kommentar,* Paradosis 43, Beiträge zur Geschichte der altchristlichen Literatur und Theologie (Fribourg, 1999).

Kreuz, G. and Petschenig, M., ed., *Iohannis Cassiani Opera,* 2nd edn, Corpus Scriptorum Ecclesiasticorum Latinorum 13 (Vienna, 2004).

Lambot, C., ed., *Sancti Aurelii Augustini Opera. Sermones de uetere testamento,* Corpus Christianorum Series Latina 41 (Turnhout, 1961).

Lardet, P., ed., *Sancti Hieronymi presbyteri Opera. Contra Rufinum,* Corpus Christianorum Series Latina 79 (Turnhout, 1982).

Laurence, P., ed. and transl., *La vie latine de sainte Mélanie par Gérontius. Édition critique, traduction et commentaire*, Collectio minor, Studium Biblicum Franciscanum 41 (Jerusalem, 2002).

McNeill, J. T., ed., *Calvin: The Institutes of Christian Religion*, transl. F. L. Battles, The Library of Christian Classics, vol. XXI (Philadelphia, PA, 1960).

Migne, J.-P., ed., *Constitutio prima Honorii Imperatoris ad Palladium Praefectum*, Patrologia Latina 48 (Paris, 1844–64).

Migne, J.-P., ed., *Decretum Constantii Imperatoris, Patris Valentiniani Augusti III, Ad Volusianum*, Patrologia Latina 45 (Paris, 1844–64).

Migne, J.-P., ed., [Anianus] *Epistola praefixa homiliis in Matthaeum*, Patrologia Latina 48 (Paris, 1844–64).

Migne, J.-P., ed., [Anianus] *Epistola praefixa homiliis de laudibus Pauli*, Patrologia Latina 48 (Paris, 1844–64).

Migne, J.-P., ed., [Anon., *Epistola ad uirginem deuotam*] in *Ad opera Sancti Ambrosii appendix. Pars prima. Complectens opera a Benedictinis in sua editione admissa*, Patrologia Latina 17 (Paris, 1844–64).

Migne, J.-P., ed., [Anon., *Epistola de uera paenitentia*] in *Sancti Eusebii Hieronymi, Stridonensis presbyteri, operum mantissa continens scripta supposititia. Epistolae. Ad quemdam qui in saeculo poenitebat*, Patrologia Latina 30 (Paris, 1844–64).

Migne, J.-P., ed., [Anon., *De uita christiana*] in *Fastidii Britannorum Episcopi De Vita Christiana Liber Unus*, Patrologia Latina 50 (Paris, 1844–64).

Migne, J.-P., ed., [Garnier, J., in] *Appendix secunda ad primam partem operum Marii Mercatoris, Complectens Dissertationes septem, Quibus integra continetur historia Pelagiana*, Patrologia Latina 48 (Paris, 1844–64).

Migne, J.-P., ed., *Libellus fidei Pelagii, ad Innocentium ab ipso missus, Zosimo redditus*, Patrologia Latina 45 (Paris, 1844–64).

Migne, J.-P., ed., *Sancti Aurelii Augustini Hipponensis Episcopi Contra Iulianum, haeresis pelagianae defensorem, libri sex*, Patrologia Latina 44 (Paris, 1844–64).

Migne, J.-P., ed., *Sancti Eusebii Hieronymi, Stridonensis presbyteri, Aduersus Iouinianum libri duo*, Patrologia Latina 23 (Paris, 1844–64).

Migne, J.-P., ed., *Sancti Eusebii Hieronymi, Stridonensis presbyteri, commentariorum in epistolam ad Ephesios libri tres*, Patrologia Latina 26 (Paris, 1844–64).

Migne, J.-P., ed., [Pelagius, *De diuina lege*] in *Sancti Eusebii Hieronymi, operum Mantissa, continens scripta supposititia. Epistolae*, Patrologia Latina 30 (Paris, 1844–64).

Migne, J.-P., ed., *Sancti Prosperi Aquitani de gratia Dei et libero arbitrio liber contra collatorem*, Patrologia Latina 51 (Paris, 1844–64).

Migne, J.-P., ed., *Vita beati Antonii abbatis, auctore Sancto Athanasio, Episcopo Alexandrino, interprete Evagrio presbytero Antiocheno*, Patrologia Latina 73 (Paris, 1844–64).

Migne, J.-P., ed., [De Montfaucon, B., transl., Athanasius' *Life of Antony*] *Vita et Conuersatio Sancti Patris Nostri Antonii*, Patrologia Graeca 26 (Paris, 1800–75).

Miller, M., ed. and transl., *Rufini Presbyteri Liber De Fide. A Critical Text and Translation with Introduction and Commentary* (Washington, DC, 1964).

Mommsen, T., *Monumenta Germaniae Historica*, Auctores Antiquissimi, 3 vols (Berlin, 1892–8).

Moreschini, C., ed., *Sancti Hieronymi presbyteri Opera. Dialogus aduersus Pelagianos*, Corpus Christianorum Series Latina 80 (Turnhout, 1990).

Morin, G., ed., *Caesarius Arelatensis Sermones*, 2 vols, Corpus Christianorum Series Latina 103, 104 (Turnhout, 1953).

Morin, G., ed., '*Fastidius ad Fatalem?* Pages Inédites du Cinquième Siècle D'Après le Manuscrit CCXXI de Reichenau', *Revue Bénédictine* 46 (1934), 3–17 [this is Morin's edition of *Ammoneo te*, also reproduced under the title *Ammonitio Augiensis* in Patrologia Latina Supplementum 1, ed. A. Hamman, cols 1699–1704].

Morin, G., ed., *Sancti Hieronymi presbyteri Opera. Tractatus lix in Psalmos*, Corpus Christianorum Series Latina 78 (Turnhout, 1958).

Munier, C., ed., *Concilia Africae A.345–A.525*, Corpus Christianorum Series Latina 149 (Turnhout, 1974).

Munier, C., ed., *Concilia Galliae A.314–A.506*, Corpus Christianorum Series Latina 148 (Turnhout, 1963).

Mutzenbecher, A., ed., *Sancti Aureli Augustini Retractationum libri II*, Corpus Christianorum Series Latina 57 (Turnhout, 1984).

Neyrand, L. and De Vregille, B., ed., *Apponii In Canticum Canticorum Expositio*, Corpus Christianorum Series Latina 19 (Turnhout, 1986).

Piédagnel, A., ed., *Jean Chrysostome. Panégyriques de S. Paul*, Sources Chrétiennes 300 (Paris, 1982).

Raspanti, G., ed., *Sancti Hieronymi presbyteri Opera. Commentarii in epistulam Pauli apostoli ad Galatas*, Corpus Christianorum Series Latina 77A (Turnhout, 2006).

Reiter, S., ed., *Sancti Hieronymi presbyteri Opera. Commentarii in Hieremiam*, Corpus Christianorum Series Latina 74 (Turnhout, 1960).

Richardson, E. C., ed., *Hieronymus. Liber de uiris inlustribus. Gennadius. Liber de uiris inlustribus*, Texte und Untersuchungen zur Geschichte der altchristlichen Literatur 14 (Leipzig, 1896).

Seeck, O., ed., *Q. Aurelii Symmachi Opera quae supersunt*, Monumenta Germaniae Historica, Auctores Antiquissimi, vol. 6, Pars prior (Berlin, 1961).

Schwartz, E., ed., *Acta Conciliorum Oecumenicorum*, 16 vols (Berlin, 1914–26).

Souter, A., ed., *Pelagius's Expositions of Thirteen Epistles of St Paul*, 3 vols, Contributions to Biblical and Patristic Studies: Texts and Studies 9 (Cambridge, 1922–31).

Turner, C. H., ed., 'The *Liber ecclesiasticorum dogmatum* attributed to Gennadius', *Journal of Theological Studies* 25 (1905), 78–99.

Urba, C. and Zycha, J., ed., *Sancti Aureli Augustini De peccatorum meritis et remissione et de baptismo paruulorum ad Marcellinum libri tres, De spiritu et littera liber unus, De natura et gratia liber unus, De natura et origine animae libri quattuor, Contra duas epistulas Pelagianorum libri quattuor*, Corpus Scriptorum Ecclesiasticorum Latinorum 60 (Vienna, 1913).

Urba, C. and Zycha, J., ed., *Sancti Aureli Augustini De perfectione iustitiae hominis, De gestis Pelagii, De gratia Christi et de peccato originali libri duo, De nuptiis et concupiscentia ad Valerium comitem libri duo*, Corpus Scriptorum Ecclesiasticorum Latinorum 42 (Vienna, 1902).

Valentin, M.-D., ed. and transl., *Sermo Sancti Hilarii de uita Sancti Honorati*, Sources Chrétiennes 235 (Paris, 1977).

Vallarsi, D., ed., *Sancti Eusebii Hieronymi Stridonensis presbyteri, Opera omnia*, 11 vols (Verona, 1734–42).

Van Banning, J., ed., *Opus imperfectum in Matthaeum. Praefatio*, Corpus Christianorum Series Latina 87B (Turnhout, 1988).

Verheijen, L. and Skutella, M., ed., *Confessionum libri XIII Sancti Augustini*, Corpus Christianorum Series Latina 27 (Turnhout, 1981).

Vogels, H. J., ed., *Ambrosiastri qui dicitur Commentarius in Epistulas Paulinas*, 3 vols, Corpus Scriptorum Ecclesiasticorum Latinorum 81 (Vienna, 1966–9).

Walker, G. S. M., ed. and transl., *Sancti Columbani Opera*, Scriptores Latini Hiberniae 2 (Dublin, 1957).

Zangemeister, K. F., ed., *Pauli Orosii Historiarum adversum paganos libri VII; accedit eiusdem Liber apologeticus*, Corpus Scriptorum Ecclesiasticorum Latinorum 5 (Vienna, 1882).

Secondary Sources

Abel, M., 'Le "Praedestinatus" et le pélagianisme', *Recherches de Theologie ancienne et médiévale* 35 (1968), 5–25.

Altaner, B., 'Der *Liber de fide*: ein Werk des Pelagianers Rufinus des "Syrers"', *Theologische Quartalschrift* 130 (1950), 432–49.

Ayres, L., 'The Question of Orthodoxy', *Journal of Early Christian Studies* 14:4 (2006), 395–8.

Bauer, W., *Orthodoxy and Heresy in Earliest Christianity*, ed. and transl. R. A. Kraft and G. Krodel (Philadelphia, PA, 1971).

Baynes, N. H., 'The Hellenistic Civilisation and East Rome', *Byzantine Studies and Other Essays* (London, 1955), pp. 1–23.

Becker, H., *Outsiders. Studies in the Sociology of Deviance* (New York, 1963).

Berlinerblau, J., 'Toward a Sociology of Heresy, Orthodoxy, and *Doxa*', *History of Religions* 40:4 (2001), 327–51.

Bohlin, T., *Die Theologie des Pelagius und ihre Genesis*, transl. H. Buch (Uppsala, 1957).

Bonner, G., *Augustine and Modern Research on Pelagianism*, The St Augustine Lecture 1970 (Philadelphia, PA, 1972), repr. in Bonner's *God's Decree and Man's Destiny: Studies on the Thought of Augustine of Hippo* (London, 1987), no. XI.

Bonner, G., 'Augustine and Pelagianism', *Augustinian Studies* 24 (1993), 27–47, repr. in Bonner's *Church and Faith in the Patristic Tradition* (Aldershot, 1996), no. VII.

Bonner, G., '*Dic Christi Veritas Ubi nunc Habitas*: Ideas of Schism and Heresy in the Post-Nicene Age', in *The Limits of Ancient Christianity*, ed. W. E. Klingshirn and M. Vessey (Ann Arbor, MI, 1999), pp. 63–79.

Bonner, G., 'How Pelagian was Pelagius? An Examination of the Contentions of Torgny Bohlin', in *Studia Patristica* 9, *Texte und Untersuchungen zur Geschichte der altchristlichen Literatur*, Band 94, ed. F. L. Cross (Berlin, 1966), pp. 350–8, repr. in Bonner's *Church and Faith in the Patristic Tradition* (Aldershot, 1996), no. III.

Bonner, G., 'Pelagianism and Augustine', *Augustinian Studies* 23 (1992) 33–51, repr. in Bonner's *Church and Faith in the Patristic Tradition* (Aldershot, 1996), no. VI.

Bonner, G., 'Pelagianism Reconsidered', in *Studia Patristica* 27, ed. E. A. Livingstone (Louvain, 1993), pp. 237–41, repr. in Bonner's *Church and Faith in the Patristic Tradition* (Aldershot, 1996), no. V.

Bonner, G., 'Rufinus of Syria and African Pelagianism', *Augustinian Studies* 1 (1970), 31–47.

Bradwardine, T., *De causa Dei contra Pelagium et de uirtute causarum ad suos Mertonenses libri tres* (London, 1618).

Brown, P., '*Gloriosus Obitus*: The End of the Ancient Other World', in *The Limits of Ancient Christianity*, ed. W. E. Klingshirn and M. Vessey (Ann Arbor, MI, 1999), pp. 289–314.

Brown, P., 'Pelagius and his Supporters: Aims and Environment', *Journal of Theological Studies* 19 (1968), 93–114.

Brown, P., 'The Patrons of Pelagius: the Roman Aristocracy between East and West', *Journal of Theological Studies* 21 (1970), 56–72.

Brown, P., *The Ransom of the Soul. Afterlife and Wealth in Early Western Christianity* (Cambridge, MA, 2015).

Brown, P., *Through the Eye of a Needle. Wealth, the Fall of Rome, and the Making of Christianity in the West, 350–550 AD* (Princeton, NJ, 2012).

Cain, A., *The Letters of Jerome: Asceticism, Biblical Exegesis, and the Construction of Authority in Late Antiquity* (Oxford, 2009).

Cameron, A., 'Apologetics in the Roman Empire – A Genre of Intolerance?', in *"Humana Sapit". Études d'Antiquité Tardive Offertes á Lellia Cracco Ruggini*, ed. J.-M. Carrié and R. L. Testa (Turnhout, 2002), pp. 219–27.

Cameron, A., *Christianity and the Rhetoric of Empire. The Development of Christian Discourse* (Berkeley, 1991).

Cameron, A., 'How to Read Heresiology', in *The Cultural Turn in Late Antique Studies*, ed. D. B. Martin and P. Cox Miller (Durham, 2005), pp. 193–212.

Cameron, A., 'Jews and Heretics – A Category Error?', in *The Ways that Never Parted*, ed. A. H. Becker and A. Y. Reed (Tübingen, 2003), pp. 345–60.

Cameron, A., 'The Violence of Orthodoxy', in *Heresy and Identity in Late Antiquity*, ed. E. Iricinschi and H. M. Zellentin (Tübingen, 2008), pp. 102–14.

Clark, E., *The Origenist Controversy: The Cultural Construction of an Early Christian Debate* (Princeton, NJ, 1992).

Cooper, K., 'An(n)ianus of Celeda and the Latin readers of John Chrysostom', in *Studia Patristica* 27, ed. E. A. Livingstone (Louvain, 1993), pp. 249–55.

Cooper, K., *Band of Angels: The Forgotten World of Early Christian Women* (London, 2014).

Cooper, K., *The Fall of the Roman Household* (Cambridge, 2007).

Cooper, K., *The Virgin and the Bride* (Cambridge, MA, 1996).

Cooper, S. A., *Marius Victorinus' Commentary on Galatians*, Oxford Early Christian Studies (Oxford, 2005).

Cooper, S. A., *Metaphysics and Morals in Marius Victorinus' Commentary on the Letter to the Ephesians: A Contribution to the History of Neoplatonism and Christianity* (New York, 1995).

Cozic, M., 'Présence de Pélage dans le *Liber ad Gregoriam* d'Arnobe le Jeune', *Revue d'Études augustiniennes et patristiques* 51 (2005), 77–107.

De Bruyn, T., *Pelagius's Commentary on St Paul's Epistle to the Romans*, Oxford Early Christian Studies (Oxford, 1993).

Dekkers, E., *Clavis Patrum Latinorum*, 3rd edn, Corpus Christianorum Series Latina (Turnhout, 1995).

De Plinval, G., 'L'heure est-elle venue de redécouvrir Pélage?', *Revue des Études Augustiniennes* 19 (1973), 158–62.

De Plinval, G., *Pélage: Ses Écrits, Sa Vie, et Sa Réforme* (Lausanne, 1943).

De Plinval, G., note under the title 'Belgique', *Revue d'Histoire Ecclésiastique* 26 (1940), 219.

Dold, A., 'Ein Aszetischer Brief aus dem 5. Jahrhundert im Codex Vindob. Lat. 54', *Revue Bénédictine* 51 (1939), 122–38.

Duval, Y.-M., 'Sur quelques manuscrits du *De uita christiana* portant le nom de Pélage', *Latomus* 64 (2005), 132–52.

Elm, S., Fabre, P.-A., Rebillard, É., Romano, A. and Sotinel, C., 'Introduction', in *Orthodoxie Christianisme Histoire*, ed. S. Elm, É. Rebillard and A. Romano (Rome, 2000), pp. viii–xxv.

Evans, R. F., *Four Letters of Pelagius* (London, 1968).

Evans, R. F., *Pelagius. Inquiries and Reappraisals* (London, 1968).

Evans, R. F., 'Pelagius' Veracity at the Synod of Diospolis', in *Studies in Medieval Culture*, ed. J. Sommerfeldt (Kalamazoo, MI, 1964), pp. 21–30.

Ferguson, J., *Pelagius* (Cambridge, 1956).

Ferrari, M., 'In margine ai codices latini antiquiores: spigolature ambrosiane del sec. VIII' in *Lateinische Kultur im VIII Jahrhundert. Traube-Gedenkschrift*, ed. A. Lehner and W. Berschin (St. Ottilien, 1989), pp. 59–78.

Frede, H. J., *Ein neuer Paulustext und Kommentar*, 2 vols, Vetus Latina. Die Reste der altlateinischen Bibel. Aus der Geschichte der lateinischen Bibel 7–8 (Freiburg, 1973–4).

Frede, H. J., *Kirchenschriftsteller: Verzeichnis und Sigel*, Vetus Latina. Die Reste der altlateinischen Bibel, 1.1, 3rd rev. edn (Freiburg, 1981).

Garfinkel, H., 'Conditions of Successful Degradation Ceremonies', *American Journal of Sociology* 61:5 (1956), 420–4.

Genest, J.-F., *Prédétermination et Liberté Créée à Oxford au XIVe siècle: Buckingham contre Bradwardine*, Études de Philosophie Médiévale 70 (Paris, 1992).

Goodrich, J. and Miller, J. D., transl., *St. Jerome: Commentary on Ecclesiastes*, The Works of the Fathers in Translation 66 (New York, 2012).

Greshake, G., *Gnade als konkrete Freiheit. Eine Untersuchung zur Gnadenlehre des Pelagius* (Mainz, 1972).

Harries, J. D., *Law and Empire in Late Antiquity* (Cambridge, 1999).

Henderson, J. B., *The Construction of Orthodoxy and Heresy: Neo-Confucian, Islamic, Jewish, and Early Christian Patterns* (Albany, NY, 1998).

Humfress, C., 'A New Legal Cosmos: Late Roman Lawyers and the Early Medieval Church', in *Late Antiquity. A Guide to the Postclassical World*, ed. G. W. Bowersock, P. Brown and O. Grabar (Cambridge, MA, 1999), pp. 557–75.

Humfress, C., 'Citizens and Heretics. Late Roman Lawyers on Christian Heresy', in *Heresy and Identity in Late Antiquity*, ed. E. Iricinschi and H. M. Zellentin (Tübingen, 2008), pp. 128–42.

Humfress, C., 'Roman Law. Forensic Argument and the Formation of Christian Orthodoxy (III–VI Centuries)', in *Orthodoxie Christianisme Histoire*, ed. S. Elm, É. Rebillard, and A. Romano (Rome, 2000), pp. 125–47.

Iricinschi, E. and Zellentin, H. M., 'Making Selves and Marking Others: Identity and Late Antique Heresiologies', in *Heresy and Identity in Late Antiquity*, ed. E. Iricinschi and H. M. Zellentin (Tübingen, 2008), pp. 1–27.

Jackson, N., *Hobbes, Bramhall and the Politics of Liberty and Necessity: A Quarrel of the Civil Wars and Interregnum*, Cambridge Studies in Early Modern British History (Cambridge, 2007).

Julia, D., 'La production de l'orthodoxie: questions transversales', in *Orthodoxie Christianisme Histoire*, ed. S. Elm, É. Rebillard and A. Romano (Rome, 2000), pp. 393–404.

Katos, D. S., *Palladius of Helenopolis: the Origenist Advocate*, Oxford Early Christian Studies (Oxford, 2011).

Keech, D., *The Anti-Pelagian Christology of Augustine of Hippo, 396–430* (Oxford, 2012).

Kelly, J. N. D., *Jerome. His Life, Writings, and Controversies* (London, 1975).

King, K. L., 'Social and Theological Effects of Heresiological Discourse', in *Heresy and Identity in Late Antiquity*, ed. E. Iricinschi and H. M. Zellentin (Tübingen, 2008), pp. 28–49.

Klingshirn, W. E., *Caesarius of Arles: The Making of a Christian Community in Late Antique Gaul* (Cambridge, 1994).

Kurtz, L., 'The Politics of Heresy', *American Journal of Sociology* 88 (1983), 1085–115.

Lamberigts, M., 'Le Mal et Le Péché. Pélage: La Réhabilitation d'un Hérétique', *Revue d'Histoire Ecclésiastique* 95 (2000), 97–111.

Lambert, B., *Bibliotheca Hieronymiana Manuscripta*, 4 vols, Instrumenta Patristica IV (Steenbrugge, 1969–72).

Le Boulluec, A., *La notion d'hérésie dans la littérature grecque IIe–IIIe siècles*, 2 vols (Paris, 1985).

Leff, G., *Bradwardine and the Pelagians*, Cambridge Studies in Medieval Life and Thought 5 (Cambridge, 1957).

Leonard, V., 'The Origin of Zealous Intolerance: Paulus Orosius and Violent Religious Conflict in the Early Fifth Century', *Vigiliae Christianae* 71 (2017), 261–84.

Leyser, C., 'Semi-Pelagianism', in *Augustine through the Ages. An Encyclopedia*, ed. A. Fitzgerald (Grand Rapids, MI, 1999), pp. 761–6.

Lössl, J., 'Augustine, "Pelagianism", Julian of Aeclanum, and Modern Scholarship', *Zeitschrift für Antikes Christentum* 11 (2007), 129–50.

Lyman, J. R., 'Hellenism and Heresy', *Journal of Early Christian Studies* 11:2 (2003), 209–22.

Mali, F., *Das 'Opus imperfectum in Matthaeum' und sein Verhältnis zu den Matthäuskommentaren von Origenes und Hieronymus* (Innsbruck, 1991).

Markus, R. A., 'Pelagianism: Britain and the Continent', *Journal of Ecclesiastical History* 37 (1986), 191–204.

Markus, R. A., *Saeculum: History and Society in the Theology of St. Augustine* (Cambridge, 1970).

Markus, R. A., 'Social and Historical Setting', in *The Cambridge History of Early Christian Literature*, ed. F. Young, L. Ayres and A. Louth (Cambridge, 2004), pp. 399–413.

Markus, R. A., '"Tempora Christiana" Revisited', in *Augustine and his Critics*, ed. R. Dodaro and G. Lawless (London, 2000), pp. 201–13.

Markus, R. A., *The End of Ancient Christianity* (Cambridge, 1990).

Markus, R. A., 'The Legacy of Pelagius: Orthodoxy, Heresy and Conciliation', in *The Making of Orthodoxy: Essays in Honour of Henry Chadwick*, ed. R. Williams (Cambridge, 1989), pp. 214–34.

Martinetto, G., 'Les Premières Réactions Antiaugustinienne de Pélage', *Revue des Études Augustiniennes* 18 (1971), 83–117.

Mathisen, R. W., '*Roma a Gothis Alarico duce capta est*. Ancient Accounts of the Sack of Rome in 410 CE', in *The Sack of Rome in 410 AD: The Event, Its Context and Its Impact. Proceedings of a Conference Held at the German*

Archaeological Institute at Rome, 04–06 November 2010, ed. J. Lipps, C. Machado and P. von Rummel, Palilia 28 (Wiesbaden, 2013), pp. 87–102.

Matsueda, R. L., 'The Natural History of Labeling Theory', in *Labeling Theory. Empirical tests*, ed. D. P. Farrington and J. Murray, Advances in Criminological Theory 18 (New Brunswick, NJ, 2014), pp. 13–44.

Mendels, D., *The Media Revolution of Early Christianity* (Grand Rapids, MI, 1999).

Mohrmann, C., 'Introduzione Generale', in *Vita di Antonio*, ed. G. J. M. Bartelink, Vite dei Santi 1 (Milan, 1974), pp. vii–lxxxiii.

Morin, G., 'Fragments Pélagiens du Manuscrit 954 de Vienne', *Revue Bénédictine* 34 (1922), 265–75.

Morris, J. R., 'Pelagian Literature', *Journal of Theological Studies* 16 (1965), 26–60.

Nuvolone, F. G. and Solignac, A., 'Pélage et Pélagianisme', in *Dictionnaire de spiritualité, ascetique, mystique, doctrine et histoire*, 17 vols (Paris, 1932–95), vol. 12.2, cols 2889–942.

Oberman, H. A., *Archbishop Thomas Bradwardine. A Fourteenth Century Augustinian: A Study of His Theology in Its Historical Context* (Utrecht, 1957).

Ogliari, D., *Gratia et Certamen. The Relationship between Grace and Free Will in the Discussion of Augustine with the So-Called Semipelagians* (Louvain, 2003).

O'Loughlin, T., 'Caesarius of Arles', in *Augustine through the Ages. An Encyclopedia*, ed. A. Fitzgerald (Grand Rapids, MI, 1999), pp. 115–16.

Österreichische Akademie der Wissenschaften, *Die handschriftliche Überlieferung der Werke des heiligen Augustinus* (Vienna, 1969–).

Pennington, K., 'The Growth of Church Law', in *Cambridge History of Christianity II: Constantine to c. 600*, ed. A. Casiday and F. W. Norris (Cambridge, 2007), pp. 380–402.

Pereira, M. J., 'Augustine, Pelagius, and the Southern Gallic Tradition', in *Grace for Grace. The Debates after Augustine and Pelagius*, ed. A. Y. Hwang, B. J. Matz and A. Cassiday (Washington, DC, 2014), pp. 180–207.

Pietersen, L., 'Despicable Deviants: Labelling Theory and the Polemic of the Pastorals', *Sociology of Religion* 58:4 (1997), 343–52.

Rackett, M. R., 'What's Wrong with Pelagianism? Augustine and Jerome on the Dangers of Pelagius and his Followers', *Augustinian Studies* 33:2 (2002), 223–37.

Rebillard, É., 'Augustin et le rituel épistolaire de l'élite sociale et culturelle de son temps: Éléments pour une analyse processuelle des relations de l'évêque et de la cité dans l'Antiquité tardive', in *L'évêque dans la cité du IVe au Ve siècle: image et autorité*, ed. É. Rebillard and C. Sotinel (Rome, 2010), pp. 127–52, repr. and transl. as 'Augustine and the Epistolary Rituals and Cultural Élite of his Time. A Processual Analysis of the Relations between Bishop and City in

Late Antiquity', in Rebillard's *Transformations of Religious Practices in Late Antiquity* (Farnham, 2013), pp. 89–114.

Rebillard, É., *Christians and Their Many Identities in Late Antiquity, North Africa, 200–450 CE* (Ithaca, NY, 2012).

Rebillard, É., '*Dogma Populare*. Popular Belief in the Controversy between Augustine and Julian of Eclanum', in Rebillard's *Transformations of Religious Practices in Late Antiquity* (Farnham, 2013), pp. 199–211.

Rebillard, É., *In Hora Mortis. Évolution de la pastorale Chrétienne de la Mort aux IVe et Ve Siècles dans L'Occident Latin* (Rome, 1994).

Rebillard, É., 'Late Antique Limits of Christianness: North Africa in the Age of Augustine', in *Group Identity and Religious Individuality in Late Antiquity*, ed. É. Rebillard and J. Rüpke (Washington, DC, 2015), pp. 293–317.

Rebillard, É., 'Sociologie de la Déviance et Orthodoxie: Le cas de la controverse pélagienne sur la grâce', in *Orthodoxie Christianisme Histoire*, ed. S. Elm, É. Rebillard and A. Romano (Rome, 2000), pp. 221–40, repr. and transl. as 'Deviance Theory and Orthodoxy: the Case of the Pelagian Controversy on Grace', in Rebillard's *Transformations of Religious Practices in Late Antiquity* (Farnham, 2013), pp. 159–77.

Rebillard, É., and Rüpke, J., 'Introduction. Groups, Individuals, and Religious Identity', in *Group Identity and Religious Individuality in Late Antiquity*, ed. É. Rebillard and J. Rüpke (Washington, DC, 2015), pp. 3–12.

Rees, B. R., *Pelagius. Life and Letters*, 2 vols (Woodbridge, 1998).

Refoulé, F., 'Datation du Premier Concile de Carthage Contre les Pélagiens et du *Libellus fidei* de Rufin', *Revue des Études Augustiniennes* 9 (1963), 41–9.

Rist, J. M., *Augustine: Ancient Thought Baptized* (Cambridge, 1994).

Rist, J. M., *Augustine Deformed: Love, Sin and Freedom in the Western Moral Tradition* (Cambridge, 2014).

Rousseau, P., 'Antony as Teacher in the Greek *Life*', in *Greek Biography and Panegyric in Late Antiquity*, ed. T. Hägg and P. Rousseau (Los Angeles, CA, 2000), pp. 89–109.

Salamito, J.-M., *Les virtuoses et la multitude: aspects sociaux de la controverse entre Augustin et les pélagiens* (Grenoble, 2005).

Scheck, T., transl., *St. Jerome. Commentary on Isaiah* (New York, 2015).

Scheck, T., transl., *St. Jerome's Commentaries on Galatians, Titus, and Philemon* (Notre Dame, IN, 2010).

Schlatter, F. W., 'The Author of the *Opus Imperfectum in Matthaeum*', *Vigiliae Christianae* 42 (1988), 364–75.

Schlatter, F. W., 'The Pelagianism of the *Opus Imperfectum in Matthaeum*', *Vigiliae Christianae* 41 (1987), 267–85.

Schur, E. M., *The Politics of Deviance. Stigma Contests and the Uses of Power* (Englewood Cliffs, NJ, 1980).

Shaw, B. D., *Sacred Violence: African Christians and Sectarian Hatred in the Age of Augustine* (Cambridge, 2011).

Smith, T. A., *De Gratia. Faustus of Riez's Treatise on Grace and Its Place in the History of Theology* (Notre Dame, IN, 1990).

Tannenbaum, F., *Crime and the Community* (Boston, MA, 1938).

TeSelle, E., 'Rufinus the Syrian, Caelestius, Pelagius: Explorations in the Prehistory of the Pelagian Controversy', *Augustinian Studies* 3 (1972), 61–95.

Thonnard, F.-J., 'Saint Jean Chrysostome et Saint Augustin dans la Controverse Pélagienne', *Revue des Études Byzantines* 25 (1967), 189–218.

Van Nuffelen, P., 'Not Much Happened: 410 and All That', *Journal of Roman Studies* 105 (2015), 322–9.

Weaver, R. H., *Divine Grace and Human Agency. A Study of the Semi-Pelagian Controversy* (Macon, GA, 1996).

Weaver, R. H., 'Introduction', in *Grace for Grace. The Debates after Augustine and Pelagius*, ed. A. Y. Hwang, B. J. Matz and A. Cassiday (Washington, DC, 2014), pp. xi–xxvi.

Wermelinger, O., 'Neuere Forschungskontroversen um Augustinus und Pelagius', in *Internationales Symposion über den Stand der Augustinus-Forschung. Vom 12. bis 16. April 1987 im Schloß Rauischholzhausen der Justus-Liebig-Universität Gießen*, ed. C. Mayer and K. H. Chelius (Würzburg, 1989), pp. 189–217.

Wessel, S., *Cyril of Alexandria and the Nestorian Controversy: The Making of a Saint and of a Heretic*, Oxford Early Christian Studies (Oxford, 2004).

Wetzel, J., 'Snares of Truth. Augustine on Free Will and Predestination', in *Augustine and His Critics*, ed. R. Dodaro and G. Lawless (London, 2000), pp. 124–41.

Williams, R., 'Does It Make Sense to Speak of Pre-Nicene Orthodoxy?', in *The Making of Orthodoxy*, ed. R. Williams (Cambridge, 1989), pp. 1–23.

Wood., S., *The Proprietary Church in the Medieval West* (Oxford, 2008).

Zito, G., 'Toward a Sociology of Heresy', *Sociological Analysis* 44 (1983), 123–30.

Translations of Primary Sources

Aside from translations included in editions, I have drawn on and adapted the following translations. I hope to have included all the translations to which I have referred but if I have omitted any, I apologise.

Bray, G. L., transl., *Ambrosiaster, Commentaries on Romans and 1–2 Corinthians*, Ancient Christian Texts (Downers Grove, IL, 2009).

Fremantle, W., transl., *Jerome: Letters and Select Works*, Nicene and Post-Nicene Fathers, Second Series, vol. 6 (Oxford, 1893).

Goodrich, J. and Miller, J. D., transl., *St. Jerome: Commentary on Ecclesiastes*, The Works of the Fathers in Translation 66 (New York, 2012).

Graves, M., transl., *Jerome. Commentary on Jeremiah*, Ancient Christian Texts (Downers Grove, IL, 2011).

Hanson, C. L., transl., *Pacian of Barcelona, Orosius of Braga*, Iberian Fathers, vol. 3, The Fathers of the Church. A New Translation (Washington, DC, 1999).

Hritzu, J. N., transl., *St Jerome. Dogmatic and Polemical Works*, The Fathers of the Church. A New Translation (Washington, DC, 1965).

Ramsey, B., transl., *The Works of Saint Augustine. A Translation for the 21st Century. Revisions* (New York, 2010).

Rees, B., transl., *Pelagius. Life and Letters*, vol. 2 (Woodbridge, 1998).

Scheck, T. P., transl., *St Jerome. Commentary on Matthew*, The Fathers of the Church. A New Translation (Washington, DC, 2008).

Scheck, T. P., transl., *St. Jerome's Commentaries on Galatians, Titus, and Philemon* (Notre Dame, IN, 2010).

Scheck, T. P., transl., *St Jerome. Commentary on Isaiah* (New York, 2015).

Teske, R. J., transl., *The Works of Saint Augustine. A Translation for the 21st Century. Answer to the Pelagians*, 4 vols (New York, 1997–9).

Teske, R. J., transl., *The Works of Saint Augustine. A Translation for the 21st Century. Letters*, 4 vols (New York, 2001–5).

White, C., transl., *Early Christian Lives* (London, 1998).

White, C., transl., *The Correspondence (394–419) between Jerome and Augustine of Hippo* (Lampeter, 1990).

Wortley, J., transl., *Palladius of Aspuna. The Lausiac History* (Athens, OH, 2015).

Index

The letter 'n' after a page number refers to the footnote number.